The Transformation of the American Democratic Republic

The Transformation of the American Democratic Republic

Stephen M. Krason

Routledge
Taylor & Francis Group

LONDON AND NEW YORK

First published 2012 by Transaction Publishers

Published 2017 by Routledge
2 Park Square, Milton Park, Abingdon, Oxon OX14 4RN
711 Third Avenue, New York, NY 10017, USA

Routledge is an imprint of the Taylor & Francis Group, an informa business

Library of Congress Catalog Number: 2011038774

Library of Congress Cataloging-in-Publication Data

Krason, Stephen M.
    The transformation of the American democratic republic / Stephen M. Krason.
        p. cm.
    Includes bibliographical references and index.
    1. United States—Politics and government.   2. United States—Politics and government—Philosophy.   3. Democracy—United States.   I. Title.
    JK31.K73 2012
    320.973—dc23

                                                        2011038774

ISBN 13: 978-1-4128-4745-2 (hbk)

This book is dedicated to the memory of my father-in-law and mother-in-law, Joseph and Catherine Walter, who were the kind of salt-of-the-earth, religious people upon whom the restoration of the American democratic republic especially depends.

CONTENTS

ACKNOWLEDGEMENTS

The author wishes to thank the following: The Witherspoon Institute and Dr. Robert P. George, Senior Fellow at the Institute, and Luis Tellez, President of the Institute, for the fellowship that enabled me to spend the 2008-09 academic year in residence researching and writing most of this book; Franciscan University of Steubenville for a sabbatical leave for that year and for financial and other assistance in bringing this book to publication; Dr. Michael Fitzgerald, of the Department of History at Franciscan University of Steubenville, for crucial historical research advice early in the project; *The Catholic Social Science Review* for permission to reprint the first chapter of this book, which appeared in an earlier version in that journal; Mrs. Toni Aeschliman for her indispensable assistance in formatting the manuscript for publication and other secretarial and computer help; Jacob Wiker for proofreading and indexing the book; my wife Therese, son Stephen II, and youngest daughter Monica for their valuable ideas for part of the final chapter, and Monica's assistance with final work on the Index; and for the support of my family generally during the more than two years that I worked on this book.

INTRODUCTION

THE AIM OF THIS STUDY

We live in a time when there has been much criticism about the United States Constitution being subverted in many ways and about the country deviating from the constitutional framework established by the Founding Fathers and having changed its character in some significant way. Is the American political order still, fundamentally, the one that was established by the Founders, or over the course of nearly two hundred and twenty-five years has it changed into something different? It is easy to make assertions about this question, but what we attempt in this book is a serious historical study and analysis in light of the thinking of the Founders themselves if, indeed, there has been such a change. Most specifically, we have considered the following: 1) Whether the Founders' thinking about the principles, practices, and conditions they believed were necessary to sustain the kind of political order they established, a democratic republic, have been upheld throughout U.S. history; and 2) If the cultural conditions of the Founding Era, when they launched the American democratic republic and that were the foundation upon which their enterprise was established, have been maintained. We believe that there has been a transformation of the American democratic republic. Our study progresses through the history of the American Republic under the Constitution from 1789 to the present, examining each historical period and considering how it compared to this thinking of the Founders and their era's cultural conditions and identifying the events, developments, and thought during each period that helped influence an ultimate reshaping of the nature of the political order. The areas of analysis in the various historical periods concern political, constitutional, and legal developments; economic and technological developments; the role of government and relations among the three branches of the federal government and between the federal government and the states; popular movements; socio-cultural (including religious) developments; demographic developments and relations among social groups; war, foreign affairs, and territorial expansion; and philosophical perspectives and currents in socio-political thought. We weigh the effects that these and other factors have had on affecting the deviation of the respective historical period from the

Founding, and which developments and periods were particularly crucial in changing the character of the American political order in the long run.

The book is divided into ten chapters, eight of which concern the historical periods and go into considerable detail. We believe that the detail is necessary to give the reader a good understanding of the respective period and to be able to secure enough information in the different topical areas to make a reasonable evaluation of the period in light of the Founding. To be sure, we do not claim to be providing a thorough, in-depth historical study of each period. We present the major events and trends, but our concern is garnering the kind of information needed to do our particular analysis. This is not the work of a historian, employing the typical method of historians of carefully studying documents and other original sources of a period to set or reset the historical facts and influences. Instead, we have tried to assemble primarily sound, respected secondary sources to give us as good and accurate of a picture of the historical periods—including the culture of the Founding Era itself—as possible to do our analysis (more general sources are sometimes used for specific factual information and statistical data). This book is the work rather of a political scientist and scholar of American politics and political thought who has sought to come to some critical conclusions about the American political order in light of historical realities. Where original sources are used it is in the manner that a scholar of political philosophy and American political thought would use them: in studying the writings of the leading Founding Fathers and other pertinent political thinkers in the beginning of the book to understand precisely and clearly their thought as it is pertinent to our inquiry. It must be kept in mind that the subject focused on here is *what the Founders thought was necessary in order to sustain a democratic republic, the kind of political order they were establishing under the Constitution—and the actual conditions, beliefs, and practices of their culture that implicitly made possible such a political order.*

The chapters proceed as follows: Chapter 1 explores the views of the Founders and the character of their culture to conclude what the standards are that we then go on to use for our analysis of the various historical periods. It gives some special attention to the crucial question of the Founding Era's understanding of the role of religion in a democratic republic. It also introduces the question of the decline of political orders, a topic focused on by many thinkers over the last two and a half millennia, which we *very briefly* consider with regard to each historical period (i.e., to determine the extent to which the factors those thinkers identify as causing decline are present). It is interesting to see that many of the very principles, practices, and conditions that the Founding upheld as needed to sustain a democratic republic are coincident with those of a good political order per se, and how departures from them signal decline. The chapter also reflects at some length on possible weaknesses in the Founders' thought and understanding that may have helped to encourage developments throughout American history that led to the undoing of their handiwork (i.e., the democratic republic of the Constitution) over time. We suggest, at the end of each historical chapter, which of these possible weaknesses may in light of developments have been operative, and consider which may have been most influential in affecting the transformation of the American political order over time. Again, there is just *brief* reflection on this subject. The prime focus of this book is the evaluation of each historical period to see its deviation from the norms of the Founding, how they led to an eventual transformation of the character of the American political order, and what the nature of that change finally has been.

Some might argue that we have painted an idyllic picture of the Founding Era. We are aware of the shortcomings of that Era—like any period and place in human history it had them, and one of its most evident ones was the existence of slavery—but it is difficult to say that its principles and ideas for the structuring of free government were anything but magnificent and had reverberating effects for the entire world over time. It is also difficult to say that the convictions and practices of its culture were, on balance, anything but exemplary in matters of social morality, community, and personal and inter-personal norms.

Chapter 2 begins the examination of the periods of American history in light of the Founding. It covers the period from 1789 to 1817, from the beginning of the new Republic after the Constitution was ratified through the first four presidents—the eras of the Federalists and the Jeffersonians. We see there what tendencies counter to the Founding may have developed very early.

Chapter 3 focuses on what we identify as a very critical period in the transformation of the American political order, the time from the end of the Jeffersonian period until the end of the Jacksonian Era (1817-1840). The key word to describe this time was democratization and, as we shall see, it features the beginnings of many crucial trends that have significant effects in the long run on the political order's character.

Chapter 4 explores the period from 1840 to 1877—a time of a major crisis in American ideals with the Mexican War and westward expansion, and then the greatest political struggle and upheaval in American history with the slavery question and Civil War and the bitter aftermath of Reconstruction. In spite of the turmoil, it is not a period where the activity of transformation gains momentum (although certain quiet cultural trends take deeper hold).

Chapter 5 focuses on the period from 1877 to 1920—the Gilded Age, Progressive Era, and First World War—when profound political, economic, cultural, and constitutional changes and changes in thought reshaped the country and markedly advanced the cause of transformation of the character of the American political order. The changes of this period served as a springboard to the more decisive changes that followed in the twentieth century.

Chapter 6 discusses the "roaring twenties," the Great Depression, and World War II (1920-1945), a time of abiding cultural changes, especially as affected the role of religion in American life and attitudes of the intelligentsia and opinion-making strata. Economic trauma and then global war, however, constrained the spread of the new secular way of thought and life among the general populace, however. The most sweeping political change was inauguration of the ongoing, substantial domestic role of the federal government by the New Deal.

Chapter 7 considers the decade and a half after World War II (1945-1960), which was mostly defined by the American role in the Cold War and as a result saw a further permanent growth of federal power. It was a time, however, that in many respects measured up well in comparison to the Founding, even while the cultural changes of the 1920s were quietly becoming more deeply implanted and spreading.

Chapter 8 examines the 1960s and 1970s, the age of veritable socio-cultural revolution, political turmoil, and the next great leap in federal and general governmental power. While many developments over a long period of time led up to this, it was a time when old certainties evaporated and ways of living were turned on their heads. It was the time when the welfare state and the activity of social engineering became permanent features of American life, and liberalism—the driving force of American politics for most of the century—was decisively transformed, with profound consequences for the character of the American political order. The transformation of the American democratic republic clearly takes place at this time.

Chapter 9 covers the period from 1980 to the present, when there is a simultaneous reaction to the developments of the previous two decades and a further ingraining of them into the American frame of life and government—capped off by an attempt at the present to carry the changes of the 1960s and 1970s even further and more sweepingly transform American politics and culture.

Chapter 10 reviews the analysis throughout the book and considers what, with the subversion of the democratic republic of the Founders, the new character of the American political order is. It makes conclusions about how the transformation happened, and what were the crucial periods and developments. It considers what the evidence of the different historical periods brought together indicates about which putative weaknesses in the Founding were particular factors in the transformation, and what can be concluded about the state of decline of the political order per se. Finally, it reflects about what might be done to restore the democratic republic of the Founders.

While our study, writing, and teaching about American politics for many years gave us a strong sense that a transformation had occurred before we started this book, a scholar must go where the evidence and sound analysis leads him. That is what we kept in mind in the course of our research. Although after nine chapters we were sure a transformation has occurred, we only resolved in the course of writing the tenth chapter what the new character of the American political order is. The evidence mustered and the argument made is clear and troubling, and all those concerned about the American Founding, our Constitution, and the future course of our political life should examine and ponder it.

"I yield slowly and reluctantly to the conviction that
our constitution cannot last."

- Chief Justice John Marshall to Justice Joseph Story (September 22, 1832)

CHAPTER 1

AMERICA'S "PARCHMENT REGIME": THE ORIGINAL CHARACTER OF THE AMERICAN DEMOCRATIC REPUBLIC AND THE CULTURE SUPPORTING IT

Introduction

We hear it said often that the practice of something does not measure up to the theory behind it. This is the case with political orders as with other types of entities, as well as with individual persons.

In Federalist 10, James Madison says that in "a pure democracy...there is nothing to check the inducements to sacrifice the weaker party or an obnoxious individual. Hence it is that such democracies have ever been spectacles of turbulence and contention...and as short in their lives as they have been violent in their deaths."[1] With such an utterly unflattering assessment by the main author of the Constitution, one wonders how we might be able to refer to the United States as a *democratic* republic? Martin Diamond, Winston Mills Fisk, and Herbert Garfinkel, in their book entitled *The Democratic Republic*, say that the U.S. is "democratic"—in the representative, not pure, sense—because it features majority rule, and is "republican" because it was intended to demonstrate such characteristics as restraint, sobriety, competence, and liberty.[2] There was intended to be majority rule, to be sure, but within the context of preserving minority rights; that is, the minority could not be suppressed or its liberty destroyed. As Diamond, et al. say, our Constitution is "faithful to the spirit and form of democracy...[but] guards against its dangerous propensities." The latter are not just the tyranny referred to by Madison, but also folly, feebleness, and ineptitude.[3] It seeks to "reconcile the advantages of democracy with the sobering qualities of republicanism," and "to render a democratic regime compatible with the protection of liberty and the requisites of competent government."[4] The consent of the governed, then, is at the heart of the American

1

/

political order, but its force is mitigated by the restraints of representative institutions, the rule of law, and social, cultural, and moral influences. This insures that the majority's will not only is not abusive, but also that the common good of the political order will be promoted.

The View Prevalent at the Time of the American Founding Fathers about the Principles and Practices Needed to Sustain a Democratic Republic

We can identify at the time of our Constitution's adoption widely held views about the principles and practices that have to be prevalent to sustain a democratic republic. They represent: 1) a mixture of institutional factors and democratic (i.e., democratic republican) practices; 2) those that relate strictly to democratic principles and practices; and 3) those involving social conditions that are necessary to sustain republican government. We can identify these views in writings of the individual American Founding Fathers (i.e., the leading figures at the 1787 Constitutional Convention and Thomas Jefferson, who is often also reckoned a "Founding Father"), major political documents of the constitutional (i.e., Founding) era, the thought of the philosophers of republican government who especially influenced the thinking of the Founders, and the retrospective assessment of the greatest commentator on the American democratic republic, Alexis de Tocqueville. These are principles and practices that from learned reflection and actual experience the leading political thinkers and statesmen of the Founding Era concluded should be present to call a political order a "democratic republic."

Regarding the first category (institutional arrangements), separation of powers, checks and balances, an independent judiciary, and federalism were particularly emphasized. Separation of powers did not happen automatically in early America, even though it was a staple of the thinking of such influential political philosophers as John Locke and Baron de Montesquieu. Indeed, after the outbreak of the Revolutionary War legislative supremacy was the order of the day in the American states, an outgrowth of the bitterness about the overbearing royal-appointed colonial governors in the years before.[5] The abuses of institutionally unchallenged legislative power became readily apparent, however, as the Federalist Papers make clear.[6] The writings of numerous Founding Fathers underscore the centrality of the notion of separation of powers. In spite of the movement toward legislative supremacy in the period 1776-1789, it also appears as a basic principle in such prominent new state constitutions as those of Virginia and Massachusetts.[7] James Madison sums it up in Federalist 47: "No political truth is certainly of greater intrinsic value."[8]

Checks and balances, of course, is a concomitant of separation of powers. Alexander Hamilton, another prominent Founder, speaks of the need for "mutual checks."[9] It had roots going back at least to Solon in ancient Athens.[10] George Dargo writes that "separation of powers, mixed with an elaborate system of checks and balances among roughly equal branches" became the cornerstone principle of American government.[11]

Probably the most famous Founding Era argument for an independent judiciary is Hamilton's Federalist 78, although the Declaration of Independence also pointedly speaks about it when it includes among the colonists' grievances against King George III that "[h]e has made judges dependent on his will alone for the tenure of their offices, and the amount and payment of their salaries."

The federal system was not something established in the Founding Era; the Constitution was erected upon the long-existing reality of it. Hamilton, representing well the general views of the Founders, insisted that the state governments had to be strong and a balance of power between them and the new federal government was as essential as the forging of a strong union.[12] Later, Tocqueville mentioned the federal system as crucial to the American democratic republic ("one of the most powerful combinations favoring human prosperity and freedom").[13] Both the Framers and Tocqueville spoke about how the federal structure in conjunction with the large land mass and population of the U.S.—large even then with many fewer states—gives rise to the notion of the extended republic. They argued that this helps protect liberty because within it dangerous factions (see below) and intense political passions are more likely to be geographically contained.[14]

It is clear that both the Founding Fathers and Tocqueville were suspicious of excessive centralization of government. The Founders state that the national government under the Constitution only has a limited range of powers and would be concerned only with matters of general concern to the whole country.[15] Tocqueville speaks of "the extreme evils which centralization can produce."[16] His conclusion that it is good for the American democratic republic that the nation (at that time) had "no great capital" seems to be connected with this concern about centralization.[17] Despite his admiration for democratic republics, he was concerned that what might happen as time goes on is that while they would continue to let individuals have some role in shaping "important affairs"—for example, by extending them the franchise—they would increasingly regiment the particular everyday aspects of their lives.[18] He sees equality as preparing men for this kind of "gentle" despotism, with enhanced centralized governmental authority, since it makes them so independent of one another that they will be only too ready to turn to the state as protector and provider.[19]

There are several factors that combine institutional arrangements and democratic practice, not fitting neatly into simply one or the other. These include the following: the notion that the makers of the laws must be subject to them like everyone else; the need for a "mixed" government, where both the propertied or leading elements of the political society and the much more numerous popular elements are represented; the presence of parties and factions to check each other so as to preserve liberty, not allowing any one group to become so powerful that it threatens the common good; and also that the laws and not the mere arbitrary whim of rulers control public affairs (i.e., "a government of laws and not of men").

The applicability of the laws to their makers was stressed by the political philosopher John Locke[20] and was commonly accepted in the political life of America almost from the beginning. Locke saw this, along with rotation in office, as being a major means of avoiding political arbitrariness.[21] This was something that obviously distinguished a constitutional regime from, say, a traditional monarchy.

Closely related to this principle, of course, was the notion that there must be a government of laws or, in other words, the rule of law must prevail. This was certainly not a new idea in the Founding period; we can find it as far back as Aristotle's writing (which indirectly influenced the liberally-educated Founding Fathers through their learning),[22] although for the most part we find that it took root in customary practice only after centuries of political struggle and constitutional development. Indeed, Aristotle delineated the fundamental elements of the rule of law (he also called it "constitutional rule"): it furthers the common interest of the community as against individualistic or singular group interests (even though the former is *mostly* derived by compromise among different specific interests); governance proceeds by means of general regulations instead of arbitrary decrees; and government is carried out by willing citizens instead of by force-wielding despots.[23]

We see many emphatic endorsements of the rule of law in the Founding Era and the thought that influenced it. Locke says that men must be "govern[ed] by *promulgated establish'd Laws…*," "to have one Rule for Rich and Poor"…[and] be designed for no other end ultimately but *the good of the People*."[24] Montesquieu says that a democratic republic requires ordered political liberty within law.[25] Such thinkers as John Milton and James Harrington, who influenced the Founders but less directly than Locke and Montesquieu,[26] also stressed the rule of law.[27] John Adams writes, "the laws…are the only possible rule, measure, and security of justice."[28] Thomas Jefferson insists on the need for "equal laws" to protect the "equal rights" of all, even minorities.[29]

In the writing of the Founding Era and the thinkers who inspired it, we find frequent references to two other points relating to law, which are part of the notion of the rule of law. While these fit more appropriately into our other categories, for the sake of continuity we relate them here. Most crucial is that the civil laws embody natural law or principles of morality not made by men (this is in the category of democratic principles and practice, without any institutional dimension; that is, it is a principle for lawmakers in a democratic republic to put into practice in their activity of lawmaking).[30] When reference is made to "good laws" in the writing of the Founding Era and in the philosophers of constitutional or republican government from the seventeenth century to Tocqueville, what is meant is the upholding of the rule of law (as defined above) and of the notion of the civil laws embodying natural law. The other point pertaining to law fits into the category of social conditions and attitudes. It is that in a democratic republic, all citizens—rulers and ruled alike—must have a respect for law. Washington and Adams say that the laws must not just be respected, but *revered*.[31]

The notion of the mixed government or mixed regime is the foundation for separation of powers. Mixed government as it appeared in the American colonies was different from the classical understanding of it and even the version that prevailed in England. The classical notion called for involving in the ruling activity monarchical, aristocratic (usually, in practice, oligarchic), and popular elements. (The latter referred to the many who were poor). This was approximated in England with the particular governmental institutions that took shape: the king or queen, the House of Lords (which represented the traditional landed aristocracy), and the House of Commons (which represented the majority who were not in the royal family or aristocracy, the commoners). The arrangement that took shape in the American colonies was necessarily somewhat different since there was no American aristocracy, and the king was present only vicariously in the person of the colonial governor (although these governors typically did not have anything like kingly powers). The U.S. Constitution also established an untraditional kind of mixed regime, although not completely different. The presidency is, in effect, the monarchical part, apparently intended to have power rivaling that of the English king—but, as the great constitutional scholar Edward S. Corwin says, without the hereditary aspect or the corruption.[32] The Senate and the Supreme Court were intended to be something like an aristocratic part, with neither elected directly by the people (this was the case with the Senate until the Seventeenth Amendment). The Senate was closer to the people—as might be expected by the fact that it comprised part of the legislative body—because it originally was elected by the people's representatives in the state legislatures. The House of Representatives was meant to be the popular body in the U.S. government, directly elected by the people. Although the U.S. had no hereditary aristocracy, the fact that this means of selecting senators brought forth the more eminent and distinguished men is clearly seen from Tocqueville's discussion of it.[33] Essentially, though, the American mixed government could not be like the English or classical one because the social framework within which the government operated was different. As Russell Kirk points out, the U.S. was a middle class country, and this helped to moderate people's attitudes and in some sense to build community. In colonial and early republican America, virtually everyone was middle class.[34] This is not to say that early America viewed property as irrelevant to politics because having the franchise was generally conditioned on either the holding of a certain amount of real property—normally quite low—or some other showing of attachment to the community.[35]

Further, in the context of mixed government, a senate—which by indirect election, long terms, or both is somewhat shielded from immediate democratic pressures—was held to be especially critical. We see this clearly in the writing of such Founding Fathers as Madison, Hamilton, and Adams. Although, as Hamilton puts it, a "broad democratic branch" is crucial in a republic, the democratic impulse must not be allowed to go unchecked (recall above the danger of a majority faction). As Federalist 63 observes, "history informs us of no long-lived republic which had not a senate."[36]

The eminent historian of the American Founding, Bernard Bailyn, writes that the early state constitutions derived the principle of separation of powers not from a specific intention to balance the powers and functions of distinct branches but from the English mixed government idea, which they in turn embodied, and from a general colonial concern about influence and corruption in government.[37]

The classic statement of the notion of the essentiality of parties and factions for holding overreaching power in check is, of course, James Madison's *Federalist 10*. The essence of his argument is that faction is inevitable in free political societies. Its causes cannot be eliminated, so its effects must be controlled. A minority faction can be checked by the vote—that is, a majority can overwhelm it. A majority faction needs to be checked by such institutional arrangements as the federal system and representative bodies that will render nationwide cabals and large-scale demagoguery (characteristic of pure democracies) unlikely. Although as indicated below the Founders in no way dismiss the importance of good statesmanship (i.e., public-spirited men able to discern and unselfishly focus on furthering the good of their political order), *Federalist 10* clearly downplays its capability to control faction.[38]

It was only three generations before the Founding Era that the principle of *Federalist 10* gained credence. Before the 1730s, parties and factions were seen as destructive of liberty and strongly discouraged.[39] This suspicion had not completely disappeared, however, even by 1800, as can be seen by Jefferson's insistence that his Democratic-Republican party—which he was the standard-bearer of in that year's presidential election—was the party to end all parties and restore the situation that had previously prevailed.[40]

Finally in this first category, we find the Founding Fathers enunciating the notion of vigorous or energetic government. That is, government must be sufficiently strong to carry out its purposes, noted below.[41] It is suggested from the above that this is part of the reason why they sought a democratic republic, instead of a pure democracy. To establish a vigorous national government in place of the weak Confederation that could not meet national needs and internal and external threats was a major objective of the 1787 Philadelphia Constitutional Convention.[42]

The items in the category of strictly democratic principles and practice are the following: that the twin purposes of government are to secure men's inherent natural rights and promote the common good; popular sovereignty; a limitation of the franchise to those who demonstrate some permanent attachment to the community; measured (i.e., ordered) liberty; political equality, but with limitations; respect for private property; and the guarantee of various political and legal rights, the most important of which were freedom of speech, freedom of the press, freedom of religion, freedom of assembly, the right to trial by jury, the right to habeas corpus, due process guarantees, and the prohibition of bills of attainder; generally, short duration in public office; civilian control of the military; and the taking of due care about public credit and avoiding excessive public debt.

Locke's natural rights of life, liberty, and property were echoed in the Declaration of Independence's life, liberty, and the pursuit of happiness. These are also seen clearly in the Virginia Bill of Rights of 1776 and the Massachusetts

Constitution of 1780. Actually, natural rights-type language is abundantly observed in the political discussion of the Founding Era. The protection of men's natural rights was not the only object of government, however. The Virginia Bill of Rights specifically speaks of attaining the common good as the other purpose. Federalist 51 states, "Justice is the end of government. It is the end of civil society."[43] Adams stresses the need for a democratic republic to motivate the citizens to "prefer the public good before their own."[44] Tocqueville states that the Founding Fathers commendably understood how the federal system would motivate citizens to take an interest in the public good.[45] The terms "public good" and "common good" are treated interchangeably here. It might appropriately be asked if for the Founding Fathers and their era it had the traditional philosophical meaning of the good of the community and of each individual person in the community. Since the education of many of Founders seems to have acquainted them with Scholastic philosophy,[46] they perhaps had this definition roughly in mind (though below we raise the question about how deep their philosophical reflection went). Even if they did not think of it precisely in this way, they were certainly trying to imply in using the term "common good" or "public good" that republican citizens must not narrowly focus on their own particularistic interests and ignore those of their political community. Indeed, their desire to establish a democratic republic to protect minorities further suggests something like this traditional philosophical meaning of common good.

The expressions of popular sovereignty in the writing of the Founding Era are numerous. Jefferson and Madison are representative. The former writes that the "mother principle" of democratic republics must be that "they embody the will of their people and execute it."[47] The latter says that the vital principle of republican government is the *lex majoris partis*, the will of the majority,"[48] which was noted above in our definition of a democratic republic. Popular sovereignty included, as the colonists' grievances against England made clear, that taxation could not be levied without the consent of the people or their representatives.

To insure popular sovereignty in practice, representation was held in the political thinking—and practice—of the late colonial and early Republican period to have to correspond to population levels and to be apportioned fairly equally among geographical areas.[49] At least Jefferson, who was more pro-democratic in his sentiments, believed it essential to conduct government in the open.[50] Interestingly, this is in opposition to the closed-door Constitutional Convention of 1787, which Jefferson was not present at.

On the question of the limitation of the franchise, as stated above, property ownership or at least some attachment to the community was generally viewed as a necessary requirement for voting in the Founding Era. Sometimes, service in the militia or simply paying taxes would substitute for property holding. The Constitution itself adopted no requirements; it strictly left the matter to the states, which is where these typical requirements were enforced.[51] There are indications, however, that the Founders wanted to leave open the issue of the further democratization of the franchise.[52]

The following statements, among others, express the Founding Era's adherence to the principles of measured or ordered liberty and restrained equality (as opposed to outright egalitarianism). Montesquieu had strongly stressed both, defining liberty not as a right to do whatever one likes, but as "a right of doing whatever the laws permit," and warning that "[d]emocracy has...two excesses to avoid—the spirit of inequality...and the spirit of extreme equality, which leads to despotic power."[53] The Federalist poses the problem of seeking ordered liberty—i.e., citizen liberty within a framework of social order—very bluntly: "In framing a government...the great difficulty lies in this: you must first enable the government to control the governed; and in the next place oblige it to control itself."[54] The Declaration of Independence cries out with the theme of ordered liberty. While liberty is one of the unalienable rights and the despotism being directed at them the reason the Americans were separating from England, the order provided by government was seen as so crucial that it is insisted that men will not change "governments long established" for "light and transient causes." When they do throw off one governing authority, they will "provide new guards for their future security" because government is vital for men. For our Founding Fathers, the need for order was a given, and completely unquestioned. The fear that it was breaking down after the Revolutionary War stimulated them to assemble in Philadelphia in 1787 to forge a better frame of government that would insure it and at the same time protect the liberty that they had fought so hard for.[55]

The notion of equality that one sees in the Founding Era is equal application of the laws, equal rights for all citizens, and a rendering of equal justice for all.[56] There was no question at all about the Founders being like contemporary egalitarians. Madison says the following in Federalist 10, regarding governmental recognition of differences in wealth: "[It is t]he diversity in the faculties of men, from which the rights of property originate...The protection of these faculties is the chief object of government. From th[is] protection...the possession of different degrees and kinds of property immediately results...".[57] Indeed, the Founders were greatly troubled by the threats to the security of property posed by the debtor class that had manifested itself in such developments as Shays' Rebellion."[58] The right of private property and the incidents thereof was fundamental for the Founding Era.[59] The Founders' sense of the folly of egalitarianism is clearly seen in the famous correspondence between the elderly Adams and Jefferson when they both state the need for a natural aristocracy of merit and virtue to be brought forth to rule in any kind of government (which is one of the necessary social conditions they pointed to).[60] There was no question in the Founders' minds about all men not being equally capable of effective rule. In emphasizing this, they were following a long line of political philosophers back to antiquity and including such moderns as Montesquieu, Milton, and Harrington.[61]

By short duration in office, the Framers did not seem to mean what we call today "term limits" (i.e., office holders not being allowed to run for office more than a stated number of consecutive times or only being permitted to hold a designated office for so many years during their lifetimes). What was meant was that the terms should be only for a limited—i.e., quite short in duration—number of years. The exception would be the Senate that they were establishing, since there would be need of a body to provide continuity and stability.

Effective civilian control over the military was a basic principle of the Framers. They knew only too well the history of the military tyranny of Cromwell in England.[62] Jefferson called for "a well-disciplined militia" and Washington cautioned, "overgrown military establishments…are inauspicious to liberty."[63] Related to this, Washington warned against America's foreign policy becoming partial to particular foreign nations and of the dangers of foreign influence on the country.[64]

The Founders also viewed the question of public debt as connected with liberty. As Jefferson writes, "We must make our election between *economy and liberty* or *profusion and servitude.*" This is because taxation follows debt, "and in its train wretchedness and oppression."[65]

As far as concerns the guarantee of the rights above (i.e., freedom of the press, freedom of religion, freedom of assembly, the right to trial by jury, the right to habeas corpus, due process guarantees, and the prohibition of bills of attainder), they are mentioned in numerous statements of the Founders, the Bill of Rights (bills of attainder are mentioned in the original Constitution itself), such important state documents as the Virginia Bill of Rights of 1776 and the Massachusetts Constitution of 1780, and *The Federalist.* Actually, most of the rights that appeared in various colonial and state documents found their way explicitly into the federal Bill of Rights. Others were encompassed implicitly in one or another provision. Again, the fact that the rights above were repeatedly singled out for mention indicates that they were seen as particularly central for a viable democratic republic. Sometimes, as in Madison's case, the Founders indicated directly that they believed these to be the most important rights.[66]

Finally, in terms of what might be called social conditions, or necessary elements that must be present in culture, our sources most frequently point to the following as particularly essential: religion (which is treated at length in a separate section of this chapter), education, morality (implied in the discussion of natural law above, and often referring in the Founding Era specifically to Christian moral beliefs), virtue (which of course is in many respects synonymous with morality), mores (closely related to morality and discussed later in this chapter), a commitment to freedom and republican principles, a condition of prosperity and certain economic factors, respect for law, respect for the common good, and the presence of a natural aristocracy (the latter three were discussed above).

The many references to education in statements and writings of the Founding Fathers and Tocqueville make one conclude that while it is crucial for the sustenance of a democratic republic, it did not have to be of the same type for everyone. They basically see two informal "levels": all citizens require a moral education and—more formally—an education in basic subjects and citizenship, but the minority who will go on to become leaders must have advanced study in the liberal arts so they can gain the deeper insights and understanding necessary to steer the ship of state (much like the education that many of the Founding Fathers themselves received).[67] In his "Bill for the More General Diffusion of Knowledge" in Virginia, Jefferson endorsed education as the means of preventing even the best form of government from degenerating into tyranny.[68] Adams says that, "[e]ducation is more indispensable, and must be more general, under a free government than any other."[69] In his famous Farewell Address, Washington says that, "[I]n proportion as the structure of a government gives force to public opinion, it is essential that public opinion should be enlightened."[70]

Regarding morality and virtue, we have seen their importance to the Founding Era by discussing natural law, the natural aristocracy, and moral education above, and below we quote Washington stressing the need for morality in conjunction with religion. The Massachusetts Constitution of 1780, which we have noted, similarly says, "the good order and preservation of civil government essentially depend upon piety, religion, and morality."[71] Hamilton insists that free government requires that "the virtue of...[the] rulers" be "strongly connected" "with their interest."[72] Adams says that "virtue, honor, and fear of the citizens" is required to secure liberty.[73] Montesquieu holds that virtue is especially crucial in a republic and entails love of the laws and country, constantly preferring the public to private interest, a love of equality and frugality (the latter seems to relate, at least in part, to what was said above about government debt), and good maxims to direct people's lives.[74] Later, Tocqueville became famous for his "doctrine of self-interest properly understood"—a kind of enlightened self-love—that he sees as motivating in Americans orderliness, temperateness, caution, self-control, and small sacrifices for the good of neighbor and community. These are not the noblest of virtues, but are virtues nonetheless and help men to both be free and work for the common good.[75]

Next, Jefferson and Madison both speak about the need for a spirit of commitment to republican principles.[76] Similarly, Tocqueville says the people need a taste for freedom.[77]

Finally, we could categorize in the realm of social conditions economic considerations. Hamilton and Jefferson also believed that government should help develop the economy, although the former heavily emphasized commerce and the latter a more balanced approach toward both commerce and agriculture.[78] Tocqueville mentions the geographical vastness of the U.S. and its great natural resources, and resulting material prosperity, as helping to sustain its democratic republic. While he does not see natural abundance as in any way a guarantee of republicanism, prosperity is crucial because it has a moderating effect on political behavior. It tempers extremism and encourages law and order.[79] This is obviously related to the presence of a substantial middle class, discussed above.

Religion in the Founding Era

Many writers have noted the centrality of religion in early America, but few have expressed it as powerfully as Tocqueville. He said that while religion "never intervenes directly in the government of American society" (viz., separation of church and state, in its proper conception) it nevertheless should "be considered the first of their political institutions."[80]

What was the religious perspective of the colonial and, especially, the Founding Era in the United States, how did it affect the life of the people, and how important was religion viewed in the shaping and sustaining of basic American political and social ideas?

We find a strong endorsement of the importance of religion for sustaining republican government in the statements of the Founding Fathers. In his Farewell Address, George Washington said that "[o]f all the dispositions and habits which lead to political prosperity, religion and morality are indispensable supports."[81] John Adams similarly wrote that "it is religion and morality alone, which can establish the Principles upon which Freedom can securely stand"[82] and that the *"general Principles,* on which the Fathers achieved Independence...were...the general Principles of Christianity...And the general Principles of English and American Liberty."[83] Dr. Benjamin Rush wrote, "the only foundation for a useful education in a republic is to be laid in Religion. Without this there can be no virtue, and without virtue there can be no liberty."[84] The Northwest Ordinance, adopted by an Articles of Confederation Congress that included many of the Constitution's Framers in it, declared, "Religion, morality, and knowledge [as] being necessary to good government."[85] Even the supposed deist, Benjamin Franklin, at a crucial impasse during the Constitutional Convention, spoke up to call for prayers, saying "that God governs in the affairs of men...without his concurring aid we shall succeed in this political building no better than the Builders of Babel."[86] He also said, "If men are so wicked as we now see them *with religion,* what would they be if *without it?"*[87] Jefferson and Madison, noted so much for their struggles for religious liberty and strong skepticism about the undue influence of religious bodies on government, echo these sentiments. In Query XVIII of his *Notes on Virginia* in 1781, Jefferson wrote: "God who gave us life gave us liberty. And can the liberties of a nation be thought secure when we have removed their only firm basis, a conviction in the minds of the people that these liberties are of the Gift of God? That they are not to be violated but with His wrath?"[88] Once, when he was confronted about his religious beliefs, Jefferson said, "'No nation has ever yet existed or been governed without religion. Nor can be.'"[89] In 1785, Madison stated that, "Religion is the basis and Foundation of Government."[90] In 1788 he said, "We have staked the future of all of our political institutions upon the capacity of mankind for self government; upon the capacity of each and all of us to govern ourselves, to control ourselves, to sustain ourselves according to the Ten Commandments of God."[91] Later in his life, in 1825, he wrote, "The belief in a God All Powerful wise and good, is...essential to the moral order of the World and to the happiness of man."[92] In his First Inaugural Address, he asserted, "We have all been encouraged to feel in the guardianship and guidance of that Almighty Being, whose power regulates the destiny of nations."[93]

Some have argued essentially that the respect accorded to religion by the

Founding Fathers was strictly utilitarian, to achieve the morality and order that republican government requires.[94] While the above quotations make clear that they believed it indeed was necessary for this, the evidence indicates strongly that this was not all there was to religion for them. While as Tocqueville says, no one can know for certain what is in the human heart,[95] we make a judgment about their religiosity on the basis of the evidence we have. M.E. Bradford's study of the fifty-five Founders established that "with no more than five exceptions (and perhaps no more than three), they were orthodox members of one of the established Christian communions."[96] M. Stanton Evans writes that "many of the framers were professing Christians—active in church affairs, engaged in prayer, avowing a belief in God and Scripture."[97] Bradford recounts the religious utterances, without reference to political concerns, and religious writings and efforts of many of them.[98] They did not just hold these beliefs privately, but the latter shaped their political thought and efforts. Charles S. Lutz and Donald S. Hyneman's well-known study of the Founders' writings from 1760 to 1805 showed that of 3,154 references they made to other sources, fully 34% were from the Bible. Another 9% were from ancient or classical writers. Thus, fully 43% came from Judeo-Christian or classical sources. Another 18% came from Whig writers, whose views were often closely intertwined with Protestantism. Another 11% came from the English common law, behind which, of course, stood the natural law and Christianity. In spite of the view of many writers that the American Founding was simply a reflection of Locke's political philosophy,[99] it should be noted that of Enlightenment era figures referred to by the Founders (only 18% of the overall total), the most frequently cited was Montesquieu (who was also one of the closest to the natural law and Christian tradition). He was mentioned three times more frequently than Locke.[100] Russell Kirk notes that studies of Americans' reading habits in the second half of the eighteenth century suggest that educated persons "often mentioned Locke on the eve of the Revolution, but seldom read his books at first hand." He says that even Jefferson cited legal thinkers such as Lord James Coke and Henry Home, Lord Kames in his Commonplace Book and public papers more frequently than Locke, and Jefferson denied that the Declaration of Independence was simply copied from Locke's *Second Treatise*. It is not surprising that Kirk observes that, "The Americans would make use of Locke, but they would not worship him."[101]

The Founders' other actions further establish that they were very serious about religion and its importance for republican government. There has been much debate and disagreement over the decades about the meaning of the religious references in the Declaration of Independence. To be sure, the reference to "Nature's God" seems to be deistic, although it was changed from an expression in an earlier draft that sounded more Christian. The statement appealing to the "Supreme Judge of the world" is essentially theistic. What use would it have been to make an active appeal to a God who could not or would not listen? In expressing their "firm reliance on the protection of divine Providence," the signers of the Declaration are clearly theistic: men can only rely on a God who can help them. This phrase, appearing near the end of the Declaration, was added by the Second Continental Congress to Jefferson's draft precisely so, in Kirk's estimation, it would sound more theistic.[102]

The practices of the Second Continental Congress, which included a number of the later Founders, give further evidence of the latter's serious religiosity. On numerous occasions, the Congress called for days of public fasting, humiliation, and thanksgiving throughout the Revolutionary War. The language of their proclamations had a distinctly Christian character. The notion of covenant, so evident in colonial American politico-religious symbolism, came across clearly in them.[103]

There was not a great deal of talk about religion at the Philadelphia Constitutional Convention of 1787, probably because the Founders knew that their concerns were with state and not church—that is, with forging a workable frame of government—and because they viewed any significant governmental involvement with religion as unacceptable. For example, as Kirk states, "no one of importance in America desired to establish a *national* church."[104] There were two noteworthy cases where it did come up, however. One concerned the oath to be taken under the Constitution by all American public officials. Framers Oliver Wolcott and James Iredell argued in favor of the exclusion of a religious test for federal officeholders (a position that the Convention agreed to) because the oath was itself such a test since it was taken before God who was thereby acknowledged to be the source of political authority and One who would be ready to punish perjury. In effect, it was a statement of the God-fearing attitudes of the Founders.[105] The other significant point of the Convention where religion came up was at the time of the impasse between the large and small states when Franklin asked for prayers. Hamilton opposed it and the Convention agreed with him. This is said by some to demonstrate the Framers' secularism. Actually, however, Hamilton said that the reason he was opposing Franklin was because he thought it would give the impression to their countrymen—who knew what they were attempting to do behind the locked Convention doors—that things were going badly.[106] This, by the way, is the same Hamilton who years later had resolved in advance of his fatal duel with Aaron Burr that he would not fire on him because his Christian scruples could not permit it.[107] Like so many things about the Convention and the Constitution, the real or full meaning is not written down or explicitly stated.

The same commitment to religion—in particular, Christianity—among the public men of the Founding Era was seen at the state ratifying conventions. One of the concerns of the Anti-Federalists—missing the very point, as so many do today, that much was unstated or assumed—was that the proposed Constitution was not religious, or Christian, enough. The responses of the Federalists sought to assure them that the Protestant Christian character of the Republic would continue.[108]

The proposal of the First Amendment, with its free exercise and establishment clauses, in the First Congress also in no way altered the prevailing view about the importance or place of religion in the American public sphere. The strong evidence about the meaning of the clauses is that that they sought to preclude the creation of a national established church (but did not affect the authority of states to have established churches), to require that the national government exhibit no sect preference (at least among Christian denominations), and to insure that free exercise of people's beliefs be guaranteed. This is apparent from the Congressional debate.[109] The final language of the Amendment was fashioned by a conference committee whose members, as we have discussed elsewhere, can hardly be said to have promoted the notion of a secular state or in any way tampered with the accepted relationship of religion and politics. The conferees included Founding Fathers William Paterson of New Jersey, who once said, "Religion and morality were...necessary to good government, good order and good laws," and Oliver Ellsworth of Connecticut, who had favored a preamble to the Constitution which would have declared belief in "the one living and true God, creator and supreme Governor of the World."[110]

How much the late colonial period and the Founding Era put into practice and policy the above expressions of the importance of religion for sound political life was seen by the following: publicly-owned lands were made available, both by the states and the Continental Congress, to religions and their affiliated religiously-oriented educational institutions and public funds provided to them;[111] the Continental Congress authorized the Commissioners of Indian Affairs to employ ministers to preach and teach among the Indians;[112] state statutes granting tax exemptions for church property existed and, apparently to aid the cause of religion, states sometimes permitted churches and church-related schools to conduct lotteries to raise building and maintenance funds;[113] both the federal and state governments employed and paid chaplains in their conventions, legislatures, armed forces, and hospitals;[114] laws made blasphemy a serious offense[115] and punished those who labored on Sunday or otherwise disrupted the Sabbath observance;[116] governmental officials frequently proclaimed days of thanksgiving to God, fasting, and prayer;[117] and prayers were also a regular feature in the Continental Congress and in the state legislatures.[118]

By as late as 1775, nine colonies had established churches to one degree or another. By the time of the Constitutional Convention, three were still in place.[119] It is clear that the First Amendment did not compel disestablishment when it is considered that Connecticut's regimen of taxing to support the established Congregational Church continued until 1818, and five New England states had established churches in some sense until different points in the first third of the nineteenth century—with Massachusetts' established church continuing the longest until 1834—without constitutional controversy.[120]

The above has discussed the official recognition of the importance of religion in the Founding Era. It remains to be asked what role it played in the life of the American people generally. Tocqueville, writing in the 1830s, speaks about "the quiet sway of religion" over America,[121] and says that it "is mingled with all the national customs and...feelings which the word fatherland evokes...[so] it has particular power." Specifically, "Christianity has kept a strong hold over the minds of Americans."[122] The Christian influence obviously continued on from early colonial times, and was rejuvenated by the Great Awakening.[123] As historian Donald J. D'Elia writes, "[t]he social way of life" in eighteenth century America was "largely based on the Christian faith...the social and political symbols of the American Founding took their meaning from it." Both the pietists and the early religious liberals among the predominant Calvinist strain of Christianity believed that government should encourage religion and morality.[124] Evangelical Protestantism had gotten a strong hold on much of American culture,[125] and reading of the Bible was widespread (with no other book approaching it in importance).[126] Tocqueville commented that even people on the isolated frontier typically had a Bible.[127] As Kirk says, "it was a biblical Christianity, this American faith, securely rooted in popular conviction."[128] American law upheld the Christian dimension of the common law. While, to be sure, Enlightenment-generated liberal ideas were being incorporated into early American law and the direct role of religious sects in government was receding, the law respected and upheld the country's Christian culture.[129]

Morality, Mores, and Culture in Early America

The early Americans' common Christianity (albeit housed in different sects) meant a common morality. There was no significant difference in moral teachings or divergence from the natural law. As Tocqueville states, this "innumerable multitude of sects...all preach the same morality in the name of God"[130]—and, as we have suggested elsewhere (and will pick up again in coming chapters of this book), except in the area of economics continued to do so until the twentieth century.[131] As Kirk writes, the Americans had "the Ten Commandments at the back of their minds, when not in the forefront" and "[m]ores and morals flowed from religious doctrine."[132] While men in early America, as at all times, fell short in practice, they accepted without much question the moral *standards* of Christianity. The virtues that the Founders emphasized were so important to the sustenance of a democratic republic were a part of this morality.

Largely connected to, and sometimes interchangeable with, morals are mores (i.e., aspects of culture, patterns of behavior). As indicated, mores were an important consideration for the Founding Fathers and the thinking of their era in maintaining a democratic republic. Mores will take a somewhat different coloration, even within the context of a common morality, on the basis of the cultural situation of a people. The culture Americans had inherited had, of course, substantially come from England. Morality was a serious matter in the life of the early republic. Tocqueville mentioned "the great severity of mores which one notices" in the U.S.[133] Nowhere were these morals/mores stricter than in sexual matters,[134] and female modesty was stressed everywhere.[135] Marital fidelity and family stability were central, and Tocqueville emphasized how critical this was for political life: "In Europe almost all the disorders of society are born around the domestic hearth and not far from the nuptial bed. It is there that men...develop a taste for disorder, restlessness of spirit, and instability of desires. Shaken by the tumultuous passions which have often troubled his own house, the European finds it hard to submit to the authority of the state's legislators."[136] Indeed, Marvin Olasky writes in our time that a major advantage the Americans had over the British during the Revolution was that leading figures in the British government and military weakened the spirit of their ranks by sexual and other moral corruption.[137]

Tocqueville was not alone among commentators in the early years of America who made clear that the concern about morality included sexual and conjugal matters. We see exhortations to self-restraint and the avoidance of a mere pleasure orientation from such thinkers as Locke, Montesquieu, and Jefferson. While not developing the connection with political life as sharply as Tocqueville, they are not oblivious to it.[138] They are also not reluctant to repudiate wayward sexual activity, as Locke implicitly does with adultery, incest, and fornication.[139]

There were other mores that, while not so directly preached by Christianity, were often rooted in the Christian and usually the classical virtues as well. The eminent American historian Gordon S. Wood mentions the frugality, industry, temperance, and simplicity of the people.[140] Kirk speaks about: "high courage in danger or adversity"; willingness to make present sacrifices for expected good in the future (which meant, among other things, that hard work would pay off in the end); a "strong inclination toward household independence," but not excluding a kind of sociality ("hospitable reception of most wayfarers and newcomers"); a "[s]hrewd practical intelligence," which helped one to know how to survive in difficult conditions; intellectual curiosity; and respect for the laws.[141] Courage, industry, and the willingness to sacrifice, especially, were considered what Wood calls the manly virtues that were often associated with the struggle to settle early America.[142] Honesty, truth-telling, fair-dealing, promise-keeping, and commercial efficiency also characterized the Americans.[143] The education of youth stressed honesty and obedience.[144]

The desire for household independence underscored the central place of the family in early America, how it was "the center of all rights and obligations." Extended, not just nuclear, families were important and a key element in most people's lives. This somewhat underscored the weakness of other social institutions in early America, such as guilds.[145] As the republic developed, however, it was not long before associational activity became abundant, as Tocqueville makes clear.[146] The sociality that Kirk says accompanied the family relation extended beyond just individuals to a general spirit of cooperativeness and a concern about the community and the general welfare;[147] maybe this stimulated the associational activity which soon followed. One result of this was that people looked out for each other; they saw themselves as having the obligation to be "their brother's keeper." Sometimes, especially in Calvinist-inspired New England, this became too close of a monitoring and interference in others' personal affairs; there was not clear enough of a public-private distinction.[148] The early Americans also did not believe that public virtue, much less enduring popular government, could result from people simply pursuing their own self-interest in the fashion of Adam Smith's invisible hand.[149] It was not necessarily that they did not subscribe to something like Tocqueville's "self-interest properly understood," but they did not believe that they could be attained without the effort to first acquire private virtue and the self-sacrifice mentioned above.

Generally, the thrust toward any kind of outright, self-serving individualism in early America was constrained by the belief in the higher moral order.[150] The hold of Christianity and its morality blunted any slippage into a Hobbesian-type atomism and resultant conflict among men that the individualistic ethos of a frontier land that came to be especially oriented to rights-thinking could have occasioned.[151] Closely related to this was the prevailing conception of liberty, which was seen in a "clearly restrictive and communal" and not "expansive and individualistic" (i.e., self-centered) sense; "it was an opportunity for the community to guide the individual toward self-regulation in the service of God, the public good, and family." The early Americans' conception of liberty stood in opposition to tyranny—hence their opposition to King George III—*and* license.[152] They did not see any intrinsic conflict between individual liberty and the general welfare, so long as the political society acted in accordance with the higher moral law (which means that it upheld the common or corporate good, i.e., the good of the community and of every person in it).[153] In this sense the early American conception of liberty emerged from the background of medieval Europe.

The social concern of early Americans reflected a sense of friendship that existed among their communities, of the sort that Aristotle said was needed for any truly good political order.[154] Indeed, William J. Bennett reminds us that George Washington "indicated that the ideal political life is to be conducted among citizens animated not just by laws or rights but also by a spirit of friendship or comity."[155] Such a spirit no doubt grew out of the myriad personal attachments that characterized the America of this time.[156] While sometimes having a dependency and paternalistic background in the colonial era, these—like the strong stress on the family—also reflected the absence of more formal institutions that would have required a more impersonal, arms-length carrying out of human interactions and affairs.[157] They also illustrated the fact that while there were social hierarchies in early America and it was a deferential society, there were no great inequalities among the people.[158] There was no nobility or hereditary aristocracy.[159] Nor, in this largely middle-class society, was there a serious poverty problem or much lower class economic and social discontent. Unlike Europe, there was a high rate of vertical mobility and a supple class structure, limited concentration of wealth, widespread land ownership, and much social and economic opportunity. Even the franchise, while not universal, was surprisingly broad.[160]

In line with this culture of relative friendship was a strong stress on the social virtue of civility, which, as Bennett puts it, "asks simply that we respect the rights and dignity of our fellow citizens." Part of what this involved was basic good manners, such as politeness. This was a dimension of basic self-restraint, learning to "become mindful of how our actions and words affect others."[161] The learned formalities over time become habitual, like the deeper virtues (e.g., temperance, justice) they reflect. As a basic example, Bennett presents George Washington's "Rules of Civility" in his book.[162] The cultivation of civility, Bennett tells us, was done and expressed by people mostly in their private interactions, but by helping to mold "domestic tranquility"—i.e., peace and harmony among persons—it had a profound effect upon politics and public life generally.[163]

There is little doubt that this stress on civility developed from the tradition of the gentleman that the Americans inherited from the British, even though the former's conception of the gentleman was a public-spirited supporter of republicanism instead of one steeped in the tradition of monarchy and European nobility. As Wood puts it, "the enlightened people of Western society had steadily enlarged the pale of civilization...Always at the center of this advance was the changing idea of the gentleman." The gentleman exhibited good behavior, amiability, high-mindedness, and acted properly in any company.[164]

This civility perhaps made possible the relatively peaceful melding of so many different nationality groups, even early in American history—groups that in Europe had sometimes been in intense conflict with each other. On the other hand, one might be able to view civility as actually being encouraged by this melding. It was a voluntary melding by self-selection—the free choice to come to America and be in a community with these other groups—and soon intermarriage. It was a "new principle of nation-building," different from the conquest and subjection that most of history had seen.[165]

Even though the early American people tried to build a community of friendship and treated each other with respect and civility—and thus related to each other as citizens on basically equal terms—and there was no nobility or significant class cleavage, they—like their leading public men above—possessed a restrained view of equality. They did not believe in egalitarianism; the equality they favored was one that acknowledged natural differences in talent, disposition, and virtue. Unlike its French counterpart, the American Revolution did not seek to destroy the social hierarchies that existed. In line with the Founding Fathers above, the American populace embraced the view that there should be an aristocracy, even if no nobility—a *natural* aristocracy "based on virtue, temperance, independence, and devotion to the commonwealth." For them, equality meant, in part, that the lowest man could climb to the top—if he exhibited these qualities.[166] It was, of course, from this natural aristocracy that our Founding Fathers—the leaders in the cause of American independence, the framers of the Constitution, and the first generation of the republic's political leaders—emerged.

The concern about the public good, the sense of people as part of a corporate whole, the widespread distribution of land and productive goods, and the middle class character of the country give some sense of the outlook about economics and economic morality in early America. There was a multitude of small producers. There were no large-scale corporations and no separation of ownership from operation.[167] The arrangement of economic life, like political and other types of institutions, was decentralized. There was not much industrialization, and its development was progressing at a very slow rate.[168] Most people were farmers of one kind or another, and most of the others were merchants or small-scale producers or manufacturers.[169] The effect of all these conditions was that in economics people tended to be independent, self-directed, and initiative-takers.[170] Even while the early Americans would not accept feudal era-type economic and property restrictions—in which the Church, state, and society each helped regulate wages, prices, quality of workmanship, working conditions, profit, interest, level of wealth, etc.—in the name of greater personal independence, social mobility, and entrepreneurial efforts, they nevertheless continued to be guided by the sense of the social obligation of property use. Private economic activity had to be carried out in a manner consistent with the general welfare. How one used one's property and wealth was a moral question.[171] Numerous laws regulated how one might use his property and put limits on economic freedom in the interest of the public good, including those which governed interest rates and forbade usury, trade restrictions, monopolies, aid to encourage new industries, and debt repayment. A broad concern—in line with the medieval tradition—seemed to be preventing unproductive investment (i.e., that which could redound to the detriment of the public).[172]

William B. Scott writes that Benjamin Franklin's views about property embodied well the view of Americans around the time of the Founding. Like a Jefferson, he strongly emphasized landholding and the ownership of productive goods. Also, similar to the later notion of the universal destination of goods in Catholic social teaching, he believed that individuals had a right to access to the resources necessary to sustain themselves. He supported a rudimentary notion of what in later labor struggles would become a just or at least a fair wage. In a departure from medieval thinking, he endorsed an acquisitive attitude and believed that people should be able to accumulate wealth without clear limits, so long as the opportunity for this was available to everyone. At the same time, ownership was subject to the needs and demands of the broader public.[173] Americans were known for thrift, sobriety, and temperance in their way of life, and there was a constant concern among their clergymen and public spokesmen about their falling prey to luxury.[174]

Bennett speaks about the meaning of justice for the Founding Fathers, and it is likely that this view represented the one in American culture more generally. He says that, while not necessarily departing from the classical and Augustinian understanding of justice as giving each one his due, justice for early America specifically meant protection *both* of people's material property and immaterial property—their safety, liberty, faculties, rights, consciences, and equality as men (even if the practice did not always measure up to their convictions).[175] The reach of justice, then, seemed to encompass both dimensions of man as understood by the twentieth century Catholic philosopher Jacques Maritain: man as individual (i.e., property and political rights) and man as person (the matters relating to his soul).[176] The presence of this dual focus seems further confirmed by the fact, stated above, that men were understood to be part of a community which had to help improve them and whose greater good they had to be ever oriented to.

A final feature to note about early American culture—and American culture mostly in an ongoing way—was the people's great faith in man's possibilities.

This was present in spite of the hard-nosed realism—even in certain instances, pessimism—that their religious background instilled in them.[177]

Possible Weaknesses in the Founding Vision

Although the focus of this book is not an evaluation of the American Founding itself, by considering what possible weaknesses may have been present in our Founders' vision or conception of a democratic republic—or, of political life more generally—we may be able to better understand the developments that have historically occurred to transform its character. We may also be able to consider later whether and to what extent those possible weaknesses played a role in its ultimate transformation.

The starting point for this examination is our previous writing on the topic of the elements of a good political order and on its reverse, the factors that have caused the decline of political orders. By noting these and making some reflection about whether they seem to be present or absent in our Founding principles above, we might be able to get a sense about deficiencies that may be at least partly the sources of later problems and harbingers of transformation. This previous research sought first to determine the elements necessary to sustain a good political order as discerned from the writings of the great political thinkers of ancient, medieval, and early modern times—when this topic was very much the concern of political philosophy and, especially in ancient (classical) thought, there was often reflection about what the best political order would be like—and from sound, realist philosophic speculation generally; second, it surveyed the writings of significant thinkers in Western history who addressed the question of what factors have caused the decline of political orders.

On the elements of a good political order, we studied the discussion of this by the following great thinkers: Plato, Aristotle, Marcus Tullius Cicero, St. Augustine of Hippo, St. Thomas Aquinas, Richard Hooker, Baron de Montesquieu, Edmund Burke, and Alexis de Tocqueville (Montesquieu and Tocqueville, of course, have been discussed in reference to the principles of the American Founding above). While these thinkers mention different elements as necessary to preserve a good political order, a number of elements appear commonly among them. The most frequently mentioned are the following of the natural law or the prevalence of virtue; the existence of the rule of law and the presence of good and just laws; the maintenance of a condition of moderation or prudence in the conduct of public affairs, or the presence of a mixed regime (which by its very nature leans to moderation); the rejection of egalitarianism, or the leveling of men or outright ignoring of differences among them; the seeking of the common good; the prevalence of good statesmanship or good legislators; the adherence of people to religion; and a properly educated citizenry. A minority of these thinkers mentioned also: the need to have private property; the need for a natural aristocracy or in some sense rule by the wise; the need for the people to consent or agree to their rulers; and the reliance on tradition or experience or custom. Only a couple mentioned specifically the need for the family to be strong, but it is probably implicit in the thinking of a number of the others (especially the thinkers from the Christian era).[178]

Sound philosophy is reasoning things out, coming to conclusions step-by-step on the basis of evidence after starting out by accepting certain basic principles of all knowledge (e.g. the principle of contradiction) that it would be absurd to reject. Philosophy is thus a science and proceeds systematically by a kind of scientific method to point to truths about reality and morality—and politics, as the classics pointed out, is tied up closely with morality. In fact, they saw it as indispensable for the shaping of the human soul. In our previous writing, we explained how the following were the principles that can be reasoned out philosophically as needed for the maintenance of a good political order: religion, the natural law, the common good, the principle of subsidiarity,[179] the principles of solidarity and social charity (which are closely related to the civic friendship mentioned above), the family, a balanced understanding of the state's role so that it is neither expansive nor minimalistic, and a condition of justice in human affairs.[180]

Next, in previous writing, we examined numerous thinkers from the ancient, modern, and contemporary (i.e., post-1900) eras who reflected in a significant way about the decline and fall of political orders: Plato, Aristotle, Cicero, St. Augustine of Hippo, St. Thomas Aquinas, Giambattista Vico, Edward Gibbon, Orestes Brownson, Brooks Adams, Oswald Spengler, Hilaire Belloc, Arnold Toynbee, Christopher Dawson, Malcolm Muggeridge, C.E.M. Joad, C. Northcote Parkinson, Carroll Quigley, and Russell Kirk. Listing here the factors these thinkers set forth as causing the decline of nations and civilizations (which does not mean just their outright collapse, but also the transformation of the character of the political order or its change into another type of political order), in the order of those receiving the most mention down to those receiving the fewest (the fewest listed were mentioned at least by two of these thinkers), perhaps provides us with a framework for consideration of the question of the transformation or decline of the American democratic republic. These factors are: turning away from religion, or at least from a people's traditional religious belief (which is the most mentioned factor); materialism or the excessive pursuit of luxury or runaway prosperity; excessive orientation to private pleasure or lack of control of the desires or passions; social conflict, turmoil, or revolution; the prevalence of a relativistic moral or ethical outlook; overcentralization or excessive bureaucratization or excessive emphasis on bigness; the dissolution of the middle class or serious economic disorders (the latter can easily relate to the former); the loss of will or the growth of a sense of purposelessness or general societal drift; the breakdown of the family; excessive urbanization or the related rise of mass culture; the prevalence of "liberalism" (which is defined by different thinkers to mean an anti-traditional viewpoint and an excessively present-oriented state of mind overrun by a moralistic sentimentality instead of reason and a false sense of benevolence, which also is intolerant of disagreement); militarism (i.e., a glorification of a military spirit and ideals); the descent of politics into essentially a struggle for power; the breakdown or absence of the rule of law; the breakdown or neglect of the common good; and the corruption of sound philosophy.[181]

It is striking how well the principles and conditions of the American Founding Era measured up to the above principles of a good political order (as can readily be noticed, the causes of decline are mostly the failure to uphold those principles). Religion, virtue, and morality were stressed, as noted above; the natural law was appealed to in the Declaration of Independence and in rhetoric of the American Revolution.[182] Both American political thinking and culture viewed the pursuit of justice as important, and civility and a spirit of friendship were present. As stated, America was a middle class country almost from the start, and was in some sense a mixed government. Promoting the common good was an objective. While equality was stressed, egalitarianism was not embraced. The need for a natural aristocracy was emphasized. Education to shape good citizenship was understood as necessary. There was a strong commitment to the rule of law, and civil laws had to conform to natural law (that is, be "good" laws)—indeed, this was a major point of the American Revolution. Private property was strongly upheld. Prosperity was sought, but temperance and sobriety prevailed. American federalism was an expression of the principle of subsidiarity, and there was not an overly strong central government. Even the colonial governments permitted their local communities much autonomy.[183] Government and other institutions were simple, on a small scale, and played a limited role in the lives of citizens.[184] The stress on civilian control of the military and bias against even standing armies insured against any kind of militarism that some writers about decline point to as a cause. The American will was certainly strong, as witnessed by the staunch effort—carried out by political entities that previously had not acted in a united fashion—made against the British, and the uncompromising insistence on the rights and liberties of Americans.

With all of these positive features, what can be said about possible deficiencies of America's parchment republic? When we consider the reflections of the thinkers above and the conclusions of realist philosophy, some points suggest themselves.

One of the most significant areas is what might be called the "privatization" of the means of creating or sustaining several of the important principles and conditions above (i.e., rendering the means informal or non-official). This is seen most vividly in the matter of natural law. Since the Founding Era probably realized that people learn their moral beliefs and practices from religion, and since the conduct of religion was outside of the reach of government, it saw natural law as something to be concerned with primarily in that realm. It clearly understood that natural law must underlie government, as we have seen, but essentially relied on the moral precepts that Christianity had traditionally taught. As a result, the Founders and their learned contemporaries engaged in no serious, substantial philosophical reflection about natural law. In spite of what was said about many of them possibly having had a Scholastic education, they probably were not sufficiently enough formed philosophically so as to know all the principles of social ethics, or how these principles should apply to the

American socio-political situation. They perhaps undersold the likelihood of commitment to certain moral principles weakening over time under the pressures of political or cultural circumstances or changing religious or intellectual movements. Indeed, they perhaps gave insufficient attention to the possibility that the hold of religion over people generally in time might weaken—not surprising in light of how the above shows the central place they saw for religion—with the ensuing weakening of traditional morality.[185]

The lack of sufficient philosophical reflection—along with such other putative problems as too much concern with individual rights, resolving public questions through a balancing of factions, and too heavy of an emphasis on the mere working of the institutional activities of government (although by no means the excessive and almost exclusive stress on these that is found in much of contemporary political science)—perhaps resulted in an incomplete public philosophy for America. Some have referred to the problem of "public purposelessness" in America.[186] In early America, individual men knew what their final end was (i.e., Christianity taught that it is to be united with God), but perhaps they did not clearly see what the role of the political society is in helping them to achieve this.[187] We can appreciate this when we consider that, in spite of their stressing its importance, we do not see in the Founding Fathers' writing a significant elaboration on or explanation of the notion of the common good (which is, at bottom line, an ethical notion and connected with man's final end). We, again, perhaps discern an inadequate philosophical understanding and formation. This may have allowed too much of an individualistic emphasis to affect the Founding.

This seeming philosophical deficiency is probably partly due to the fact that from its earliest times America historically has been a nation of practical people—men of affairs—not philosophers. Perhaps it also betrays the influence of the Calvinist version of Christianity which was so strong in early America—whose fideism made it suspicious of and mostly uninterested in philosophical reflection—and of the Enlightenment, which like Calvinism downplayed the ability of reason to know moral truth and whose extolling of individualism emasculated such traditional notions as common good. Further, the Protestant notion of all religious truth coming from Scripture discouraged the consulting of anything but the Bible—e.g., classical philosophical texts—about matters dealing with or at least touching on the transcendent. Clearly, the Founding Fathers were not reluctant about philosophical reflection or unwilling to consult the classics, nor were they thoroughgoing imbibers of Enlightenment thought (although influenced by it to some degree).[188] Still, these factors might explain their failure to go *deeper* into certain philosophical and ethical principles.

Perhaps the Enlightenment influence that was present to at least some degree was also seen in the way that natural law in the Founding Era comes to be talked about so much in political discourse in terms of natural rights (even while, of course, Christian morality—i.e., the natural law—was endorsed by the Founders and reigned supreme in the conduct of men's lives). Almost certainly we see here the effects of the Enlightenment's individualism. It seems as if in official public discourse there is a lessened tendency to speak about natural law as what it most fundamentally is: a set of moral obligations. Indeed, this individualism was probably at least somewhat responsible for the privatization mentioned above (i.e., because of government's heavy concern with securing natural rights it was viewed as having a very limited formal role in the moral formation of men).

The Protestant Reformation, along with (again) the Protestant notion of individual interpretation of Scripture, insured the next aspect of privatization as related to natural law. That is, the decision about how to discern some of the more difficult points of natural law and how to apply them to current types of situations or circumstances—even as they concerned points of social morality and morally-charged social issues—was left essentially to private judgment. Even if ardent Protestants believed that a divinely-inspired source external to themselves—the Bible—was the source of morality, some points were not addressed by it, or not clearly addressed, or how to apply them was not apparent. It is a basic point of Catholic teaching that the Church's magisterium—the Pope and the bishops in union with him—are the divinely-appointed interpreters/arbiters of the natural law and how to apply it (i.e., given the authority to do so by Jesus Christ Himself). Protestantism, of course, rejected this. It did so apparently without thinking that it would make any difference. The perspective seen in the Founding Era above that Christian morality would simply be permanently in place was apparently firmly believed throughout the early centuries of Protestantism. Without realizing it, early America perhaps was living off the accumulated moral capital of the Catholic Middle Ages, maintaining a commitment to natural law principles surprisingly well—in both private and public life—until the twentieth century in all areas except, after awhile (as will be discussed later in this book), economics. Actually, the multiplication of sects almost inevitably would lead to different moral teachings. Shades of difference in beliefs about ultimate things would certainly tend to result, at some point, in differences about the teaching concerning conduct and way of living needed to reach the ultimate. While empirical proof of causation may be difficult, one can certainly wonder if the absence of an authoritative moral interpreter did not finally catch up with America—that if the Church had been looked to for that purpose the erosion of traditional moral principles might have been attenuated. If this role of the Church had been widely acknowledged in America, it might have provided a "backstop" to check the erosion of sound morality. There was no provision for this—for even an informal consideration of the magisterium's teachings—in the Protestant-generated American political order. The result over time was both the elevation—obviously this happened not just because of the original Protestant idea, but also because of other influences—of the law of the state as the determiner of social morality and of the private conscience (without any expectation of or certain provision for its proper formation) as its judge and, in a sense, its ultimate arbiter. Positive law became the main formative force, but the stress given to individual conscientious objection both led to legal reform efforts and the tradition of civil disobedience. Reacting to the latter, the American Catholic political philosopher Orestes A. Brownson argued that the Protestant idea of individual conscience as the basic arbiter of social morality and the justice of positive laws, without reference to the authority of the Church, leads to chaos.[189]

It could further be said that once the hold of natural law weakened and secularization advanced, the very fact of American religious pluralism—implicitly accepted as the model for political pluralism in Federalist 10, since it was viewed as promoting peace after the Age of Religious Wars—stimulated positivism. If a common morality was no longer accepted, and different sects now had different moral positions and could no longer speak with one moral voice—with the consequence that religion could play less of a role in insuring social order—then the law of the state had to play a more central role. It should be added that the state would have to become more powerful to enforce its law.

Actually, in spite of the embracing of this Protestant idea of the primacy of individual judgment, fairly quickly after the formation of the Republic—at least as soon as the U.S. Supreme Court case of *Calder v. Bull* (1798)[190]—it became apparent that there would have to be, in effect, some authoritative interpreter/arbiter of the natural law (even if, over time, people preferred not to say that is what was happening or even that the natural law actually exists). By and large, the Supreme Court came to do this. This was, however, in fact not a true departure from the Protestant principle because the Court is a strictly human institution without any claim to a divine mandate. What happened was that instead of all people having the power of making private judgments—at least, those judgments that would be authoritative and of social consequence for the U.S.—it was a small, elite group. Apart even from the enhanced state power that would be necessary to maintain order as the interior restraint of religion eroded, the power of the state would certainly increase when one of its institutions became the *de facto* arbiter of the natural law!

The insufficient philosophical reflection, avoidance of publicly embracing theological precepts, and Enlightenment-inspired individualism of our Founding Era—to the extent that they existed—may have weakened America in another way. The Declaration of Independence mentions the pursuit of happiness as one of the central natural rights of men to be secured by government. Sound, serious philosophical reflection, especially when guided by Revelation, makes clear what true human happiness is: it pertains to higher things, and ultimately to man being united to God and thereby achieving his eternal happiness. What we suggest here is that although this was understood by a religious population at the Founding, the fact that it was perhaps not uppermost in the minds of our Founders or at least not brought enough into the Founding project may have opened the door to problems later on.

The Protestant foundations of the U.S. (and specifically their strong Calvinist component) in the later era of secularization would give rise to a different kind of morality and, more politically significant, a public moralism that would bring the threat of governmental despotism over the everyday things of life that it was noted Tocqueville feared.[191] Again, the absence of a truly authoritative moral arbiter—with the divine protection enjoyed by the Church's magisterium—has perhaps made such moralism more likely, since there is nothing to restrain both substantive moral errors and excessive or immoderate moral claims.

As there was no formal means to interpret the natural law in our parchment Republic, there was none to insure that the natural aristocracy they thought crucial would be brought forth. It has sometimes been said that the Founding Fathers realized that their political generation was an outstanding one and tried to insure that by fashioning a solid institutional framework the democratic republic they forged would survive lesser men in the future. Nevertheless, as we have seen, it is clear that they believed that capable and virtuous leaders were always needed. However, in another example of privatization, they seemed to believe—or hope—that these leaders would be spawned by the broader American culture. As they apparently believed that the extant moral framework would continue, they perhaps thought that the related cultural one would too—thereby insuring that this function would be successfully performed.

Not only was it a problem that there was no formal way to bring forth a natural aristocracy, but there was no a formal mechanism in the new frame of government for shaping virtue in the citizenry overall. As we have seen, the Founders certainly believed virtue important—but thought that it would and should be done "privately" by the churches, family upbringing, community efforts, and to some extent the laws on the state level. To be sure, this perspective is valid in light of both the principle of subsidiarity in social ethics and the simple reality of how such a thing is best done. Indeed, the argument has even been made that "[f]ree institutions"—as in America—"go a long way to form the virtuous citizen."[192] It is also valid in light of the concern about individual liberty and the realization that government cannot impose virtue. This may all be so, but it probably presumes a strong culture behind the institutions and sees the inculcation of virtue as almost a side effect. The latter may not be enough, and when the nongovernmental forces above are not working effectively it almost certainly will not be enough. Moreover, even in regimes that are genuinely serious about liberty law always plays a role, in some sense, in shaping virtue (i.e., among other purposes, it seeks to redirect behavior in a manner that is deemed socially good and desirable)—even if it is understood that the state is not the primary means for doing this. The point is that removing the new national government from the shaping of virtue, and downplaying the role of government in it generally—indeed, effectively diminishing virtue as an avowed public or political concern—was perhaps a problem with the new republic.[193]

Related to the question of natural law is popular sovereignty (which we said is essentially governmental decisionmakers embodying the will of their people and executing it). We saw above how popular sovereignty was a central— perhaps *the* most central—theme of the Founding. On one hand, this seems completely appropriate and utterly uncontroversial. What is a democratic regime if not one that embodies the notion of popular sovereignty? At the same time, we saw above that America was not simply majoritarian (i.e., not simply a democracy). Regarding the nature of American constitutionalism, Corwin states the following: "The attribution of supremacy to the Constitution on the ground solely of its rootage in popular will represents…a comparatively late outgrowth of American constitutional theory. Earlier supremacy accorded to constitutions was ascribed...to their embodiment of an essential and unchanging justice."[194] So, the Founding Fathers did not simply embrace popular sovereignty as their unchallenged ruling principle; men were understood always to be subject to the limitations of natural law. Still, perhaps too much stress was put on popular sovereignty, instead of on the upholding of the truth irrespective of popular sentiments (or at least within the obvious limits of prudence, as Aristotle or Aquinas would have understood it) with the effect being a decline in the hold of natural law over time.

It is possible that this excessive stress on popular sovereignty in the Founders' thinking reflected the Enlightenment's emphasis on man as the center of things; at least this was one of the ways this general perspective may have influenced them—even if they did not embrace it wholesale. God as the source of political authority was downplayed; it was seen as being grounded completely in human consent. Indeed, Brownson made this point emphatically. He believed that the phrase, "Governments derive their just powers from the assent of the governed," in the Declaration of Independence was a telltale indication of this.[195]

It was mentioned that, while early Americans were associational, there was a lack of more formalized social institutions at that time of the Founding— which almost certainly reflected the fact that this was a new nation carved out of the wilderness. As noted, this was to soon change. That the Founders' political thought is silent about the role of intermediary institutions or associations probably follows from their absence. Still, their knowledge of European history and the European situation means that they would have been familiar with guilds and the like, and one wonders if this silence in their writing and in the Constitution was the result of both insufficient philosophical reflection (i.e., on social ethics) and the undue influence of Enlightenment individualism.

At the core of any discussion of intermediary institutions is the only natural and specifically necessary one—the family.[196] As noted, the Founding Era had strong respect for family ties and conjugal morality, but the family does not figure sufficiently—and not directly, at all—into the political thought of the Founding Fathers. They perhaps failed to see clearly enough its centrality for a political order. Again, their (likely) insufficient formation in social ethics rendered them perhaps unable to appreciate *sufficiently* the family's foundational role for political life. Perhaps they just took the family's role for granted and so did not believe it necessary to mention[197] (as stated above, many things were simply assumed by them). Still, traditional ethical analysis and classical political philosophy—consider the discussions in Plato's *Republic* and Aristotle's *Politics*[198]—both explicitly recognize the family as having a crucial importance for politics and all social life.

Federalist 10 embraces the notion of having numerous factions so they can effectively balance themselves off, averting the possibility of any one of them becoming too powerful and endangering liberty. There is much truth to this, and it suggests the value of a pluralistic political society in the best sense of the word. Still—tied in with our suggestion that the Founders had an insufficiently developed notion of the common good—their strong stress on this may betray too minimal of a notion of what was needed for good government. Just as the notions of deterrence and balance of power among nations can help to secure international peace, they are minimal and probably by themselves cannot be successful for the long run.[199] To secure true, abiding international peace requires justice among nations. So, true good government—even perhaps a truly peaceful domestic political order—requires more than just a "balance of power" among factions; it requires a sound conception of the common good in which both justice and social charity prevail. We have shown that justice was indeed a concern of the Founders and that both justice and civility and friendship—tied in with social charity, as stated above—were etched into their culture. Perhaps the lack of an avowed emphasis on justice in the political and constitutional theory present in the Founding, however, was a shortcoming, and helped spawn the sense of public purposelessness mentioned above.

Perhaps the latter signals another possible deficiency in Founding thought: despite the fact that, as noted, Americans were communal, there is too little discussion of the importance of community and our constitutional framework does little to promote it or insure its vitality. This, again, may reflect the effects of Enlightenment individualism or, more likely, was something that was just taken as a given by the Founders. It may also reflect the fact, as Fr. John Courtney Murray, S.J. thought, that the religious pluralism above—even more as it advanced to a kind of moral pluralism, and aggravated by the aforementioned philosophical deficiency—meant disagreement about ultimate human questions, which in turn made deep-seated consensus and community very difficult.[200] Regardless, we wonder if the lack of formal attention to community in the political reflection of the Founding Era, as with other points above, did not leave America susceptible to an intensified individualism over time.

While we do not notice in the Founding Fathers' statements any mention about the value of good statesmanship, *The Federalist* suggests that they believed it important. Federalist 10 implicitly recognizes the value of statesmanship when it laments that in dealing with the problem of faction, "enlightened statesmen will not always be at the helm."[201] The value of statesmanship is further implied in Federalist 10's discussion of representatives. It says that when citizens can vote freely, they will be more likely to select "men who possess the most attractive merit and the most diffusive and established characters."[202] It also speaks of the important role of representatives in a republic once they are selected: "the public views" will be "refine[d] and enlarge[d]" because they will "pass…through the medium of a chosen body of citizens, whose wisdom may best discern the true interest of their country, and whose patriotism and love of justice will be least likely to sacrifice it to temporary or partial considerations."[203] Still, the very paucity of the Founders' direct discussion of statesmanship and their obvious stress on institutional factors and the above balance of power among factions and interests to restrain excesses, protect liberty, and avert tyranny, shows that the Founders downplayed its role. Maybe this reflected their overriding concern about protecting liberty and the fact that this typically involves a negative conception of government (i.e., stop it from doing certain things, instead of insuring that it actively do certain other things for the good of the community). Statesmanship, on the other hand, implies essentially a positive conception of government's role. That is, the great statesman has a sound moral vision and, with much prudence, tries to guide his political order, however tentatively, toward it. He tries, with a humble instead of a crusading attitude, to nudge his political order toward the moral ideal, but realizes that it will never be attained fully.[204] So statesmanship involves an understanding of the common good, which is most fundamentally a philosophical notion that we have noted our Founding Fathers may have lacked a clear, deep understanding of. Furthermore, while institutional restraints are crucial and to be sure take on a "life of their own" in making government and its accoutrements work as they should, ultimately government functions only as well as the people manning it. Thus, good statesmanship—as the above thinkers held—is a vital condition for truly good government, and the Founders' de-emphasis of it may have paved the way to future difficulties.

The Founders' confidence in the "new political science," featuring such notions as representation and the extended republic, probably reflected the influence of the Enlightenment. Men could now derive from reason and theorizing about politics new approaches that were more reliable than such old ones as statesmanship—while the "old" approaches were not dismissed, the new ones played the more prominent role.

The Founders' strong emphasis on institutional or structural factors seemingly laid the groundwork for another problematical development that is suggested by what is said above. The smaller scale governmental and other institutions, the greater willingness to operate informally, and the carrying out of even public tasks through personal contact gave way increasingly to an arms-length, impersonal, less flexible, and eventually bureaucratic regimen. Perhaps at the root of this was simply the very constitutional order built on institutional norms that they established.

The Founders' desire to check the dangers of faction was apparently behind their desire to have a large commercial republic. Federalist 10 says that there are many reasons for faction, but historically "the most common and durable source...has been the various and unequal distribution of property."[205] They reasoned, it seems, that if property—economics—is the main culprit, then economics must be the main solution. The conflict between the rich and poor—the "haves" and "have-nots"—had been the kiss of death for republics—which had mostly been on a small scale—in the past. In a large commercial republic, as Martin Diamond puts it, "the hitherto fatal class struggle is replaced by a safe, even salutary struggle among different kinds of propertied interests....a man will regard it as more important...to further the immediate advantage of his specialized trade...than to advance the general cause of the poor or the rich." The result would be that larger, class-type economic interests would be "fragmented into sundry narrow, more limited interests, each seeking immediate advantage." The justification for this, from the standpoint of preserving republican government, was that it would render unlikely the emergence of a majority faction that would oppress the rest of the citizens and thwart the common good in order to advance itself. In the context of a federal system, it would be especially unlikely that a nationwide majority faction would emerge.[206] Thus, the Founders essentially believed that if men would be diverted into commercial pursuits it would be conducive to the preservation of free government in this geographically large and federated nation. This notion presumed a regimen of equal opportunity to pursue commercial interests,[207] in the manner of Franklin's thinking above. The commercial republic's notion of the common good being protected by individuals pursuing their own economic interest rings of Adam Smith's invisible hand—and thus bears the influence of the Enlightenment. Diamond says that Madison shared Smith's understanding of the connection between "a very large area of trade and the possibility of division of labor," which forms the basis for the protective "multiplicity of faction."[208]

One wonders if the Founders' strong advocacy of the notion of the commercial republic did not open the door, as with other things mentioned, to an increasing individualism as time went on. It effectively liberated the passion of acquisitiveness (as associated with Franklin above). As a moderate desire this was acceptable enough and even helped men to develop certain virtues,[209] but may ultimately have led to the destructive passions of greed and avarice—which, as we shall consider in this book, in turn may have later on led to a laissez faire social condition which still later spawned a reaction of tighter government control and regulation.[210]

The commercial republic notion may also have signaled the transformation of economics from a moral to a utilitarian matter in the American mind. It may have weakened the late colonial era beliefs above of the social obligations accompanying property and the need to carry on economic activity in conformity with the general welfare that had considerable implications both for American economics and politics later on.

As far as early American culture was concerned, it was mentioned that people's conception of themselves as "their brother's keeper" led sometimes to a too-close monitoring of their fellow citizens.[211] One wonders if this attitude did not pave the way, in secular times later, for an unwarranted or excessive intrusion of the state into people's personal and family affairs.

Finally, we suggest possible deficiencies in two specific institutional areas. One is the understanding of federalism. As stated above, the Founding Fathers viewed the new national government as one of distinctly limited powers, and this is essentially what strong defenders of federalism in our own day insist upon. Precisely what the Founders meant by this and the point about the national government being concerned only about general matters, however, was not made—and probably *could not have been made*—completely clear.[212] As soon as the Constitution was put into effect there was a debate between "strict" and "loose" or "liberal construction" positions.[213] The former "reads the grants [of powers to the national government] literally and attempts to adhere to the letter of the express words of the document"; the latter "reads the grants in broader terms of ends desired, which allows a great latitude of implied powers."[214] The Founders believed that the new national government "was not to deal with the vast bulk of political matters,"[215] but also that its "governing powers" would have to be "broad" in order "to achieve the blessings of union."[216] According to Diamond, Fisk, and Garfinkel, "the country has never actually been governed under the strict constructionist view."[217] Still, as we go on to say in this book, problems have developed in some periods of American history because there has been an insufficiently flexible understanding of federalism, that did not acknowledge enough national power, and at other times—especially starting in the second half of the twentieth century—there has been a sharp imbalance in the opposite direction so that centralization has advanced rapidly and the limitations of federalism ignored. While forging the proper balance in practice between federal and state power is not without difficulty, one wonders if maintaining it would have been consistently easier and the historic clashes between the two sides in the loose versus strict constructionist debate narrowed if there had been a better sense of the principle of subsidiarity. It would have perhaps provided a better understanding from the beginning of both what areas government would have to become involved in and whether they could be addressed well or justly at the state or local level without federal government involvement. Since subsidiarity avers that matters should be dealt with at the lower level unless there is a clear need to do so at more distant levels, using it as a guideline would have provided a greater flexibility and reasonableness without violating the strong fundamental bias—on most matters—toward more localized action. As above, this deficiency may have been due to the Founders' insufficient philosophical reflection. Again, they may not have been schooled enough in social ethics or understood how such a principle applied in their situation.[218]

Numerous people in our time have commented about the second institutional deficiency: that the Founding Fathers did not have a good sense about how powerful the independent, co-equal judicial branch—and judiciaries across the country, in general—could become (as seems clear in Federalist 78).[219] They certainly could not foresee how they would become major shapers of public policy under the color of constitutional interpretation. It is hard to fault the Founders for this, however, since at that time there had been little experience with judiciaries playing a political role or being leading governmental institutions. In a sense, though, it might have been foreseeable from what was said above about the Supreme Court becoming the American magisterium. If the Court, in effect, would be looked to as the interpreter of the natural law—since the Church's magisterium was not accepted to do this—should it be surprising that it and inferior judicial bodies that are called upon to play the same role but less definitively, would become so powerful?

This chapter has set out the principles and practices that America's Founding Fathers and their era believed necessary to sustain a democratic republic, explained the importance of religion at the time of the Founding, and identified the important aspects of American culture in the Founding Era—all with the aim of providing the elements that will be used for the evaluation of whether the United States has been transformed from the democratic republic that was established by the Constitution. It has also identified possible areas of weakness in the Founding conception, as determined in large part by significant reflections about the elements of a good political order and the conditions that have resulted in the decline of political orders. As we progress through the various periods of American history in the coming chapters and find indications of transformation we shall look back on these areas and consider if they may not have influenced it.

Notes

1. James Madison, Federalist 10, in Alexander Hamilton, James Madison, and John Jay, *The Federalist* (N.Y.: Modern Library, n.d.), 58.

2. Martin Diamond, Winston Mills Fisk, and Herbert Garfinkel, *The Democratic Republic: An Introduction to American National Government* (2nd edn.; Chicago: Rand McNally, 1970), 89-91.

3. Ibid., 11.

4. Ibid., 10.

5. George Dargo, *Roots of the Republic: A New Perspective on Early American Constitutionalism* (N.Y.: Praeger, 1974), 52.

6. See James Madison, Federalists 48 and 49; Alexander Hamilton, Federalist 71, 73, and 78, in *The Federalist*.

7. Constitution of Virginia—1776. Source: Ben Perley Poore, compiler, *The Federal and State Constitutions, Colonial Charters, and Other Organic Laws of the United States* (second edn.; Washington, D.C.: U.S. Government Printing Office, 1878), II, 1910-1920 and I, 957.

8. Madison, Federalist 47, in ibid., 313.

9. Alexander Hamilton, "Speech on the Senate of the United States," in *The Works of Alexander Hamilton* (ed. John C. Hamilton; N.Y.: Charles S. Francis, 1850), II, 444.

10. See Russell Kirk, *The Roots of American Order* (Malibu, Calif.: Pepperdine U. Press, 1974), 65.

11. Dargo, 52.

12. Hamilton, "Speech on Compromises," in J.C. Hamilton, II, 44; remarks in the New York ratification convention, June 21, 1788, in Jonathan Eliot, ed. *The Debates in the Several State Conventions on the Adoption of the Federal Constitution* (Philadelphia: J.B. Lippincott, 1901), II, 257, 258.

13. Alexis de Tocqueville, *Democracy in America* (ed. J.P. Mayer; Garden City, N.Y.: Doubleday [Anchor Books], 1969), I, i, 170.

14. See Madison, Federalist 10, 61-62; Hamilton or Madison, Federalist 51, 340-341; Tocqueville, I, i, 162-163. It should be pointed out that in asserting that a large, heavily populated political entity was more likely to sustain republican government than a small one, the Founding Fathers were going against the thinking of Montesquieu and the tradition of political thought before them (see Baron de Montesquieu, *The Spirit of the Laws* [tr. Thomas Nugent; N.Y.: Hafner, 1949], I, viii, 120). This perspective, along with such principles and practices as the notion of representation, separation of powers, and checks and balances, was part of their new political science that they believed advances in political understanding had made possible.

15. Madison, Federalist 14, in *The Federalist*, 82.

16. Tocqueville, II, iv, 693.

17. Ibid., I, ii, 279.

18. Ibid., II, iv, 693-694.

19. See ibid., II, iii, 671-674, 690-695.

20. John Locke, *Second Treatise*, in *Two Treatises of Government* (ed. Peter Laslett; rev. edn.; N.Y.: Cambridge University Press, 1960), xi, 138, 19-23, 407.

21. Locke makes an exception for what he calls the prerogative power, in which a political executive at his discretion, when the public good demands it, can act without sanction of the law and even against its provisions. The prerogative power is necessary because sometimes the laws may be too inflexible to address serious or exigent needs, or simply make no provision for doing so (see ibid., xiv, 160, 1-14, 422).

22. Aristotle, *Politics*, IV, iv, 1292a; IV, vi, 1293a. The liberal learning of our Founding Fathers is briefly discussed in Peter V. Sampo, "Educating the Man and the Citizen in Higher Education," in Stephen M. Krason, ed., *The Recovery of American Education: Reclaiming a Vision* (Lanham, Md.: University Press of America, 1991), 101-110.

23. Discussed in George H. Sabine, *A History of Political Theory* (N.Y.: Henry Holt, 1937), 95.

24. Locke, xi, 5-10, 409. Emphasis is in the book.

25. Montesquieu, I, xi, 150. We talk about the meaning of "ordered liberty" in the text below.

26. See, e.g., Kirk, *The Roots of American Order*, 281, 315-316 (on Harrington); Bernard Bailyn, *The Ideological Origins of the American Revolution* (Cambridge, Mass.: Harvard University Press [Belknap Press], 1967), 34-35, 45 (on Harrington and Milton).

27. John Milton, *A Defence of the People of England*, in *Political Writings* (ed. Martin Dzelzaninis; Cambridge, Eng.: Cambridge University Press, 1991), 166-167; Sabine, 502-503.

28. John Adams, *Defence of the Constitutions of the United States of America*, in *The Works of John Adams* (Boston: Little & Brown, 1851), IV, 295.

29. Thomas Jefferson, First Inaugural Address, in Saul K. Padover, ed., *The Complete Jefferson* (N.Y.: Duell, Sloan and Pearce, 1943), 384.

30. On the civil law embodying natural law, see: Adams, *Defence*, in *Works*, IV, 293-295; Virginia Bill of Rights of 1776, Massachusetts Constitution of 1780 (incorporating natural rights notions), in Poore, II, 1908, 957; George Washington, *Farewell Address* (N.Y.: General Society, Sons of the Revolution, 1963, 1982), 24 (stating that morality—i.e., transcendent moral principles—is an "indispensable support" for good political life). Consider also the great stress on natural law in Blackstone (see Krason, *Preserving a Good Political Order and a Democratic Republic: Reflections from Philosophy, Great Thinkers, Popes, and America's Founding Era* [Lewiston, N.Y.: Edwin Mellen Press, 1998], 128-129), who was a significant influence on the American patriots and an even more overwhelming one on the early American legal profession (the latter is mentioned in Kirk, *The Roots of American Order*, 192, 369, 373-374).

31. Washington, 16; Adams, VI, 208.

32. Edward S. Corwin, *The President: Office and Powers 1797-1957* (4th rev. edn.; N.Y.: New York University Press, 1957), 14-15.

33. Tocqueville, I, ii, 200-201.

34. Kirk, *The Roots of American Order*, 94.

35. Diamond, Fisk, and Garfinkel, 363-366.

36. Hamilton or Madison, Federalist 63, in *The Federalist*, 410.

37. Bernard Bailyn, *The Origins of American Politics* (N.Y.: Alfred A. Knopf, 1968), 79.

38. Madison, Federalist 10, 57.

39. See Bailyn, *Origins of American Politics*, 125-127.

40. See Donald V. Weatherman, "Endangered Guardian: America's Two Party System and Progressive Reform," lecture at the Heritage Foundation, Washington, D.C., May 1, 1988, published as Heritage Lecture #156; available from http://www.heritage.org/Research/GovernmentReform/HL156.cfm; Internet; accessed Aug. 14, 2008.

41. See Washington, 18; Jeffferson, First Inaugural Address, in Padover, 386; Hamilton, Federalists 23, 25, and 70, 141-146, 153-158, 454-463.

42. See, e.g., Diamond, Fisk, and Garfinkel, 36-42.

43. Hamilton or Madison, Federalist 51, 340.

44. Adams, *Defence*, in *Works*, Six, 208.

45. Tocqueville, II, ii, 511.

46. See James J. Walsh, *Education of the Founding Fathers of the Republic: Scholasticism in the Colonial Colleges, a Neglected Chapter in the History of American Education* (N.Y.: 1935), and Bernard Bailyn, *Education in the Forming of American Society: Needs and Opportunities for Study* (N.Y.: Vintage, 1960), 89-90 (he takes a more restrained view of the extent of Scholastic influence on colonial and Founding Era education than Walsh, but agrees that it was significant).

47. Jefferson, letter to Samuel Kercheval, July 12, 1816, in Padover, 287-288.

48. James Madison, letter to an unknown correspondent, 1833, in Marvin Meyers, ed., *The Mind of the Founder: Sources of the Political Thought of James Madison* (Indianapolis: Bobbs-Merrill, 1973), 530.

49. Bailyn, *Origins of American Politics*, 81.

50. Jefferson, First Inaugural Address, 386.

51. See U.S. Constitution, Art. I, Sec. 2.

52 See the discussion in Krason, *Preserving...*, 105-106.

53. Montesquieu, I, xi, 150; viii, 110.

54. Hamilton or Madison, Federalist 51, 337.

55. The notion of ordered liberty at the time of the Founding seems to have been very much tied up with "freedom from arbitrary, despotic, or autocratic rule or control"; it did not embrace extreme individualism. The eighteenth century view of liberty was in no way seen as exempting behavior from social oversight, and in fact the individual was understood as having to use his liberty within the context of and to further the public good (or his moral obligations as made known by religion). With the importance of the family at the time, it also involved a notion of familial independence, which meant in substantial part family economic independence. (See Barry Alan Shain, *The Myth of American Individualism: The Protestant Origins of American Political Thought* [Princeton, N.J.: Princeton University Press], 1994, 163, 170, 179, 186, 191. He takes the quoted phrase from the *Oxford English Dictionary*, which is referring to the meaning of liberty among Americans and Europeans at the time of the Revolutionary War.)

56. See, e.g., James Madison, Letter to Dr. Jacob de la Motta, Aug. 1820, in William J. Bennett, ed., *Our Sacred Honor: Words of Advice from the Founders in Stories, Letters, Poems, and Speeches* (N.Y.: Simon & Schuster, 1997), 333; Thomas Jefferson, First Inaugural Address, March 4, 1801, in William J. Bennett, 348; Jefferson, Letter to Samuel Kercheval, July 12, 1816, in Padover, 289.

57. Madison, Federalist 10, 55.

58. See Diamond, Fisk, and Garfinkel, 40-42.

59. Krason, *Preserving...*, 98.

60. Jefferson, Letter to Adams, Oct. 28, 1813, in Padover, 283; he responds to Adams's letters of July 9 and Sept. 15, 1813.

61. For a summary of these thinkers' comments about the need for a natural aristocracy, see Krason, *Preserving...*, 93-95, 123-124, 127.

62. Kirk, *The Roots of American Order*, 266-267.

63. Jefferson, First Inaugural Address, in Padover, 386; Washington, 12.

64. Washington, 30, 32.

65. Jefferson, Letter to Samuel Kercheval, July 12, 1816, in Padover, 290-291.. Emphasis is in the original.

66. For a more thorough discussion these rights, see Krason, *Preserving...*, 97-99.

67. Stephen M. Krason, "Higher Education in a 'Democracy of Worth': A Perspective and Some Proposals for Restoration," in Krason, *The Recovery of American Education*, 135-136. It must be understood that by the term "levels," we are not at all referring to anything like the grade or class levels that characterize institutional schooling.

68. Jefferson, "A Bill for the More General Diffusion of Knowledge," in Padover, 1048.

69. Adams, *Defence*, in *Works*, Six, 197-198.

70. Washington, 26.

71. Massachusetts Constitution of 1780, in Poore, I, 957.

72. Hamilton, "Speech on the Senate," in New York ratification convention, 1788, in J.C. Hamilton, II, 453.

73. Adams, *Defence*, in *Works*, Six, 208.

74. Montesquieu, I, ii, 34, 40-41.

75. Tocqueville, II, ii, 526-527.

76. Jefferson, Letter to Samuel Kercheval, July 12, 1816, in Padover, 288; Federalist 57 (Madison), 373.

77. Tocqueville, I, ii, 284.

78. Hamilton implemented a policy of aiding commerce as the country's first Secretary of the Treasury under Washington. Jefferson enunciated his "balanced" principle in his First Inaugural Address (see Padover, 386) and tried to follow it in his administration.

79. Tocqueville, I, ii, 280-281, 287-288, 306.

80. Tocqueville, I, ii, 292.

81. George Washington, *Farewell Address*, 24.

82. John Adams, Letter to Zabdiel Adams, June 21, 1776, in William J. Bennett, 371.

83. John Adams, Letter to Thomas Jefferson, June 28, 1813, in William J. Bennett, 377. Emphasis is in the original.

84. Benjamin Rush, "Of the Mode of Education Proper in a Republic" (1798), in William J. Bennett, 412.

85. Northwest Ordinance, Article 3 (July 13, 1787), in William J. Bennett, 383.

86. "The Question of Representation: Benjamin Franklin's Invocation for Prayer at the Constitutional Convention," June 28, 1787, in William J. Bennett, 385. There is some question about whether Franklin was a thoroughgoing deist (see Donald J. D'Elia, "We Hold These Truths and More: Further Catholic Reflections on the American Proposition," in Donald J. D'Elia and Stephen M. Krason, eds., *We Hold These Truths and More: Further Catholic Reflections on the American Proposition* [Steubenville, O.: Franciscan University Press, 1993], 66.

87. Quoted in Donald J. D'Elia, *The Spirits of '76: A Catholic Inquiry* (Front Royal, Va.: Christendom Publications, 1983), 140. Emphasis is in the book. See the book for sources.

88. Jefferson, Notes on Virginia (1781), quoted in William J. Federer, *America's God and Country: Encyclopedia of Quotations* (Coppell, Tex.: Fame Publishers, 1994), 323.

89. Jefferson, quoted in: Michael Knox Beran, "Behind Jefferson's Wall," in *City Journal* (Spring 2003), available from http://www.city-journal.org/html/13_2_behind_jeffersonswall.html; Internet; and Joseph Loconte, "The Wall Jefferson Almost Built," (Dec. 27, 2001), available from http:////www.heritage.org/Press/Commentary/ed122701c.cfm; Internet; both accessed Aug. 16, 2008.

90. Madison, June 20, 1785, quoted in Federer, 410.

91. Madison, 1778, quoted in ibid., 411.

92. Madison, letter to Frederick Beasley (Nov. 20, 1825), quoted in ibid., 412.

93. Madison, First Inaugural Address (March 4, 1809), quoted in ibid.

94. See, e.g., Walter Berns, "Religion and the Founding Principle," in *The Moral Foundations of the American Republic* (ed. Robert H. Horwitz; Charlottesville, Va.: University of Virginia Press, 1977), 157-182.

95. Tocqueville, I, ii, 293.

96. M.E. Bradford, *A Worthy Company: Brief Lives of the Framers of the United States Constitution* (Plymouth, Mass. & Marlborough, N.H.: Plymouth Rock Foundation, n.d.), viii.

97. M. Stanton Evans, *The Theme is Freedom: Religion, Politics, and the American Tradition* (Washington, D.C.: Regnery, 1994), 274.

98. M.E. Bradford, *Original Intentions: On the Making and Ratification of the United States Constitution* (Athens, Ga.: University of Georgia Press, 1993), 89-92.

99. See, e.g., Chuck Braman, "The Political Philosophy of John Locke and Its Influence on the Founding Fathers and the Political Documents They Created," available at: http://www.chuckbraman.com/Writing/WritingFilesPhilosophy/locke.html; Internet; accessed Aug. 16, 2008; Robert A. Goldwin, "John Locke," in Leo Strauss and Joseph Cropsey, eds., *History of Political Philosophy* (3rd edn.; Chicago: U. of Chicago Press, 1987), 510; Walter Berns, "American Presidency: Statesmanship and Constitutionalism in Balance," *Imprimis* (Jan. 1983), available from http://www.hillsdale.edu/news/   imprimis/archive/issue.asp?year=1983&month=01; Internet; accessed Aug. 16, 2008; Morton G. White, *Philosophy, The Federalist, and the Constitution* (New York : Oxford University Press, 1987).

100. These results of the Lutz and Hyneman study appear in Robert R. Reilly, "The Truths They Held: The Christian and Natural Law Background to the American Constitution," in D'Elia and Krason, 87. For a discussion of the connection of Whig thinking with Protestant Christianity, see Ellis Sandoz, *A Government of Laws: Political Theory, Religion, and the American Founding* (Baton Rouge, La.: Louisiana State University Press, 1990), 130; Mark A. Noll, "The Bible in Revolutionary America," in *The Bible in American Law, Politics, and Political Rhetoric* (ed. James Turner Johnson; Philadelphia: Fortress Press/Chico, Calif.: Scholars Press, 1985), 43, 49-51.

101. Kirk, *The Roots of American Order*, 291-292.

102. Ibid., 404. Jefferson is also often thought of as being a deist, "a child of the Enlightenment," in James David Barber's phrase (Barber, *The Presidential Character: Predicting Performance in the White House* [2nd edn.; Englewood Cliffs, N.J.: Prentice-Hall, 1977], 14). Sandoz quotes historians Samuel E. Morison and Henry Steele Commager as saying, however, that Jefferson was "[d]eeply religious without being a churchman," and relates that he believed in God (although he would not assent to the Trinity), the moral teachings of Christ, and personal immortality, and in the last thirty or

more years of his life made a "resolute study of the Bible, Biblical scholarship, and mastery of theological literature" in classical and modern languages (Sandoz, 148-149).

103. Sandoz, 136-138.

104. Kirk, *The Roots of American Order*, 435. Emphasis is in the book.

105. Bradford, *Original Intentions*, 92.

106. Evans, 270.

107. Evans, 270; D'Elia, "We Hold These Truths...," 110-112.

108. Gerard V. Bradley, *Church-State Relationships in America* (Westport, Conn.: Greenwood, 1987), 74-78.

109. See Stephen M. Krason, *The Public Order and the Sacred Order: Contemporary Issues, Catholic Social Thought, and the Western and American Traditions* (Lanham, Md.: Scarecrow Books, 2009), 206-214, for a brief discussion of the history of the drafting of the First Amendment that leads to this conclusion.

110. Quoted in Paul C. Ford, *Essays on the Constitution of the United States of America* (Brooklyn: 1892), 168-172, which is referred to in Chester James Antieau, Arthur T. Downey, and Edward C. Roberts, *Freedom From Federal Establishment: Formation and Early History of the First Amendment Religion Clauses* (Milwaukee: Bruce, 1964), 189, 195. The work of the conference committee is discussed in Krason, *The Public Order and the Sacred Order*, 210-211.

111. Antieau, et al., 62. It should be pointed out that there were few tax-supported schools at this time and that even the ones that were not religiously affiliated had curricula that emphasized the three R's and *religion*.

112. Ibid., 72.

113. Ibid., 73-74.

114. Ibid., 75.

115. Ibid., 78.

116. Ibid., 80-81.

117. Ibid., 67.

118. Charles C. Rice, *The Supreme Court and Public Prayer: The Need for Restraint* (N.Y.: Fordham University Press, 1964), 31; Antieau, et al., 75-77. For more specific examples of governmental assistance (both state and federal) to religion during the Founding Era, see Bradley, chaps. 2, 4.

119. Evans, 275-276.

120. Antieau, et al., 69; George Brown Tindall and David E. Shi, *America: A Narrative History* (5th edn.; N.Y.: W.W. Norton, 1999), 439.

121. Tocqueville, I, ii, 295.

122. Ibid., II, i, 432.

123. Kirk, *The Roots of American Order*, 336-342.

124. D'Elia, "We Hold These Truths...," 67, 68.

125. Noll, 48-50.

126. Sandoz, 129, 131.

127. Tocqueville, I, ii, 303.

128. Kirk, *The Roots of American Order*, 343.

129. James R. Stoner, Jr., "Christianity, the Common Law, and the Constitution," in Gary L. Gregg II, *Vital Remnants: America's Founding and the Western Tradition* (Wilmington, Del.: ISI Books, 1999), 204.

130. Tocqueville, I, ii, 290.

131. Stephen M. Krason, "The Murray Thesis, Abortion, and the American Political Order," in D'Elia and Krason, 209.

132. Russell Kirk, *America's British Culture* (New Brunswick, N.J.: Transaction, 1993, 72.

133. Tocqueville, I, ii, 291.

134. See ibid., 291-292; II, iii, 594-603.

135. Curtis P. Nettels, *The Roots of American Civilization: A History of American Colonial Life* (2nd edn.; N.Y.: Appleton-Century-Crofts, 1963), 450.

136. Tocqueville, I, ii, 291. Still, writing primarily about colonial America, David Hackett Fischer argues that the severity of sexual morality, at least in practice, varied by region, with rates of pre-marital pregnancy and illegitimacy lowest in the Delaware Valley area (where Quakerism was strong) and New England (where Puritanism was predominant) and rather high in the Tidewater South and the frontier ("Backcountry") areas. (See Hackett, *Albion's Seed: Four British Folkways in America* [N.Y.: Oxford University Press, 1989], 813.)

137. Marvin Olasky, *Fighting for Liberty and Virtue: Political and Cultural Wars in Eighteenth-Century America* (Washington, D.C.: Regnery, 1995), 141-169.

138. For examples of these thinkers' views on sexual virtue, see Stephen M. Krason, *Abortion: Politics, Morality, and the Constitution: A Critical Study of* Roe v. Wade *and* Doe v. Bolton *and a Basis for Change* (Lanham, Md.: University Press of America, 1984), 478-481.

139. See John Locke, "First Treatise of Government," in *Two Treatises of Government* (ed. Peter Laslett; N.Y.: Cambridge University Press, 1963), sec. 59, 220.

140. Gordon S. Wood, *The Creation of the American Republic 1776-1789* (N.Y.: W.W. Norton, 1969), 52.

141. Kirk, *America's British Culture*, 72-76.

142. Wood, *The Creation of the American Republic*, 52, 53.

143. Kirk, *America's British Culture*, 75; Gordon S. Wood, *The Radicalism of the American Revolution* (N.Y.: Vintage, 1991), 41.

144. Nettels, 452.

145. Wood, *The Radicalism of the American Revolution*, 44.

146. Tocqueville, II, ii, 513-517. Even if associations were not abundant in late colonial and immediate post-revolutionary America, they seemed to multiply in number fairly quickly as the Republic got underway. (See Robert A. Nisbet, *The Social Impact of the Revolution* [Washington, D.C.: American Enterprise Institute for Public Policy Research, 1974], 19.)

147. Wood, *The Creation of the American Republic*, 61, 118; Harold Underwood Faulkner, *American Political and Social History* (6th edn.; N.Y.: Appleton-Century-Crofts, 1952), 55. Wood specifically says that the root of this concern for the general welfare was the religion of the people.

148. Wood, *The Radicalism of the American Revolution*, 59.

149. Wood, *The Creation of the American Republic*, 68-69.

150. Barry Alan Shain, "Liberty and License: The American Founding and the Western Conception of Freedom," in Gregg, 212.

151. Kirk, *The Roots of American Order*, 270, 274.

152. Shain, 215-216, 220.

153. This is the upshot of Wood's discussion in *The Creation of the American Republic*, 60-62.

154. See Aristotle, *Politics*, IV, xi, 1295b.

155. William J. Bennett, 147 (commentary on the chapter on "Civility and Friendship").

156. Wood, *The Radicalism of the American Revolution*, pp. 57-58.

157. Ibid., 57-58.

158. Jack P. Greene, "Introduction," in Jack P. Greene, ed., *The Reinterpretation of the American Revolution 1763-1789* (N.Y.: Harper and Row, 1968), 30.

159. Wood, *The Radicalism of the American Revolution*, 112.

160. Greene, 29.

161. William J. Bennett, 146 (commentary on the chapter on "Civility and Friendship").

162. Ibid., 152-155.

163. William J. Bennett, 146 (commentary on the chapter on "Civility and Friendship").

164. Wood, *The Creation of the American Republic*, 194. For a good discussion of the nature of the republican-oriented "American gentleman," see Kirk, *The Roots of American Order*, 312-323.

165. Nettels, 383.

166. Wood, *The Creation of the American Republic*, 71.

167. Nettels, 454-455, 415.

168. Wood, *The Radicalism of the American Revolution*, 111, 59.

169. Nettels, 413-415.

170. Ibid., 454-455.

171. William B. Scott, *In Pursuit of Happiness: American Conceptions of Property from the Seventeenth to the Twentieth Century* (Bloomington, Ind.: Indiana University Press, 1977), 9-11.

172. Nettels, 456.

173. Scott, 22-23. About the earlier Christian notion that there were ethical limits to wealth accumulation, seen vividly in medieval times, see Amintore Fanfani, *Catholicism, Protestantism, and Capitalism* (Notre Dame, Ind.: University of Notre Dame Press, 1984 [originally published by Sheed and Ward, 1953]), 21-26.

174. Olasky, 216; Wood, *The Creation of the American Republic*, 108-110.

175. William J. Bennett, 314-316 (commentary on the chapter on "Justice").

176. Daniel J. Sullivan, *An Introduction to Philosophy* (rev. edn.; Milwaukee: Bruce, 1964), 159.

177. D.W. Brogan, *The American Character* (N.Y.: Vintage, 1954), 79.

178. Krason, *The Public Order and the Sacred Order*, 67.

179. The classic definition of the principle of subsidiarity is as follows: "It is an injustice and at the same time a grave evil and disturbance of right order to assign to a greater and higher association what lesser and subordinate organizations can do." (See E.F. Schumacher, *Small Is Beautiful: Economics as if People Mattered* [N.Y.: Perennial Library, 1973], 244; Pope Pius XI, encyclical *Quadragesimo Anno* [*Reconstructing the Social Order*], 1931, #79-80.) Thus, if some activity *needs* to be done and can be successfully carried out by the private sector starting with the individual and the family, and then going on to other private associations it should be before any level of government should become involved in it, and if the private sector can do it and can do it on a local level this should be attempted instead of doing it at some more distant level. If government must undertake a needed task in order to successfully complete it, it should do so at the level of government closest in proximity to the people affected. It is only when this is not possible that levels of government more distant from the people should carry out the task. It is understood that some activities by their nature—like national defense—have to be carried out by the highest level of government.

180. Krason, *Preserving...*, 5-29.

181. Ibid., 135-172.

182. See Kirk, *The Roots of American Order*, 402-412; Robert P. George, "Natural Law, the Constitution, and the Theory and Practice of Judicial Review," in Gary L. Gregg II, ed., *Vital Remnants: America's Founding and the Western Tradition* (Wilmington, Del.: ISI Books, 1999), 160. For numerous examples of the rhetorical references to the natural law in the period of the Revolution, see Charles S. Hyneman and Donald S. Lutz, *American Political Writing during the Founding Era, 1760-1805* (2 vols.; Indianapolis: Liberty Press, 1983).

183. Kirk, *The Roots of American Order*, 330.

184. Wood, *The Radicalism of the American Revolution*, 81-82, 111, 128.

185. It is a basic teaching of the Catholic Church—which, of course, very few of the Founding Fathers would have known about—that man does not keep the natural law for long without the benefit of religion (see *General Catechetical Directory* #61).

186. See Benjamin R. Barber, "The Compromised Republic: Public Purposelessness in America," in Horwitz, 19-38.

187. Essentially, the state must: maintain order; help in the securing of justice; encourage religion; help in the moral formation of the individual by good laws, sound education, and fashioning a good public moral atmosphere; help bring about public prosperity (this basically means making available equal opportunity—it is up to the individual and the family to secure private prosperity or personal/family temporal well-being); and promote the common good. It does not just focus on man's temporal well-being or satisfaction, but is concerned—within the limits appropriate to it—with his spiritual good broadly understood. For a further explanation of realist philosophy's understanding of the state's role, see Thomas J. Higgins, *Man As Man: The Science and Art of Ethics* (rev. edn.; Rockford, Ill.: TAN Books, 1992), chaps. XXI (discusses the notion of human society—of which the state is a natural one), XXIV, XXV.

188. Scholars such as Henry F. May trace the various dimensions and degrees of the Enlightenment's influence in America, even on American religion (see Henry F. May, *The Enlightenment in America* [N.Y.: Oxford University Press, 1976]). As indicated above, the case that the Enlightenment was not the overwhelming influence on the thinking of the Founding Fathers is made ably by writers such as Russell Kirk and Robert R. Reilly (see: Kirk, *The Roots of American Order*, 291-293; Reilly, 87-89).

189. See Orestes A. Brownson, "The Higher Law," *The Works of Orestes A. Brownson* (ed. Henry F. Brownson; Detroit: Thorndike Nourse, 1885), XVII, 7-16.

190. 3 Dall. 386. *Calder v. Bull* was one of the Supreme Court's first cases involving constitutional limitations on governmental power. The Court's decision limited the application of the constitutional prohibition of ex post facto laws to criminal matters, excluding civil matters from its reach. There was a debate among the justices, as seen in their opinions, about whether unenumerated rights or natural law should be resorted to by the Court in making decisions because of a concern about men disagreeing about the content of natural law or principles of justice. (See H. Jefferson Powell, "Calder v. Bull," in Kermit Hall, ed., *The Oxford Companion to the Supreme Court of the United States* [N.Y.: Oxford University Pres, 1992], 174-175.)

191. Tocqueville, II, iv, 691-695.

192. Sampo, 105.

193. Martin Diamond argues that this absence of focus on the new government securing virtue and, as we go on to say, justice was deliberate on the part of the Founding Fathers: "The American political order was deliberately tiled to resist, so to speak, the upward gravitational pull of politics toward the grand, dramatic, character-ennobling but society-racking opinions about justice and virtue" (Martin Diamond, "Ethics and Politics: The American Way," in Horwitz, 56).

194. Edward S. Corwin, *The "Higher Law" Background of American Constitutional Law* (Ithaca, N.Y.: Cornell University Press, 1955), 4.

195. Orestes A. Brownson, "The Democratic Principle," in Russell Kirk, ed., *Orestes Brownson: Selected Political Essays* (New Brunswick, N.J.: Transaction, 1990), 195. This essay was originally published in *Brownson's Quarterly Review*, April 1873.

196. For a discussion of the natural character of the family, see Austin Fagothey, *Right and Reason: Ethics in Theory and Practice* (St. Louis: C.V. Mosby, 1953), 428-435. We have already seen Tocqueville's comments about the importance of conjugal stability to the political order. For further brief discussions, see Krason, *Abortion*, 458 (referring to Aristotle's thought) and E. Cahill, *The Framework of a Christian State* (Fort Collins, Colo.: Roman Catholic Books, n.d., [reprint of 1932 edn.]), 320-324. The state, of course, is also a natural institution, but it is not—by the very definition of the term—an *intermediary* institution (i.e., one that stands between the state and the individual). By the way, the Church is not a natural institution, but a *supernatural* one.

197. Allan C. Carlson seems to have this interpretation. He says, "the family was deeply embodied in the unwritten constitution of the new United States, in the social views that the Founders held." (Allan C. Carlson, *From Cottage to Work Station: The Family's Search for Social Harmony in the Industrial Age* [San Francisco: Ignatius Press, 1993], 7.)

198. Regarding *The Republic*, see Allan Bloom's discussion of Plato's understanding about the importance of the family for the city in his "Interpretive Essay" at the back of his translation of that dialogue (Allan Bloom, ed., *The Republic of Plato* [N.Y.: Basic Books, 1968], 379-389), and also Leo Strauss, "Plato," in Leo Strauss and Joseph Cropsey, eds., *History of Political Philosophy* (3rd edn.; Chicago: University of Chicago Press, 1887), 48-52. Regarding Aristotle's view, see Aristotle, *Politics*, II, iii, 1261b; II, iv, 1262a-1262b.

199. On this point about the balance of power and international peace, see Pope John Paul II, "Negotiation: The Only Realistic Solution to the Continuing Threat of War" (speech to the UN General Assembly, read for the Pope by Cardinal Agostino Casaroli, June 11, 1982), #8, 11.

200. See the discussion in Peter Augustine Lawler, "Murray's Transformation of the American Proposition," in D'Elia and Krason, 103.

201. Madison, Federalist 10, 57.

202. Ibid., 60.

203. Ibid., 59.

204. We have discussed this more elsewhere. See: Krason, *Abortion*, 493-501; Stephen M. Krason, "Toward a Catholic-Realist Perspective for International Political Life," in *The Catholic Social Science Review*, vol. iv (1999), 291-295.

205. Madison, Federalist 10, 56.

206. Martin Diamond, "The Federalist," in Strauss and Cropsey, 677.

207. Ibid., 678.

208. Ibid., 677.

209. To satisfy acquisitiveness requires what have been called "bourgeois" virtues, such as venturesomeness, hard work, the ability to still immediate desires to achieve long-term goals, honesty in commercial relations, and some sense of justice in order to accommodate oneself to others' interests in a political society where acquisitiveness reigns widely. These are more examples of virtues, even if not the highest ones—a further expression of Tocqueville's "self-interest properly understood." (See Diamond, in Horwitz, 63-65.)

210. Daniel J. Sullivan writes that "the 'liberal,' laissez-faire state...has never been realized except at the cost of exploitation, and its issue is either in some form of economic totalitarianism or in social anarchy. Both these tendencies are compensated for...by such a complicated series of social structures—laws, price controls, cartels, trade unions, employer associations, government bureaus, etc.—that in time the citizen becomes a slave to the very machinery set up to ensure his freedom." (Sullivan, *An Introduction to Philosophy* [rev. edn.; Milwaukee: Bruce, 1964]. 138-139.) Sullivan here echoes Pope Pius XI's assessment of the course of modern economic life (see Pope Pius XI, *Quadragesimo Anno* [*Reconstructing the Social Order*], #101-110]).

211. This likely was reflected in such things as the child-saving philosophy and efforts that have characterized, in one fashion or another, most of American history. (See Allan C. Carlson, *Family Questions, Reflections on the American Social Crisis* [New Brunswick, N.J.: Transaction, 1988], 241-256.)

212. Diamond, Fisk, and Garfinkel, 138.

213. Harry V. Jaffa, "The Case for a Stronger National Government," in Robert A. Goldwin, ed., *A Nation of States: Essays on the American Federal System* (Chicago: Rand McNally, 1961), 120. Jaffa uses the term "liberal construction," and Diamond, Fisk, and Garfinkel (at 139) the term "loose construction."

214. Diamond, Fisk, and Garfinkel, 139.

215. Martin Diamond, "What the Framers Meant by Federalism," in Robert A. Goldwin, ed., *A Nation of States: Essays on the American Federal System* (2nd edn.; Chicago: Rand McNally College Publishing Co., 1974), 31.

216. Ibid., 39.

217. Diamond, Fisk, and Garfinkel, 141.

218. It should be pointed out that the principle of subsidiarity did not exist under that name in social ethics at the Founders' time—and, for that matter, the philosophical sub-field of social ethics did not exist either—but the notion was present in ethical reflection.

219. Good examples of the abundant literature on this topic are: Edward S. Corwin, *The Doctrine of Judicial Review: Its Legal and Historical Basis and Other Essays* (Princeton, N.J.: Princeton University Press, 1914); Alexander M. Bickel, *The Least Dangerous Branch: The Supreme Court at the Bar of Politics* (Indianapolis: Bobbs-Merrill, 1962); and Christopher Wolfe, *The Rise of Modern Judicial Review: From Constitutional Interpretation to Judge-Made Law* (N.Y.: Basic Books, 1986).

CHAPTER 2

1789-1817: THE FORMATIVE YEARS, THE FEDERALIST PARTY ERA, AND JEFFERSONIANISM

History, Politics, and Culture in the First Decade of the New Republic, 1789-1801

The period from 1789, when the new national government under the Constitution was organized, to 1801, when America's first political party, the Federalists, was ushered out of power and Thomas Jefferson's Democratic-Republicans took over has often been called the Federalist Period or Era. By examining developments at this time, we can see how the new political and constitutional framework took form and how the practice, most immediately, measured up to the theory. This is an issue to consider, even though several (although a minority) of the figures in the early government were also Framers of the Constitution, because the transition from theory to practice is always difficult; political and social pressures, much less circumstances, can always move people away from their original intentions; and simply most of the people in the new government were not at the Philadelphia Convention and some did not even initially favor the Constitution.[1] We shall determine if in the first decade or so of the Republic, even if the beginnings were in complete accord with the Founders' vision, stirrings occurred that already were moving the nation away from that vision. In the second part of this chapter, we shall see if the sweeping Jeffersonian election of 1800—which was in large part a reaction to and repudiation of the Federalists, and had a democratizing tone to it—and its aftermath signaled at all a departure from that vision.

The subjects that emerge for examination during the Federalist Period and comparison with the various points set forth in Chapter 1 are: federalism and the growth of federal government power; the powers of the executive branch; criteria for appointments to that branch and conduct of governmental officials; judicial power; military power; the rise of political parties and voluntary associations; democratization, citizen rights, and the question of a natural aristocracy; economic developments; socio-cultural developments; and changing intellectual currents.

Federalism and the Growth of Federal Government Power. One of the most noteworthy events of the Federalist Period was the Whiskey Rebellion of 1794. President Washington raised a force made up of state militiamen to put down this small uprising of whiskey makers against a tax imposed by the federal government. The resistance to the tax then collapsed fairly quickly.[2] This was not an enhancement of federal power from what the Constitution envisioned because one of the main factors motivating its drafting was the sense, after Shays' Rebellion of 1786-87, that the states and the Confederation government were not strong enough to subdue domestic insurrections.[3] As far as the tax itself was concerned, there does not seem to have been a serious question about its being outside the realm of federal power—the issue of constitutionality was not raised and both the early Federalists and Democratic-Republicans in Congress voted for it—even though it was strongly opposed in what was then the West.[4]

Other federal government initiatives in the 1790s *did* raise questions of whether the actions were within its constitutional powers. Most of these concerned the new government's economic policies, spearheaded primarily by Washington's Treasury Secretary Alexander Hamilton. The first of these was the establishment of the Bank of the United States, which was the subject of controversy for most of the first half-century of the new Republic until its final demise in 1841. In defending his proposal for the Bank, Hamilton acknowledged that he was making what has been called a "broad construction" of the Constitution, through the use of the necessary and proper clause. He believed that the Bank was necessary to help the government collect taxes, regulate trade, and provide adequately for the country's defense. He insisted, as John C. Miller puts it, that the federal government had "the right to employ all the means 'necessary and proper' to the attainment of such objectives as were not forbidden by the Constitution or not contrary to the essential ends of society." This set a precedent that became enshrined in the constitutional doctrine of the Supreme Court under another leading Federalist, Chief Justice John Marshall.[5] James Madison, the main author of the Constitution, in spite of previous nationalizing tendencies opposed Hamilton's position. He did not find in the Constitution either an express or implied power that would permit Congress to charter a bank. Actually, he had proposed at the Constitutional Convention to specifically allow Congress to charter corporations, but this was not acted on. Now he expressed the opposite sentiments, apparently concerned that the balance of power should tilt toward the states and not too much federal power should be inferred from the Constitution.[6]

The decision to establish the Bank ended up helping the early Republic's economy in many ways, so it truly was a prudent and pragmatic undertaking and the constitutional argument against it in any event was tenuous. The Bank played a significant role in stimulating business enterprise, motivating sound financial practices in other banks, and helping the government's foreign exchange operations.[7] It thereby became a means to help keep intact the principle of the Founding Era of avoiding damaging public debt. In fact, Hamilton made it clear that—while he understood that government would take on debt—it had to meet its obligations for servicing it and dealing fairly with its creditors.[8]

Even before John Marshall, Hamilton's broad interpretation of federal government powers—and of governmental power more generally—began to gain support on the Supreme Court. In *Hylton v. U.S.* (1796),[9] the Court gave Congress some leeway in taxing with a somewhat loose interpretation of what an indirect tax was. It held that a tax on carriages was not a direct tax and so—this was, of course, before the Sixteenth Amendment—did not have to be apportioned among the states according to their populations. Then in *Calder v. Bull* (1798),[10] the Court, while holding that the ex post facto prohibition of the Constitution applied only to criminal statutes, stated that private rights had to yield to public exigencies. This meant that if acts of government had a retroactive effect, courts would sustain them even if they interfered, say, with private property rights.[11] The decision paved the way for statutory and legal innovations in the decades ahead as a means of promoting internal improvements and achieving economic development.

In 1798, another federal tax was imposed, which was more far-reaching than the whiskey tax of 1794 and perhaps as controversial. This tax was imposed on houses, land, and slaves and—along with the Alien and Sedition Acts of the same year—paved the way for the defeat of the Federalist party in 1800. While the tax may have been constitutional, and did not represent an overreaching of federal authority, the Fries case involving the prosecution of a major resister perhaps did. The government expanded the charge from what traditionally at common law it would have been—a high misdemeanor—into the capital offense of treason.[12] It was perhaps an early example of a new crime based on a theory, as opposed to a clear-cut statutory provision.

Miller writes that during the Federalist Period, Hamilton's "grand design" for the U.S. economy was "the centralization of governmental authority and the industrialization of the United States by means of government aid to business."[13] In his famous Report on Manufactures he proposed government encouragement and assistance in the developing of a manufacturing sector in the U.S. He called for government: to promote emigration to overcome the labor shortage in the country, the further development of banking, and investment from abroad; to impose taxes to service the national debt so that government bonds could then be sold, even overseas, to bring in capital that would in turn be invested to stimulate manufacturing; to enact protective tariffs; to waive duties on certain raw materials from abroad needed for American industry; and to provide bounties and premiums on specific manufactured products and awards for inventions. He made it clear that he was not undercutting agriculture; in fact, he held it to be the preferred sector of a nation's economy. He rather sought a mixed economy that he believed would redound to the benefit of all citizens.[14] The Report did indeed assert a definite, "proactive" economic role for the federal government, but according to Stanley Elkins and Eric McKitrick "[t]he proposals…were modest."[15]

The final development that signaled a significant—and probably the most controversial—exertion of federal power was the Alien and Sedition Acts of 1798. What motivated the Acts were: the foolish efforts of French Ambassador Edmond-Charles Genet ("Citizen Genet") to recruit American fighters and rouse public sentiment to support French hostilities against Britain and Spain; the conflict between the pro-French and pro-English "parties" (i.e., partisans) in the U.S.; the virulent, scurrilous partisan attacks on leading public figures in certain parts of the American press; and the increasingly bitter division between Federalist and Democratic-Republican sympathizers. The statutes gave the president the power to imprison or deport aliens he judged dangerous, substantially increased the length of time before a resident alien could seek naturalization and imposed alien reporting requirements, and made it a crime to utter or publish false, scandalous, or malicious statements against the U.S. government (though it required proof of malicious intent, made truth a defense, and gave juries the power to decide what the law was). In fact, the standards of the Sedition Act were more liberal than the common law standard, and were much more restrained than the recently enacted British Treasonable Practices Act (1795).[16] So, whether the Acts represented an expansion of federal power—much less governmental power in general—is questionable, at least unless one reads the First Amendment free speech clause in an absolute, literal way. In fact, the Democratic-Republicans seemed to have no problem with enforcing seditious libel so long as it was done at the state level.[17] Also, it is clear from the Constitution that Congress has control over immigration by its powers to make the rules for naturalization.

The final versions of the Alien and Sedition Acts were much moderated over some of the proposed provisions. These, along with the political conflicts that formed part of the background to the Acts (noted above), perhaps are more instructive about a compromising of the Founding vision of a democratic republic than the Acts themselves. On the alien question, some in the Federalist party pushed to disqualify naturalized citizens from holding federal office. One leading Federalist politician seemed to have favored shutting off immigration. There was strong Federalist sentiment for wholesale deportation, believing that some groups were subversive and naturally attracted to the Democratic-Republicans and—anticipating nativism later on—that they threatened the American character. The original legislation called for sweeping registration, surveillance, and permits for aliens, and any alien returning after deportation would have been subjected to life imprisonment. The leading Federalist promoters of the Sedition Act in both the Senate and the House of Representatives initially pushed for a law so broad that it would essentially have reached any statements of opposition to the federal government even if true, and proposed the novel notion that a person could be punished for treason even if the U.S. were not at war. To be fair, it was the Federalists—who controlled both chambers—who were responsible for staving off these extreme provisions.[18] Still, in spite of the untruths being hurled back and forth between the two early parties, the fact that the Federalists were in control and prosecuted only

Democratic-Republicans does not make it appear that the spirit of free speech and free press was much embraced.[19]

As far as concerned outright competition between the federal and state governments—which some in the Constitution's ratification debates feared would result in a weakening of the latter[20]—during the Federalist Period, Leonard D. White writes that, except possibly for the area of revenue-raising, it "failed to materialize." This was because "[t]he range of federal activities was small." Hamilton was aware of the danger that competition for revenue would develop, and his response was to have the federal government corner certain subjects for taxation and create such conditions that the states would not see the need to tax much or at all in those areas.[21]

When we consider how the points discussed in this section on "Federalism and the Growth of Federal Government Power" comport to the principles mentioned in Chapter 1, we observe the following: We have already noted above that the constitutional balance of power between the federal and state governments does not appear to have been affected by establishing the Bank of the United States, the federal whiskey excise tax, the Alien and Sedition Acts, and federal revenue-raising initiatives. More generally, these developments did not signal in any way an over-centralization of power or activities, which is a sign of the decline of regimes. They probably should be read just as giving substance in practice to the Founders' vision of a sufficiently strong national government. As noted, Hamilton was concerned that the balance of power could easily tilt in the direction of excessive state power. Quite the opposite of inviting serious economic disorders, the above suggests that Hamilton's economic policy initiatives had a positive effect on the economy of the early Republic. Further, the policies were in line with the cultural norm of frugality in early America and while accepting a need for some government debt, sought to avoid a reckless use of public credit. While the Sedition Act did not per se pose a challenge to the traditional views of press and other freedoms at the backdrop of the Founding, its selective, and partisan-oriented, application, probably did. The Founding vision in this respect was blurred. The Fries case also seemed to deviate from traditional legal norms and so, arguably, violated the rule of law and in some sense perverted justice. This situation, however, was to be quickly rectified after the election of 1800, when the Jeffersonians won and repealed the Alien and Sedition Acts.

The Powers of the Executive Branch. There were numerous developments regarding the powers of the executive branch of the new government during the Federalist Period. This was perhaps to be expected, since precedents were going to be established as theory was transformed into practice and there were so many eminent public men in the early executive branch. There is no doubt that the presidency and the executive branch were able to establish their strength and prominence—even though the Framers believed that Congress was the first among co-equal branches[22]—because of the fact that George Washington first occupied the office. As White writes, "Members of Congress were the more ready to accept the essential implications of an independent executive when discretion was to be exercised at the outset by a man whose integrity and patriotism were beyond question."[23] The question was, however, did executive power or the actions of the executive during the Federalist Period—in spite of its being headed by the president of the Constitutional Convention and having a number of other Framers as part of it—deviate or start to deviate in any significant way from the "big" principles of the Founding Era? The pertinent Founding principles and practices that should be considered here—in this and the section to follow—are: the maintenance of separation of powers (both in actual practice and in spirit); checks and balances; the upholding of the rule of law and the role of an independent judiciary; the concern for popular sovereignty, which included insuring the responsibility of those in power to the people; the bringing forth of good men to positions of authority (i.e., a natural aristocracy); and a focus on the common good.

During his administration, Washington made all the significant executive decisions, even many minor ones; no Cabinet secretary—much less inferior officials—resolved important questions without getting his approval.[24] Under both Washington and John Adams, the precedent took root that the President consulted with the Cabinet collectively, "but without any implication that the President was either bound to consult or to accept the advice that he received."[25] As a way of keeping full control of its power of the purse, Congress specified that the Secretary of the Treasury—even while a presidential appointee and unlike other Cabinet members—make reports and render other information, when sought, directly to it. It also asserted its right to examine Treasury documents. Congress took other measures to limit the Secretary's power; according to Miller, it did not want the office to become like the British Chancellor of the Exchequer. In imposing these limits, some in Congress were concerned more fundamentally that the presidency was already a too powerful office under the Constitution.[26]

Generally speaking with reference to the powers of the top executive branch officials, however, Congress "left substantial freedom of action" to them and "kept...out of most administrative details." It was nevertheless understood that the executive branch was responsible to Congress.[27] It tended to trust the President with substantial discretionary powers, but not his subordinates. It was accepted, however, that the President could delegate to his immediate subordinates the power to act in his name, so long as they followed his directives. Going down the line in the early executive departments, this spirit of limiting the discretion of subordinates was also evident. In the Treasury Department, Hamilton refused to accept any discretionary powers in tax officers; otherwise, he thought that personal passions and predilections would enter in and become a foundation for governmental oppression. He realized that there had to be room for discretion since no statute could foresee all possible contingencies, and varying circumstances would always have to be taken account of. He sought to place it in higher officials, however.[28] A system of checks and counterchecks was in place to prevent subordinate Treasury officials from making unauthorized expenditures.[29] Executive officials would not have the finality of judgment, since their actions were understood as always being subject to judicial review.[30] In line with the desire to avoid excessive administrative discretion leading to abuses and oppression, the federal government was careful not to punish citizens for making inadvertent errors—even when it came to something so essential to it as taxation—and even set up procedures to remit fines and forfeitures in order to insure needed flexibility in enforcement.[31]

Also in reference to dealings with Congress, Washington set the permanent precedent for the practice of "advice and consent," which was specified for treatymaking in the Constitution. In 1789, Washington went to the Senate chamber and sought advice about negotiating an Indian treaty. The senators were reluctant to provide him the answers he sought—maybe because he expected too much of them too quickly. After that, he refused to undertake such consultations with the full Senate, and set the standard for the future.[32] By and large, the "advice" part of advice and consent has been ignored as a formal practice—although Presidents generally do it informally with individual important senators and even include some on negotiating teams.

Criteria for Appointment to the Executive Branch and Standards of Appointee Conduct. On this subject, we can see that Washington quickly set down standards of both competency and integrity for people who occupied positions under him, and this by and large continued under Adams. Washington gave some preference in filling federal appointments to those who had held state office. He believed that those who had served commendably at that level deserved to be elevated to the service of the entire country. He declined to allow something like mere military service in the Revolution to give a man the "inside track" for a federal appointment. Certainly, citizens were preferred over aliens, although aliens were appointed as unsalaried U.S. consuls abroad—perhaps reflecting the fact that at this early time there were not many accomplished U.S. diplomats. Persons were not appointed just because of financial need, although Washington was cognizant of this factor in setting salaries. Family relationship (i.e., nepotism), indolence, and alcohol problems were disqualifying. Washington carefully secured information about the qualifications of prospective appointees from certain Cabinet members, some military officials, and just private citizens whom he trusted.[33] Some immediate subordinates, especially in the Adams administration, seemed to engage in some degree of favoritism of family members in making lower level appointments,[34] but White tells us that the "number was...comparatively small" and the Federalists compiled a "relatively good record" in this area.[35] Actually, White argues that the practice of seeking high quality people for executive appointments was perhaps an outgrowth of the Federalist notion that those who were "superior in education, in economic standing, and in native ability" were the ones who should conduct the affairs of government.[36] It was perhaps their version of the ruling of a natural aristocracy.

As far as remaining in office was concerned, a "high standard of integrity" generally prevailed.[37] When people were removed—which did not happen often—it mostly happened "for serious delinquency or for failure to account for public funds." There were a few instances in Adams's administration where removals were made because of differences in political philosophy, but that was definitely the exception. Washington had set the precedent of appointing men of divergent perspectives, and a consensus developed among both the Federalists and the Democratic-Republican party—that emerged as their opposition—that removals "should be made only for cause."[38] Perhaps the most noteworthy removals of officials during the Federalist Period were Edmund Randolph by Washington and Timothy Pickering by Adams, both from the position of Secretary of State. The former actually resigned under pressure for divulging confidential U.S. government information to the French and proposing that they bribe certain American politicians;[39] the latter was removed at least partly for exerting influence on behalf of his relatives.[40]

Still, even if there was no impropriety, one wonders if already during the Federalist Period a coziness of government and economic interests can be observed from the fact that, as Miller states, "[l]arge tracts of land had been sold at giveaway prices to land companies" even though the federal treasury was disadvantaged as a result.[41] Further, the country began to see government actually taken financial advantage of by arms suppliers who sold it inadequate and deficient weaponry.[42] On the state level, favored treatment of government for certain economic interests and public officials using their offices for their own pecuniary benefit was hardly unknown—in fact, sometimes it was blatant and substantial. One example was the Georgia legislation that transferred huge tracts of land under the state's control in what is now Alabama and Mississippi to the Yazoo Land Companies very inexpensively. Many members of the Georgia legislature had shares in the companies and profited from the sale. The public outcry that prompted a newly elected legislature to repeal the sale led to the famous U.S. Supreme Court case of *Fletcher v. Peck*.[43]

We evaluate the above two areas, relating to the executive, in the following manner: The above indicates that separation of powers and checks and balances were carefully upheld during the Federalist Period. Congress was unwilling to permit the exercise of too much authority by the executive and worked to insure accountability to it, especially in financial matters. It had a wariness of accelerating executive power. From his standpoint, Washington was cautious about letting executive power grow by permitting too much discretion by appointees under him. Both of these things and the additional concern about treating citizens properly under the tax and other laws also indicate attentiveness to the principle of popular sovereignty. The principle of checks and balances was further carved into these early arrangements by the judicial oversight of the executive that was mentioned. Perhaps the only exception to this close attention to separation of powers was Washington's unwillingness after the above treaty episode to abide by the "advice" aspect of the Constitution's "advice and consent" provision, and its subsequent narrowing in meaning in American history (though one could hardly say that this had a significant adverse effect on the viability of separation of powers in the federal government). The upholding of the rule of law was evident in this fact and in the realistic approach taken to the question of discretion: it was limited to be sure, but Washington knew he had to permit it to some degree. The rule of law can be offended not just by allowing too much official discretion, but also by strictures that are too inflexible. As mentioned, the criteria employed in making executive appointments indicates that the Federalist Period sought to bring forth a kind of natural aristocracy into government that was envisioned in the Founding Era. The standards of integrity indicated an acute awareness of the need to avoid letting those with lack of control of their desires for wealth—a factor that can cause regime decline—to serve in government. On the other hand, developments like the Yazoo land case indicate that that spirit and the concomitant factor of decline of the pursuit of runaway prosperity and materialism—were present in a significant way during this time. They also, of course, indicate obliviousness by some to the common good.

The Judicial Power. While the solidification of the power of the Supreme Court as a co-equal branch had to wait for John Marshall's Chief Justiceship and the growth of its power for decades after that, there were some distinct early stirrings of its strength. A federal district court for the first time declared an act of Congress unconstitutional in 1792,[44] anticipating the Supreme Court's clearly establishing such a power in *Marbury v. Madison*[45] eleven years later. Also, the Supreme Court's willingness to give substantial leeway to federal action—i.e., a broad interpretation of federal power under the Constitution—was seen before the Marshall Court, as noted above in the *Hylton* decision. Interestingly, the practice of assessing the judiciary through a political lens—which has become so common in our day—also emerged at this early time. The Democratic-Republicans cheered the 1792 decision because it seemed to accord with their view of restraining federal power vis-à-vis the states, but later, after the *Hylton* decision and Jefferson's election and the ensconcing of Federalists on the Supreme Court, their eagerness to embrace it cooled considerably. In 1792, they had even called for the Court to strike down the First Bank of the United States.[46] In short, with political considerations at the forefront they switched from initially being what we today call "judicial activists" to "judicial restraintists."

In light of Founding principles, the above makes clear that judicial independence was well respected in the Federalist Period; this is seen in the fact that courts began in a small way to exercise the power of judicial review—even against Congress.[47] This was only the distant beginning of the courts as powerful institutions, and represented little more than their struggling to establish themselves as a co-equal branch of government. More ominously, the Democratic-Republicans' aforementioned flip-flopping in their view of court power depending on whether they agreed with the outcome began the practice of treating the courts as basically a political institution, which in some sense compromised the integrity of the notion of rule of law.

The Military Power. During the Federalist Period, the American military increased in size. The size of the post-Revolution military increased first during the Washington administration in 1792 due to ongoing hostilities with Indian tribes on the western frontier. This gained the support of the early Democratic-Republican party in spite of their dislike of high governmental expenditures—a larger army, of course, was costlier—and suspicion of standing armies. It had become clear that local militias were inadequate to deal with the Indian problem.[48] During the Adams administration, further increases occurred because of the fear of war with France, which heightened in 1798 because of the XYZ Affair and the French declaration that any ship carrying British goods, which most American ones did, was subject to confiscation on the high seas.[49] At that time, the Federalists in Congress had pushed through an increase in size much larger than Adams wanted.[50] Miller argues that once war with France did not materialize, there was what would today be called "mission creep" regarding the increase in the size of the military. The "most compelling reason" now "was to back up Federal tax collectors, district attorneys, and judges in the enforcement of unpopular laws." The result was opposition in the civilian population, taxpayer unhappiness, "the resentment of the champions of civil rights," and strong criticism from the Democratic-Republicans, and it contributed to the 1800 defeat of the Federalists.[51]

By way of assessment, there is no doubt that the military power was strictly subjected to the civilian power as the government got started in the Federalist Period. The increase in the military's size in no way indicated the rise of even a limited militarism; it was a realistic response due to foreign and domestic threats. Still, the view of the Federalists in Congress of increasing the size of the military for internal control and, especially, to secure acceptance of unpopular laws was unsettling. It presented a challenge to popular sovereignty and, since support for this divided along partisan lines, raised the specter of using the military in a partisan way. It was a development which makes one think of the descent of politics into a power struggle that characterizes decline. It betrays a weakening of social charity and civic friendship and damage to the common good.

The Rise of Political Parties and Voluntary Associations. We have spoken about inter-party conflict between the Federalists and the Democratic-Republicans; it seemed as if partisanship and partisan attacks became very strong and bitter rather quickly in American history. It went even to the point of criminal prosecutions under the Sedition Act that had at least *some* partisan motivation behind them. While one might see the roots of the struggle between these two early parties in the Federalist-Antifederalist conflict over the Constitution's ratification, Madison perhaps laid the immediate theoretical foundation for it in 1791 when he expanded his viewpoint in Federalist 10 that factions were simply a reality of politics to be reckoned with into one which saw them as at least somewhat desirable. To be sure, he was not prepared to wholeheartedly and enthusiastically embrace them; the old idea that factions damaged the "organic whole" of society, created disharmony, and could pave the way to instability and tyranny was still present in the general political outlook.[52] Most immediately he and Jefferson were becoming increasingly disenchanted with the political and policy successes of Hamilton. They were troubled by what they saw as a heightened concentration of federal government power. In a series of articles in 1791-92, Madison set out the following points: 1) If in Federalist 10 he had argued for a "multiplicity of interests," he now said that two parties was the natural arrangement—a kind of equilibrium, where one would check off the other (thereby justifying the emerging Democratic-

Republican party as a check to Hamilton's Federalists); 2) He said that those who favored a limited government, a narrow interpretation of the Constitution, and a republican as opposed to a monarchial and aristocratic spirit were more faithful to the terms of the American constitutional union (i.e., he was drawing an implicit contrast between his and Jefferson's Democratic-Republicans and the Federalists); 3) He viewed the "anti-republicans" as seeking to enhance the monied interests, and believed their vehicle was their political party (he speaks about this in a way to evoke the old suspicion of parties, even though what he essentially calls for is support of another political party to oppose it); 4) Even though it is implicitly support for the Democratic-Republicans that he is seeking, it is only for the sake of defeating the anti-republicans once and for all and with the triumph of the true republicans all parties would become "superfluous" (this certainly foreshadowed Jefferson's understanding that the Democratic-Republicans were the "party to end all parties"); 5) In Jeffersonian fashion, the yeomanry are the backbone of a republic and a good political order, and urban life takes on a corrupting character; 6) He opens the door to the Jacksonianism of a generation later by suggesting a majoritarian idea and indicating that the people can safely be trusted to make the best decisions for themselves. To be sure, some of these points departed from the more restrained republicanism of the Madison of the Founding Era, but Elkins and McKitrick say they were "undiluted polemic" and that Madison was now speaking as a "partisan."[53] If this is so, it illustrates clearly the extent to which political party considerations were coming to dominate American politics only four to five years after the Constitution was drawn up. One should not think that Madison was a mere opportunist, however, as he had come to believe that the Democratic-Republican party was needed to act as a kind of "intermediate entity," an "opposition force" to protect the people from this other party that had emerged to defend privilege;[54] the people as a mere mass could not protect themselves without this kind of organized entity.

Along with the rise of parties was the related development of political associations. As noted in Chapter 1, early America did not yet see the plethora of voluntary associations that Tocqueville commented so pointedly about in the 1830s. The decade after the revolution began to see the growth of voluntary associations, although they were "still a novel form of social action."[55] The growth of the phenomenon of voluntary associations, Elkins and McKitrick tell us, "is usually seen as a series of transformations, each with reference to some sort of dichotomy: from stability to movement and change, from localism to cosmopolitanism, from local to supra-local systems of marketing and communication, and so on." Relationships changed from a status to a contract basis, from natural to financial, from communal/organic to abstract/impersonal. Communities no longer "moved as a unit to achieve their purposes," and individuals changed the focus of their efforts.[56] Political associations—clubs, of a sort—took shape in the 1790s, in a post-revolutionary atmosphere of enhanced political debate and engagement and a sense that the French Revolution—which initially was thought to be an emulation of America's—should be supported. The clubs were called either democratic societies—the term apparently suggested by Citizen Genet—or republican clubs, and as time went on came to view themselves as something like defenders of republican principles in the face of the apparent attempts to crush them by the *ancien regime* in Europe and also monitors of American public officials to insure that they upheld the Constitution and republican principles.[57] While the societies were not adjuncts of the Democratic-Republican party, most of their members identified with it even though they were not very prominent members of it. The societies stirred up much controversy, but their rhetoric was probably more significant than their actual efforts.[58]

The above developments point out even more strikingly what was noted above: There was erosion, at least in the public domain, of civic friendship, social charity, and civility. It was seen even in the theory of such a great American statesman as Madison, when he viewed the Federalists with such suspicion that he asserted the need for a countervailing political party to, in effect, protect republicanism. As the American outlook passed from one that saw factions as threatening to a harmonious community to one that viewed them as necessary to sustain liberty, the tensions and clashes that so quickly emerged still underscored that if factional competition were not restrained the common good could be threatened. Maybe this is why people like Jefferson, as seen below, never quite subscribed to the Madisonian exultation of the value of faction. It is thus fair to say that with all of this much of the Federalist Period, especially during Adams' presidency, was a time of social conflict (one of the indicators of societal decline). This new regime of factionalism, at a deeper level, helped to diminish the notion of the community as an organic whole— with individuals and families oriented to and seeing their efforts as directed to furthering the good of the whole (as discussed in Chapter 1)—and further advanced individualism.

Democratization, Citizen Rights, and the Question of a Natural Aristocracy. What was said about Madison, the Democratic-Republican party, and the democratic or republican societies makes clear that there is a prodding of the early Republic toward more democratization. As Elkins and McKitrick state, "as early as the mid-1790s…one already sees a clear turn in the direction of popular politics…a 'populist impulse' became discernible."[59] Still, it was not so clear that the principles that the societies—much less the new Democratic-Republican party—were advocating were truly democratic. Indeed, the claim of the societies to be concerned about upholding the Constitution and laws, protecting liberty, opposing maladministration, stressing the importance of discussion and the exchange of views, and promoting citizen vigilance did not seem to depart from the perspectives underlying the democratic republic forged by the Founders a few years before.[60] Moreover, most of the societies disappeared by the mid-1790s, and never seemed to command substantial popular support.[61] Another indicia of democratization is the expansion of the franchise and access to office-holding. This happened to some degree during and right after the Revolutionary War in a number of states with a loosening of property-holding requirements, along with the limiting of the powers of state governments. The 1790s actually saw something of a reversal of this, with a tightening of property-holding requirements. This was counter-balanced, however, by the additions of bills of rights and other protections of the individual to the state constitutions to insure that the propertied did not dominate the common person.[62]

Another expression of democratization in the 1780s and 1790s, though outside of the political realm, was the abolition of primogeniture. Also, the equalization of daughters' property rights was occurring at the same time.[63]

Perhaps the most evident expression of an extreme democratic impulse was the Whiskey Rebellion above. As we saw, though, few people actually took part in it, it commanded limited popular support, and it was put down almost without resistance. While the Americans of the Federalist Period were less reluctant about mob action in light of their revolutionary experience, the "presumption was that a normally law-abiding people did not take mob action without good cause, that if they did there must be injustice somewhere, and that within reason it behooved the authorities to do what they could to correct it."[64] As stated above, the ability of government to quell civil disorder was a motivating concern for the Constitution. What the Founders had in mind was that ochlocracy (i.e., a regime of mob rule) should be restrained and that a democratic republic meant that peaceful, constitutional means were made available to address citizen grievances.

Hamilton believed that businessmen, the educated, and the professional class should man the new government. Not only did they have competence, but they also could look beyond parochial local interests and be focused on the good of the Union.[65] This was a kind of natural aristocracy that the Founders looked to. The Federalist party generally reflected that view, but with the large landowners thrown in—and their general focus on leadership by the economically well-off—their idea of a natural aristocracy perhaps slid toward oligarchy. They were consistent with Founding principles in favoring republican government while opposing outright democracy, and being very fearful of the latter leading to the emergence of demagogues. Republicanism distinguished between liberty and licentiousness and resisted uncontrolled power in the masses—in short, it embraced ordered liberty. The Federalists said that the masses—the many—should be represented in a well-ordered government, and were in line with the classical notion of a mixed government with democratic, aristocratic, and monarchic elements on an equal footing. Outright rule by the people would destroy liberty. They also believed, contrary to what might have seemed the case with Hamilton's federal economic initiatives above, that liberty would also be decimated if government became too powerful. It is possible, however, that with the Federalist party, the realism of the Founders was transformed into a cynicism or pessimism about the people—the common people were held to be more incapable and untrustworthy than perhaps they really were.[66] The result was, as John C. Miller says, "[t]he authoritarian element became progressively stronger in the party [and] distrust of the people became more pronounced."[67] This was probably reflected in their selective opposition to the limiting of civil rights in some states in the 1790s—opposing the curtailing of property rights, which would have hurt their economically advantaged leaders, but not of free speech and religious liberty—and in their adopting of the Alien and Sedition Acts.[68]

In spite of the noise made by the democratic societies, democratization did not really advance much during this period. To be sure, the populist impulse was there, but with the renewed tightening of property requirements for the franchise and, even more, the cynicism the Federalists exhibited toward the common people, one could even say that the trend was slightly in the opposite direction. It might be that with the Federalist attempt to curtail rights by the application of the Sedition Acts and their push in an oligarchic direction, they challenged the "democratic" part of the democratic republic established by the Framers. Again, however, when the new state bills of rights, to say nothing of the federal Bill of Rights, and such developments as abolishing primogeniture are factored in, things remained as they had been with this exception: Perhaps culturally, with Shays' rebellion in the background, the American psyche may have become a touch more ochlocratic. Could this time period, then, have laid the mental groundwork for the later nullification crisis and then the Southern succession? As far as a furthering of the related question of equality is concerned, it can be seen along with this concern for the common man, by the new bills of rights, daughters' property rights, and again abolition of primogeniture—but it was very restrained. It concerned mostly legal rights, which would be expected in any republic to be equal.

The Federalists might have further harmed republican government if they had in the long run been successful in their selective application of rights guarantees: emphatic about property rights, but willing to compromise other rights also held as crucial by the Founding Era. These attitudes and actions could reasonably be said to have challenged popular sovereignty and the Federalists' increasing oligarchic ethos may have compromised both the Founding notions of mixed government and the need for a natural aristocracy (i.e., since an oligarchy is not the same thing as a natural aristocracy).

Finally, the hardening of the Federalists' thinking about the common man was another expression of a weakening of civic friendship and solidarity and regard for the common good during this period, and almost certainly over time would have incited social conflict.

Economic Developments. We have discussed the federal economic role, as fashioned by Hamilton. We mentioned his attempt to control the federal debt, which was something that the Founders—of which Hamilton himself was one— thought important to sustain a democratic republic. Growing prosperity characterized America during the Federalist Period; this was something that Tocqueville would say was critical for democratic republics. If the country had been edging problematically toward excessive luxury during the late colonial and Founding Era—which, as we have noted, some believed was the case—the strains of the Revolution and the economic problems of the Confederation period quelled that for many citizens.[69] Hamilton's policies helped stimulate expanded trade, the bringing in of foreign capital that helped markets to grow, and the developing of manufacturing and other industries. The agricultural economy was aided by the overseas demand for American foodstuffs caused by the British-French war.[70] The economy was further stimulated by the states' undertaking of various internal improvements. As Paul Johnson puts it, during Washington's presidency "America achieved takeoff into self-sustaining industrial growth."[71] All this helped continue the cultural norm of economic self-sufficiency for people.

Socio-Cultural Developments. Along with the economic depression of the 1780s, came some socio-cultural problems in the U.S. While there was increasing economic strain for some, for others—as happens in almost any era of economic downturn—there was wealth. The agrarian elements—the large majority of people—suffered while land speculators and some of the coastal-based merchant class did well. As Henry F. May writes, the effect was a weakening of "traditions of frugality and equality." There was also an increase of crime, social conflict, weakening religiosity, and a diminished moral tone. Maybe this is not surprising in the aftermath of the Revolution. Any politico-social upheaval—even a relatively restrained one like the American Revolution—is likely to cause some social dislocation and turmoil. It was even more likely when coupled with economic problems. Emigration was also increasing. In the 1790s, this caused a renewed effort by religious authorities and government—the federal response to the Whiskey Rebellion and the Alien and Sedition Acts might be understood as an expression of this—to make sure "the center held."[72] The efforts of religion came in the midst of changes occurring within it: trying to adapt itself to the changed situation of post-revolutionary America, struggling to come to grips with the influences of the Enlightenment and to moderate or transform them to make them compatible with basic Christian beliefs, and a rise of internal factionalism as traditional and liberal beliefs competed with each other.[73]

These changes should be commented on; more will be said later about the substantial changes that issued forth from them in the nineteenth century and the implications they had for the American political order as time went on. A noteworthy point that May makes about the developments of the 1790s is that "the more conservative elements in American religion," despite being "the more literate and the more organized, lost all chance they may have had of channeling or controlling the great and chaotic religious energies of American society."[74] While the early liberals were not deists, their views bore some marks of deism. While they talked of God's fatherhood, they emphasized more that he was the Architect—a deistic notion—and Governor of the universe. Their notion of fatherhood was not a fully Christian one, however; they saw God as a benevolent and understanding Father, not as one who would deal with men as a just—and if need be—harsh judge. Still, men would merit their eternal place depending entirely on their free-willed efforts. They also were increasingly turning away from a belief in the possibility of eternal damnation. While they surely wanted to liberate themselves from any lingering Calvinist notion of predestination, they seemed also—even while upholding the doctrine—to downplay the role of grace. They were edging toward a view of human nature associated with utopianism. Man was slowly being made the center, displacing God. They generally sought to downplay the necessity of accepting a doctrinal formulation for church membership—in so doing, and whether they fully realized it, they were perhaps diminishing the importance of doctrine per se. In New England, the liberals of the last decade of the eighteenth century were paving the way for Unitarianism.[75]

The encroaching utopianism of the religious liberals was tied up with the spirit of the new American nation, which they saw as a representing not just political advancement for man, but social and economic as well. As Sydney E. Ahlstrom puts it, "The idea prevailed widely that 'this new man, this American' was a new Adam, sinless, innocent—mankind's great second chance."[76] May notes that for "many" Americans, the millennium, the Second Coming of Christ, "tended to be vaguely identified with the success of American institutions"[77]— as if America was to play a central role in Christ's ultimate New Creation. In a less apocalyptic vein, May tells us that there was a close identification of America, republican principles, and Protestantism. He says that at least up to 1795, Protestantism, republicanism, and the Enlightenment seemed to most New Englanders to belong together."[78] They had a positive view of the Enlightenment—a matter we shall not explore here—which they identified with moderation, compromise, order, and tolerance (elements that we have noted were part of the Founding Fathers' thinking), although they vigorously opposed, via the Federalist party, the *radical* Enlightenment of the French Revolution.[79] Some Americans embraced the French Revolution, seeing no incompatibility with it and Protestantism or American constitutional principles because it advanced republicanism.[80]

Even with these problematical developments, organized religion had a markedly salutary effect on American culture. As Henry Adams writes in one of his classic works, *The United States in 1800*, except for the matter of temperance America was a moral society.[81] If a movement away from traditional Christianity and doctrine was gaining strength, it was not yet affecting morality (and would not for some time, as Tocqueville's observation about that in Chapter 1 indicated). Perhaps this also reflected the "Second Great Awakening," which like the first had its greatest impact among average citizens.[82]

Otherwise, the movement west in America continued and with it the loosening of extended family and community ties that began happening in the Founding Era. The flip side of this was that the urban population—which troubled both Jefferson and John Adams, both of whom worried that a large urban population would diminish the possibilities of sustaining republican government—was small.[83] There were no extremely large cities.

On another subject, we saw that education was important in the thinking of the Founding Fathers in helping to sustain a democratic republic. It apparently was not accorded the same kind of importance in the popular mind, however, nor was it readily available in a formalized way. As Henry Adams says, "The labor of the land had precedence over that of the mind throughout the United States."[84] He posited that, "[u]ntil they were satisfied that knowledge was money, they would not insist upon high education" (which essentially meant any kind of formal education in academic subjects).[85] Even books, outside of those privately owned, were not abundant. There were some libraries, though not a large number; a number of these were connected with colleges. Even though Benjamin Franklin had founded the first library in 1732, by 1800 all the libraries in the U.S. together "could hardly show fifty thousand volumes, including duplicates, fully one third being...theological."[86] The stirrings of educational reform were underway, however. The democratic societies promoted the cause of free education for the public above any other. Their rationale was to be echoed many times in the future of the U.S.: they sought to use a newly-created school system to "reform society." The schools they sought would be "soundly republican, secular, and practical." An early ideologist of this republican-oriented educational reform movement was Robert Coram, a Democratic-Republican party activist in Delaware. He was a supporter of French Enlightenment thinking, an egalitarian, and something of a utopian. He believed that social wrongs could be eliminated by putting in place republicanism, just laws, and equal schools. Like most egalitarians, he wanted uniformity: the schools had to be uniform. Further, schools had to be free, public (i.e., governmentally-controlled), should embrace or convey no religious perspectives or "systems of manners," and essentially should not encourage competition among pupils. The aim rang of egalitarianism, utopianism, and the later socialism: to make it possible for everyone to earn an equal living. May says that Coram's views "had a big future in American educational reform," even while they did not advance far in the 1790s. The most fertile ground for such educational ideas was New England, whose public school systems— commended by Coram—were already taking shape.[87]

We can see that in the socio-cultural area there were in the 1790s stirrings of a number of things that would have important implications for the sustenance of Founding principles over time. There was an increasing optimism about human nature that contrasted with the hard-nosed realism of the Founding (the latter was seen in the stress on such institutional mechanisms as separation of powers and checks and balances). The fact that this new perspective afflicted elements in the American religious world—especially in highly influential New England—was particularly portentous because their religious perspective is what primarily shapes most people's outlook about man and society.[88] American religion began to change from having a traditional Christian perspective to one influenced by the Enlightenment. These changes began at this point; the implications for American political life would be off in the future, since changes in thought take awhile before they affect the activities of persons and cultures. One of the crucial subjects religious change is profoundly connected with is morality and virtue, which were nearly at the top of the principles in Chapter 1. This, in turn, opened the door for the expansion of individualism, especially because of the Enlightenment influence. We consider in later chapters how ongoing religious changes affected morality and individualism over time. The early changes seen in the philosophy animating American education gave further impetus to the downplaying of traditional religion, a loss of realism about human nature, and the growth of the egalitarian idea—challenging the Founding Era's much more restrained view of equality and the value of a natural aristocracy. Moreover, the very view of education that people like Coram started to espouse was sharply different from that of the Founding Fathers, which stressed moral and citizenship education and, for those who would be leaders, the liberal arts.[89] While in some sense, Coram can be said to have embraced the notion of citizenship education, his focus on "practical" studies would seem to have left little room for the liberal arts. Secular education, such as Coram called for, was largely unknown in the Founding Era and, as stated, it would have scarcely conceived of a notion of moral training apart from religion.

Intellectual Currents. Although some of what has been said above suggests intellectual currents afoot in the U.S. in the Federalist Period, we can say a bit more about this that has some implications for the maintenance of the principles in Chapter 1. Jefferson figures in this, even though he came into full prominence after the Federalist Period. A "child of the Enlightenment,"[90] he had a "confidence in progressive change." He believed that morality would carry the day in political life, that government in the future would be conducted without force[91]—as if no one would ever need to be coerced, even though the whole notion of governmental authority involves it rightly being able to compel men to cooperate toward the attainment of the common public good.[92] With some aid from good leaders—as opposed to an elevated cadre of rulers mistrustful of the people, as with the Federalists—the people would make right choices. As Henry Adams said about him, he "held the faith that men would improve morally with their physical and intellectual growth." Jefferson did not say what would stimulate this improvement, however.[93] It was not religion,[94] nor was it scientific and technological progress (as some Enlightenment figures thought).[95] Adams suggested that it was perhaps simply man's nature,[96] as if human nature could be improved by some inner force. This contrasted with the view of the Federalists, as indicated by the above, but was possibly the wave of the future. As May states, Jefferson's distinctions between progress and perfectibility and between scientific and moral progress—a kind of distinction between a moderate American version of the Enlightenment and the radical European version—were mainstays of American culture—profoundly influencing even American religion—for a long time.[97] Even if Adams dismissed the influence of religion on Jefferson, May observes that Jefferson's perspective really comes forth from his religious thinking: there is "[a] benign God, a purposeful universe, and a universal moral sense."[98]

When assessing these intellectual currents, we can see the same slippage from realism as above. With his belief in the common man's ability to act rightly and his optimism about man generally, the one Founder Jefferson seems to deviate from the realism of the Founders generally (recall that in spite of being grouped among their number, he was not at the 1787 Convention). This is one of the first in a long history of American expressions of faith in the people. His belief that human improvement could be achieved without the force of religion—despite his insistence, seen in Chapter 1, that it is essential for nations—was not a view that would have been embraced in the American thought or culture of the Founding Era. While Americans have believed in the possibility of human progress since John Winthrop's famous "city upon a hill" sermon,[99] it had not been seen as anything that could be achieved without great effort or without the guidance of Providence. Jefferson's almost automatic view of it—even if his unrealism was inconsistent throughout the years—bespeaks the Enlightenment, something like Adam Smith's "invisible hand" reaching well beyond economics. This perspective would become more common in future times.

History, Politics, and Culture During the Jeffersonian Era (the Administrations of Jefferson and Madison), 1801-1817

The 1800 election, which permanently ushered the Federalists out of power and brought Thomas Jefferson and his Democratic-Republican party—which he only reluctantly embraced—into control of the executive and legislative branches of the federal government, has been called by some "the revolution of 1800."[100] This may be overly dramatic, but still it did represent in some sense an acceptance of ideas identified with Jefferson's version of republicanism, or Jeffersonianism. While there were differences, as we shall see neither Jefferson nor his successor and the last of the Founding Fathers to be President, James Madison, sharply turned away from the policies of Adams, Hamilton and the Federalists generally. The major historical and political developments of the period 1801-1817 were as follows: 1) The Jeffersonian challenge to the federal courts, which included the repeal of the Federalist-passed Judiciary Act of 1801 that had established many new judgeships and the attempted removal of Justice Samuel Chase; 2) The U.S. Supreme Court's firmly establishing its power, in spite of the initial Jeffersonian assault, by the 1803 *Marbury v. Madison* decision in which it clearly asserted its prerogative to declare acts of Congress unconstitutional; 3) The Louisiana Purchase of 1803 and the ensuing Lewis and Clark expedition; 4) The ongoing struggles with the Barbary pirates that were crippling American trade in the Mediterranean; 5) The Aaron Burr conspiracy to supposedly bring about the severing of some western lands from the Union; 6) The trading boycott actions against Great Britain culminating in the Embargo Act of 1807 caused by the impressments of American sailors at sea and other harassment of American shipping, which seemed to backfire and cause considerable damage to American commerce;[101] 7) The end of the Indian wars in the old Northwest, as signaled by General William Henry Harrison's victory at the Battle of Tippecanoe; 8) The War of 1812, as the culmination of the nearly decade-long tensions with Britain and the result of early American nationalism,[102] which was by far the most significant event during the Madison Presidency; 9) The Hartford Convention of 1814, which was the most dramatic expression of New England's frustration at economic disadvantages from the War of 1812 and the first significant assertion of the sucessionist idea; 10) The developing "National System" under Madison, in which the federal government consolidated its Federalist-inaugurated economic policies and augmented them with substantial funding for internal improvements and a protective tariff; and 11) The enhanced migration of Americans westward and increasing settlement west of the Appalachians. Against this background of the basic historical developments of the Jeffersonian Era, the subjects that seem particularly pertinent for examination and comparison with the points set forth in Chapter 1 are: Jeffersonian principles; federal and state power and powers of the branches of the federal government; economics and government economic policy; parties, interests, and democratization; the growth of American nationalism; military power; and socio-cultural developments.

Jeffersonian Principles. The main principles that animated Jefferson, his party, and this era—and which must in some sense be said to have been embraced by the majority of the electorate in the 1800 election—were the following: 1) Stress on the individual and on natural rights; 2) Consent as the basis for political legitimacy; 3) Majority rule, but protection of minorities; 4) The securing of liberty as the basic purpose of government; 5) Limited governmental power in general; 6) Education as a necessary means of producing the kind of enlightened electorate a democratic republic requires; 7) Stress on agrarian life as the most conducive to the shaping of virtue, but encouraging a kind of balance among agriculture, commerce, and manufacturing; 8) Free enterprise, private property, and economic self-sufficiency; 9) A suspicion of power and privilege; 10) A more equal distribution of wealth; 11) Stress on economic development and western settlement, but in an orderly fashion so as to avoid political tensions; 12) Equality of treatment and equal opportunity for social and economic advancement; 13) The dignity of the common man, although Jefferson himself also favored a natural aristocracy of merit and there is much question as to whether the Jeffersonians favored democracy (as discussed below); 14) A pacific approach—at least characterizing Jefferson himself—in trying to solve international disputes and problems, which was reflected by the embargo policy (Harold U. Faulkner calls the approach "peaceable coercion"); 15) Opposition to centralized governmental power and strict construction—i.e., narrow interpretation—of federal authority under the Constitution; and 16) The right of revolution if government became oppressive.[103] The last of these principles, except for the American Revolution itself, operated at the philosophical level, although one wonders—particularly with the view of some scholars that Jeffersonianism fed sectionalism and strong anti-centralization sentiment in the South[104]—if it did not in some way help to stimulate the later nullification and successionist movements that culminated in the Civil War.

In his famous First Inaugural Address, Jefferson added some other principles that will be helpful in our comparison of the Jeffersonian Era with the Founding principles: equal justice for all; avoiding "entangling alliances" with other nations; free elections; eliminating government debt; preservation of the federal system, which involved both a solicitousness for state government power but also a vigorous national government; "a well-disciplined militia"; the "diffusion of information" (i.e., more readily available education), and the rights of religious liberty, press freedom, habeas corpus, and trial by an impartial jury.

Freedoms, Rights => Success

Actually, he emphasized that these were not just Democratic-Republican (i.e., Jeffersonian) principles, but ones that all Americans embraced.[105]

Don E. Fehrenbacher makes an observation about Jeffersonian principles that has pertinence for the inquiry undertaken in this book. He says that not long after the Jeffersonian Era the "Jeffersonian tradition separated into two distinct and contrary strains of thought. One stressed freedom through restraint of power, or minority rights; the other stressed democratic use of power, or majority rule." The result was that as American history unfolded, both sides in controversies such as the sectional struggle over slavery, the extent of economic freedom, and the legitimacy of the welfare state appealed to Jeffersonian principles.[106]

We shall see how well President Jefferson carried out Jeffersonian principles in practice and how greatly his chief policies differed from the Federalists he so ardently opposed. We should consider first how these principles measured up to those of the Founding Era. Most of them, especially (as should be evident) those that Jefferson enunciated above in his First Inaugural Address, conform to those that we spoke of in Chapter 1. A few observations are in order, however. A stress on the common man, a republican spirit, and a belief in the need for greater equality run through this corpus of Jeffersonian principles. To be sure, stressing the value of consent is part of the principle of popular sovereignty. The suspicion of power and privilege, while it may be seen as consistent with popular sovereignty, may also jeopardize the civility and civic friendship characteristic of American culture in the Founding Era and the solidarity that social ethics indicates a good political order needs. It is also possible that it gave rise to a heightening inter-class hostility that was seen in the Jacksonian Era and later. Also, one wonders if this was consistent with other views of Jefferson in favor of qualifications for suffrage (at least to show some attachment to the community, if not to have to have property outright)[107] and in support of a natural aristocracy. There is no doubt that the Founding Era upheld a kind of equal treatment—seen in equality under the law—and perhaps the stress on economic self-sufficiency and initiative, the middle class character of early America, and the perceived value of widespread land ownership suggested equal opportunity and a condition of relative equality in the distribution of wealth. Moreover, the classical tradition that America emerged from (e.g., Aristotle)[108] emphasized a relative equality of wealth—that is, avoiding extremes of wealth and poverty—as needed for civic peace. Still, one wonders if this emphasis on equality in the area of wealth does not go beyond the thinking of the Founders—one thinks even of the Jeffersonian Madison saying in Federalist 10 that unequal property grows out of the innate inequality of talent[109]—and may not have laid the groundwork for an ever-greater stress on economic equality as American history unfolded.

There is no question that the Founding Era viewed liberty as a main object of government, but for the Jeffersonians to say that it is its *basic* purpose—that is, essentially its only purpose—was probably not consistent with that era. After all, the Preamble of the Constitution effectively says that the purposes of the country, *besides* "secur[ing] the Blessings of Liberty," are "to form a more

Embrace of individual
&
Rule by people

perfect Union, establish Justice, insure domestic Tranquility, provide for the common Defence"—all these essentially relate to achieving order and security—and "promote the general Welfare"—which might be said to help achieve what social ethics calls public prosperity.[110] We also saw in Chapter 1 how the Founders viewed the securing of natural rights *and* the promoting of the common good *both* as the purposes of government. The Jeffersonians' heavy focus on liberty points the way to the views of classical liberalism late in the nineteenth century and also to the avowed position of liberalism from the 1930s to the 1960s with its strong civil libertarian bent, even while the latter repudiated a sweeping adherence to liberty in the economic realm.

Virtue was certainly seen as essential by the Founders, but they—or most of them, at any rate—would not have been willing to agree with the Jeffersonians that agrarian life was necessarily the most likely to promote it. They did not address the question of a balanced development of the different sectors of the economy, but the practice of doing this of course began very quickly after the new government was put in place—which might be expected in light of political pressures from each of these sectors. Also in economics, the stress on free enterprise, private property, and economic self-sufficiency certainly conforms to the principles and practice of life in the Founding Era.

While the Founding Fathers do not make western settlement one of their basic principles, Article IV, section 3 of the Constitution certainly anticipates it. The desire of the Jeffersonians to accomplish it without political conflict certainly conforms to the need for civility, civic friendship, and solidarity.

The pacific foreign policy tendencies were not something specifically embraced by the Founders; they did not address this directly. It does seem, though, that they thought that a nation would have to be prepared for military action to insure its security. By the same token, realists that they were, it is not likely that they would have wanted to rush into military ventures and would have favored other means of resolving foreign policy problems short of that. Jefferson was the major Founder to speak against entangling alliances, but that practice started right away with the Washington administration where Jefferson served as Secretary of State.

Certainly, the Founding Era opposed over-centralization of power, but not necessarily a narrow construction of federal power. The federal government would do what it had to do and do it energetically. If a narrow interpretation meant there would be less than a vigorous federal government, this would not have accorded with what the Framers sought. All the other principles Jefferson stated in his First Inaugural are to be found among the Founding Era's beliefs about factors needed to sustain republican government in Chapter 1.

Federal and State Power and Powers of the Branches of the Federal Government. As noted, the Jeffersonians opposed excessive federal power and centralized power in general; they advocated state power and states' rights. One of the first things the Jeffersonians did when they got into power was to repeal the Judiciary Act of 1801, as noted above, which they viewed as further consolidating federal power. This demonstrated not just or perhaps most basically an anti-centralization emphasis, but their desire to keep intact what

State > Fed.

they understood to be the proper balance between federal and state power mentioned in Jefferson's First Inaugural. Both Jefferson and Madison were concerned that the limited-powers character of the federal government, as made clear in the Federalist Papers,[111] be maintained—with specific alterations to be done only through constitutional amendment. Jefferson was fond of denouncing the notion of implied powers. Still, when confronted with Napoleon's offer of the Louisiana Territory, in spite of personal anguish about its constitutionality, he went ahead and did it. He was concerned that a constitutional amendment would take too much time, and was confronted by the possibility that Napoleon would withdraw the offer.[112] His constitutional reluctance when confronted with questions like this may not have been shared by most Jeffersonians who, after all, were in favor of more U.S. territory and westward expansion.[113] Jefferson's constitutional scruples about his trade embargo were similarly submerged by his judgment of what political realities necessitated.[114] In his administration, Madison opposed popular legislation because he thought it unconstitutional. He vetoed the so-called Bonus Bill near the end of his second term because it provided federal funding for internal improvements. In doing so, he rejected the broad interpretation of the general welfare and interstate commerce clauses used to justify it. He distinguished this from questions about the constitutionality of the Bank of the United States and tariff policy; some in an ongoing way charged that both were unconstitutional. He insisted that there was never any question about the latter's constitutionality, and that the former's was established by "open debate and cumulative precedent."[115]

Another point about governmental power that should be noted concerns the treatment of individual liberty during the Jeffersonian Era. The noted constitutional scholar Leonard Levy has written about the "darker side" of civil liberties under Jefferson. He says that the embargo was put in force with very insufficient national and Congressional debate, and that Jefferson did not even explain the need for it and why some loss of liberty and economic sacrifice were needed to accomplish the goal of protecting America from foreign danger. Levy indicates that liberties were violated in a substantial way; in fact, he says that enforcement of the embargo "carried the administration to the precipice of unlimited and arbitrary powers as measured by any known American standards." As passive resistance to the embargo intensified, his administration used increasingly coercive measures, and he secured legislation that permitted questionable searches and seizures—though Congress would not grant the sweeping, virtually unlimited warrantless search and seizure powers he sought—and violations of self-incrimination and other due process protections.[116] Levy suggests that his actions were perhaps motivated by "his conviction that the great American experiment in self-government and liberty was in nearly constant danger."[117] In effect, some civil liberties had to be violated some of the time to preserve republican government. Abraham Lincoln took a similar position later during the Civil War. One wonders, however, if Jefferson's condoning of similar acts violating constitutional liberties by General James Wilkinson, who was embroiled in the Aaron Burr treason case, did not reach such a principled level. He was perhaps willing to allow political considerations, public opinion, and his belief that those he thought guilty should not necessarily have the full protections of law override his commitment to the rule of law.[118]

Some developments during the Jeffersonian Era affected the power relations among the three branches of the federal government. One concerned the powers of the presidency, which first waxed during Jefferson's terms, then waned during Madison's. As Marshall Smelser puts it, "Jefferson quietly preserved the Federalist conception of presidential power."[119] He seemed to be able to skillfully handle and manage Congress,[120] and it was during his administration that the president began to take an active part in shaping legislation.[121] He consolidated his power within the executive branch by an early version of the spoils system. Fehrenbacher says that this "partly offset the formal separation of powers" and achieved "a degree of operating unity in the federal government." He "completed the general framework of the modern presidency," with its activism and policy leadership with which we are familiar.[122] Other examples of this were the presidential deployment of U.S. forces abroad without Congressional approval (the conflict with the Barbary pirates) and a continued substantial federal economic role (including funds for the internal improvements that Madison later opposed), as discussed below.[123] This was, of course, in addition to the Louisiana Purchase and the Embargo Act. Then there was the attempt to undo the judicial reforms of the Federalists and to curb the power of the courts, which, while carried out by his party in Congress, had Jefferson's quiet support. During Madison's terms, Congress enhanced its power at the expense of the presidency—in spite of the fact that the Democratic-Republicans still controlled Congress. Congress took more policy initiative and was less cooperative about presidential appointments. It even got into administrative details, which is a particular prerogative of the executive. Perhaps this occurred because of Madison and Jefferson having different personas, but perhaps it was also because of Madison's firm convictions about the constitutional roles of the two branches—which, as his Bonus Bill veto indicates, he was less willing than Jefferson to compromise on.[124]

It is interesting to note that as Congress's power was heightening during this period, its members began to look out for their personal pecuniary interests. With the Bill of Rights provision prohibiting Congressional pay raises to take effect for the Congress approving them not having been ratified—it had to wait 200 years until it became the 27th Amendment in 1992—they voted themselves a salary increase in the final days of the Madison administration.[125] Promoting economic self-interest in the Jeffersonian Era and strident, unmeasured rhetorical attacks during the Federalist Period were not the only examples of political opportunism during these early decades of the Republic. Some were already twisting the obvious meaning of language for political purposes. When the time came to bar the slave trade in 1808, as specifically provided for in the Constitution, some argued that this provision also forbade the movement of slaves *within* the boundaries of the U.S. because, they claimed, the terms "importation"—used in Article I, Section 9—and "migration" were synonymous. According to one of his present-day biographers, Drew R. McCoy, Madison, who was the primary drafter of the Constitution, "found this interpretation astonishing, even incomprehensible,"[126] and there was no basis for it in the Constitutional Convention's deliberations. Apparently, the early anti-slavery crusaders felt justified in altering the meaning of the Constitution. Interestingly, one of the supporters of this strained interpretation was John Jay, the former Chief Justice and one of Madison's co-writers of the Federalist Papers. One is led to think that, even though he was no longer on the Court, his view presaged the novel interpretations of constitutional provisions of justices later in history.

Even while the courts were under assault during at least the early part of the Jeffersonian Era, they were effectively establishing their power that would make them in the distant future—in the minds of some—the most powerful branch. The *Marbury* decision was not during the Jeffersonian Era followed by other decisions—or, for that matter, during Marshall's entire long tenure as Chief Justice—that declared acts of Congress unconstitutional. That was to happen in future times. In fact, there were hardly any cases that struck down state statutes or expanded federal power. The latter would have to wait for *McCulloch v. Maryland*[127] shortly after the end of the Jefferson-Madison period. It was as if the politically-astute Marshall knew he could push only so far: The Court merely had to act to establish its power, in practice as well as theory, to declare federal laws unconstitutional—which the Founders anticipated would emerge in some fashion—in order to firm up its position as a serious co-equal branch of government. With this foundation, Marshall made the obvious jump seven years later in *Fletcher v. Peck* (1810) (mentioned above) to apply judicial review to state legislative enactments. That posed no problem, in light of the Supremacy Clause of the Constitution. The problem was that—while not exactly making the kind of novel, twisted interpretation of constitutional wording that Jay, et al. did above—he read a meaning into the contract clause that was probably not intended by the Founding Fathers. What Marshall probably did was to use the clause to justify a decision that, in essence, involved an unenumerated right (i.e., a right grounded in natural law or the traditions of a free people)—this may not have been problematical, but his loose reading of the contract clause and the very *notion* of contract perhaps was.[128]

We can add the following to the above. It is obvious that for the most part Jefferson's and Madison's pragmatism—as would be the case throughout American history—won out in their personal struggles about upholding Jeffersonian principles. While, as stated, constitutional principles might be sacrificed in the short run to, in effect, save the Constitution (at least in time of exigency)—the same could not be said about basic moral principles—it is doubtful that this was the case here. Perhaps they set too easy of a standard too early about permitting deviation from civil liberties and other constitutional principles. Moreover, Jefferson's apparent political opportunism in the cases mentioned harmed the rule of law. It did not exactly signify that he was allowing politics utterly to descend into the mere power struggle we spoke of, but it certainly made politics seem to be more central even than the rule of law. This was reinforced by the Jeffersonians' abortive assault on the Supreme Court. There was no particular abuse of power by the Court as an institution or by

Justice Chase or Chief Justice Marshall (who they might also have gone on to try to impeach). Arguably, political considerations—even if masquerading as Jeffersonian principles—crowded out the rule of law and judicial independence. In a different way, the worst side of politics trumped principle when Democratic-Republican-controlled Congresses voted themselves pay raises, continuing the practice of legislative self-enrichment, if more subtly, of the Yazoo affair. The tradition of American politicians advancing themselves economically by their official actions—so much in opposition to the public spiritedness of the Founding Era—was becoming firmly implanted.

If separation of powers may have been directly jeopardized by the Jeffersonian attack on the Court, a subtler transformation of it may have occurred with Jefferson's steps to become a policy leader. Yet, it also occurred in the other direction under Madison—who was less willing or less capable of playing this role than his predecessor—when Congress got involved in running the executive branch. Probably, Jefferson's presidential policy role was not anticipated by the Founders—Madison's disagreement with it signaled that— and while Congress was meant to be the paramount branch, the level of its administrative meddling almost certainly was not either. The precedent of back-and-forth advancement and then diminishing of the powers of one or the other political branch was established. It is possible that we could just view this as an ongoing expression of the tension of a separated powers system, but one thinks that the limits could have been more readily and logically understood (especially regarding limitations on Congress). One could argue, thinking back to the above, that they *were* under Washington. In any event, probably the most enduring alteration of the separation of powers doctrine under Jefferson was his expansion of presidential power.

Finally, we noted the beginnings of the relativization of language for the purpose of promoting a socio-political agenda—with a moralistic justification, as we continue to see today. Part of this involved the creating of a constitutional-legal fiction—the understanding given to contract—which serves as a kind of early, if inauspicious, precedent for judicial actions of the twentieth and twenty-first centuries. So, curiously, as the Supreme Court's power was being illegitimately threatened by the Jeffersonians, it was more quietly—but also illegitimately, at least in terms of the justification for its action—expanding it.

Economics and Government Economic Policy. Even though Jefferson had opposed the Bank of the United States when the Federalists were in power, under the influence of his well-regarded Treasury Secretary Albert Gallatin he came to view it as an economically valuable institution. He saw it as working along with the state-chartered banks, which the Jeffersonians were more disposed to, to bring about economic development. Unlike Hamilton, however, he strongly opposed deficit spending and, following the sentiment of his First Inaugural, sought to retire the federal debt as quickly as possible. He believed that a permanent government debt drained capital from the private sector in taxes, thereby harming the primary forces for economic advancement. While not opposed to trade, his policies—even before the embargo—stressed economic self-sufficiency. Also, in line with his First Inaugural and in spite of the agrarian bias of the Jeffersonians, he sought a balance in the economy among the agricultural, commercial, and manufacturing sectors. He may have sought particularly to help farmers, but saw the need for development of the overall economy. In contrast to the Federalists (as suggested above), Jefferson's administration worked to develop the West by making it easier for settlers to purchase lands and by increasingly pushing the Indian tribes out. The western settlement was not to be a ragtag affair; he sought an orderly development that, for example, was impatient with illicit squatters. An orderly development was necessary to avoid political tensions and the multiplication of a class of subsistence farmers who would become the agrarian poor. By the time of his Second Inaugural in 1805, Jefferson was also strongly promoting federal assistance for internal improvements and called for a constitutional amendment to make it possible. Gallatin proposed an elaborate plan for it.[129]

As far as Madison is concerned, besides pushing through the chartering of a new Bank of the United States—the Second Bank was established in 1816—the centerpiece of his economic program was the tariff. In fact, incongruously, it went beyond the Hamiltonian tariff to not just raise revenue but also protect, of all things, manufacturing.[130] In spite of both Jefferson's and Madison's constitutional reluctance about the federal role in internal improvements, in fact the federal government was involved during this era—as in the Federalist Period—in subsidizing them to some degree.[131] This included the financial support for the building and extension of the National Road.[132] This was only part of the economic activity generated by the federal government, which also included the Post Office—already a large national enterprise—social insurance and hospitals for disabled sailors, Indian trading posts, and the purchase of arms.[133]

As might be expected, the states and their local governments (where the Jeffersonians were especially strong) were even more active in economic life—both as stimulants to its development and regulators. Besides a heavy involvement in internal improvements—which even featured outright ownership of canals and later railroads—and school construction, they provided bounties, tax exemptions, and subsidies; engaged in public-private ventures; got some control over banking and early corporations by the power to charter; licensed trades and professions; set standards for products; and legislated about creditor-debtor relations. After awhile, their substantial efforts especially in internal improvements got them into financial difficulty.[134]

This all gives us a picture of the role of government in economic life during the Jeffersonian Era. Even if the Jeffersonians believed that economic activity was best left to private initiative, this did not mean that is was an age of laissez faire. As Fehrenbacher writes, "few Americans subscribed to the doctrine of minimal government...On the contrary, believing that the state was their servant, the people repeatedly invoked its aid in the economic development of the country."[135]

As far as the overall economic prosperity of the people was concerned, it continued to grow throughout the Jeffersonian Era for most of the country.[136] Just prior to the War of 1812, economic woes afflicted the agricultural sector because of British and French actions; this probably motivated many in Congress to vote for the declaration of war against Britain.[137] New England suffered economically during the embargo, but was actually helped economically by the War.[138] The demise of the First Bank of the United States in 1811 and the War stimulated a serious inflation, which was stemmed only after the establishment of the Second Bank. Still, it was in general a period of rising prosperity and, with the opening of western lands, the notion of America as an "opportunity society" took deeper root. An important part of the opportunity society, which was so much tied up with the Jeffersonian pro-agrarian vision, became firmly implanted at this time: some measure of economic self-sufficiency, self-employment, and owning real property outright.[139] Later, of course, this vision extended beyond people on the land—the family farm—to people in other sectors of society.

We can make the following observations about this subject area in light of the principles and practices from Chapter 1. Restraining government debt was certainly consistent with both Founding and Jefferson's own principles, although it is not so clear that the Founders believed there should be no government debt. It was already mentioned that Jefferson's approach to western settlement, with its desire to avoid creating a polarized situation regarding wealth, showed a concern for the common good and civic friendship. Similarly, in a cultural sense, the Jeffersonian Era continued the spirit of the colonial and Founding periods in maintaining a communal orientation—instead of a laissez faire one—in economics. However, some of the state regulatory policies above and the corporate chartering power opened the door to the transformed economy of the decades ahead. Like the Founding Era, the prosperity sought was not excessive; people were not fixated on material consumption and luxury.

Parties, Interests, and Democratization. We have listed the basic Jeffersonian principles and discussed how the Jefferson and Madison administrations adopted a number of the policies of the Federalists before them. Still, one should not assume that somehow there was limited political conflict or that a cross-party consensus reigned during this period. While the nastiness of political rhetoric may not have reached the levels of the 1790s, it was still evident. The opposition of the Federalists to westward expansion was a chief example of this.[140] Another, of course, was the harsh opposition of Federalist New England to, first, the embargo and then the War of 1812, both of which hurt New England economically. Faulkner says that Jefferson's embargo gave "declining [F]ederalism a new lease on life."[141] Partisan politics seemed to be a pervasive point of controversy; Smelser indicates that many people were almost defined by their party. Party competition was probably more intense than even in the 1790s because the parties were now clearly defined and established. This led to a large jump in electoral turnout, at least in Congressional and legislative districts where party competition was strongest. The first refinements of political campaigning occurred in the Jeffersonian Era. Mass popular appeal started to become important, with both parties now using democratic-sounding rhetoric, techniques to reach the masses, and developing stronger organizations. The spoils system to reward party loyalty, which Jefferson began to use in a restrained way in his administration, was already in place in a much more free-wheeling way on the state level—paving the way for the age of Jackson.[142] Local government institutions generally took on a more democratic tinge.[143]

Madison was quite well aware of the increasing democratization that was going on. A few years after he left the presidency, he wrote that he saw universal suffrage and short terms for all federal offices looming in light of the new attitudes. He was concerned that a property-less majority would become a threat to the rights of the propertied minority. He did not believe that protection of the rights of property could any longer be achieved by suffrage restrictions or institutional changes, and seemed to place his hope in the reality of the extended republic, the popular sense of justice reinforced by sound education, and—somewhat contrary to the weakening sense of deference mentioned above—to the authority he thought those of great property would automatically command.[144] Two of Jefferson's Cabinet members and lieutenants, Henry Dearborn and Levi Lincoln, diminished the importance of property as a basis for protecting liberty. The former said it needed no special protection, agreeing with Madison that it almost automatically generated respect. The latter held that an enlightened citizenry and not property was what most insured republicanism, and so property-holding should not at all be the basis of representation.[145] He was certainly very much at odds with Edmund Burke on this.[146] As it was, the large landholdings of many old families had disappeared after 1800, as a result of the abolition of primogeniture and entail.[147] This was an obvious indication of greater democratization and advancing equality.

The orientation and actions of the parties and the increasing democratic character of political attitudes were further significant indications of the greater democratization taking place. It was suddenly not so popular, at least in common understanding, to think in terms of a natural aristocracy—in spite of the fact that toward the end of their lives, as we noted in Chapter 1, Jefferson and Adams would commiserate about the perennial need for it. American life was becoming less hierarchically ordered and more individualistic; the deferential attitudes mentioned in Chapter 1 were less evident. Even the Federalists were not willing to suggest, simply, that the best people should govern, but in effect that the best people should "come to power through the whole people."[148] Still, in the midst of this the colonial era American gentleman did not disappear, but was somewhat transformed into the husbandman—mostly yeomen but whose outlook spread to the town-based artisans, as well—who like his colonial forebears was staunchly republican-oriented but with a more intensely independent and democratic tinge.[149] They were, one might say, the gentlemen of a less deferential and more democratic era.

Interestingly, part of the impetus for this advancing democracy may have been the Protestant religion. In spite of its being the basis, as discussed below, for individual self-restraint—perhaps with an excessive sternness—it stimulated "broad participation in decision-making and a sense of equality among...lay [church] members."[150]

Still, in spite of this new democratic impulse and both political parties taking on a more democratic, common-man character—setting the stage for

Jacksonianism—they both also were increasingly aligning themselves with and seeking support from eastern monied interests.[151] These were the same monied interests that had been the flashpoint of opposition between the two parties in the 1790s and that were still the target of attack in Jeffersonian rhetoric.

In terms of comparison with the points of Chapter 1, we can say the following: First, regarding the inter-party tensions, especially pertaining to New England, the same observations made in the section on "The Rise of Political Parties and Voluntary Associations" in the part of this chapter about the Federalist Period apply here, except in a more limited way. To summarize otherwise: democratization advanced, with Founding notions about a natural aristocracy, property rights, the representation of property in government, and restrained equality challenged or debunked—though such ideas as the gentleman do not disappear, but were transformed and further democratized. The organic, hierarchical, deferential character of American culture receded and individualism advanced. As noted above, money affected politics more—as seen with the continuing potency of monied interests, regardless of which party and socio-politico-economic perspective ruled.

Growth of American Nationalism. There were several factors that caused the War of 1812,[152] but many historians have identified American nationalism as the primary one.[153] This certainly demonstrated that, in spite of growing sectionalism, American pride and national identity were strong. To be sure, it almost swept the U.S. toward a potentially disastrous defeat and featured such destructive manifestations as an imperialistic effort to seize Canada[154] and mob violence against anti-War critics.[155] The nationalist fervor continued with the close of the War[156]—perhaps accompanying the sense of confidence that Americans now had in their strength (noted above), despite the War's ending essentially in a draw. It prompted Madison to push aggressively for a sweeping agenda of an enhanced federal role in economic development and internal improvements and a permanently strengthened military—all initiatives that went against the traditional Jeffersonian grain. Part of this was the country's first protective tariff and the reestablishing of the Bank of the United States.[157] In short, the War had a permanent effect on the nature and activities of the federal government. This was to be buttressed in the decade after the Jeffersonian Era by a series of Supreme Court decisions opening the door to the greater exercise of federal power. The expansionist spirit of the War also seemed to become a permanent feature of the American psyche. It expressed itself after the War— prompted by the general westward orientation of the Jeffersonians—in the first stirrings of Manifest Destiny, and was to culminate almost a century later in the extension of American sovereignty to lands away from the continental U.S. after the Spanish-American War.

Military Power. As noted, the Jeffersonians had a dislike of large military establishments, even if in practice the War of 1812 seemed to change their sentiments. Under Jefferson, the military was drastically retrenched, which helped him to substantially reduce the federal debt. He associated standing armies with aristocratic power and saw them as threatening to liberty. Even though he had a pacific approach to foreign policy and preferred to negotiate solutions to problems, he showed that he was also a realist. The pacific side of him was seen clearly when—despite his insistence in his First Inaugural that there would be "not a cent for tribute"—his administration paid a substantial sum to the Barbary pirates to protect American shipping in the Mediterranean.[158] As mentioned, however, when he saw this did not work he sent American forces into action in one of the first examples of a presidential foreign military action without a declaration of war. His attempt to avoid war was also seen by the Embargo Act—although it is not clear that one should read that as a reflection of his—or the Jeffersonians'—basic pacific orientation or simply the fact that he realistically understood that the U.S. could not successfully prosecute another war with Britain. It was also under the "pacific" Jefferson that the U.S. Military Academy (West Point) was founded. Madison, as noted, pushed for an expanded and better funded military after the War of 1812; he and the Jeffersonians perhaps had learned their lesson about the need for sufficient military strength. He had shared Jefferson's fear of militarism, to be sure, and he and the Democratic-Republican Congress had not been willing to adequately fund the military even during the War.[159] Still, after the War the size of the standing military was permanently enlarged.

The first wave of outright American nationalism seemed to feed on the advancing democratization, and expressed itself in imperialistic desire, a larger and more permanent military establishment, and a touch of ochlocracy. The military changes, however, seemed in line with the realistic spirit of the Founding and the shrewd practical intelligence of American culture—overcoming a fundamental Jeffersonian bias in the opposite direction—and in no way betrayed militarism.

Socio-Cultural Developments. American religion in the Jeffersonian Era was in agreement about morality, even among the deists. It was also accepted that morality was rooted in God, although reflecting the more voluntarist Protestant tradition it was seen typically as based in the divine will instead of the divine intellect.[160] As things proceeded through the Federalist Period into the time of Jefferson, American religion waned in fervor. The Second Great Awakening, which had begun in the 1790s, continued, however, and evangelical revivalism took root. In some sense, this was a reaction against the perceived threat of the French Revolution. A significant portion of this revival, conservative in character, took place in the agrarian class—even though many of these people were Jeffersonians, the party that had been most supportive of the French developments and whose leader was not viewed as a traditional Christian.[161] Separation of church and state came to be increasingly accepted, even though in New England—where paradoxically the most liberal theology was found—there were still established churches (see Chapter 1). Such separation did not mean eliminating the state, much less the culture, from religious influence (in Chapter 1, Tocqueville's claim that religion was the first of America's political institutions was noted). The prevailing political viewpoint was that a moral order grounded in religion was necessary for limited, constitutional government. The sentiment of Jeffersonian theorists was that the common law did not uphold Christian principles, but the greatest early

American jurists and the broader public disputed this.[162] From within this revivalism began to stir the religiously-based social reform movements that would flower in the decades ahead, such as anti-slavery and pro-temperance.[163]

If the mainstream of American culture and religion had a Christian view of man, certain elements within American religion and thought were propounding a different view: Unitarianism and Universalism. They already had made headway "among opinion leaders"[164] and would become more influential over time. They had an overly optimistic view of man; they were the scions of the Enlightenment. As Smelser says, the former "was an institutionalized deism," saying that "God was too good to damn man"; the latter was "much the same except...that it emphasized the doctrine of universal salvation...man was too good to be damned." To be sure, they gained strength as a reaction to the rather dark picture of man presented by Calvinism—and gained their foothold in once-staunchly Calvinist New England. The notion of ethics separated from revelation—not in the sense of ethical norms rooted in a nature that God always stands behind and which expresses His very nature, but of naturalism—began to appear in theological writing. Thus, the opposite of the predominant voluntarism above was about to gain a foothold in American culture and religious thought. A more fundamental part of the philosophical structure of naturalism—materialism—was also gaining expression thanks to thinkers such as Joseph Priestley. While it would be a century before it would gain any traction even among the American intelligentsia, it would eventually manifest itself—especially when later influenced by other intellectual currents—in "environmentalism" (which held that social problems essentially result from institutions and practices in the social environment and not from human nature or in immoral choices made by men). It gave rise readily to secular humanitarianism—that is, a human response to social evils without a religious orientation.[165]

It is said, "the fish rots from the head." These troublesome ideas—the very framework of moral relativism—in the early 1800s had captured few people's minds. America was a fairly moral nation. As Daniel Walker Howe puts it, "This was not a relaxed, hedonistic, refined, or indulgent society....The prevailing versions of Protestantism preached a stern morality and self-control."[166]

Individualism in a moral sense, then, had not yet afflicted very many Americans. We saw above that it had not yet consumed most people in the economic realm, either. They did not seek to escape from demands—they did not define freedom as avoidance of responsibility—but aimed, as Howe says, "to act purposefully in the service of goals." Sometimes, admittedly, the goals came from their personal objectives, but they also came from their families, their religion, and their communities. Regarding the latter, Americans retained the communal character they had in the colonial and Founding Eras, even as they moved west into the frontier. If anything, their local communities continued to impinge on personal and family freedom as they had in the colonial period. In the small locales where most lived there were pressures to conform, consensus was stressed, and differences of opinion were not well tolerated. Small communities also were often not welcoming of cultural differences.[167] The groundwork for the tyranny of majority opinion that Tocqueville and John Stuart Mill were to write about a generation later was in place.[168] A mindset of conformity—which was perhaps obscured by the political disagreements between Federalists and Jeffersonians—was taking hold that a century later, under a different set of socio-economic-demographic influences, would bring forth mass culture.

Although significant changes in two other main socio-cultural areas, the family and education, would not begin to take place until after the Jeffersonian Era, there were some anticipatory developments. Chapter 1 noted that Tocqueville—speaking about ongoing conditions a generation later—said that American sexual morals and the integrity of the marital state were exemplary in the U.S. As an early historian of the American family, Arthur W. Calhoun, writes about the entire period from the Revolutionary to the Civil Wars, "the wife's managerial capacity" was "recognized and rewarded with full sway over the domestic hearth" and she also "exerted an exceptional influence in the larger world as the adviser of her husband and the arbiter of social standards, of morals, of propriety."[169] Sometimes wives were even essentially partners with their husbands in family businesses.[170] The norm was that "husbands treated their wives with notable tenderness." The relationship tended to be free of shallow sentimentality. Women were exempted from heavy-duty labor and the messiness of the marketplace. Women in society were treated with an "extreme courtesy...based on a genuine and growing respect and deference." Women were "not sheltered...but were free to travel in safety and to know the world." When there were cases of husbands physically abusing their wives, the law and public opinion would generally support the woman.[171] While divorce was not common, it had become easier to get after the American Revolution.[172] Its incidence increased as the nineteenth century wore on, and the increase was most pronounced after 1860.[173] Calhoun makes a striking statement of the root cause of this: "Even at the dawn of Independence, while each community firmly upheld matrimony, the Protestant repudiation of Catholic doctrine was already portending freedom in marriage and divorce that threatened to produce further laxity."[174] While feminism had to wait a few decades for its first substantial flowering in the U.S., a few early nineteenth century writers started to focus on women's rights. While "they did not gain a great following," they espoused "the nucleus of the modern point of view."[175] This was a version of individualism, putting the focus on the individual members of the family and diminishing the nature of the family as a unit. We also observe during the Jeffersonian Era the early stirrings of economic strains on the family. The Industrial Revolution had not yet descended with full force on America, but the factories that did exist were typically manned by women and children. Most of the women were not married, to be sure,[176] but a pattern was set for women regardless of marital status to be diverted from the family in the future—and, of course, children were already being separated from it. It also signaled a beginning shift away from the family as the center of economic life, a development that by itself divides people in the family from each other and weakens the central role of the family in society.

Regarding education, it still remained largely a private and church-controlled affair for youth who would even be able to take advantage of it in any formal way. By 1800, a solid minority of American states had constitutional provisions for education, and the others provided financial and other support for it. In 1789, Massachusetts had already mandated that each town maintain a common school, but the results were mixed.[177] Throughout the Jeffersonian Era and beyond, the Commonwealth struggled to establish an adequate public education arrangement. New York made similar initial efforts, establishing a common school fund and following New England by establishing school districts.[178] Public—i.e., government-controlled—schooling had to await further developments later in the century to come into its own. The same was the case with educational innovation and ideology. Still, what was developing during the Jeffersonian Era was the attitude that education was the way to perfect man. Smelser calls this, in effect, a very early expression of the environmentalism above; it was derived from the views of the French *philosophes*, an example of how the Enlightenment influenced America. The American environment would be perfected by, specifically, *rationalistic* education, democracy, and science.[179] This incipient perspective was another force prodding the country in a more democratic direction and one eager to make a major cultural change by stripping education from its traditional religious moorings and secularizing it. While Jefferson and others close to him sought a secularization of education, at least to a certain extent, educators and clergymen were mostly opposed to them.[180]

Again, the changes brewing among the intelligentsia in religion, philosophy, education, and even the family deviated from the thinking of the Founding Era and laid part of the foundation for later significant developments that would have definite implications for American political life. The religious changes, which gained more force than in the Federalist Period, were occurring among a new, increasingly secular elite. This set the standard that would be followed throughout American history, eventually spreading a watered-down version of secularism to the masses. The influence of the changes—which were definite departures from Christian tradition—was enhanced by the fact that they now became institutionalized into new denominations. As we saw happening in other, related developments in thought, they had particular implications for politics because they included a changed—i.e., more optimistic—view of human nature. If in government policy—e.g., economics and the military—the realism of the Founders was reinforced, in these brewing areas of culture it was weakening. At least, the cracks were starting to noticeably widen. To be sure, the age of moral relativism was in the future, but with the project of undermining—even if the secularizing elite was not fully aware of it—the twin pillars of philosophy and revelation, the erosion of the virtue so emphasized in Chapter 1 could only follow in time. This would be even more the case once the new thinking about education took hold. All this meant that, in the final analysis, individualism was gaining. The very self-reliance and practical wisdom of the American character were unwitting allies in helping such a strain of thought find fertile soil—and it would grow and eventually flourish from there. Even the practice and thinking (e.g., incipient feminism) about the family would be affected. If, however, individualism was gaining, so were the lineaments of mass culture taking shape as the cultural force of the majority over the minority was intensifying. It was aided, paradoxically, by the ebbing of a communal orientation in American life that actually—in spite of the excessive community monitoring in places like Calvinist New England—had enhanced the dignity of the individual.

In summation, we can say the following about how well the two earliest periods of the American Republic conformed to the principles of the American Founding, the beliefs and practices of the culture supporting it, and the principles of a good political order discussed in Chapter 1, and the ways in which the beginnings of transformation were occurring. On the governmental level, the balance of power between the state and federal governments was maintained—even with the determined federal role in economics. The doctrine of separation of powers saw some challenges, but the only enduring change was an enhancing—only modestly by 1817—of presidential power. The developing political life set some serious negative precedents: intense factionalism that threatened civility, civic friendship, and the common good; public office used for personal financial benefit; the tie-in of public officials with monied interests; the corruption of language—an early example of relativism in the public arena—in the interest of advancing socio-political and moralistic agendas; and even using the coercive powers of government to further policies not necessarily widely embraced by the citizenry. While standards for appointment were fairly high, the spoils system was advancing—especially under the Jeffersonians—so the future would jeopardize them. America, to be sure, was not and never has been militaristic, but it gained realism about the size and role for a military in a potentially great nation. If militarism was not present, the spirit of nationalism and expansionism was—fed in part by the Jeffersonian desire for western development. By the end of the Jeffersonian Era, democracy clearly had advanced and such Founding principles as those concerning a natural aristocracy, a restrained franchise, and the role of property in government were in retreat. Even the rule of law suffered some bruises, and government showed a willingness to weaken rights guarantees (at least selectively). In economics, the norms of the Founding Era were still in place, though the growing role of government—both state and federal—in encouraging and taking part in economic development would in time herald a departure from the communal orientation of earlier economic thinking. The pursuit of luxury, the dangers of which were earlier feared, had not set in. The Founders' concern about government indebtedness was well addressed. Changes in religion accelerated as the country moved through these periods, with a new, more optimistic view of human nature—promoted by changing philosophical and educational ideas— that challenged the realism of the Founding the result. Moreover, the very religious changes in question actually slowly helped begin a movement—to be traced in this book—that would in the distant future advance secularism and actually undermine the religious commitment that the Founding Fathers deemed essential to sustain a democratic republic. Individualism became more and more implanted—even if not radically—in the American psyche and influenced politics, culture, and religion as this time period wore on. Along with this, individual rights stressed by the Founding became more secure and emphasized, although contrastingly, the specter of majority domination of minorities became more apparent. Actually, the proper relationship of majority to minority of the Founding was being corrupted in two opposing ways: there was a slight movement toward majoritarianism, but the ideas of Jeffersonianism eventually perhaps helped encourage a sectionalism wherein disenchanted regional minorities sought to advance their own economic interests irrespective of the majority will.

While we shall wait until the last chapter to consider at some length the significance of the possible weaknesses in the Founding thought suggested in Chapter 1 in affecting socio-political developments in America, we would only note that a number of them may have been in play during these earliest periods of the Republic (we shall suggest which of these seem to be pertinent in each period studied in this book): the lack of a sound understanding of the common good, the seeds of expanded individualism, the lack of a means to bring forth a natural aristocracy, possibly too much stress on popular sovereignty, the lack of a sufficient emphasis on community, the lack of a sense that religion might weaken and with it a sound worldview, and, to a very limited degree, the failure to see the centrality of the family for the political order.

Notes

1. Of the members of Congress and leading officials of the executive branch— President, Vice President, and Cabinet members—from 1789-1801, 29 of 122 had been at the Constitutional Convention (see: "1st United States Congress," http://en.wikipedia.org/ wiki/1st_United_States_Congress; Internet; "Presidency of George Washington," http:// en.wikipedia.org/wiki/Presidency_of_George_Washington; Internet; "John Adams," http://en.wikipedia.org/wiki/John_Adams; Internet; all accessed June 14, 2010).

2. See John C. Miller, *The Federalist Era, 1789-1801* (N.Y.: Harper, 1960), 156-159.

3. Carol Berkin, Christopher L. Miller, Robert W. Cherny, and James L. Gormly, *Making America: A History of the United States* (Boston: Houghton Mifflin, 2003), 191.

4. Miller, 155-156.

5. Ibid., 58-59.

6. Ibid., 57.

7. Miller, 60-61.

8. Ibid., 39-40.

9. 3 U.S. (3 Dall.) 171.

10. 3 U.S. (3 Dall.) 386.

11. This interpretation of the importance of these decisions is found in Miller, 180-182.

12. Miller, 247-248.

13. Ibid., 63.

14. Alexander Hamilton, *Report on Manufactures* (Dec. 5, 1791), IV, VII (excerpts available from http://history.sandiego.edu/gen/text/civ/1791manufactures.html; Internet; accessed July 1, 2008); Miller, 64-65; Stanley Elkins and Eric McKitrick, *The Age of Federalism* (N.Y.: Oxford University Press, 1993), 260-261.

15. Elkins and McKitrick, 161.

16. See Miller, 230-232; Elkins and McKitrick, 592-593.

17. Miller, 237.

18. Miller, 230; Elkins and McKitrick, 591-592.

19. Tindall and Shi, 364.

20. See Herbert J. Storing, *What the Anti-Federalists Were For: The Political Thought of the Opponents of the Constitution* (Chicago: University of Chicago Press, 1981), 11-12, 15, 28, 35, 69, 90-91.

21. Leonard D. White, *The Federalists: A Study in Administrative History—1789-1801* (N.Y.: Free Press, 1948), 404.

22. See Hamilton or Madison, Federalist 51, 338.

23. White, 17.

24. Ibid., 27.

25. Ibid., 48.

26. Miller, 26-27.

27. White, 512.

28. Ibid., 449-450.

29. Miller, 27.

30. White, 455.

31. Ibid., 456.

32. Miller, 13-14.

33. White, 260-263.

34. See ibid., 280-284.

35. Ibid., 284.

36. Ibid., 508.

37. Ibid., 285.

38. Ibid., 284-285, 290.

39. Miller, 169-170.

40. White, 250-252.

41. Miller, 38.

42. Elkins and McKitrick, 272.

43. Alpheus Thomas Mason and Donald Grier Stephenson, Jr., *American Constitutional Law: Introductory Essays and Selected Cases* (14th edn.; Upper Saddle River, N.J.: Pearson/Prentice Hall, 2005, 324-325). The citation for *Fletcher v. Peck* is 10 U.S. (6 Cranch) 87 (1910).

44. Miller, 181.

45. 5 U.S. (1 Cranch) 137 (1803).

46. Miller, 181.

47. The Founding Fathers seemed to have expected that judicial review in some form would emerge. See, e.g., Corwin, *The Doctrine of Judicial Review*; Charles A. Beard, *The Supreme Court and the Constitution* (N.Y.: Macmillan, 1926). Federalist 78 (Hamilton) also distinctly suggests it.

48. Elkins and McKitrick, 272.

49. Ibid., 582.

50. Ibid., 593.

51. Miller, 249-250.

52. Elkins and McKitrick, 264-265.

53. Ibid., 267-270.

54. Ibid., 488.

55. Ibid., 454-455.

56. Ibid., 454.

57. Ibid., 456-457.

58. Ibid., 457, 459, 461.

59. Ibid., 451.

60. Ibid., 456-457.

61. Ibid., 461.

62. Berkin, Miller, Cherny, and Gormly, 184.

63. Richard D. Brown, *Modernization: The Transformation of American Life 1600-1865* (Prospect Heights, Ill.: Waveland, 1988 [originally published by Hill and Wang, 1976]), 99.

64. Elkins and McKitrick, 465.

65. Miller, 39.

66. Miller, 112-115.

67. Ibid., 118.

68. Ibid., 117.

69. George Brown Tindall and David E. Shi, 341.

70. Berkin, Miller, Cherny, and Gormly, 208.

71. Paul Johnson, *A History of the American People* (N.Y.: HarperCollins, 1997), 227.

72. Henry F. May, *The Enlightenment in America* (N.Y.: Oxford University Press, 1976), 182.

73. This is discussed in ibid., passim.

74. Ibid., 277.

75. Sydney E. Ahlstrom, *A Religious History of the American People* (New Haven, Conn.: Yale University Press, 1972), 391-393.

76. Ibid., 392.

77. May, 251.

78. Ibid., 196.

79. Ibid., 275-276.

80. Ibid., 251.

81. Henry Adams, *The United States in 1800* (Ithaca, N.Y.: Cornell University Press [Great Seal Books], 1955; consists of the first part of Adams' *History of the United States of America during the First Administration of Thomas Jefferson*, published by Charles Scribner's Sons in 1889), 35.

82. Ahlstrom, 387.

83. Ibid., 42.

84. Henry Adams, 93.

85. Ibid., 52.

86. Ibid., 43.

87. May, 235-236.

88. On this point, see the reflections of such deep and astute thinkers as Henry Edward Cardinal Manning, Irving Babbitt, and Christopher Dawson.

89. Sampo, 106.

90. James David Barber, *The Presidential Character: Predicting Performance in the White House* (2nd edn.; Englewood Cliffs, N.J.: Prentice Hall, 1977), 14.

91. May, 287.

92. This is the basic understanding of social ethics about the purpose of the state (see Higgins, 438).

93. Henry Adams, 129.

94. Ibid.

95. May, 360.

96. Henry Adams, 129.

97. May, 340-341. May does say, however, that even the more extreme version of the Enlightenment—that human nature could be perfected outright—has consistently influenced some in America (May, 360-361).

98. Ibid., 302.

99. See Kirk, *The Roots of American Order*, 12-13.

100. See "United States Presidential Election, 1800," http://en.wikipedia.org/wiki/United_States_presidential_election,_1800;Internet; accessed Aug. 25, 2008.

101. Harold U. Faulkner, *American Political and Social History* (6th edn.; N.Y.: Appleton-Century-Crofts, 1952), 169-170.

102. Morton Borden, *Parties and Politics in the Early Republic, 1789-1815* (N.Y.: Thomas Y. Crowell, 1967), 99.

103. A.J. Beitzinger, *A History of American Political Thought* (N.Y.: Dodd, Mead, 1972), 308; Borden, 69; Don E. Fehrenbacher, *The Era of Expansion, 1800-1848* (N.Y.: John Wiley and Sons, 1969), 18; Richard E. Ellis, "The Political Economy of Thomas Jefferson," in Lally Weymouth, ed., *Thomas Jefferson: The Man, His World, His Influence* (N.Y.: G.P. Putnam's Sons, 1973), 90, 92, 94; Faulkner, 169, 171 (the quotation is from 169); Christopher Lasch, "The Jeffersonian Legacy," in Weymouth, 232, 233.

104. Lasch, 232-233.

105. Faulkner, 157.

106. Fehrenbacher, 31.

107. See Jefferson, "Draft of a Constitution for Virginia," in Padover, 112. On the other hand, the second most prominent Jeffersonian, Madison, was more democratic in his view about the franchise, completely opposing any kind of property qualification and supporting a movement toward universal suffrage (see Madison, speech of August 7, 1787 at the Constitutional Convention, redone in 1821 for planned posthumous publication of his Convention notes, in Myers 506-508).

108. See Aristotle, *Politics*, VII, x, 1330a; II, vii, 1266b-1267a. Kirk discusses at length how the classics were an intrinsic part of the long cultural heritage behind the American Republic (see Kirk, *The Roots of American Order*, chapters iii and iv).

109. Madison, Federalist 10, 55.

110. "Public prosperity" is defined as "the sum total of those helps and facilities which must be available to put private well-being within the reach of all: it is an abundance of social, economic, and industrial *opportunities* which will help all classes of citizens to use their initiative and industry and thus secure a desirable competence for themselves" (Higgins, 423; emphasis is in the original). In the case of the U.S., with its federal system, it would have been intended that the central government could legislate and otherwise affect this only in certain areas pertaining to general nationwide concerns (i.e., that concern its enumerated and implied powers).

111. See Hamilton, Federalist 17, 101-104; Madison, Federalist 45, 303.

112. Borden, 69; Fehrenbacher, 17.

113. Faulkner, 161.

114. Fehrenbacher, 18.

115. Drew R. McCoy, *The Last of the Fathers: James Madison and the Republican Legacy* (NY.: Cambridge University Press, 1989), 94-96. The quotation is from 95.

116. Leonard Levy, "Jefferson as a Civil Libertarian," in Weymouth, 198, 200.

117. Ibid., 209.

118. Ibid., 197-198.

119. Marshall Smelser, *The Democratic Republic, 1801-1815* (N.Y.: Harper & Row, 1968), 317-318.

120. Ibid., 318.

121. Fehrenbacher, 32; Faulkner, 158.

122. Ibid.

123. Borden, 65-66. He mentions that this was Henry Adams' assessment.

124. Smelser, 317-318.

125. Daniel Walker Howe, *What Hath God Wrought: The Transformation of America, 1815-1848* (N.Y.: Oxford University Press, 2007), 87.

126. McCoy, 109-110.

127. 17 U.S. (4 Wheat.) 316 (1819).

128. See Mason and Stephenson, 325; note 47 above (Founders and judicial review).

129. Ellis, 89-90.

130. Howe, 83.

131. Fehrenbacher, 75.

132. McCoy, 94.

133. Fehrenbacher, 75-76.

134. Ibid., 76.

135. Ibid., 75.

136. McCoy, 179.

137. Faulkner, 176.

138. Ibid., 182.

139. Howe, 44.

140. Smelser, 321.

141. Faulkner, 170.

142. Smelser, 321-322.

143. Howe, 40.

144. McCoy, 195-197.

145. Beitzinger, 317.

146. See Edmund Burke, *Reflections on the Revolution in France*, in Edmund Burke, *Reflections on the Revolution in France*/Thomas Paine, *The Rights of Man* (bound together in a single volume; Garden City, N.Y.: Anchor Press, Doubleday, 1973), 63.

147. Arthur W. Calhoun, *A Social History of the American Family*, vol II, *From Independence through the Civil War* (N.Y.: Barnes and Noble, 1918), 136.

148. Smelser, 322.

149. See Howe, 37-38.

150. Ibid., 39.

151. Faulkner, 184.

152. See Faulkner, 175-177.

153. Borden, 99.

154. Ibid., 100; Faulkner, 176-177, 182.

155. Howe, 90.

156. Faulkner, 182.

157. Ibid., 182-184.

158. Ibid., 158-159.

159. Howe, 90.

160. Beitzinger, 316.

161. See ibid.; Smelser, 25.

162. Beitzinger, 316.

163. Ahlstrom, 426-428.

164. Smelser, 32.

165. Ibid., 32-33.

166. Howe, 38.

167. Ibid., 40-41.

168. See Tocqueville, I, i, 246-261; John Stuart Mill, *On Liberty* (Harmondsworth, England: Penguin, 1974; originally published in 1859), chap. 1.

169. Calhoun, 110.

170. See, e.g., Howe 44.

171. Calhoun, 110.

172. Tyndall and Shi, 283.

173. Kermit L. Hall, William M. Wiecek, and Paul Finkelman, *American Legal History: Cases and Materials* (N.Y.: Oxford University Press, 1991), 278.

174. Calhoun, 32.

175. Ibid., 116.

176. Ibid., 172-175.

177. S.E. Frost, Jr., *Historical and Philosophical Foundations of Western Education* (Columbus, O.: Charles E. Merrill Books, 1966), 319-320.

178. Ibid., 392-393.

179. Smelser 31.

180. Ibid., 25.

CHAPTER 3

1817-1840: THE ERAS OF "GOOD FEELINGS" AND JACKSONIAN DEMOCRACY

The periods of the James Monroe presidency—hailed as the "Era of Good Feelings" because of the restoration of American confidence after the War of 1812, the cessation of inter-party rancor after the functional collapse of the Federalist party, and the almost unanimous electoral college vote for Monroe in his reelection of 1820—and that of John Quincy Adams and the "Jacksonian" presidents—Andrew Jackson himself and his chosen successor Martin Van Buren—are not, to be sure, a continuum. Monroe was formally a Jeffersonian, although one who continued and expanded the Hamiltonian-type policies that Jefferson ironically embraced in spite of his philosophical opposition (as we saw in Chapter 2). In doing this, he effectively laid the groundwork for Jacksonianism. In any event, the political, social, and cultural trends that become so clear during the time of Jackson's presidency were already clear. The second Adams, while hardly an insignificant political figure (although he had his greatest influence when he returned to the national political stage later as a member of the House of Representatives), was in a "holding pattern" presidency awaiting a rematch with an infuriated Jackson who believed a corrupt deal in 1825 had robbed him of the office. Adams held the office while Jacksonianism implanted itself in the politics and culture around him before Jackson finally won the office in 1828. In fact, some authors hold that the Jacksonian Era actually began with the War's end in 1815 and the two periods we have distinguished are really one.[1] While that may overreach, the fact is that the Jacksonian movement, if one can call it that, overshadows the developments of these two earlier presidencies. So, our analysis of the subjects focused on in this chapter, unlike the more clearly and meaningfully delineated Federalist and Jeffersonian periods, will examine together the entire time period above—taking care to note how developments proceeded during the times of Monroe and Adams, even while those during Jackson's administration and after are by far the most important and given the greatest attention.

The general subject areas that the history of the period 1817-1840 indicates for our purposes should be considered are these: governing socio-politico-economic principles; federalism, sectionalism, and the growth of federal and overall governmental power; growth of executive branch power; democratization, citizen rights and law, and developments in political life; economic and technological developments, economic policy, and the rise of the working class; military power, nationalism, and expansionism; socio-cultural developments and intellectual currents; and voluntary associations, popular movements, and the emergence of the Whigs.

Governing Socio-Politico-Economic Principles. Monroe's first inaugural address set out his basic principles for governance. Deviating from his predecessor James Madison, he embraced the newly discovered "nationalism" of the Democratic-Republican party (i.e., federal support for internal improvements and protective tariffs to help American industries develop). He believed in strong efforts at domestic conciliation, elimination of discord (this fit the basic political atmosphere of the "Era of Good Feelings"), and the need to stress unity and the common interest. Internationally, he insistently sought the furtherance of American national interest.[2] The high point of his foreign policy, of course, was the Monroe Doctrine, which warned European powers to refrain from further colonization in the Western Hemisphere. Constitutionally, he took a broad view of federal power under the general welfare clause and of implied powers generally.[3] Like Jefferson—and like all of America's first six presidents, according to Daniel Walker Howe—Monroe maintained a suspicion of political parties and sought to end parties.[4] (Arguably, even the Jacksonians were not enthusiastic about parties; they simply saw the Democratic party as needed as a countervailing force so that economic elites would not take control of the country.[5]) Monroe was unsuccessful in this, of course, and had to be contented with limiting parties to one broad-based one, the Democratic-Republicans—the only one left standing after the dissolution of the Federalists—that soon developed factions within it.[6]

The Jacksonians viewed themselves as the inheritors of the Jeffersonian tradition, but they went beyond it. It was with Jacksonianism that "democracy," which had been held to be a perverted form of government by the classics and (as Chapter 1 noted) was criticized by *The Federalist*, came to be seen as a positive force. As Sean Wilentz puts it, they saw democracy as "the fulfillment of republicanism."[7] Like the Jeffersonians, they saw themselves as on the side of the "producers," but they expanded that group to include not just the agrarian elements but mechanics, the members of the new working class, and entrepreneurs.[8] Both were focused on attacking privilege, and Arthur M. Schlesinger, Jr. says that the Jacksonians saw themselves as avowedly elevating "human rights" over the property rights that were so central to Jeffersonianism.[9] They still favored a kind of laissez faire, but they thought that government had to intervene as a kind of referee among persons and groups and to check such excesses of the growing business community as monopoly.[10] According to Schlesinger, the Jacksonians believed that they were at the forefront of what would become a new international movement of democratization. The era of the people was coming;[11] the common man could and would rule. There was an extolling of majoritarianism.[12] They saw themselves as promoting both political and social equality, at least for adult Caucasian males (in fact, they took active steps to disenfranchise free Negroes in the North).[13] Nevertheless, Wilentz tells us that they were not per se a pro-slavery party. They were simply concerned about furthering such other of their principles as national harmony and upholding constitutional order[14] (even if, as we see below, they were not reluctant about stretching the Constitution's provisions when it came to funding internal improvements, resettling the Indians, and executive power).

What was the Jacksonian thinking about economics? It was fundamentally Jeffersonian, with the kinds of practical compromises Jefferson made—e.g., opposing a protective tariff, but tolerating it in practice—and a more interventionist stance by government. The Jacksonians seemed to believe—in the manner of Catholic social teaching—that the natural arrangement for economic interests is to work together harmoniously. They favored economic competition, and the attempts at monopoly by some in the business community upset this and had to be countered by government. They saw the Second Bank of the United States—which, of course, Jackson after a long effort effectively destroyed—as part of this. Otherwise, they believed that government should be simple, frugal, and avoid debt.[15] Instead of a tariff or significant taxes, they favored initiatives like the sale of public lands to raise federal revenue.[16] They favored a "hard money" regimen; that is, they favored that transactions, such as the purchase of public lands, be in gold or silver coinage. This was because average people had trouble affording paper money since it was inflated due to land speculation and government-funded internal improvements (Jackson's Specie Circular is discussed below).[17] Also like Catholic social teaching, Jacksonian democracy was a kind of "spread the wealth" movement; while opposing economic privilege, it did not oppose enterprise. In fact, it sought to enable more to become entrepreneurs.[18] The Jacksonians were also America's first "pro-labor" political party, only because the rise of manufacturing, the beginnings of the separation of ownership and production, and the growth of economic privilege had started to produce an urban-based working class—as noted, a new element of the common men that the Jacksonians were devoted to defending and advancing. They did not advocate a labor theory of value, but believed that workers were entitled to the full enjoyment of the fruits of their efforts.[19]

One other area in which we can discern distinct Jacksonian principles is law. The Jacksonians were suspicious of the common law. They believed that it gave too much discretion to judges and saw it as too conservative, opposed to democracy, and protective of the interests of a privileged few. They embraced the nascent law codification movement. They fell under the influence of Jeremy Bentham, who they saw as a democratic reformer[20] and who proposed to draw up an entire legal code for the U.S. (even though he had never even visited the country).[21] Some of their spokesmen hailed the "greatest good for the great number" standard of utilitarianism, which implicitly embraces moral relativism and can be ready to sweep away deep-seated principles or permit obvious

injustices for reasons of expediency.[22] The typical Jacksonian perhaps did not
fathom the meaning or implications of this standard, but it arguably permanently
influenced the approach to reform in the U.S.—which we see culminating in the
New Deal and afterwards (as this book goes on to show): pragmatic decision-
making rules, especially to solve a perceived substantial immediate problem or
help dispossessed elements in political society, with traditional socio-politico-
legal-economic principles left more or less intact although possibly weakened or
transformed in some way. The law for the Jacksonians should be used to combat
privilege, promote greater democracy, and further economic justice. This was
seen in their view of corporation law. Unlike the old practice of granting
corporate charters in a very limited way, they now made them readily available
if certain minimal requirements were satisfied.[23] Even though, to be sure, the old
practice had turned into a means of furthering monopolistic ends, stopping it
meant ending the notion that one—in principle, at least—could receive a
corporate charter only if he was serving an identifiable public interest. It was
one more signal (discussed in Chapter 2) of the now sweeping shift away from
viewing society as an organic whole with the prime focus the overall good of the
community.

Finally, as we discuss more below, the Jacksonians extolled the executive
power and—in a seeming contradiction to their democratic agenda—
downplayed the legislative. This was because they saw the executive as a kind
of tribune—the spokesman for and defender of the people.[24]

Now we consider how the principles discussed in this section compare to
the elements, principles, and points discussed in Chapter 1. First, we can
certainly say that the spirit of Monroe's presidency—irrespective of the question
of whether these conditions actually prevailed to a significant degree—was in
accord with the concern about the common good, civility, and civic friendship
that was seen in the Founding Era. The broad view he took of federal power
under the general welfare clause and implied powers, while subject to debate,
did not clearly violate any of the principles put forth by the Founding Fathers as
necessary to sustain a democratic republic. In fact, as far as the principles of
social ethics discussed in Chapter 1 are concerned, it may have been warranted
since the states—as mentioned below—did not seem able to fund internal
improvements on their own and private interests were not likely to fund public
instrumentalities. We consider the Monroe Doctrine and American foreign
policy and the country's role in the world below. As far as basic views about
political parties were concerned, neither Monroe nor the Jacksonians embraced
the positive view of political parties and factions that had gained credence by the
time of the Founding; as noted, even for the Jacksonians parties were a kind of
needed nuisance.

To turn specifically to Jacksonian principles, their vigorous advocacy of
democracy, common man rule, and majoritarianism certainly went against
Founding principles. They emphasized the "democratic" part of the American
democratic republic and sought to leave the "republican" part behind. As
indicated, they seemed to now see America as going beyond republicanism to
democracy. This was underscored by the fact that their party was now called just

the "Democratic," instead of the "Democratic-Republican" party. Common man rule meant that the natural aristocracy stressed by the Founders—and perhaps even the spirit of the gentleman upheld in earlier American culture—was no longer pertinent. This was underscored by their push for not just political, but social equality (at least for Caucasian males). While not embracing the sweeping egalitarianism of the French Revolution and its ilk, this dismissal of natural aristocracy and the interest in social equality had a distinct echo of it. The concern about restraining potentially destructive majority factions was a major reason why the Founders rejected outright majoritarianism. The Jacksonians' insistent attacks on "privilege," both in their theory and in their political rhetoric, may have compromised civility and the common good. Their objective seems to have been the *dethroning* of the "privileged"; they seemed inattentive to the need to "reach out" and forge the civic friendship that was so stressed in the culture of the Founding Era. The Jacksonian democratization/anti-privilege ethos was no doubt behind their view about "human rights" taking precedence over property rights. Besides the obvious fact that property rights, like all rights, are rights of human persons, this position was basically contrary to that of the Founding Fathers who, it will be recalled from Chapter 1, believed property rights and a number of other legal and political rights—the Jacksonians would have exclusively included the latter under "human rights"—to be "preeminent" rights. On this, the Jacksonians went in the opposite direction of the extreme Federalists of the 1790s, who wanted to assert the supremacy, at least in practice, of property rights over such rights as free speech and religious liberty (see Chapter 2). Thus, the selective protection of rights (further evidenced with certain other Jacksonian practices below) was a feature of American politics from early in the Republic. It showed both the early tendencies to political opportunism and, more deeply, the difficulties in keeping different rights—and different basic principles— in a proper tension with each other.

We analyze Jacksonian economic policies below. On the level of principle, we can definitely say that their belief that a harmonious, cooperative inter-working of different elements in the economic order and their strong opposition to monopoly conforms to such cultural norms as cooperativeness, concern for the general welfare, limits on economic freedom in the name of the public good, and decentralization of economic institutions of the Founding Era. Certainly, their support for simple, frugal government that avoided debt met the spirit of the Founders—although, in practice (as suggested below), they may have been more austere than the Founders required. The "spread the wealth" perspective, with more people being able to be landowners and entrepreneurs, certainly conformed to the culture of the Founding Era. So did their insistence that the new working class that they embraced be permitted to have a sufficiency of the fruits of their labor.

The Jacksonians' spurning of the common law was certainly against the tradition behind the Founding. The Founders recognized that the common law was the basis of the rights and liberties that they held as central.[25] The Jacksonians did not seem to understand it very well, thinking that it left judges unfettered when in truth they were bound by precedent and the entire common law system had the natural law and Christian morality behind it. They opened the door, wittingly or not, to legal positivism and to the kind of majoritarian threats to citizen liberties that legislatures bent on codification could bring forth. In doing so, they also seemed oblivious both to the pitfalls that sweeping legislative power (which is implied in codification) had brought about during the Articles of Confederation period and to the contradiction this posed to their avowed desire to diminish legislative power in preference to executive. Their embracing of Bentham and, of some, of the utilitarian calculus was sharply contrary to the Founding stress on natural law, virtue, and religion—as well as to the centrality of the natural law to the great thinkers of Western political philosophy and the tradition that the Founding had emerged from. While few of the Jacksonians would have thought of themselves as moral relativists, they perhaps did not see that that is precisely what Benthamite utilitarianism meant. As we also saw in Chapter 1, moral relativism—along with the sense of purposelessness, moralistic sentimentality, and condition of politics as power struggle that it tends to breed—were major factors in societal decline. The way the Jacksonians changed corporation law went contrary to those of their economic principles that seemed to uphold the economic outlook of the American culture of the Founding Era. The fact that they no longer expected corporations to aim to further the public interest seemed to open the door to more of the kinds of business abuses that they railed against. With the new corporation law, they were taking one more action that transformed the former organic character of society; implicitly for them, culture and morality were no longer the means of insuring proper economic behavior. Now they would rely overwhelmingly on governmental and legal restraint; this paved the way for the regulatory state of a century later. They accepted the new terms of the market, instead of believing that the new economic changes should be incorporated into the older social order and restrained by it on the latter's terms. In a certain sense, this legal change conformed to the notion that Chapter 1 suggested might be a weakness of the Founding itself—an unwillingness to have government embrace an overarching conception of the common good or public interest (even while a certain, less ambitious conception was definitely present in the Jacksonians' aims to restrain privilege and monopoly, etc.).

Finally, the Jacksonian embellishment of the executive and diminishment of the legislative, on balance, is problematical in light of the thinking of the Founders. On the one hand, the Founders sought to establish a truly strong executive;[26] on the other, they held the legislative to be, one might say, the first among co-equal branches.[27] One wonders if the Jacksonians' view was fashioned merely as a grounds of promoting (before his election) and then defending (when in office) the one man Jackson, and that they were largely oblivious to the twin dangers of abuse and mediocrity among political executives. One also wonders if in their zeal to promote majoritarian democracy via a president as tribune, they were ready to downplay separation of powers and checks and balances. We evaluate Jackson's actual carrying out of the powers of the office below.

Federalism, Sectionalism, and the Growth of Federal and Overall Governmental Power. 1817 to 1840, in spite of the Jacksonian espousal of states' rights, was essentially a time of consolidation of federal power. The decisions of the Marshall Court in this period, starting with *McCulloch v. Maryland*[28]—which definitively upheld the constitutionality of the Jacksonians' despised Bank of the United States—supported implied powers, took a reasonably broad view of federal power under the commerce clause, and gave security to federal powers from diminishment or encroachment at the hands of the states. Even though the Jacksonians did not like some of these decisions, they accepted them. When one of their own, Roger B. Taney, became Chief Justice after Marshall's death, he did not attempt to reverse the federalism jurisprudence of the Marshall Court (though the Taney Court did give the states more power to regulate in matters of interstate commerce).[29] In fact, actions of the Jackson administration itself helped to permanently reinforce federal power. While Jackson ultimately sank the Bank, which seemed to bolster the state interest within the federal system, he did not change Monroe's direction by eliminating federal funding for internal improvements (as George Dangerfield puts it, his views were "rather expedient than constitutional").[30] He also carried out what was arguably the most forceful projection of federal power onto a state before the Civil War by putting federal forts on alert and sending a warship into Charleston Harbor during the Nullification Crisis in 1832. As Charles M. Wiltse says, during the crisis "Jackson was saying with [Daniel] Webster and Marshall that the nation was superior to the states."[31] The tariff was promoting sectionalism, drawing the South together as an aggrieved part of the country economically disadvantaged by the success of tariff-protected manufacturing industries in the North. Wiltse argues that Jackson's strong response to the crisis even further promoted Southern unity and deepened sectionalism (which, of course, would reach its height with the slavery question), ultimately paving the way for the Civil War.[32] Even before 1840, however, slavery was forging sectional conflict in light of the greater dependence of the Southern economy on slave-sustained cotton production, growing Northern abolitionism, and a hardening of Southern views in defense of the institution.

Jackson was a defender of states rights to be sure, but he shared John Marshall's—and *The Federalist's*[33]—belief that the Constitution gave the federal government powers that were not dependent on the states.[34] On this, he fundamentally clashed with John C. Calhoun, his vice president, whose argument for nullification—i.e., that a state constitutional convention could be called to declare a federal law null and void within that state—held that the federal government exercised sovereignty only as a agent of the states which could, effectively, reign in that sovereignty. Essentially, he held that sovereignty rested only in the states. While Calhoun asserted this position to sidetrack more radical elements in South Carolina who were suggesting succession, the implication of his theory was that a state had the right to secede.[35]

Nullification theory was not the only novel interpretation of the Constitution that Calhoun put forth. Relating to the question of internal improvements, he contended—seemingly at odds with his strong states' rights convictions—that the Framers had intended outright to empower Congress to appropriate money for anything they denominated a worthy national purpose. Madison, the Constitution's main drafter who was President at the time, completely rejected this (although it influenced Monroe).[36] Henry Clay, the great Speaker of the House of Representatives, bluntly called for loose constitutional interpretation to deal with America's changing demography, economy, and technology.[37]

If nullification was a frontal, theoretical attack on national supremacy, such a challenge on the practical level was frequently occurring in the South. Howe writes that "inconvenient federal laws" were ignored, sometimes with the acquiescence of federal officials, as in the routine refusal to deliver abolitionist mail to Southern addresses.[38]

Moving in the opposite direction of the sectionalism percolating in the South was the sentiment of a growing anti-slavery element in the North that held, with nineteenth century Catholic thinker Orestes A. Brownson, that the American nation preceded the states as a historical, if not political, fact.[39] They obviously went farther than the Jacksonians, although this perspective conformed somewhat to the ethos suggested by Jackson's actions in the Nullification Crisis.

Apart from questions of federalism, there was a growth of governmental powers in general during the period 1817-1840. A tendency developed that would repeatedly manifest itself in the course of American history: in times of national economic hardship people looked to government for help.[40] Different interests began to go to government for assistance and satisfaction of their wants; Monroe-style Republicanism, with hefty federal spending for internal improvements and the like, had convinced them "that prosperity depended on public policy."[41] The precedents were thus established on both of these points for the much more sweeping governmental, and especially federal government, power—prodded by interest group demands—of the twentieth and twenty-first centuries. If the Taney Court did not reverse the federalizing actions of the Marshall Court, it did enhance the powers of state governments to regulate private matters according to what they deemed the public interest (i.e., gave a green light to the exercise of what came to be called state "police power"). It slightly weakened the Marshall Court's contract clause jurisprudence by holding that ambiguities regarding private property rights would be resolved in favor of government.[42] During this period, America witnessed such an everyday expansion of governmental power as the development of regular police forces;[43] it also saw the beginning of the operation of institutions of higher learning by state governments.[44] It also experienced the threatening extension of governmental power with such practices as the refusal to deliver abolitionist mail above and the imposition of the Congressional "gag rule," whereby members were forbidden to present petitions regarding slavery on the floors of the houses.[45]

Let us consider how the historical developments in this section compare with the points put forth in Chapter 1. First, Jackson's strong action against South Carolina in the Nullification Crisis in no way went against the Founding thinking. One of the major concerns that the Founding Fathers had in framing the Constitution was that a strong national government was needed to, *inter alia*, stop domestic insurrection. It was basically correct that the nation was seen as superior to the states—the supremacy clause indicates as much. With the Constitution, the states could now be characterized as *semi-sovereign*. Second, the growing abolitionism in the North and the hardening of the pro-slavery position in the South both presented problems. While the Founders accepted slavery in order to forge a national government, they saw it as an evil, were aware of the contradiction it presented to the principles they enunciated, sought to limit it to the extent they could, and looked to its gradually dying.[46] So, the increasingly uncompromising pro-slavery Southern position was contrary to the Founders. On the other hand, abolitionism—irrespective of the moral truth of its opposition to slavery—had the ring of a moralistic crusade to it, especially with the obliviousness of some abolitionists to the grave political consequences of seeing America as utterly corrupt because of slavery and seeking to achieve their end whatever the cost.[47] The tendency to such moralism—as we shall see—was repeatedly expressed both domestically and in foreign policy as American history went on. It also will be recalled that moral sentimentality as a substitute for reason—which is not unrelated to moralism—is a factor causing the decline of regimes. As both sides became more extreme and uncompromising, the common good was threatened—which, at once, the Founders (despite their possibly insufficient conception of it) saw as necessary to sustain a democratic republic, the great Western thinkers and realist philosophy hold to be an element of a good political order, and the thinkers addressing the subject hold the absence of to be a cause of a political order's decline. The resulting sectional-based social conflict—which was slowly growing during this period—could ultimately upset the balance of federalism established by the Founders and is a factor in the decline or dissolution of a political order. The latter, of course, is what almost resulted from this in the Civil War. Expressions of the absolutism of the Southern position were the disruption of abolitionist mail, which was a kind of violation of freedom of the press, and the Congressional "gag rule" that had implications for the freedom of debate in Congress and the broader rights of free speech and to petition for a redress of grievances which are enshrined in the Bill of Rights.

The growth of interests seeking things from government perhaps represented a self-interested orientation that was at odds with what both the Founders themselves and their era's culture stressed, and possibly also represented a de-emphasis of the common good. It may also have signaled a greater pursuit of material well-being and the luxury that the Founding Era feared and the Federalist and Jeffersonian periods, as we saw, were able to avoid. Politically speaking, it may have represented the stirrings of interest group power that would come to dominate American politics later on—with some of the dangers of faction that Madison warned against. It may also have indicated the beginnings of an excessive turning to the federal government to solve problems, which went against the spirit of federalism, and a slowly increasing centralization of political authority. On the state level, the development of publicly-controlled colleges certainly violated no constitutional provisions, but one wonders if they were justified under the principle of subsidiarity—especially in light of the success of private colleges in providing higher learning and their ready availability even in the newer states of, say, the old Northwest.

Growth of Executive Power. At the beginning of the period of our inquiry, we witness Monroe continuing and even enhancing the presidential legislative leadership that took shape with Jefferson with his aggressive push for federal funding of internal improvements.[48] As Howe writes, however, it was Jackson's administration that "would witness novel assertions of presidential power."[49] He summarizes these: Jackson "extended the circle of presidential advisors, expanded the patronage to be dispensed, and broadened the use of the veto power. He [also]...combined the office of the presidency with leadership of his political party."[50] We have seen how he and his movement believed the president to be a tribune of the people, and downplayed legislative authority. Jackson's presidency was not—contrary to the claims of some of his political opponents—an attempt "to substitute executive tyranny for balanced government of the Founders."[51] Jackson was not utilizing powers that were unstated in the Constitution or outside the realm of what would have been anticipated for a president. It was just that he was willing to use them when previous presidents had not been. For example, he was only the second president to use the pocket veto. He certainly acted no more extravagantly on federal internal improvements funding than his predecessors; in fact, the projects funded were often in federal territories instead of states and so were less subject to constitutional criticism.[52] While Jackson's readiness to violate federal obligations under Indian treaties was troublesome, in light of moral principles and the cultural norms of America of the Founding Era (as discussed below), the Jacksonian-controlled Congress's efforts to cut off the Supreme Court's jurisdiction to hear appeals from state courts on Indian cases and even his unwillingness to enforce the Court's decision in the Cherokee case were not excessive exertions of power.[53] Article III of the Constitution clearly gives Congress the power to alter the appellate jurisdiction of the Court and the doctrine of separation of powers—reinforced by Federalist 78—implies that one of the ways the Court can be checked is by presidential refusal to execute its decisions.[54]

The violation of the Indian treaties and the tribes' forced relocation flatly went against the central Founding principle of the rule of law—it should be understood that treaties are of the nature of legal documents and, in fact, in the U.S. take on a status similar to the Constitution itself (i.e., they become part of "the law of the land")—and the cultural norms of the Founding Era, regardless of whether the people of that time universally had good relations with the Indians. Recall that promise-keeping, civic friendship, and basic justice were among these norms. The first of these was just pushed aside. Civic friendship certainly was not extended to the tribes. Justice was clearly violated, since the rightful property of the tribes as well as their immaterial property—i.e., their rights, safety (many died on the forced migration westward),[55] and equality as men—were taken from them. In addition, this demonstrated a lusting—on the part of the Caucasian population in those areas, at least—for *more*, a materialism or quest for luxury whose dangers we have noted.

During the Bank controversy, Jackson dismissed his Secretary of the Treasury William J. Duane for refusing to withdraw the federal government's deposits in the Bank. The criticism of Jackson as acting outside of his powers in dismissing a Cabinet member had no merit; he acted within the limits of Article II of the Constitution.[56] Similarly, the claims of Whigs that Jackson conducted his whole anti-Bank campaign with his small cohort of close presidential advisors and thereby undercut checks and balances and mixed government carried little weight. Presidents are always going to rely on their most trusted advisors, especially when undertaking their most crucial actions, and he was certainly not isolated from Congress in opposition to the Bank. The majority in the House of Representatives were Jacksonian Democrats, who supported him; while the Senate, with the opposition in charge, censured him. The censure was reversed once the Jacksonians got control.[57]

Where Jackson does seem to have acted excessively was in his ordering Duane—who was not a Bank supporter[58]—to do what apparently was forbidden by the law by removing the deposits.[59]

What we certainly can say is that Jackson's actualization of presidential powers that existed in potency and his extension of presidential leadership—as was the case to a more modest degree with Jefferson—made it easier for future presidents to exercise more sweeping powers and set a new norm for what was the acceptable reach of presidential authority. On the negative side, his being willing to violate the law regarding the Bank deposits provided an early precedent and created a kind of hidden momentum in the presidency for ignoring a law if a president thought the ends important enough to justify it. This reached its full flowering with the "imperial presidency" of the twentieth century where presidents did such things as routinely committing American troops abroad—even for extended wars—without declarations of war or even clear Congressional authorization, sweepingly expanded and misused government secrecy regulations to hide their miscues, stretched the pocket veto power to an unprecedented extreme, and invoked executive privilege to try to stop criminal investigations.[60] To be sure, it is accepted that there would be uncommon occasions when the executive prerogative power discussed by Locke would justify a president's acting outside of the law for the sake of the public good.[61] While these would mostly be situations of exigency and serious national crisis—such as when Abraham Lincoln had to take extraordinary measures at the outbreak of the Civil War—they would not necessarily be limited to these.[62] It is not so clear, however, contrary to Jackson's ideological perspective, that the public good demanded that the Bank be destroyed or that the Bank was not good for the U.S. economy.[63] In any event, the Lockean prerogative notion does not countenance the executive acting against the law blithely. It must also be remembered that Locke sought to embellish the legislative power and to establish the rule of law; that suggests that barring a truly serious need, the president must uphold the laws of the people's representatives. Thus, Jackson's action seemed to circumvent the rule of law that was, of course, a central feature of the Founding, in order to achieve an objective that he thought necessary to advance "the cause of the common man." One wonders if this set a standard for later reform efforts by bending, weakening, or reinterpreting constitutional principles or provisions—and often getting courts to go along with them—to "meet the new needs of the time" and advance democracy and new notions of rights.[64] If the rule of law could selectively be avoided, the further related condition sought by the Founders, actual reverence for the laws, could not be advanced.

Was the mixed government of the Constitution weakened by this strong stress on the executive? Probably not, but the spirit of commitment to the principle was certainly not strong among the Jacksonians. It was perhaps the beginning of the recurring cycle of the waxing and waning of the power of one branch or another—usually the legislative and the executive alternating—that has characterized American political history. The real challenge to mixed government came from the larger tide of democratization, as noted below.

Democratization, Citizen Rights and Law, and Developments in Political Life. The period in question, especially the administrations of Jackson and Van Buren, is known for its expansion of democracy in America—the era of "Jacksonian democracy." Jackson, as the above makes apparent, saw himself as the champion of what he termed "the people," and saw government as something to be used to promote the "common man." The Jacksonians believed that America could be a shining light for the rest of the world in the movement for democratization.[65] There were many examples of democratization in America after 1815: the franchise was broadened and came to be regarded distinctly as a right (at least for adult Caucasian males), as property requirements—and even taxpayer status requirements—were largely abolished;[66] local officials began to be elected instead of appointed in a number of states (even the local governments of the largest cities, New York and Philadelphia, had been appointed before this time); most states went to secret ballots (which eliminated the supposed danger of intimidation or excessive influence by elites); property requirements for office-holding were reduced or eliminated;[67] the practice of using caucuses as the means of nominating candidates for office was ended and meetings at which the mass of people could select candidates took their place;[68] by the 1830s, all but one state had direct popular voting for the electoral college in presidential elections;[69] electioneering was increasingly being geared to everyday people and politicians were finding that it pays to focus the public's wrath on elites;[70] there was a high level of popular enthusiasm for campaigns and elections and much discussion of campaigns and issues;[71] there was a growth of political organizations, with publicity, rallies, and the heavy use of printed campaign materials;[72] and the notion of the president as "tribune" of the people answerable only to them—noted above—gained currency.[73] Some Jacksonians would have gone even farther, such as those in Massachusetts who sought to substantially curtail the power and independence of the state judiciary.[74] Fehrenbacher writes that one of the problems that John Quincy Adams faced in his reelection bid was that, whether true or not, he "gave the impression of a disdainful patrician sniffing at the common people."[75]

The utter democratization of the franchise to the degree that it was done was clearly contrary to the Founders' beliefs; as we have noted, they intended the franchise to be broad but not universal even for Caucasian male adults. To be sure, it was the culmination of a broadening that began in the Jeffersonian period. There was no mistaking the democratic nature of the developments above and the fact that they reflected—and perhaps did their part in helping to spawn—the rising mass culture that so much contrasted with the Founding Era. The Jacksonians' overwhelming faith in the people bespeaks a version of egalitarianism. The readiness to see in Adams just another elitist underscores the discarding of the notion of natural aristocracy and even any seeming sense that some men might actually be more virtuous and capable than others to rule. They do not even stress the notion of the gentleman—not even its Jeffersonian counterpart, the husbandman. The Jacksonians had a naïve confidence in the capability of the masses that was given its fullest expression by some of the democratic theoreticians of the time, as seen below.

In spite of the dawning democratic future, there were also countercurrents and darker dimensions. First, in spite of the fact that the expansion of the franchise was taking place in general, it was being eliminated or restricted for free Negro males who had had it previously.[76] In the South, while the democratic trend could not be stifled, it did not advance as far as elsewhere and the plantation-based gentry still controlled the region's politics. They informally manipulated the majority—e.g., by making small political reforms that satisfied the Caucasian masses—in order to reinforce its support for the slavery system.[77] Further, democratization became a means of further deepening sectionalism—to some degree it was as a result of calculated political manipulation. Democratizing trends in the North helped to promote opposition to slavery.[78] Besides fortifying slavery within the South itself, as just noted, it enabled people like Calhoun to try to protect it nationally by sharpening sectional divisions. He could successfully appeal to the masses both North and South to oppose the Northern financial interests, reconstitute the Democratic party into what he saw as a more pro-states rights post-Jackson stance, and enable it to maintain control of the national government so Southern sectional interests could be protected.[79]

The darkest side of democratization at this time, which the Federalist and Jeffersonian periods also saw to a very limited degree, was mob action, rioting, vigilantism, and the dangers of demagoguery—it was the old notion of democracy as ochlocracy. Mobs targeted abolitionists, Catholics (with the developing nativist sentiment), Mormons, free Negroes, and banks (the latter no doubt stimulated by the Jacksonian political vitriol directed against Eastern financial interests). As Howe says, "Ethnic, racial, and religious animosities provided the most frequent provocation to riot."[80] Labor tensions also led to rioting and violence.[81] Vigilantism was seen not just on the frontier, but in the old northeastern states and in the South (where it was fueled partly by fears of slave insurrections).[82] Abraham Lincoln's raising the specter of the demagogue emerging from the violence and vigilantism of 1830s America in his Young

Men's Lyceum Speech (1838) is noteworthy.[83] These developments were probably the clearest example of the breakdown of: civility and the easy melding of different social groups, civic friendship, and an orientation to the common good that are identified with the Founding Era.

It is not surprising that Wilentz observes that as Jackson left political life, he came to realize that the democratic idea he had so ardently championed, for better or for worse, "brought not peace but further conflict."[84] Indeed, the Founding Fathers emerge as profoundly wise and prescient in restraining the democratic dimension of our political order with the institutions, norms, and practices of republicanism so that stability and civic peace could prevail. The Jacksonians, we have to conclude, were less attentive to this problem.

Howe mentions a few factors that stimulated democratization, besides the obvious propagandization for the principles of democracy by the Jacksonians: 1) The western settlement, wherein the new states on the then frontier typically opened up the franchise in order to attract immigrants. 2) The influence of churches and church organizations was important. First, they helped to spawn a more democratic outlook through the work congregants did "through the creation, administration, and financing of churches and other voluntary societies"; this was effectively a "widespread direct democracy." (We already saw in Chapter 2 how American Protestantism influenced the development of democracy because it encouraged participation within congregations by their members.) Also, leading preachers, such as Lyman Beecher (the father of Harriet Beecher Stowe), continued the evangelical spirit of the Second Great Awakening and stressed especially the "universal appeal" of Christ to "every race, nation, sex, and class." Beecher also stressed—and this theme in no small way helped to spawn the religious-inspired social reform movements of the nineteenth century discussed further below—that Christianity meant not just saving individual souls but also transforming society.[85] Moreover, the more liberal elements of the influential Congregational Church in New England— influenced by the Enlightenment (see Chapter 2)—were strongly stressing notions of human rights and freedom.[86] These things obviously had a strong democratic ethos to them. 3) Advances in transportation and communication, which made information generally and politically-oriented publications in particular more readily available—we noted above the intense discussion of politics and political issues—and made it easier to ship and distribute publications and for people to get to polling places.[87] The easier dissemination of publications, of course, would only have an influence with a literate and educated public. Jack Larkin writes that during this period, "Americans were strikingly literate, surpassing most of the nations of Western Europe."[88] Even before the 1830s, more children received formal schooling for longer periods of time.[89]

We have already noted the Jacksonian views about legal reform as part of their overall democratization effort. The push for codification met its greatest success in the newer western states where Jacksonian democracy had its strongest support.[90] Also as mentioned, the Taney Court opened the way for the state exercise of police power that in turn paved the way for the social (i.e., economic regulatory) legislation of the post-Civil War era. The era 1817-1840 saw American courts—whether manned by Jacksonian, pre-Jacksonian, old Federalist, or Whig judges—modify the law and alter traditional common law doctrines, such as those relating to private property rights, in the interest of economic development and new entrepreneurial, manufacturing, and corporate demands.[91] This was in line with the Jacksonian view that the common law should be pushed aside since it was an obstacle to democratization and modernization, but it ironically occurred largely because common law judges were able to take advantage of that system's historic adaptability to new circumstances. Among the changes made were: an expansion of the eminent domain powers of the state, a putting aside of the traditional common law restraint on excessive profit-making, and a movement away from the traditional requirement that contracts be equitable and capture the fair value of a good or service toward a complete freedom of contract.[92] The result was a kind of severing of ethics and economics as far as the law was concerned, and a further diminution of the notion of the social use of property referred to Chapter 1. This represented a further breaking down of the traditional notion of an organic community pursuing common moral and social norms. The stress now was on freeing the marketplace from social constraints buttressed by the law, so that individual economic actors—and agglomerations of actors in the newly-refashioned corporation—could advance themselves and prosper.[93] Even though the Jacksonians embraced the cause of workers in a time of increasing labor ferment and the beginnings of unionization (see below),[94] changes in labor law to address workers' concerns and to make organizing even legal largely had to wait for the 1840s.[95]

It is worth recalling that the readiness to alter the common law to address political and social conditions—even, one is inclined to say, beyond the normal understanding of it as being inherently adaptable and flexible to meet new needs—happened both in the Federalist and Jeffersonian periods. We suggested above that certain of Jackson's and the federal government's actions hurt the rule of law by selectively applying it; this, too, as Chapter 2 indicated, was not new. It seems as if Jackson just followed unfortunate precedents.

One other area of the law was the focus of a clash between the Jacksonians and the remaining defenders of older arrangements. The Jacksonians sought separation of church and state, and it was in this period that the few remaining legally established or preferred churches were eliminated on the state level. The Jacksonians sought to go beyond ending formal preferences by eliminating state legal requirements favoring preferences for individual believers as opposed to unbelievers, such as those stating that the latter's testimony could not be accepted in court. While the mainstream of the Jacksonians did not go this far, some among their ranks anticipated the radical church-state separation of post-World War II America and most of the "professional agnostics and atheists of the day...were active Jacksonians."[96] In other words, the Jacksonians did not outright disassociate themselves from these people. One wonders if by this and by their pushing for this more sweeping church-state separation—both probably motivated by their democratization ethos—they were not preparing the ground for twentieth century secularization. More, by including the secularists and unbelievers in their ranks, were they opening the door to the notion that the whole range of opinion deserves respect—i.e., that all positions are to be treated with equal validity, even belief and unbelief—that became predominant in the twentieth century? Were they setting the groundwork for the later view that politics should—officially at least—avoid truth claims? Were they also perhaps nudging the country in the direction of the ultimate removal of religion from the public square? The evidence overwhelmingly is that framers of the First Amendment—some of whom had been at the Constitutional Convention, as stated in Chapter 2—had absolutely no intention that it should require any of the latter,[97] and it is very clear from Chapter 1 that religion was necessary in the Founders' estimation to sustain a democratic republic.

The question of rights is related to law. The gag rule and the suppression of anti-slavery mail were mentioned above. There were other significant examples of the interference with or manipulation of rights during this period. The Jacksonian Democratic party was generally intolerant of anti-slavery sentiment within its ranks, even repudiating a Democratic journalist for running editorials not promoting abolitionism but condemning censorship and mob violence against abolitionists.[98] (This was much like the unwillingness of today's Democratic party to accept anti-abortion elements.[99]) While there was generally a free press,[100] pro-abolitionist newspapers and books were legally suppressed in the South,[101] and even the North witnessed mob attacks on abolitionist newspapers.[102] While there were efforts to clearly separate church and state and not disadvantage nonbelievers, journalists faced legal punishment for openly anti-church or anti-religious propagandizing.[103] If this time witnessed a lot of discussion of public issues, the newspapers themselves did not always exhibit the spirit of free exchange that must reinforce free speech. This was seen when the local town-based newspapers opposed legislation to grant free postage to all newspapers for fear that it would give an advantage the city press, and when the Jacksonian editor contracted to publish the official Congressional debates of the time suppressed opposition speeches.[104] The Jackson administration itself hardly encouraged the spirit of free political exchange when it switched the contracts for most federal government printing from opposition to pro-administration newspapers.[105] We see here the same compromising or selective embracing of rights noted above (i.e., freedom of the press and free speech when the content is not agreed with). More, the lack of the spirit supporting these rights, at least in same cases, is troublesome because ultimately, as the Founding Fathers recognized, the key to maintaining republican government and the different aspects of it is the spirit of commitment to it in the minds and hearts of the leaders and the people. There is also seen here, again, a lack of civility.

Besides the democratic changes and reforms above—reflecting the same democratizing currents—there were many new developments in the politics of the time. These fell into four general areas: changes in practice of the constitutional order; the long-term shaping of the character of political parties, the implanting of the spoils system, and the means of campaigning and making electoral appeals. The one significant development in the first category that took hold in this period was the attempted direct control of the U.S. senators from a state by the state's legislature. If the legislature passed a resolution directing its senators to vote a certain way on legislation, they were expected to follow the directions or resign.[106] Such a practice is nowhere mentioned by the Founding Fathers, and one wonders if it constitutes an attempt by the states to exercise an excessive control over national decision-making, upsetting the proper understanding of federalism. Concerning the second category, the efforts at nonpartisanship by the party-skeptic Monroe that led instead to one broad-based political party gave way, it might be said, to the institutionalization of the party system with the rise of the Jacksonians (even though, they themselves had a kind of reluctance about parties, as noted, and justified theirs as a kind of protective device for "the people"). The Democratic party—the transformed Democratic-Republican party of Jefferson—was the first mass democratic political party.[107] It was during Jackson's presidency that Tammany Hall in New York City became affiliated with the Democratic party and emerged as the first of the American urban political machines.[108] The roots of the spoils system, as mentioned in Chapter 2, were in the time of Jefferson. In spite of the usual association of Jackson with the spoils system, it was still used in a relatively limited way by him with only 10% of carried-over federal employees replaced during his administration (and the new people on balance were the same quality as the ones replaced).[109] Still, the standard set by the Washington administration (see Chapter 2) was hardly being matched, and Jackson firmly established the system on the national level that, Fehrenbacher insists, over time "inevitably lowered the quality of public service."[110] Regarding the fourth category, we already notice these practices and tendencies that became typical of the history of American campaigns: the attempt to pander to the people's distrust of the "elite" (already mentioned), specific appeals to ethnic and other identifiable groups in the electorate[111] (this included negative appeals by putting down other groups as the nativist era heated up[112]), "campaigning against Washington,"[113] a "carnival atmosphere" where issues and proposals were little discussed,[114] strong distortion and scurrilous characterization of the political opposition[115] (we noted a lot of this in the second half of the 1790s, but it found a regular place in campaigning by this time), and melodramatic political speechmaking—as opposed to reasoned appeals—to get points across (Wilentz calls this "political theater," and it was first perfected by the Whigs in 1840).[116] In these political party, spoils system, and campaign-related developments, we observe: (again) the decline of the natural aristocracy idea—even the basic merit needed to man governmental positions that Washington was so fastidious about upholding was compromised—and a kind of egalitarianism; the rising mass culture that both weakened the notion of community of the Founding Era and is a sign of societal decline; and the decline of civility, respect for the common good, and commitment to truth-telling that was so much a part of Founding Era culture. While the forms of the mixed government the Founders sought remained, democratization meant that in practice it was weakened with the democratic aspect taking on more prominence.

Economic and Technological Developments, Economic Policy, and the Rise of the Working Class. The period 1817-1840 was one of considerable change in the nature of economic life. It was, in some sense, a time of transition. Business and production organization was changing. Machine operations were replacing production done by hand, with the result that more volume could be turned out.[117] Ownership and management were not yet separated, except in the largest business entities,[118] but the rise of the nineteenth-century corporation—with its very attractive feature of limited liability for the investor—was slowly changing that.[119] As the scale of production increased, so did the reliance upon credit.[120] While during this period the notion of the state conferring a corporate charter to an entity it believed would act in the public interest continued to prevail, this too was changing. This change was actually motivated by public attitudes, as the old individual craftsmen resented what they saw as favored treatment by bestowing a charter and because more people wanted to become investors. So, the practice took hold of granting a charter to any entity that complied with certain incorporation procedures.[121] In general, old ways of thinking and acting were giving way to market imperatives. The uncertainties and insecurities that the market brings became evident, as did a greater concern about luxury.[122] The old "more episodic" rhythms of labor of an agrarian and craftsman-oriented economy were altered.[123] Now they were both more regular—and thus more monotonous and all-absorbing—and more intense; manufacturing workers averaged twelve to fourteen hours per day six days per week.[124] The family was still essentially the center of most economic life since the country was still predominantly agrarian.[125] The advancing manufacturing age, however, was starting to take its toll. As children went out of the home to work in factories and the like, parental authority weakened.[126] The household was transforming, as Western society slowly was, from a producing to a consuming unit, and the roles of husband and wife were becoming more sharply distinguished as the former became the exclusive off-site wage-earner and the latter reigned over the private, domestic sphere.[127] Much has been made about the legal vulnerability of the wife in earlier America, although as we saw in Chapter 2 this is not quite accurate. Regardless, in practical terms "mutual affection and respect often moderated the severity of legal tradition."[128] There were economic contrasts: While there was overall greater material abundance and a rising standard of living, there were also more property-less workers in both urban and rural areas.[129] The wage system was now becoming the norm, with the result that the status, independence, sense of solidarity, and economic restraint characterizing a spirit of self-regulation of skilled tradesmen and artisans was disappearing.[130] The latter was a reflection of the old kind of organic, more cooperative, community built around a common ethical vision with attention to the overall public good. The wage system and increasing proletarianization of workers began to spawn unionization (as noted), intensify class-consciousness and working class discontent,[131] and stimulate America's first taste of economic radicalism.[132] While social mobility continued to characterize American life[133]— this was always a great point of difference between America and Europe— economic inequality was growing (due not just to industrialization and the dynamic of a market-based economy, but also to the arrival of increasing numbers of poor immigrants, the departure of unpropertied young men from the homestead to make their own life in the West, etc.).[134]

The period 1817-1840 was overall one of growing prosperity, but it had distinct peaks and valleys, the latter being especially the Panic of 1819—which was probably America's first experience of the effects of the modern boom-and-bust business cycle[135]—and the Panic of 1837, a depression that lasted for the course of Van Buren's term and helped to usher out the Jacksonians in 1840.[136] Probably federal economic policies played an important role in bringing about both panics (especially 1837's). The heavy government borrowing for the War of 1812, along with actions of the Second Bank of the United States and new interconnected economic relationships—spreading internationally even at this stage—were causes of the first.[137] Jackson's sinking of the Bank, his insistence on paying off the federal debt without having an alternative mechanism to stabilize the money supply after the Bank's demise, his Specie Circular, public land sales which fueled speculation, the failure of the federal government to manage America's foreign trade balance (which involved tariff considerations), and actions of the Bank of England (somewhat in response to the trade problems) and other international influences were the main factors in the second.[138] The upheavals did not seem to deflect Americans from the increasing focus on luxury noted above.

It was not the shaping of a market economy per se that was responsible for the period's prosperity, however. This was the time of an early explosion of technology and internal improvements, which *in turn* helped to mold the new market economy and spawned prosperity. There were advances in transportation and communications, as mentioned. The Erie Canal was completed in 1825. Howe says that it was "the first step in the transportation revolution that would turn an aggregate of local economies into a nationwide market economy."[139] There were other canals built: between 1815 and 1840 a total of 3,000 miles of canals were constructed.[140] Harbors were improved.[141] The National Road (i.e., Cumberland Road) was completed across much of Ohio by the end of the 1830s and many other "turnpikes"—gravel roads—were built during this time.[142] Steamships came into use in the 1820s, which especially aided in the settlement of the Mississippi-Ohio River region. The steam railroad, which had enormous implications for the westward expansion of the country, appeared around 1830 and by 1840 over 3,000 miles of track—mostly in the North—had been laid. American domestic and foreign trade was accelerated from 1820 onward.[143] Investment in transportation infrastructure was done by a combination of private entities—made possible by the changes in corporation law—state appropriation, and federal subsidies from the sale of public lands—with one or the other the primary source of funding for the different kinds of internal improvements.[144] Meanwhile, outside of internal improvements other technological innovations were being developed, in such areas as industrial machinery, textiles, agriculture, firearms, and printing.[145] Fehrenbacher tells us that these occurred because of the practical ingenuity that had continued to be an American strength since before the Founding Era, instead of any new developments of scientific theory.[146]

As Chapter 2 made clear, Americans had never been supportive of laissez faire in economics. This was reinforced by the Panic of 1819. People from all over the spectrum of economic thinking argued for government involvement and regulation of some kind.[147] The very idea of a democratic republic meant that government was a servant. As "their servant, the people repeatedly invoked…[government's] aid in the economic development of the country."[148] We mentioned Monroe's basic economic policies above. He gave a broad interpretation to federal spending powers on internal improvements and lined up the federal government squarely on the side of encouraging economic development.[149] Moreover, the Era of Good Feelings saw in a limited way a return to paper money—to the "soft" or fiat currency that the colonial and Revolutionary periods had used—which created various problems.[150] This would be something Jackson later would put a stop to, causing still other problems. Adams continued the Monroe policy of protective tariffs,[151] even while negotiating early versions of "most-favored nation" trade treaties with various countries.[152] He essentially continued Monroe's program of federal funding for internal improvements and even enhanced it to further develop the postal distribution network.[153] He also strongly stressed federal land sales.[154] The general Jacksonian economic principles are discussed above. A few main features of the Jackson administration's economic policy were: a strong support for economic competition, refraining from government intervention to favor certain economic interests[155] (even though Wilentz says that Jackson's policies actually *increased* government control over the economy[156]); opposition to the Bank, which he saw as harmful to the average citizen; continued federal funding for internal improvements, with some reluctance and restraint[157]; the complete elimination of the federal debt (but, as noted above, the way he went about it adversely affected the economy); a reluctance to lower tariffs (even though it hurt some states and he finally did lower them after the Nullification Crisis); proposed revenue sharing with the states after the debt was retired;[158] the issuing of the Specie Circular, an executive order that required that payment for the purchase of public lands be made exclusively in gold or silver, supposedly to reduce land speculation and the amount of paper money in circulation (though this too hurt the economy, as noted above, by causing deflationary pressures and a credit crunch);[159] and, in line with the intent of the Specie Circular, making it easier for people to purchase public lands[160] (this corresponded with the Jacksonian "spread the wealth" perspective above). Van Buren's economic policy corresponded with the general view of Jackson of opposing the privileged and supporting the people.[161] Faced with an unprecedented economic downturn in the form of the Panic of 1837, he kept the Specie Circular intact and tried to move further toward hard money policies.[162] He also sought liberalization of land policies.[163] While state governments started to regulate state-chartered banks more,[164] he proposed to have the federal government do the same[165]— even as he also proposed to disinvolve the federal government from banks by setting up a separate U.S. Treasury depository.[166] Like Jackson and Jefferson, he proposed this moderately interventionist governmental role while insisting that federal constitutional power was limited.[167] Even though his policies were not successful in ending the Panic, his rhetoric about economic life paralleled perspectives from the Founding Era: he called for economy and frugality in government, cautioned the public to practice simplicity and avoid indulgence, admonished people not to turn to the federal government to make up their economic losses, said that government did not have the role of helping men enrich themselves, and made clear that government should work for the public good in economic life.[168] The Whigs, who emerged at the end of this period, began a transformation of thought about the place of wealth in the American nation that, as we shall see, became prominent later on. As Wilentz puts it, they characterized the "search for profit and power" by men of "property and standing" as "a moral and patriotic impulse."[169] The time would come when it would be said that "the business of America is business"[170] and the "American dream" would be identified essentially with temporal well-being. Further, the Whigs made it sound—as would political spokesmen of the future—as if this were a defining notion of this new democracy.[171]

By way of evaluation, we can say the following. We have already noted that the Jacksonian concern about frugal government and avoiding debt concurred with the Founders' thinking, but—like the socio-cultural movements of this time (see below)—they carried it too far when they sought to do things like *completely* avoid public debt. While Jackson wanted to remove federal regulation of banks, the continued tendency throughout this entire period of people looking to the federal government for help with the economic situation and for funding for internal improvements and the like makes one wonder if the balance that the Founders sought to maintain between the federal and state governments was not already slowly shifting toward the former. At the same time, the back and forth character of Jackson's and Van Buren's actions made it clear that these presidents did not yet seem to see the proper and necessary role for federal policy in dealing with economic problems. The inattention to the international influences on the American economy further demonstrated this. The other developments that we observe in this section on economic life betray a slow departure from the cultural norms of the Founding Era: 1) a much-enhanced concern with material accumulation and temporal well-being (to the point where, by the end of this period, the Whigs were indirectly extolling it by making a kind of moral defense of moneymaking); 2) the greater concern about self-interest and less about the public interest as the market economy expanded; 3) the decrease of a spirit of cooperation, at least in economic life, as competitive advantage became the focus; 4) the widening of economic inequalities; 5) the compromising of civic friendship and to some degree the weakening of the middle class character of America as class consciousness increased; 6) the development, in some cases, of outright social conflict engendered by economic developments (we have already seen how ethnic, racial, and religious tensions also affected this); 7) the attenuation of the regime of widespread property ownership; 8) the substitution of government policy for ethics, cultural norms, and the common law as a means of regulating economic life (where it *was* being regulated); 9) a reduction in the possibility of vertical mobility for a time by at least a certain portion of the population, especially those in the new industrial working class and immigrants; and 10) some weakening of the family due to economic pressures and the slow transformation of its economic role and the roles of its members. As we saw, the legitimacy of the notion of wealth accumulation without limits had already implanted itself in the culture of America's colonial and Founding periods. The Jacksonians perhaps just continued the spirit of Franklin of wanting everyone to have a chance to partake in it, and sought to use government to help insure that. The Whig promotion of wealth accumulation—it was the same with the Republican party later in the nineteenth century—featured a lessened concern about everyone having a chance to take part in it—or at least they were more inclined than the Jacksonians to let everyone make their own opportunities for it without government help. Even if the earlier culture had this view, it had many other practices and mores that limited the potentially adverse effects of it (as if it were open to the benefits of wealth accumulation—to say nothing of stressing the personal characteristics that made it and many other achievements possible, such as self-sacrifice and industriousness—but able to minimize its detriments). As American culture and politics progressed, the means or willingness to continue to limit these effects diminished. To be sure, even while all these developments were clearly perceptible and advancing, their full flowering was still off in the future.

Military Power, Nationalism, and Expansion. Wiltse writes that at the end of the War of 1812 there was overwhelming sentiment within the U.S. to move in "the direction of consolidation, of national self-sufficiency, of world power."[172] This no doubt fueled or intensified efforts such as internal improvements, economic development, the movement westward (in spite of what was considered the annoying presence of the Indian tribes), and the Monroe Doctrine. It perhaps helped overcome any constitutional reluctance about the federal government's funding internal improvements. Nations like individuals are shaped by their experiences, and the sense of vulnerability Americans felt from the war almost certainly forged their determination in these areas. It probably went deeper that this, however, because Americans did not seem just to want to be sure of their place for defensive reasons; they desired expansion, and Manifest Destiny signaled just ahead in the 1840s. Wiltse says that even after the war, they still desired to annex Canada and had an interest in Cuba. In fact, the Latin Americans were suspicious of the U.S.'s intentions.[173] As far as the Monroe Doctrine was concerned, the Latin Americans "resented its presumption of U.S. hegemony."[174] To be sure, Howe tells us that the American nationalism of this period was not exclusively focused on expansion or establishing American influence abroad; it "developed a variety of permutations." There was the "judicial nationalism of Marshall and Story," which stressed a "nationalist program of banking and internal improvements."[175] That was also the nationalism of the post-Madison Democratic-Republican party, and was adopted—in whole or in part, and to different degrees—by all the presidential administrations of the period. Then there was Jackson's brand of nationalism, which was squarely based on territorial expansion (although focused on what would become the continental United States).[176] Part of this involved his Indian removal policies.[177]

As far as the military during this period was concerned, it remained small (although large enough to carry out the Indian removals and to help motivate a backing off of South Carolina during the Nullification Crisis). Also during this period, the country witnessed the decline of militias. The Militia Act of 1792 had mandated the enrollment of all able-bodied male citizens in their respective state militias,[178] but the militias declined because many men did not want to serve or did not take them seriously. State politicians did not want to press the case because as times became more democratic more of these men became voters and could turn them out of office.[179] So, large standing armies and the over-militarization of the nation—the fears of the Founding Fathers—were no threat, but the decline of a spirit of service and commitment, needed in the final analysis to maintain liberty, perhaps were. At the root of this probably were a concern about convenience and a loss of public-spiritedness.

The expansionistic impulse of this period, of course, continued the earlier American attitude—actually, it probably intensified it since the Jacksonians were so much oriented to the people on the frontier. As we have seen, it exhibited an especially ugly side with the Indian removal (in that case, it was not westward expansion, but expansion into territory that European-Americans coveted right within the original states). The continued American desire to annex Canada, etc., after the near disastrous outcome of that effort in the War of 1812 signaled not just a moral blindness—for Americans should have apprehended the injustice of such an objective—but a lapse in their trademark practical intelligence we spoke about in Chapter 1. Moreover, it also showed a deficiency in the old American spirit of friendship, since after all Canada was a neighbor. One is led to speculate that the push for expansion—even to the point of violating Indian treaties and forcibly dislodging and moving the tribes—was driven by democratization. The people wanted that and their leaders responded. This push in a small way could even have helped further advance the slow accretion of power by the federal government and the notion of strengthening governmental power generally; after all, expansionism requires forceful government to achieve or at least to back it up. The effects of democratization were also seen, as stated, in the decline of the state militia. It enabled people to escape responsibility; it seemed to weaken both the socio-cultural and the legal pressures that could be brought on them to act for the good of the community. Indeed, this suggests that in some sense democratization compromised such earlier cultural norms as concern for the good of the community and the willingness to sacrifice.

Socio-Cultural Developments and Intellectual Currents. There were many different social changes and new ideas that occurred or were beginning to take hold during the period 1817-1840. The eighteenth century belief that the education of youth was never to be controlled or even influenced by government was rapidly giving way. The movement to embrace government (i.e., public) education was led by Massachusetts and given a boost by new western states such as Ohio that were given grants of public land to use for education. The shaping of the new norm of bureaucratically-structured state-run education was imported during this time from Germany. Further, it was in the 1830s that the decision was made to aim for universal education, at least at the elementary level, for children at government expense; the argument justifying this, that carried the day, was that national unity and the perpetuation of what had now become the American democracy required it.[180] Increased immigration seemed to heighten the urgency of these objectives. The ethos of the public schools, to some degree until the 1950s, was common denominator Protestant. The ardent early promoters of public education, like Horace Mann, had no intention of removing religion from them (as happened completely later in American history). Bible-reading was a common practice in schools in the nineteenth century, and Protestant religious instruction also often took place until Catholic parochial schools also sought state funds. The solution to this dilemma was just to eliminate such instruction altogether.[181] We already have noted that state-run colleges began at this time.

American religion was undergoing many changes. Calvinism, so influential in American Protestantism, was undergoing a profound transformation. The old, central notion of predestination in Calvinist theology gave way to a strong emphasis on free will, which then was expanded to mean that one was responsible not only for himself but also others. A Christian humanitarianism thus developed, which—as Wiltse says—had "its arms wide to receive the best of German rationalism, of French humanism, of Jacksonian democracy."[182] It was an early example of the melding of Christian and secular thought—even with secular thought which had been hostile to Christianity and whose presuppositions were often at odds with Christianity. While Fehrenbacher writes that the change in Calvinism was precipitated by the democratic and optimistic spirit of the age[183]—this grew out of the secular Enlightenment, which had influenced American Protestantism—it likely went on to help stimulate further secular trends as time went on. These developments were led by intellectually pace-setting New England.

Even utopian ideas began to gain circulation in America during this time, no doubt also motivated by Enlightenment-based optimism about the possibilities of human nature and the sense of American exceptionalism. Religion probably had a role in this, too: Besides its more optimistic tinge in general (as just noted), there were new Christian theologies like Charles Grandison Finney's perfectionism—that man could be reborn and live without sin.[184] Full-fledged utopianism was a notion that did not take hold in America. The New Harmonys, the Brook Farms, and the like were short-lived. Utopian communities were a kind of escapism; as Wiltse says, Americans on the contrary wanted to engage society and change it.[185] Although modern utopian thought had its roots in the Enlightenment, the fact that the notion of progress instead of it caught on in the U.S. probably is a reflection of how the Enlightenment played out differently here as opposed to Europe.

If American religion was embracing secular trends, this was also a time of "vigorous revivalism."[186] The Second Great Awakening and its aftermath resulted in religion coming to be more and more identified with causes of social reform, including abolitionism, temperance, mental health and insane asylum reform, prison reform, and reform of the debtor laws. The early feminist movement was even stirring by the mid-1830s.[187] This reform idea, when carried out either by people with religious or secular motivations, reflected a growing belief that personal virtue was in some way shaped by one's social environment.[188] Thus, efforts had to be made to improve society. After 1840 and until the end of the Civil War, much of the reforming zeal was focused on the anti-slavery cause.[189] This religious revival included a millenarian strain that influenced its social action and, to some degree, its politics.[190] This millenarian thinking produced a particular religious version of American exceptionalism, although Howe tells us that both the religious and secular strains saw America as exempt from the kind of history of other nations—including, it would seem, susceptibility to the factors causing decline in Chapter 1—and having a unique destiny.[191]

One of the outright secular intellectual currents that made its initial appearance in America in the 1830s, imported from Europe, was socialism. Its biggest proponents were associated with the radical element of Jacksonian democracy.[192] Part and parcel of the mechanics of socialism—although motivated by other ideological perspectives as well—is social engineering, which America first saw during this time. According to Howe, colonization of freed slaves in Liberia "constituted one of the most grandiose schemes for social engineering ever entertained in the United States."[193]

Mobility and westward migration continued to bring about social change and the weakening of traditional institutions, as we noted they had since late colonial times. Cultural ties were also weakened, and organized religion became fragmented (due also to the various developments occurring within it and the very essence of Protestantism of rejecting central authority). Immigration added to these developments, even though it was relatively light until the 1840s (still, the nativist movement was making its appearance). These factors, along with the advancing democratic ethos, helped necessitate the new mass appeal politics discussed above. The weakening of the old institutional framework and the isolation, the increasing enmassment, and the social impotency of each individual caused by the advance of equality that Tocqueville spoke of helped to stimulate the rise of voluntary associations.[194]

The increase of immigration, the changes in the institutional framework and religion, the weaker hold of the family, and the rise of urbanization brought about such social pathologies as the increase of prostitution.[195] This happened even though it has been argued that sexual morality became more severe (reflecting what Tocqueville observed in this period).[196] Change was also occurring in the family due to a different view about childrearing, particularly among the more affluent in urban areas and in the towns. Responding to evangelical ministers and emerging child-rearing "experts," who told them that the health of the Republic or at least success in the new socio-economic order depended upon self-control, character, and virtue, mothers suddenly came to view themselves as having a heavy burden of responsibility and anxiety for something that had previously been taken in stride as a natural thing. They devoted increasing attention to the rearing of their children, maybe too much.[197] So began a regimen in middle and upper class child-rearing that continues even today: a kind of doting, overprotective presence, and a reluctance to allow child-rearing to proceed in a more natural, rough-and-tumble manner where children would learn the lessons of life in a perhaps more profound way on their own.

We have talked about Jacksonian principles and the practice of Jacksonian democracy. In the realm of thought, there were several democratic theorists in this period whose writing helped advance the philosophical case for democracy. Most prominent among them were George Bancroft, Richard Hildreth, Frederick Grimke, and Walt Whitman (who is the best known of the group, but more as a poet than a democratic theorist). Brought together, these are the main features of their thought: the necessity of political and legal equality, while recognizing the inevitability of social and economic inequality; the view that government has a limited role—i.e., removing "artificial legal restraints and privileges" (this was in the spirit of Jackson's attack on the Bank and monopoly)—and laissez faire in economics should be the norm; majority rule was extolled, but (except for the utilitarian Hildreth) they were not outright majoritarians and believed in "the primacy of moral law"; and, finally, instead of extolling the executive over legislatures—as Jacksonian principles did—they extolled public opinion. So, while upholding the moral law, in some sense they made public opinion—i.e., the majority—the arbiter of it. As A.J. Beitzinger puts it, public opinion became "an infallible indicator of the content of moral law." To insure that this would work, they believed that the cause of democracy must be advanced; the larger the public—i.e., the more who were guaranteed the right to political participation—the more certain we could be of such infallibility. They certainly favored protecting minority rights, but believed that such "an informed public" would necessarily "have regard for the interests of minorities."[198] Attributing *infallibility* to the moral judgment of public opinion reminds one of Rousseau's belief that the general will—the collective of all the people—necessarily knows what is best for a political society. Their view also seemed to be an extrapolation—applied to the collectivity—both of Jefferson's belief in human improvement inevitably occurring just perhaps because of some force in human nature and Finney's perfectionist theology. They believed that the long-run effect of allowing public opinion to rule would be the improvement of the human race.[199] It perhaps could also be said that—even though a secular notion—their view had roots in the Protestant idea of the validity of individual interpretation of Scripture, which at this period of time in the religious realm was expanding beyond the latter to broader doctrinal judgments. If the individual could be his own religious and even moral authority, how much more reliable of an arbiter many individuals could be. These democratist thinkers exuded not just an overpowering confidence in public opinion, but assigned to it an almost mystical character. Indeed, it was a secularized version of gnosticism: it was not some small, select group that knew the truth, but in these new democratic times it was the people.

Now, we evaluate the developments discussed in this section. First, over time the increasing emphasis on formal (i.e., institutional) education diminished yet another traditional role of the family—and correspondingly reduced the family's social importance. To be sure, the greater stress on education was in conformity with the Founders as long as it provided training for citizenship, liberal learning, and character formation.[200] The shrinking of the role of religion in the public schools not too long after they became widespread—due to the Catholic question above—was an early stirring—along with the aforementioned Jacksonian push for more complete church-state separation and acceptance of skeptics and atheists into their ranks—of the minimizing of religion in American public life. This, of course, was contrary to the Founders, Tocqueville, the great Western political thinkers, and the commentators on societal decline surveyed in Chapter 1. Perhaps, more precisely, it could be said that it began a momentum in this direction that was almost imperceptible as long as the culture was fundamentally religious and public leaders acknowledged the importance of religion (Tocqueville, we recall, made clear the overwhelmingly religious character of American life in the 1830s). Moreover, the entire project of government-run education and the claim of its proponents that it better prepared young people for democratic citizenship than private, essentially religiously-controlled education was without parallel in the Founding Era and not advocated at all by the Founding Fathers (except at higher levels with Jefferson's founding of the University of Virginia).

It might be observed that the displacement of religious instruction from the new government schools because of Catholic demands was a clumsy way to deal with religious pluralism. Maybe not much better could be expected in light of lingering Protestant-Catholic hostility and a lack of experience in dealing with such pluralism, but if a spirit of civility, friendship, and accommodation had been employed instead of constricting the religious dimension of the schools it might have slowed down the path of secularization.

It was not just these educational and political developments that set a long-term course for limiting religion in American public life, but the changes in American religion itself. By opening itself to secular influences and a secular-based outlook about the world, it was slowly beginning to make itself—i.e., religion *per se*—a less significant force. One wonders too if its newly found social-reform orientation, while having a definite influence—often for the good—on the subjects in question did not further set the stage in the long-run for limiting its influence *as religion*.

The new optimism, shared both by secular and religious forces, was arguably a further slippage from the realism of the Founding Fathers and the "shrewd practical intelligence" of their culture. That utopianism even made an appearance in 1817-1840 America is a testament to how far this optimism had advanced. The millenarian dimension of American religion likely furthered the weakening of realism and practicality in the general outlook of Americans about the above social reform matters and other socio-political questions over time. Indeed, this was perhaps illustrated even in the short course by the social engineering of the Liberian enterprise.[201]

The further loosening of cultural and institutional bonds continued a development begun in colonial times. This, plus the ascendancy of mass culture, weakened community and perhaps helped aggravate the diminishment of civility, sense of public purposelessness, and resulting insufficient attention to the common good that has been noted. The weakening of religion that began at this time almost certainly added to these developments over the course of American history and blazed the path to a departure from the natural law, the sound moral norms that the Founders thought so important. The first expressions of the latter were already happening during this period with the removal of economics from an ethical context and the increasing unwillingness of some economic actors to be attentive to the public interest and the moral norms that shape it.

Voluntary Associations, Popular Movements, and the Emergence of the Whigs. We have already made reference to the increasing presence of voluntary associations, especially with reference to the emerging reform movements of this period. We have also mentioned that early labor unions formed. Among the first successful voluntary associations were temperance societies; Howe says that they "served as a model for other movements."[202] This movement had very deep religious roots, like so many of the voluntary associations of the time. There were, however, also civic, occupational, and political (i.e., besides political parties) organizations.[203] As suggested above, many of these were broadly popular organizations, involving not just prominent individuals but also many average people; there was a lot of involvement in voluntary associations, as Tocqueville observed.[204] The leaders of the early temperance movement— Lyman Beecher was probably the most prominent among them—set a certain pattern and standard of what today we would call socially-activist or "advocacy" organizations: taking an absolutist position on the cause or issue they were advocating for. Beecher and the others moved from seeking moderation and restraint in drinking to calling for its total repudiation. Howe suggests that this shift may have been motivated, at least partly, because it "made a more effective appeal."[205] Voluntary associations, at least advocacy ones, tended to be popular or "mass" phenomena not only because they enlisted large numbers of citizens in their ranks but also because they had to gear their appeals to a mass audience. In this sense, they mirrored the developments in politics discussed above and, it will be recalled, even in the Jeffersonian Era. This reflected the new democratic ethos. The emergence of advocacy-type voluntary associations was a new expression of the notion of faction that would eventually become the norm in the form of the contemporary interest group.

Wilentz's discussion of the Whigs, who emerged during the Jacksonian period and prevailed in the 1840 election, shows that they accepted Jacksonian democratic and limited government ideas,[206] but also embraced more eagerly the new reform movements. The latter, while popular movements in their composition, embraced a kind of elite set of judgments about what was good for people, increasingly relied on expert opinion—as seen in the reliance on the emerging field of psychiatry in the mental health reform and asylum movement—and were ready to employ the coercive powers of government to achieve their objectives. Like the Jacksonians, the Whigs sought social, economic, and political progress. The Jacksonians viewed government as playing the role of eliminating what they saw as such private-sector impediments to progress as monopolies. The Whigs were less likely to support government economic intervention and regulation—though they did favor its chartering and sustaining the Bank—but they were ready to let it "coerce individuals toward what they considered personal improvement" in the name of advancing social progress.[207] The willingness to publicly coerce to achieve personal improvement was, to be sure, not a new feature on the American political landscape.[208] In this regard, the Whigs were in line with the country's Calvinist background,[209] but sought to achieve aims that could be seen as either Christian or secular. As Wilentz says, "Whig self-reform adapted ethical precepts from across the spectrum of post-Calvinist American Protestant belief." Their views spanned a range from the new revivalism to Unitarianism. They reflected the new Christian humanitarianism spoken of above. They contrasted themselves to the Jacksonians, who they said believed that the socio-politico-economic order was the cause of problems; the Whigs believed that the individual was exclusively responsible for his situation, so change and improvement should occur there.[210] Nevertheless, they embraced institutions—in fact, they helped bring about a veritable revolution in the role of certain institutions in the U.S., such as public schools and reformatories—to achieve this self-improvement.[211] In a sense, both the Whigs and the Jacksonians practiced a moralistic politics; as Wilentz points out, they just saw different groups in the roles of victims and victimizers. Both embraced an early version of the "politics of victimhood," and so stand as a precedent for what has become common in contemporary America. For the Jacksonians, the farmers and the workers were the victims (although the Whigs also tried to forge alliances with labor), and the Eastern monied interests and the Bank were the victimizers; for the Whigs, the victims included slaves, families tormented by alcoholic husbands-fathers, and the insane; the victimizers were the slaveholders, the intemperate, people who did not understand mental illness and the like.[212]

   Essentially, the same assessment of the rise of the leading types of voluntary associations and the Whig party during this period can be made. First, the mass character of many of these organizations illustrated the rising mass culture of America that we have been discussing (which, of course, was contrasted with the local-community orientation of the Founding Era) and all the pitfalls that that represented. Next, in the views of both the issues-oriented voluntary associations and the Whig party—with their absolutist positions on such questions as temperance and unwillingness to accommodate or forge common ground with those who disagreed with them—one sees a lack of the realism, moderation, civility, and spirit of cooperativeness identified with the Founding Era. These absolutist positions were on issues that certainly had a moral dimension, but did not involve uncompromisable moral truth. As such, their stance arguably hurt the common good, a large part of which in any political order involves compromise among different groups and different positions. Further, their taking such absolutist moral positions without a solid ethical analysis to back them up and their spirit of crusading zeal bespoke a kind of moralistic sentimentality. When it came to alcohol consumption, their position was also anti-traditional—which made it seem even more intolerant. Moralistic sentimentality and an anti-traditional attitude are, of course, elements that the thinkers in Chapter 1 identified with societal decline. Most central for our analysis, however, is the fact that moralism represented a twisting of natural law and virtue that put it at odds with the Founding. The readiness to coerce people to get them to achieve what others thought was improvement for them— even more, when a questionable moralism was behind it—seemed to violate liberty, irrespective of whether it occurred to some degree in the colonial and Founding periods. In addition, the political calculating of some voluntary associations to forge absolutist positions because they made for more effective mass appeals demonstrated the kind of opportunism and cynicism that we saw during the Federalist Period. It was a further undercutting of civility and civic friendship. The same kind of practice and, again, moral sentimentality were seen in the victimization politics that both political parties took part in, with more negative implications for the common good. Next, if the Jacksonians began the public marginalization of religion for the reasons mentioned, the Whigs contributed with their "big tent" framework above for fashioning public ethical norms. Finally, while on the one hand the Whigs' greater reluctance to accept government economic regulation was contrary to the Founding Era's use of law for this purpose, it also suggested an unease—in the manner of that era—with simply turning over sweepingly to government the role of restraining economic waywardness. The latter was more likely to be the Jacksonian position, even though they were essentially laissez faire and the grounds they thought justified governmental action were in no way as expansive as those of the Democratic party a hundred years' later. Still, the Whigs' reluctance did not mean that they instead sought to place a greater emphasis on ethics, culture, attitudes, or the community acting in other ways to restrain economic life. Rather, they too embraced laissez faire. What this meant, on a more fundamental philosophical level, is that both the Jacksonians and the Whigs embraced individualism.

To summarize, we can say the following about how the period 1817-1840 upheld or deviated from the principles and conditions the Founders thought necessary for republican government and the culture of the Founding Era. Regarding the former, the conception—and certainly the arrangements—of federalism were upheld, but there were developments (intensifying sectionalism on the one hand, and a greater expectation that the federal government address problems on the other) that were moving in both centrifugal and centripetal directions that in time would upset the delicate tension between the national and state levels. The power and reach of government in general expanded. The spreading of democracy and embracing of majoritarianism—especially by the Jacksonian movement—were certainly against Founding principles. Along with this were the disappearance of the notion of a natural aristocracy and an advancing egalitarianism. Expressions of ochlocracy—the mob—were increasingly frequent. Separation of powers, checks and balances, and mixed government were not outright weakened by Jackson's actions, but the theoretical thrust of Jacksonian principles went in that direction by overembellishing executive power. The view of political parties, contrary to the Founders' thinking about faction, as at best a necessary evil continued—even while parties became highly developed and the central force in American politics. The advocacy group-type of faction also emerged, which was something unknown to the Founding Era. The Jacksonian dislike of the common law and compromising of the rule of law certainly went against Founding beliefs. The culture was certainly still strongly religious, and specifically Christian, but the long-term weakening of religion—especially in the public arena—began. The Jacksonians' openness to Benthamite thought signaled a challenge not only to America's common law heritage, but also to the Founders' stress on the need for natural law and virtue. During this time, we saw the first significant departures from a traditional natural law-based moral framework in the economic realm and with the moralistic positions taken on such public questions as alcohol consumption. The commitment to the common good appeared weakened on several fronts. The value placed on property rights diminished somewhat, both in the views of the Jacksonians and in the new exercise of state police power to advance economic development and market imperatives. Other rights stressed by the Founders, while largely intact, were sometimes selectively upheld. As far as the changes from the cultural outlook and practices of the Founding Era were concerned, we can observe the following. In addition to a compromising of the common good or the good of the community, there was a weakening of community in general and the acceleration of mass culture. Civility, civic friendship, cooperation, and a willingness to accommodate ebbed on many fronts. The norms of promise-keeping and truth-telling were compromised, especially in politics and in dealing with the Indians. Basic justice was grossly affronted with the Indian removal. Many of these developments show that the realism of the Founding Era was diminished. The Jacksonians believed in restraining economic freedom in the name of the public good and promoting a regimen of widespread property-holding and a spreading out of wealth, as did the Founding Era. However, their acceptance of a *fundamentally* laissez faire perspective, an essentially instrumental and ethically-neutral view of the market, and—in seeming contrast to these—the beliefs in government-stimulated economic development and complete substitution of government regulation for ethical-cultural restraints on the economy (even though the latter was done to only a modest degree in practice) were in contrast to the Founding Era. Socio-economic mobility became somewhat more difficult with the rise of an industrial working class and more immigration, and the universally middle class character of earlier American political society seemed less evident (even if, in the long-run over the course of American history, such mobility and the middle-class character prevailed as the normal condition). Still, as with certain periods in the decades ahead, as the industrial era unfolded—and in an extended way for some groups through American history—these problems manifested themselves. The culture of luxury that the Founding Era was so fearful of advanced. There were signs of a weakening of a spirit of self-sacrifice and of public-spiritedness due no doubt to democratization and the growth of individualism.

During the 1817-1840 period, we witness some of the factors (at least in a developing stage) that the thinkers in Chapter 1 said caused the decline of political orders: moralistic sentimentality (approximated by the moralism of the time), politics descending into essentially a power struggle, the stirrings of social conflict (with sectionalism), the declining of community, the growth of purposelessness (seen in the weakening of the willingness to sacrifice), the neglect of the common good in different ways, the slow growth of mass culture, the increasing desire for luxury, the ignoring in certain ways—some significant, as with the Indian treaties—of the rule of law, and the changes in traditional religious belief and the beginnings of a turning from religion in some quarters.

Of the aforementioned possible weaknesses in the American Founding itself, the ones that perhaps manifest themselves in light of the developments of the period we have studied in this chapter are these: an incomplete public philosophy, a sense of public purposelessness, and a lack of a sound understanding of the common good (all due to an insufficient philosophical reflection in the Founding Era and its background); the beginning of the difficulty of discerning the natural law because of the lack of an authoritative moral interpreter, which planted the seeds of positivism; the corresponding heavy stress on popular sovereignty perhaps at the expense of natural law; the groundwork for an expanded individualism, and the corresponding insufficient emphasis on community; the lack of a formal way to bring forth the natural aristocracy that the Founders said was needed; (in a limited way) the failure to see the family as central for the political order; and—this period particularly causes one to think this one is pertinent—the emphasis on a commercial republic led to more individualism and laissez faire.

Notes

1. See, e.g., Charles Sellers, *The Market Revolution: Jacksonian America, 1815-1846* (N.Y.: Oxford University Press, 1991).
2. Howe, 92.
3. Sellers, 150.
4. Ibid., 93-94.
5. Sean Wilentz, *The Rise of American Democracy: Jefferson to Lincoln* (N.Y.: W.W. Norton, 2005), 516.
6. Howe, 94.
7. Wilentz, 425.
8. Beitzinger, 323.
9. Arthur M. Schlesinger, Jr., *The Age of Jackson* (Boston: Little, Brown, 1945), 312.
10. Ibid., 517.
11. Ibid., 319.
12. Beitzinger, 323.
13. Wilentz, 512-513.
14. Ibid., 512.

15. Beitzinger, 323.

16. Sellers, 149. In contrast to reinstituting taxes they opposed, Jacksonians in Congress even cut back the military. Even while they figured that public land sales would be a source of revenue, they cut the price of them as much as possible.

17. See: http://en.wikipedia.org/wiki/Specie_Circular; Internet; accessed Sept. 23, 2008.

18. Charles M. Wiltse, *The New Nation: 1800-1845* (N.Y.: Hill and Wang, 1961), 143.

19. Schlesinger, *The Age of Jackson*, 316. He points out that Van Buren stated this quite directly.

20. Ibid., 330.

21. Kirk, *The Roots of American Order*, 372.

22. See Daniel J. Sullivan, *An Introduction to Philosophy* (rev. edn.; Milwaukee: Bruce, 1964), 167-168.

23. Schlesinger, *The Age of Jackson*, 336-337.

24. Beitzinger, 323.

25. See Kirk, *The Roots of American Order*, 191, 372-373.

26. See Edward S. Corwin, *The President: Office and Powers* (N.Y.: New York University Press, 1957), 14-15, 147-148, 153, 168; Russell Kirk, *America's British Culture* (New Brunswick, N.J.: Transaction Publishers, 1993), 64-65; Sir Henry Maine, *Popular Government* (Indianapolis: Liberty Classics, 1970; originally published in 1885), 212-213.

27. Hamilton or Madison, Federalist 51, 338.

28. 17 U.S. 316 (1819).

29. Fehrenbacher, 95.

30. George Dangerfield, *The Awakening of American Nationalism: 1812-1828* (N.Y.: Harper and Row, 1965), 200.

31. Wiltse, 113.

32. Ibid., 75, 123.

33. See Hamilton, Federalist 32, (mentions division of sovereignty between states and the federal government), 197; Madison, Federalist 44 (argues that for the Constitution, federal laws, and treaties not to be the supreme law of the land would have been "an inversion of the fundamental principles of all government...a monster, in which the head was under the direction of the members," 295, 296 (the quotation is from 296).

34. Wilentz, 382.

35. Howe, 397-398.

36. Sellers, 150.

37. Dangerfield, 201-202.

38. Howe, 430.

39. Wilentz, 227. See also Orestes A. Brownson, *The American Republic: Its Constitution, Tendencies and Destiny* (ed. Americo D. Lapati; New Haven, Conn.: College & University Press), 156-157.

40. Wiltse, 72.

41. Sellers, 148.

42. Fehrenbacher, 95.

43. Howe, 432.

44. Ibid., 457.

45. Willentz, 451-452.

46. See Herbert J. Storing, "Slavery and the Moral Foundations of the American Republic," in Horwitz, 224-225.

47. Tindall and Shi, 664. About these likely consequences of the uncompromising push of the abolitionists, see Orestes A. Brownson, "Abolition Proceedings" and "The Fugitive-Slave Law," in Henry Brownson, ed., *The Works of Orestes A. Brownson*, vol. 15, 81-82

48. Sellers, 150.

49. Howe, 283.

50. Ibid., 483.

51. Ibid., 390.

52. Ibid., 359.

53. Ibid., 355.

54. Concerning Federalist 78 on this point, see Krason, *The Public Order and the Sacred Order*, 568-569.

55. See Howe, 416.

56. See James Madison, "Speech in Congress on the Removal Power, June 8, 1789, in Jon Roland, ed., *Selected Works of James Madison*, http://www.constitution.org/jm/jm.htm; Internet; accessed Oct. 16, 2008. Contrary to Jackson's critics, this had been the prevailing view up until the Reconstruction controversies after the Civil War when President Andrew Johnson was impeached for violating the Radical Republican-crafted Tenure of Office Act by dismissing his Secretary of War Edwin M. Stanton. The Senate's refusal to remove him vindicated the historical understanding, which was given constitutional force in the Supreme Court decision of *Myers v. U.S.*, 272 U.S. 52 (1926).

57. "United States House of Representatives Elections, 1834," http://en.wikipedia.org/wiki/United_States_House_of_Representatives_elections_1834; http://www.senate.gov/artandhistory/history/minute/Senate_Censures_President.htm; Internet; both accessed Sept. 30, 2008.

58. Schlesinger, *The Age of Jackson*, 100.

59. Howe, 390.

60. See, e.g., Arthur M. Schlesinger, Jr., *The Imperial Presidency* (N.Y.: Popular Library, 1973).

61. See John Locke, *Second Treatise*, in John Locke, *Two Treatises of Government* (rev. edn.; ed. Peter Laslett; N.Y.: Cambridge University Press, 1963), para. 160, p. 422.

62. See Edward S. Corwin, *The President: Office and Powers* (N.Y.: New York University Press, 148.

63. See, e.g., the points made in Wiltse, 143-144.

64. See, e.g., Jean M. Yarbrough, "Progressive Conservative?' in *Claremont Review of Books* (Fall 2008), 27, discussing the progressivism of Theodore Roosevelt; Charles R. Kesler, "The Audacity of Barack Obama," in ibid., 14, discussing how Franklin D. Roosevelt sought to expand the range of rights in the Bill of Rights and changed the Supreme Court's personnel so that statutory law effectively doing this was upheld. The Court did this partly by stretching the meaning of the interstate commerce clause, as it also did to accommodate the objectives—even if meritorious—of the civil rights legislation of the 1960s spearheaded by Lyndon B. Johnson.

65. Wiltse, 118.

66. Howe, 489, 491. Howe says that these changes were not entirely because of the embracing of more democratic principles; the newer states were eager to attract settlers and saw the absence of suffrage limitations as an incentive (490).

67. Sellers, 107.

68. Wilentz, 516.

69. Howe, 395.

70. Sellers, 166-167.

71. Fehrenbacher, 78-79.
72. Howe, 276.
73. Ibid., 94.
74. Wilentz, 189.
75. Fehrenbacher, 82.
76. Wilentz, 186, 194-195, 431, 468.
77. Ibid., 347, 431.
78. Ibid., 226-228.
79. Ibid., 461.
80. Howe, 431-435. The quotation is from 431.
81. Wilentz, 422.
82. Howe, 435.
83. Ibid., 438.
84. Wilentz, 455.
85. Howe, 166.
86. Ibid., 245.
87. Ibid., 231.
88. Jack Larkin, *The Reshaping of Everyday Life, 1790-1840* (N.Y.: Harper Perennial, 1988), 35. See also Sellers, 365-366.
89. Ibid., 53-54. See also Sellers, 366.
90. Schlesinger, *The Age of Jackson*, 332.
91. Sellers, 51-52.
92. Ibid., 53-54.
93. Ibid., 54.
94. Wilentz, 358, 423.
95. Howe, 549.
96. Schlesinger, *The Age of Jackson*, 354-356. The quotation is from 356.
97. See, e.g., Gerard V. Bradley, *Church-State Relationships in America* (N.Y.: Greenwood Press, 1987).
98. Howe, 511.
99. See, e.g., Nat Hentoff, "Life of the Party," in *The New Republic*, June 19, 2000, http://groups.csail.mit.edu/mac/users/rauch/nvp/civil/hentoff_casey.html; Internet; accessed Oct. 14, 2008; Mark Shields, "Intolerant Democrats Finally Waking Up," CNN.com, Jan. 31, 2005, http://www.cnn.com/2005/ALLPOLITICS/01/31/intolerant.democrats/index.html; Internet; accessed Oct. 14, 2008.
100. Howe, 493.
101. Wilentz, 732-734.
102. Ibid., 466-467.
103. Howe., 495.
104. Ibid., 494.
105. Wilentz. 316.
106. Wiltse, 148.
107. Wilentz, 516.
108. "Tammany Hall," http://en.wikipedia.org/wiki/Tammany_Hall; Internet; accessed October 2, 2008.
109. Paul Johnson, *A History of the American People*, 341.
110. Fehrenbacher, 83-84.
111. Howe, 276.
112. Wilentz, 511; Fehrenbacher, 102.
113. Howe, 276.

114. Paul Johnson, *A History of the American People*, 358.
115. Wilentz, 487.
116. Ibid., 504.
117. Wiltse, 147.
118. Howe, 542.
119. Fehrenbacher, 67.
120. Ibid.
121. Howe, 558.
122. Sellers, 152-153.
123. Larkin, 61.
124. Sellers, 153.
125. Fehrenbacher, 105.
126. Ibid., 106.
127. Howe, 556-557. As Fehrenbacher says, "Many a wife, far from being an abjectly subservient creature, was the real ruler of her household" (105). Tocqueville put it similarly: "although the American woman never leaves her domestic sphere and is in some respects very dependent within it, nowhere does she enjoy a higher station" (Tocqueville, II, iii, 603).
128. Fehrenbacher, 105.
129. Larkin, 61.
130. Wilentz, 210.
131. Schlesinger, *The Age of Jackson*, 339; Howe, 539.
132. Wilentz, 458.
133. Howe, 542.
134. Ibid., 538-539; Larkin, 61.
135. See: "Panic of 1819," http://en.wikipedia.org/wiki/Panic_of_1819; Internet; accessed Oct. 4, 2008.
136. Howe, 505.
137. Howe, 144; "Panic of 1819."
138. Howe, 502-503; Wiltse, 149-150
139. Howe, 118.
140. Fehrenbacher, 62.
141. Sellers, 151.
142. Fehrenbacher, 61.
143. Ibid., 60, 62.
144. Ibid., 61-62, 65.
145. See ibid., 65-67.
146. Ibid., 66.
147. Dangerfield, 268-269.
148. Fehrenbacher, 75.
149. Sellers, 150-152.
150. Ibid., 171.
151. Howe, 274.
152. Ibid., 252.
153. Ibid., 252-255.
154. Ibid., 252.
155. Ibid., 501.
156. Wilentz, 440.
157. See ibid., 358-360.
158. Wiltse, 108-109.

159. Http://www.britannica.com/EBchecked/topic/558645/Specie-Circular; Internet; accessed Oct. 5, 2008.

160. Schlesinger, *The Age of Jackson*, 346-347.

161. Wilentz, 459.

162. Ibid.; Howe, 503.

163. Schlesinger, *The Age of Jackson*, 347.

164. Howe, 507.

165. Wilentz, 459.

166. Faulkner, 213.

167. Howe, 505.

168. Ibid.; Wilentz, 459.

169. Wilentz, 492.

170. Calvin Coolidge made this statement in the 1920s.

171. Wilentz, 492-493.

172. Wiltse, 55.

173. Ibid., 89-90.

174. Howe, 116.

175. Ibid., 124.

176. Ibid.

177. Ibid., 412-423.

178. "Militia (United States)," http://en.wikipedia.org/wiki/Militia_(United_States); Internet; accessed Oct. 6, 2008.

179. Howe, 491.

180. Wiltse, 129-132.

181. Howe, 453-455.

182. Wiltse, 133.

183. Fehrenbacher, 107.

184. Sellers, 235.

185. Wiltse, 135.

186. Fehrenbacher, 107.

187. Ibid., 136.

188. Ibid., 110.m,

189. Wiltse, 185.

190. Howe, 285-286.

191. Ibid., 304.

192. Wiltse, 184-185.

193. Howe, 265.

194. Fehrenbacher, 102-103. For his discussion on this point about equality, see Tocqueville, II, ii, 514-515, 537.

195. Howe, 528-529.

196. Larkin, 199-200.

197. Ibid., 52-53.

198. Beitzinger, 334-335.

199. Ibid., 335.

200. See Sampo, 106.

201. Still, one must be cautious about being too ready to dismiss the Liberian colonization and resettlement as impractical social engineering, since even the "realist" Lincoln supported it (see: Alexander M. Bickel, *The Least Dangerous Branch: The Supreme Court at the Bar of Politics* [Indianapolis" Bobbs-Merrill, 1962], 66).

202. Howe, 168.

203. Ibid., 191.

204. See Tocqueville, II, ii, 513-514.

205. Howe, 166-167. The quotation is from 167.

206. Wilentz, 489.

207. Ibid.

208. See, e.g., Allan C. Carlson, *Family Questions: Reflections on the American Social Crisis* (New Brunswick, N.J.: Transaction Books, 1988), 242; Thomas Jefferson Wertenbaker, *The Puritan Oligarchy: The Founding of American Civilization* (N.Y.: Grosset & Dunlap, 1947), 159-182, passim.

209. Wilentz, 488.

210. Ibid., 488, 490. The quotation is from 488.

211. Ibid., 489.

212. See ibid., 491-492.

CHAPTER 4

1840-1877: EXPANSION, SECTIONALISM, THE CIVIL WAR, AND RECONSTRUCTION

The period from 1840 to 1877 was, of course, momentous and tumultuous. It featured the intensifying sectional conflict over slavery through the 1840s and 1850s, the fractionalizing and collapse of political parties and the fashioning of new ones in the same decades, the complete breakdown of national unity in 1860 and the bloodiest war in American history, the tragic assassination of the president who had led the country through the war shortly after its conclusion. Then came the great political conflict both on the national political stage and between sections occasioned by Reconstruction, the political scandals that rocked the country during the 1870s, and the political turmoil caused by the impeachment and near removal of one president and the division brought about by an inconclusive presidential election at the end of the period and the political wheeling and dealing that finally resolved it. The realities of the pageant of American history during this period could have provided the plots for several melodramatic political novels. It also gives us much historical material to measure against the thinking and culture of the Founding Era. Before beginning our analysis, we should recount the main events and developments of this period, many of which will be referred to in that analysis.

1840 represented the year that the first political party other than the Democratic or Democratic-Republican party won a presidential election since the Federalist Era. It was a short-lived success for the Whig party, however, as its newly elected president, William Henry Harrison, lived only a month after his inauguration and was succeeded by a vice president, John Tyler, who was at best a nominal Whig and repeatedly battled with the Whig party in Congress. During his administration, the U.S. annexed Texas, which of course set the stage for the Mexican War during the presidency of his successor James Knox Polk. It also saw the beginning of organized anti-immigrant efforts with the rise of the nativist American Republican party and the destructive anti-Catholic Kensington riots in Philadelphia in 1844. The Dorr Rebellion broke out in Rhode Island against the limited suffrage permitted by the state's still-intact colonial charter, but changes were made before serious violence erupted. The "gag rule," which had forbidden anti-slavery petitions in the House of Representatives was finally repealed. The Polk presidency that followed was a period of unabashed American expansionism. The major expression of this was the Mexican War, which culminated with the invasion of Mexico by American forces and Mexico's cession to the U.S. of about half of its territory. Polk also concluded a treaty with Britain, sidestepping armed conflict, which secured for the U.S. the territory of present-day Oregon, Washington, and Idaho—even though it was less territory than some expansionists wanted.[1] The proposed Wilmot Proviso, which would have banned slavery from any territory acquired from Mexico, helped intensify the simmering sectional tensions in Congress. Polk also sought, unsuccessfully, to purchase Cuba from Spain. Congress also approved the Walker Tariff, which substantially reduced tariff rates, and enacted a law restoring the Independent Treasury System, under which government funds were held in the Treasury rather than in banks or other financial institutions. This continued until the establishment of the Federal Reserve in 1913. The Compromise of 1850, the last major effort by the "Great Compromiser" Henry Clay, sought to diffuse the heightening slavery tensions by, *inter alia*, permitting California to enter the Union as a free state, terminating the slave trade in the District of Columbia, and tightening enforcement of the Fugitive Slave Law. In spite of the Compromise, the slavery issue reached a fever pitch in the 1850s, as many northern states resisted the mandate to enforce the Fugitive Slave Law and the Kansas-Nebraska Act of 1854 (which had created the territories of Kansas and Nebraska, repealed the Missouri Compromise of 1820,[2] and allowed settlers in those territories to decide if they wanted slavery or not) caused a miniature civil war among pro- and anti-slavery elements in Kansas. After the "Bleeding Kansas" turmoil died down, the *Dred Scott v. Sandford* decision of 1857,[3] which held that Negroes could never be citizens, reignited Northern anti-slavery sentiment, and John Brown's attempt to seize a federal arsenal in Virginia and set off a slave revolt left the South feeling that it was on a precipice.[4] The 1860 election divided the vote among four major candidates as the Union stood on the verge of splitting apart, and resulted in the first Republican president. The election of Abraham Lincoln—who opposed the extension of slavery, but did not seek to abolish it where it existed—was followed quickly by secession and the formation of the Confederacy. The ensuing standoff at Fort Sumter led within weeks after Lincoln's inauguration to the outbreak of war. What followed were four years of bloody battles—largely inconclusive until the last year and a half[5]--and the near devastation of much of the South. The triumph of the North, however, was followed by the tragedy of Lincoln's assassination on April 14, 1865; it happened only five days after General Robert E. Lee's surrender to General Ulysses S. Grant, which was the effective end of the war. The Thirteenth Amendment, ending the "peculiar institution" of slavery that was at the core of the sectional controversy that led to the Civil War, was ratified late that year. The accession to the presidency of Vice President Andrew Johnson, a Democrat who had run on a national unity ticket with Lincoln in 1864, quickly resulted in deep conflict over Reconstruction policy between him and the

Republican Congress. Many of the particulars of Reconstruction are discussed below. The conflict finally led to steps by Congress to limit presidential power, including the Tenure of Office Act that forbade the president from dismissing any of his appointees whose positions had required senatorial confirmation unless the Senate agreed. The Act was specifically aimed at protecting Secretary of War Edwin M. Stanton, who had sided with Congress on Reconstruction policy against the President. After Johnson suspended Stanton at the end of a Congressional session, the president was impeached in 1868 but spared from removal by a single vote. About a month after Johnson's acquittal, one of the key elements of the Congressional Reconstruction effort, the Fourteenth Amendment, was ratified. Later that year, Grant was elected as the second Republican president. The Fifteenth Amendment, which gave Negroes the right to vote and was the final of the "Civil War Amendments," was ratified in 1870. With it, all of the former Confederate states were readmitted to the Union—the final four only after meeting the condition of ratifying the Fourteenth and Fifteenth Amendments.[6] Reconstruction continued throughout Grant's presidency and he worked to protect the freed Negroes in the South, although he loosened military rule there.[7] His administration was rocked by scandals—involving fraudulent gold speculation, the stealing of tax monies from the federal Treasury, and the Crédit Mobilier of America scandal in which members of Congress who supported railroad construction funding for the company were permitted to purchase shares of its stock below-market cost.[8] While Grant was not involved in the financial and political corruption, he refused to act decisively against the people in his administration who were, even after the scandals came to light.[9] Grant's administration and Reconstruction ended with the disputed presidential election of 1876. The election, between the Republican Rutherford B. Hayes and the Democrat Samuel Tilden, was unresolved due to conflicting election returns from three Southern states and a disqualified elector from Oregon. Congress ultimately established an electoral commission (made up of five senators, five House members, and five Supreme Court justices) to sort this out, which decided that the disputed electoral votes should go to Hayes—with the result that he won the election by one electoral vote. There apparently was an understanding worked out between Hayes and the Southern Democrats to the effect that they would acquiesce in his election and accept the resolution with no attempt to oppose it in Congress if he ended the remaining military occupation of the South. He did this upon taking office, amidst criticism from within Republican circles that it would result in the weakening of the new rights of the Southern Negroes.[10]

The above, then, is a brief sketch of the period from 1840 to 1877. Several subject areas emerge from the history of this period for the purpose of making our comparisons with the points in Chapter 1: political developments, expressions of democratization, and conflict; the distribution of powers between the federal government and the states, and the growth of overall governmental power; the powers of the branches of the federal government; military power and foreign affairs; Manifest Destiny, westward movement, and expansion; social, cultural, and demographic developments and reform movements;

intellectual currents; legal developments, the maintenance of the rule of law and the politicization of law, and citizen rights (including the position of the Negro); and economics, government economic policy, labor and class questions, and technological developments. We fill in more details about the history as needed to enable us to carry out our analysis of these subject areas. Since this period clearly breaks down into three distinct sub-periods—the antebellum period of rising sectionalism (1840-1860), the Civil War (1861-65), and Reconstruction (1865-1877)—for each of the subject areas we shall look at how developments progressed in each of the sub-periods and make our comparisons with reference to the situations of the sub-periods where pertinent.

   Political Developments, Expressions of Democratization, and Conflict. As Howe states, after the events of the 1840s (especially the Texas annexation, the Mexican War, and the most intense abolitionist efforts seen up to then)—as the country stood on the threshold of the much more divisive 1850s—"North and South found themselves more divided than ever by the institution of chattel slavery" which was also "defended more stridently" than it probably had ever been.[11] These two opposing positions—the immediate abolition of slavery (no longer was gradualism acceptable) versus a new defense of it as a positive good (no longer was it seen as a necessary evil)—hardened in the 1830s (as indicated in Chapter 3).[12] (Besides such absolutism becoming, as previously noted, the standard of American social movements, it had become the standard of the two sections about slavery.) The moderation that the great thinkers said was necessary for a good political order—and whose absence Chapter 1 noted is a typical cause of political decline—was dissipating. Obviously, this intensified the perpetual tensions that exist between states and the national government in the federal system, and between the individual states. The challenge to the federal structure of the Constitution, as noted in the next section, was becoming increasingly apparent in the 1840s. The conflict between two distinct regions, with a heightening sense of unity within each and each seeing a greater differentiation between itself and the other, was put into sharper focus. The spirit of cooperation, civic friendship, and a concern for the general instead of just particularistic welfare that characterized the culture of the Founding were diminishing.

   There were many other political developments during the 1840s and 1850s, which were not as momentous as this basic division although some were related to it and an expression of it. Chapters 2 and 3 discussed many facets of the changes in how politics was being "carried out" (especially in light of democratization). Further examples were observed during this period. The 1840 campaign was distinguished by its populist appeals—coming now from the party that previously had been associated more with privileged elements than the "have-nots." The Whig campaign of retired General William Henry Harrison ("Tippecanoe") evoked images of the log cabin and hard cider to connect with the voters. They even included these visual symbols in their campaign paraphernalia. This was in spite of the fact that they still favored a soft money policy and government economic intervention, positions not then seen as "democratic" in their character.[13] Politics was already coming to be seen, in

Howe's words, as a version of "mass entertainment"—a condition associated with democracy.[14] In line with the democratization of elections was the need for highly developed campaign organizations, careful strategies for party speakers, the publication of a substantial number of tracts directed to voters, and a careful targeting of campaign appeals to different local situations and battleground states.[15] Besides tracts, there were also campaign periodicals.[16] Candidates started to appeal to particular groups of voters, such as evangelical Protestants.[17] Campaigns featured exaggeration, truth-stretching or outright false claims about the opposition, and personal attacks on opponents; in the 1840s the Democratic party was especially deft at this.[18] How ugly the 1844 race became was seen by the Democratic attacks on Clay, the Whig nominee, as debauched, womanizing, irreligious, and an abolitionist (which he never was).[19] Howe writes that in New York, voter fraud—the Democrats "voted large numbers of ineligible (noncitizen) immigrants"—helped tip the close election to Polk.[20] Even though sectionalism was to characterize the decade, it did not really manifest itself in the election of 1840 as the winning Harrison did well in both North and South.[21] Sharp sectional division, both between and within parties, began later in the decade in the 1848 election.[22] Democratization seemed to vulgarize politics in the way campaigns now seemed to have to be carried out. The populist appeals, even by the Whigs, underscored how unpopular a notion such as a natural aristocracy would have been by this time. The ugly political attacks showed that politics had deviated sharply from the principles characterizing the Founding Era's culture. Recalling Chapters 2 and 3, this kind of politics was not new, but further democratization and perhaps the existence of the earlier precedents caused it to expand well beyond what was seen before. Respect, civility, honesty, justice (i.e., in terms of respecting men's reputations, one of their immaterial assets), and the need for civic friendship were ignored. The rule of law was outright flouted by the Democrats' allowing non-citizens to vote. The blatant appeals to different social groups were a subtle downplaying of community. The sectional division that started to overlay partisan politics was another expression of the gradual decline of civic friendship and orientation to the general good of the nation.

There were other indications, positive and negative, of the new democratic way of life and politics. The face of ochlocracy, which was first seen way back in the Federalist Era and intensified in the Jacksonian Era with mob action and rioting, manifested itself in the following ways in the 1840s. The aforementioned Dorr Rebellion took place in Rhode Island in 1841-42, agitated by the Democratic party. In an attempt to overturn the colonial charter still in effect, which limited the right to vote and other citizen liberties primarily to property-holding adult males, the Dorrites circumvented the state legislature and staged a rump convention and referendum. They then elected their leader Thomas Dorr "governor" in an illegal election, set up a "shadow government," and threatened violence if anyone tried to stop them. When Dorr tried to seize a state arsenal, his support dissipated and the legitimate authorities suppressed the rebellion. After that, a referendum adopted most of the changes the Dorrites sought.[23] Second, in its 1848 platform the Democratic party officially

commended the various revolutions in Europe of that year. In 1851, when exiled
Hungarian revolutionary Lajos Kossuth—who "embodied the spirit of European
popular radicalism"—toured the U.S., he was greeted by "a tumultuous public
response."[24] Third, during the California Gold Rush that started in 1848, in spite
of the fact that a functioning state government existed, "mining camps governed
themselves as informal democracies" with "kangaroo courts," "notorious
lynchings," and a violent environment.[25] Fourth, the Philadelphia anti-Catholic
riots were the most violent outburst of nativism, and as the nineteenth century
went on "Protestant mobs sporadically indulged in open conflict." In the 1850s
"Protestants burned a dozen churches in different towns," and there were many
riots that grew out of clashes between nativists and Catholic immigrants.[26]
Catholic mobs also violently disrupted nativist meetings.[27] Fifth, American
violence and the ochlocratic spirit extended beyond the nation's borders during
the time of the Mexican War. As Howe puts it, "The young men [new volunteers
who joined regular U.S. Army troops] who responded to the call to fight for
America's manifest destiny brought with them the fierce individualism,
propensity to violence, and racial antagonism so widespread in civilian society."
Besides having fights within their ranks, Howe says they "pillaged" the Mexican
civilian population, committed murders (sometimes senseless ones), and even
massacred a group of Mexican civilians in retaliation for the killing of one of
their number. With the exception of the eminent General Winfield Scott, neither
top Army commanders nor American politicians tried to rein them in. The Polk
administration even "encouraged harsh treatment of occupied areas in an effort
to press the Mexicans to sign a peace treaty ceding land."[28] Howe argues, "the
ideology of American expansion seemed to legitimate the assertion of force by
the strong and the destruction or expropriation of those who resisted." Episodes
such as these highlighted what the Founding Fathers saw as the consequences of
democracy, how they "have ever been spectacles of turbulence and
contention."[29] That only begins to state the problem with the above. The Dorr
Rebellion—however valid the Dorrites' criticisms of Rhode Island's colonial
charter might have been—implicitly repudiated such Founding ideas as
limitations on the franchise and equality. Dorr's actions, the practices in
California, the nativist riots, and certainly the outrages of the Mexican War
volunteers and the political officials who excused them made respect for law and
the rule of law a farce. By the same token, the Rhode Island authorities'
willingness to allow a political marginalization of a substantial part of the
population showed an imperviousness to the common good—after all, the
political order that the Founders established was a *democratic* republic. Most of
these episodes also demonstrate a breakdown of civic friendship and a spirit of
community. The Mexican War volunteers' behavior would have been
considered utterly criminal and loathsome by the standards of the Founding
culture, even if the latter were not always realized in its practice; it violated the
most basic standards of morality, self-restraint, justice, and fair-dealing. They
made a mockery of the principle of protecting life, liberty, and property that was
central to the Founders. Even though the Founders saw these as natural rights of
men, the Mexican War volunteers seemed to think that they did not extend to

those who were not Americans. The democratic impulse, once unleashed, proceeded into destructiveness and readily subverted principles of the Founding that involved self-control and virtue.

More peacefully, the mid-1840s continued the wave of democratic constitutional reform at the state and local levels that had reached a fever pitch during the Jacksonian Era.[30] Even while the country was reaching universal adult male Caucasian suffrage, in fact in much of the South the politics was dominated by the large landholding and slaveholding elements.[31] In fact, Wilentz states that by the second half of the 1850s the Democratic party nationally came to be dominated by slaveholding interests.[32] They paid enough attention to the aspirations of the Caucasian population down the socioeconomic scale to garner most of their support, which included agreement—in an ever more ardent and uncompromising way—of the regime of slavery. In the North, on the other hand, a norm of *greater* popular participation—but clearly having its limits—was taking hold. Also, the 1850s featured the democratization of matters that by their very nature should not be reduced to popular preference with the rise of the movement for squatter sovereignty (i.e., determining whether the new territories seeking to come into the Union should have slavery—that is, the question of whether some men should be allowed to own and outright control other men—by means of popular vote). Lincoln hammered home this very point in his famous debates with Stephen Douglas in 1858.[33] This bore a similarity to referenda on abortion and homosexual "marriage" in the twentieth and twenty-first centuries. The ultimate attempt by the Supreme Court to remove slavery from the political realm and "resolve" it in *Dred Scott* also paralleled contemporary judicial actions to resolve the latter—by, essentially, favoring one side in the controversies by proclaiming or upholding ersatz rights that did violence to natural law. In all these cases, the nature of man was assaulted—something that neither votes nor courts should have sought to effect. Actually, as it was, many slaveholders still supported the arrangement of the Missouri Compromise of 1820 whereby slavery could expand into certain areas even if the populace did not want it. In other words, they were really not interested in a democratic resolution of the question at all.[34]

In any event, squatter sovereignty was not a great testimony to the democratic idea in the Kansas Territory. The struggle featured extensive voter fraud, an attempt to prosecute the members of a free-state territorial government that was elected and to suppress anti-slavery newspapers, regular armed clashes, an armed siege of the town that was the center of anti-slavery activity, the promulgation of the pro-slavery Lecompton Constitution that was produced by a constitutional convention of highly dubious legality, competing state governments at one point, and murder and pillaging. The latter included the Pottawatomie Creek massacre perpetrated by John Brown and his followers, who brought fanatical bloodlust to the national slavery struggle and were later outrageously held to be heroic by many in the North who saw themselves as holding the high moral ground.[35]

Thus, we witnessed the progression of the effects of democratization: it took hold during Jefferson's time, became entrenched in the Jacksonian Era with slippages into ochlocracy (see Chapter 3), then within less than a generation after that a range of abuses manifested themselves. There was only a small reaction in thought and reform movements against democratization late in the 1840-1877 period. Democracy and its discontents were completely in place.

Significant conflict also was engendered by the intensified enforcement of the Fugitive Slave Law after the Compromise of 1850. This was met with widespread resistance in the North, sometimes resulting in violence. Even among moderate northerners, the Fugitive Slave Law helped to harden antislavery sentiment—and thereby further aggravated the sectional conflict—because of its harshness and seeming readiness to compromise citizen liberties to uphold the putative rights and interests of slaveholders (see below).[36]

Numerous questions relating to Founding Era principles and cultural mores were presented by the above. Lincoln suggested, in effect, that squatter sovereignty infringed on the inherent rights of men. It also represented a significant early case of departing from the natural law foundation of the Constitution. In a certain way, it sought to enshrine positivism: the will of man was held to be supreme in lawmaking, irrespective even of questions involving the constitutional tradition or basic human dignity. The above suggested that the *Dred Scott* decision was also essentially an exercise in positivism. *Dred Scott* also challenged the principles of separation of powers and checks and balances. The former can be said to have occurred because the Court entered the political realm—in fact, in an overwhelming way—reserved to Congress and the presidency. The latter was affronted because of the very fact that the Court went ahead and did this, knowing the great difficulty of overturning its decisions. In almost magisterial fashion, it sought to impose an essentially final resolution of the slavery question figuring it could not be checked even if wrong. To the contrary, the principles of separation of powers and checks and balances embody the notion that power must be checked because men are wounded and thus they overreach, can be self-aggrandizing, and can also be wrong in their judgments and conclusions. This understanding was obviously grounded in the Founders' view of human nature. So in a curious way—no doubt without awareness of it—the Court, like the squatter sovereignty advocates, challenged fundamental aspects of Founding thought. One wonders if the example of the embellishing of presidential power under Jackson helped embolden the Court to overreach on its behalf in *Dred Scott.* An additional reason to wonder that is that Chief Justice Taney, who authored the opinion, played a major role in Jackson's sinking of the Second Bank of the United States.

The conflict in Kansas bore some resemblance to the outrages perpetrated by the volunteers in the Mexican War. In addition to its being an affront to basic morality and creating a condition like a Hobbesian state of nature, it contrasted with Founding Era culture by its lack of fair-dealing, a spirit of compromise and moderation, civility, and civic friendship.

The deep sectional divisions over the slavery question were mirrored in Congress. While the "gag rule" showed the extent to which the Congressional leadership and majority—mostly Democratic—would go to try to preempt debate about slavery on the national political stage, it could not hold back the heightening tensions. These culminated in two physical assaults perpetrated by slave state members of Congress on northern members. One was the famous 1856 clubbing in the Senate chamber of Senator Charles Sumner of Massachusetts by three southern House members a few days after he made intemperate speeches attacking slavery and a southern senator who was one of its leading defenders.[37] The other was an 1857 melee on the House floor involving over thirty Congressmen.[38] Wilentz says that the passing of the two prominent compromise-oriented Whig figures in 1852, Henry Clay and Daniel Webster (both of whom played a crucial role in the last great sectional compromise effort, the Compromise of 1850), helped to break down the sectional rapprochement that had previously prevailed in Congress.[39] The times and the people in American politics in the 1850s were becoming increasingly intemperate. As stated, sectional and political conflict and political nastiness were not new; however, they markedly intensified in many ways during the 1840s and 1850s.

While the episodes in Congress were "minor league" compared to Bleeding Kansas, they underscored the same absence of civility, moderation, and civic friendship. They also showed how the slavery conflict and the times corrupted the statesmanship and gentlemanliness that the Founders and their era viewed as necessary for republican government and which, in fact, characterized the Founders themselves. The lack of statesmanship was also seen in a practical way by the fact that "great compromisers" were no longer left to try to solve or diffuse the deepening conflict—if, indeed, that was still possible. On the other hand, the prominent statesmen who helped craft the renewed commitment to the Fugitive Slave Law in 1850 perhaps should have seen the challenge it would likely pose to the Founding principle of respect for law. In spite of the issue of prudential considerations, it seemed to fail also on another aspect of the rule of law—its failure to embody the natural law, a necessary component of the rule of law (although one could also say that about the fugitive slave clause in Article IV of the Constitution itself). Those northerners who treated the Fugitive Slave Law so dismissively also were undercutting the rule of law, however. As Brownson said, by making themselves the arbiter of the morality of law without reference to any more authoritative interpreter (see the brief discussion below), they laid the foundation for disorder. We further discuss the question of the Fugitive Slave Law and the rule of law later in this chapter.

There were other political developments that pertained to the parties. The Democrats, who in spite of their domination had previously viewed parties as a necessary evil, seemed now to accept the notion that they were a positive good, and essentially fell in line with the "new political science" of the Founders. The Whigs, on the other hand, seemed not to. Effectively, they embraced the former Democratic view that parties existed to defend the strata in political society that they represented from the threatening Democrats.[40] Perhaps in line with the still early stage of the party system and the fact that they were as yet a long way from achieving a kind of quasi-public status in law, it was easier to start a party in the nineteenth century. Election law generally was also in an infant stage; the parties and any group could print their own ballots to distribute them to the voters.[41] These realities, the fact that that no solid second party had yet shown its staying power, and the fluidity of the political situation—stimulated increasingly by sectionalism built around the slavery question, but secondarily by the nativist controversy[42]—led to the rise and fall of several new parties in the 1840s and 1850s. Finally, in the 1850s the strongest of these second parties, the Whigs, collapsed and the rapid accession of the modern Republican party followed. This occurred, of course, because of the heightening anti-slavery sentiment in the North. Slavery, of course, was a point of deep conflict within the "majority" party, the Democratic, even while there was no strong abolitionist movement within it. Most of the controversy within it concerned how to deal with the slavery expansion question and whether to uphold the moral righteousness of slavery in principle.[43] Finally, of course, in 1860 the Democratic party split into northern and southern wings, with each putting up its own candidate and thus insuring Lincoln's victory. Less dramatically than events like Bleeding Kansas, these party developments were nevertheless a consequence of the lack of civic friendship.

Obviously, the tensions of the 1850s were eclipsed by the struggles and devastation of the Civil War in the next decade. A chronicle of the war is not germane to our purposes in this book, except to say that it represented a complete breakdown of civil order and civic friendship within the country—at least between the two main sections of the country. Social conflict within the North, due to the tensions generated by the larger conflict and war, was also present, however. This was seen by the anti-Negro riots across the North in 1862 and by the Copperhead and other anti-war activity in the North, which even went to the point of seeking a further severing of the Union to enable the Midwest to forge a separate peace with the South.[44] Thus, the common good was much challenged even within the North. Social conflict and revolution, of course, are main reasons for the decline of political orders. Maybe in a certain sense, Lincoln understood this when he said that the war tested "whether government of the people, by the people, for the people" could survive.[45] The Union, of course, did overcome the worst of the conflict and survived.

With the conflict raging, the period of the Civil War not surprisingly did not see much in the way of changes in the basic functioning, structure, or practices of politics in the country. Obviously, the Confederacy constructed a government, but that is outside the focus of our attention. Reconstruction brought some changes. The public's demands on government, especially in the northern states, caused the Republican party—which was solidly in control—to shift from the ideological orientation that had characterized it up until that time—i.e., opposition to slavery and disunion—to an "organizational mode of politics." The organization itself, instead of issues, now commanded loyalty. A result was that patronage—the spoils system—became very important for the party. This was like the earlier Jacksonian Democrats but on a much larger scale, and would be paralleled in the developing Democratic party urban political machines. Many people were actually working full-time for political organizations. The new areas (see below) that especially state governments got involved in during Reconstruction made for cozier government-business relationships. Such coziness, it will be recalled, began in the Federalist Period with land companies; the practice deepened and expanded in this period. There was much conflict of interest, many favors doled out, and corruption.[46] So, we had the scandals of the Grant era. Government's increased social welfare functions were both the *result* of the activity of interest groups—the reform movements that we have discussed—and established the framework for an *ongoing* regime of interest group influence on government, as the new government or government-funded workers who would have to staff the programs now became an institutionalized lobby to keep them in place. The substantial growth of the spoils system, the burgeoning of the demands on government, and the corruption resulted in calls for reform (discussed below). Interest group self-interest—a form of individualism—had begun to take hold. After the sectional crisis of the Civil War was partially mended (but not entirely, as this chapter indicates), this was a new challenge to the common good from within. The corruption of this time showed how compromised the ethic of honesty, truth-telling, fair-dealing, and the need to restrain luxury (and even wealth accumulation unless all could take part) had become only a hundred years after the Founding Era. The rise of organizational politics and decline of a "principle" orientation, especially within the Republican party, makes one think of two of the indices of a political order's decline: a descent of politics into a power struggle and a sense of public purposelessness. The new demands of interest groups and staff depending on the existence of programs for their own benefit—which would expand more in the future as government would undertake more activities—was a dimension of societal-corrosive materialism. The new demands on government—slowly growing since the reform movements of the Whig period began to demand that government address various social problems—would begin, of course, to compromise the notion of limited government, at least at the state and local levels (although as we note below, there was some retraction of this after Reconstruction).

The Distribution of Powers between the Federal Government and the States, and the Growth of Overall Governmental Power. In the antebellum period, one of the main national issues, of course, was the exclusion of slavery in the new western territories. The most important pieces of federal legislation about this were the Missouri Compromise of 1820, the Compromise of 1850, and the Kansas-Nebraska Act. Although Congress's actions, especially respecting the latter two acts in the 1850s when the slavery issue was at a fever pitch, were controversial, there is not much question in light of Article IV, Section Three, Sub-Section 2 of the Constitution that it was within its authority to legislate on matters concerning the territories (nothing in that provision excluded slavery as a topic of legislation, despite the Supreme Court's holding in *Dred Scott*).[47] So, its legislation was not an expansion or an unconstitutional exercise of federal power. On the other hand, the U.S.'s Manifest Destiny expansionist policy of the 1840s probably did enhance federal government power. Howe writes, the policy "required conscious deliberation and energetic government action to bring it into being...Power politics, diplomacy, and war proved as much a part of America's 'manifest destiny' as covered wagons."

Polk and the other heirs of Jackson "demonstrated eagerness to exploit the authority of government in expanding the American empire."[48] Ironically, however, the federal government ultimately weakened itself—which perhaps emboldened secessionists in the decades ahead and made more possible the breaking away of the South in 1861—by the very fact that "[t]he North and South fell to quarreling over the spoils" of the Mexican War.[49] That weakness or at least lack of will was manifested in the initial federal tepidness in response to the South's actions, with President James Buchanan denying that states had the right to secede but insisting that he could not force a seceding state back into the Union.[50] An insurrection was brewing, however, and there was no question that he could have used strong federal power to stop it—as Lincoln proceeded to do—in light of Article I, Section Eight, Sub-Section 15 and Article I, Section Nine, Sub-Section 2 of the Constitution, which make clear federal power to suppress insurrections within the country's borders, and the very fact that a strong national government was established by the Constitution partly because of a perceived deficiency of the Articles of Confederation government to do that in light of Shays' Rebellion.[51] More fundamentally, the same observation that was made in Chapter 3 about Jackson's response to the Nullification Crisis would certainly apply to secession: Jackson had the constitutional power to stop a milder challenge to federal supremacy that could have led to a state seceding, so *a fortiori* Buchanan or Lincoln could rightfully have acted to stop outright secession by several states. There was no question at all of an overreaching of federal power.

As far as other examples of the expansion of federal power before and during the Civil War were concerned, we witness, curiously, a continuation of Jacksonian reluctance about federal funding of internal improvements in Congress's slowness to agree to provide a grant to establish telegraph infrastructure.[52] (Interestingly, if the Whigs had been able to hold onto power long enough, the federal government on this point might have become more powerful and the federal-state balance tilted toward the former since they were favorable to central economic planning—in the nineteenth century notion of the term—and government economic intervention.)[53] Otherwise, the main activities of the federal government before the Civil War were national defense, foreign affairs, Indian affairs, public land sales, the post office, and collection of import duties; Fehrenbacher says this was "about the same as 1800," and there were only about 5,000 civilian employees.[54] Moral questions aside, the unwillingness of northern state governments, often by putting legislative obstacles in place, to enforce the Fugitive Slave Law both before and after the Compromise of 1850 showed a weakness of federal power vis-à-vis the states and perhaps tilted the balance in the federal system. Prior to the U.S. Supreme Court's 1842 *Prigg v. Pennsylvania* decision,[55] some states actually tried to overturn the Fugitive Slave Law with their own enactments. While the Court declared this unconstitutional, it effectively said that states were not actually obliged to enforce the law.[56]

It is also questionable if the Civil War itself caused a permanent expansion of federal power—at least immediately. To be sure, the Thirteenth Amendment ended a prerogative of the states—whether to have slavery—and thereby nationally preempted that matter. The Fourteenth Amendment, of course, set the stage for the nationalization of most of the Bill of Rights, race relations, the protection of minority groups, and the rights of business in the decades and century ahead, but its practical applications were limited during the Reconstruction Era. Indeed, the Founders viewed some of the rights that it ultimately nationalized as necessary for a democratic republic (even though they saw them as essentially being enforced on the state level). The Fifteenth Amendment nationalized one part of the question of voting rights, but again in practical terms in an ongoing way this did not happen until the next century. Obviously, the projection of the military power of the Federal forces onto the Confederate states during the Civil War—where most of the battles occurred— and the imposing of military governments on the South during Reconstruction created a sharply unbalanced relationship of federal and state power in that part of the country. This was not ongoing, however, and could be expected since the South had engaged in a violent rebellion against the federal government. Moreover, the South invited the strictures of Reconstruction when rebellious attitudes still seemed widespread, the pre-war political elites tried to muscle themselves back into power on their own terms, and some southern state "black codes" kept the freed slaves in a position just a little above their previous condition.[57] Federal power was enhanced in the North during the war by Lincoln's suspension of habeas corpus—even in some of the states where rebellion against the Union was not likely—the general militarization of the nation to win the war, and the federal conscription law. Still, all this lasted only for the war years or part of them. Richard D. Brown tells us that, contrary to the modern war experience of European countries, it was even the case that "no great bureaucracy was permanently established, nor was national centralization achieved."[58]

In the final analysis, an argument can be made that during the period of the 1840s and 1850s the balance between state and federal power tilted toward the states. There was a centrifugal tendency. If anything, federalism was distorted by federal government power not being strong enough. The Civil War and Reconstruction years outright reversed this as respects the South, but by 1877 it can probably be said that while the federal government clearly established its supremacy—at least by decisively establishing that no state could secede— essentially what happened was that a *proper balance* was restored in the relationship. What this means was illustrated by such constitutional provisions as the Supremacy Clause (Article VI, Section Two) and the requirement that public officeholders at all levels take an oath to uphold the Constitution (Article VI, Section 3). The states, as stated previously, were meant to be semi-sovereign, not to challenge the federal government's sovereignty. However, the Civil War constitutional amendments and the later abandoned federal Reconstruction efforts to protect civil rights and improve the situation of the freed slaves—no matter how justified and commendable—may have served as a precedent for an unwarranted future expansion of federal power in many areas.

In various ways, we can say that overall governmental power increased during the period 1840-1877. First, as discussed, the very fact of American expansionism during the period of Manifest Destiny required enhanced governmental power. As Howe says, the supposedly small-government "Jacksonian Democracy... demonstrated eagerness to exploit the authority of government in expanding American empire."[59] The Civil War conscription laws—both in the Union and the Confederacy—were the country's first experience with such legislation. In sharp contrast to the efforts to resist the fugitive slave laws, a few northern state legislatures passed laws actually forbidding Negroes from settling within their territory.[60] Public pre-college education was expanding and more public institutions of higher education were also being established.[61] The first state compulsory school attendance law was enacted in 1852 and many other states followed in the 1860s and 1870s.[62] The states also "greatly expanded" their role in public health, care of the blind and deaf, and public works.[63] The states began to enter the mental health field, as public asylums were established across the country.[64] While the balance in the federal system may have tilted toward the states in these antebellum years, a harbinger of the federal government's social welfare role of the next century was seen when Congress passed a bill to set aside public lands to fund these asylums (which was vetoed by President Franklin Pierce).[65] During the Civil War, the federal government took the first step toward its heavy twentieth and twenty-first century involvement in public education by the first Morrill Land Grant College Act, which granted every state public lands to sell to get funds for the establishment of public colleges. The federal Civil Rights Act of 1875 would have been a major, unprecedented expansion of governmental power in general and federal power in particular if the U.S. Supreme Court had not struck down most of its provisions. It would have projected federal regulatory power and federal criminal law directly onto private citizens and entities in an unprecedented way. It prohibited racial discrimination in jury selection, public transportation, and public accommodations (including restaurants and theaters). An earlier version, which did not receive final Congressional passage, had even sought to forbid racial discrimination in schools. Congress's authority to pass the law was premised on Section 5 of the Fourteenth Amendment. Initially including schools in the law's reach, however, aimed—in utilitarian fashion—to achieve a desired end without regard to the intent of the Amendment, since in the same year that Congress proposed the Fourteenth Amendment it established a segregated school system for the District of Columbia.[66] This was perhaps another early example of novel constitutional interpretation to achieve an end like that concerning the slave importation clause early in the century (see Chapter 2).[67] As it turned out, such new federal prerogatives would have to wait about ninety more years to become part of American law. Finally, the Reconstruction period saw the beginning—at least in a limited way—of the economic regulatory state (what traditionally was called "social regulation"), occasioned by disenchantment with railroad rate practices. This occurred on the state level, but an unsuccessful effort was also made in Congress in 1873 to do it nationally.[68] This was another harbinger of the centralization of power—and distortion of the federal system—of the next century. The increased role of government in general had been foreshadowed since the Republic's early decades by the public's turning to it to aid in economic development. The Jacksonian Era's efforts at economic regulation and the growth of public schools, government-run asylums, and the like at that time considerably enhanced the trend. Still, the scope and degree of the expansion during the 1840-1877 period was unprecedented (again, with most of it happening in the states).

The Powers of the Branches of the Federal Government. During the period 1840-1877, there were considerable developments respecting the powers of the three branches of the U.S. Government. There was at different times a waxing and waning of the powers of the individual branches in respect to the others and sharp shifts in the locus of federal power (such waxing and waning went on to become an occasional feature of American politics). The period began with a weakening of presidential power after Tyler assumed the executive office. With the initial uncertainty of his presidential status, his ongoing battle with the Whig party in Congress (who controlled both houses during the first two years of his term), and becoming the first president to face an impeachment investigation, he was able to accomplish little beyond the annexation of Texas in the last days of his presidency.[69] Things immediately moved in the opposite direction with Polk's presidency as he took the lead on America's expansionist policy and war-making. The Mexican War was probably America's first presidential war. Howe writes that "[t]he president had essentially made the war." John Quincy Adams at the time wrote that Polk had infringed on the Congressional prerogative to declare war.[70] It set a decisive precedent for the last half of the twentieth century and beyond. After Polk, until Lincoln, there was a succession of what are generally considered to have been weak presidents—Zachary Taylor, Millard Fillmore, Franklin Pierce, and James Buchanan (who, as we have seen, would not even interpose federal power to stop southern secession)—although during that time it cannot be said that Congress waxed in power since it was crippled by the sectional conflict in the nation. If anything, the weakness of both political branches allowed the Supreme Court to flex its muscles—possibly asserting political supremacy for the first time—in the *Dred Scott* case. As stated, it sought to resolve the most crucial and divisive political question confronting the country, something the political branches—where compromise is more typically the order of the day—repeatedly had been unable to accomplish. When one considers Federalist 78—the Court is called "the least dangerous" branch—it is clear that this assertion of judicial supremacy was a deviation from the Founders' intent.[71] In any event, it also failed to solve the slavery problem, and contributed to the bringing on of the great cataclysm of 1861-1865.[72] As a result, its power and position in American political life also suffered grave damage.[73] It did not make a revival until well after the Reconstruction Era. The Court was probably weakened mostly by the loss of respect for its authority in the public's eye. This perhaps led it to be less likely to render potentially controversial decisions and emboldened the political branches to challenge it. The former was seen in the Court's reluctance to accept sensitive cases challenging the constitutionality of Reconstruction legislation;[74] the latter in Congress's withdrawing the Court's jurisdiction to hear the case of *Ex parte McCardle*, which concerned the power of federal courts to issue writs of habeas corpus in the Reconstruction South.[75]

With Lincoln's accession, of course, the presidency's fortunes were reversed, and its powers probably reached a high point up to that time. After his death, it fell fairly quickly to one of its lowest points. Lincoln's role as Commander-in-Chief during a period of domestic insurrection and war resulted in a substantial expansion of executive power.[76] Andrew Johnson's ongoing struggle with Congress, the wrestling away from him by Congress of much of Reconstruction policy,[77] and his impeachment and near removal from office, followed by Grant's scandal-ridden administration, lack of political experience, and philosophical commitment to legislative supremacy[78] weakened the presidency's place in American politics. Along with scandals, Grant's time in office brought significant patronage abuses. He tentatively sought to institute reforms, but did not have the will to follow through with them.[79] Congress's power grew so strong that by 1885 the young scholar Woodrow Wilson spoke of the existence of "Congressional government."[80] Still, as Civil War historian James M. McPherson puts it, the events of this period "temporarily altered but did not destroy the balance of powers among the three branches of the federal government."[81] That might have happened had not Edmund Ross and the handful of other Republican senators not voted against Johnson's removal even though it meant sacrificing their political careers,[82] and had the Supreme Court's justices not wisely decided to avoid a direct constitutional confrontation with Congress in *McCardle* and other Reconstruction cases.[83] Such crucial principles and practices of the Founders for sustaining republican government as separation of powers, checks and balances, judicial independence, and mixed government might have been permanently weakened had not a few key, but now obscure, political actors deeply embraced certain qualities of Founding Era culture. Those senators showed courage and concern for the common good over party interest, and the justices perhaps demonstrated shrewd practical intelligence and a sense of when to compromise.

Military and Foreign Affairs. The militias had fallen into disuse in the years before the Mexican War, and the U.S. made little use of them in the war. The professional army was small and so to supplement it volunteers were relied upon and trained and equipped at U.S. Government expense.[84] It was stated above that many of these volunteers were unruly and even bloodthirsty. Polk injected politics into the military during the war. According to Howe, Polk was aware of the fact that most regular army generals were Whigs and "once they had served his purposes he did all he could to disparage their accomplishments and derail their careers." He also established numerous new general officers to lead the volunteer units, and made sure every one of them was a Democrat—mostly former Democratic officeholders. Lesser officers for the volunteer units were chosen by state governors—mostly Democrats—or elected by the men directly. Polk even proposed to put the overall command of the army in the hands of Democratic Senator Thomas Hart Benton of Missouri.[85] After the Mexican War ended, Polk's unwarranted military court of inquiry of the heroic and principled General Scott, undertaken partly for political reasons, represented more undue political interference with the military.[86] It is reasonable to think that the principle of civilian control of the military that the Founding Fathers believed essential to sustain republican government implied a corollary: that to guard against the possibility of the principle being upset the political authorities should not inject politics into what are essentially military affairs. This was exactly what Polk was doing. While the war was not generally popular, Wilentz tells us that the country, especially the North, did become afflicted by "war fever" and a "militarist clamor."[87] It was not, however, deep-seated or enduring nor did it give the military a more prominent place in American life. In fact, by the eve of the Civil War the U.S. Army can only be said to have been in a weak state. The regular army had fewer than 16,000 men, based in small units across the country. About a third of its officers resigned upon secession to join the Confederacy. Almost all of the top officers were aged, and there was little coordination among them. It lacked sufficient resources once the war broke out. The U.S. Navy was not in much better shape. Under half of its ships were even in commission, and it lacked the background and preparation for the "coastal and inshore work" that the war would involve. The militias continued to be in disarray.[88] Within a fairly short period of time in 1861, however, 700,000 men had enlisted in the Union army. Patriotism, a sense of honor, and a belief in principles of liberty motivated many to join the Union army (interestingly, those who joined the Confederate army tended to have the same motivations, but with a very different twist on the notion of liberty).[89] This was a very different spirit than was noted in Chapter 3 with the state militias; the will and courage that had typified the Founding Era were evident. During the war, Lincoln demonstrated that he was clearly in command of the Union forces as he was not hesitant when the war was not going well to sack his generals. The army exhibited other features of a republican army: initially, as mentioned, officers were elected (they were in the Confederate army also); many generals were appointed because of political connections or sponsorship; and by far most of the soldiers were drawn from the ranks of civilians instead of being professionals.[90] When the war ended, there was a rapid demobilization. The U.S. Army reduced its size by over 65% within eighteen months after the Confederate surrender, although it was definitely larger than before the war (at 65,000). There was a considerable military presence in the South during Reconstruction, initially about 200,000 troops. During the war, there was, of course, the conscription law. After the surrender, the Union army paraded through Washington with a grand spectacle of its power and within three years the public elected the top Civil War general (Grant) as president. If these things resembled militaristic nations the similarity stopped there, however. As McPherson writes, "The army did not become a power in American life."[91] There was no question that the Founding Fathers' principle of civilian control of the military was maintained—even if the country was left with a somewhat larger military after the war—or that an enduring spirit of militarism, which Chapter 1 mentioned as one of the symptoms of a declining culture, did not set in. During the Mexican War and before the Civil War, if anything, the country witnessed the effects of a too weak military, with the state militias having fallen into disuse and the military so small that the Mexican War was prosecuted with the large number of often undisciplined volunteers who perpetrated the outrages mentioned. The excessive weakening of the military was a legacy of Jeffersonian-Jacksonian thinking, even though the development did not seem to be in line with the continuing objective of territorial expansion (discussed more below).

The leading foreign affairs questions during the period from 1840 to 1877, other than the Texas annexation and the Mexican War, were these: the Webster-Ashburton Treaty (1842) between the U.S. and Britain, which settled a long-standing dispute about the Maine-Canadian boundary; the Oregon Question, which finally resulted in an acceptable division of disputed territory in the far northwest between the U.S. and Britain in 1846 (mentioned above); the Clayton-Bulwer Treaty (1850), in which the U.S. and Britain jointly agreed not to seize control of any Central American nation and to permit international access to any isthmian canal that would be built (this did not stop the 1855 seizure of Nicaragua by American filibusterer William Walker, whose new government was diplomatically recognized by the Pierce administration); Lincoln's intimations of war against any country recognizing the legitimacy of the Confederate government during the war (none did); the attempt by the French Emperor Napoleon III to gain control of Mexico in 1864-65, which President Johnson responded to with a military build-up on the Mexican border; the Alaska purchase from Russia in 1867; the Burlingame Treaty (1868) which established friendly relations with China and encouraged (for a time) Chinese immigration; and the Grant administration's success in settling damage claims in an international tribunal against Britain for wartime destruction caused by the *Alabama* and other British-built Confederate ships.[92] When one considers this history, it is apparent that throughout this entire period the U.S. dealt roughly equally with each of the countries in question (i.e., treating them toughly or favorably as U.S. objectives indicated), without apparent favoritism. The one exception was Mexico whose land the U.S. targeted for expansionism. In any event, it appears that the U.S. *basically* upheld Washington's admonition, mentioned in Chapter 1, of not allowing its foreign policy to become partial to particular foreign nations. The Kossuth affair, mentioned earlier, suggests that the U.S. may have been less faithful in following his other admonition—at least when swept up in emotional and ideological support for a cause—of being watchful of the dangers of foreign influence on the country. Kossuth did not, however, succeed in getting the U.S. to deviate from its usual policy of neutrality to embrace revolutionary elements in the Austrian Empire.[93]

Manifest Destiny, Westward Movement, and Expansion. The annexation of Texas was the first significant territorial expansion of the U.S. during the period 1840-1877, as mentioned above. After the annexation, there were tense relations between the Texans and Mexico. The latter had warned that annexation would result in its going to war with the U.S.; in addition, Texas—supported by the Polk administration—claimed all the land between the Nueces and Rio Grande Rivers. Polk also sought for the U.S. territory all the way to the Pacific, and viewed Mexico's declaration of war as a pretext to have the U.S. Navy seize California's ports. Polk tried to purchase the Texas territory that was in question, but political sentiment and conditions in Mexico made that impossible. When Polk ordered the U.S. Army into the territory, Mexico attacked and then the U.S. declared war.[94] Howe calls Polk's Mexican policy "provocative"; he suggests that Polk wanted war with Mexico simply because he sought more territory. Much more important to Polk than the disputed territory in Texas, however, was California. He believed the U.S. had to get California to deny it to Britain—even though it appears that she was not seeking it—and to get access to the Pacific so as to boost the U.S. commercially. Howe says, "Polk was fully prepared to persuade the Mexicans to cede California by whatever means it took": purchasing it, fomenting a Texas-type rebellion by the American settlers there, or war.[95] Polk's aim was "continental expansion."[96] He sought not only these territories, but Oregon and New Mexico as well.[97] He also had ideas about taking even more of Mexico, although his aim was not to absorb the entire country. Some in his administration and the Democratic party advocated this, however. His party strongly embraced the cause of expansion and imperialism, and overall Polk was among the most imperialistic of Democratic politicians.[98] Some Democrats even wanted to take over Cuba and territory in Central America (Pierce later attempted to get Cuba from Spain).[99] The Webster-Ashburton Treaty was not motivated by an attempt to take more territory to the north, although Polk had imperialistic concerns in mind in negotiating it as "he wanted to resolve tensions with the British in order to minimize their opposition" to Texas annexation.[100] Even while, as mentioned, the Mexican War was not generally popular in the U.S., the policy of Manifest Destiny and expansionism that triggered it was.[101] Various groups had an interest in supporting Manifest Destiny: Western land speculators, railroad promoters, small farmers who wanted to move west and get a new start, northern workingmen who saw new economic opportunities, old Jacksonians with the vision of extending Jefferson's agrarian republic, the Democratic party generally which saw it helping its political interests (the Whigs generally opposed territorial expansion), and those who coveted Mexico's silver and other natural resources. It is thought that pro-slavery elements may have supported it as a way of extending their peculiar institution into more areas.[102] On a loosely philosophical level, Manifest Destiny was justified on different grounds, even if it "might otherwise have simply been called American expansionism or imperialism": white supremacy, expanding freedom (Jefferson's "empire for liberty"), the extension of Jefferson's "agrarian republic" (as just noted), biological necessity ("expand or die"), and geographical determinism (it was claimed that the natural boundary of the U.S. was the Pacific Ocean).[103]

With the acquisition of the territory from Mexico after the war, the addition of California, the resolution of the Oregon question, and national attention increasingly turned to the sectional controversy in the 1850s, American ardor for expansion cooled somewhat after 1848. The Gadsden Purchase—a strip of what is now southern Arizona—from Mexico in 1853 to provide needed land for transcontinental railroad construction was the only noteworthy territorial acquisition until after the Civil War, though there was an initial move for annexation of the Hawaiian Islands in the 1850s.[104] Imperialism in a small way resumed with Secretary of State William Seward, who engineered America's next significant, but largely unwelcome, territorial acquisition of Alaska in 1867. Mostly, however, according to Faulkner, American policy focused on commercial instead of territorial expansion during the remaining years of the period focused on in this chapter.[105] A good example of this was the treaty to facilitate trade, mostly involving sugar, with Hawaii in 1875 (though it paved the way for the later successful annexation). Minor efforts at territorial expansion were attempted by the Johnson and Grant administrations in the Dutch West Indies and Santo Domingo, but were spurned by Congress.[106] The next great effort at American expansionism would not come until the Spanish-American War of 1898.

The movement of settlers westward, of course, aided Manifest Destiny and the formal policy of expansion. The movement along the Oregon Trail and settlement in the Pacific Northwest had been going on for some time before it led to the tensions with Britain. Even before the Gold Rush, many settlers were attracted to California and Oregon—passing up the semi-arid and arid plains region—because of land and climate more conducive to farming. Migration to California intensified during the Gold Rush, which was accompanied by a "boom town" phenomenon. In the 1860s, more people became interested in settling in greater numbers in the plains despite the opposition of hostile Indian tribes. In time, the U.S. Army defeated the Indians, however, and permanent settlement occurred. Ranchers followed the prospectors to California, Colorado, and other territories in the Rockies.[107] Another great westward migration was that of the Mormons under Brigham Young in 1846. Two major events of the 1860s further stimulated westward movement: the Homestead Act (1862), which encouraged the development of unoccupied western lands if settlers just improved them, and the completion of the transcontinental railroad (1869), which made relocation to the West much easier.[108]

The Manifest Destiny and expansionism policy highlighted a sharp change from the spirit of the Founding Era's culture, even if it saw western settlement as a "natural" expansion of the country.[109] The desire to have *more* was a lust for the luxury that that culture was so wary of. It also showed a lack of moderation, simplicity, and self-sacrifice. The readiness to go to war against a neighboring country to satisfy this desire showed anything but the communal, cooperative spirit and orientation to the common good—which is not confined just to one's own people—that was also part of that culture. Further, such imperialism was an aspect of militarism and materialism, factors in regime decline—even if, as discussed below, there was no significant advancement of a militarization of American life during the Mexican War or even later in the much more enveloping military situation of the Civil War.

The willingness to use aggression to achieve expansion was not started by Jefferson. If he sought an "empire for liberty," he did not develop an aggressive policy to make it happen. He purchased the Louisiana Territory—he did not fight or pressure France for it—and in foreign affairs he was known for his pacific approach (as discussed in Chapter 2). While the attempt to seize Canada during the War of 1812 may have been a precedent for the policy of the 1840s, probably the most direct one was Jackson's illegitimate nullification of the Indian treaties and seizure of their lands. Indeed, as indicated, Polk was a faithful Jacksonian. The level of aggressive expansionism of the 1840s, however, was well beyond anything that had preceded it.

   Social, Cultural, and Demographic Developments and Reform Movements. Socially and culturally, the period 1840-1877 saw many crucial developments, some of which had their origins in the earlier periods discussed, that permanently reshaped aspects of American life. First, we consider the status of the family. The family still continued to be the main economic unit for both production and consumption.[110] The major reason for this was that family farming remained the chief source of income for the majority of Americans into the twentieth century.[111] Various pressures on the family were intensifying, however. As noted, the mobility of the population weakened extended family ties from early in American history, and this was probably furthered by the increased western movement during this period.[112] There was a trend away from the family's central economic role, however, with the progress of industrialization and urbanization. Industrialization meant that the father's work outside of the home would remove him more from family matters. Women's entry into industrial employment stimulated in them a greater attitude of independence from the household.[113] These developments, children's leaving the home for school and work—it was a time of increasing child labor, which was necessary for the income of working class families[114]—and the kind of doting attitude of increasingly affluent parents that was mentioned caused parental authority to weaken during this period. Accompanying this was a breakdown of juvenile reserve and modesty. This was much commented about at the time. Juvenile crime rose. Increased urbanization caused the birth rate to steadily decline, although in mid-century it was still relatively high.[115] Such family pathologies as divorce, contraceptive use, and even abortion became increasingly frequent.[116] The feminist movement, which emerged publicly with the Seneca Fall Convention of 1848, advocated easier divorce.[117] Contributing to marital breakdown were the practices of entering "easily and lightly" into marriage and early marriage (the latter often involved young teenage girls marrying men well into adulthood). It is not surprising, according to Arthur Charles Cole, that "[t]he family...seemed to many in the process of disintegration."[118] While the family still was central, then, it continued to weaken. This seems to have been a progressive development in American history, although the number and intensity of family-related problems seemed to noticeably increase during this period.

   It was thus a time of declining morality, one of the things the Founding Fathers held critical for a democratic republic. We also see here the enervating of marital fidelity, the integrity and stability of the family (and adequate moral formation of children within it), and respect for law (with the rise of youth crime). With the increasingly "soft" childrearing practices among the affluent we observe one aspect of the troublesome effects of luxury and perhaps another subtle expression of weakening of the will.

There were some quiet developments in education during this period, but the really momentous changes would occur later in the century. First, the common school—i.e., elementary school—was the extent of most people's education at this time, although the high school was gaining in importance.[119] Still, by as late as 1878 there were only 5,500 high schools in the entire country, largely in urban areas.[120] The notion of the common schools was that they would seek to inculcate patriotic virtue, responsible character, and democratic participation, all to be developed through intellectual discipline and the nurture of the moral qualities," and this program would include religion.[121] Its ambience for a long time was essentially common denominator Protestant.[122] Even while the South lagged behind in making formal schooling available for even Caucasian children until Reconstruction—and it was scarcely available for Negro children at all until then[123]—overall American educational attainment and literacy rates were high even in comparison to western Europe.[124] As public education expanded, so did nonpublic education (thanks especially to the development of the Catholic parochial school system). This occurred from the elementary school to the college level.[125] Along with the aspects above that were stressed in the common schools—which conformed to the Founding Fathers' view about the necessary focus of education—most Americans also received the technical sort of education that Tocqueville said was most appropriate for the masses.[126] Similarly, higher education conformed to the liberal arts vision that the Founding Fathers thought was necessary for those who would lead a democratic republic, but the beginnings of change were occurring. With some Americans going to Europe to earn their doctorates from German universities, a "new model" for the budding American university began to take hold that focused on more specialized, technical training. Training in the natural sciences and mathematics was emphasized more, and philosophy and history less. The old, leading American colleges (e.g., Harvard, Yale, and Princeton) followed this,[127] and they were the pacesetters for the rest of higher education in the country. There was an expanded stress on applied programs, stimulated partly by the Morrill Act. Also, the elective system was slowly instituted.[128] Over time, there would be a weakening of the character of liberal arts education. So, the seeds were sown in this period for the decline of the type of education that the Founding Fathers and their era believed necessary for the proper formation of future leaders.

There was a continuing increase of associational and reform activity. Fehrenbacher says that associations were "vehicles of cooperative effort" that partially compensated for the loss of the organic, communal-oriented, interlocking functional-based culture of colonial America. They did not overcome the more individualistic ethos of nineteenth century American life, however. In fact, to get a sense of how far Americans had deviated from this spirit of the eighteenth century it is worth noting that one of the points of contention between the Yankee New Englanders and the immigrant Irish was that the latter, according to Richard D. Brown, "represented the traditional network of values and relationships that [for] the natives…represented regression."[129] Another point that Fehrenbacher says about the rise of voluntary associations is that it underscored a trend toward specialization occurring because of the changing economy. Still, that trend was slow in developing.[130] Just as the liberal arts were only beginning to weaken and giving way to specialization in higher education, so specialization in occupations and social roles and activities was happening only gradually. As far as reform movements were concerned, two general types had emerged: the philanthropic and the protest types. The former was discussed in Chapter 3 and further developed during this period. Philanthropic groups (such as the mental health and prison reform groups) were the major type before the Civil War; the protest groups became more prominent later in the nineteenth century (as we shall see in the next chapter).[131] The abolitionist movement was one of the first of this latter type. The tendency of some social reform movements (e.g., the temperance organizations) to take absolutist positions, setting a pattern for later public advocacy groups, has been noted. This development in the temperance movement occurred only after an internal struggle between moderate and extreme factions, with the latter winning.[132] The efforts of the ultimately absolutist temperance movement bore fruit in the fashioning of public policy during this period. Maine enacted the first state prohibition statute in 1846 and a dozen more states followed suit within a decade. Even though most of these were later repealed or struck down by state courts,[133] the road to the Eighteenth Amendment was being paved. The perspectives that emerged during the Jacksonian Era shaped reform efforts. In the face of such phenomena as increasing urban poverty, enhanced unemployment during economic downturns, and even well accomplished men slipping into financial want, many Americans revised their thinking about whether individuals in the face of a transforming economy were completely responsible for their socio-economic situation. Still, the division deepened between those who continued to firmly believe that, in Fehrenbach's words, "a worthy man could overcome the handicaps of his environment and that the struggle would only strengthen his character," and those who believed that social reforms and governmental action were necessary to help people to deal with conditions spawned by the new industrial order.[134] Both viewpoints stimulated a conviction about the need for social reform, but the type and focus were different. The former focused on changing the individual, even while as time went on it sought to do it through establishing institutions—in many cases, run or supported by government—to reform him, instead of punishing him. The latter sought to alter social and economic conditions or at least foster equal opportunity for economic well-being, with government assistance if necessary. These were an extension of the Whig and Jacksonian Democrat positions, respectively. In this immediate post-Jacksonian Era period, the approach to reform became a bit more secular. The "reform impulse"—which may have been enhanced by the very democratization previously discussed, with its great stress on equality—"absorbed strong influences from Europe," where a more thoroughgoing Enlightenment influence than took hold in America (see Chapter 2) "had partly secularized traditional religious imperatives."[135]

A new kind of reform movement emerged in the Reconstruction period, which aimed at governmental reform. For a number of years after the Civil War, there were Congressional efforts to establish a professional civil service, based somewhat on the British model, and to make appointments to federal employment on merit. A few basic steps were taken under Grant, but serious civil service reform would have to wait until later in the century.[136] An interesting twist was taken by some in this movement, which sharply deviated from the humanitarian and democratic ethos of the century's previous reform efforts. They wanted to reverse the scope of government's activities and to begin to insulate it from popular demands, both of which we saw had multiplied after the Civil War. Out of nativist sentiment, or weariness with the ongoing struggles with the South, or concern about where the increasing democratization of the century had led, they called for a reintroduction of educational and property qualifications for voting (they may not have been aware of how literacy tests were beginning to be abused to stop southern Negroes from voting). This group of reformers saw both continuing violence in the South and corruption and machine politics in the North to be symptomatic of the same problem: a kind of natural aristocracy—men of great capability—was no longer able to rule. As noted, this was the legacy of democratization. The solution in the North was civil-service reform, and in the South it was finally permitting the former leading figures of the antebellum period to re-enter politics.[137] These reformers idealized the old southern plantation-based gentry—who as we saw above and is apparent below, often did not act with wisdom, prudence, or a spirit of the common good—and did not seem to understand that just having a professionally-trained civil service cadre would not insure public-spiritedness. With the ring of both those among the earlier reformers who thought men had to look inside themselves to correct their situations and the later disciple of Negro self-improvement, Booker T. Washington, they said that all that could be done for the freedmen by government had been done and now it was up to them themselves. So, they called for an end to Reconstruction efforts. Completely ignoring the realities in the South, they did not even want the federal government to any longer intervene to protect the former slaves from the Ku Klux Klan and other violence.[138] These political reformers, as mentioned, achieved their goals of civil service reform only later in the century. They did see some government retrenchment in the wake of the Panic of 1873, as states and localities imposed budget limits. The franchise was not restricted and it is doubtful if politics thereafter typically featured the highly capable men they sought.[139]

We commented before about how the tendency of the early advocacy organizations to take absolutist positions, especially on matters that by their nature are given to compromise, showed a lack of the realism, moderation, civility, and spirit of cooperativeness of the Founding Era. The tendency on the part of some who continued to believe that the individual was necessarily responsible for his economic hardship and that he should pull himself out of it perhaps illustrated a departure from the Founding Era's view that the community should be willing to help its members. It epitomized the thinking of the new, individualistic mass culture where men tended to be isolated and unsupported. It also showed a deviation from that era's belief that all should have a sufficiency of goods. The more secular viewpoint of many of the reformers was one more small step in the direction of religious decline. The views of the early breed of governmental reformers represented to only some degree a return to the thinking of the Founding (and, as it was, the reformers' view did not appear to spread to the larger political society). While their seeking to bring forth a kind of natural aristocracy and limit the franchise concurred with the "republican" side of our democratic republic, it did not seem sensitive to the "democratic" side. Perhaps these reformers aimed to limit suffrage too much. As noted in Chapter 1, the Founders expected eventually that suffrage would broaden even if they were hesitant about it being universal. More generally, the reformers seemed to give short shrift to the Founders' principle of popular sovereignty. Secondly, the reformers perhaps had a confused notion of what a "natural aristocracy" is. Establishing merit in the sense of functional or technical expertise as would be the case with a civil service does not insure the moral character or prudential judgment that is required for political leadership. Anticipating the Progressive Era, they wrongly believed that political rule could be successfully carried out by apolitical technicians. Confusion of a different sort was seen by their wanting to resurrect the old plantocracy in the South. While it is true that the Washingtons, Jeffersons, Calhouns, et al. who were part of it, in spite of their shortcomings, could be said to have been a true natural aristocracy of sorts—a republican-oriented one, to boot—there was no necessary identification of that element with a natural aristocracy. In some respects, most of them may have been closer to the European hereditary aristocracy that the Founding Era disdained. Further, in these reformers' oblivion to the abuses in the South, they short-changed the civic friendship, civility, respect for the rule of law, and basic justice that was part of Founding culture.[140]

The above dissipation, in spite of the high level of associational activity, of a communal orientation that was occurring in American culture was an aspect of the sectional division between North and South before the Civil War. The North emphasized personal liberty, hard-work, opportunity, competition, and a cosmopolitan outlook; the South was more like classical Greece and Rome, making prominent such principles as honor, loyalty, valor, tradition, trust, benevolence, generosity, and fidelity, and had a more aristocratic and localistic outlook and relaxed, gentleman-like attitude about affairs. To be sure, it was not as if the principles of the one section were not at all present in the other, but this division depicts the different general cultural norm in each. Many northerners disliked not just slavery but the hierarchical, aristocratic-type culture that they believed had spawned it.[141] As Richard D. Brown puts it, the "traditionalism of..[the southern] social outlook...was joined to a political vision looking back to an earlier, more traditional republicanism."[142] It might be said that the South did not yet embody the post-Calvinist New England ethic that had already largely transformed the North since the time of the Founding. After the war, things changed. According to Brown, the war was a "modernizer of immense proportions"—the characteristics of the North mentioned tend to be associated with cultural modernization—for both regions, advancing these characteristics in the South and even more than before in the North. Localism and regionalism, for example, survived, but declined.[143] The war, in his estimation, was a decisive defeat for traditional culture in the U.S.[144] Thus, there were elements of the Founding Era's culture remaining in the cultures of both North and South—although probably more in the South. The rejection of the hierarchical dimensions of southern culture by the North underscored its turning away from the non-democratic aspects of the Founding; the decline of localism signaled centripetal, centralizing tendencies that were, of course, at odds with the Founding culture.

In many ways, moral corruption afflicted America in the antebellum and Civil War periods. First, the luxury orientation so feared by moral spokesmen of the colonial era and early Republic seems to have deeply set in before the War. This was the case with material comforts in the home, amusements, trips, and the like. As traditional culture was passing away in the North; a "new aristocracy of wealth," increasingly based on commercial success, replaced it. In the South, the comforts of wealth were not as widespread but the old plantocracy—in its final days—indulged in their lavish balls and other social affairs and trips to northern resorts.[145] Some commentators of the time talked about "the growing inclination toward extravagance and dissipation."[146] The pathologies afflicting marriage and the family were already mentioned. Other public problems related to sexual morality included increased prostitution and, during the time of the California Gold Rush, even human trafficking from abroad for that purpose.[147] Gambling exploded, oftentimes given police protection in the large cities of the Northeast.[148] A crime wave swept across the major cities in the 1850s, fueled in part by economic distress and poverty. As mentioned above, juvenile crime increased significantly.[149] Alcohol was a major problem stimulating crime, and liquor trafficking activity was high.[150]

Such moral conditions continued during Reconstruction. The Reconstruction period, in the North at least, was perhaps a time of even greater luxury than 1840 to 1865. It was the period when "[a]n economy of local producers was turning into a national market of consumers."[151] We noted that the luxury orientation took firm root during the Jacksonian Era, paralleling the growth of the market-based economy. It became more intense after that. Sexual immorality was a problem, especially with men. While the serious problems of urban prostitution continued (in fact, prostitution became more open in large cities), women were seeking to set a new moral tone for the culture by trying to promote Victorian moral norms and end a double standard that found sexual licentiousness more acceptable for men. Unlike the feminists of the second half of the twentieth century, however, they would not let women sink to the level of many men, but sought to elevate manhood to the standards of sexual purity of most women. Apparently, even within marriage a kind of "macho" attitude prevailed, with men lacking self-control and moderation in their sexual demands on their wives; efforts were made to change this attitude. On a more public level, the neo-Calvinist Comstock movement emerged to address the weakened morality. It sought to "evangelize" the higher standards of sexual virtue and to advocate legal and public policy that would buttress it. As this was occurring, however, a seemingly contrary anti-natal attitude seemed to be developing among the middle class, with the declining birth rates of 1840 to 1865 continuing.[152] Another dimension of moral decay in the Reconstruction period, of course, was political corruption discussed elsewhere in this chapter. It ranged from the Grant scandals to the corruption in the southern Reconstruction governments to the regime of urban political scandal by the likes of the Boss Tweed ring in New York City.[153]

Besides the luxury orientation, we see above many other deviations from the cultural norms of the Founding Era. The notion of wealth without apparent limits, with an imperviousness to others being able to take part in it, was becoming ingrained at least among some elements. The first emergence of a kind of consumer culture in the U.S. demonstrated also the unpopularity of the notion of willingness to make present sacrifice for future good.. The decline of sexual morality was another factor in weakening the norms of marital fidelity and family stability. The above gives many indications of a lessening of a sense of temperance or moderation, at least in personal behavior (which, as we saw in Chapter 1, is not disconnected with public behavior). We have already discussed how the Founding Era's norms were affronted by political corruption. All of these developments seemed to advance considerably over what had been seen even in the periods examined in Chapters 2 and 3. We can only speculate as to the causes of these deviations, in light of what else began to happen in those periods and was continuing in this one: democratization, religious change (discussed below), economic change, an ignoring of the need for a natural aristocracy, the decline of the notion of the gentleman, and the general weakening of the norm of moderation (which was traditionally understood to be central for morality).

In religion, pluralism—at least within Christianity—became the norm during the antebellum period because of the increased number of Catholics after the annexation of formerly Mexican territory and heightened Catholic immigration (which was to be even more the case after the Civil War, for the rest of the century). Even within Protestantism, there was deepening division, as new break-off sects emerged and some denominations split along sectional lines because of the larger slavery-sectional split in American politics.[154] It was because of Catholic-Protestant conflict—the specific context was the Catholic school funding conflict in New York City—that one of the earliest claims of the need for a rigid view of church-state separation was made. This appeared in a widely disseminated report of the City's Board of Assistants' committee on schools.[155] In the report, the Board anticipated a common separationist argument of the twentieth century that divisiveness would result in the absence of rigid separation.[156] Some nativist groups picked up on the demand for separationism—even claiming that the Bible taught it—understanding that by doing so they were constraining churches, but reasoning that that only meant Catholicism because it was a unified church and Protestants were separate sects. So, even though they clamored for separationism, they understood it to not affect common-denominator Protestantism in the public schools.[157] Interestingly,

Protestant clergymen from the 1840s increasingly embraced separationism and were reluctant—contradictorily, since they often got involved in politics—even about the principle of religion exercising influence on government in the absence of any kind of legal establishment.[158] In the 1850s, Henry P. Tappan, the first president of the University of Michigan, provided a foretaste of the sweeping secularization of universities in the twentieth century by discouraging even student prayer meetings. He advocated separation in even those higher education institutions that were not publicly funded.[159] Around the same time, religious liberals permanently joined the ranks of separationists because they saw it as reinforcing the individual's freedom from "the constraints of a creed." They anticipated two common features of all-too-typical thinking about religion in contemporary America, nurtured by the long period of twentieth century separationism: that a person can call himself religious, even attach himself to a sect, but determine for himself what beliefs he will embrace; and that religious belief should retreat to a private domain, and become disconnected from other aspects of one's life. They also anticipated a typical practical objective of the contemporary separationist: to use the notion of separation of church and state as a way of restraining the social or cultural influence of more traditional denominations.[160] By the 1870s, liberal religionists were insisting that, specifically, a "secular theory" of the state was needed, which seemed to mean that religion should not influence the state at all.[161] By that decade, separationism had come to be accepted as a part of the American creed, irrespective of whether it had been a principle of the Founding Era. Even many Protestant clergy and laity who were reluctant to espouse a *sweeping* separationism adhered to a more moderate version of it. They tried to discourage the view that it meant that religion and politics were in two distinct domains, never to interact, with the implication that religion could not or should not shape public morality.[162] This, however, was exactly part of what the newly emerging secular liberalism of the 1870s sought. They said that government could not enact any laws that "coincided with the morality of a distinct religion, such as Christianity." Only "natural" morality and secular notions of equal rights and liberty should influence law. They also believed that such things as church tax exemptions, public appropriations for church-related charitable and educational institutions, and "blue laws" should be eliminated. The very fact that religious institutions were precisely religious should be enough to exclude them from public benefits they would otherwise be eligible for.[163] By the end of this period, in 1876, secular liberals were saying that even obscenity laws—which, in essence, were nothing more than laws promoting a standard of basic public decency—should be repealed. How much the secularists were in control of this new American phenomenon called "liberalism"—vis-à-vis the believers who joined the liberal ranks (in such organizations as the National Liberal League)—is seen in the fact that the latter went more than halfway in meeting the objections of the secularists about obscenity laws by holding that obscenity should be prosecuted only if there were clear, unambiguous laws. It should be noted that some of the secular liberals were "free love" advocates.[164]

Interestingly, in light of how twentieth-century separationists often tried to claim that the original intent of the First Amendment mandated their position, the secular liberal separationists of this time recognized that the Amendment was "insufficient" from their standpoint. They sought to "enlarge" it by proposing a new version of the First Amendment in 1874.[165]

We have seen that a progressive secularization took place in the first ninety years of the American Republic. First, American religion changed after the Founding Era from traditional Christianity to an Enlightenment-influenced Christianity. Then the Jacksonian Era featured the first stress on outright separationism and equal treatment of believers and unbelievers (even welcoming the latter as "good Jacksonians"). The post-Civil War period witnessed a more sweeping separationism, increasing acceptance of the notion of a secular state, and even a serious push to strip public morality of a religious basis. We also see below a turning away from a traditional Christian view about man by leading thinkers of the latter period. A Christian culture still continued in the America of the 1870s, but it—in fact, any kind of religious culture at all—was now under organized attack. The separationist viewpoint, which would ultimately help to undermine it, was now broadly accepted (even if in an attenuated form) and secularism was advancing. The framework for the rigid separation of church and state in American law, politics, and culture in the twentieth century was now in place.

A number of other observations can be made about the above developments in religion and church-state relations. First, the Catholic-Protestant tensions that helped spawn separationism certainly exhibited a lack of civic friendship. It was not as much the case as with the intense anti-Catholic, nativist activity of the 1840s or even the milder version discussed below, but was still so. Second, the initial steps toward secularizing higher education and the later call for an outright secular state essentially signaled that religion was coming to be seen as not so important any longer as a public or social concern. Third, the emergence of the notions of belonging to a church but thinking that one can shape his own personal beliefs regardless of its teachings and that sound morality does not require religion represented an embracing of relativism and, effectively, a minimizing of the importance of religion. Fourth, the separationist push to eliminate the influence of religion on the shaping of law and public policy was a clear departure from the Founding understanding of its necessity for the sustenance of republican and, even more basically, all good government. Fifth, aiming to do things like strip churches of tax exemptions raised the specter of a threat to religious liberty, which was both a central right for the Founders and a purpose of the First Amendment.[166] Some have even said that the Founders viewed it as our "first freedom," which means that it had a special place in our constitutional scheme.[167] It also evoked hostility to religion, which of course the Founders saw as so important. Indeed, the separationists' attempt to formally have the First Amendment changed underscores how significantly their view deviated from the Founding period. Finally, the separationists' insistence on repealing obscenity laws and the advocacy of free love by some of them shows both how they distorted such central Founding rights as free speech and press and underscores their imperviousness to the importance of sound sexual morality and the principle of marital fidelity of the Founding Era's culture. More basically, it was another expression of the acceptance of moral relativism, which undercut the Founders' and their era's commitment to natural law and to the entire belief that along with religion morality—sound morality—had to undergird republican and any good government. It also was a harbinger of what would come in the twentieth century.

Nativist activity, in response to heightening immigration and particularly the increased Catholic presence, has been noted. In 1860, the percentage of the American population that was foreign-born reached 13.2%. This prompted economic nervousness in the native-born population—it was feared that in the new less secure industrial order immigrants would take jobs away—as well as ethnic stereotyping and blaming of the immigrants for deteriorating urban conditions. Like the extreme Federalists in the 1790s (who were reacting to the fear of political radicalism instead of economics), the antebellum nativists sought not to curtail immigration but to place obstacles on immigrants' gaining citizenship, voting rights, etc. The nativist movement, which was at first locally based, soon became national and expanded. As mentioned, nativism affected the political party arrangements.[168] In the 1840s, the American Republican or Native American party was organized, which in the 1850s became simply the American party (often called the "Know Nothing" party).[169] It had considerable success in some states and cities, but by the end of the decade declined.[170] Both ethnic and religious divisions—the increasing religious divisions even among Protestants were noted above—significantly influenced politics.[171] California's ethnic diversity increased in the years before and during the early part of the Gold Rush, and the different groups initially got along. As time went on, however, there was conflict.[172] In the Reconstruction period and after, immigration continued to increase, although most immigrants still came from western, central, and northern Europe (which was different from earlier in American history only in the number); late in the century, there was much immigration from eastern and southern Europe and this further enhanced the country's ethnic diversity. There was also immigration starting early in the 1840-1877 period from China, and enhanced Jewish immigration toward the later part of the period. These latter groups faced considerable hostility, including anti-Chinese rioting in California in the 1870s. Organized anti-immigrant activity tailed off during the Civil War and Reconstruction—probably because the country's focus was on other things—but resumed late in the 1880s with the formation of the strongly anti-Catholic American Protective Association.[173]

Besides the native born-immigrant conflict, there was anti-Negro violence. In addition to the Civil War era riots mentioned above, rioting directed against the recently freed former slaves occurred during the early Reconstruction period in the South. After the military occupation suppressed such activity, the anti-Negro violence was carried out on a smaller, but still widespread, scale by groups such as the Ku Klux Klan.[174] Anti-Negro rioting was seen again late in Reconstruction in Mississippi after the occupation had ended, and intimidation was also used there as a political tool to force Caucasian Republicans not to vote or to abandon their party.[175]

Obviously, the above developments were contrary to such Founding cultural norms as civility, civic friendship, concern for the common good, and the melding of different groups together. All of the rioting and intimidation of different groups that we have noted violated respect for law and also the protection of life, liberty, and property that were basic principles of the Founding Fathers for sustaining a democratic republic.

Intellectual Currents. Perhaps the leading intellectual currents in the antebellum and Civil War periods were the views of the friendly critics of democracy (coming on the heels of Jacksonianism), Unitarianism, transcendentalism, Calhounism, and American nationalistic thought. In the Reconstruction period, a rudimentary social evolutionary idea emerged, which laid the foundation for the social Darwinism that emerged in the period after this one and will be examined in Chapter 5.

Friendly critics of the new American democracy of the Jacksonian Era, such as the famous novelist James Fenimore Cooper and political thinker Orestes A. Brownson (both of whom wrote in that era and the current period), accepted the new broad suffrage and the political and legal equality of citizens but feared—in the manner of John Stuart Mill and Tocqueville—the tyranny of the majority and conformism induced by public opinion.[176] Unlike (it seems) the extreme pro-democratic thinkers of the Jacksonian Era (see Chapter 3) and the transcendentalists below, these thinkers "retained the concept of original sin." They did not believe that men, either individually or collectively, were necessarily going to make choices conducive to the good for themselves or their fellow men. Both recognized a tendency in democracy to slip into demagogy and to trample on individual rights, and saw that the conditions of liberty and equality that democracy spawned had to be rightly limited. A democratic polity can be "viable and just" only within a checks-and-balances system and when good, public-spirited men—like the class of republican gentlemen that the Founding Fathers were part of—ruled. It also required a commitment to natural law. Brownson believed that even this was not enough, however; what was also needed was the acceptance of the Catholic Church as the authoritative interpreter and arbiter of the natural law, which was part of her divinely-appointed mission. This did not mean establishing her as the official church, but just recognizing this authority. Otherwise, the sovereignty of individual judgment about moral questions affecting politics—which, it would seem, would be particularly embellished in a democracy due to what was just said about liberty and equality—could have anarchic consequences.[177]

Unitarianism, which was founded earlier in the century, was mentioned in Chapter 3 as a major expression of a new Christian humanitarianism. It was a major force in helping the notion of the possibility of human perfectibility to become further implanted in the American mind. Its founder, William Ellery Channing, who died shortly after the beginning of the period focused on in this chapter (in 1842), inspired many religious liberals and reformers of his time (we have seen how important both groups became). Channing saw the divine reflected in human dignity; the stress was already on man, and the way this would play itself out as American history went on was that man increasingly could rely just on himself and leave God behind. This could easily be anticipated from the nature of his thought itself, which bore a heavy imprint of the Enlightenment. Channing's thought influenced a whole array of nineteenth century reform concerns, including the anti-slavery cause, anti-imperialism, the cause of workers, and women's rights.[178]

Transcendentalism, associated especially with Ralph Waldo Emerson and Henry David Thoreau, brought an antinomianism to American thought. It believed that men were fundamentally apolitical, and believed that "coercive government" might ultimately be eliminated. As such, it probably paved the way later on for the openness of American intellectuals to Marxism, the belief of the Reconstruction Era government reformers above and the later Progressive Era that hitherto political problems could be solved without politics by means of mere technical expertise (e.g., running local government was seen as an efficiency problem to be handled by technically-trained city managers instead of politicians), and a subversion of the importance of the political (usually to the economic)—and also led to a turning away from politics in preference to other endeavors by many prominent men. While the pro-democratic thinkers of the Jacksonian Era attributed almost infallibility to public opinion in general, the transcendentalists thought that each *individual* could give authoritative answers to moral questions—without even presuming any particular moral formation—which could then provide answers to political questions (which they considered to be always essentially moral in character). They thus represented the next step in thought after the latter thinkers. Transcendentalism profoundly influenced the history of later American protest movements—not just in the obvious way by Thoreau's presumed doctrine of passive resistance to unjust laws (even though Howe says he did not actually embrace this and is wrongly credited with it[179])— but also in their new notion of individualism seen above (i.e., that the dissenting individual necessarily can better understand politics than institutions, the mass, or received wisdom).[180] The latter made their viewpoint akin to the thought of Marx—that was being independently formulated at about the same time—by the fact that, like Marxism, their view was fundamentally gnostic. The transcendentalists' belief that the individual could be so all knowing was essentially rooted in their theological belief that every person can be "directly in touch with the divine." This meant, of course, that the individual really does not need an institutional church. This, plus their religious syncretism—holding that all religions have an equal truth claim—are views that are often found in contemporary American life They also perhaps furthered the American tendency, mentioned above, of fashioning one's own creedal formulations.[181]

Calhoun, of course, was a strong defender of slavery and states' rights. Not surprisingly, then, his theory asserted the fundamental inequality of men, the inevitability of social exploitation, and the view that the Constitution was basically a compact among sovereign states that retained their sovereignty when they entered it. Calhounism also held, however—in line with the culture of the Founding Era—that the community was organic and not a mere collection of individuals brought together, even if it was made up of groups that sometimes had conflicting interests. The latter made compromise a basic need of politics.[182] He also rejected majoritarianism, and embraced his famous notion of the concurrent majority: that the different groups or interests or classes that make up the community would have to separately agree to proposed laws or at least have a veto over them—to insure that they would not be victimized by the action of the overall majority.[183] In taking this position, Calhoun actually believed that he was seeking to restore the intent of the Founding Fathers, who saw their vision of a balance between national and state power—as embodied by the need for both the "national-oriented" House of Representatives and the "state-oriented" (i.e., representing the states) Senate to have to both agree to pass a law— distorted by the aim that quickly took hold in American history of just capturing control of the entire national government. He sought to achieve this by, in effect, improving upon the political arrangements the Founders established.[184]

Before and after the Civil War, writing appeared which promoted national supremacy and a notion of American nationalism. The old story of American exceptionalism and a "sense of mission" was seen in this writing, although some of it under Hegelian influence carried this to the extreme of seeing America as "a mystical entity whose vocation and obligation were from God directly."[185] Lincoln expressed a more mainstream view: that there was a "perpetuity…inherent in the fundamental laws of all national governments"—in America's case, the Constitution—which forbade secession. He also said—like Brownson—that the Union or American nationhood predated the Constitution, going back to the Articles of Association of 1774; the Constitution provided for a "more perfect Union."[186] A number of thinkers held that any nation had an organic unity—making one think of the culture of the Founding Era—and that the fundamental law that Lincoln spoke of came forth from it.[187]

What we are calling a rudimentary social evolutionary strain of thought was put forth by such thinkers as John W. Draper and Lewis H. Morgan. It was early American social science, seeking—in the manner of Marx—to provide "scientific" explanations of society and politics. There was a deterministic dimension to their thought. Draper had a pessimistic tilt to his thought, Morgan an optimistic one. Draper saw "social advancement" as controlled by natural forces, just as is bodily growth. Reformers were wrong to think that such advancement or the improvement of all men (e.g., that all can be educated to a high degree) is possible by human devices; this could not overcome natural limitations. Nature has smiled favorably on the U.S.: it has provided the conditions under which American political ideas could thrive. It also seems to have destined that the American nation stretch from the Atlantic to the Pacific. Thus, he gave a natural sanction to expansion and imperialism, like the biological justification others gave it above. His view was by no means *entirely* deterministic. Men could overcome, say, climatic factors by the use of science. This very science on one hand made possible an equality of opportunity, and on the other would insure a hierarchy of "superiority and subordination."[188] His thought, while not rigid in how it saw society, clearly set a framework for social "survival of the fittest" theories after it. Morgan, on the other hand, viewed humanity as having definitely advanced over the course of its existence. This was seen in scientific discoveries and inventions and in the development of the ideas of government, the family, and property (it should be noted that, partly in line with the social contract thinkers, the latter are not natural to man but had to be developed). These great developments came out of primitive, inchoate notions. There was a kind of symbiotic relationship between the human mind and these institutions: they came from basic notions in the mind, but as they developed they helped the mind to expand. Morgan seemed to be influenced by Locke in thinking that property was the especially important development, and "technological advancement" was crucial in helping it to emerge. Property is also the cause of change in politics and culture. Similar to Marx—in a curious way this also was the case with the great ideological defenders of the economic liberalism that Marx so despised—economic institutions were seen as the foundation on which politics and culture were erected, and technological development was the foundation of both. There was the unmistakable ring of American exceptionalism in Morgan's thought: the "American society based on private property and the politics of representative democracy was the highest stage of civilizational development" possible. As with Draper, there was also a sense of American mission and destiny. For Draper, nature ordained America to spread its democratic way of life across the continent. For Morgan, the American democratic idea and all the reform ideas that came with it would save the human race.[189] It was not just a secular humanistic perspective—i.e., a human idea that purported to bring a kind of salvation to the world—but a *hubristic* one. It was a moderated version of the secularized Christian eschatology of Marx. Morgan saw progress—defined in terms of the promulgation throughout the world of American socio-politico-economic ideas—as inevitable. In spite of its utter optimism and embracing of the reform spirit of the age, however, his theory like Draper's also provided a foundation for the period of laissez faire, "survival of the fittest" economic liberalism that was to come. It did this by making private property relations the basis of everything else, making man the measure of all things, and treating economics, politics, and culture as amoral developments of human evolutionary activity. Their laissez faire perspective was erected on the foundation laid in the Jacksonian Era—it was to help provide the intellectual justification for the further development of economic liberalism as the country progressed into the Gilded Age.

The friendly critics of Jacksonian democracy, Cooper and Brownson, were very much in line with the Founding Fathers, although as the developments of this period show they were increasingly out of step with the drift of American political and social life. The Founders, of course, did not acknowledge the need for the Catholic Church as the authoritative moral teacher—which was something that Brownson insisted on. We suggested in Chapter 1 that this is a possible fundamental weakness of the Founding. Unitarianism, while still upholding religious belief (although since it was not trinitarian, not in a traditional Christian way), was a major early force in advancing secular humanism. It began to move man to the center of things. As such, it helped to cause the decline of religion—traditional theism—that the Founding saw, as we have emphasized, as essential for free and good government. Some of the criticisms above of the separationists in the Reconstruction period apply to the transcendentalists also. The rise of transcendentalism showed how religious viewpoints in the antebellum period departed even further from the early American religious understanding than had some in the previous periods examined (that is, the departures built on each other). Transcendentalism, with its utter optimism about man and seeming belief that moral principles could easily be known and almost automatically adhered to, was flatly contrary to the realism of the American Founding. It also opposed the Founders' understanding that politics is natural for man, that man needs political life. The transcendentalists were like the social contract thinkers in taking the opposite position. Their exultation of the powers of the individual expressed an utterly extreme individualism, which was also an expansion of the philosophical legacy of the social contract thinkers. Their belief that the individual could stand all by himself apart from any church in his relationship to God was a religious expression of the egalitarianism rejected by the Founding. If the Founding Fathers were influenced by many aspects of, say, Locke's thought, these points were certainly not among them. Calhoun's view embodies a number of the principles of the Founders, but like the post-Civil War government reformers above he ignored the democratic side of their democratic republican idea. In his desire to oppose majoritarianism, he downplayed majority rule with his notion of the concurrent majority. He rejected equality outright, while it was only egalitarianism or equality without any limitations that they opposed. As far as the national supremacist thinkers are concerned, a Hegelian-inspired view of American nationalism obviously was not in line with the Founding Fathers. The kind of abstract notion of the state featured in Hegelian thought had no place in their thinking. They were realists, not abstract theoreticians or ideologues. Government for them was a practical endeavor that was shaped by the men's actions, not something that descended from beyond them and was essentially out of their control.[190] Draper's and Morgan's moderate determinism was similarly at odds with the Founding's realism and the more balanced Christian-inspired understanding (despite the predestination doctrine of traditional Calvinism) that men, both individually and as a collective, can largely control their lives and future direction. Draper conformed to the Founders in believing in equality of opportunity, but his view of hierarchy betrayed a rigidity, inevitability, and artificial claim of naturalism that made it more like later twentieth-century fascism than their notion of natural aristocracy. Like the governmental reformers mentioned and Calhoun, his perspective downplayed the democratic dimension of the Founding. Morgan followed the transcendentalists in essentially subverting the political to the economic. His perspective was a further affront to the realism and balance of the Founding view by attributing a messianic aura to America; the Christian worldview of the Founders gave them the wisdom to realize the folly of that. This was a reckless view of American exceptionalism, much beyond the example for liberty that the Founders saw America as providing for the world. Draper's and Morgan's laying the foundation of laissez faire went contrary to the restrained economic freedom, sense of social obligation of property, and orientation to the communal well-being of the Founding culture's economic relations. Perhaps because of the transformation that had taken place in the Jacksonian period, where the notion of natural aristocracy had vanished from people's minds, the connection of ethics and economics had become muted, and economic laissez faire became so prominent, Draper, Morgan, and the governmental reformers mentioned above were no longer intellectually equipped to recover the true understanding of the Founding. They saw certain problems, but could only resurrect facsimiles of the old principles—convoluted or distorted notions of them—even though they thought they had the real thing. In short, the intellectual currents of this period for the most part—apart from the friendly critics of democracy—in spite of certain points of conformity deviated overall from the Founding perspective. This was seen especially with the decline of realism, the departure from a traditional religious outlook, an increasing (in some ways, almost extreme) individualism, an inability to maintain a proper balance between the democratic and republican aspects of the Founding, and a distortion of such notions that are part of this balance as equality and natural aristocracy.

Legal Developments, the Maintenance of the Rule of Law and the Politicization of Law, and Citizen Rights (including the Position of the Negro). The main legal developments and questions of citizen rights during the antebellum period related to the slavery question, Texas annexation, and the fallout from the Mexican War; during the Civil War period to the prosecution of the war; and during Reconstruction to trying to secure the position of the freed slaves. It was already mentioned that the "gag rule" was lifted in the House of Representatives in 1844. Chapter 3 discussed the serious implications the rule had posed for both free debate in Congress and free speech in general. Texas annexation was brought about possibly by extra-constitutional means in 1845. The annexation treaty negotiated by the Tyler administration with the Lone Star Republic—which was a sovereign nation—to bring it into the Union as the State of Texas was defeated in the Senate in 1844 (the opposition of some in the North to the extension of slavery was probably the key reason[191]). The Democrats in Congress, quietly spearheaded by President-elect Polk with President Tyler's support, then pushed through a joint resolution to bring about the annexation (which required only a majority in each house, instead of the two-thirds in the Senate needed for the treaty).[192] Historically, some scholars have argued that since Texas was an independent country, annexing without a treaty was a violation of international law.[193] Polk's military court of inquiry of General Scott that was mentioned above, with the political motivations behind it, was a misuse of the judicial process—thereby offending the rule of law—in addition to being a potentially problematical example of political interference with the military. In the aftermath of the Mexican War and the U.S. annexation of the formerly Mexican territory, the rule of law and property rights were flouted as most Mexican landowners lost title to their property. Greedy, unethical newcomers were able to legally maneuver to grab their holdings, apparently violating the provisions of the Treaty of Guadalupe Hidalgo that had ended the war. The Treaty was further violated when the existing inhabitants were refused American citizenship. Thus, even though Mexicans had inhabited this territory for three hundred years they were considered foreigners after the cession occurred. In parts of east Texas, they were even forcibly expelled. Howe tells us that in California, the Indians—who had been helped and protected historically by the Spanish missions—were treated even worse than the Mexicans; the new state would not even allow the federal government to establish reservations to shelter them. This was the case even though the Treaty had also provided that they should automatically become American citizens.[194] This lack of respect for legal norms in California under the early days of massive American settlement and statehood was also seen above in the meting out of "justice" in the mining towns during the Gold Rush. Not only did the outright disregard of the Treaty provisions represent a shocking abuse of the rule of law that was such a central principle of the Founding, but also a spurning of the cultural norm of the Founding Era of keeping promises. As suggested also by what was said above about it, the Mexican War era saw much besmirching of the heritage of the Founding.

The new commitment to the enforcing of the Fugitive Slave Law in 1850 actually prompted a weakening of the rule of law, with challenges coming from both sides of the controversy. Many northern states, in light of the *Prigg* decision, would not enforce the law, which increasingly led to slave hunters and kidnappers being hired by slaveowners to quietly come North to try to capture runaways (sometimes they even seized free Negroes to bring into slavery). The opposition to the law had become so intense in parts of the North that mobs sometimes tried to stop official efforts to enforce the law, in addition to the northerners who violated the law by assisting runaways to flee to freedom via the underground railroad.[195] We noted other problems earlier in this chapter. In addition to the rule of law implications, the Fugitive Slave Law raised problems of civil liberties. The apprehended persons—even if they were actually free Negroes—had no legal recourse. The federal commissioners who oversaw its enforcement had an incentive to promote as many apprehensions as possible because they received a payment for each slave—or presumed slave—to be returned to his master. Citizens—even if they morally objected to slavery—were required under threat of imprisonment to actually assist in slave recoveries.[196]

McPherson says that the violations of civil liberties were relatively mild during the Civil War—at least, compared to some government policies later during World Wars I and II—and we can see that from the following (even though we also notice that there definitely *were* violations). There was press censorship as far as reporting about the war was concerned. Initially, news dispatches about battles had to be cleared by U.S. Government censors and some journalists were arrested for their reports; later reporters were sort of left on their honor to file only reports that did not hurt the Union cause.[197] It can be expected that a government during wartime would regulate the flow of military-related information. Still, it is always a question of manner and degree, and arresting reporters probably went too far in compromising free speech. The northern colleges experienced suppression of free expression. Students were forbidden to wear Democratic party badges, newspapers sympathetic to the Copperhead position were banned from college libraries, students were forbidden to give what were judged to be disloyal talks, and boards of trustees tightened their control over administrators and professors who might take stands seen as disloyal to the Union.[198] In other words, as often happens in such periods, a kind of self-censorship occurred within private institutions. Other than direct government censorship, northern mobs ransacked the offices of several Copperhead newspapers. At least two of the mobs were led by Union soldiers, and the federal government looked the other way.[199] So, in the North during the war there was not intense suppression—officially or unofficially—of the press, except for that of the Copperheads. The most noteworthy question of civil liberties during the war, however, was Lincoln's order suppressing habeas corpus and mandating military trials for treasonous or disloyal activity (the latter included "discouraging" enlistments and "resisting militia drafts"). The U.S. Government also set up "a secret network of agents and informers whose zeal frequently exceeded their discretion," according to McPherson. Men were detained without trial or even without learning of the charges. In Maryland, numerous public officials were among those held. The intensity of the semi-martial law regimen—held *post hoc* by the Supreme Court to be unconstitutional in places where civilian courts were in operation—was essentially determined by how successful the North's military effort was at any particular time. Some people were arrested just for writing or speaking against the Lincoln administration's war policies or calling for accommodation with the South. The detentions were generally brief, however. Free elections were not interfered with and, in fact, many of Lincoln's political opponents were elected.[200]

In the South, property and economic rights were infringed upon partly because of policies aimed to influence foreign opinion. For example, hundreds of thousands of bales of cotton were destroyed not just to prevent their falling into the hands of the advancing Federals but also in the hopes of swinging England's and France's views about the Confederacy.[201] The former could be judged, in light of republican principles, to be an acceptable reason for such an action in a time of war, but the latter likely could not. Also, when farmers balked at the price the Confederate government offered them for their crops—to be used to feed the army—the government just seized them.[202] This would likely be acceptable only in an extreme situation. Openly pro-Union newspapers like the *Knoxville Whig* were suppressed, but "a moderate amount of freedom of the press" seemed to survive in the Confederacy (although, in fact, most newspapers readily supported the rebellion). As in the North, schools were expected to show to pupils support for the Confederacy and educational materials were altered to that end.[203] Midway through the war, the leaders of the Confederacy proclaimed "defeatist" talk to be seditious and gave President Jefferson Davis the power to suppress it by copying Lincoln and suspending habeas corpus. One former Confederate Congressman was arrested for opposing this, but such actions did not blunt the criticism.[204] Then, there was the notorious Confederate treatment of Union prisoners at the prison camp in Andersonville, Georgia (although there is dispute among historians about whether *in general* there was deliberate mistreatment of Union prisoners other than Negro soldiers in Confederate prison camps).[205]

Overall it should be concluded that while such crucial rights in the Founders' pantheon as freedom of the press and speech and property rights were violated—sometimes outrageously—on both sides, in light of the wartime situation there was not a threat to republican government, especially since—this obviously pertains only to the North—once the war was over they ceased. Suspension of habeas corpus is, by itself, not a violation of Founding principles. After all, Article I, Section Nine, Sub-Section 2 of the Constitution—referred to above—specifically permits this "when in cases of rebellion or invasion the public safety may require it." The extent to which it was applied may have gone too far at times, even considering Lincoln's valid belief that the slowness of civil justice could have hampered the war effort and that he needed at times to violate certain specific provisions of the Constitution in order to save constitutional government.[206]

The Reconstruction period spanned all the topics contained in the title of this section: it witnessed important legal developments, challenges to the rule of law, the politicization of law, issues of citizen rights, and of course crucial questions concerning the position of the Negro under American law. The most significant legal changes were the adding of the Thirteenth, Fourteenth, and Fifteenth Amendments to the Constitution, briefly discussed above. The Civil Rights Act of 1875, near the end of Reconstruction (also discussed above), would have been a sweeping legal change if it had stood up. The rule of law in the South during Reconstruction was seriously threatened by the rise of the Ku Klux Klan, which sought "social and economic control of the black population" with intimidation and violence. The Republican authorities in the South tried to control the Klan, but could not partly because it used intimidation against them also. The state militias were unreliable and the occupying U.S. Army troops were ill-equipped to deal with the Klan's guerilla tactics. Civil justice also was ineffective because of Klan intimidation, which included murdering witnesses.[207] In light of all this, something approaching martial law seemed to be the only solution. Although this seemed to step outside of the rule of law, it was done so the rule of law could be provided for. As stated above, the suspension of habeas corpus was constitutionally permitted during times of insurrection; this was virtually a continuation of the insurrection after the official surrender at Appomattox. Such suspension was authorized in Congress's Ku Klux Klan Act of 1871, which gave teeth to an 1870 statute passed to enforce the Fifteenth Amendment. The Act also gave the president the authority to use the army to enforce voting rights. Grant instituted a vigorous enforcement action, with the aim of destroying the Klan. The Klan was effectively suppressed for a period of years and the South was peaceful during the rest of the Reconstruction period.[208] In spite of this, the right of Negro suffrage was not effectuated in practice.

As the 1870s went on, support for the Reconstruction policy within the Republican party—which was its main political champion, as the Democrats, even in the North, were consistent opponents of Reconstruction legislation—and in the North generally waned. In this changing political climate, federal funding for enforcement lessened and the Supreme Court made it more legally difficult. The stage was set for: rendering ineffectual the Fourteenth and Fifteenth Amendments as tools to insure Negro equality, the federal government's almost completely turning away from southern race relations questions, the onset of the Jim Crow regime, and the actual repeal of most of the Reconstruction era enforcement legislation late in the century—all of which meant a substantial loss of the rule of law respecting the Negro.[209] Overall, when we consider the situation of the Negro's rights during the Reconstruction period, we must say that they were tentative, incomplete, and precarious—even at their best. Morality, concern for the common good, civic friendship, civility, a spirit of justice, appropriate freedom, even the basic spirit of the gentleman were greatly lacking in the Reconstruction South and afterwards (as we shall see) regarding treatment of the Negro and those who defended him. Of course, the failure to apply these principles to the Negro during the Founding Era (when most were enslaved) was *its* great deficiency.

Apart from the realm of legal rights, Negro education took hold and made slow but definite gains throughout the rest of the century—in spite of its being segregated, first de facto then later de jure.[210] As the years of Reconstruction progressed, the economic situation of southern Negroes—at least in terms of per capita income—increased markedly (although that could be expected since they had no place to go but up from their slavery situation). Still, their standard of living was only half as good as that of southern Caucasians (who were much poorer after the War than before). A significant minority of southern Negro farmers owned their land.[211] As far as northern Negroes were concerned, the federal constitutional and legal changes, directed especially to the South, helped them as well. Eric Foner tells us that the Reconstruction period "witnessed astonishing advances in the political, civil, and social rights of Northern blacks," even though their economic situation was not very good.[212] Things were improving for Negroes economically, but they shared with an increasing number of the working class an insufficiency of material well-being caused by an inadequate distribution of wealth—conditions that the Founding culture opposed.

Probably the overriding political event during Reconstruction was the impeachment and trial of Andrew Johnson. The Tenure of Office Act was, in light of what was said about the removal power in Chapter 3, a clear-cut case of politicizing the law. It violated the historic understanding of presidential power and was without constitutional foundation. It was a hammer to hold over Johnson's head to make him accept and implement Congressional Reconstruction policy; it was a law aimed at achieving a pure political objective.[213] Its enactment despite the long-standing constitutional understanding makes it appear also as an exercise of arbitrary legislative power, offensive to the rule of law. These were the very kind of political and legal practices that the Founding conception of government repudiated.

The cases of selective application of law, twisting of the law, and ignoring of established constitutional principles and of treaty provisions to achieve political ends had precedents that went back to the Federalist Period, as we recall from the earlier chapters. The Jacksonian Era had provided the most outrageous previous examples with Jackson's ordering of the withdrawal of the federal deposits from the Second Bank of the United States and his unilateral abrogation of the Indian treaties, the latter even involving the repudiation of a Supreme Court decision. The flouting of the rule of law in this period—e.g., the blatant refusal to honor the terms of the Treaty of Guadalupe Hidalgo and the poor treatment of the Mexicans now in American territory—almost directly built upon that precedent. While Lincoln's suspension of habeas corpus seems to receive the most criticism during the Civil War, it is the actions surrounding the Mexican War that were the most abusive of the rule of law. Concerning situations where liberties were truly compromised, we have seen that both the Federalist and Jeffersonian periods provided precedents for the selective upholding of rights that—along with the fervor of wartime—may have made such actions easier in this period.

Economics, Government Economic Policy, Labor and Class Questions, and Technological Developments. In the antebellum period, there were economic ups and downs with a general increase in prosperity, significant technological developments, and improvement both for agricultural interests and labor. There were good harvests and crop prices in the 1850s and machinery was improving. The increased value of farmland holdings also benefited agricultural prosperity.[214] The strength of the industrial labor movement was increasing, partly because of labor organizing experience brought by new immigrants. Immigrants also helped boost prosperity by providing needed labor for economic development, stimulating land sales, and helping business and industry in other ways. The workday began to be reduced.[215] There were many negative developments regarding the economy and labor, however. First, in spite of the advantages just mentioned, the number of immigrants entering the U.S. tended to depress wages. Overall, increases in wages in the 1850s were not significant. While technology had its economic advantages, it also had its detriments, as seen in he fact that new machinery was eliminating certain categories of jobs. There was much land speculation, particularly with the expansion of railroad construction. There were numerous strikes around the middle of the 1850s because of low wages. The Panic of 1857 caused much unemployment and the fear of unrest.[216] The number of the landless was increasing, and a "system of tenantry" was taking shape that some feared would cause more class division and weaken both patriotism and "the spirit of independence" in the country.[217] In the 1840s New York State was hit by the "Anti-Rent War," which was directed against a leasehold tenure system that Stephen Van Rensselaer had maintained. Basically, in *noblesse oblige* fashion, he had long allowed tenant farmers to occupy his vast Hudson Valley lands even though they could not pay the rents. When his heirs tried to collect long-overdue rents, a veritable rebellion broke out. After much turmoil and violence and the election of local political leaders favorable to the tenants, a settlement was reached.[218] So, one of the last remnants of the hierarchical, organic culture of the colonial and Founding periods—rooted ultimately in an older, medieval ideal— passed away. The tenants wanted to be on their own. They wanted to claim the land as theirs by right, even if they had not met their financial obligations. On the other hand, the Rensselaer heirs were no longer willing to be tolerant of the people their ancestor had traditionally "looked after." The relationship was now seen as one at arm's length; they were two sides in a market arrangement. This was all in line with the democratization, individualism, and market-oriented motivations that had taken deep root in the Jacksonian Era.

When the Civil War began, stock prices soared and speculation increased even further. The latter was stimulated by currency inflation caused by the flooding of the country with paper money (this was done in both North and South, but was worse in the latter).[219] This was not sufficient to enable the North to meet the costs of the war, however, and the first personal income tax was imposed in 1861 and remained in force until well into Reconstruction.[220] The war, as might be expected, stimulated mineral industries, livestock production, and railroad building. It also "accelerated the spread of mechanization and the factory system."[221] By the end of the war decade, fully two-thirds of the American workforce was working for someone else or another economic entity, instead of being self-employed.[222] The Civil War saw a continuation of the labor unrest and strike activity of the 1850s, although once wages caught up with the price increases of the war the strikes tailed off. The labor movement came out of the war with an enhanced strength and spirit of solidarity, at least among skilled workers.[223] Larger railroads absorbed smaller ones, and the first signs of oligopoly and monopoly that would rear their heads later in the century were seen.[224] A corrupt practice developed between some politicians and businessmen wherein the former passed on inside information about political and military developments that enabled the latter to reap massive—and excessive—profits. War profiteering caused public resentment, particularly in the West where people judged—in Jacksonian fashion—that they were facing eastern exploitation. They believed that wartime federal taxation and tariff policies were further evidence of this. The war brought a certain prosperity—as wartime production usually does—but at the cost of unprecedented inflation.[225] While the workforce in the North was becoming modernized, adapting to new technology and new occupations, that of the South lagged behind. The old manorial idea typified the South's plantation-based economy, so that even updated agricultural practices were unknown.[226] The manorial system was related to Van Rensselaer's leasehold tenure system—except for the crucial difference that one used free labor and the other slave—and it persisted as the standard in the South when the latter was an almost isolated remnant in the North. Of course, after the Civil War ended the plantation system declined and the last substantial connection with the economic arrangements of the colonial and Founding Eras was broken. Also after the war, the South gradually joined the commercial and—much later on—industrial orders fashioned around the principles of the modern market economy that had implanted themselves decisively in the Jacksonian Era.

The economic momentum of the wartime North continued after the war. By 1873, U.S, industrial production was 75% above where it stood at the war's end—mostly because of expansion in the North. During this same period, there was an enormous increase in railroad construction and, of course, in 1869 track was finally connected from coast to coast.[227] Real wages continued to increase, and so did the strength of organized labor. Large-scale factories had emerged, but were a long way from dominating the economy since there were still a multitude of small enterprises (although as noted below a stronger push toward monopoly began after 1873).[228] The postwar labor movement, which focused on skilled workers, was based on the traditional belief in artisan independence (in spite of the fact that, as noted, such artisans were shrinking in number). Against the deepening laissez faire ethic, the labor unions tried to promote—in line with the Founding Era's culture—the notions of "mutuality," or cooperation, and that ethics cannot be divorced from economics. Some labor spokesmen even talked of a "family wage" and "worker-owned cooperatives,"[229] anticipating Catholic social thought and arrangements such as employee stock-ownership plans in the next century. There was further progress, both in legislation and the early collective bargaining, in achieving a shorter workday.[230] After these positive results came the Panic of 1873, which "ushered in...a downturn that lasted, with intermittent periods of recovery, nearly to the end of the century." Foner calls it the "first great crisis of industrial capitalism." It caused major urban unemployment and heightened class conflict.[231] The labor movement's cooperative aims were replaced by confrontation and demands for an expanded governmental role in the economy. For their part, major business leaders moved more toward monopoly to lower costs.[232] What Foner calls the "proliferation" of vagrancy laws—which, effectively, made unemployment a crime—seemed to be another indication of inter-class hostility, as well as presenting possible civil liberties problems.[233] The Panic also affected the agrarian sector, badly hurting small farms and prompting the beginnings of the "protest" type of reform movement referred to earlier with the Grangers, etc.[234] The Panic was caused by the overexpansion of railroad building, paid for by speculative credit (which is often the culprit in causing economic crises). When railroads began defaulting on their bonds it had a ripple effect in the economy, affecting other industries that in some way—even if distantly—were connected to the railroads.[235] In the South, in spite of the overall decline of the plantation system, cotton plantations continued. Various forms of tenancy developed, especially sharecropping (although as we have stated, a sizable minority of southern Negroes owned their own land). In fact, cotton continued to dominate southern agriculture. Sharecropping was not slavery, and agricultural workers' income increased because of good cotton prices, but practically speaking it tied the former slaves to another's land, kept them in debt, and made it difficult for them to get land of their own.[236] Industrial growth developed slowly in the post-war South, and did not come into its own until the 1880s.[237] Changes in law in the South by Reconstruction Era state governments to make it more hospitable to corporate development no doubt helped to spur this on.[238]

The above economic developments of this period—i.e., economic relationships becoming almost exclusively defined by the market, the increasing loss of independence of most economic actors, the rise of increasingly distinctive and rigid economic classes, the trend toward bigness, and the appearance of frequent economy-wide "crises" due in substantial part to speculation—implanted themselves in a decisive way as economic features, in differing degrees, of American economic life up to the present time.

We can mention certain highlights of economic policy during the antebellum and Civil War periods. When they briefly held power in the early 1840s, the Whigs had sought to reestablish a national bank. Tyler proved to be an immovable obstacle to this.[239] The Whigs and Tyler joined to enact a bankruptcy act and a homestead act that paved the way for the much more sweeping homestead act enacted during the Lincoln administration.[240] Polk opposed a protective tariff and, as noted, signed the Walker Tariff bill to sharply lower the rates of the existing revenue-raising tariff.[241] It was also mentioned that he agreed to a law restoring the Independent Treasury System. During the 1840s, technological advancements in transportation and communications aided the causes of the economy, national integration, expansionism, and even reform. Goods, military forces, and ideas all moved and were disseminated more easily.[242] During the Civil War, of course, much economic policy on both sides was geared to the war effort. The reliance of the Confederacy on printing money—fiat currency—to finance its military effort caused crippling inflation. Taxes played only a small role and could not be effectively collected.[243] The Union avoided an excessive reliance on fiat currency, effectively imposed taxes (including an income tax, as noted above), and was successful at war bond sales. The result was that it largely avoided inflation, and while real wages declined they quickly recouped after the war. It also successfully avoided shortages of civilian goods; it was able "to produce both guns and butter."[244] This is why McPherson concludes, "Unsound financial policies were one cause of Confederate defeat."[245] The beginnings of the economic or social regulatory state during Reconstruction were noted above. The start of a movement, which would culminate late in the Progressive Era with the establishment of the Federal Reserve System, to have the federal government regulate the money supply began with the "Inflation Bill" of 1874, a reaction to the Panic of 1873. It would also have provided for the circulation of more paper money or fiat currency. Grant vetoed it, however. Some say his veto signaled the beginning of the Republican party's alignment with big business interests.[246] It was noted that southern Reconstruction governments made pro-business legal changes. They worked hard to attract northern capital and extended various kinds of aid to railroads to help further develop the transportation infrastructure that manufacturing would need.[247] Both taxes and the public debt considerably increased in a number of northern states because of the new responsibilities above.[248] This was a departure from both the reluctance about debt by the Founders and the outright frugality of both the Jeffersonians and Jacksonians.

While the economic developments of this long period featured certain things that called to mind the cooperative, communal spirit and orientation of the Founding Era that all have a sufficiency of material goods (e.g., the initial "mutuality" approach of the labor movement and the increasing wage levels before the Panic), its predominant thrust was a deepening of the contrary trends that became firmly implanted in Jacksonian times. So, episodes like the Anti-

Rent War, the woes of the working class, the fact that most workers were now wage earners employed by others, and an increase in monopoly illustrated the loss of the sense of the social obligation of property, the moral limit on economic freedom and the belief that all should be able to take part in wealth accumulation, the ability of the individual to shape his economic destiny, and a decentralized condition of economic life. Many could not share in property ownership, the economic norm of the Founding culture, although the advent of homesteading would help restore that. The actions of both sides in the Anti-Rent War and in the mostly conflictual ongoing character of labor-business relations underscored the loss of: civic friendship, concern for the general welfare, civility, fair-dealing, and even the norms of promise-keeping, industry, and honesty. The class differences that first began to appear during the Jacksonian Era became the norm as the market economy continued to develop in the direction of economic liberalism and laissez faire. The situation of conflict between business and labor and the haves and the have-nots that was by now the usual feature of American economic life may not have developed just because of the breakdown of the Founding Era's economic and other cultural norms, but also because of a suspicion that slowly was engendered between these different classes by the political rhetoric that began in the Jeffersonian period and intensified during the Jacksonian Era. The excessive profit-making and business-government collusion affronted the public morality of the Founding culture. The readiness of the Confederacy to turn to fiat currency and the strong push in that direction in the reunited country after the Civil War suggests a loss of the Founding Era's mores of sobriety and responsibility. The higher wartime public debt was understandable, but its growth on the state level after the war demonstrated the same problem and directly went against the Founding Fathers' admonition against excessive public debt.

We have seen how a substantial number of the principles and conditions the Founding Fathers set forth as necessary to sustain a democratic republic and the mores of their culture from which that kind of political order emerged were downplayed or ignored, to at least some degree, during 1840-1877 in the topical areas examined. The former included separation of powers and checks and balances (threatened for a time, but not permanently, even while the period ended with Congressional supremacy); judicial independence (largely because of the Supreme Court's own actions, although again not permanently); and federalism (a centrifugal threat before the Civil War and a centripetal one afterwards). These institutional norms and arrangements in the end survived intact, and in the next period examined (1877-1920) the weakened presidency and Supreme Court decisively reasserted themselves. The matters of strictly democratic principles and practice in the Founders' thought (as categorized in Chapter 1) suffered ongoing damage: promotion of the common good, popular sovereignty and other dimensions of the democratic side of the regime (too expansive in the Dorr Rebellion and, in a sense, in southern secession and too restrictive in some of the intellectual currents and reform movements), equality (again, embraced too sweepingly or downplayed), the need for a natural aristocracy (either ignored entirely—as started to be the practice in the Jacksonian Era—or convoluted by certain thinkers or governmental reformers), and the embodiment of a higher law in the laws of the state (we noted the stirrings of positivism in the *Dred Scott* opinion and the views of the church-state separationists). In terms of rights, we saw that freedom of speech and press were violated in some instances, but not in a serious or enduring way (the foundation for a future distortion of them, however, was present in certain of the views of the church-state separationists). The protection of the rights of life, liberty, and even property were especially threatened in the case of the Negro, and after the cessation of the Reconstruction regime would be an ongoing reality. The most outrageous case of the subversion of property rights involved the landholders of the former Mexican territories. The specter of a threat to religious liberty emerged from the views of some of the separationists. In terms of the conduct of government, the public debt became a problem. On social conditions, we saw the declining sense of the importance of religion and the realization of its necessity in public life in American thought and popular movements, as well as a relativization of religious truth. The outright insistence on a secular state was seen for the first time. We witnessed the beginning of a decline of the type of education that shaped leaders in the Founding Era. The beginnings of moral relativism also were noted, and for the first time America saw the strong advocacy of the notion that morality without religion was possible. America witnessed a level of political corruption and politics-business collusion not previously seen. The decline of morality in terms of urban crime and conflict, family breakdown, and sexual immorality was more manifest than at any previous time. Respect for law and the rule of law faced attack on many fronts throughout this period (from the Mexican War developments, to urban riots, to the different expressions of vigilantism, to the flouting of the law by urban juvenile delinquents). We saw that these cultural norms of the Founding Era were weakened or not paid sufficient attention to: the four related norms of sexual morality, marital fidelity, family stability, and respectfulness and obedience of children; the avoidance of luxury (in many ways); temperance or moderation; the willingness to engage in self-sacrifice; the related norms of honesty, truth-telling, and promise-keeping; a spirit of cooperation and community; respect for the general welfare and the maintenance of a community of friendship; a constraining of any tendency toward individualism; civility and the spirit of the gentleman; a voluntary melding of different groups of people; a respect for social hierarchy within the context of a relative economic equality and a middle class condition; such related economic conditions as widespread land ownership and a sharing in needed material goods, a decentralized structure of economic enterprise, economic independence and the ability to shape one's economic destiny (but with a realization that there must be limits on economic freedom); the norms of social obligation of property use and an equal opportunity of all to accumulate wealth; sobriety and industriousness; and justice. We have also noted a veering away from the realist perspective about man and life of both the Founding Fathers and their culture. While the intense American faith in man's possibilities, notwithstanding this realism, continued—

the intellectual currents and the reform movements of the period deviated from this in both directions of excessive optimism and pessimism.

We have also noted how a number of these deviations from the Founding continued developments from the two previous historical periods examined.

In terms of the factors the thinkers identified in Chapter 1 as causing the decline of political orders, we can say that while only one was acutely evident—social conflict and revolution, because of the conflict over slavery and the Civil War—a number were seen either in an incipient or limited way that would flourish later in American history: changes away from traditional belief in religion, the pursuit of luxury, a relativistic moral outlook, an emphasis on bigness (seen in economics), urbanization (developing progressively), and the descent of politics into a struggle for power (enhanced over what had previously been seen in American history).

The points of possible weakness in the Founding vision suggested in Chapter 1 that were evident by developments in the period 1840-1877 were these: the lack of a sound understanding of the common good due to insufficient philosophical reflection; the seeds of an expanded individualism; the discernment of the natural law and its application left to private judgment and the ensuing implantation of the seeds of positivism; orientation to the higher things not brought into the constitutional order; the absence of a reliable way to bring forth a natural aristocracy; the lack of a reliable means to shape virtue and its downplaying as a concern of politics; an insufficient emphasis on justice and community (in the Founders' thought, even if the slack was picked up by the broader cultural norms); the stress on a commercial republic leading to economic laissez faire; the downplaying of statesmanship due to an excessive stress on institutional factors; too rigid of a view of federalism (although what was seen was more of a confused view that erred in both centripetal and centrifugal directions at different times); the failure to see the centrality of the family to the political order (to a limited degree, at least); and a lack of sufficient awareness of the likelihood of the hold of religion weakening so that the resultant worldview and morality would also be prone to weaken.

Notes

1. See "James K. Polk," http://en.wikipedia.org/wiki/James_K._Polk; Internet; accessed Nov. 18, 2008.

2. The Missouri Compromise had forbidden slavery in the Louisiana Purchase territory above 36° 30′ north latitude.

3. 60 U.S. 393.

4. James M. McPherson, *Ordeal by Fire: The Civil War and Reconstruction* (3rd edn.; N.Y.: McGraw-Hill, 2001), 128-129.

5. Ibid., 348.

6. Ibid., 589.

7. "Ulysses S. Grant," http://en.wikipedia.org/wiki/Ulysses_S._Grant; Internet; accessed Nov. 18, 2008.

8. "Crédit Mobilier of America Scandal," http://en.wikipedia.org/wiki/Crédit_ Mobilier_of_America_scandal; Inter-net; accessed Nov. 18, 2008.

9. "Ulysses S. Grant."

10. McPherson, 645-646.

11. Howe, 836.

12. McPherson, 44-46, 51-52.

13. Howe, 574.

14. Ibid., 577.

15. Wilentz, 701.

16. Howe, 577.

17. Ibid., 579.

18. Wilentz. 701.

19. Ibid., 572.

20. Howe, 688-689.

21. Ibid., 578.

22. Ibid., 796.

23. Ibid., 599-602. The quotation is from 601.

24. Wilentz, 661.

25. Howe, 819.

26. Philip Hamburger, *Separation of Church and State* (Cambridge, Mass.: Harvard University Press, 2002), 216-217.

27. Ibid., 211.

28. Howe, 771-772, 781. The quotations are all from 771-772.

29. Madison, Federalist 10, 58.

30. Wilentz, 586-587.

31. Ibid., 770.

32. Ibid., 717.

33. See, e.g., Harry V. Jaffa, *Crisis of the House Divided: An Interpretation of the Issues in the Lincoln-Douglas Debates* (Chicago: University of Chicago Press [Phoenix Books], 1959, 1982), 347-349.

34. Wilentz, 770.

35. Ibid., 686-687, 692, 716-719, 751.

36. Ibid., 645-653.

37. Ibid., 690-691.

38. Ibid., 718.

39. Ibid., 666.

40. Howe, 584.

41. Ibid., 827.

42. Ibid.

43. Wilentz, passim.

44. McPherson, 295-298.

45. See Abraham Lincoln, "The Gettysburg Address."

46. Eric Foner, *Reconstruction: America's Unfinished Revolution, 1863-1877* (N.Y.: Harper & Row, 1988), 484-486, 466-468. The quotation is from 484.

47. The pertinent passage of this constitutional provision reads as follows: "The Congress shall have the power to dispose of and make all needful rules and regulation respecting the territory or other property belonging to the United States..."

48. Howe, 707-708.

49. Ibid., 796.

50. McPherson, 146.

51. The language of these constitutional provisions—the first specifically gives Congress the power "[t]o provide for calling forth the militia to...suppress insurrections and repel invasions," and the second restricting the power of Congress to provide for the suspension of habeas corpus "unless when in cases of rebellion or invasion the public safety may require it"—implicitly, but clearly, indicates that the federal government has the power to act to put down insurrection of any sort. On the intention of the Founding Fathers to forge a national government strong enough to deal with insurrections like Shays' Rebellion, see Ryan J. Barilleaux, *American Government in Action: Principle, Process, Politics* (Upper Saddle River, N.J.: Prentice-Hall, 1996), 31.

52. Howe, 693.

53. Ibid., 583.

54. Fehrenbacher, 7.

55. 41 U.S. 539.

56. "Personal Liberty Laws," http://en.wikipedia.org/wiki/Personal_liberty_laws; Internet; accessed Nov. 27, 2008.

57. McPherson, 542-544, 552-553.

58. Richard D. Brown, *Modernization: The Transformation of American Life 1600-1865* (Prospect Heights, Ill.: Waveland Press, 1976), 176

59. Howe, 707-708.

60. Wilentz, 652.

61 "History of Education in the United States," http://en.wikipedia.org/wiki/History_of_education_in_the_United _States; Internet; accessed Nov. 27, 2008; Donald G. Tewksbury, *The Founding of American Colleges and Universities Before the Civil War* (Hamden, Conn.: Archon Books, 1965), 167-168 (chart).

62. "Compulsory School Attendance," http://www.faqs.org/childhood/Ch-Co/Compulsory-School-Attendance.html; "State Compulsory School Attendance Laws," http://www.infoplease.com/ipa/A0112617.html; Internet; both accessed Dec. 3, 2008.

63. Foner, 469.

64. Howe, 604-605.

65. Ibid, 605.

66. McPherson, 620-621.

67. The best scholarly evidence indicates that the framers of the Fourteenth Amendment were unable among themselves to resolve whether the amendment was intended to outlaw all forms of racial discrimination, including in public education, and left the matter open for later constitutional development (which happened in the 1950s) (see: Alexander M. Bickel, "The Original Understanding and the Segregation Decision," *Harvard Law Review*, vol. 69, no. 1 [1955]; Robert G. McCloskey, *The American Supreme Court* [Chicago: University of Chicago Press, 1960], 246). The point here is that very shortly after the Amendment's ratification, it would have been difficult to claim that its framers intended to end public school racial discrimination.

68. Foner, 384-389 474-475.

69. "John Tyler," http://en.wikipedia.org/wiki/John_Tyler; Internet; accessed Nov. 27, 2008.

70. Howe, 812.

71. Hamilton, Federalist 78, 504.

72. Walter Ehrlich, "Scott v. Sandford," in Kermit L. Hall, ed., *The Oxford Companion to the Supreme Court of the United States* (N.Y.: Oxford University Press, 1992), 759.

73. McCloskey, 96. McCloskey's comment about the Court's fall after the decision is striking: "In 1850 the Court enjoyed popular support as nearly unanimous as can ever

be expected in a diverse democratic society. It was playing a modest but significant part in the affairs of the nation. Eight years later, it had forfeited that position, and its role in the American polity was nearly negligible."

74. McPherson, 576.

75. *"Ex parte McCardle,"* http://en.wikipedia.org/wiki/Ex_Parte_McCardle; Internet; accessed Dec. 8, 2008.

76. Brown, 182.

77. See "Reconstruction Era of the United States," http://en.wikipedia.org/wiki/ Reconstruction_era_of_the_United_States; Internet; accessed Nov. 28, 2008.

78. Sidney M. Milkis and Michael Nelson, *The American Presidency: Origins and Development, 1776-1998* (3rd edn.; Washington, D.C.: CQ Press, 1999), 170-171.

79. Ibid., 171-173.

80. See Woodrow Wilson, *Congressional Government: A Study in American Politics* (N.Y.: Houghton Mifflin, 1885).

81. McPherson, 577.

82. See John F. Kennedy, *Profiles in Courage* (N.Y.: Harper & Row, 1955, 1961), 142.

83. McPherson, 576-577.

84. Howe, 491.

85. Ibid., 750.

86. Ibid., 791.

87. Wilentz, 604-605.

88. McPherson, 179-180.

89. Ibid., 184-186.

90. Ibid., 191-192.

91. Ibid., 523.

92. "Timeline of United States Diplomatic History," http://en.wikipedia.org/wiki/ Timeline_of_United_States_diplomatic_history; Internet; accessed Nov. 29, 2008.

93. Wilentz, 661-662.

94. "Mexican-American War," http://en.wikipedia.org/wiki/Mexican-American_War; Internet; accessed Nov. 30, 2008.

95. Howe, 735-737. The first quotation is from 735 and the second from 736.

96. Ibid., 702.

97. Ibid., 708, 757.

98. Ibid., 683, 798-799, 830, 852.

99. Ibid., 811; Wilentz, 669.

100. Howe, 675.

101. Ibid., 762.

102. Ibid., 705-706, 798.

103. Ibid., 703-704; Fehrenbacher, 121.

104. Faulkner, 250, 550.

105. Ibid., 546, 543.

106. Ibid., 552-553.

107. "Westward Migration," http://www.answers.com/topic/westward-migration; Internet; accessed Dec. 2, 2008.

108. "Timeline of Western Migration and U.S. Expansion," http://www. flowofhistory.org/themes/movement_settlement/westerntimeline.php; Internet; accessed Dec. 2, 2008. About the Homestead Act, see "Homestead Act," http://en.wikipedia. org/wiki/Homestead _Act; Internet; accessed Dec. 2, 2008.

109. Patrick J. Buchanan, *A Republic, Not an Empire: Reclaiming America's Destiny* (Washington, D.C.: Regnery, 1999), 61.

110. Fehrenbacher, 105.

111. James M. Volo and Dorothy Denneen Volo, *Family Life in 19th Century America* (Westport, Conn.: Greenwood, 2007), x.

112. Fehrenbacher does point out, however, that while this mobility weakened the ties of the extended family, it also had the effect of "broaden[ing] the scope of family connections" as the members of (especially) prominent families tended to have significant influence, almost independently of each other, in different parts of the country (Fehrenbacher, 105).

113. Ibid., 106.

114. Volo and Volo, 316.

115. Fehrenbacher., 105; Arthur Charles Cole, *The Irrepressible Conflict, 1850-1865* (N.Y.: Macmillan, 1934), 153-154.

116. Cole, 171-172.

117. Ibid., 172-173.

118. Ibid., 169-170. The quotation is from 169.

119. Ibid., 208.

120. Berkin, Miller, Cherny, and Gormly, 553.

121. Howe, 453.

122. Ibid., 455,

123. "History of Education in the United States"; accessed Dec. 3, 2008.

124. See Brown, 138-140.

125. Fehrenbacher, 109.

126. Brown, 139.

127. "Liberal Arts Colleges—History of Liberal Arts Colleges, Characteristics of Liberal Arts Colleges," http://education.stateuniversity.com/pages/2179/Liberal-Arts-Colleges.html; Internet; accessed Dec. 3, 2008; Brown, 103.

128. Berkin, Miller, Cherny, and Gormly, 553.

129. Brown, 153.

130. Fehrenbacher, 104.

131. Ibid., 111.

132. Ibid., 112.

133. Ibid.

134. Ibid., 110.

135. Ibid.

136. McPherson, 594-595; Foner, 493.

137. Foner, 492-493, 499.

138. Ibid., 498-499.

139. Ibid., 519.

140. Even if the Founders upheld—or, it might be more correct to say, tolerated—slavery (where justice was even more offended by men owning other men than in the post-slavery Reconstruction Era where free Negroes were facing intimidation and abusive treatment), they and even the southern slaveholders did not at their time defend slavery as a positive good (as we have said before). There also was not the kind of viciousness as was seen with the Ku Klux Klan activity, lynchings, and widespread vigilante violence at this time.

141. Brown, 170-171.

142. Ibid., 173-174.

143. Ibid., 175.

144. Ibid., 186.
145. Cole, 198-201.
146. Ibid., 156.
147. Howe, 819.
148. Cole, 156, 157, 158.
149. Ibid., 153-154.
150. Ibid., 160.
151. James A. Morone, *Hellfire Nation: The Politics of Sin in American History* (New Haven, Conn.: Yale University Press, 2003), 224.
152. Ibid., 225-227.
153. About the Tweed ring, see Sean Dennis Cashman, *America in the Gilded Age: From the Death of Lincoln to the Rise of Theodore Roosevelt* (3rd edn.; N.Y.: New York University Press, 1993), 151-158.
154. Howe, 795-796; Fehrenbacher, 108.
155. Hamburger, 222.
156. See Krason, *The Public Order and the Sacred Order*, 193, 196.
157. Hamburger, 228-229.
158. Ibid., 233, 243.
159. Ibid, 253.
160. Ibid., 254.
161. Ibid., 256.
162. Ibid., 270-275.
163. Ibid., 304-306. The quotation is from 306.
164. Ibid., 330-331.
165. Ibid., 296-297.
166. Krason, *The Public Order and the Sacred Order*, 274; Peter J. Ferrara, *Religion and the Constitution: A Reinterpretation* (Washington, D.C.: Free Congress Foundation, 1983), 42.
167. See William Bentley Ball, *Mere Creatures of the State? Education, Religion, and the Courts—A View from the Courtroom* (Notre Dame, Ind.: Crisis Books, 1994), 8-9.
168. Howe, 826-827.
169. "Know Nothing," http://en.wikipedia.org/wiki/Know-Nothing_movement; Internet; accessed Dec. 5, 2008.
170. Ibid.; Faulkner, 345.
171. Howe, 581.
172. Ibid., 818.
173. Berkin, Miller, Cherny, and Gormly, 543-546, 588-590; Cashman, 95.
174. Foner, 262-264; McPherson, 585-586,606-607.
175. McPherson, 636-637.
176. See: John Stuart Mill, *On Liberty* (Middlesex, England: Penguin [Pelican Classics], 1974); Tocqueville, I, ii, 246-261; II, i, 435-436.
177. Beitzinger, 337-341, 348-353, 360-361. The quotations are from 360.
178. Howe, 613-615.
179. Ibid., 624.
180. Beitzinger, 346.
181. Howe, 620 (he particularly attributes these latter views to Emerson).
182. Beitzinger, 384-385.
183. Ibid., 282; "Concurrent Majority," http://en.wikipedia.org/wiki/Concurrent_majority; Internet; accessed Dec. 6, 2008.

184. Beitzinger, 383-384.

185. Ibid., 391, 392.

186. Ibid., 387-388.

187. Ibid., 391. These thinkers included Francis Lieber, Brownson (whose view was noted in Chapter 3), and John A. Jameson.

188. Beitzinger, 400-401.

189. Ibid., 400-402. The quotations are from 400 and 401.

190. See Kirk, *The Roots of American Order*, 397-400.

191. "Texas," http://en.wikipedia.org/wiki/Texas; Internet; accessed Nov. 20, 2008.

192. Howe, 698-699.

193. "Texas Annexation," http://en.wikipedia.org/wiki/Texas_Annexation; Internet; accessed Nov. 20, 2008.

194. Howe, 809-811.

195. Cole, 268-269, 273-274; Wilentz, 645-647, 676.

196. Wilenz, 648, 651.

197. Cole, 373.

198. Ibid., 370-371.

199. McPherson, 317.

200. Ibid., 317-319. The quotations are on 317. The Supreme Court case referred to is *Ex parte Milligan*, 71 U.S. 2 (1866).

201. Cole, 384.

202. McPherson, 411.

203. Cole, 389-390.

204. Ibid., 402.

205. McPherson, 485-487.

206. Ibid., 318.

207. Ibid., 606-608. The quotation is from 607.

208. Ibid., 609-610.

209. Ibid., 635-638; 659. This assessment of the Democratic party is seen consistently throughout McPherson's discussion of the Reconstruction period in Part Three of his book, 531-661.

210. Ibid., 617-620.

211. Ibid., 623-624.

212. Foner, 471-472. The quotation is from 471.

213. The latter is clearly indicated by what McPherson says. See McPherson, 566.

214. Cole, 101, 106-107,112,

215. Ibid., 140, 148, 150, 151.

216. Ibid., 114, 150-151, 153.

217. Ibid., 117.

218. Wilentz, 591; Eric Ford, "New York's Anti-Rent War," *Contemporary Review* (June 2002), http://findarticles.com/p/articles/mi_m2242/is_1637_280/ai_88702710/pg_1?tag=artBody;col1; Internet; accessed Dec. 10, 2008.

219. Cole, 346-348.

220. "Income Tax in the United States," http://en.wikipedia.org/wiki/Income_tax_in_the_United_States#Early_Federal_income_taxes; Internet; accessed Dec. 9, 2008.

221. McPherson, 402.

222. Ibid., 407.

223. Ibid., 406-407.

224. Cole, 351-353, 355.

225. Ibid., 347, 359-360.

226. Brown, 146,
227. Foner, 461.
228. Ibid., 475.
229. Ibid., 477-479.
230. Ibid., 481.
231. Ibid., 512-513. The quotations are from 512.
232. Ibid., 513-514.
233. Ibid., 519.
234. Ibid., 515-516.
235. Ibid., 512.
236. Ibid., 404-409.
237. McPherson, 652-653.
238. Foner, 381.
239. Wilentz, 524.
240. Howe, 592-593.
241. Wilentz, 579-580.
242. Howe, 703-704, 835, 851-852.
243. McPherson, 220-222
244. See ibid., 222-226.
245. Ibid., 222.
246. Foner, 521-522.
247. Ibid., 381
248. Ibid., 469.

CHAPTER 5

1877-1920: THE GILDED AGE, THE PROGRESSIVE ERA, AND WORLD WAR I

With the end of Reconstruction, America went through a period of massive industrialization, economic transformation marked by the growth of large-scale corporate enterprise, unprecedented levels of foreign immigration and internal migration, the growth of a new urban-based culture, attendant socio-economic problems, and a resulting strong impulse to address these with major reforms pushed by a new political movements. The overwhelming focus on domestic concerns was interrupted briefly by the Spanish-American War and a renewed American policy of expansion—this time outside of the continental U.S.—and then was pushed aside completely by the outbreak of the Great War in Europe. At the end of this forty-three-year period, the large-scale changes that had taken place in many ways had reshaped the face of American life and fashioned the nation of the twentieth century. We examine in this chapter how these profound changes affected the character of the democratic republic of the Founding and if the cultural norms sustaining it were still viable. As in previous chapters, we focus on several important topical areas—many the same or similar as previously—for our inquiry: economics, economic policy, employer-labor relations, and technological developments (which have a particular prominence in this period since so many of the changes are economic in character); politics, political movements, and political and governmental reform; relations among the three branches of the federal government, federal-state relations, the role and powers of government; foreign affairs and expansionism; legal developments and citizen rights; immigration and inter-group conflict, urban life, western settlement, and the frontier; socio-cultural developments; and currents in political thought.

Economics,   Economic   Policy,   Employer-Labor   Relations,   and Technological Developments. Fundamental changes in economics and financial transactions took deep hold during the Gilded Age. The following are some of these, according to Thomas C. Cochran and William Miller. The corporation was now "the dominant type of business organization." Corporate property was "represented not by land or other physical assets, but by negotiable paper easily convertible into other types of negotiable paper." Business transactions were increasingly being carried out in stocks and bonds, "in *rights* to property rather than in physical property." Negotiable instruments, such as "checks cancelled through central clearinghouses, were used rather than cumbersome commercial paper." The means of "contract making" was considerably streamlined and made easier.[1] The separation of ownership and control became the norm for business corporations. Effectively, the managers became the controllers and the true owners; the stockholders, who were spread far and wide, could do little to control them or change their decisions. Further, as the large corporate arrangements of the Gilded Age developed and before government tried to significantly regulate their activities the public was unable to have any influence over them except to not patronize them (which was not always a feasible course of action).[2] Competition became cutthroat. Initially, pooling agreements administered by trade associations sought to remedy this and insure sufficient profits for all the member firms by such efforts as controlling output, dividing the market among the members, establishing consolidated marketing outlets, and controlling patents. This failed probably because, according to Cochran and Miller, such arrangements flew in the face of Anglo-American law, which viewed them as a restraint on trade.[3] Ultimately, bankers became the arbiters. Since the scale of production and activity demanded large amounts of funds, credit became increasingly important and bankers "could impose order"— taming reckless and destructive competition—in exchange for credit.[4] As time went on, bankers came to exercise considerable influence over many corporations. Large corporations sought to combine with each other as another way of escaping the "competitive anarchy." They often "overcapitalized" the new merged corporation. In some cases, financiers such as Jay Gould got control of companies—what nowadays would be called "hostile takeovers"—forced mergers, and overcapitalized them purely for the sake of enhancing his profits. These were clearly examples of what ethicians would call unproductive investment. Bankers had to come into the picture, in a sense, to "rescue" these overcapitalized corporations, and demanded some control over their management. The result was many interlocking directorates and large holding companies controlled by many of the same giants of banking, such as J.P. Morgan.[5] In a related fashion, the trust also appeared. In the strict sense of the term, it was a device to concentrate the management of a group of companies in the hands of a single board of directors.[6] The stock speculation that was rife in these overcapitalizations helped—along with railroad overbuilding, as with the Panic of 1873—to bring on the Panic of 1893.[7]

Corporate consolidation became standard procedure for the great bankers; as far as they were concerned, it was the only way to insure "order in mature capitalist society." They even were willing to make damaging economic choices for companies—such as forcing profitable ones to take on bankrupt properties— or to get involved in "endless litigation" if it meant achieving a perceived needed consolidation.[8] Even though they knew only banking, they came to exercise more and more control over the production, transportation, and service sectors of the economy. Cochran and Miller argue that they contributed little to the development and advancement of these other sectors. Among other things, they "bureaucratized" them in such a way as to stymie innovation.[9]

By way of analysis, we can make several points. First, while popular sovereignty still ruled in terms of leaders being brought forth by elections, in a broader sense popular sovereignty was harmed by the fact that until government regulation began the public, as noted, could not even check the activities of the great corporate entities that shaped such an important part of American life, the economy. Moreover, one might also say that the spirit of popular sovereignty certainly did not seem to carry over to the economy much, as seen by the separation of ownership and control within corporations (i.e., the stockholders were the corporate equivalent of voters in political life, but as noted had virtually no influence). At least, this went directly contrary to the economic arrangements of the Founding culture. Second, the big corporations and their managers seemed focused merely on their own ends, on profit, not at all on the common good that the Founding Fathers said had to be stressed to sustain a democratic republic. What was apparent was the kind of self-serving individualism that the Founding and its culture had rejected. Third, this also meant—as what follows makes even clearer—that there was an absence of a sense of the social obligation of property so evident in Founding times. Fourth, the deliberate overcapitalization machinations of people like Jay Gould seem offensive to the Founding culture's insistence on fair-dealing. There was an air of manipulation that seems even to be against the standards of honesty and propriety. The Founding Era's economic views rejected things that were of the nature of unproductive investment. Fifth, the bigness of economic entities and increasing centralization—discussed more below—was completely contrary to the economics of the Founding Era. Sixth, the whole approach to economics and the very obsession with bigness suggests a disregard of the temperance of Founding culture. Seventh, allowing these kinds of economic changes to take place without any significant opposition from government until later in the 1877-1920 period was contrary to the role understood for government in the Founding Era. Eighth, the apparent suppression of innovation by the sometimes banker-imposed bureaucratization of business was contrary to the spirit of initiative fostered in the Founding Era's culture. Finally, in spite of all of these troublesome points of comparison, there is no doubt that much industry, sacrifice, self-directedness, initiative, courage, and practical intelligence—other qualities characteristic of the Founding culture—were exhibited in abundance by the usually self-made men who built up their companies and areas of the economy and became captains of industry.

The general push toward consolidation and "bigness" in economic enterprise did not happen just because of the desire to restrain excessive competition or speculative intentions. Among other advantages, bigness or monopolistic/oligopolistic position within an industry made possible: control over supply and demand (and prices and profits); savings in purchasing raw materials and capital goods; and ease in getting credit, marketing products, and overcoming seasonal fluctuations.[10] Thus, efficiency, keeping costs low, and economizing became key considerations—utilitarian, to be sure, but understandable. Cochran and Miller contend that such a utilitarian mindset about the conduct of business and economic affairs, coupled with the general prevalence of laissez faire ideas, helped to intensify labor-management conflict and eventually paved the way for a regime of government regulation and intervention. In spite of some of major strikes in the 1870s and 1880s— discussed below—they argue that the two sides might have worked out a somewhat more cooperative set of arrangements after the 1890s had not the next serious economic downturn, the Panic of 1907, intervened and widened the gap between profits and wages, reduced productive investment, and threatened jobs because of more efficient productive processes. In addition, the consumer-oriented economy was advancing further, at the expense of a production orientation. This demanded higher wages in order to create a wide enough distribution of consumer purchasing power. Contrary fundamental trends in the economy were on a collision course: some employers saw the utilitarian value of higher wages, but it was negated by the equally utilitarian efficiency focus that increased productivity faster than wages; production was increased, but consumption of what was produced lagged because workers could not afford to buy it; employers tried to curb job turnover, but their laissez faire perspective made them oppose unionization that almost axiomatically would have been the pathway to greater work force stability.[11] Some employers sought labor harmony by "scientific approaches" to management (i.e., as developed by Frederick W. Taylor, American business history's first management "guru")—just as we shall see that "scientific" and technical approaches were brought into politics and government administration in the Progressive Era—but that failed. So did "welfare capitalism," where employers half-heartedly set up profit-sharing and bargain stock-purchase programs for workers but in return cut wages and regimented the workers more. This was hardly in the spirit of concern for worker welfare and employer-worker cooperation.[12] These efforts were probably doomed from the start because the laissez faire perspective of the employers— i.e., the economic liberalism that shaped their understanding—made them unable to see, first, that the problem was not fundamentally a scientific and technical one, but a *moral* one, and as such they were not free to be cavalier, conditional, or insufficiently sincere in their concern about employee welfare. Parenthetically, employers' captivation by scientific management was little more than an extension of their stress on efficiency; they could not appreciate that process was less important than moral ends. In the end, the employers circled the wagons even more tightly, any hopes of a more cooperative spirit went by the boards, and instead of economic and labor problems being largely worked out amicably in the private sector, government would ultimately be turned to. The New Deal would come along later to make government the arbiter and substitute provider for the workers and the dispossessed that secure employment and a just wage would have been able to take care of.

Laissez faire and the efficiency orientation aside, perhaps the very bigness that had come to dominate much of the American economy made unlikely the forging of a true cooperative arrangement. The employer-employee relationship was no longer a personal one in large-scale industry. Plant managers did not even have much authority over their individual plants, since geographically distant executives—or even bankers, as noted—wielded the true authority and set personnel policies for the company or even a set of consolidated companies.[13] Under such circumstances, it is not difficult to see how workers come to be viewed as essentially factors in production.

We have noted that labor organizations developed much earlier in the nineteenth century. With the sweeping industrialization, corporate consolidation, and breakdown of close employer-employee relationships above one would expect that attempts at unionization would have expanded in the Gilded Age. At the beginning of the period examined in this chapter was the Railway Strike of 1877; labor historian Joseph J. Rayback calls it "the most violent and significant labor upheaval in the nineteenth century."[14] It started when a series of developments, including a *35%* wage cut over three years by the Reading Railroad, "combined to produce a bitter resentment among eastern railway workers." The strike spread from one line to another in the East and Midwest, witnessed massive confrontations, battles between strikers and militias and federal troops, and widespread disruption of rail traffic and destruction. By the time it was finally put down, ten million dollars of property damage and hundreds of deaths had occurred.[15] During the next several years, the cause of workers was tenuous. In the wake of the strike labor struggled for public support. No labor organization gained substantial strength, and while there were some localized strike victories most were failures. Labor turned to political action, and had some successes on the local level but could not exert broader influence.[16] The Knights of Labor, formed in the 1860s, finally—for a time—emerged as the predominant force in the labor movement. After achieving considerable success in a series of strikes in 1884 directed especially against the railroads, they consolidated the disparate elements of American labor with the aim of establishing one all-encompassing union for all types of workers. They were able to capitalize on deep frustration among the industrial working class. The Knights advocated arbitration for labor disputes, an eight-hour workday, worker health and safety legislation, and also sought fundamental change in economic life by establishing various cooperative ventures in order to free workers from the wage labor system. They did not achieve much success in the latter, but it gained them further support as workers struggled during the Panic of 1884. While they reached a membership of over 700,000 by the following year, they and the fortunes of labor once more declined.[17] The Haymarket Affair of 1886—when a bomb exploded in Chicago during a massive strike, and killed a policeman—turned the tide, again, against labor.[18] The Knights, who were not involved in the criminal act, were one of the casualties. Unskilled workers also believed that the Knights' leadership did not help them enough. The Knights declined and virtually disappeared by 1900.[19] The American Federation of Labor (A.F. of L.) succeeded the Knights as the most prominent force in the labor movement. This happened during the last decade of the nineteenth and first decade of the twentieth centuries, amidst a series of major setbacks for the labor movement. These included the Homestead Strike of 1892 and other mostly unsuccessful steel strikes, the mining strikes in the West and South in 1892, the Pullman Strike of 1894, and Supreme Court decisions that held that both labor boycotts of company products and strikes that disrupted interstate commerce violated the Sherman Anti-Trust Act (which had been enacted ostensibly to check business monopolies). There were some labor victories, however. Perhaps the most noteworthy of them was the Anthracite Coal Strike of 1902. The A.F. of L.'s membership fluctuated during these two decades, but by 1910 it was still much larger than the Knights' membership had ever been, and it grew considerably more by the time of American entry into World War I.[20] Rayback catalogs the poor conditions of workers during the pre-World War I period: "unbearably long hours, intolerably low wages, unhealthful and unsafe working conditions, lack of sanitary facilities, brutal and avaricious foremen, exploitation through company stores."[21] He also details the way employers responded to labor organizing and strikes: the routine use of strikebreakers (sometimes recruited from overseas), routine use of injunctions and state and local militia to put down strikes, incarcerating strikers in crowded jails and bull pens and herding them into rail cars and depositing them in the middle of the desert during western mining strikes, brutality by hired company guards, even murder. Some of the most serious clashes occurred in the mining industry in both the eastern and western U.S.[22] Of course, not all employers acted this way or companies featured these conditions. Nor were the actions of strikers and union organizers always above reproach. Some elements of the labor movement were anarcho-syndicalist, socialist, and Marxist and predisposed against corporate enterprise and even private economic activity in general.[23] For example, Philip Taft and Philip Ross chronicled the history of labor violence in this and following periods in a study for the National Commission on the Causes and Prevention of Violence in 1969.[24] Still, during the pre-World War I period, in general, management treatment of workers can at best be said to have been unsatisfactory, unjust, and undignified. It was a period of intense conflict in labor-management relations.

Progressivism, or the Progressive Movement, of course, was one of the new reform movements of this period. George Brown Tindall and David E. Shi write that it was "so varied and comprehensive that it almost defies definition." They "crusade[d] against the abuses of urban political bosses and corporate robber barons," seeking "greater democracy and social justice, honest government, more effective regulation of business, and a revived commitment to public service."[25] Its ranks were heavily made up of the educated classes of America.[26] While the Progressive Movement was not coterminous with the labor movement, it joined the efforts of the latter in helping to enact a substantial amount of labor legislation, especially on the state level. This included such subjects as child labor, women's working conditions, minimum wages and maximum hours, workplace safety, and workmen's compensation. Enforcement was often uneven or ineffective, however, and unfavorable judicial decisions became obstacles.[27] Progressive efforts also helped forge federal legislation on such matters as child labor, labor conditions in the District of Columbia, an eight-hour workday and workmen's compensation for federal employees and contractors, an eight-hour workday for railroad workers, railway disputes and labor conditions generally, the establishment of a Department of Labor which provided conciliation services for labor disputes, and clarification of the Sherman Anti-Trust Act to provide that it did not apply to labor unions.[28] During the years of American involvement in World War I, the Wilson administration was intent on insuring that labor problems not disrupt war-related production. It was very responsive to union requests; adopted the wage, hours, and working conditions standards of localities where contract work was being done; established acceptable pay scales and other compensation for seamen in the shipping industry; recognized the right of collective bargaining; and set up mechanisms to address labor disputes.[29] At the same time and after the conclusion of the War in 1919, the federal government cracked down on the more radical elements in the labor movement, as part of a general suppression of political radicals, on loyalty grounds (mentioned below). The 1920s were to bring a decline in the fortunes of organized labor. This will be discussed in the next chapter.

Meanwhile, the period from 1877 to 1920 presented serious problems for the agricultural sector of the economy. The last thirty years of the century experienced a long-term decline in commodity prices, which Tindall and Shi say was "the product of domestic overproduction and growing international competition for world markets." Overproduction was caused somewhat by the opening up of more and more western lands to farming, and by new technologies in transportation and communications that made it possible to bring more and more output to an increased number of markets. The effect was lowered farm prices. Other factors contributing to the troublesome economic situation of the farmers were high railroad rates and processing costs, high tariff rates (which resulted in higher costs for farm equipment and tighter circulation of U.S. currency abroad so that foreign buyers had a more difficult time purchasing American crops), and the persistent problem of farm debt. Farmers argued that as individual operators they could not get the favorable price treatment from railroads and other entities that big business enterprises could exact.[30] They also claimed that they were hampered by an insufficiency of currency in circulation, which is why they became advocates of paper money. This became a major focal point of their discontent and they saw creditor interests as behind the tight money policy.[31] Like labor, their response was to organize as best they could in their situation as individual family farmers. There were three main expressions of the farmers' organizing effort at different periods: the Granger Movement, which lasted mostly for the roughly twenty-year period from 1867 to 1884; the Farmers' Alliance, which picked up from the Granger Movement and lasted for the next five years or so; and the Populist party, which took over from the Farmers Alliances, reached its high point in the 1890s, and survived through most of the first decade of the twentieth century.[32] The Grangers promoted farmer-owned cooperatives for buying and selling, somewhat along the lines of what the Knights of Labor tried to do for workers. They became indirectly involved in politics in the Midwest through different third parties like the Greenback party, which briefly showed political strength, and secured passage of railroad rate regulation—"Granger Laws"—in certain states.[33] The Farmers' Alliance was especially strong in the South and the Great Plains. The Alliance was a movement concerned about fostering personal virtue among rural people, as well as economic justice. They picked up on the cooperatives idea of the Granger Movement as a way of securing farmers' independence from financial institutions, but did not succeed. They unsuccessfully sought legislation to receive federal government loans at very low interest and to store their crops in government warehouses. They worked mostly within the Democratic party—with some success in the South—until the emergence of the Populist party.[34] Major meetings of representatives of various farm, labor, and reform organizations in 1891 and 1892 brought the party into existence. Their platform called for the federal loan and warehousing legislation just mentioned, free and unlimited coinage of silver (which they believed would elevate the economic condition of the masses and provide jobs for western miners), nationalization of the hated railroads and of telephone and telegraph systems, the eight-hour workday, and restrictions on immigration (which was popular with many workers and unions because of the belief that new immigrants threatened their jobs and wage levels.).[35] The Populist party had some limited success in the elections of 1892 and 1894, but did not succeed in winning over the urban-based workingman and—not surprisingly, in light of the latter views—immigrants.[36] In 1896, they supported the Democratic presidential candidate, William Jennings Bryan who supported most of their agenda and made silver availability a central theme. The Populist party sharply declined after this.

The following points of comparison are in order. First, while we said that the Founding Era certainly embraced a norm of commercial efficiency, this period's excessive fixation on efficiency and narrowly technical and amoral treatment of economics was in opposition to its principles. Second, the intense labor-employer conflict was also contrary to it in many ways: the lack of cooperativeness, the lack of concern for the community, and the absence of civic friendship and civility (and in many of the strikes and clashes, the lack of even basic self-restraint). Third, the employers' frequent unwillingness to provide a just wage and attend to workers' welfare and their tendency to treat them essentially as a factor in production specifically offended the belief that all had a right to secure needed goods, the notion of a social obligation of property, the concern for basic justice, the opportunity to allow others to share sufficiently in material goods, and the spirit of being one's brother's keeper that animated Founding Era culture. The fact that these conditions were allowed to occur underscored how far American culture had deviated from the understanding that economic freedom must have proper limitations. Fourth, the fashioning of a consumer culture, or a consumption-driven economy, seemed likely to undermine the old norm of thrift. The disregard of the agrarian sector would have been unthinkable to the Founding Era, since most people then were farmers. It further exhibited the absence of community, civic friendship, understanding of the common good, attentiveness to the "brother's keeper" ethic and the dangers of great wealth disparity, and beliefs that there are proper limits to economic freedom, that all should be able to secure needed material goods, and that all should have the opportunity to accumulate wealth. It is noteworthy that—in contrast to the direction that many reform efforts went later in the 1877-1920 period (see below)—the Grangers did not just engage in social protest and even the fostering of economic self-help, but tried to promote the personal virtue of their members. This was in line with the thinking of the Founding Fathers and their era—which was at the foundation of their understanding of what insured the viability of the American and any democratic republic—that men's souls must be kept in the proper order.

Illustrating the marginalization of workers, farmers, and immigrants was the vast wealth disparity of the time. Around 1900, the overwhelming amount of wealth in the U.S. was in the hands of about 10 per cent of the population.[37] This, of course, strikingly went against the arrangements of the Founding culture, where there were no great inequalities and no significant concentration of wealth. Indeed, it seemed to offend the very principle of limited equality that the Founders themselves held to be necessary for a democratic republic. The middle class society of the Founding Era seemed to have at least greatly diminished. What this also meant was that many were property-less. This was a condition very much against the convictions of the Founding Era. There seemed to be little attention to the Founding Fathers' awareness, mentioned in Chapter 1, that conflict between the rich and poor—the "haves" and "have-nots"—had historically been the kiss of death for republics.

The period from 1877 to 1920 was, of course, a time of rapidly expanding technology, which was much of the basis for the fast growing economy. Rayback says that the period beginning in 1890 was one of "ever-growing domination by the machine." Such sources of power as coal, natural gas, petroleum, and hydroelectricity became standard.[38] The early part of this period saw the substantial expansion of the telegraph network,[39] and around the same time the telephone, electric lights, the phonograph, and typewriters were beginning to gain circulation.[40] The gasoline motor was already patented around this time,[41] and by 1915 nearly a million cars and trucks were manufactured annually.[42] The motor vehicle, of course, would revolutionize transportation. Railroads blanketed the country, and urban rail transit systems flourished.[43] By the end of the century, telephone communication had spread significantly.[44] Radio was invented as early as 1896, and by 1920 had begun to "mushroom…into a great industry."[45] Even by 1890, American "transportation and communication facilities and industry had become…overwhelmingly mechanized."[46] Water transportation declined until around World War I, when new technologies for mechanical loading and unloading helped stimulate its revitalization.[47] Refrigerated railroad cars appeared, corrugated rollers helped stimulate the flour milling industry, new farm implements were invented (we mentioned above how mechanization caused a great expansion of farm output), and the motion picture was developed.[48] In consumer industries, innovations in meat-packing eliminated much wasted meat, bread production became mechanized, the "tin can" was developed to advance food preservation, new machinery substantially increased textile production, innovations in rubber and glass production expanded those industries, and toward the end of the period the mass production of major household appliances began.[49] This is only a small listing. As Tindall and Shi say, "the list of innovations can be extended indefinitely." The face of everyday America was truly remade by the technological innovation of this period, and while it stimulated national wealth and individual and family economic well-being,[50] workers often suffered from it. Mechanization (specifically, the physical dangers presented by the machines themselves and the monotony that came with a highly mechanized production process) led to an explosion of job-related injuries. Employers often would not address this until union pressure and workplace safety laws required them to do so.[51] When new technologies were introduced that could speed up production with fewer workers, workers were let go or reduced to lesser jobs.[52] Thus, more negative features of technological advance became apparent than had been the case in the 1840-1877 period. The fact that they were not readily addressed illustrated many of the same problems that were mentioned above about the treatment of labor in comparison with the principles of the Founding Era culture.

When speaking about government economic policy so far, we have spoken mostly about labor legislation. We now briefly consider the other major types of government economic policy of this period. These can be placed into seven different categories: regulation of business, currency, taxation, tariffs, land and other grant programs, conservation, and other kinds of state and local regulation.

Regarding the regulation of business, we have mentioned already the Sherman Anti-Trust Act, which made illegal any combination or monopoly in restraint of interstate trade or commerce.[53] How effective of a tool it was in stopping monopoly, however, depended on the willingness of individual presidential administrations to enforce it and federal courts to apply it. The Progressives initially were enthusiastic about breaking up big corporations, but later—when they saw the difficulty of doing that and making small firms truly competitive—they moved toward regulation.[54] The problem with that presented itself very quickly, however, and continues to bedevil regulatory efforts until today: people who have been in an industry are the ones who best know about it, so they either get appointed to the regulatory bodies or are heavily consulted in drafting the regulations.[55] In the pre-Progressive days, President Grover Cleveland began the federal regulatory effort by establishing the Interstate Commerce Commission to stop railroads from discriminating in pricing among different customers and commodities and from establishing secret agreements among each other to fix shipping rates.[56] President Theodore Roosevelt undertook the first major federal economic regulatory effort, which included barring rebate arrangements between shippers and railroads; giving the Interstate Commerce Commission the power to set maximum railroad freight rates; regulating pipelines, express companies, bridges, and ferries; meat inspection; and pure food, medicines, and alcohol.[57] Under President William Howard Taft, the federal government initiated telephone and telegraph regulation, and set up agencies to examine mining and child welfare as a prelude to regulation in those areas.[58] Then under President Woodrow Wilson, the Federal Trade Commission was set up to enhance anti-trust enforcement, deal further with the matter of price discrimination, and restrict interlocking directorates among big companies and corporate acquisitions of competing companies' stock.[59] World War I went well beyond regulation to near federal government direction of the economy through the War Industries Board. It set priorities, planned production, fixed prices, and made decisions about allocating raw materials, plant construction, and product design.[60]

There was nothing about business regulation, per se, that offended Founding principles. We saw in Chapter 1 how many laws regulated economic matters in the Founding Era, including restraining monopolies. In fact, a couple of early state constitutions forbade monopolies.[61] One difference between the Founding Era and the period we are examining is that in the former the regulation was local, whereas in the latter it was by states and, increasingly, by the federal government. The situation was different by this time, however, as industrial concerns were often no longer local and many were interstate. It will be recalled that in the name of entrepreneurial freedom, etc., the early Americans would not accept feudal-type restrictions on economic activity, but the regulations of the 1877-1920 period were hardly as sweeping as those. Railroad rate regulation perhaps was close to the latter, but the monopolistic character of the railroads as a shipping agent and their direct effect on the public welfare—especially in agricultural areas—would seemingly have justified such regulation within the Founding economic perspective. While government regulation, then, would have been acceptable, it is questionable that its being the *exclusive* means to control big corporations was—which in the final analysis was the program urged by the Progressives and adopted by the federal government from this time forward. The Founding belief in a decentralized economy and also, in effect, the elimination of monopoly—this would almost certainly include oligopoly, as well—was abandoned (while the economy by this period could not reasonably have been expected to be as decentralized as in the Founding Era, it cannot truly be said that bigness to the degree it existed was inevitable). The sweeping government direction of the economy during World War I *might* have been accepted by the people of the Founding Era, with their practical bent, because of the exigent circumstances—although since the country itself was not in danger of foreign invasion they might not have considered it *enough* of an exigency. When one looks ahead, however, to the New Deal and to the unparalleled federal government attempts to control the economy during the presidencies of George W. Bush and Barack Obama, to address an even less serious economic downturn than the Great Depression, one wonders if the World War I policies did not set a precedent for government action sharply at odds with Founding principles.

As far as currency was concerned, it was mentioned that at different times reformers, representing agrarian interests, called for more readily available silver and paper money. The country went from a limited expansion of silver in 1878 due to too little money in circulation, to a much more readily available silver currency supply in 1890, to a sharp restriction of silver and a restoration of the gold standard in 1893, to the big issue of silver availability in the 1896 election (Bryan's famous "cross of gold" speech) and the federal government's concession that a strict gold standard limited its ability to met its obligations (and its having to take on more debt to do so).[62] The "free silver" issue declined in importance after the 1896 election, but under Wilson currency questions were addressed in a different way. The Federal Reserve System was established to address the nagging problem of lack of a sufficient money supply, with its effects on purchasing power. To sustain the money supply, it established a paper currency—Federal Reserve Notes—backed up by a combination of government gold reserves, commercial paper, and promissory notes signed by borrowers. Effectively, this was the beginning of the notion of a currency whose value was maintained by the very confidence people had in the government to back up its money. It stabilized banking by requiring banks to maintain a certain level of reserves and permitted the new Federal Reserve Board to tighten or loosen credit as the national economic situation dictated.[63]

There seems to be nothing in the Founding understanding that would have precluded an economic policy geared to managing currency. In fact, if the objective was to put the government on a sound financial footing and help insure sound banking and financial practices in general then it was very much in line with Founding concerns. If the Federal Reserve Board's regulation of credit would have the effect of encouraging people to turn to credit too much and encourage individual and family debt, it would go against Founding cultural practices of thrift and frugality. As far as the existence of the Federal Reserve itself was concerned, it was like the Bank of the United States, although with more sweeping powers. Chapter 2 argued that the Bank raised no constitutional problems, although the question that might be raised here is whether the creation of the Federal Reserve offended popular sovereignty and even checks and balances, since it was removed from politics and direct political control and given such substantial monetary and other economic powers.

As far as taxation was concerned, the main development during this period concerned the federal income tax. As mentioned in the last chapter, an income tax had been enacted during the Civil War to raise funds for the Union war effort and expired afterwards. The revenue problems that Cleveland encountered prompted him to turn to that precedent to enact a peacetime income tax. Its 2% rate fell on only 10% of households. However, it was declared unconstitutional by the Supreme Court in 1895 because it was not apportioned among the states on the basis of population.[64] The decision was effectively overturned in 1913 by the Sixteenth Amendment to the Constitution. Faced with increased federal responsibilities in light of Progressive Era legislation, the federal government needed another, regular source of revenue.

As far as the states were concerned, income taxes were a thing of the future. They and their local governments relied heavily on the property tax, mostly on real property but with some personal property taxed also. All property owners were subject to it, although enforcement was often uneven and not always fair. For example, favored business corporations often received exemptions. Also sometimes county assessors undervalued property in their areas and let more of the burden be borne by other parts of the state. The taxing of interstate businesses, like railroads, was complicated, and their tax burden varied greatly at different points along their systems.[65]

In light of these additional revenue needs, it was not surprising that tariff policy was a concern throughout this period. It was also an issue because some believed that the prevailing high tariffs were raising prices and hurting the economy. This motivated President Chester A. Arthur to set up a commission on tariff revision in 1882. Cleveland strongly advocated tariff reduction, but was unsuccessful in bringing it about during his first term. When Benjamin Harrison came to power (Cleveland's two terms were separated by Harrison's presidency), he raised rates so high on some goods that the federal government went into deficit.[66] Congress finally passed what he considered a compromise-ridden, and thus inadequate, reduction bill during his second term. After his election in 1896, McKinley—a firm believer in the economic advantages of tariffs—raised the rates again. After his reelection in 1900, he called for an international movement toward something like "free trade," but that rang hollow.[67] Finally, under Wilson the Underwood Tariff of 1913 cut rates in the face of weakened trade during World War I, but the institution of the income tax made tariffs less important as a federal revenue source.[68]

Nothing made a federal income tax, per se, problematical in light of the Founding. One might even argue that since it initially fell only on the highest income groups it helped advance the Founding Fathers' restrained notion of equality and limit the potential for have/have-not conflict (and, thereby, in the long run perhaps encourage civic friendship). Nevertheless, there is another line of analysis about this: True, the federal government needed a more reliable income stream, but once the tax was enacted and current needs met, there was nothing that stopped the federal government to keep adding to the matters it spent money on and raising the tax rates and expanding the elements in the population it taxed to get it. Indeed, that is what happened as American history progressed. One wonders if this did not open the way as time went on for, first, more debt which the Founders were so concerned about (since once ongoing spending commitments are made, standing revenue sources often prove inadequate to meet them) and, second, more and more taxation to deal with that debt (the Obama administration, for example, called for increased taxes specifically for this purpose[69]). We should recall from Chapter 1 that Jefferson said that what followed from government debt was "wretchedness and oppression." The carelessness about economic policy was seen further in the tendency for most of this period to persist with high tariffs even though they had a negative economic effect.

Land grants, as had been the case for decades, and other grants played an important part in government economic policy. The grants under the Homestead Act continued and, in fact, the Enlarged Homestead Act was passed in 1909.[70] In 1877, the Desert Land Act helped to claim desert lands for agriculture with grants to prospective farmers. Other federal land grant programs to miners and settlers who planted timber on part of their land, which were enacted in the decade or so prior to 1877, were also continued.[71] Wilson's administration also saw the beginning of the federal grants-in-aid programs that are so abundant in the present-day—and have probably been the main basis for the federal government's regulation of so many areas of American life. Wilson set up grants for farm demonstration programs under the control of land-grant colleges, and matching grants to states for highway construction. He also established direct loan programs for farmers.[72] Still, while the federal role was increasing (for example, by 1920 eleven grant programs had been created and $30 million of federal funds were being expended),[73] over 60% of governmental spending and taxing was by state and local governments and over 75% of all public employees worked for the latter levels of government.[74]

Over time, however, the federal grant programs helped diminish state power and arguably have weakened the federal system that obviously was such a central feature of the American democratic republic and that the Founding Fathers believed it played a crucial role in sustaining it. They have increasingly helped to bring about the kind of political centralization that the Founders eschewed. Many grants go to state governments, which they have a hard time refusing even though attached conditions often restrict their decision-making authority. Grants that go directly to individuals or private entities may withdraw an area of regulatory or policy oversight from the states. Some over the years have even gone to local governments directly, which has limited states' political authority over what their instrumentalities do. Moreover, with grants over time going to so many types of activities we have witnessed the federal government stretching itself well beyond the large national concerns that the Founding Fathers anticipated. These crucial developments began with the Wilson administration.

While the federal government had begun establishing national parks (i.e., areas protected from development) with Yellowstone in 1872, it was Theodore Roosevelt who began federal conservation efforts in earnest. He substantially expanded the national park and wildlife refuge system, used legislation passed under Benjamin Harrison to protect millions of acres from development, and set up a National Conservation Commission that then became a prototype for state commissions. He showed that the full weight of the federal government was behind conservation by his convening of the 1908 White House Conference on Conservation.[75] Taft followed up on this by gaining from Congress broad presidential authority to protect public lands. He also intervened to stop oil exploration on public lands and engineered passage of a law to protect land in Appalachia.[76]

As far as other types of state and local regulation were concerned, this period saw the burgeoning of professional licensure laws in the states. The first ones appeared in the decade after the Civil War, and they were becoming standard for professions such as medicine by the 1890s. The first municipal building code was enacted before the Civil War. Concerns about both worker and fire protection caused local governments to tighten up on these codes during the period from 1877 to 1920.[77] Probably the most sweeping and personally regimenting and intrusive government regulation of the Progressive Era was the ratification of the Eighteenth Amendment (Prohibition) in 1919, which culminated a century of efforts by temperance and prohibition advocates. In a contrary direction, state power to invoke eminent domain was subjected to constitutional restraint when the Supreme Court held that the "takings" clause of the Fifth Amendment applied to the states by virtue of the Fourteenth Amendment.[78]

While we have said that the Founding Era stressed the social use of property and such matters as eminent domain seem to be sanctioned by the Constitution, there has been an odyssey at the state and local level—beginning in this period—of attempts at tight control of private property use through building codes, zoning (mentioned below), and the like. This arguably has gone beyond what the Founding Era considered acceptable regulation and arguably compromises the fundamental right to property so cherished then. By the late nineteenth century, state and local governments were expanding the use of eminent domain[79]—and were arguably utilizing it for purposes that went beyond traditional common law restraints. Recently in U.S. history, we have even witnessed the practice of governmental taking of private property for private uses (claiming, with the sanction of the Supreme Court,[80] that since the uses will help the economy and thus redound to the public welfare the traditional requirement of a "public purpose" for a taking is met). This is a distortion of the meaning that the Founding Era had of the public welfare or public good. The problem with the notion of alcohol prohibition was discussed in Chapter 4. The use of law to shape moral behavior—even though the behavior frequently enough, but not necessarily, had social implications—was not unknown in the Founding Era, but such a sweeping restraint on a national scale was unknown in the Founding Era and would have been rejected as an excessive exercise of governmental, and certainly federal, power.

In closing this section, it must be said that while the 1840-1877 period set down the basic character of the later American economy the 1877-1920 period solidified and substantially expanded it. It also established the modern American regulatory state, especially at the federal level, and the positive role of government to act to secure the general welfare in some sense. The New Deal was to expand that considerably and the Great Society even more.

Politics, Political Movements, and Political and Governmental Reform. The above discussion of economics has already noted a number of things about the politics of the 1977-1920 period. The Republicans controlled the presidency throughout most of this period, interrupted only by Cleveland in the middle and Wilson at the end. Nevertheless, the Democrats did well in losing presidential elections, partly because after 1876 they monopolized politics in most southern and border states. Further, from the mid-1870s until the mid-1890s Congress changed hands several times.[81] Divided government was as much the norm as not during the Taft and Wilson presidencies. Perhaps this relatively competitive situation between the two parties was what led to the high voter turnout around the country during this period (70-80%).[82]

The Reconstruction Era corruption and influence peddling discussed in the last chapter continued into the Gilded Age, and the business-government collusion added to it. In 1877, the investigative John Jay report of the New York Custom House "substantiated widespread allegations of bribery and corruption."

The troublesome spoils system kept defying reform until things reached a breaking point with the assassination of President James Garfield in 1881 by a disappointed, unbalanced office seeker. In the same year, revelations came out about bribery in the awarding of contracts for western mail delivery. In 1884, a pattern of corruption and extortion in the U.S. Marshal Service came to light.[83] At that time, state legislatures still elected U.S. senators. Party leadership gained increasingly tight control over the legislatures, and they exacted payoffs from wealthy men seeking Senate seats. The Senate came to represent well-heeled economic interests. Large companies poured substantial funds into political campaigns. Corporations extended all sorts of financial rewards to politicians for supporting them. What today would be understood to be conflict of interest was rife.[84] As Leonard D. White puts it, "The decline in public esteem of the party system was alarming."[85] White argues that corruption at the federal level grew out of local corruption, caused especially by the local party machines, since both state and federal officials depended upon these machines to get elected.[86] Government-business corruption was also abundant on the local level, through such practices as the use of inspectors or threats to withhold services to harass businesses into making illegal payments and the granting of franchises and special favors in return for payoffs.[87] Obviously, corruption of any kind in politics damages the common good, frustrates the cause of frugality in government, is an official embodiment of the disregard for honesty, fair-dealing, and promise-keeping (i.e., the implicit promise of public officials to the people to carry out their duties with integrity), makes private advancement as opposed to the public welfare paramount, and shows pathetically how the desire for personal luxury overrides all else. It was an utter affront to the character of the early Republic at the Founding. The collusion with business additionally underscores the primacy given to greed and naked private advancement over the general good. In any event, all these corrupt political developments stimulated a movement toward limiting party influence by ending or restricting the spoils system and establishing a well-functioning civil service system, an aim of reformers for some time. The last chapter pointed out the problematical character of thinking that apolitical technicians could necessarily conduct the affairs of government correctly, but this is what was sought. The Garfield assassination gave the final impetus to significant civil service reform. In 1883, the Pendleton Civil Service Act was enacted. It established an independent civil service commission to oversee a federal merit system and insulate it from political party pressure. Initially, it covered only a small minority of federal positions, but allowed presidents to extend the coverage.[88] This occurred regularly through a succession of administrations, until by 1909 fully two-thirds of federal employees were under civil service.[89]

The literal buying of Senate seats simply undermined popular sovereignty and the functioning of the republican side of the American democratic republic, which depended upon the Senate in particular to have the wisdom and long-range vision to restrain the democratic impulses of the moment. The result was an institutional diminishment of this crucial role of the institution and a transformation of it into more of a democratic body by the Seventeenth Amendment.

It is striking how politics descended into a kind of struggle for power or the pursuit of money during this period, instead of being focused clearly on the public good and having greater ends for man in mind.[90] This was illustrated by Senator Roscoe Conkling of New York who said about politics, "'Nothing counts except to win.'"[91] Still, there were substantive differences between the two major parties. Republicans for the most part were the party of a high or relatively high tariff, believing that it promoted economic growth. They were the party of temperance and then prohibition, and of public morality and decency— this grew out of the social reform ideas of earlier in the nineteenth century, which were discussed previously. They favored tighter immigration and naturalization controls, as they had absorbed some of the nativist sentiment of the earlier movements. They were the party most supportive of southern Negro concerns, but after 1876 neither party gave much attention to this. They were also more willing to support the concerns of large corporate interests, but neither party until the Progressive Era opposed these.[92] The Democrats, continuing the Jacksonian tradition, were the party of no governmental interference in the economy—they were more laissez faire than the Republicans—or in social relationships and social behavior. To be sure, they did not embrace twenty-first century libertinism (e.g., on sexual questions and reproductive freedom), but believed that such a scheme as alcohol prohibition—which actually represented moralism, instead of something that was per se immoral—was, in the words of one historical source, "a violation of personal liberty." They opposed a protective tariff and strongly favored federal land grants. They opposed activist government of any kind because they believed it furthered the position of the privileged. They continued to see themselves, rightly or wrongly, as the party of the common man. They were strongly for states' rights, including on racial matters (i.e., segregation for them was strictly a state matter).[93] On the latter, they permitted the subversion of basic justice and the main obstacle to civic friendship among the two leading racial groups in the country.

The scurrilous, low political campaigning and emotional appeals to different electoral groups that was seen throughout earlier American history— and intensified with the Jacksonian Era—continued, as illustrated by the 1884 presidential campaign. Senator James Blaine of Maine, the Republican nominee, tried to gain Irish-American votes by using anti-British rhetoric. Cleveland faced the accusation, which may not have been true, that he had fathered an illegitimate child earlier in his political career when he was single. Some Republicans called the Democrats the party of "rum, Romanism, and rebellion."[94] The internecine Republican party conflict between the Stalwarts and the reform-minded Half-Breeds over a period of years can only be called nasty. All this showed a lack of the civic friendship, civility, and honesty that America's Founding culture stressed.

While democratization was the uncontested order of the day, the negative side of it continued to be apparent. Besides the political party manipulation that has been discussed, the lack of the political sophistication of the masses was seen in how the votes of entire electoral blocs shifted because of small comments taken out of context that were made during campaigns.[95] Sean Dennis Cashman refers to a comment by James Bryce, the eminent English commentator on American politics and culture during the Gilded Age, to show how undistinguished the members of Congress were and how much it was at the whim of popular opinion (and, we might add, how far its members had slipped from being anything like a natural aristocracy): "'Europeans think that the legislature ought to consist of the best men in the country, Americans think that it should be a fair average sample of the country. Europeans think that it ought to lead the nation, Americans that it ought to follow the nation.'"[96] White comments that structures and practices of Congress—discussed further below— were somewhat responsible for undercutting the very possibilities of statesmanship.[97] The Progressives had "great faith in democracy,"[98] as was apparent from the political reforms they successfully over time brought about: direct primaries (even the first presidential primaries took place during this period, in 1912), popular election of senators (this was achieved with the Seventeenth Amendment, noted above, which was ratified in 1913), initiative, referendum, and recall (the latter three innovations were adopted in numerous states in different forms).[99] All these things—ultimately widely adopted— weakened the republican character of the U.S., the restraint upon democracy that it will be recalled Federalist 10 insisted was necessary to keep a political order intact. Their support for the Australian (i.e., secret) ballot[100] also might be viewed as a democratizing development—since the masses could now be free to vote without the undue influence of employers and others above them—though it should probably be understood simply as a way to insure basic fairness. On the other hand, such other Progressive reforms as the short ballot—which overturned the Jacksonian scheme of electing as many public positions as possible, and shifted some from elective to appointive—and the commission and council-manager forms of local government seemed to go against the democratic grain.[101] While these latter notions rightly sought to remedy the problem of unqualified people in governmental roles that increasingly required functional expertise, they also reflected the Progressive penchant to seek efficiency. They shared the efficiency perspective of scientific management theory in business and, more fundamentally, of employers (noted above). They saw politics and government—in spite of its claims to be seeking "the moral regeneration of public life"[102]—as an amoral, merely technical matter. In this sense, the Progressive Movement was also not unlike the perspective of the Conkling-type of machine politicians that it claimed to oppose, who divorced politics from moral and human ends. The Progressives thought they could solve the problem of integrity in government by, in some sense, removing integrity as a consideration. The further enhancing of associational activity during the Progressive Era could also be understood as a democratizing development, but it might also be seen as something that further gave rise, over time, to the kind of corrupt and elite-dominated politics that the Progressives decried. This is because some of these associations were, effectively, political interest groups or led to such—in fact, people during this time increasingly "related to politics through organized interest groups" instead of political parties[103]—which the history of American politics has made clear do not necessarily act for the public good. In fact, already during Wilson's presidency there was a Senate investigation of lobbying.[104] The same counter-democratic tendency was the case with the very emphasis on developing a professional civil service. White says that this reform was resisted partly because the spoils system, where a new president brought his own people who shared his political perspective into government, "to many...appeared [to be] the natural order in a republic. It seemed to be one means by which the people ruled." Also, like the jury system, it was a way in which people "participated in the art of government...a school of citizenship."[105]

It is curious that the Progressives never seemed to consider the more moderate change of continuing the spoils system, but specifying minimum background and qualifications for holding different positions. Further, the civil service reforms sought provided for access to government employment on the basis of competitive exams, which one could take right out of college. Was it not possible, however, that people could be highly competent for government service on the basis of previous practical expertise, in politics and otherwise, even if they could not score well enough on an examination? Might they also not be more capable for that employment than the recent untested and inexperienced college graduate? The rigidity of the Progressives' position may actually have achieved less in terms of the competence sought than it might have, and also may have resulted in the substitution of a new "elite"—based upon education and functional expertise, which may not always be the things most needed in government—for the one made up of the political party warhorses who they regarded as corrupt. Indeed, as the Progressives submerged the moral ends of politics with their efficiency obsession, they also sought to solve the problems of politics by ignoring politics and (as stated) treating it as a technical undertaking. The politician should be pushed aside so the technician could master the problems of government.

The supposedly democratically-oriented Progressive reformers could not even bring themselves to embrace the notion of a set term for civil service employment, which was pushed for some years and eluded enactment in 1912 only by virtue of Taft's veto pen. Again, democratic concerns were pushed aside in the interest of the focus on efficiency. The norm of expertise again superseded the norms of representativeness and responsiveness. The complete repudiation of the spoils system, in principle as well as practice on the federal level, arguably went against popular sovereignty. Later, in 1920, the notion of such a limited term for federal employment permanently went by the boards with the enactment of a federal pension system.[106] With that, federal civil servants became, in effect, an interest group seeking to preserve their own jobs. Bureaucratic power, at all levels of government, went from there to become increasingly powerful as American history went on.

Relations among the Three Branches of the Federal Government, Federal-State Relations, and the Role and Powers of Government. We have mentioned the weakness of the presidency over the last third of the nineteenth century, continuing on from its grievous wounding by the near removal of Andrew Johnson. None of the presidents of that time was willing or able to exercise policy leadership, and believed that their role was "simply to administer the government." Congress's role was often excessive even regarding the latter function,[107] though with the Pendleton Act the president gained greater control over executive personnel matters.[108] The president was virtually sidelined in budgeting,[109] and Congress was even "in *de facto* command of the appointing power."[110] Theodore Roosevelt finally reclaimed the lost presidential authority. He asserted "vigorous executive action,"[111] developing a stewardship notion of the presidency where he saw himself as acting directly for the people. He insisted that, "he might do anything not expressly forbidden by the Constitution."[112] He vigorously but carefully enforced anti-trust laws, and showed that he could effectively use both the carrot and the stick to solve problems and accomplish objectives, as when he used the combination of a White House mediation effort and a threat to take over mines to settle the Anthracite Strike of 1902.[113] He was also an assertive and effective legislative leader.[114] His successor, Taft, on the other hand, was not a strong legislative leader, even though (as noted) his presidency was not without legislative accomplishments. He was more inclined to follow the view of the other post-Lincoln Republican presidents that essentially Congress should be the one to craft legislation. This probably helped lead Progressive-inclined Republicans in Congress to revolt against him.[115] Wilson reverted to TR's practice of more vigorous executive leadership, which he had long philosophically believed in. He readily stepped up to a position of legislative and Democratic party leadership. He, of course, had to show foreign policy and military leadership as well later in his presidency. He did not show the same effectiveness in foreign policy leadership in dealing with Congress after the war as he had in passing domestic legislation in his first term, perhaps because by that time he showed less willingness to compromise and less capability in dealing with the opposing party.[116]

Belief about the president's limited role was not the only reason why Congress's power eclipsed his during this period. The presidency was also hampered by an insufficiency of resources and certain practices that had taken hold. The presidential staff was very small, and the Cabinet was not used collectively as a way to advance a national agenda or even as a sounding board about national issues or policy.[117] Actually, presidents may not have had enough time to devote to the serious, ongoing consideration of large issues because they were day-in and day-out confronted by much trivial business—this, in spite of the fact that they generally did not interfere in the everyday affairs of executive branch departments where most executive business was conducted.[118] Then, there were simply temperamental considerations: some presidents by nature were less assertive and willing to be combative than others.

The back-and-forth pattern of American history of one branch of the federal government having preeminence over the others continued.

In spite of the low state of presidential power during much of this period, it was a time when the presidential veto power solidified itself. The Jacksonian view that the president was free to veto measures even if there was no question of constitutionality or threat to executive prerogatives had firmly been accepted at least since Polk's time, but a number of the presidents of this period still were sparing in their use of the veto. In fact, for the first time—as Congress got more and more into the practice of pork barrel spending—there was serious discussion about a presidential line item veto.[119] Overall, however, it was only with TR that separation of powers, in practical terms, was restored with the re-establishment of presidential leadership. The federal government was taking on the character of a mixed government again.

It should be noted that Congress's preeminent power vis-à-vis the executive developed despite its own lack of "order and discipline," at least until it was whipped into shape by powerful Speaker of the House Thomas B. Reed near the end of the century. This concerned the institutional factors that were referred to above as hurting the cause of Congressional statesmanship. White lists them as: excessively decentralized decision-making authority, the same lack of a national outlook that hampered the presidency (which, in its case, may have been due to the excessive influence of the local political machines noted above), an inadequate means of insuring the flow of information, an inability to act in a timely manner, insufficient opportunity for debating alternatives, a weak sense of responsibility, an inability to develop long-term goals, and a lack of confidence in being able to reach solid conclusions.[120] With the liabilities of both political branches, one is lead to think—reinforced by what has been said about excessive political party and big business power—that there was a crisis of national governance during the first half or more of this period. A picture is created of something like the conditions of the Articles of Confederation period that the Founding Fathers sought to remedy.

The political branches also confronted the courts during this period, on both the state and federal levels. Melvin I. Urofsky says, there was a "generally favorable attitude of both state and federal courts toward reform legislation," but "the few major cases that went the other way captured the headlines and made it appear as if all courts stood opposed to the Progressive agenda."[121] He mentions specifically the Supreme Court's weakening of the Sherman Act and the Interstate Commerce Commission, invalidating labor statutes in *Adair v. U.S.*, and striking New York's maximum hours statute in *Lochner v. New York*, discussed below. In 1908, TR attacked the courts "for obstructing badly needed reforms.[122] At the same time, the Court received more public criticism than it had probably since the *Dred Scott* case. Some even attacked the very doctrine of judicial review. There was a move in the Senate to require a Court majority of at least 6-3 to declare any acts unconstitutional. No constitutional or other changes were made to restrict the Court's power. A federal law passed in 1914 permitting discretionary Supreme Court review of decisions of a state's highest court whenever a federal claim was raised; this primarily had the effect of limiting state judicial power. Also on the state level, several states passed judicial recall provisions as a way to check overreaching power in their courts.[123] In some cases, the courts were perhaps overstepping separation of powers, and the mild resistance showed a desire to keep viable the principle of checks and balances and perhaps laid the general groundwork for the more decisive challenge to the judiciary during the New Deal.

As far as federal-state relations during the period from 1877 to 1920 were concerned, two different general approaches were discernible. The first—evident since the beginning of the Republic—was what was called dual federalism, the notion that the national and state governments were equal partners with separate and distinct spheres of authority. Federal power had expanded during the Marshall Court era, as noted, by broad interpretations of the "necessary and proper" clause and implied powers. The two levels of government did not collaborate much and, of course, an ongoing tension occurred over the questions of federal and state prerogatives and, until the Civil War, of the freedom of states to secede from the Union. The second approach, called cooperative federalism, began about halfway through this period (around the turn of the century) and persisted until the 1960s. It was marked by greater cooperation between the levels of the government and saw the beginning and then the continuing expansion of the federal grants-in-aid programs, as mentioned.[124] In the waning decades of dual federalism, the federal government increasingly involved itself in regulatory areas that had previously been exclusively within the purview of the states, as seen in the business regulatory efforts above. When it came to something like protecting racial minority groups, however, there was actually a restricting of federal action from what had occurred in the Reconstruction Era. This was solidified near the end of the era of dual federalism by the Supreme Court's *Plessy v. Ferguson* decision upholding segregation. Cooperative federalism was made more viable by the enhanced federal largesse made possible by the Sixteenth Amendment. TR stressed national power, contending that the approaches to some matters were too decentralized. Wilson sought more active federal-state cooperation, but in a deferential way toward the states.[125] Perhaps the most significant development in the federal-state relationship during this period was the Seventeenth Amendment. In addition to diminishing the Senate's role as a check on popular excesses (as noted), it also weakened the federal character of the Senate. It was sometimes said that under the original Constitution senators were something like ambassadors of their states to the national government. Now, they were no longer elected by the main governmental institution of each state—its legislature—but by the people directly. It could not so clearly be said that they any longer were representatives of the government of a state to Washington, like the ambassadors of the U.S. Government to foreign countries. They were now simply elected officials providing national representation for the people of their state, just as House of Representatives members did for their state or part of it. The Senate now became another national body, not so much a federal one. The drive for the Amendment was understandable, however, in light of the corruption that had set in. Senators had long since ceased to be anything like the natural aristocracy that the Founding Fathers had envisioned and that Tocqueville, in some sense, had observed about them in the 1830s. This underscores the fact that institutions will retain their vitality, charism, and strength only if they are part of a sound culture that brings forth people of solid character into them. Nevertheless, the Amendment might be viewed as signaling the end of one of the two institutional features of the American constitutional order—the electoral college is the other—that held out at least the *possibility* of providing a regular mechanism for bringing forth a natural aristocracy. This is because *in theory* at least they both set up a filtering arrangement to make possible deliberation to bring forth accomplished, worthy men. Also, if the restoration of presidential power reinforced the mixed government character of the American political order, the Amendment somewhat weakened it by making the Senate a more democratic institution.

The Progressive Movement believed that the "scope of local, state, and federal government authority should be expanded" to achieve its objectives stated above.[126] As such, the period witnessed the sharp expansion of the governmental regulatory role discussed above. In a sense, this represented a return to a role seen for government in the Founding Era, but in another way it deviated from that time by expecting that it would *primarily* be government that could be relied upon to solve economic and social problems. In addition to the other areas of regulation, Progressives "wanted municipal or state regulation of public utilities." Although socialism did not advance in the U.S., some Progressives pushed municipal ownership of utilities. Some communities undertook this.[127] While expansion of the role of government and, specifically, the federal government was more substantial than seen before, it is clear from what was said in Chapter 4 that this was not a new phenomenon. It had been slowly taking place through much of the nineteenth century and these developments built on it.

Foreign Affairs and Expansionism. Prompted by an expanded American trade presence in the world, the social Darwinism (discussed below) that took hold among enlightened opinion, and such writings as Josiah Strong's *Our Country* (which promoted previously uncommon missionary activity among Protestants), Alfred Mahan's *The Influence of Seapower Upon History, 1660-1783* (which argued, contrary to long-prevailing opinion, that controlling seaborne commerce was the key to success in war and that this required far-flung naval bases and colonies), and John Fiske's *The Destiny of Man* (which argued, although not because of innate racial reasons, for the superiority of the Anglo-Saxon race) a renewed push for Manifest Destiny took hold.[128] American expansion during the time from 1877-1900 focused on the Pacific region, the Far East, and Latin America, often in competition and conflict with European powers (who were in the midst of an intense race for colonies). In 1878-79, the Samoan islanders entered treaties with the U.S., Britain, and Germany to promote trade, permit them to establish naval bases, and give them rights to intervene diplomatically in case of disputes with other nations. In 1887, the Germans tried to extend their power to establish a protectorate, but ultimately the three countries set up an "uneasy partnership" in the form of a "tripartite protectorate."[129] The American experience in Hawaii had actually begun as early as 1795 when missionaries and agricultural interests started to settle there. In 1875, an agreement favoring Hawaiian sugar imports in the U.S. in exchange for exclusive American naval access and other influence in the Islands was concluded. A series of events occurred in the 1880s and 1890s: American settlers pressured the king to accept a constitution, U.S. withdrawal of the favored treatment for sugar, a rebellion against Queen Liliuokalani by the settlers that was backed up by U.S. Marines, an ensuing proposed treaty of annexation that was rejected by the Cleveland administration when a special commission learned that American sugar interests unhappy about the loss of favored treatment engineered the coup, the proclamation of an independent republic by the rebels after this spurning by Washington, and finally McKinley's maneuvering of the ratification of the treaty in 1898 in the backdrop of the Spanish-American War.[130] In the 1880s and 1890s, there were tensions between the U.S. and Britain about dominion over the Bering Sea, which the U.S. claimed in 1889 as a way of curtailing Canadian seal hunting, and over the Venezuelan-British Guiana boundary dispute (which had some importance because of the discovery of gold in the area, and motivated the U.S. to invoke the Monroe Doctrine). Arbitration treaties ultimately solved both problems.[131]

Of course, the Spanish-American War overshadowed other American foreign policy and expansionistic undertakings during the pre-World War I period. A history of the former is beyond the scope of our inquiry. All we shall say is that American public opinion—encouraged by "yellow journalism"—and economic interests supported the anti-Spain insurrection in Cuba that raged through the second half of the 1890s, and elements in McKinley's Republican party were eager for intervention. Tindall and Shi argue that public opinion, whipped into frenzy for war, may have been the major force in bringing it about. As they say, "Until the 1880's, a certain ambivalence about overseas possessions had checked America's drive to expand. Suddenly, in 1898 and 1899, the inhibitions collapsed." They add that the "chief motive was a sense of outrage at another country's [Spain's] imperialism,"[132] though one wonders, in light of what was said above about the *weltanschauung* that had been developing, if that was just a pretext. The other part of the history that is important is the aftermath. The 1898 Treaty of Paris that ended the war left the U.S. with far-flung colonial possessions, including Cuba (which was granted independence shortly thereafter, in 1900), Puerto Rico, the Philippines (where the war had extended to), and Guam. The U.S. also laid claim to Wake Island in the Pacific and outright annexed some of the Samoan Islands.[133] Typically, what the U.S. sought to do was to spread representative institutions and constitutional government to these new acquisitions, though somewhat contradictorily she put down indigenous independence movements in the meantime and did not hesitate to insure that her military and strategic interests would be satisfied (e.g., establishing bases).[134] McKinley summed up American aims in this policy of imperialism: to vindicate national honor, to open up new commercial opportunities (which European countries in a more "'discreditable'" way would take advantage of if the U.S. did not), to help the colonized peoples become fit for self-government and save them from anarchy, and to "'uplift and civilize and Christianize them'"—especially the Filipinos (ignoring the fact that they were already thoroughly Catholic, thanks to the Spanish).[135] The other example of the expansion of the American presence in Asia during McKinley's administration concerned China, which was the target of European and Japanese imperialism. The British had proposed to the U.S. a common front to protect China from the other powers, but the Senate balked at what it saw as an entangling alliance. The administration came back with the Open Door Policy, which was essentially a unilateral version of the British proposal. It basically called for open trade with China, but not interfering with the "spheres of influence" established by the various powers. According to Tindall and Shi, it was essentially an American admonition without standing in international law, which satisfied American business interests seeking trade and anti-imperialists who were concerned about maintaining "China's territorial integrity." Then the Boxer Rebellion erupted, and the U.S. joined the other European powers and Japan in a military intervention to rescue the besieged foreign embassy compound in Peking.[136]

The critique in light of Founding principles in Chapter 4 of the Manifest Destiny policy applies to the American expansionism of this period. As stated, the desire to have *more* territory represented a kind of lust for the luxury that Founding Era culture was so wary of. It also showed a lack of moderation, simplicity, and self-sacrifice. Further, such imperialism—and we have indicated that in spite of the justifications given, that is what it was—was an aspect of militarism and materialism, factors in regime decline.

TR's administration was known for its "walk softly but carry a big stick" approach in foreign affairs, which included the Roosevelt Corollary to the Monroe Doctrine: the U.S. would intervene first in a problem in the Western Hemisphere to ward off an intervention by outsiders. The U.S. would now become an international policeman, and became more involved in Latin America than ever. Probably the major international undertaking of his administration was commencing the building of the Panama Canal. It occurred after the administration pressured Colombia into a favorable deal for the land to build the canal, which came on the heels of American plotting with disenchanted elements in Panama Province to separate it from that country. Tindall and Shi say that the episode "needlessly offended Latin American sensibilities.[137] Cochran and Miller contend that it "creat[ed] a profound suspicion of American 'justice' and American 'righteousness' in the nations of the western hemisphere."[138]

TR also assumed the role of negotiator in the Russo-Japanese War. Japan had gained the upper hand, but "neither side could score a knockout blow." In the Treaty of Portsmouth, which resulted from the TR-sponsored peace conference, "the concessions all went to the Japanese."[139] This raised questions about American neutrality. Another Founding Era—or, at least, Federalist Era—foreign policy principle that was compromised by another TR mediation effort was non-involvement in European affairs and disputes. With evident tensions among Germany, France, Britain, and Spain over Morocco, TR interposed the U.S. and helped fashion the Act (i.e., Treaty) of Algeciras to diffuse a possible war.[140]

During this period, we must conclude that the country's commitment to the Founding Fathers' principle of impartiality in foreign relations was inconsistent.

According to Tindall and Shi, Wilson sought to "help create a new world order governed by morality and idealism rather than by crass national interests." He and his first Secretary of State William Jennings Bryan, the former presidential candidate, "believed that America had been called to advance democracy and moral progress in the world." For example, Wilson denounced Taft's "dollar diplomacy," which sought to further foreign policy aims through the use of economic power by guaranteeing loans made to other countries, and in the tense international atmosphere just before World War I he had Bryan negotiate numerous treaties whereby nations agreed to take their disputes to international arbitration (which, of course, were completely ignored).[141] Wilson's high-minded international moralism and orientation to peace did not stop his continuing the policy of intervention in Latin America, nor did it make him open to the peacemaking initiatives during the War of Pope Benedict XV or the overtures for a settlement from the Austro-Hungarian Emperor Charles (Wilson refused to deal with Charles' government in its existing form, even though he was probably the most conciliatory of the belligerent rulers).[142] Wilson's elevation of democratic rule to the level of a moral principle, overriding even the traditional American stress on neutrality, was seen with his foreign policy stance of recognizing only duly elected governments. He applied this vigorously after Victoriano Huerta seized power in Mexico in 1913. Wilson put diplomatic pressure on Huerta, quietly supported the rebels under Venustiano Carranza who opposed him, and even insured that the rebels but not Huerta would get arms from outside. During the ensuing political turmoil in 1914, a small incident led to an American intervention. A group of American sailors were wrongly arrested in Tampico and the Mexican government quickly ordered their release and apologized to the U.S. The ship's commander brushed the apology aside and ordered the Mexicans to salute the American flag, which was an attempt to rub the whole incident in their faces. Wilson backed him up and sent a naval and Marine Corps force into the country and toppled the incumbent Mexican government. Ultimately, Huerta had to leave office and Carranza assumed power. Mexican resentment at the American actions, however, helped fuel the rebellion of Pancho Villa, his attacks in the American Southwest, and civil strife as Carranza's government struggled to defeat him. Carranza's coming to power brought a new secularist constitution,[143] which paved the way for one of the most intense anti-Catholic persecutions in modern times in the 1920s. Elsewhere in Latin America, Wilson continued the American military occupation of Nicaragua begun as part of the Taft dollar diplomacy that Wilson had so excoriated. He also sent American forces to Haiti and the Dominican Republic, interventions that lasted for twenty and ten years respectively. As Tindall and Shi say, these actions "exacerbated the Yankee phobia among many Latin Americans."[144] Again, the analysis here is the same as in Chapter 4: The interventions into neighboring countries went against the communal, cooperative spirit and orientation to the common good—which extend beyond one's own people—that was also part of Founding Era culture. America's conduct respecting elements in Mexico certainly went against the impartiality that the Founding Fathers exhorted. It also exhibited a lack of honesty, fair-dealing, civility, and even—in the case of the forced flag salute and then the Wilson administration's backing this up—of basic good manners and gentlemanliness. These were all part of the Founding culture.

The Wilson administration held back from entering World War I, tolerating violations of freedom of the seas by both the Allied and Central Powers while taking steps toward military preparedness. It tried to remain neutral.[145] Ultimately, the Zimmermann Telegram, in which the Germans clumsily tried to incite the Mexicans to march against the U.S. in the Southwest, and Germany's unrestricted submarine warfare drew the U.S. into the war. Preparedness brought forth anti-war sentiments from some segments of the population, who enunciated traditional American opposition to large standing armies. In 1916, Wilson sought to increase the army to 400,000, but was forced to accept a gradual increase only to 223,000. He did succeed in getting Congress to agree to a considerable enlargement of the navy. To fund this, the income tax doubled (from 1 to 2%), and estate and corporate taxes were enacted. These were promoted by Progressives and received popular support because they would fall mostly on the wealthy.[146] As he made last efforts for peace in late 1916 and early 1917, Wilson said there had to be "'peace without victory'" and a "'peace among equals'" and enunciated some of the Fourteen Points that he later put forth to the Versailles Peace Conference. When he finally called for a declaration of war on April 2, 1917, of course, he said that the U.S. had to enter the war to make the world "'safe for democracy.'"[147] The war saw the largest American military build-up to date, with army (including National Guard) strength up to 3.7 million men (Wilson also allowed women into the armed forces, although strictly state-side).[148] For the first time, the U.S. massively mobilized, even on the home front. As mentioned above, the economy was largely directed by the federal government in the interest of war production. With immigration largely curtailed and many men in uniform, women for the first time moved significantly into the workforce (although this ended upon the war's conclusion).[149] One wonders if both these developments—especially with the precedents they established for the future—did not ultimately weaken the family, which was so strongly emphasized in Founding culture. One also asks whether, with the Sangerian movement for contraception heating up at this time, they did not help pave the way for a weakening of sexual morality, which was also so much a part of that culture. The federal government established a substantial war propaganda machine and, even though its aim was supposed to be persuasion to sustain public support for the war effort instead of censorship,[150] censorship and other dimensions of the suppression of civil liberties in fact were common (see below). In many ways, a militaristic atmosphere—a sign, again, of decadent cultures—took hold for the duration of the war.

Although the vast increase in the military size would only be temporary and it would shrink after the war, the size still remained larger than it was before 1916.[151] Also, the size first was increased upon Wilson's request before the U.S. had entered the war; it was peacetime for the U.S. Thus, the Founders' principle about standing armies may have been offended to at least some degree.

Wilson's Fourteen Points called for numerous international principles and practices that went against the whole history of international relations and in some cases against the very nature of how it could reasonably be conducted. These included stopping "conquest and aggrandizement"; ending "private international understandings of any kind" and always conducting diplomacy "in the public view" (he here seemed oblivious to the fact that in any context compromising is unlikely when under the public eye and nations are unwilling to compromise when they will look weak publicly); complete "equality of trade conditions"; arms reductions (which have historically been achieved only when a number of very difficult to attain conditions are met[152]); the "impartial adjustment" of colonial claims (as if nations would not try to gain advantage in this at the expense of others' disadvantage); a guarantee of autonomous development of the ethnic groups under the former Austria-Hungary (even though nations have almost never relinquished parts of their domains easily and peoples with little or no self-governing experience have usually not been able to automatically develop themselves as nations successfully and justly); and that nations should no longer be "separated in interest." Topping all this off, of course, was his proposal for a League of Nations (ultimately at the Versailles Conference, seeing the difficulties of having such objectives accepted, he jettisoned all the other objectives except for the League).[153] In spite of his suggesting that nations needed to compromise internationally, Wilson's intransigence in yielding or compromising anything in the Versailles Treaty as it was finally drawn up caused its defeat in the Senate in 1920.[154] Ironically, despite its emergence as the linchpin of Wilson's whole program for post-war peace, the U.S. was never to join the League of Nations.

In light of the Founding, Wilson must be faulted both for wanting the U.S. to crusade for democracy around the world—both before the war and at Versailles afterwards—and for his unrealistic expectations about international politics. As we have said throughout this book, the Founding Fathers fashioned a democratic republic, not an out-and-out democracy. His unreasonableness about this even caused him to further disregard the Founders' principle of impartiality in foreign dealings when he refused to negotiate with Emperor Charles. We have also said that they, like the people of their time generally, were hard-nosed realists. This realism, grounded in their Christian worldview, is made abundantly clear in their reflections about human nature in *The Federalist*.[155] The moralism that he—and Bryan—brought to international affairs was akin to the moralism of many of the nineteenth century's reform movements, especially the prohibitionists. As such, it pushed aside the natural law of the Founding tradition for principles that were less than morally necessary. They were also imprudent and immoderate, and so contrary to the Founders and their culture; thus, they and their moralism compromised statesmanship.

Legal Developments and Citizen Rights. There were many developments in law during the period from 1877 to 1920. We discussed above labor laws, business and other social legislation (e.g., the Interstate Commerce Commission and the Sherman Act). We also noted that while courts at times opposed such laws, mostly they were upheld. The Supreme Court seemed to follow TR in making distinctions between "good" and "bad" monopolies, and allowing the federal government to break up the latter.[156] The vagueness of the Sherman Act—an early example of Congress's delegating the role of providing clear meaning to statutory provisions to the executive and the courts—perhaps invited the back-and-forth judicial enforcement it received.[157] More to our purpose, such vagueness also weakened the rule of law that the Founders said was crucial to a democratic republic and compromised separation of powers. Such specific matters as federal attempts to regulate child labor through its interstate commerce power were disallowed by the Supreme Court, which held it to be a state question.[158] State courts invariably upheld child labor legislation, however.[159] Maximum hours laws for women employees were mostly upheld by state courts and passed constitutional muster by the Supreme Court in 1908.[160] Maximum hours laws for male employees, in the states that enacted them, were also mostly upheld by state courts.[161] Courts were less accepting of legislation seeking to strengthen the bargaining power of workers vis-à-vis their employers, at least in the absence of health and safety questions. Beginning in the 1870s, the courts readily granted injunctions to halt strikes.[162] The Supreme Court was particularly assertive in this area, irrespective of questions of federalism. It embraced the notion of substantive due process—perhaps seen most vividly in the *Lochner* decision above—which held that corporations were persons under the Fourteenth Amendment and that their "substantive" rights to property would be violated by social regulation. Part of substantive due process—which was, in effect, a skewed notion of natural law that absolutized private property rights— was the liberty of contract. This was particularly pertinent in labor cases, as the Court claimed that state regulations enacted to protect the worker interfered with his putative liberty to accept the terms of employment set out for him by his employer.[163] The Court somehow overlooked the fact of the typically extreme disparity in bargaining power between employer and worker, such that the worker's only "liberty of contract" was to take and maintain a job on the employer's terms or leave. The employer could even arbitrarily terminate the worker. As indicated, the Court was not consistent with this doctrine, upholding some social regulatory legislation. Urofsky says that when it came to union cases, however, "freedom of contract truly reigned supreme."[164] Private property rights, particularly of corporations, gained "the highest legal protection,"[165] without being linked with social obligations. While the right to property was a central right of the Founding, this absolutization distorted its meaning. Much of the analysis of the section on economics and labor above in light of the Founding Era is pertinent here. We see here an early example of a lack of a desperately needed spirit of accommodation in American law that, first, parallels the aforementioned uncompromising positions taken by reform movements and, second, appears again on very different questions later in the twentieth century (partly because of a similar absolutist stance of later reform and interest groups).

If courts worked to protect corporate property rights in the areas mentioned, they were not nearly so concerned in the intellectual property area. In 1879, the Supreme Court ruled that Congress could not enact legislation providing trademark protection, declaring that it was authorized neither by the constitutional power to grant patents or to regulate interstate commerce. This seemed incongruous, in light of Lawrence M. Friedman's saying that "[t]he trademark is essential in a mass-production economy, based more or less on free enterprise."[166] Perhaps the Court could not quite see the connection, or else in all these areas was simply reluctant to permit any extension of federal or general governmental power.

Another kind of social legislation, especially in agricultural states, which courts typically struck down concerned mortgage foreclosure protection. Following *Dartmouth College v. Woodward*, the courts ruled that such laws violated the contract clause to the U.S. Constitution since they effectively altered the terms of the mortgage agreements.[167] This involved upholding property rights, so seemed to be in line with the Founding. There would have been other ways for governments to deal with such a problem, such as using a carrot and acting as a bargainer.

Another area of property law developing at this time concerned land use and conservation. We mentioned federal conservation efforts. State-level efforts paralleled these, in some cases through adding provisions to state constitutions. Land use laws did not always have high-minded conservation objectives in mind. Residents in "fashionable" neighborhoods in eastern cities sought them as protections of property values—a frequent defense of these and related types of laws even in our time—and to "maintain the prevailing patterns of segregation by income and class."[168] This hardly conformed to such Founding Era norms as civic friendship, concern for the general welfare, and avoidance of individualism. As the twentieth century progressed, zoning (i.e., restricting the use of real property in different parts of a city or town to particular purposes, such as residential, commercial, or industrial) was perhaps the major way to control land use. New York City enacted the first comprehensive zoning ordinance in 1916.[169]

The growth of social regulation during this period meant the expansion of economic crimes, in which the state—as typifies the criminal law—regarded certain economic-related actions as offenses against the community and sought to suppress and punish them, without relying on private efforts for legal redress (i.e., private lawsuits). In other words, "white-collar crimes" were established that, if committed, would garner criminal punishment (fines and imprisonment). These laws, of course, were enacted mostly at the state level and ranged from such things as selling articles as "sterling silver" that were composed of less than a certain amount of pure silver to marketing impure food. Criminal laws relating to matters such as elections and voting also appeared. These white-collar crime statutes were often not enforced, however.[170] There were implications for the rule of law here. Inconsistent enforcement always undercuts the rule of law. On the other hand, the law may have tried to reach too many things, the subject matter may have been too complicated to easily adapt the criminal law to, and the lack of enforcement may have reflected the basic difficulty of doing so—all these issues also have the effect of compromising the rule of law.

A couple of developments in law relating to the family during this period should be mentioned. While child labor was indeed a significant problem at this time, it is worth noting that the child labor legislation referred to represented not just—or perhaps fundamentally—economic regulatory legislation but a substitution by the state of its authority for that of parents. No longer would the parents determine—probably according to their understanding of their family's needs—if their minor child could and should go to work, but the state would.[171] Perhaps restricting or outright forbidding child labor was indeed necessary, but it may have set a precedent for the undermining of parental authority that would in time further weaken the family. It was mentioned that as the century went on divorce law was progressively becoming liberalized in many states; from 1850 to 1870, many states enacted liberal laws. After 1870, the momentum went in the opposite direction as significant national figures such as the famous newspaper publisher Horace Greeley (near the end of his life in 1872) and Yale University president Theodore D. Woolsey vigorously spoke out against divorce (it would be hard to imagine a major New York newspaper editor or an Ivy League university president today leading the fight for tighter divorce laws). Woolsey helped organize and led the New England Divorce Reform League in 1881, which helped secure the tightening of the state laws in New England. Some feminists and utopian reformers, on the other hand, clamored for more permissive divorce laws. Despite the laws' tightening, the number of divorces kept rising in the last third of the nineteenth century, reaching 55,000 nationally in 1900. Obviously, however, in contrast to the present time this number was miniscule. The phenomenon of "migratory divorce," in which people traveled to a state with more permissive laws to divorce and had their decree respected back home by the Constitution's full faith and credit clause, appeared even before this period and continued.[172] If there is doubt about child labor laws weakening the family, there was not much about more divorce weakening it. There were also implications for the communal norms of the Founding. Could one readily develop an orientation to his community and to civic friendship if he were brought up in a fractured family community?[173]

The law codes of the time featured many offenses against public morality, which were enforced in some states and not in others. Liquor control was a particularly contentious one, and of course at the end of this period prohibition was enshrined into national law—albeit, as it turned out, for only a short time. Lotteries were decisively suppressed by federal law. There was a renewed effort to enforce Sunday closing laws in some places, although sometimes because union labor pushed it instead of concerns about piety.[174] This perhaps illustrated a tendency of the time to keep the forms of religion, when in reality—as the comments below show further—religious commitment was diminishing. By contrast, the Founding Fathers obviously were not talking just about mere forms when they said that religion was essential for a democratic republic.

There seemed to be a dissonance about the treatment of children under the law. On the one hand, they were in many ways treated like adults in the way they were part of the workforce in substantial numbers. On the other hand, in the streets of the big cities where they congregated to play, the authorities readily brought the hand of the law down on them for petty things, such as playing baseball in the streets, throwing snowballs, shooting craps, and loafing. Sometimes, they would sleep out in the street, in a manner similar to "homeless people" today. Girls would be treated more severely by the authorities than boys in such cases for fear that they might become prostitutes. They would likely be sent to "reform schools," where they would also be sent if they had been exposed to "sexually illicit behavior"—a broad, catch-all term—in the home, befriended "low" persons, run away from home, etc. Sometimes poor parents claimed their daughters were behavior problems so they could have them committed and insure that they would have adequate food and lodging.[175] It seemed as if the law was used not just to punish juveniles who committed actual crimes, but also to instill morals and what the authorities considered good manners and civil behavior. It was this era's version of what family historian Allan C. Carlson has called "child saving."[176] The state's efforts seemed to be an inadequate—and overreaching—substitute for the family. Perhaps working with private entities like churches to build up families would have been better.

The late nineteenth century, of course, saw the consolidation of the "separate but equal," race-based system of law in the southern and border states (it is often called "Jim Crow"). The compromise to resolve the 1876 election, as noted in the last chapter, paved the way for this, and the Supreme Court gradually gave it its imprimatur. After initially holding in 1878 that states could not prohibit segregation in transportation organs,[177] it switched, in 1890, to upholding a state law *requiring* segregation on interstate carriers.[178] Then in 1896, in the famous *Plessy v. Ferguson* decision, it clearly declared that state-mandated segregation did not violate either the Thirteenth or Fourteenth Amendments.[179] If Congress and the executive had withdrawn from racial civil rights after 1876, the Court now did so as well. As Urofsky puts it, the Court "seemed only too willing…to leave the fate of minorities to state and local governments."[180] The result of the latter was sometimes Ku Klux Klan activity—which made a comeback—vigilantism, and lynch laws. This was the very "stuff" of lawlessness.[181]

The Supreme Court was only somewhat more accommodating to the West Coast Chinese, in spite of their being a target of much hostile feeling there. In *Yick Wo v. Hopkins* (1888), the Court invalidated a San Francisco ordinance because of "obviously discriminatory intent." The city had granted licenses to operate laundries in wooden buildings to all but one non-Chinese applicant, but turned down all two hundred Chinese applicants. Urofsky says that the Court would act if the discrimination were obvious, as here, but if a law looked good on the surface the Court would not investigate to see if it was applied discriminatorily.[182] The bottom line is that all three branches of government were impervious to promoting the civic friendship, reasonable equality, civility, respect for people's immaterial property, and simple justice that were among the norms of the Founders and their culture. Whether the norms were sufficiently respected for the Negro of the Founding Era was a different question. The important point for our analysis is the fact is that the norms at least were in place. Also, the Court's insufficient treatment of legal discrimination—barring it only where obvious on the surface—challenged the rule of law.

Next, World War I and its immediate aftermath created many civil liberties issues. Under the newly passed Espionage and Sedition Acts, "criticism of government leaders and war policies was in effect outlawed." The Espionage Act of 1917 severely punished insubordination, disloyalty, refusal of duty in the armed forces, and the circulation of false reports and statements with intent to hurt the war effort. It barred from the mails anything in these categories or that advocated treason, insurrection, or resistance to any law. The Sedition Act of 1918 punished doing or even saying anything to obstruct the sale of war bonds, advocating cutbacks in war production, or communicating anything "disloyal, profane, scurrilous, or abusive" about the American form of government, the Constitution, or the military. These laws were aggressively enforced, with socialists and labor radicals not surprisingly the most frequent targets. One of the most noted prosecutions was of the Socialist leader Eugene V. Debs. Even a Socialist Congressman from Milwaukee received a twenty-one year prison sentence for writing editorials in one of that city's main newspapers calling the war a capitalist conspiracy.[183] Right after the war, the Red Scare of 1919— coming on the heels of the Bolshevik Revolution, the attempted Communist coups in other places in Europe, and the domestic mailing of bombs to prominent U.S. citizens—led to: over 5,000 people being taken into custody in their residences without arrest warrants; the deportation—without any judicial process—of about 250 political radicals (almost all aliens who were legally in the U.S., but at least two of whom were naturalized citizens) to the U.S.S.R.; and the expulsion of five duly elected Socialist party members from the New York legislature.[184] There was no evidence that any of these people were tied to the mailed bombs, by the way. Such central rights of the Founders as freedom of the press, freedom of speech, freedom of assembly, and due process guarantees were jeopardized here, even if part of this occurred during wartime.

Finally, one of the most significant, enduring developments in law in this period concerned legal and jurisprudential philosophy. The central figure was Oliver Wendell Holmes, Jr., who was appointed to the Supreme Court by TR in 1902. He laid the groundwork for what came to be called legal realism, the view that the only source of law was human making. As far as the common law was concerned, judges were the ones who made it; they did not "discover" it (i.e., discern what it was from a legal tradition rooted ultimately in immemorial principles not fashioned by men). Judges, he said, decided cases on the facts, and then wrote opinions afterward presenting a rationale for their decision. The true basis of the decision was often some principle or premise outside the law, fashioned in society.[185] His view of law was fundamentally historicist: legal principles always had their origin in some human decision or action made at some historical time.[186] He also sharply distinguished between law and ethics, essentially holding that notions of ethics should not shape law. Morton White says about Holmes that he believed that if one had a "moral duty" to do something, it "is of no interest to the lawyer."[187] This obviously did not conform to the natural law background of the Founding; it was positivistic. It also became highly influential on American legal thinking and judicial decision-making, as we note in coming chapters. This is so completely contrary to the Founding notion that morality was crucial for a democratic republic and the reality of its permeating every aspect of the culture of Founding times. Holmes' thought was part of the larger trend of the time, seen also with the separation of ethics from economics and the treating of both business management and public governance as mere technical questions. The judge for Holmes was like a legal technician. Science—physical, natural, and social—was seen as having precise truths, but ethics—"the laws of a world order," to use Robert H. Wiebe's expression—was not.[188] Further, even while there was optimism about progress, the understanding about human ends was lost—except for vague humanitarian sentiments. Perhaps because of the latter, legal realists like Holmes believed that law should work to promote social welfare.[189]

   Immigration and Inter-Group Conflict, Urban Life, Western Settlement, and the Frontier. The 1877-1920 period saw the most substantial levels of immigration in U.S. history. In 1907, it reached an all-time high of almost one million arrivals. From then until the outbreak of World War I, it hovered around 650,000 per year.[190] Between 1880 and 1914, around 21 million immigrants came.[191] In 1890, *four-fifths* of New York City's residents were foreign-born.[192] The last chapter mentioned the "new immigration" that began after the Civil War, with a much greater number of immigrants coming from eastern and southern Europe. Many of these immigrants crowded into big city slums. In the first decade of the twentieth century, at a time of substantial urban growth, 41% of the newcomers to American cities came from abroad.[193] Along with Negroes who had migrated from the South, they were heavily concentrated in unskilled and semi-skilled jobs; native-born Caucasians dominated skilled and lesser administrative jobs, to say nothing of high-level corporate jobs. The former groups were simply refused better positions in an age before anti-discrimination laws.[194] Jacob Riis's noted 1880 book, *How the Other Half Lives* detailed the squalid conditions of the urban slums, and called for a renewed "Christian sense of justice" to stop the divisions between the poor slum dwellers and the upper classes.[195] Tindall and Shi mention that a massive "urban proletariat," which was "landless, tool-less, and homeless," had arisen. The situation that Jefferson had feared as undermining republican government—large numbers of people jammed into the cities instead of a nation of independent, largely self-sufficient yeoman farmers—had come to pass.[196] The cultural and economic conditions of the cities—the many property-less, the great inequalities among the people, and the divisions within the community and lack of civic friendship—were far from the conditions of the Founding Era.

   If the population of the country overall grew substantially in the Gilded Age, the "cities grew many times as fast."[197] In 1860, one-sixth of Americans lived in communities of at least 8,000 people; by 1900, one-third did. During the same forty-year period the rural population doubled, but the urban population quadrupled.[198] By 1910, nearly 50% of the population was urban-based. Most major present-day U.S. cities had emerged by 1910.[199] While American cities traditionally had developed where there was some kind of port, railroads and industrialization proved to be the main stimuli for urban growth in the final decades of the nineteenth century. The railroad influence was seen especially in the plains, the South, and the Far West. Tindall and Shi tell us that by the 1880s, "[m]uch of the westward movement...was...an urban movement."[200] If industry helped to spawn city growth during this period, cities also helped to further industrialization. This was because the growth required more housing and commercial buildings, more lighting, and new infrastructure.[201]

Besides the expansion of railroads and the growth of cities, the advance of communications and other new technologies stimulated settlement in the West. What was once considered the "Great American Desert"—the Great Plains, extending into the Rocky Mountain area—was made conducive to farming by new inventions and agricultural processing technologies. Meat-packing and processing advances, along with technological advances that rendered usable livestock parts previously discarded (these were alluded to above), made western ranching an increasingly profitable business. The availability of railroads made it possible for large numbers of livestock to get to stockyards and processing plants relatively quickly.[202] As Cashman says, "The final settlement of the West was one of the most dramatic stories of the Gilded Age."[203]

The heavy immigration of this period caused a resurgence of nativism and considerable inter-group hostility. As mentioned, the anti-immigrant American Protective Association (APA) appeared in the 1880s and 1890s. It was especially strong in the interior of the U.S.[204] They mostly opposed the immigrants because so many of them were Catholic. As Tindall and Shi state, nativism "now surfaced mainly in anti-Catholic, and secondarily, anti-Semitic, sentiments."[205] The latter was a response to the new wave of Jewish immigrants from eastern Europe. The rejuvenated Ku Klux Klan expanded outside the South and became anti-immigrant, anti-Catholic, and anti-Jewish in addition to anti-Negro.[206] Other factors besides religion, however, shaped the suspicion of the new immigrants: greater cultural differences and more significant language barriers than were found with the older immigrants from western and northern Europe; the fact that so many were illiterate peasants; criminal and gang activity among some of them; the presence of social and political radicals among their number; and the fact that some had been brought here by anti-labor employers as strikebreakers.[207] Anti-Chinese feeling—racial prejudice and the hostility of workers who saw the Chinese as competitors for jobs were factors in this—has already been mentioned. They led to the Chinese Exclusion Acts of 1882 and 1902—the first suspended and the latter just halted Chinese immigration.[208] It was the first significant stoppage of immigration in American history, and it set the precedent for the era of restrictive immigration that began with the Emergency Immigration Act of 1921. Anti-Japanese sentiment gained strength in the first decade of the twentieth century, especially in California.[209] John Higham says that amidst the backdrop of the labor and social conflicts of the 1890s and the new social Darwinism, "racial nativism became more...widespread."[210] By this he means not just racial sentiments against non-Caucasian groups like the Chinese and Japanese, however, but also other Caucasians who were not Anglo-Saxon; thus, "race" seemed to have a broader definition than is generally the case today. The mixing through intermarriage of colonial and Founding Era America was no longer typical; the differences for some were now too great to digest. Among the proponents of this racial nativism—who thought that the Anglo-Saxon Americans, whether by background or temperament, were more suited to liberty and free government— were many New England intellectuals and patricians.[211] After World War I, eugenicist Madison Grant developed a more elaborate, systematic argument about this in his widely read book *The Passing of the Great Race*. It helped to shape the new restrictive immigration policy.[212]

The 1877-1920 period did not see nativism translate as readily into rioting against despised groups, as earlier in the nineteenth century. There were some, however, such as the anti-Jewish riot in New Jersey in 1891[213] and Independence Day Protestant-Catholic riots involving the APA in Montana in 1894[214] and Boston in 1895.[215] There were also many episodes of physical intimidation and attacks.[216] It seemed for the most part, however, as if the hostility was expressed in more subtle but still generally blatant ways. However, there were several anti-Negro riots in both North and South during and right after the World War I.[217] This was in addition to the targeting of Negroes with the vigilantism and lynching mentioned above. Nativism and this type of treatment of racial, ethnic, and religious minority groups offended such principles of the Founding and Founding culture as reasonable equality, respect for the common good, a spirit of cooperativeness, civic friendship, civility, basic justice, and the need for good manners. The official tolerating of violence against the Negro also deeply offended the norms of respect for law and the maintenance of the rule of law.

Socio-Cultural Developments. The period from 1877 to 1920 saw further changes in religion, church-state questions, education, family life, associational activity, and moral conditions. In religion, the greater diversity noticeable in the post-Civil War period further increased due to the stepped up immigration and urbanization. The diversity was occurring mostly because the Protestant hegemony was giving way to a substantial Catholic minority and the percentage of Jews increased (although it was still very small). There was nothing like the even greater diversity of the present-day, however. This enhanced diversity within the Judeo-Christian spectrum muted Protestant denominational differences. The first stirrings among Catholics and Jews of the desire to become "Americanized"—i.e., essentially fitting into the attitudinal framework established by the predominant Protestant culture—became apparent.[218] The nature of the Protestant-oriented culture was itself changing, however. "Liberal theology" was changing the face of American Protestantism. In it, "the world was seen as a fundamentally good and benevolent place, not as a battleground between good and evil." What emerged from this was the "Social Gospel movement," which put the focus of the religious person on "improv[ing] social conditions."[219] The roots of this, of course, were in the religious changes earlier in the nineteenth century discussed in Chapter 4. On one hand, Protestants— particularly the middle class—attempted to make religious devotion a greater part of their everyday lives at home; on the other hand, religion became less a set of seriously held beliefs and more a matter of sentiment. Protestantism increasingly came to be defined less by a specific creed and more by— essentially—family morality, civic responsibility (which was especially in line with the Social Gospel idea), and the "social function" of church-going.[220] The influence of the Unitarianism earlier in the century, with its downplaying of dogma and theology on behalf of just "ethical living" and stress on "improv[ing] social conditions," was clearly discernible.[221] The rise of fundamentalism— which stressed doctrinal strictness and the inerrancy of the Bible, even in matters about which it does not speak authoritatively such as science and history—was a reaction to liberal Protestantism.[222] Certainly, liberal Protestantism's perspective about human nature was counter to the hard-nosed realism of the Founding Era (which also, of course, was nurtured by a Protestant worldview). Liberal Protestantism was now at the center of American religion and this fact illustrates how sharply the mainstream American religious perspective had been transformed in the course of the nineteenth century. At the extreme of this transformation (in terms of perspective, but not necessarily the types of adherents since it attracted many people of wealth) was Christian Science, which essentially denied the reality of evil.[223] These religious developments show the loss of religious commitment, at least in the sense of believing that religion has a set of specific teachings that must direct one's life. For mainstream Americans it was giving way to a kind of half-Christian, half-secular humanitarianism rooted in a general sense of Christian belief. Besides being seen decades before in Unitarianism this was a feature of the earlier nineteenth century reform movements, as noted in Chapter 4. What happened by the current period was that it had become normative. It was religion, however, not a vague humanitarianism that the Founders said was necessary for a democratic republic and that their culture embraced.

The increased religious diversity did not mean less conflict between Protestants and Catholics over the public schools. Some spokesmen outright insisted that the public schools were, in effect, Protestant schools (a position which, as mentioned, was first asserted during the church-state controversies of the 1840-1877 period). Others, as a way of avoiding Protestant-Catholic conflict, essentially called for their secularization, removing religion entirely.[224] As far as church-state issues in general were concerned, the battle lines essentially had been drawn in this previous period and the momentum for separationism intensified. As was seen, different groups with different objectives came together to advocate church-state separationism in various degrees. In addition to the Protestant elements and secularists that had been part of it, Jews, Masons, Seventh-Day Adventists, the Ku Klux Klan, and the APA and other nativists (who were mostly Protestant) embraced it.[225] The different elements advocated different approaches to bring about separationism. For example, nativist Protestants and liberal secularists gave up on trying to get a separationist substitute for the First Amendment adopted.[226] The former turned to working on the state level to get separationist amendments to state constitutions, blocking funding for sectarian schools, and—in a spirit of *suppression* of religious freedom—opposed allowing orphans and prisoners to have access to religious services of other faiths than Protestantism in state institutions.[227] The latter turned to lobbying to change laws they believed violated church-state separation and to "cultural agitation" to change public perspectives.[228] Interestingly, the separationists became less honest about American history than in the previous period. Protestant denominations started to claim that strict separationism had been their tradition (when in fact some of them had used the state to enforce their doctrines).[229] The Seventh-Day Adventist writings distorted the views of Jefferson and other Founding Fathers and even misrepresented their historical actions. They falsely claimed that the First Amendment resulted from a struggle for rigid separationism. They overemphasized the influence of early colonial separationist Roger Williams on the later Bill of Rights, even trying to present him, anachronistically, as a Founding Father.[230] All this ostensibly set the stage for the later distortion of the views of the Founding Fathers by the post-World War II separationists. We saw that separationism had taken firm hold toward the end of the 1840-1877 period. Now, the crusading for it took on one of the worst characteristics—with the same negative comparison to Founding cultural norms—that we have noted of political campaigns: telling untruths to gain advantage. As stated in Chapter 4, the Protestant-Catholic conflict in the public schools and elsewhere showed the absence of civic friendship and civility.

In education, there were many important developments, but for the purpose of our analysis perhaps the ruling attitudes about it and the reform efforts were especially noteworthy. More people were going to college[231] and the colleges took on a more vocation-oriented focus;[232] this followed from their greater focus on specialized training in the 1840-1877 period. Another outgrowth of the latter was the new stress on professionalism and credentialism, which saw the expansion in number and authority of professional associations to regulate entry into learned professions and the beginning of regional educational accrediting agencies.[233] Compulsory attendance requirements at the elementary school level became almost universal, with the present-day view taking hold that the aim of education should prepare people to meet the imperatives of the changing workplace. School populations increased sharply between 1890 and 1920, and high schooling continued to expand and saw revised curricula along these lines and to prepare students for college.[234] Continuing a pattern that began during the 1840-1877 period, educational bureaucracy grew (especially within urban systems). The refrains so common today were already heard then: bureaucratic rigidities, inefficiency, funds not channeled in a sensible direction, and the lack of tangible results despite ever increasing expenditures.[235] Advances were made in literacy, including among the Negro population.[236] The increase in education would have been welcomed by the Founders, but—continuing and consolidating the trend seen in the 1840-1877 period—the nature of it for those who would be of the group who would go on to become leaders would not have been. This was because the vocational focus minimized the liberal arts. The increasing bureaucratization in education and the rise of credentialing bodies betrayed an over-centralization that the Founders would probably have been skeptical of.

The reigning attitudes among educators, of course, shaped American education. On the one hand educators embraced traditional ideas, such as the need to instill personal virtues (e.g., temperance, industriousness, thrift) and good manners, in order to promote sound morality (which they thought was the key to solving all the new social problems they saw around them). They believed that these were all needed to sustain a sound republic.[237] Here, they continued the outlook of earlier American educators. Perhaps in Jeffersonian fashion, they believed that even amidst urban squalor, education had to connect with the rural, pastoral vision that had been so much a part of the American tradition.[238] On the other hand, educators abstracted themselves from the reality around them and had an overwhelming optimism about what education could accomplish. They were oblivious to the weakness of human nature and the intractable character of some social problems because of their belief that improvement was inevitably occurring in the human condition. The abundance of scientific and technological progress was insuring this. They thought that schools, for their part, were helping to bring this about just because they were efficiently educating increasing numbers of students.[239] In all this, they reflected the view about progress that had taken hold earlier in the nineteenth century, the quasi-utopian optimism of some of the earlier thinkers surveyed, and the perspectives of the leading educational reformers of their time. In this sense, they were in conflict with Founding realism, much as many other reform movements were. They were also influenced by the other prominent strain of thought of the last third of the nineteenth century: social Darwinism.[240] While this tempered, on a practical level, their expectations for education, it did not necessarily move them closer to the principles of the Founding Era. (This was in spite of their commendable stress on shaping virtues for the good of the Republic.) Rather, it contrastingly tainted them with a kind of cynicism about man and a kind of over-rigidity in the distinctions they made between the different groups in society (thereby undercutting the possibilities of civic friendship and the other communal norms of the Founding culture). This was like the problem of the post-Civil War thinkers who reacted to the difficulties caused by excessive democracy by subverting the "democratic" dimension of the American democratic republic. Educational thought seemed more like an uneasy amalgamation, in moderated form, of the two great clashing ideologies—that actually had a common root—of the first half of the twentieth century, communism/socialism and fascism, than a return to the understanding of the Founding and the Western philosophical and Judeo-Christian tradition which stood behind it.

S.E. Frost, Jr. says that the main thinkers who inspired social Darwinism—Herbert Spencer, Thomas Henry Huxley, and Charles Darwin himself (the former two wrote on education specifically)—"attacked the humanistic, classical education" (that is, the liberal arts, the kind of education the Founding Fathers had). Frost says that these thinkers "found fertile soil for their point of view" in America because of our "democratic approach to schooling and a growing willingness to look at new ideas," and because of the undermining earlier in the nineteenth century of traditional religion —which would have been resistant to their thought—by Unitarianism.[241] Their thought, then, both emerged because of the corruption of Founding ideas about democracy and religion and ultimately helped to further undermine the founding belief in natural law. A new philosophy called pragmatism came forth from the attempt to apply social evolutionary thought to different fields, and in turn reinforced these thinkers' subversion of classical education. It saw education "as depending not on the authority of the past but rather on its ability to accomplish what is desired." For pragmatism, truth is not a settled thing but is "dependent upon the consequences of men's actions."[242] John Dewey during the current period and the next one to be considered (1920-1945) was the main thinker promoting both this philosophical pragmatism and its application to education. It is evident that pragmatism, like Holmesian legal thought, would readily subvert the notion that morality is not made by men—and with it a condition that the Founders saw as utterly essential for a democratic republic. It would naturally tend to also undermine religion and, for that matter, the rights that the Founding Fathers held as central for a democratic republic because both relied upon inherited tradition (for the latter, it was the tradition of the common law). The fact that pragmatism was to form the intellectual ambiance of education meant that this notion would be propagated to new generations, and would persist and thereby have implications for the future character of the American democratic republic.

Dewey was perhaps the dean of educational reformers of these two periods. The above optimism about human nature and belief in the likelihood of progress—in a secular humanistic sense, simply by man's own effort alone—were seen in his views that the child should be at the "center" of schooling and be allowed to be "creative," that "indoctrination" should be avoided, that the purpose of education should be "eliminating the selfish ambitions that presumably generated social conflict" and "obvious social evils," and that education should be "an agency of progressive social change."[243] Christopher Lasch tells us that in an impractical fashion—especially considering that they were adherents to a philosophy called "pragmatism"—most educational reformers gave little heed to how to put their reforms into place. A figure such as Edward A. Ross did, thinking that the essentially independent and idea-generating universities would become the engines of reform. He was impractical in a different sense, however, by not foreseeing how they would succumb to the same bureaucratization of the rest of education and come under governmental pressure.[244] This all, of course, was so contrary to the prudence of the Founding Fathers and the "shrewd practical intelligence" of their culture.

It was contradictory for educators and educational reformers of this period to be pushing what at bottom were their "own conceptions" of what constituted "good education,"[245] while at the same time believing themselves to be stressing what was good for the Republic and promotive of more democracy.[246] This is especially underscored by their increasing hostility to classical and traditional humane learning that, after all, had descended to modern men from the greatest minds of the past and been worked out and refined through the ages. (Obliviousness to the latter, of course, was completely to be expected by men formed in the cauldron of pragmatism since it involved acknowledging the value of authority.) It was essentially their *own* theories that the reformers were espousing. There was nothing about them that indicated they were a natural aristocracy of the sort that a Plato and Aristotle or the Founding Fathers had in mind—i.e., with the kind of wisdom, deep understanding, and prudence that that implied (indeed, their impracticality and lack of realism indicated quite the opposite). Educational historian William A. Bullough writes about their "elitism and paternalism" and high "self-evaluation."[247] One wonders if they had this self-conception because they were part of what, in essence, was a new "aristocracy"—an artificial not a natural one, to be sure—spawned by the new regime of specialized education, professionalism, and credentialism, and simply by membership in "the new industrial and commercial classes."[248] There was, then, a gnostic dimension to these reformers and, as such, it was not surprising that they should favor centralized authority in education. Even if, as indicated, bureaucracy sometimes thwarted their reform ideas, controlling things from the center was the way that their "true" understanding about education could be universally implemented. These changes in American education took deep hold, even though many as noted had previously gained a foothold. Most critical for our analysis, perhaps, was the weakening of the liberal arts.

Regarding family life, we have already mentioned the tightening up of divorce laws and the contrary continuation of the trend toward more divorces. There were other developments. Some women began to get college educations and became career women afterwards (generally in education and the new social service agencies). This resulted in a lower marriage rate and later marriages.[249] Feminists throughout the nineteenth century complained about women being limited to the domestic realm. We saw earlier that that was not an entirely correct characterization even very early in American history, and throughout the period from 1877 to 1920 many women worked outside the home.[250] The early part of this period saw the Comstock Laws, which checked the availability of contraceptives. In spite of growing opposition to abortion in the medical community, it continued to be resorted to as in the 1840-1877 period.[251] One might speculate that this reflected the weakening hold of doctrinal religion and the continued creeping secularization generally. In the second decade of the twentieth century Margaret Sanger launched her movement to crusade for contraception, which in the next period considered (1920-1945) gained widespread acceptance among Protestants and eventually saw a practice historically universally condemned in Christianity and viewed as a "private vice" transformed into a "public virtue."[252] All these developments put new stresses on the family—which, again, the Founding tradition had seen as so central—and likely weakened it. As noted, World War I brought unprecedented numbers of women into the workforce. The notion of "companionate marriage" advanced during this time among the middle class, perhaps under this feminist influence. It "emphasized gender equality, mutual respect, and emotional intimacy," and downplayed the notion of the natural rights and duties of each partner within marriage.[253] Contrary to how it sounded, it may have introduced individualism into marriage and thus undercut the notion of the family as a unit. Its focus seemed to be on women being in control of *their* bodies and *their* destinies. It probably confused the traditional notions of husband-father as the head of the family and wife-mother as the heart. The Founding Era rejected individualism even in politics and economics—now, here it was in the family. In the 1877-1920 period, the family pathologies of earlier in the nineteenth century continued and even expanded, and the stirrings of their becoming legitimized and acceptable were now evident.

It is worth noting Christopher Lasch's observation that the social reformers of this period—some of whom were included among the educational reformers above, and also included such people who significantly shaped ideas of social service as Jane Addams—believed the family to be a kind of "tyranny."[254] While the "child saving" activity of the state that Carlson writes about stretched throughout American history[255]—and we recall from Chapter 2 that community interference generally with the family began back in the colonial period—it is likely that these reformers helped to shape a suspicion of the family that was ongoing in the social service professions.[256]

As noted above, this period saw a burgeoning of associational activity of various kinds. We have already mentioned labor unions, different kinds of politically active interest groups, and social reform and professional organizations. Many religious, fraternal, veterans, charitable, sports, and special interest organizations also made their appearance. The membership of existing associations also burgeoned and they "increasingly federated into state and national organizations." Also, many associations that emerged in this period "proved to be among the longest lasting in the history of the United States." Fraternal organizations provided life and disability insurance to their members that as workers they could not get from their corporate employers.[257] These associations provided a reference point, a means of helping to address temporal needs, and generally helped men to navigate through the isolation of mass, industrial culture.[258] What they did was, in a limited way, to make up for the absence of the communal culture of the Founding Era.

As far as morals of the period were concerned, we have already spoken of family and sexual morality questions. We also mentioned laws regarding public morality. The widespread problems of gambling, excessive liquor consumption, and prostitution of the period from 1840 to 1877 continued, as did bribery and payoffs of big city police forces from the interests behind them.[259] Drug abuse also emerged in the last third of the nineteenth century, as opium dens arrived with Chinese immigration to the West and medicinal drug abuse, often involving the opium derivative morphine, occurred (especially among women).[260] We said in the last chapter that official corruption compromised the ethic of honesty, truth-telling, fair-dealing, and the need to restrain luxury, along with just affronting basic morality. To the moral decline of this period was added a new nemesis that was to be such a malaise a century later, drug abuse.

Finally, during the 1877-1920 period the eugenics movement emerged. It grew out of genetics research being done at the time, but was influenced by social Darwinism and nativism. Some raised the concern that the mass immigration of the time permitted many "unfit" people to enter American society. Also, while it predated this,[261] it was not unrelated to the new effort to propagandize for contraception (in fact, Margaret Sanger, the leading contraceptive propagandist—mentioned above—was a supporter of the eugenics movement).[262] Some eugenicists, riding the democratic reform spirit of the time as projected internationally during World War I, believed that the way to control the growth of despotism might be to somehow regulate marriages—say, among the increasingly discredited European hereditary aristocracy—so that political despots would not spring from them. We see here one example of the political dimension of the eugenics movement. Its proponents were not hesitant—very much in line with the Progressive mentality about social regulation in other areas—to use government coercively to achieve their ends[263] (in fact, Carlson states that "leaders within the Progressive movement...embraced the eugenics campaign[264]"). Richard Hofstadter mentions that this was an expression of collectivism, but he does not necessarily judge it harshly. He merely says that it, like so many other reform movements of this era, "was based upon an increasing recognition of the psychological and moral relatedness of men in society."[265] It seems as if it is deserving of condemnation, however, because it violated the natural rights of the family in being prepared to forcibly dictate reproductive choices to it and in the name of a purported collective good—which it determined with reference only to human-concocted social theory, as with the educational reformers above—was prepared to subvert human dignity. If reproduction does not go to the heart of human dignity, it is hard to see what does. It was utilitarianism pure and simple. This strikes at the very foundation of the natural law tradition undergirding the Founding. The collective it was promoting was one in which the individual and the family were subsumed into a scheme deemed desirable by some—by the kind of "reform" elite discussed above. It was not synonymous with the good of the community understood in Founding culture, where the integrity of individual and family, of course, were held to be central. Also, of course, the fact that an elite was promoting it put it at odds with the democratic dimension of the American democratic republic.

Currents in Political Thought. We have talked above about the leading intellectual currents of the time, so in this final section of the chapter we shall just highlight some of the main perspectives in, specifically, political thought. To be sure, as will be apparent, they were often related to and grew out of the economic conditions of the time and either embraced or reacted against the broader social Darwinist socio-economic thinking above. Some of those who reacted against it helped influence the Progressivism of which we have spoken so much about (Progressivism itself was a politico-economic movement and not a school of political thought).

Perhaps the preeminent intellectual defender of social Darwinism was William Graham Sumner. Social Darwinism believed that life most fundamentally was a struggle for existence, and Sumner said that "the greatest forward step" in that struggle was the production of capital, which was "the necessary means of an advance in civilization" since it "increase[d] the fruitfulness of labor." Further, "[s]ocial advance depends primarily upon hereditary wealth" because such a person can pass along the entrepreneurial virtues to his offspring. That's why the family is so important for Sumner—a rather limited rationale for defense of the family, to be sure. He believed that since they help society so abundantly with their "organizing talent," the "captains of industry" rightfully should be able to amass vast fortunes. Interestingly, here Sumner is the "flip side" of Marx, both absolutists about opposing positions: Marx thought that labor generates all wealth, and Sumner thought that, at least for the most part, it was great entrepreneurs and corporate administrators. In a kind of convoluted Calvinism—actually, bordering on a crass economic materialism—he believed that "money is the token of success."[266] Accordingly, he extolled inequality. If true liberty exists, those who best exemplify the entrepreneurial virtues "will come out at the top." He criticized the notions of equality and natural rights that shaped the American Founding. He was a historicist and legal positivist like Holmes: rights were not grounded in nature, but "were simply evolving folkways crystallized in laws."[267] He said that if by "democracy" one meant "a principle of advancement based on merit" (i.e., a politico-cultural condition upholding something like the principle of equal opportunity), it was good; if it meant "equality in acquisition and enjoyment" (i.e., something like guaranteeing equal results and equal wealth), it was "thoroughly impracticable." He thought that the "democratic ideal"—essentially, the Jacksonian notion—was transitory and would pass with the next stage of "social evolution." He argued that the democratic "dogma" and the "democratic temper of the people" that had been passed down at least from the Jacksonian Era was opposed to the "constitutional framework" of the Founding Fathers.[268]

Many thinkers and writers reacted against social Darwinism and the growth of economic power. Brooks Adams, a scion of the famous Adams family (i.e., John and John Quincy Adams) who it will be recalled was one of the thinkers mentioned in Chapter 1 who wrote about the decline of political orders, essentially saw a kind of sovereignty in the industrial age being exercised by business interests, by "capitalism." They essentially utilized the courts as their agency to exercise that sovereignty. This enabled them to get favorable treatment under the law and to avoid their rightful public responsibilities. By using the courts to further their ends, they subverted both the rule of law that the Anglo-Saxon tradition had struggled so long to achieve and the arrangements of the Constitution. In acting for them the courts assumed a kind of "judicial prerogative," in which they nullified legislative enactments and "perverted" their own role from a judicial to a political one. Effectively, then, they made themselves "superior to the Constitution."[269] Adams sounded curiously like Karl Marx in that he lamented the modern focus on the economic crowding out all other concerns, even the religious.[270] His analysis rightly saw the problem of distortion of separation of powers and the rule of law in the Gilded Age.

Edward Bellamy sounded similar themes. He said that a "wise political economy"—i.e., one that "shall satisfy both our ethical ideals and our material needs"—is needed by democracy "if it is not to perish."[271] Democracy—and he had no sense that in America there was to be anything but this—had not advanced far enough historically to insure that the people were truly sovereign. Sounding a theme similar to the British Catholic thinker Hilaire Belloc in the first half of the twentieth century (Bellamy died in 1898), he insisted that the mass of people were not completely free because they were economically dependent on the rich. The successful struggles to throw off kingly rule had not brought true democracy, but "plutocracy" with the "capitalists"—i.e., the big business entrepreneurs—in control.[272] Democracy requires economic equality, but what existed was "wage-slavery" that both thwarted human dignity and undermined the rights to life, liberty, and the pursuit of happiness in the Declaration of Independence." Bellamy followed the Declaration in seeing the securing of these rights as the purpose of government.[273] To make this possible he believed that socialism was necessary—government had to "control and direct" the means of production and distribution. This did not mean, to be sure, that there would be no private property, but that "the exact line between public and private rights be marked off." He also thought the state had to eliminate the possibility of poverty. Bellamy's stress on the need to rediscover the social use of property, the sense of the obligation of the community to help its members in a brotherly fashion, the need for cooperation and an orientation to the common welfare, and his belief in how enlightening people about social ethics and a better culture would play a major part in bringing about this new order all ring of the Founding Era. His desire for state control; his outright rejection of such basic features of economic life as rent, interest, profit, and competition; his seeming egalitarianism; his utopianism, and his outright endorsement of democracy do not.[274] It is also not so clear that his private-public property distinction would not really undermine the right to private property.

Walt Whitman, known mostly as a poet, echoed Adams and Bellamy about America not being a true democracy; he said it was a "*bourgeois* capitalistic society."[275] Like Bellamy, he did not believe that democracy had advanced to the stage that it should be at. He found fault with the Jacksonian conception of democracy: it exalted individualism and ignored the community, and its laissez faire orientation led to a kind of anarchy. It was true that democracy had to stress individual liberty and equality, but it also had to promote solidarity. This, for him, was a kind of vague notion of brotherhood, mutual charity, and comradeship.[276] Whitman's disregard of both traditional religion and its ethical norms resulted both in these notions having an insufficient substance and in the absence of specific moral restraints on human conduct. Thus, they could easily lead to the anarchism that he criticized in Jacksonianism. Like Bellamy he reached for a utopianism, and was somewhat taken with the thought of Marx and Engels[277]—completely oblivious to the fact that their prescriptions required sweeping, centralized state power and easily led to a dystopia. So, while like Bellamy aspects of his thought conformed to Founding thought and culture, it sharply departed from them as well. The centralization, attachment to democracy, disregard of religion, and broad meaningless ethical platitudes would have been rejected by the Founding, even as his communal focus conformed to it.

While Henry George was more an economic thinker than a political one, his views were a throwback to Jeffersonianism and—perhaps more basically, in many ways, to the Founding culture. He stressed the importance of land ownership, decentralization, economic theory coming to grips with life as it really was for the common man, the notion of the social dimension of property, and the need to be concerned about the common welfare.[278] He rejected Marxism with its view of the necessary hostility between workers and owners—cooperation, as in the Founding culture, was the proper arrangement of things—and rightly saw it as leading to tyranny. Still, there was a similarity between Marxism's notion that workers were robbed by the capitalist of the surplus value of a good that they had created and his view that workers were being denied the fruits of their effort by means of a "measured increment" taken from them in the form of profit and rent.[279] He saw monopoly as "the prime source of social injustice," and when it came to natural monopolies like utilities he thought that the state at some level should own them.[280] His main public policy idea was a single tax on land, which he believed would cure the problem of the measured increment.[281] In spite of his similarities to Founding culture, his skepticism about profit and rent and the economic determinism in his thought[282] would be foreign to it (i.e., it would only reject extremes of the former and with its Christian character would shy away from any kind of determinism).

Two other thinkers also believed that the U.S. was not democratic in the right way, although they did not see a flawed economic order as the source of the problem. George William Curtis believed that "more adequate democratic machinery must be provided." He believed that the basic problem within American political life was the Jacksonian spoils system and he was a main intellectual spokesman for the civil service reform movement discussed above.[283] Edwin Lawrence Godkin saw the main problem not as the economic order, but an important long-standing aspect of American economic policy. He thought that Clay's "American System," in which government was expected to help economically develop the country by internal improvements had led to a situation where "favored interests" kept lining up to get publicly-funded goodies. The closeness of business and politics that had begun back in the Federalist Period needed to end and government had to revert to focusing just on its basic function of keeping the peace.[284] While the laissez faire oriented social Darwinists like Sumner and corporate leaders favored minimalist government, this was a new take on it. Curtis' ready acceptance of democracy and overly eager advocacy of a civil service system had problematical implications for both dimensions of the democratic republican idea: favoring too much popular control on the one side, and—in light of the critique of the Progressives and civil service above—an inattentiveness to its hurting popular sovereignty on the other. Godkin may have been too extreme in his criticism of government and too minimalistic in his view about the role of government, in light of the Founding Era experience.

To the contrary of these thinkers who saw democracy as a good thing, James Russell Lowell—like Whitman, known primarily as a poet—was skeptical of democracy and believed that the problem in America was not too little of it but too much. He called for a return to the spirit of the Federalist Period, where leadership would be carried out by "the better elements of society." Instead of sympathy with the growing agrarian and labor demands discussed above, he saw in it an expression of the dangers posed by democracy.[285] He certainly upheld the republicanism of the Founders and their belief in natural aristocracy, but may have had too little sense of the character of their culture as regards economic justice, widespread wealth and property-ownership, and civility. He perhaps also downplayed the democratic dimension of the American democratic republic.

While it is not clear how much direct effect the above thinkers had on the shaping of American socio-politico-economic life, it is likely that one or the other provided an intellectual buttressing for competing positions: the defense of a relative laissez faire arrangement on one side, and the attitudes that supported Progressivism and paved the way for the later more sweeping changes of the New Deal on the other.

In this chapter, we have seen how a number of the principles of the Founding Fathers were insufficiently upheld during this period, although the deviation from the supporting norms of the Founding Era culture was even more apparent. Regarding the former, we saw the following: In different ways popular sovereignty was compromised by not initially subjecting great economic power to public control, and then perhaps by such notions as a politically insulated civil service system and a Federal Reserve System as responses to it. While democracy was religiously promoted abroad, and formally adhered to domestically in principle in the popular mind and among most political thinkers, great economic power in practice challenged popular sovereignty. Among the political thinkers of the time democracy was either unquestioningly embellished or, by contrast, the democratic side of the American democratic republic submerged—in other words, the proper balance between the democratic and republican dimensions was seldom attained, even in theory. Correspondingly, the old notion of a natural aristocracy was strikingly absent even among the highest governmental figures and what substituted for it were politicians oriented mostly to power, a new financial plutocracy, and elitist reformers. Separation of powers and checks and balances were both strengthened in this period by the restoration of presidential power and the American version of mixed government was also restored along with this. As the period went on, however, these were to some degree to be weakened again by the Seventeenth Amendment, the new exertion of judicial power, and the emergence of institutions like the Federal Reserve. The Seventeenth Amendment and the development of federal grants-in-aid programs damaged federalism. The rule of law was compromised by the vagueness that began to appear in the new regulatory law and white-collar crime statutes and in the refusal to afford protection to minority groups and to restrain great economic power. The natural law tradition of the Founding gave way to domestic and foreign policy moralism (which further represented a loss of Founding realism), rising positivistic jurisprudential notions, the philosophy of pragmatism, and the developing eugenics movement. Morality in practice was affronted by public corruption and in theory by the positivistic jurisprudence that saw it as having no rightful relationship with law and politics. The Founders' stress on the common good gave way to a new norm of individualism (seen especially in economics, but also in how people typically used politics to gain something for themselves and in the "new thinking" about the family). The restrained sense of equality of the Founding Fathers was distorted, with sharp disparities in wealth and situation broadly evident in the new industrial age. This new inequality was not just economic, however, but also in a significant way political—for even though all male citizens now had the vote, the average citizen could not attempt to have the public influence that the wealthy or political machine operatives did (nor, indeed, in an age when Senate seats were bought could good men of limited means easily gain political offices). There was appearing carelessness about public debt. The period ended with a permanently larger standing military, contrary to the Founders' principle. In spite of the attempts at neutrality in the early years of World War I, there were many disturbing cases of the violation of the Founders' insistence on foreign affairs impartiality. A number of basic political and legal rights stressed by the Founding Fathers were seriously undermined during World War I, and the rights of property distorted by the loss of a sense of social obligation regarding its use and chipped away at by the emergence of certain real property regulations on the local level. Religious commitment discernibly weakened and as the nature of mainstream religion lost its doctrinal focus a sound—realist—understanding of human nature was also lost. A vague humanitarianism emerged to refashion men's relationships to different aspects of culture and public life. The political thought of the time became increasingly secular, and for the most part stood at the extremes of too much or too little government.

This period saw the diminishing of almost the full range of Founding Era cultural norms. The root was perhaps the individualism mentioned above. As mentioned, in economics we witnessed the sweeping loss—developing throughout the nineteenth century as laissez faire took hold and coming to a head in the Gilded Age—of the principle of the social obligation of property. Economics was shorn of the ethical framework seen in the Founding, so that it was now viewed, essentially, as an amoral and merely technical matter. Thus, great disparities in wealth so contrary to the middle class culture of the Founding became deeply entrenched, economic freedom saw no limitation, and the old anti-monopolistic convictions were completely overturned. Also, instead of those who were advantaged acting as their brother's keeper they sought to suppress the legitimate demands of marginalized workers and farmers for reasons of their own interests. Deep divisions developed between the wealthy and the dispossessed, the immigrant and the native-born, different religious groups, minorities and the mainstream. The result was that the incivility, lack of civic friendship and a cooperative spirit, and damaging of the common good of the 1840-1877 period continued—with less intensity and violence, perhaps, and the absence of a cataclysmic conflict of the nature of the Civil War, but involving larger numbers of people and with more of a basis in economics. Basic justice was offended in the treatment of some groups. Also, involved in the economically generated developments of the time was the loss of the spirit of temperance and a drive for luxury. The latter and the lack of moderation, simplicity, and self-sacrifice were also seen in the renewed imperialism of this time. The absence of civility, respect for the common good, and even the spirit of gentlemanliness were evident in America's relationship with its Mexican neighbor. Ever increasing centralization—in economics with the rise of corporate giants and monopolies spanning the entire country, and in government with a greater reliance on federal power to counter it and to undertake twentieth-century war—was the new reality, so contrary to the Founding culture of smallness and the early spirit of federalism. The growth of centralization, bureaucratization, and mass culture and the erosion of communal life was counterbalanced in part by the increase of associational activity. Such basic, everyday cultural norms of the Founding, which loomed large even in the carrying out of economic and political affairs, as honesty, truth-telling, and fair-dealing, flagged in this time. The moral downside of Gilded Age economics was only partly compensated for by the stress on Founding-like qualities of industry, sacrifice, self-directedness, initiative-taking, courage, practical intelligence, and other entrepreneurial virtues of the self-made men of industry. The type of education stressed by the Founding Fathers as so critical for future leaders—the liberal arts—continued its decline from the previous historical period. This further helped to weaken the realist outlook characteristic of Founding times and encouraged both the contrasting perspectives of quasi-utopianism and social Darwinism and also the philosophy of pragmatism with its effective denial of truth. The family, which the Founding era saw as at the center of culture and the foundation for sound political life (see Tocqueville's comments), had continued to suffer from the likes of rising divorce. While the period may have seen a tightening of sexual norms overall—as witnessed by the Comstock laws and tighter divorce laws to counter the greater incidence of divorce—the family was on the verge of facing an unprecedented assault and weakening as the twentieth century rolled on by socio-cultural movements and the waning hold of religion that became evident in the 1877-1920 period.

It seems, overall, that many of the socio-cultural trends deviating from the Founding cultural norms that were visible in the 1840-1877 period were enhanced and deepened, and spread more widely. The principles the Founding Fathers themselves stressed did not face the big, dramatic challenges that they did in that period (e.g., the substantial overreach of judicial power in the *Dred Scott* decision), but were perhaps more numerous and permanent (e.g., the growth of federal government power). Basic citizen rights also faced perhaps the greatest challenge in American history. Possibly most profound were the socio-cultural and philosophical changes (e.g., pragmatism and Holmesian thought) that saw natural law increasingly pushed from the mainstream of American thought and that transformed religion—particularly mainline Protestantism—and affected even the life and perspective of the average person. We need to go no further than Washington's Farewell Address to realize how central religion and morality are to a democratic republic.

As indicated, this period in the U.S. witnessed the appearance of most of the factors the thinkers who wrote on this subject saw as causing the decline of political societies: a weakening religious commitment and a change in traditional religious belief, materialism and the excessive pursuit of luxury, social conflict and turmoil, the prevalence (at least increasingly, in thought) of a relativistic ethical outlook, over-centralization and an excessive emphasis on bigness, a weakening of the middle class and serious economic disorders, excessive urbanization and the rise of a mass culture, the glimmers of an anti-traditional viewpoint (seen in such things as the education reform movement), an increasing moralism, the growth of militarism in at least a limited way (around World War I), the descent of politics into a struggle for power, the weakening in certain—but definite—ways of the rule of law, the breakdown or neglect of the common good, and the corruption of sound philosophy (seen in the social Darwinism, pragmatism, and political and legal thought of the time). As the previous chapters make evident, more of these factors were seen in this period than in any previous one—in fact, most of them were visible (see Chapter 1).

Finally, the points of possible weakness in the Founding vision from Chapter 1 that perhaps are suggested by the period from 1877 to 1920 were these: an incomplete public philosophy, lack of a full awareness of the principles of social ethics, and a good understanding of the common good all due to insufficient philosophical reflection; the seeds of an expanded individualism; the roots of positivism because interpretation of the natural law was left to private judgment, without a reliance on the Catholic Church; the lack of a reliable way to bring forth a natural aristocracy; too rigid of—or, more correctly, an insufficiently flexible—view of federalism, which like the 1840-1877 period saw too much federal government action in some areas and too little in others; an insufficient stress on intermediary associations, justice, and community; the downplaying of statesmanship; emphasis on the notion of the commercial republic eventually giving rise to more individualism and laissez faire; a lack of realization of how much the hold of religion would weaken and with it the worldview and morality shaped by it; failure to see the family's centrality to the political order; a lack of awareness of how powerful the courts would become; and how so much of a stress on institutional and structural factors helped lead to bureaucratization.

Notes

1. Thomas C. Cochran and William Miller, *The Age of Enterprise: A Social History of Industrial America* (rev. edn.; N.Y.: Harper & Row, 1961), 142, 151. Emphasis is added.
2. Ibid., 202.
3. Ibid., 140-141.
4. Ibid., 140.
5. Ibid., 148-150.
6. Ibid., 142.
7. Ibid., 150; "Panic of 1893," http://en.wikipedia.org/wiki/Panic_of_1893; Internet; accessed Jan. 28, 2009.
8. Cochran and Miller, 192-193.

9. Ibid., 198-200.

10. Ibid., 189-190.

11. Ibid., 228-229.

12. Ibid., 244, 247.

13. Ibid., 230.

14. Joseph G. Rayback, *A History of American Labor* (rev. edn.; N.Y.: Free Press, 1966), 133.

15. Ibid., 134-135.

16. See ibid., 135-140.

17. Ibid., 158-163.

18. Ibid., 167-168.

19. Ibid., 174, 178; "Knights of Labor," http://en.wikipedia.org/wiki/Knights _of_Labor; Internet; accessed Jan. 29, 2009.

20. See Rayback, 194-226.

21. Ibid., 261.

22. Ibid., 233-234, 241, 244, 245, 248, 256-258.

23. See, e.g., ibid., 226-249; Tindall and Shi, 922-926; Cochran and Miller, 237.

24. See Philip Taft and Philip Ross, "American Labor Violence: Its Causes, Character, and Outcome," *The History of Violence in America: A Report to the National Commission on the Causes and Prevention of Violence*, ed. Hugh Davis Graham and Ted Robert Gurr, 1969; http://www.ditext.com/taft/vio-con.html; Internet; accessed Feb. 22, 2009.

25. Tindall and Shi, 1073.

26. Rayback, 260.

27. Ibid., 262-265.

28. Ibid., 266-272; Tindall and Shi, 1114.

29. Rayback, 273-274.

30. Tindall and Shi, 1013-1014.

31. Ibid., 1015.

32. See ibid., 1016-1023; "Farmers' Alliance," http://en.wikipedia.org/wiki/ Farmer's_Alliance; Internet; accessed Jan. 30, 2009; "Populist Party (United States)," http://en.wikipedia.org/wiki/Populist_Party_(United_States); Internet; accessed Jan. 30, 2009.

33. Tindall and Shi, 1016-1017.

34. Ibid., 1017-1021.

35. Ibid., 1022.

36. Cashman, 325.

37. Tindall and Shi, 908.

38. Cochran and Miller, 187.

39. Paul Johnson, *A History of the American People*, 580.

40. Cashman, 143; Paul Johnson, *A History of the American People*, 581.

41. Cochran and Miller, 181.

42. Rayback, 189.

43. Ibid., 188.

44. Tindall and Shi, 896.

45. Rayback, 189.

46. Ibid., 188.

47. Ibid., 188.

48. Tindall and Shi, 895-896.

49. Rayback, 190.

50. Tindall and Shi, 908-909. Some might dispute the latter statement, by pointing to such facts that, despite a 20 per cent increase in per capita income in the U.S., price increases caused the average American worker's purchasing power to decline 5 to 6 per cent from the turn of the century to the start of World War I (Cochran and Miller, 234-235). Still, most would agree that this is a correct assessment. As time went on, most workers became better off.

51. Cochran and Miller, 231-232.

52. Rayback, 304. Rayback discusses this in the portion of the book that speaks about the early 1920s, but it is clear from how he speaks about it that it is a general assertion about the effects of new technologies that applied to the previous period as well.

53. Cashman, 360.

54. Tindall and Shi, 1080.

55. See ibid., 1080.

56. Ibid., 1005.

57. Ibid., 1089-1091.

58. Ibid., 1098-1099.

59. Ibid., 1109-1110.

60. Ibid., 1138.

61. Poscoe Pound, *The Development of Constitutional Guarantees of Liberty* (New Haven, Conn.: Yale University Press, 1957), 84. It might even be argued that indirectly this protection against monopolies found its way into the U.S. Constitution as part of the privileges and immunities clause.

62. Tindall and Shi, 997; Cashman, 251, 271-273.

63. Tindall and Shi, 1108.

64. Cashman, 273; "Income Tax in the United States," http://en.wikipedia. org/wiki/Income_tax_in_the_United_States; Internet; accessed Feb. 1. 2009. The Supreme Court case was *Pollock v. Farmers' Loan and Trust Co.*, 157 U.S. 429, aff'd on reh'g, 158 U.S. 601.

65. Lawrence M. Friedman, *A History of American Law* (N.Y.: Simon and Schuster [Touchstone], 1973), 497-500.

66. Cashman, 256, 264-265, 268.

67. "Tariffs in American History," http://en.wikipedia.org/wiki/Tariff_in_ American_history; Internet; accessed Feb. 1, 2009.

68. Ibid.

69. "Obama's Budget Balances Deficit Reduction and Stimulus Spending," Bloomberg.com;http://www.bloomberg.com/apps/news?pid=20601103&sid=atVV2FPW lH4&refer=us; Internet; accessed Feb. 23, 2009.

70. "Homestead Act," http://en.wikipedia.org/wiki/Homestead_Act; Internet; accessed Feb. 1, 2009.

71. Cashman, 285, 290.

72. Tindall and Shi, 1112-1113.

73. Eugene Boyd, "American Federalism, 1776 to 1997: Significant Events," http://usa.usembassy.de/etexts/gov/ federal.htm#dual2; Internet; accessed Feb. 7, 2009.

74. Tindall and Shi, 992-993.

75. Ibid., 1091-1092.

76. Ibid., 1098.

77. Ibid., 1083.

78. "Eminent Domain," http://en.wikipedia.org/wiki/Eminent_domain; Internet; accessed Feb. 1, 2009. The case was *Chicago, Burlington & Quincy Railroad v. Chicago*, 166 U.S. 226 (1897).

79. See, e.g., Friedman, 315.

80. See *Kelo v. New London*, 545 U.S. 469 (2005).

81. Cashman, 247.

82. Tindall and Shi, 992.

83. Leonard D. White, *The Republican Era: 1869-1901* (N.Y.: Macmillan, 1958), 378-379.

84. Cashman, 253-257; Tindall and Shi, 992. The quotation is from Cashman, 253.

85. L. White, 13.

86. Ibid., 383.

87. Ibid., 383-384.

88. Tindall and Shi, 999.

89. "Civil Service," http://en.wikipedia.org/wiki/Civil_service; Internet; accessed Feb. 2, 2009.

90. Cashman, 246.

91. Quoted in Tindall and Shi, 996.

92. See Berkin, Miller, Cherny, and Gormly, 516; Tindall and Shi, 994.

93. Berkin, Miller, Cherny, and Gormly, 516.

94. Tindall and Shi, 1001-1003.

95. Cashman, 262, 266.

96. Ibid., 260. The quotation is from James Bryce, *The American Commonwealth*, I, xiv.

97. L. White, 48.

98. Albert C. Ganley, *The Progressive Movement: Traditional Reform* (N.Y.: Macmillan, 1964), 27.

99. Richard Hofstadter, *The Age of Reform: From Bryan to F.D.R.* (N.Y.: Vintage, 1955), 257.

100. Ganley, 31.

101. Hofstadter, *The Age of Reform*, 257.

102. L. White, 295.

103. Berkin, Miller, Cherny, and Gormly, 640.

104. Ganley, 77.

105. L. White, 18.

106. Ibid., 316-317.

107. Ibid., 45.

108. Ibid., 97.

109. Ibid., 99.

110. Ibid., 295.

111. Tindall and Shi, 1084.

112. Ibid.

113. Ibid., 1085-1086.

114. See ibid., 1089-1092.

115. Ibid., 1095-1096; .

116. See, e.g., Ganley, 76-80.

117. L. White, 100-102.

118. Ibid., 93-94, 392.

119. Ibid., 39-40.

120. Ibid., 48.

121. Melvin I. Urofsky, *A March of Liberty: A Constitutional History of the United States* (N.Y.: Alfred A. Knopf, 1988), 575.

122. Ibid. The citation for *Adair* is 208 U.S.161 (1908), and for *Lochner* is 198 U.S. 45 (1905).

123. Ibid., 576-578.

124. Boyd.

125. Ibid.

126. Tindall and Shi, 1073.

127. Cashman, 372.

128. Cochran and Miller, 204. On Strong, see "Josiah Strong," http://en. wikipedia.org/wiki/Josiah_Strong; on Mahan, see "Alfred Thayer Mahan," http://en. wikipedia.org/wiki/Alfred_Thayer_Mahan; and Tindall and Shi, 1036; on Fiske, see "John Fiske (philosopher)," http://en.wikipedia.org/wiki/John_Fiske_(philosopher); all these Internet sources were accessed Feb. 9, 2009.

129. Tindall and Shi, 1039.

130. Ibid., 1039-1041.

131. Ibid., 1041-1042.

132. Ibid., 1042-1048. The quotations are from 1042-1043.

133. Ibid., 1053.

134. Ibid., 1055-1058.

135. Ibid, 1053, quoting a talk McKinley gave to a Methodist group.

136. Ibid., 1059-1060.

137. Ibid., 1063-1066. The quotation is from 1066.

138. Cochran and Miller, 210.

139. Tindall and Shi, 1068.

140. Ibid., 1069.

141. Ibid., 1118. On dollar diplomacy, see "Dollar Diplomacy," http://en. wikipedia.org/wiki/Dollar_Diplomacy; Internet; accessed Feb. 14, 2009.

142. Warren H, Carroll, *1917: Red Banners, White Mantle* (Ft. Royal, Va.: Christendom Publications, 1981), 108.

143. Tindall and Shi, 1119-1121.

144. Ibid., 1121-1122. The quotation is from 1122.

145. Ibid.,

146. Ibid., 1129-1130.

147. Ibid., 1132-1134. The quotations from Wilson are from 1133 and 1134.

148. Ibid., 1136; Brian Mitchell, *Women in the Military: Flirting with Disaster* (Washington, D.C.: Regnery, 1998), 3 (on the point about women in the World War I military).

149. Tindall and Shi, 1138-1139.

150. Ibid., 1140.

151. "U.S. Army," http://www.spartacus.schoolnet.co.uk/USAarmy.htm; Internet; accessed Feb. 24, 2009.

152. About the historic problems of arms control and disarmament, see, e.g., Hans J. Morgenthau, *Politics Among Nations: The Struggle for Power and Peace* (6th edn.; N.Y.: Alfred A. Knopf, 1985), 419-439.

153. These principles are stated in Wilson's "Fourteen Points" Speech, as it appears in *War, Labor and Peace* (Washington, D.C.: Committee of Public Information, 1918).

154. Tindall and Shi, 1154-1155.

155. See, e.g., Hamilton or Madison Federalist 51, 335-341.

156. Urofsky, 534. The key decision on this was *Standard Oil v. U.S.*, 221 U.S. 1 (1911).

157. Friedman, 406.

158. Urofsky, 548-549. The most pertinent decisions were *Hammer v. Dagenhart*, 247 U.S. 251 (1918) and, shortly after the period under consideration, *Bailey v. Drexel Furniture Co.*, 259 U.S. 20 (1922).

159. Urofsky, 547.

160. Urofsky, 550-551. The Supreme Court decision was *Muller v. Oregon*, 208 U.S. 412.

161. Urofsky, 552-553.

162. Ibid., 562-563.

163. See McCloskey, 131-135.

164. Urofsky, 563.

165. Ibid., 501.

166. Friedman, 382. The Supreme Court's decision was *Trade-Mark Cases*, 100 U.S. 82 (1879).

167. Ibid., 374-375.

168. Ibid., 366-367

169. Ibid., 584.

170. Ibid., 510. The citation to the 1819 *Dartmouth College* case is 4 Wheat. (17 U.S.) 518.

171. This was by no means the first example in American history of the state's supplanting of parental authority (see Allan C. Carlson, *Family Questions: Reflections on the American Social Crisis* [New Brunswick, N.J.: Transaction Press, 1988], 234-235, 242-243).

172. Friedman, 136-139.

173. See Aristotle, *The Politics*, II, iv.

174. Friedman, 510-512.

175. Julie Husband and Jim O'Laughlin, *Daily Life in the Industrial United States, 1870-1900* (Westport, Conn.: Greenwood Press, 2004), 129-130.

176. See Carlson, 241-256.

177. Urofsky, 481. The case was *Hall v. DeCuir*, 95 U.S. 485.

178. Urofsky, 481. The case was *Louisville, New Orleans & Texas Railway v. Mississippi*, 133 U.S. 587.

179. Urofsky, 481. The citation for *Plessy* is 163 U.S. 537.

180. Urofsky, 482.

181. Friedman, 349.

182. Urofsky, 482.

183. Tindall and Shi, 1141.

184. Ibid., 1160.

185. "Oliver Wendell Holmes, Jr.," http://en.wikipedia.org/wiki/Oliver_Wendell_Holmes,_Jr.; Internet; accessed Feb. 20, 2009.

186. Morton White, *Social Thought in America: The Revolt Against Formalism* (Boston: Beacon Press, 1957), 64.

187. Ibid., 65.

188. Robert H. Wiebe, *The Search for Order: 1877-1920* (N.Y.: Hill and Wang, 1967), 147.

189. "Legal Realism," *West's Encyclopedia of American Law*, http://www.answers.com/topic/legal-realism; Internet; accessed March 21, 2010.

190. John Higham, *Strangers in the Land: Patterns of American Nativism 1860-1925* (N.Y.: Atheneum, 1975 [originally published by Rutgers University Press, 1955]), 110, 159.

191. Cochran and Miller, 230.

192. Tindall and Shi, 937.
193. Ibid.
194. Cochran and Miller, 230.
195. Higham, 40.
196. Tindall and Shi, 932.
197. Cochran and Miller, 250.
198. Cashman, 135.
199. Tindall and Shi, 932.
200. Ibid., 931-932. The quotation is from 931.
201. Cashman, 136.
202. See ibid., 284-291.
203. Ibid., 283.
204. Tindall and Shi, 946.
205. Ibid., 945.
206. Ibid., 1166.
207. Ibid., 946.
208. Ibid., 946-947; Friedman, 444.
209. Higham, 166.
210. Ibid., 138-139. The quotation is from 138.
211. Ibid., 139.
212. Tindall and Shi, 1165; "Madison Grant," http://en.wikipedia.org/wiki/
Madison_Grant; Internet; accessed Feb. 16, 2009.
213. Higham, 92-93.
214. Ibid., 84.
215. Husband and O'Loughlin, 229-230.
216. See, e.g., Higham, 84-93.
217. Tindall and Shi, 1138, 1158-1159.
218. Husband and O'Loughlin, 224-225.
219. Ibid., 225-226.
220. Ibid., 225.
221. S.E. Frost, Jr., *Historical and Philosophical Foundations of Western Education*
(Columbus, O.: Charles E. Merrill Books, 1966), 424.
222. Husband and O'Loughlin, 226-227.
223. Ibid., 233.
224. Ibid., 230.
225. Hamburger, 356, 366-369, 391-397, 399-400.
226. Ibid., 337.
227. Ibid., 338-339.
228. Ibid., 338, 343.
229. Ibid., 345-346.
230. Ibid., 356-358.
231. Tindall and Shi, 951.
232. Cashman, 367.
233. Ibid.
234. Ibid., 367-368.
235. William A. Bullough, *Cities and Schools in the Gilded Age: The Evolution of
an Urban Institution* (Port Washington, N.Y.: Kennikat, 1974), 142.
236. Urofsky, 487.
237. Bullough, 95-96.
238. Ibid., 97.

239. Ibid., 90-91, 145.

240. Ibid., 82-85.

241. Frost, 424.

242. Ibid., 425.

243. Christopher Lasch, *The New Radicalism in America, 1889-1963: The Intellectual as a Social Type* (N.Y.: W.W. Norton, 1965), 159-160.

244. Ibid., 175.

245. Bullough, 93.

246. Tindall and Shi, 971.

247. Bullough, 92.

248. Ibid.

249. Husband and O'Loughlin, 143-144.

250. See Tindall and Shi, 981-982

251. Husband and O'Loughlin, 143-144.

252. See James Reed, *From Private Vice to Public Virtue: The Birth Control Movement and American Society Since 1830* (N.Y.: Basic Books, 1978). On the almost universal moral condemnation of contraception in traditional Christian teaching until the twentieth century, see: "Birth Control," http://www.catholic.com/library/Birth_Control.asp; Internet; "Christian Views on Contraception," http://en.wikipedia.org/wiki/Christian_views_on_contraception; Internet; both accessed Feb. 28, 2009.

253. Husband and O'Loughlin, 139, 144.

254. Lasch, 142.

255. Carlson, 241-256.

256. This is indicated by Carlson at 246-248.

257. Husband and O'Loughlin, 234-235.

258. See ibid., 234.

259. Cashman, 140.

260. Husband and O'Loughlin, 164.

261. Richard Hofstadter, *Social Darwinism in American Thought* (rev. edn.; Boston: Beacon Press, 1955), 161, 163.

262. See Robert Marshall and Charles Donovan, *Blessed Are the Barren: The Social Policy of Planned Parenthood* (San Francisco: Ignatius Press, 1991), 275-281.

263. Hofstadter, *Social Darwinism in American Thought*, 166-167.

264. Carlson, 237.

265. Hofstadter, *Social Darwinism in American Thought*, 167.

266. Ibid., 58.

267. Ibid., 59.

268. Ibid., 60.

269. Verson Louis Parrington, *The Beginnings of Critical Realism in America, 1860-1920*, vol. 3, *Main Currents in American Thought* (N.Y.: Harcourt, Brace & World, 1930), 233-234. The quotations are from 234 and 233, respectively.

270. Ibid., 235.

271. Ibid., 307.

272. Ibid., 308. See also Hilaire Belloc, *The Servile State* (Indianapolis: Liberty Classics, 1977).

273. Parrington, 309-310. The quotations are from 310.

274. Ibid., 311-313. The quotations are from 311.

275. Ibid., 82. Emphasis in the original.

276. Ibid., 76.

277. Ibid., 84, 76.

278. Ibid., 130, 131, 135.

279. Ibid., 134-135.

280. Ibid., 136; "Henry George," http://en.wikipedia.org/wiki/Henry_George; Internet; accessed Fen 21, 2009.

281. "Henry George."

282. Parrington, 136.

283. Ibid., 138.

284. Ibid., 138-139.

285. Ibid., 138.

CHAPTER 6

1920-1945: THE "ROARING TWENTIES," THE GREAT DEPRESSION, AND WORLD WAR II

A great cataclysm such as World War I could not help but to change American culture, although as will be noted many of the developments that emerged were part of longer range trends already seen previously. This twenty-five-year period proceeded from disillusionment, cultural upheaval, retreat from the world, and a prosperous but really mixed economic situation in the 1920s; to the deepest economic depression in American history, an unparalleled (to that time) expansion of federal government power and responsibilities to respond to it, and the rise of a new, more fearsome international threat and specter of war in Europe and the Pacific; to an unprecedented American military effort in history's most destructive conflict and the concomitant further expansion of federal power in order to carry it out. Cultural upheaval, massive federal government expansion, and participation in large-scale warfare have obvious implications for Founding principles and the mores needed to sustain them, as they have been discussed in this book. Our examination in this chapter focuses on the following eight areas, which are similar or virtually identical to those considered in previous chapters: economics, economic policy, and labor questions; relations among the three branches of the federal government and the role and powers of the federal government; constitutional change, constitutional law developments, and citizen rights; significant political developments and socio-political movements; immigration and relations among racial, ethnic, and religious groups and economic classes; foreign affairs and war-making; socio-cultural developments; and currents in political and social thought. Since economics was such a prominent feature of most of this period, we start our discussion with it and treat it at some length. As with previous historical periods, we do not treat the developments in great detail but provide a sufficiency of information to enable us to make our comparison with the Founding Era and its principles.

This period began by the final defeat of the Treaty of Versailles, insuring an American retrenchment from significant international political involvement, in

1920 and the election of Warren G. Harding later that year (the international retrenchment was a significant part of Harding's "return to normalcy"). The U.S. signed separate peace treaties with its World War I adversaries in 1921. The 1920s were the only complete decade to experience the regimen of Prohibition, and women's suffrage also began to be implemented. Both the Eighteenth (Prohibition) and Nineteenth (women's suffrage) Amendments went into effect in 1920. The Harding administration was wracked by the Teapot Dome Scandal, which involved favoritism and bribery in letting out oil exploration leases on federal land, and ended prematurely by the death of the president. Vice President Calvin Coolidge then became President. The twenties seemed to be the era of business in America. It was also a time of unprecedented immigration control; organized gangsterism (encouraged by Prohibition); the spread of new technologies, such as the automobile and radio, throughout the culture that changed American life; unrealistic attempts to abolish or outlaw war culminating in the Kellogg-Briand Pact; and a weakening of sexual restraint. Herbert C. Hoover came to the presidency in 1929 after a campaign that featured strong anti-Catholic sentiment directed against the Democratic nominee, and first major party Catholic candidate, Al Smith. Hoover's presidency was quickly throttled by the stock market crash of October 1929 and the onset of the Great Depression. He faced the political repercussions of it—having been blamed for insufficient federal government intervention to address it—in the realigning election of 1932, which swept Franklin D. Roosevelt into the White House and began a Democratic hold on the presidency and Congress for most of the next five decades. Roosevelt inaugurated massive federal legislative efforts—the New Deal—to correct and regulate the economy, support labor, and construct a federal social "safety net," as is discussed below. Prohibition was also repealed by the Twenty-first Amendment late in 1933. (Near the very end of Hoover's term the Twentieth Amendment, whose main importance was that it moved the presidential inauguration day from March 4 to January 20, was ratified, but did not go into effect until 1937.) Some important New Deal legislation was struck down by the U.S. Supreme Court that, after FDR's sweeping reelection victory in 1936, led to his ill-fated court-packing plan below. Although he suffered politically for that, he was then able to make a string of appointments to the Court that insured more favorable rulings and shifted its direction (also discussed below). His domestic initiatives waned in the later 1930s, as war clouds gathered abroad and he turned his attention to foreign affairs and eventually to building support in a reluctant nation for efforts to help the Allies. With the likely prospect of U.S. entry into the war, FDR was reelected in 1940—becoming the first president to be elected to a third term. Then came the Pearl Harbor attack in late 1941, which thrust the U.S. into complete war mobilization and a massive military effort in a two-front war. FDR was elected to a fourth term in 1944, but died on April 12, 1945. Vice President Harry S. Truman became president. The war in Europe ended a few weeks later. The Pacific war, of course, ended formally on September 2, 1945, after the dropping of the atomic bombs on Hiroshima and Nagasaki.

With this brief overview of the main historical developments of the period, we proceed to look more at the specifics of the areas above.

Economics, Economic Policy, and Labor Questions. At the end of World War I the U.S. had become, for the first time in her history, a "creditor" nation—that is, foreigners owed American investors much more money than was owed abroad.[1] The 1920s saw a significant economic expansion, with prosperity largely continuous until the stock market crash. William E. Leuchtenburg says that the U.S. "achieved the highest standard of living any people had ever known."[2] Per capita income "soared" from where it had been before the war, workers received the highest wages in U.S. history, and there was an "enormous increase in efficiency of production." This sharp productivity increase was achieved by "more efficient management, greater mechanization, intensive research, and ingenious sales methods."[3] Such industries as the automotive, petroleum, chemicals, steel, construction, telecommunications, power, consumer goods, and financial services expanded greatly. There was also a real estate boom, which reached its highest levels in Florida and California.[4] The bigness and merger activity of the Gilded Age continued and expanded, as seen in such industries as power and utilities generally, banking, automobiles, meat-packing, and retail sales. By the end of the decade, "the consolidation movement in American business reached boom proportions."[5] Even farming was becoming a larger scale enterprise in the 1920s, and shared in the mechanization of production industries.[6] Of course, the bigness, which had long since become the norm of American economic life, went against the decentralization typical of Founding Era economics. The economic expansion—and to some degree corporate desire to stymie union-organizing—led to a flourishing of the welfare capitalism mentioned in Chapter 5. Factory buildings with more safety features and employee cafeterias were constructed. The shorter workday and workweek were becoming more typical. Profit-sharing, employee stock-ownership plans, bonuses, pension programs, health programs, company recreational activities, and personnel departments were established.[7] Even if 1920's welfare capitalism did not have entirely positive motivations behind it—and if it was likely to continue only in prosperous times—it did seem more sincere than when attempted in the Gilded Age. It was not now an excuse to cut wages and the like. It conformed to the Founding culture's spirit of being one's brother's keeper and being concerned about the general welfare, and exhibited some sense of the social obligation of property.

There were significant weaknesses in the economy also, however, which led ultimately to the collapse that began late in 1929. In spite of the overall unprecedented high wage levels, many Americans suffered low wages and irregular employment. Anthony J. Badger tells us that, "[m]ost working-class males and many in the middle class were not paid enough to support their families above a subsistence level" (this makes one wonder if the supposed middle class was really a middle class).[8] Indeed, profit levels were disproportionately high compared to wages and ran well ahead of productivity.[9] The high level of profits proved to be a major factor in instigating the stock market crash, as many companies had so much excess profit that they poured it into the market and caused "a runaway speculation."[10] Further, the wage gains were unevenly distributed in the economy. The rise in farm income was only half of the rise in non-farm income.[11] Farming was generally a troubled sector of the economy throughout the 1920s—and its situation became even worse during the Depression.[12] Farm tenancy and the number of farm mortgages both increased, as the value of farm products plummeted.[13] Besides farming, certain other industries suffered: mining, railroads, shipping, textiles, shipbuilding, and shoe and leather production.[14] The per capita income increase of the top 1% of the population almost doubled, while that of the lower 93% went up only 6%.[15] There was also a considerable geographical disparity. The Northeast and West Coast were the most prosperous regions, and the Midwest and South lagged behind.[16] The real estate boom in places like Florida was partly fueled by speculation—which accompanied the stock market speculation—until the bubble burst in 1926.[17] There was an overproduction of consumer goods,[18] but with the higher profits not translating into sufficiently higher wages for most people there was not a large enough of a market for them.[19] The banking sector was also in difficulty. There were nearly 5,000 bank collapses in the 1920s,[20] and most banks were "pitifully undercapitalized."[21] By 1927, various measures of economic activity were declining.[22] They were insufficiently heeded, however, possibly because the speculation-driven stock market continued to gain and an excessively optimistic attitude had taken hold in the early 1920s that economic growth would be permanent.[23]

A number of points present themselves when comparing to the Founding Era. First, the lack of a sufficient wage for many people would have offended that era's stress on notions of what later came to be called a just wage and the universal destination of goods. Second, and following from this, the concentration of wealth and great disparities of wealth—as we also said when discussing the Gilded Age—would have clashed with the prevailing principles of the Founding culture. Even if the standard of living was increasing in the 1920s for many, it was in no way the middle class culture of Founding times. As such, even if the Founders' notion of equality was accepted formally, the economic disparities make one think that *in practice* it was much compromised. People may have had the equal right to accumulate wealth in a theoretical sense, but there were most likely practical obstacles to that for most of them. Obviously, the economic disparities among regions showed a condition where the general welfare was not being furthered. The inattentiveness of government to the various kinds of economic disparities at this time perhaps showed that it was not willing adequately to uphold the Founding Fathers' principle that part of government's purpose was to promote the common good. While, to be sure, there might have been legitimate federalism concerns, state governments were not addressing such matters any more than the federal government was and it could hardly have been expected that the states could adequately address problems of a nationalized economy or problems such as regional differences. Overall, the relative unwillingness of government to put restraints on economic freedom was counter to the Founding period, where it will be recalled there were many laws imposing such limits. Finally, the substantial speculation of the period represented a kind of unproductive investment rejected by the Founding culture.

Virtually all of these conditions had been seen at different times in the nineteenth century, and had become especially evident in the last quarter of that century. They all came together and considerably mushroomed in the 1920s and 1930s.

The 1920s saw organized labor's fortunes decline. David J. Goldberg says that the combination of an open-shop drive, capital flight, and technological developments caused big losses in A.F. of L. membership in the early 1920s. Unions in mining, brewing, textiles, and railroads—"among...[its] most militant and progressive unions"—were the hardest hit. Further, the fastest growing industries—such as the automotive, rubber, chemicals, and power—"remained almost totally union-free."[24] Overall, from 1920 to 1923, A.F. of L. membership declined 1.4 million.[25] United Mine Workers (UMW) membership declined 80% in the 1920s.[26] There were also some serious labor conflicts in the decade. The Great Railroad Strike of 1922, which involved a walkout by railway shop workers, was halted when the U.S. attorney general got a court injunction. This was not an uncommon response. Almost half of the injunctions issued by federal courts to end strikes over a 130-year period came in the 1920s.[27] 1922 witnessed other strikes in textiles (which followed from a 20% pay cut) and coal mining (which saw deadly violence on both sides, including ritualistic murders of strikebreakers by a mob).[28]

Some of the federal economic policies of the 1920s helped pave the way for the eventual economic collapse. Most noteworthy were the high tariff rates, consistently increased throughout the decade. The U.S. insisted in the early part of the decade that its World War I allies repay all that they had borrowed during the war. The only way the Allied nations could do that was through the trade of goods and services with the U.S., but the high tariff barriers made that difficult. Some of the pressure was taken off by the Dawes Plan of 1924, which defused the financial and international crisis caused by France's occupation of the Ruhr Valley after Germany defaulted on its war reparations payments—which were mandated by the Treaty of Versailles—by committing the U.S. to lend money to Germany to enable them to continue the payment. That, in turn, enabled the Allied powers to continue making debt payments to the U.S. The U.S. got its money back not by lowering tariff barriers and trading more with the Allies, but by Germany's reparations payments that were funneled to the U.S.—from money the U.S. lent to Germany in the first place. Actually, European financial strength was increasingly dependent on American investment and tourism dollars. Later in the decade, shortly before the stock market crash, American investment tailed off. After the crash, it was drastically cut, and with that Leuchtenburg says that "the underpinnings of the international economy were pulled out and the whole system collapsed."[29] Even after this, decisionmakers in Washington did not comprehend the problem presented by high tariffs. In 1930, the Hawley-Smoot Tariff was enacted and raised rates even further.[30] There was nothing in the Founding Era that militated against tariffs, and as we saw in Chapter 2 even protective tariffs were proposed by Hamilton in the 1790s and implemented during Madison's presidency. The ever-increasing tariff levels of the 1920s, however, would seem to have offended the temperate, self-controlled spirit of the Founding Era and its emphasis on commercial efficiency. The spirit of friendship and concern for the common good of the Founding also seemed to have been harmed, since as we saw in Chapters 3 and 4 these extended beyond the boundaries of the nation. Other harmful federal policies, according to Leuchtenburg, were those in the areas of taxing (which encouraged over-saving by the rich and aggravated the maldistribution of income), anti-trust (which "added to the rigidity of the market and left business corporations too insensitive to changes of price"), farm (which promoted imbalance among sectors of the economy), fiscal (which tended to favor business interests too strongly), and monetary (the Federal Reserve lowered the discount rate too much and over-stimulated the stock market).[31] When one considers all this, he gets the sense of the great complexity of the American economy and governmental economic policy by the 1920s. Although greater complexity is to be expected as things go on and develop, its contrast from the simplicity of the Founding period was striking. The strong pro-business bias of fiscal policy was duplicated in the regulatory agencies, which were led by Harding and Coolidge appointees.[32] In fact, Tindall and Shi recall a *Wall Street Journal* article of the time that stated that under Coolidge, "'Never before…has a government been so completely fused with business.'"[33] The latter was a problem in itself: if government becomes too closely tied in with one element in the community or one sector of the economy it compromises its responsibility to promote the common good. Other federal government policies of the 1920s seemed in line with the basic principle of the Founders of avoiding excessive public debt. Under Secretary of the Treasury Andrew Mellon government expenditures were reduced, the budget was balanced for a time, and the Bureau of the Budget (later the Office of Management and Budget) was established to bring greater efficiency, professionalism, and nonpartisanship to budget preparation.[34] Some might argue that the Founding admonition about public debt was taken too literally during the period, that maybe a less abstemious approach and at least a bit more federal spending might have helped the economy (they should have heeded the lesson of the Jackson administration about this). For example, the Harding administration resisted the demands of farm interests for subsidies to help them overcome the slump in prices caused by wartime overproduction.[35] Federal grant-in-aid programs continued, however, and federal highway funding stimulated substantial state and local road construction.[36] Nor was federal regulation of important interstate industries in the economy absent—for example, federal railroad and electric utility regulation was substantial. In fact, the Tennessee Valley Authority was almost enacted before FDR.[37]

Hoover's record on the economy is often misunderstood; his economic ideas actually show an affinity to those of the Founding Era. While adhering to the gold standard and an insistence on a balanced budget, he actively prodded the leading banks to pool their efforts to loosen up on credit, secured legislation to expand the money supply by releasing large amounts of gold from the government reserve and to secure loans to enable average homeowners to forestall mortgage foreclosures, and set up the Reconstruction Finance Corporation which made public funds directly available to financial institutions in the form of loans.[38] Hoover set the stage for the New Deal. As David M. Kennedy puts it, he "embraced direct government action," and "now stood ideologically shorn before a storm of demands for unemployment relief"[39]—if corporate entities could be "bailed-out," why not average citizens? Hoover had philosophically accepted federal intervention. If, as we said, the Progressive Era established the regulatory state and an activist federal economic role and the New Deal sharply expanded it, the Hoover period kept its momentum going in between. When he was Secretary of Commerce (1921-1929), Hoover had sought "a stiff graduated tax on legacies and gifts," and opposed Mellon's tax cuts for the wealthy.[40] This was in the character of the Founding Era of avoiding great economic disparities and the concentration of wealth, and preserving middle class culture. He urged the Federal Reserve Board "to curb speculation by restricting credit."[41] This is consistent with the Founding culture's concern about unproductive investment and general stress on the need for sobriety and self-restraint. He pushed for higher wages, better labor standards, a shorter workweek, and even worker participation in workplace decisionmaking. As we recall, the Founding culture admonished an inchoate version of a just wage and also a cooperative spirit. He called for changes in Southern agriculture so tenants and sharecroppers could come to own their own land. This was consistent with the preference of the Founding culture for widespread distribution of land and ownership. He worked for the establishment of trade associations in which businesses could exchange information about pricing and inventories, standardize products, and plan sensibly for their industries—he thought that these practices could eliminate cutthroat and destructive competition.[42] Such trade associations would help insure that the economy would remain more decentralized—in the spirit of the Founding Era—since to coordinate in this kind of manner would help to keep the constituent firms healthy and intact so as to stave off consolidation. These trade associations bore some resemblance to the occupational groups or industrial councils advocated by some Catholic social thinkers in the twentieth century. He believed that those who were economically disadvantaged should not be neglected, but should be assisted by private charities and local government.[43] Hoover's sentiments overall showed agreement with the Founding Era that economic freedom had to be *properly* limited. His emphasis on the solution of public issues by technocrats,[44] however, signaled an attempted diminishment of politics that had more in common with the Progressive Era than the Founding.

Besides the collapse of stock prices, the Great Depression resulted in grossly reduced production by major industries, massive unemployment (reaching nearly a quarter of the workforce in 1932, but much higher in some cities), a severe drop in the already-flagging farm income, and substantial problems of mortgage foreclosures, homelessness, and lack of money for basic necessities.[45] We will not resolve here the question of whether Hoover's policy of limited intervention was insufficient to combat the Depression, or how much government intervention generally was needed, or whether government intervention at all was a reliable way to do it. We only briefly note below the situation of the economy on the eve of World War II after nearly eight years of an interventionist New Deal. The point here is that Hoover's efforts did not succeed, and his decisions like calling in troops to clear out the World War I "Bonus Army" from Washington only deepened dislike and opposition to him and paved the way for his decisive defeat in 1932.

FDR's early administration, of course, is known for the legislative activity of his First Hundred Days, which projected the federal government decisively into the economy to try to end the Depression. The roll call of legislation just of this short period—to say nothing of the entire Roosevelt administration through the 1930s—was dizzying. These were some of the major New Deal legislative initiatives: the Emergency Banking Relief Act, which provided federal managers for troubled banks; the Federal Emergency Relief Act, which provided outright grants to the states for the first time for unemployment compensation and public assistance (this was done further through other initiatives later on); the establishment of the Civilian Conservation Corps, which provided government-funded jobs for young men on government lands; the abandonment of the gold standard; the Emergency Farm Mortgage and Farm Credit Acts, which provided loans to farmers to refinance their mortgages at lower interest rates; the Home Owners' Loan Act, which did the same for home owners generally; the Glass-Steagall Banking Act, which extended the powers of the Federal Reserve Board and set up the Federal Deposit Insurance Corporation to insure bank accounts; the Federal Securities Act, which began federal regulation of certain activities of the stock markets; and the National Industrial Recovery Act, which became the linchpin of the early New Deal program by setting up a structure of self-regulation within individual industries under federal supervision (utilizing codes for the conduct of business and labor relations) and also set up a public-works job program (the NIRA was struck down by the Supreme Court); the Agricultural Adjustment Act, which subsidized farmers to cut back production so prices could rise (interestingly, though, in an example of the unintended consequences of government policies, it encouraged large farmers to drive tenants off the land and helped cause the migrant problem captured in John Steinbeck's *The Grapes of Wrath*; the Court initially invalidated part of the act); and the Tennessee Valley Authority Act, which got the federal government into the power-production business.[46] FDR generally acted pursuant to statute, but also sometimes acted unilaterally and issued many executive orders. In 1933 alone he issued seventy-one.[47] His major unilateral actions in the economic area were probably his ordering the four-day "bank holiday" shortly after his inauguration and forbidding the private ownership of most gold.[48] He also sought, and received, broader executive authority from Congress. A good example of the latter was his aggressive moves to tighten executive branch spending and reorganize agencies, pursuant to the passage of the Economy Act in the First Hundred Days.[49] The so-called "Second New Deal," FDR's legislative program in the second half of his first term, focused on labor legislation and constructing a social "safety net." Its key legislation was the National Labor Relations Act (Wagner Act) and the Social Security Act, both enacted in 1935. The former gave workers a right to bargain collectively and form unions without management interference, obliged management to bargain in good faith, and set up a National Labor Relations Board to enforce its provisions. It stimulated union organizing activity,[50] and for the first time gave organized labor a solid footing in national law. By 1936, there were over four million trade union members; by 1940, 7.28 million.[51] Social Security was, of course, a federally administered pension fund primarily for the elderly. FDR's second term did not feature such an explosion of new legislation. The main initiatives were the Wagner-Steagall National Housing Act, which got the federal government into slum clearance, public housing, and rent subsidization; the Farm Tenant Act, which provided loans to help poor farmers and tenants to own farms; an expanded Agricultural Adjustment Act (by late in the New Deal, however, federal agricultural policy had evolved to the point that it intruded on the freedom of individual farmers and their families by forbidding them to even grow food for their own consumption if that went beyond federal crop cultivation limitations); the Pure Food, Drug, and Cosmetic Act, which expanded legislation from the Progressive Era; and the Fair Labor Standards Act, which established national minimum wage and maximum hours standards and child labor prohibitions (all of which, as stated below, the Supreme Court now gave a "green light" to).[52]

With all these new programs, it might be expected that the balanced-budget orientation of the Republican 1920s would not continue. From the beginning, the New Deal downplayed budget balancing, in spite of FDR's 1932 campaign promises to the contrary. Deficit spending prevailed throughout the 1930s and, while FDR made a renewed effort at budget balancing in his second term, in the end he was essentially won over to the new Keynesian perspective that government deficit spending was good if it stimulated the economy. Once World War II spending kicked in, federal deficits exploded to over twelve times more than their high in the 1930s.[53] The wartime spending was twice as high as the *total* of all the previous federal spending in the Republic's history.[54] Indeed, if there was an obvious repudiation of a Founding principle during the New Deal it concerned a restrained public debt. While, in some sense, groundwork had been laid for this in the 1877-1920 period by the federal government's greater willingness to run deficits and the temptation to spend more because the income tax provided an enhanced funding stream, this was precedent shattering. Initially, New Deal tax policy was regressive, featuring excise taxes and the new Social Security tax. The income tax touched only a small percentage of the population. Only in the Second New Deal did FDR push through income tax change so that both rates on the wealthy and corporations were hiked, as were estate taxes (which especially hit the wealthy). An excessive profits tax was also imposed on business. As Badger states, FDR decided in 1935 "to side with the advocates of soak-the-rich taxation."[55] The New Deal deficits proved Jefferson's point that taxation follows from them. Late in the 1930s, the FDR administration became aggressive about anti-trust enforcement; it was part-and-parcel of the anti-business tone of the later New Deal. In fact, Kennedy speaks about FDR's "antibusiness campaign" that started in 1936, and gives examples of his harsh rhetorical attacks.[56] His administration saw big companies, among other things, as erecting distribution roadblocks to increase their gains. It pioneered the use of consent decrees, which halted anti-trust actions in exchange for a company or industry setting out detailed plans for reorganization. These anti-trust efforts, however, did not have much effect in changing the structure or scale of American industry.[57] Trying to restore some balance in wealth distribution, alleviate wealth concentration, and encourage decentralization was in the spirit of the Founding culture, but a kind of anti-wealthy persons attitude that seems in part to have animated these policy initiatives—made evident by FDR's rhetorical attacks—violated that culture's norm of civility. The violation was even more serious since it came from public decision-makers, including the main decision-maker—the president.

Even though labor legislation made significant advances during the 1930s, there were some major labor conflicts. The conditions of the Depression and the John L. Lewis-led break-off of several militant unions from the A.F. of L. and formation of the new Congress of Industrial Organizations (C.I.O.) led to a new labor aggressiveness.[58] San Francisco was almost shut down by a longshoremen's strike in 1934. In 1934 deadly clashes in Minneapolis-St. Paul (Teamsters) and New England (textile workers) occurred.[59] In 1936, rubber workers in Akron, Ohio staged a sit-down strike and the new United Rubber Workers union developed from it.[60] Later that year, the United Auto Workers (UAW) began a lengthy sit-down strike against General Motors, which had ignored the Wagner Act, and ultimately forced labor concessions from the company after some minor violence and when it was clear that neither FDR nor the state authorities in Michigan would act against the strikers.[61] Within a few years, all the other major auto companies also recognized the UAW. A 1937 strike against smaller steel companies to gain national union recognition led to the most violent union clash of the decade, the Republic Steel massacre in Chicago. Police killed ten marchers and beat up numerous others, including strikers' wives. Cashman says that there were strikes that year in "all of the nation's key industries"—a total of over 4,700 involving almost five million workers.[62] By the way, a number of unions in the 1930s were infiltrated by Communists—who were sometimes welcomed by union leadership.[63] It is clear from the continuing labor clashes of both the 1920s and 1930s that both the civility and spirit of cooperation of the Founding culture were lacking in this important area of economic life. This also underscored the basic inequalities in American life—largely absent at the Founding—that were noted above. To be sure, economic disparities would be addressed to some degree by the legal recognition of labor rights in the New Deal, but the conflictual attitude that had become increasingly ingrained with the economic transformations of the nineteenth century would continue. There was no "community of friendship" among labor and managers.

It probably cannot be said that per se the growth of government regulation of the economy went against Founding ideas. After all, we mentioned how laws restrained economic freedom in many ways during the Founding Era. Obviously, however, there was never any regulation on the scale of the New

Deal or a reaching over the whole national economy. It raised at least some problems of decentralization and federalism, although the answer to that was that a nationally organized economy required a national response—and the New Deal did try to work through state and local government when it could.[64] The New Deal seemed, by and large, to accept the reigning bigness and complexity of the modern U.S. economy—which was anything but in the spirit of the simplicity of the Founding. While, again, times change and it was probably too much to expect a whole economy to display that earlier simplicity, if the NIRA had held up it might have provided the basis for an ongoing policy and effort aimed at restoring some measure of decentralization.

The U.S. began to mobilize for World War II before her entry into the war, as a result of the Lend-Lease Program (discussed below) and the increased American preparations following the fall of France in 1940. Legislation that year gave the president more authority over the economy to allocate materials and facilities as needed for defense. In 1942, the War Production Board was established to direct industrial conversion—which was almost completely in the private sector—to war production. The government also financed war materiel factories. With most production oriented to war goods, the government imposed strict price controls to stop the prices of scarce consumer goods from exploding. An Office of Price Administration was set up to enforce these price controls. Food and consumer goods had to be rationed. Congress gave the president the power to control wages and agricultural prices. Feelings of patriotism ran somewhat thin among business, labor, and other groups in the midst of this. Tindall and Shi tell us that the former two "chafed at the wage and price controls" and that economic stabilization generally was "subject to constant sniping by special interests." At times, the government actually operated certain companies because of their lack of cooperation. To finance the war effort, the federal income tax was expanded to cover more of the population—it was now a "mass" tax. Most of the needed revenue, however, came from government borrowing (e.g., war bonds), so that by the war's end the federal deficit was six times larger than before Pearl Harbor.[65] Cashman says that the result in terms of level of production of war materiel was "truly astounding."[66] Obviously, the kind of outright centralized management of the economy carried on during World War II was contrary to the decentralized practices of the Founding Era, but as we said about the similar conditions during World War I the Founding Fathers and their era were practical and could be adaptable to exigent circumstances such as major wars. As far as the unhappiness of different groups were concerned, one is let to wonder if that did not manifest a lack of the spirit of sacrifice of the Founding culture. The transformation of the income tax during the war remained in place afterwards,[67] and one wonders if that did not show a lack of the ethic of honesty and promise-keeping on the part of federal policymakers after the war since it was done specifically for the war effort (though this criticism might be somewhat softened by the rise of the Cold War right after World War II ended).

We might ask, overall, how the New Deal changed the government role vis-à-vis the economy, and whether the FDR program helped end the Great

Depression. Tindall and Shi tell us that by the end of the 1930s "the power of the national government was vastly enlarged...[It] had taken on the duty of ensuring the economic and social stability of the country." The New Deal "had experimented for a time with a managed economy under the NRA," but thanks to the Supreme Court that approach ended and the New Deal moved "toward enforcing competition and priming the economy with government spending."[68] It solidified and then expanded the modern regulatory state, not directing the economy but controlling it with regulations enforced—and even partially made—by a centralized bureaucracy. The notion of "pump-priming" signaled a new approach of government to deal with the economy: seeking to promote full capacity production and full employment.[69] The New Deal changed the approach to the economy in another way: government now aimed to provide security for everyone involved in the economy. Kennedy says it sought, "security for capitalists and consumers, for workers and employers, for corporations and farmers and homeowners and bankers and builders...[j]ob security, life-style security, financial security, market security."[70] Even if it could not achieve it to a universal degree, the spirit behind the New Deal, then, was one of the welfare or paternalistic state where the "old scourges of mankind" would supposedly be eliminated and man's temporal well-being insured.[71] The New Deal did not seek to abandon capitalism, but to transform it into a "relatively riskless capitalism."[72] In doing this, it may have weakened such Founding norms as self-reliance and household independence (government would now be relied on more to protect people from even the basic challenges of a market economy), and perhaps even to some degree the entrepreneurial spirit. Did the New Deal end the Depression? That is an unresolved question. After the first two years of the New Deal, more than 20% of the workforce was still unemployed.[73] By early 1938, after some improvement, unemployment was still at 19%, there was a 40% decline in industrial output, a minor stock market crash took place with stocks losing one-third of their value, and corporate profits sank 80%[74]—and it must be kept in mind that none of these indicators had risen very high since before the Depression started. Even as late as 1940, with war production getting underway, the unemployment level was 14.6%. By 1942, with war production going at full tilt, the unemployment rate was only 4.7%.[75] So while Tindall and Shi's conclusion that with war production "only massive government spending had finally been able to end the depression" is correct,[76] it is not at all clear that that result would have happened in the absence of the outbreak of the greatest war in history—or, in other words, that substantial government intervention per se can reverse a deep economic decline.

Relations Among the Three Branches of the Federal Government and the Role and Powers of the Federal Government. During the 1920s, the relationship between Congress and the presidency reverted to the one that had been more traditionally identified with Republican administrations between Lincoln and TR. While Harding could in no sense be considered an activist president, he did take some initiatives during his short time in office to move the country away from the legacy of Progressivism.[77] This was somewhat like Ronald Reagan's activism in stepping back from "liberal" government sixty years later. Harding actually got the opportunity to appoint four Supreme Court justices—with the aim of reversing what he saw as decisions too accepting of economic regulation. He did likewise with appointees to federal regulatory bodies. Like Reagan later, he slashed taxes and the growth of the federal government, and as noted above tried to get control of budgeting to control federal spending. Unlike many of his predecessors who thought the president should be deferential to Congress, he worked "in shepherding legislation through Congress."[78] Coolidge, on the other hand, was not activistic even to scale down government. As Tindall and Shi state, he "brought to the White House a clear conviction that the presidency should revert to its Gilded-Age stance of passive deference to Congress."[79] Hoover, by contrast, probably took more legislative initiative even than Harding. He pushed a plan to reduce taxes for those at lower incomes, took some very minor initiatives to support the Negro, pushed through a special session of Congress the Agricultural Marketing Act to support the efforts of farm cooperatives and to buy up surpluses, and as stated undertook some interventionist moves as the Depression deepened. Still, no one would have said that Hoover was renowned as a legislative leader or circumvented any Congressional prerogatives. He could not even bring himself to oppose his party's majority in Congress to defeat the troublesome Hawley-Smoot Tariff.[80]

FDR, of course, epitomized legislative leadership. During roughly the first five years of his presidency, Congress largely cooperated in passing New Deal legislation. As Badger puts it, "Not only was Congress persuaded to pass laws that fundamentally altered the relationships between government, the economy, and the individual, but Congress also vested extraordinary powers in the executive branch." Further, in the early New Deal Congress "delegated vast, unencumbered authority to the president."[81] As he further says, "the dire nature of the economic crisis...persuaded...congressmen to handover power and responsibility to any leader willing to accept them."[82] FDR's personal qualities in dealing with members of Congress and his dangling of patronage also helped secure such sweeping deference.[83] Also, as mentioned, he heavily used executive orders. In his second term, despite FDR's massive reelection victory in 1936, he sustained several major defeats as the renowned "conservative coalition" of southern Democrats—many of whom were in key committee chairmanships in Congress—and Republicans began to get the upper hand.[84] This resulted from the resurgence of long-subverted concerns on the part of some members about the dangers of big government, Congressional "resentment of presidential whip-cracking" and FDR's sometimes cavalier attitude, FDR's tendency at times to refuse to compromise, the Congressional belief that some legislation was not well-prepared, and a reaction to the court-packing plan (discussed below).[85] Still, as Tindall and Shi state, the result of the New Deal and World War II was that "[p]residential authority and prestige increased enormously at the expense of congressional and state power."[86]

By way of evaluation in light of Founding principles, we are inclined to say that during the 1920s presidential power may have ebbed too much and in the period from 1933 to 1945 it grew too much. Still, the imbalance between president and Congress did not go to an extreme in either direction—during the

1920s presidents were exerting their authority and during the Great Depression the president was only exerting the strong leadership that the Lockean prerogative notion would expect in exigent circumstances, as stated earlier in this book. During the time of the most restrained of the 1920's presidents, Coolidge, it was not so much a problem of a weak president vis-à-vis the Congress as it was that the federal government generally did not seek to be activistic. While a better balance could have been achieved, the principle of separation of powers was not threatened. These periods were in line with the history of waxing and waning of the two branches discussed earlier. What we can say is that in the long-term the president was now looked to as a legislative leader and problem-solver. TR and Wilson's administrations had set precedents for this, and FDR expanded on them; without that background FDR almost certainly could not have undertaken the substantial legislative leadership that he did. Presidential power permanently increased, though probably not beyond what the Founders would have thought acceptable.

Before the middle of FDR's second term, the Supreme Court had struck down New Deal legislation in seven of nine cases that had come before it. After this, in 1937 FDR was concerned that perhaps Social Security and the Wagner Act—which would become his two most enduring legislative achievements—were going to suffer the same fate.[87] With the record as it was, FDR's attorney general, Homer Cummings, advocated taking steps against the Court.[88] FDR himself had lamented that the "horse" of the judicial branch was not pulling to solve the problems of the Depression as the other two horses on the team—the executive and the legislative—were.[89] What he came up with was the famous court-packing plan. This idea was originally developed in the Wilson administration, additionally shaped by the eminent Princeton University constitutional scholar Edward S. Corwin, and promoted by Cummings.[90] The plan would have permitted FDR to appoint a new justice for each sitting justice who had reached the age of seventy, up to a total of six new justices. So, the Court would have been enlarged to up to fifteen members. It also would have permitted him to appoint up to fifty new lower federal court judges for the same reason.[91] He claimed that the justices on the Court because of their advanced age were unable to keep up with the workload.[92] As Tindall and Shi point out, there was "ample precedent and power" for such a move.[93] Congress clearly had the power to expand or reduce the size of the Court, within constitutionally prescribed limits. The Court's size, in fact, had varied at different times throughout American history. Congress is also free to establish or eliminate lower federal courts as it sees fit, or even to eliminate all federal courts except for the Supreme Court. The president, of course, is constitutionally free to propose legislation about the courts. Nevertheless, the plan ran into immediate, intense opposition. Some of it came from unlikely quarters, such as pro-New Deal members of the Court and prominent members of FDR's own party. In light of FDR's statements about the Court's unfavorable decisions, the plan seemed "too contrived." It never came up for a vote in Congress, but it is still often said that FDR "lost the battle, but won the war" since afterwards one justice regularly switched his vote to uphold New Deal legislation and a closely-divided Court now sustained his programs.[94] Later in 1937, FDR began to get the opportunity to make appointments to the Court, and by 1938 it changed almost one hundred eighty degrees to give sweeping deference to Congress in passing economic regulatory legislation of virtually any kind. The only requirement was that the legislation had to have a rational basis—a very broad standard indeed.[95] As the Court established a new pattern of deference to Congress in the regulatory arena, it continued a historic pattern of granting "very broad discretion" to the executive in foreign affairs (e.g., the 1936 decision in *U.S. v. Curtiss-Wright Export Corporation*[96]). With the onset of World War II, this went even to the point where the Court would not interfere with the presidential order authorizing internment of American citizens of Japanese descent and the stripping of their basic rights in the supposed interest of national security.[97] The Court clearly spelled out its new stance of legislative deference in *U.S. v. Carolene Products Company* in 1938.[98] Curiously, especially in light of its action—or inaction—regarding the Japanese internment, a famous footnote in its *Carolene Products* opinion pointed the way to the role the Court would emphasize for itself in the future, which would ultimately result in its once again greatly enhancing its power at the expense of the other branches (see Chapters 7 and 8). It said that the Court would subject to a heightened standard of judicial review governmental actions aimed at "discrete and insular minorities" which might not be able to gain protection from the normal "political processes."[99]

The Founding principle of judicial independence was probably not threatened by FDR's court-packing plan, as popular and even scholarly opinion at the time had claimed.[100] As noted above, it was well within the constitutional prerogatives of Congress to enact. Indeed, it can strongly be argued that the Court itself for some time had been overreaching on *its* rightful role and perhaps threatening separation of powers when it frequently struck down social legislation and tried to erect rigid constitutional doctrines to stymie it. This is even further evident when one considers what has been said about how the relative laissez faire direction of the U.S. economy before the 1930s was at odds with the Founding culture, and how there was little constitutional or historical basis for the Court's absolutist defense of property rights and corporate interests.[101] If anything, the court-packing plan could be considered as a legitimate assertion of checks and balances to restore a sound arrangement of separation of powers. We are even tempted to stretch this to say that FDR's effort helped to vivify the particular American version of mixed government by enabling the democratic demand for legislative action in the crucial economic area to be met when the Court had been suppressing it—i.e., it was seeking to let the broad, democratic masses have their part in governance on the central political questions of the time. The Court with its obstructionism may have been acting not as the "aristocratic" institution that the Founding scheme of mixed government in some sense called for, but as an oligarchic one as it acted to uphold big economic interests. By letting the popular will be better expressed on crucial economic questions, the court-packing plan may also have helped further the Founders' principle of popular sovereignty.

As indicated above, the New Deal entered areas previously carried on by the states—particularly in social welfare (public assistance, unemployment compensation, and old-age protection) and labor legislation, and generally enhanced the role and power of the federal government in American life. Michael Barone writes that before the New Deal, the federal government "'was remote from the life of ordinary people,'" but then it became a "'living presence across the country.'"[102] As indicated above, it would not be correct to say that the New Deal supplanted state functions—many programs were set up along the lines of a federal-state partnership and involved grants-in-aid.[103] As we saw, the latter notion dated back to the Wilsonian period; the previous practice was now substantially expanded upon. Now, however, methods such as tax-offsets were devised to pressure states to join into partnerships if they were reluctant. FDR apparently was insistent that states be involved and that programs not be strictly federal or that all power be centralized—even though he would have liked to have had a standardized nation-wide safety net.[104] The effect of these federally generated, partnership-oriented social welfare programs, then, was not so much the expansion of federal power at the expense of the states, but the growth of governmental power across the board.[105] Still, the New Deal abandoned the "principle of decentralized administration" in the U.S., and projected itself more directly onto individual concerns and into matters that if government addressed at all it previously had done so only on a more localized level.[106] Federalism was certainly not destroyed, but weakened—New Deal programs were a decisive further, big step in the erosion begun by grants-in-aid programs. Further, many of FDR's advisors were ready to centralize even more—they seemed to lack the spirit of support for federalism.[107] The federal government's stepping in to attack the Great Depression did not necessarily thwart the ethical principle of subsidiarity—which stands behind federalism—but the new mind-set of readily transferring matters to the federal government did. What was clear was that what Federalist 17 said about "[t]he variety of more minute interests" being "under the superintendence of the local administrations," and the federal government's "falling less immediately under the observation of the mass of citizens" and "[r]elating to more general interests," was no longer the case.[108] There is no question that the New Deal embodied what the Founding Fathers had in mind about "energetic government,"[109] but it went well beyond their thought about the scope and reach of national power.

As indicated previously, World War II added to the expansion of the federal government. In fact, Michael C.C. Adams writes that it was "vastly increased" by the war. The "central bureaucracy more than tripled," and "big government worked closely with big business" because of military production needs. This continued after the war—in large part because of the onset of the Cold War—"forming the embryo of the military-industrial complex" that President Dwight Eisenhower later warned about when he left office. The combination of the New Deal's federal domestic efforts and the U.S.'s massive new international and military role spawned by the war, then, cemented an ongoing big centralized government. Adams tells us about one other development that came out of this: the "organization society." The greater dominance of bigger institutions than ever along with the expected upsurge of American nationalism in the circumstances of war—and later a seemingly "permanent crisis" with communism—led to a kind of regimen of conformity. Adams says that "the roles of individual intellect and conscience were diminished and loyalty to the group, being a team player, was emphasized."[110] This became a theme of much critical commentary during the 1950s, when such conformity seeped more deeply into American culture.[111] More will be said about this later. What we can observe here is that this new norm of conformity seemed to be at odds with the spirit of liberty of the Founding and the spirit of initiative and courage that were part of that culture. The big institutions that spawned this new attitude, of course, were contrary to its norm of decentralization. Further, the organizational society was not synonymous with the communal orientation of Founding Era culture—the former involved a diminishment of individuality, while the latter involved an associational emphasis that respected each individual person and reflected his fundamental social nature.

Constitutional Change, Constitutional Law Developments, and Citizen Rights. As mentioned, there were four constitutional amendments that came into force during the period from 1920 to 1945: the Eighteenth (imposing Prohibition); the Nineteenth (women's suffrage); the Twentieth (changing the presidential inauguration day from March 4 to January 20 and setting January 3 as both the date when Congressional terms commence after election and for each session of Congress to begin, giving formal recognition to the de facto practice that the vice president actually becomes president upon the latter's death or resignation during his term, and empowering Congress to determine by law who shall act as president or vice president until either shall have electorally qualified in the case of a disputed election); and the Twenty-first (repealing the Eighteenth Amendment, and ending Prohibition).

The clash of the Prohibition movement—with its moralism, elevation to the level of an intrinsic moral evil something that was not, lack of moderation and prudence in its outlook and objectives, and seeking of an unprecedented reach of central government power—with the Founding Era's outlook was discussed in Chapter 5. This centralization of power was even more evident in light of the fact that its enforcement was heavily the responsibility of the federal government. For awhile, the country officially embraced this perspective—with unfortunate consequences, as seen in the serious difficulties of enforcement and the rise of crime that it caused.[112] So, when Prohibition was repealed it was an expression of an outlook more in line with the Founding. It should be noted, of course, that while government retrenched in the area of alcohol control it was expanding in unprecedented ways in other areas.

The fact that the Nineteenth Amendment enfranchised women was not contrary to Founding thinking, even though at hardly anytime and in any place in early America could they vote. A question could be raised about whether the further democratization of the franchise—in a sweeping way, since this was the largest expansion of the franchise in American history, extending to more than double the number of people previously eligible to vote—was problematical. It probably was not, since as Chapter 1 mentioned the franchise in early America was surprisingly broad—we must remember it was meant to be a *democratic republic*—and the Founding Fathers probably expected its further democratization. Moreover, women could be landowners and taxpayers and could show attachment to the community in other ways, so the Founding criteria for a limited franchise could be theoretically upheld. The problem was that the limited franchise in actuality had gone by the boards with the utter democratization of the Jacksonian Era, long before women received the franchise. It was no longer even considered that once a certain group was granted the vote—after women received it, the next group in the 1920s was American Indians[113]—that any of these criteria would be applied to it. Nor did the enfranchisement of women significantly alter American politics in the period examined in this chapter. As Leuchtenburg says, it "caused scarcely a ripple."[114] Women did not initially vote in large numbers,[115] and when they did they did not divide much differently than men and married women tended to vote as their husbands did.[116]

The Twentieth Amendment raised no questions pertinent to this book's inquiry, and in the final analysis the constitutional changes of the period compromised neither the Founding principles nor the cultural norms that we have discussed.

The leading constitutional law developments of the period regarding economic regulation were discussed above. As indicated in Chapter 5, the Supreme Court's absolutist defense of property rights was nagging but never consistent. In the face of the attempts at federal regulation during the New Deal, the Court's obstructive stance perhaps reached its high point, it initially refused to permit much Congressional flexibility to legislate under the interstate commerce clause. Then, as noted, after FDR's ill-fated court-packing plan, it abruptly went in the other direction and seemed to allow virtually any Congressional regulation in the name of interstate commerce. The Court had stymied subsidiarity in both ways, first by not allowing sufficient federal intervention if needed and then—when it essentially abandoned any standard as to what fell into "interstate commerce"[117]—by opening the door to a progressive centralized authority foreign to the Founding. It seemed as if for the post-1937 Court the suddenly desirable end of government supervision of the economy justified the constitutional means. This abandonment of constitutional standards was inimical to the Founding perspective because it weakened the rule of law that is so essential to avoiding the governmental arbitrariness that can undermine liberty. While we have seen that there had been many instances of the rule of law being pushed aside in American history, the Court had not often been the one responsible. Maybe here it got swept along in the *weltanschauung* of the New Deal era's toppling of old restraints, in the face of what were seen not only as unprecedented problems but also a changed political consensus. More likely perhaps it was influenced by the pragmatism and Holmesian legal realism that had become implanted in prior decades (see Chapter 5). The Court seemed oblivious to any concern about the Founders' intent regarding the commerce clause. Perhaps the stretching of the commerce power, by the FDR administration and Congress as their rationale for enacting much New Deal legislation and by the Court in accepting it, ultimately harkened back to the actions of Jefferson and Jackson in "reinterpreting" constitutional provisions to advance the cause of democracy or supposedly meet new needs or benefit the nation.[118] Before its changeover in 1937 to uphold New Deal legislation, the Court had utilized the delegation doctrine to strike down much of the First New Deal's regulatory scheme (i.e., Congress could not "delegate" what were essentially governmental powers to non-governmental entities, as it attempted to do when it permitted industries to formulate legally enforceable regulatory codes in the NIRA).[119] This doctrine continues to stand as constitutional precedent, even though it made it difficult for government, at least, to utilize the carrot and the stick to motivate the norms of cooperation and the social use of property by industry that had typified the economic life of the Founding Era.

There were other significant cases in which the Supreme Court of the 1920-1945 period established precedents "nationalizing" certain important rights (i.e., affording nationwide federal constitutional protection for them, and applying the pertinent provisions of the Bill of Rights to the states as well as the federal government—it is also called "incorporation"). Even before seriously implementing the dictum of footnote #4 of *Carolene Products* above, the Taft, Hughes, and Stone Courts—referred to as such after the Chief Justices of the period—took a fairly aggressive stance in defense of civil liberties. In *Meyer v. Nebraska* (1923) and *Pierce v. Society of Sisters* (1925), the Court invalidated state statutes that, respectively, forbade instruction in school in a language other than English and the teaching of foreign languages before high school, and required parents to send their children to government-run schools. In both cases the Court reached back into common law—and implicitly, in some sense, to natural law—to defend, in the interest of liberty protected under the Fourteenth Amendment, parental rights to control the upbringing and education of their children.[120] In *Gitlow v. New York* (1925) and *Near v. Minnesota* (1931), the Court announced that the First Amendment's freedom of speech and the press clauses were applicable to the states, and in *Gitlow* embraced the "clear and present danger" standard that had the effect of expanding individual freedom of speech.[121] In the famous *Powell v. Alabama* decision (the "Scottsboro Case"), the Court held that the Sixth Amendment's right of counsel applied to the states—via the Fourteenth Amendment's due process clause—as well as the federal government, and required counsel to be appointed for indigent criminal defendants in capital cases.[122] This also was an important early step in insuring equality under the law for American Negroes, since the young men convicted in the case were probably the victims of racial prejudice.[123] An early, dim foreshadowing of the judicial activism on behalf of Negro civil rights in the 1950s and 1960s was seen in the 1944 decision of *Smith v. Allwright*. It invalidated Texas's "white primary"—in this one-party Democratic state where winning a primary election was tantamount to election, Negroes were excluded from primary election voting—on Fifteenth Amendment grounds.[124] In 1937, the Court applied the First Amendment rights of assembly and petition to the states in *DeJonge v. Oregon*.[125] The Court initially refused protection to individual rights, but then reversed itself and extended such protection in the significant areas of marriage and procreation and religious liberty. In *Buck v. Bell* (1927), it upheld a state statute permitting compulsory sterilization of persons of low intelligence—a result of the coercively-oriented eugenics movement discussed in Chapter 5, which by the 1920s had succeeded in influencing the law in some states.[126] In 1942, however, it struck down compulsory sterilization even for criminals in *Skinner v. Oklahoma*.[127] The Court first refused to entertain a religious liberty claim by Jehovah's Witness parents in 1940 after they were prosecuted for truancy when their children were expelled from a public school for refusing—for religious reasons—to salute the flag (*Minersville School District v. Gobitis*), but then afforded such protection in 1943 (in *West Virginia State Board of Education v. Barnette*) on free speech grounds.[128] Yet another reversal—even quicker than the latter—occurred in another religious liberty/free speech matter involving the Jehovah's Witnesses. After first upholding a tax on literature distributed by the Jehovah's Witnesses in *Jones v. Opelika* in 1942, the Court struck such a tax in its 1943 decision in *Murdock v. Pennsylvania*.[129] So, while economic liberty—at least after 1932—was being limited civil liberty was gaining more protection.

These decisions certainly upheld the rights of freedom of speech, assembly, press, and religion, the protection of life and liberty, and the upholding of due process guarantees and equality under the law that the Founding Fathers believed are crucial for a democratic republic. They also showed the respect for the family that was so central in Founding culture. In the parental rights decisions, the Court also showed a willingness to follow the natural law tradition that was part of the Founding—even though it did not refer to natural law explicitly. The ultimate rejection of compulsory sterilization in *Skinner* was an extension of this respect for the family and natural law, since the Court held that such action ran afoul of the rights to marry and procreate. As stated in Chapter 5 about the eugenics movement that was behind it, if the Court had allowed *Buck v. Bell* to stand, it would have been promoting the opposite positions, which would have been against Founding principles: damaging the family, violating human dignity, and undercutting the natural law by embracing a utilitarian perspective. If until 1937, the Court embraced what Chapter 5 called a skewed version of natural law—substantive due process—that was also out of line with Founding notions in the property rights area, throughout most of this period its decisions in these other areas accorded with the common law tradition and the pre-modern notion of natural law behind it. Nationalizing rights probably did not undercut federalism in light of the Fourteenth Amendment and because the Founders, as suggested, probably did not view federalism in an utterly rigid way.

Along with the FDR administration's anti-trust effort, in 1940 the Federal Communications Commission (FCC) attempted to address the oligarchic situation of radio broadcasting. There were only four national networks. The FCC sought to issue regulations that would have limited the networks' requirements that their affiliated stations air network programming, network ownership of stations, and network-newspaper cross-ownership, among other things. Presumably, the FCC sought more access to the airwaves and more diversity of programming and opinion. The coming of the war shelved the initiative, however.[130] When the war began, there was both formal and informal censorship. The military censored all news reports from the front, and war correspondents refusing to cooperate were sent back to the U.S. Embarrassing information or information about morally unacceptable conduct was suppressed. There was much self-censorship by journalists. Public and private communications were all reviewed. The Office of War Information had the role of propagandizing to support the war effort. Top American military officials stage-managed dramatic moments to forge an image for themselves, and they sometimes manufactured facts about the success of operations.[131] Adams contends that the "manipulation of news during the war created a permanent trend," with various public figures and institutions and even the media itself continuing to try to shape news-reporting in a way favorable to themselves.[132] A kind of self-censorship occurred in education, continuing a wartime trend begun during the Civil War (see Chapter 4). In 1943, the American Association of University Professors (AAUP) issued a report that said wartime patriotism was hurting academic freedom as professors with unpopular views were being fired and military needs were dictating curriculum. In high schools the quality of debate suffered, and sometimes citizen group pressure forced the revision of social studies textbooks to eliminate references to anything in American history that might be embarrassing and arguably cause disunity in time of war.[133] The conformist-oriented "organization society" above that began in the New Deal got a big boost by the war, and became a fixture for some time afterwards.[134] Still, Cashman argues that while FDR went along with "tight controls on freedom of speech and association," he "diffused" efforts that "might have further erodedy free speech, curbed dissidents, and deprived aliens of civil liberties"[135]—notwithstanding the Japanese internment, of course.

Besides the Japanese internment, the war also did not result in a dramatic and large-scale suppression of political and religious groups if they were seen as threatening to the war effort in some—even remote—way. Conscientious objectors whose claim was rejected by the Selective Service System were sent to prison; the largest number were Jehovah's Witnesses. Those whose claim was accepted were either given non-combat assignments in the military or sent to work in civilian public-service camps, where they typically faced strict military discipline and harsh conditions and were not only not paid by the government but required to reimburse it for their food and clothing.[136] Less problematical perhaps were the 1944 charges brought against a small number of fascist sympathizers (including Lawrence Dennis, discussed below), but the government could not secure convictions during a trial characterized by extreme "irreverence and showmanship."[137] The latter set a pattern for future manipulation of judicial proceedings in cases involving political dissidents— even a turning of them into public spectacles—which demonstrated in a certain way a loss of respect for the rule of law. The Smith Act of 1940 imposed strict alien registration and fingerprinting requirements, and permitted deportation of aliens who had held a membership at any time in their lives in a fascist or Communist organization. Congress required careful screening of persons seeking entry into the country and registration of any organization advocating violent overthrow of the government and having foreign connections. Some states barred Communist-connected parties from the ballot, and the Justice Department moved against Communist or fascist organization leaders—sometimes on overblown charges.[138] Although the wartime suppression of liberties, except for the case of the Japanese internment, was not as pronounced as in World War I, that period and even the Civil War before it served as precedents for these developments.

When considering citizen liberties in the World War II period, one cannot forget conscription. The country's first-ever peacetime draft was put into effect in 1940, reaching men between twenty and thirty-six. After Pearl Harbor, men between eighteen and forty-four were liable to the draft, and men from forty-four to sixty-five could have been liable for labor service if another provision of the law had ever been activated. With local draft boards administering conscription, the law was administered somewhat unevenly across the country.[139]

By way of evaluation of the above policies and practices, we cannot say that they signaled a general regimen of suppression during the war. Some, however, were abuses. While censorship in the interest of national security during the country's greatest war was to be expected and fully compatible with the Founders' realism, its use to cover up bad or immoral military actions or to enhance the image of generals compromised the Founders' commitment to free speech. It is difficult to see how the Japanese internment—which effectively was detaining innocent people for the duration of the war and in most cases causing the forfeiture of their property and businesses—could in any way be judged as compatible with the Founding Era principles of liberty, equality, respect for due process, property rights, fair-dealing, civility, civic friendship, and a cooperative spirit. The monitoring of aliens and fascist and Communist sympathizers would not only be compatible with Founding principles during wartime, but during peacetime as well. The Founders' realism and concern about government providing security—a major motivation behind forging the Constitution[140]—readily permits the government to protect its democratic republican character from ideologies and groups that advocate undermining it. On the other hand, stretching the law to nail leaders of repugnant groups affronts the Founding Era's commitment to the rule of law and fair-dealing. The treatment of conscientious objectors challenged Founding notions of freedom of religion, civility, civic friendship, and fair-dealing. Conscription certainly raised liberty questions, and such an extreme step as this would have seemed justified—even in the exigent situation of World War II—only if the FDR administration could have demonstrated an inability to raise a sufficient volunteer force. While starting the draft in 1940 could have been viewed as acceptable as part of war preparations with American entry into the war likely imminent, the very fact that the U.S. was not yet in it seemingly would have made the administration's burden of justification greater. The disparities in the implementation of the draft law compromised the rule of law, equality, honesty, and fair-dealing. The never-implemented "industrial draft"—i.e., the "labor service" mentioned above—

would have been difficult to justify in any event under the Founders' understanding of liberty, to say nothing of the Fourteenth Amendment's forbidding of "involuntary servitude." The latter has generally only been viewed as inapplicable to convicted criminals. Still, the fact that such a provision could even have been enacted probably illustrates how prepared the New Deal had made public policy-makers to suppress individual liberty for a greater good or even a perceived greater good.

Significant Political Developments and Socio-Political Movements. Some of the significant political developments of the 1920-1945 period have been stated above, such as the "return to normalcy" election of 1920, the Teapot Dome Scandal, the Hoover election of 1928 with its anti-Catholic undertones, the realigning FDR election of 1932 that made the Democrats the majority party, the sweeping FDR reelection of 1936, FDR's third-term election of 1940, and the New Deal itself. We here comment on a few of these developments and discuss others. The Teapot Dome Scandal was on par with the scandals of the Grant administration, and like them developed because of government-business relationships. As we have also seen, such relationships have been the source of corruption back to the earliest years of the Republic. As with the Grant scandals, the president was not part of them but they involved his top aides. Grant's problem was that he refused to act once the scandals became known, Harding's that he excessively trusted his friends. As we have said about all political scandals involving money, they compromised the Founding norms of honesty, truth-telling, fair-dealing, and the eschewing of luxury. The anti-Catholicism of 1928 showed a lack of civic friendship and civility. That election was significant not just because it saw the first major-party Catholic candidate, but also because the country's large cities for the first time shifted into the Democratic column.[141] This was a harbinger of the realignment of 1932. Certainly, the Depression was the great factor in the Democrats' victory in the latter election, but the long-term trends were in their favor. The 1936 election brought overwhelming Democratic control to the executive and legislative branches, with FDR winning all but two small states and his party emerging with a three-to-one majority in the House of Representatives and a four-to-one majority in the Senate.[142] Shortly, as seen above, he was also to acquire a "working majority" on the Supreme Court to uphold his programs. The question arises here about whether there was enough of a political opposition to FDR to insure the functioning of checks and balances. That was a legitimate issue, even though as noted by the middle of FDR's second term a functioning opposition emerged with the informal coalition of the southern wing of his party with the Congressional Republicans after the 1937 court-packing plan (even before that, the southern Democrats had increasingly opposed FDR).[143] After the 1938 mid-term elections, when the Republicans rebounded solidly, the new coalition was further strengthened.[144] In some sense, the extreme weakness of the Republican party in the mid-1930s might be seen as a weakening of the situation of factions available to check each other off that the Founders believed was necessary to preserve liberty. Even while political liberty was not being threatened by FDR when he was riding high, such things as the policy upheld in *Wickard v. Filburn* above make one wonder if economic freedom was sometimes being excessively curtailed. FDR had attempted to "purge" members of his own party in the 1938 primary elections who he thought were insufficiently supportive of the New Deal;[145] one can wonder if that was not a step toward the suppression of opposition. Also one wonders if FDR's insistence, when his power was at its peak after the 1936 election, that all three branches should work together to achieve his New Deal program as stated above was not an expression of a belief that the mixed regime character of the American political order was now irrelevant (even if the *actual* restraining of the Supreme Court's overreaching that gave unwarranted protection to great economic power could be viewed, as mentioned above, as a kind of restoration of a mixed government notion). FDR's statement has the ring of a sweeping notion of democracy, where no branch should restrain the people's will.

Kennedy tells us that the new opposition to FDR signaled a "resurgent conservatism."[146] He says that it was comprised of many groups of people: Republicans and people fearful of the strong executive power just referred to, corporate managers and middle-class property owners suspicious of his embrace of labor unions, investors who saw his policies hurting business on many fronts, taxpayers concerned about new burdens, businessmen and farmers unhappy with government regulation, and Caucasian southerners concerned about the stirrings of Negro civil rights (although the South was more restrained in its support of the New Deal generally).[147] Some conservative figures within the Democratic party who had formerly supported FDR formed the Liberty League in 1934 to oppose what they saw as the New Deal's increasing statism and FDR's accumulation of excessive power in the executive. It included such noted figures as former Democratic presidential nominees Al Smith and John W. Davis.[148]

Throughout much of the New Deal period, there was another political movement—of a populist stripe, which gained the support of many in the masses—that sought more sweeping economic and political reform than FDR offered. Some elements of this had national and some essentially regional followings. These included the Wisconsin-based Progressive party, led by Robert LaFollette, Jr. and Philip LaFollette; the League for Independent Political Action, an organization mostly of intellectuals spearheaded by economist and later U.S. Senator Paul H. Douglas and prominent philosophical and educational thinker John Dewey (who is further discussed below); Francis Everett Townsend and his tax reform movement; muckraking novelist Upton Sinclair and his EPIC (End Poverty in California) program; the radio priest Fr. Charles Coughlin and his National Union for Social Justice; and most prominently Louisiana governor and then U.S. Senator Huey Long and his Share Our Wealth Society. The LaFollettes, who formed the briefly successful Wisconsin Progressive party,[149] promoted the idea of a "cooperative society," without really defining it.[150] The League for Independent Political Action advocated a kind of democratic socialism "with a systemic egalitarianism under pervasive state control." They called for "national economic planning."[151] Townsend called for a national value-added tax to be used to make monthly payments to everyone over sixty to encourage them to retire. Besides supporting them, he claimed it would raise wages by shrinking the labor pool. "Townsend Clubs" sprang up around the country to support the idea, even though economic analysis showed that it would massively increase the national tax burden and was economically untenable.[152] Sinclair, who was the Democratic candidate for governor of California in 1934, sought in EPIC to have the state seize idle lands and factories and turn them over to farmers' and workers' cooperatives to put them back into use. Inspired by Edward Bellamy (see Chapter 5), he had a vision of an eventual "cooperative commonwealth," where private ownership of production as we know it would cease.[153] While initially Coughlin discussed the principles of the papal social encyclicals on his radio program, he later turned to continual attacks on the "Money Power"— by which he meant Wall Street and international bankers. Some writers have alleged that his attacks also had an anti-Jewish tone to them,[154] but he defended himself in writing against those charges. His National Union, which may have had several million members, called for protecting labor, nationalization of key industries, monetary reform, and opposition to American entry into the World Court. His criticism of FDR, whom he had initially supported, was often harsh and polemical.[155] Ultimately, he was ordered by his archbishop to cease his political commentary and activities. Kennedy refers to Long as "the radical most likely to succeed."[156] His rhetoric was "always a language of resentment" and "raw class antagonism," as he contrasted the virtues of the masses with the vices of those he called the elite.[157] Badger refers to his "vitriolic personal abuse of his opponents."[158] His ruthless treatment of opponents even included an effort to put a special tax on newspapers and to forbid them to publish what he considered to be slanderous material (i.e., that which criticized him).[159] He had a record of putting in place social welfare and public works programs, and restraining corporate power as governor of Louisiana, though Kennedy says his political "grip" on the state made it "the closest thing to a dictatorship that America has ever known."[160] There was much corruption in the state government. His Share Our Wealth Society called for confiscating large fortunes and levying steeply progressive income taxes, and then distributing the revenue to every American family in the form of a "household estate" to enable each one to own a house and car. It also sought a guaranteed family income (the level called for was almost double the median family income at the time), educational subsidies, old-age pensions, shorter working days, and better veterans' benefits.[161] Long was assassinated in 1935. There were also the socialists, now led by Norman Thomas, and the Communists. The latter never gained much popular support, though they achieved influence in some unions.[162] The Socialist party polled nearly 900,000 votes in 1932, but that was still far below the major parties and by 1936 it fell to below 200,000.[163] Badger points to the contradictory attitudes of these populist movement leaders of the 1930s: "They all hated the extension of bureaucracy and state power by the New Deal. Yet they all advocated schemes that would have dramatically increased state power. They condemned the New Deal for not doing enough for farmers and the poor, yet at the same time denounced the AAA and the welfare programmes for doing too much."[164] Badger's assessment of most of them as "demagogues"[165] appears to be accurate in light of their harsh, relentless attacks on the elements they believed were behind the economic calamities of the time, and their presenting themselves as men on white horses who had the ready, simple, sweeping, and decisive solutions.

There is little question that the Founding Fathers saw demagogic figures as a threat to the kind of political order they had fashioned. As noted in Chapter 2, Shays' Rebellion had been a significant factor in leading them to believe that a Constitution with a stronger central government was needed. The demagogue is a threat to liberty, and a figure like Huey Long who established himself as the overwhelming political power in his state and bowled over opposition can hardly be said to have had regard for such principles as separation of powers and checks and balances. Kennedy writes that when his administration was developing ideas for Social Security legislation, FDR made it clear that if it placed all control in the hands of the federal government he dreaded to think what would happen if Long were to become president.[166] The demagogues of the 1930s were an extension of Jacksonianism, which had brought about the triumph of democracy. For them, there was nothing beyond the perceived will of the people—which they, in a gnostic-like fashion, believed themselves uniquely qualified to interpret. (We saw above, however, that even FDR fell into this line of thinking at times.) They were oblivious to the Founders' insistence on the need for a mixed regime, to say nothing of a natural aristocracy. In fact, they would have been disdainful of a notion like the latter, even while figures such as Long established themselves as a kind of elite, but without any indication that they were men of great virtue, capability, and statesmanly qualities. Their views challenged the rights of property that were central to the Founders, and their general spirit of intolerance hardly betrayed a respect for free speech. Long's actions showed his readiness to disregard freedom of the press and the rule of law. They had a hollowed-out notion of virtue, which seemed to see it as class-determined—although one wonders if FDR did not to some degree share in that by his heightened polemics as time went on against big business. Their distance from Founding realism is seen by their seeming obliviousness to the political and economic consequences of their views—as seen in how they would expand government which they had criticized as supposedly having expanded too much, and in their silence about such matters as the danger of excessive public debt. Even while they seemed to want to promote such Founding cultural norms as household independence, achieving a middle class kind of existence for Americans, widespread distribution and ownership of property and productive goods, the social obligation of property, and trimming inequalities, they were ready to compromise such other ones as economic freedom, temperance, truth-telling (viz., by distorting the truth about who was to blame for the economic crisis of the time), civic friendship, cooperation, and civility (viz., by their appeals aimed at dividing groups and desire to "put it" to the wealthy and corporate interests). As extreme democrats, there was also little in their rhetoric that suggested that they were concerned about the mass of people assuming the responsibilities suggested by such Founding cultural norms as frugality, industry, simplicity, commercial efficiency, sobriety, and restraining luxury.

We indicated above that the groundwork for such extreme socio-politico-economic movements and beliefs—even while they did not prevail—had been established by the democratization and rise of class-consciousness of the Jacksonian Era. Other influences proceeded from this. That era spawned the first significant group of extreme political thinkers, the pro-democracy ideologues discussed. We said earlier that transcendentalism proceeded from them and in turn opened American intellectuals to Marxism. We noted also that Marxian and related ideas became apparent in the thought of the 1877-1920 period, and that was also when the Socialist party of Debs became politically active. The radicalism of a minority in the labor movement during the latter period provided another historical forerunner. The radical activity and violence of the Red Scare was a recent backdrop for the radicalism of the 1930s. In addition to this background in earlier thought and historical events, radical ideas gained greater strength when they were brought to the U.S. by some late nineteenth and early twentieth-century immigrants.[167] When the dire economic conditions struck, all this led to the strongest expression yet, for a time, of egalitarian and even socialist perspectives.

The other significant political development of the 1920-1945 period was FDR's running for a third term in 1940, and being the first president to be elected to a third term—and then, of course, a fourth one that was cut short by his death less than three months after it began. For some who saw him as aggrandizing excessive power throughout his first two terms, this was confirmation of his reach for despotism. The Founding Fathers, however, put no constitutional restraint on the number of times a president could be reelected. Washington established the two-term tradition, which had always been followed.[168] Further, FDR's running again in 1940 must be put into the context of the start of World War II which most people figured the U.S. would be drawn into at some point. With the American mobilization already going on one might conclude that it was already a wartime situation for the U.S. When FDR was reelected in 1944, of course, the U.S. had long been in the war and was closing in on victory. It has long been said that Americans are reluctant to change leaders in the midst of a major war. It does not seem that checks and balances and the underlying concern about checking concentrated or excessive power was violated by FDR's third term. It is likely, however, that it was in some sense the next step in the long growth of presidential power that began with Jackson or even Jefferson—manifesting itself dramatically, however, only with some presidents. It was also perhaps another manifestation of the prerogative tradition noted in Chapter 3, since FDR's whole presidency took place in a crisis time.

Immigration and Relations Among Racial, Ethnic, and Religious Groups and Economic Classes. Immigration, which had primarily been from Europe, slowed to a trickle during the time that World War I engulfed that continent. In 1919, there was a trend for immigrants to return home with money earned here during the war, but in 1920 immigration substantially picked up again.[169] The landmark Immigration Act of 1924 ended the historic regime of mostly open immigration and sharply restricted the opportunities for immigration. It established an annual quota, which was only 2% of the number of foreign-born persons from each nationality living in the U.S. in 1890—this later was adjusted to the number of persons of each ancestry living in the U.S. in 1920. It prohibited immigration from the Far East and south Asia, but placed no limits on Latin American or Canadian immigration—even though Congress apparently did not expect the upsurge in Hispanic immigration that followed. To give an idea of the impact of the act, Italian immigration in the first decade of the twentieth century was 200,000 per year, but after the act it was limited to 4,000 per year.[170] After the act, overall immigration to the U.S. averaged only about 300,000 during the remainder of the decade, and slid to an average of about 50,000 in the 1930s with the added pressure of the Depression. The act was probably motivated by a combination of eliminating job competition from foreign workers, maintaining a national ethnic status quo, the belief that the new national problems could better be solved with a relatively static population, a crime upsurge that came with Prohibition and involved many young immigrants, a new nationalism carrying over from World War I, and the writing of eugenicists such as Madison Grant (see Chapter 5) and Lothrop Stoddard who saw many immigrant nationalities as genetically inferior.[171] The long history of nativism in America going back to the Jacksonian Era and the eugenicist sentiments of some in the Progressive Movement were in the background of the latter attitudes.

As far as the eugenicists were concerned, by the way, they were increasingly accepting racial supremacist attitudes as the framework of their work, which increasingly came to be accepted by the intelligentsia in America as hard science and were popularized by such events as the Second International Congress of Eugenics in New York City in 1921.[172]

In addition to the tight restricting of immigration in the 1920s, the decade saw a revived nativism with the aforementioned reemergence of the Ku Klux Klan. As noted, the new Klan was not only anti-Negro, but also anti-Catholic, anti-Jewish, and anti-immigrant. With its new nativist emphasis, the Klan gained appeal outside of the South. It was especially strong in the Midwest. In 1925, it staged a large march in Washington, D.C., though its influence had crested with the passage of the 1924 immigration law.[173] Still, it was responsible for many violent attacks and became a political force in various states in the 1920s.[174] Even apart from the Klan, lynchings of Negroes in the South continued, with the perpetrators seldom brought to justice—even while Negro crimes (or mere allegations of crimes) against Caucasians were "punished swiftly and brutally,"[175] as the Scottsboro case demonstrated. Congress attempted to pass an anti-lynching bill, but almost all southern members were against it and it was killed by a Senate filibuster.[176]

In the period from 1920 to 1945, there were a number of race and ethnic riots: Tulsa in 1921; Levy County, Florida in 1923; Harlem in 1935 and 1943; and Detroit and Los Angeles in 1943.[177] Tindall and Shi say that with the onset of World War II, there was a "growing militancy" by Negroes to end segregation and claim their civil rights, and suggest that this may have "aroused antagonism" from some Caucasians that led to violence. While the emergence of the major successes of the civil rights movement had to wait for the 1950s and

1960s, there were such achievements as an executive order from FDR ending racial discrimination in defense industries and the Supreme Court's declaring the white primary unconstitutional (see above).[178]

We have already touched on some aspects of the relations among religious groups and economic classes by discussing the anti-Catholicism in the 1928 presidential election, the Klan's newly-found anti-Catholic and anti-Jewish views, the labor conflicts in the 1920s and 1930s, and the demagogic appeals of the 1930's populists. Regarding anti-Catholicism, Higham also says that its upsurge in the 1920s was closely related to the growth of Protestant fundamentalism.[179] In seeming contradiction to the U.S.'s struggle against the Nazis in World War II, anti-Jewish views were apparent in American culture in this period. Besides the Klan, Higham says that in the 1920s they were seen within the agrarian sector and among some prominent figures. Charges of a Jewish world conspiracy and manipulations by Jewish international bankers gained prominence, and the strongly anti-Jewish fantasy "Protocols of the Elders of Zion" that had been made up by the Czarist Russian secret police at the beginning of the century was circulated.[180] We already mentioned the possibly anti-Jewish views among the populists of the 1930s. Cashman writes that a "belief that Jews were not contributing fully to the war effort persisted throughout the war." Reports from the government's Fair Employment Practices Committee "indicated widespread discrimination against Jews on the labor market." Around Boston, gangs of youth desecrated synagogues and intimidated Jewish businessmen. Most outrageous was the U.S.'s refusal to accept Jewish refugees from Nazi-controlled regimes in the late 1930s. American public opinion lined up strongly against Congressional efforts to raise immigration quotas to allow more Jewish *children* to emigrate from Germany and Austria.[181] The U.S., along with other Western Hemisphere countries, handed the Nazis a propaganda victory by refusing to accept any of the Jewish refugees who tried to flee Germany aboard the *MS St. Louis* in 1939.[182] The imprisonment of conscientious-objecting Jehovah's Witnesses and the reprisals against them in the school flag salute matter were mentioned above. There were also attempts by local governments to interfere with their activities. Anti-Jehovah's Witness riots also occurred in Little Rock and in Springfield, Illinois. Cashman writes that there was "a deep-seated popular distrust of the sect."[183] To be sure, apart from any dislike of them because of their men's refusal to serve in the military, the Jehovah's Witnesses were sometimes provocative in their proselytization tactics.[184] Thus, there was probably intolerance on both sides.

Except for labor conflicts, the cases of protest by the economically dispossessed were not as dramatic, violent, or probably as frequent as the above. Perhaps the economically dispossessed were too busy struggling to survive day to day. The best-known protest action was probably the march and encampment of the unemployed World War I veterans demanding the bonuses that Congress had voted in 1924 to give them (the "Bonus Army"). Some squatted in vacant government buildings, and when the Hoover administration ordered police and then the military to clear them there was some violence and a few deaths.[185] Then there were also the "Hooverville" shantytowns in such cities as New York and St. Louis,[186] which were probably as much residences for unemployed homeless men as symbols of protest. There were also mobs in different places that stopped foreclosures, and strikes of militant farmers in Iowa and Nebraska that blocked produce deliveries.[187] Cashman concludes about the 1920s and 1930s that the U.S. was distinctly divided on class, racial, and ethnic lines, and that there was not much movement across class lines.[188] The latter was a phenomenon that had showed up increasingly in the nineteenth century, as noted in previous chapters.

The analysis in light of the Founding Era that we have made in previous chapters on inter-group hostility and nativism is pertinent here. While rioting and large-scale inter-group violence was not as great as during, say, the 1840-1877 period—which was perhaps the high point of, especially, religiously-based nativism—it occurred in each of the historical periods we have so far examined. It has been a repeated feature of American life, at high levels in some and low ebbs in others. Always it illustrates a breakdown of civility and the rule of law, the absence of civic friendship, and a loss of respect for equality, the common good, and the rights to life, liberty, and property. The same is obviously true of lynching, to which additionally one could add that it represented an abdication of governmental authority to a mob in the way that the kangaroo courts of the California Gold Rush days did—except that it was an even uglier spectacle. The repeated inter-group hostility, in general, violated not only civic friendship, but also the spirit of cooperativeness, basic justice, equality, and the ready melding of different groups seen in Founding culture. While it is true that melding would always be more difficult in a country of many more and more diverse groups, the *weltanschuung* perhaps changed in American history after the Founding. The hostility toward certain religious groups, and especially state actions such as against such groups as the Jehovah's Witnesses—when their actions in question could hardly be said to have adversely affected the common good—challenged the central Founding right of freedom of religion. The hostility, from whichever source or religious group it emanated, also signaled the same absence of civic friendship and spirit of equality as with ethnic and racial group hostility. As stated in Chapter 5, the eugenicists were undercutting the family and the dignity of the individual, both of which were central to the culture and spirit of the Founding. The substantial economic disparities of the Great Depression period underscored the decline of the middle class norm of Founding culture and the reality of a have and have-not division that the Founders saw as destructive of a political order. The rigidities of class evident even before the Depression underscored an absence of the social mobility of the Founding Era.

Foreign Affairs and War-making. If two words could capture American foreign policy in the 1920s, they would be isolationism and idealism. One must always be careful in using terms such as these because the U.S. was in no way completely isolated from international developments during that time—any nation that engaged in trade and had foreign embassies would not be strictly isolationist—and while it pursued some big objectives that might be called idealistic it was not as if its leaders and diplomats did not understand how foreign affairs worked. It was in a *relative* sense that the U.S. was isolationist and idealistic—in reference to how it had acted before, what might be the expected normal course of policy for a developed and powerful country particularly in the era it was part of, and how reasonable its expectations were for the success of particular policy choices or international arrangements it sought to fashion in light of how international politics normally works. Harding's foreign policy was one of contrasts with regard to these two key terms: while it aimed at isolationism as far as concerned America's role in world power politics and in having a political and military presence in Eastern Hemispheric affairs and sought to retreat from Wilsonianism, it demonstrated an idealism similar to his with its policy initiatives in 1920s. In fact, Leuchtenburg tells us that "[m]easured by prewar standards, American participation in world affairs was considerable." The U.S., of course, took no part in the League of Nations and even strongly criticized the League's attempts to institute a collective security arrangement as potentially threatening to the U.S. The U.S. emphasized the rights of neutrals, like itself.[189] A neutral stance by the U.S. regarding conflicts among other nations seems to be in line with the Founders' perspective, but it is not so clear—even if it is perhaps an understandable further development of this—that they viewed the U.S. as having an obligation to uphold *other nations'* rights as neutrals. The U.S. took two major peace initiatives in the 1920s, one essentially in line with foreign policy realism and the other perhaps even a farther stretch than Wilsonian idealism. The former was the Washington Naval Conference of 1921-22, which resulted in three treaties including an agreement to limit the size of the navies of the major powers to an agreed upon ratio made acceptable because it appealed to the parties' sense of their national interests.[190] It helped to defuse the possibilities of an arms race for a decade, until militarists prodded the Japanese government to start rebuilding its arsenal and resume its expansionistic designs. The Kellogg-Briand Pact of 1928 was the exercise in idealism, in which most countries of the world supposedly renounced war as an instrument of national policy except for self-defense. This was completely in line with the ruling view of American foreign policymakers that power, instead of something that was morally neutral and could be used for good or bad, "was in itself evil."[191] This completely contrasts with the realism about politics of the Founding Fathers.[192] Within three years, Japan turned its back on the Pact and attacked China and, of course, within a decade World War II effectively began with the Anschluss in Austria. In the pact the U.S. "reserved freedom of action under the Monroe Doctrine,"[193] and it did not motivate her to retrench from a policy of either economic or military intervention in Latin America. In fact, by the beginning of the Coolidge administration the U.S. "was running the financial policies of ten Latin-American nations." Harding had militarily intervened in Honduras, and Coolidge continued a military presence in Nicaragua.[194] The U.S. imposed heavy tariffs that "aroused great antagonism" in Latin America and had "devastating effects" on its economy, and continued economic strictures on Haiti and the Dominican Republic until the 1940s.[195] Still, changes in Latin American policy were definitely in the wind. In fact, by the end of the Hoover administration Leuchtenburg asserts that, "relations with Latin America were better than they had been at any time in...[the] century."[196] Harding resolved the long-standing Colombian grievance with the U.S. by paying an indemnity for the Panama Canal territory. Coolidge resolved an oil rights dispute with Mexico, withdrew American forces from Haiti, and made a personal appearance at the Pan-American Conference in Havana in 1928. Hoover made a goodwill tour in Latin America and circulated a State Department memo that seemed to foreswear American military intervention in the region. FDR continued on the same course by ending the remaining American military presence, renouncing the right to intervene in Cuba, and went to the 1936 Pan-American Conference in Buenos Aires.[197] In place of military intervention and in spite of the cold shoulder the U.S. had long given it, both Hoover and FDR turned to the League of Nations to mediate Latin American disputes. The most notable example was the resolution of the Paraguay-Bolivia Chaco War.[198] FDR's policy toward Latin America has often been called the "Good Neighbor Policy."[199] The efforts at better relations with Latin America were a furtherance of such Founding norms as fostering a communal and cooperative spirit, civic friendship, and an orientation to the common good—it was in contrast to how American imperialism in that region in the 1840s had thwarted those norms. Its efforts to mediate disputes were a further effort to promote the common good and insure civility within the community of Western Hemispheric nations.

During his administration, up until Hitler attacked France, FDR went back and forth between isolationism and interventionism. His personal sentiments were internationalist, and Kennedy describes him as a Wilsonian.[200] During the 1932 campaign he abandoned his earlier support for American membership in the League of Nations and announced that international trade was secondary to domestic economic revival. He refused to take part in serious negotiations about currency stabilization at the 1933 London Economic Conference because of his desire to pursue his own course on monetary policy. Early on, he signaled his intent to stay away from international military engagements by cutting the already small U.S. Army. He laid the groundwork for Philippine independence and a thus an end of American presence in the Far East. On the other hand, he pushed for new trade agreements, concluded a separate currency agreement with Britain and France, and recognized the Soviet Union, in addition to his "Good Neighbor" initiatives in Latin America.[201] Even in 1939 and 1940, before and after the attack on Poland, FDR took the diplomatic initiative, unsuccessfully, to dissuade Germany and Italy from their aggressive posture.[202]

Throughout the 1930s and up until Pearl Harbor, the U.S. proclaimed her neutrality. This was backed up by strong popular isolationist sentiment.[203] As tensions in Europe first rose in the mid-1930s, Congress forbade American arms shipments to any belligerents.[204] A number of policy changes and actions near the end of the decade and, especially, the beginning of Nazi aggression called American neutrality into question, however. The U.S. lifted the arms embargo to help the Allies, increased defense appropriations, instituted a peacetime draft, began an embargo against Japan of goods needed for war production, started the Lend-Lease program with Britain (in which the U.S. received long-term leases for military base facilities in British possessions in the Western Hemisphere in return for fifty supposedly over-aged American destroyers; a version of Lend-Lease was later extended to the U.S.S.R.), occupied Greenland after its mother country Denmark (it was a Danish colony) fell to the Germans so the latter could not take control of it, froze Japanese assets in the U.S., and forged the Atlantic Charter with Britain (which, in effect, proclaimed joint war aims).[205]

It is clear that on its surface, the above actions from 1939 to 1941 did not show the impartiality in foreign matters that the Founders commended. By the same token, it is not so clear that with their strong sense of realism such functional abandonment of neutrality would have merited condemnation by them. A central reason for the new government in 1787 was to insure security for the nation,[206] and it was certainly reasonable to conclude that American security would have been threatened if Britain had fallen to the Nazis and by further aggressive expansion by Germany and Japan even if an attack on America did not seem imminent. Further, there was no question at all that the partial American mobilization before December 7, 1941 represented some kind of sudden militarization of American life. The American problem had been quite the opposite: insufficient military strength. This led to neither Germany nor Japan taking American power seriously, and stimulated greater aggressiveness on their parts.[207] However, the large-scale drafting of men may have had another unexpected internal consequence with implications for Founding cultural norms. The fact that military life, as Adams describes it, had a depersonalizing effect (i.e., made so many men a kind of cog in a machine)[208] may have helped encourage—along with the continued growth of urbanization, discussed below—an increasingly mass society. This, as we have said before in this book, went against the situation of the Founding culture.

As World War II was ending, three events will be noted and briefly evaluated in light of Founding principles: the Yalta Agreement, in which the U.S., Britain, and the Soviet Union agreed on actions to be taken in Europe at the conclusion of the war; the saturation and incendiary bombing of civilian populations in places like Berlin, Dresden, and Hamburg, Germany and Tokyo, Japan by American and other Allied aircraft;[209] and the dropping of the atomic bombs on mostly a civilian population. In the Yalta Agreement, the Allied Big Three promised to put in place free elections, representative governments, and constitutional liberties in the areas of Europe they occupied at the end of the war.[210] The U.S. and Britain did this, but the Soviets did not. One wonders if the American expectation that the latter would have gone along with this, in light of the disdain of such "bourgeois freedoms" in Communist ideology and the Soviet record at home, was reasonable and did not in some sense offend Founding realism. Moreover, one wonders if the U.S.'s effectively making such a secret deal to shape the destiny of millions of persons in different countries without their involvement in some way (i.e., at least seriously consulting with underground Allied collaborators and governments in exile)—even given the constraints of wartime conditions—could be reconciled with such Founding notions as popular sovereignty, fair-dealing, respect for the general welfare, and even basic justice.[211] As far as the above military actions were concerned, they offended basic justice and certainly deviated from the precept of the Christian tradition that shaped Founding Era morality of doing no harm to the innocent. Even if morally unjustifiable, one might be prompted to understand the dilemma that President Truman faced in deciding to use the atomic bombs—i.e., there would be virtually certain massive loss of both American military men and Japanese civilians in the planned invasion of the Japanese home islands.[212] The bombing of the civilian sections of Berlin, Dresden, Hamburg, and Tokyo, perhaps largely for reasons of destroying civilian morale[213]—a form of psychological warfare—deserves no such indulgence. James Turner Johnson suggests that these actions were undertaken partly because there had been an insufficiency of moral reflection about warfare during the century before technology made possible the practice of "unlimited war" in the early twentieth century.[214] One wonders, too, if the saturation into the culture of the philosophy of pragmatism discussed in this and the last chapter was not also a factor in shaping such war strategies. A philosophy geared so much to accomplishing what is desired (as stated in Chapter 5) struck a chord in a country that always had a strong practical bent (recall that "shrewd practical intelligence" was a Founding Era norm). Practical considerations—in warfare or in peace—were more easily twisted toward an amoral or immoral direction at a time when the restraint of religion had been so eroded by the secularization discussed below.[215]

Socio-Cultural Developments. The 1920s can only be said to have been a time of cultural upheaval—Walter Lippmann referred to the "'vast dissolution of ancient habits'" that was taking place[216]—although, in fact, this was not as sweeping as was to be the case in the 1960s. Intellectuals and artists turned decisively in a counter-cultural direction, and despair and a sense of meaninglessness pervaded their thought, writing, and artistic creations.[217] Their focus—and in many respects of the broader culture which became increasingly consumerist, self-indulgent, luxury-focused, and oriented to forgetting about thrift and living for the moment—was an individualistic one. There was a turning away from a focus on the good of the broader community.[218] The intellectuals rejected Progressive politics and social reform ideas; as Leuchtenburg says, for them "Progressivism had become a kind of orthodoxy." They were about rejecting orthodoxies of all sorts, and "middle-class values" generally.[219] There was not much fervor for social reform generally; those so inclined just accepted whatever social and economic gains had been achieved in the past.[220] Among many writers there was a strong anti-American ethos; they saw American culture as "in a desperate and perhaps hopeless state" and some just left the country.[221] The counter-cultural ethos spread out from the intelligentsia to affect people generally, especially youth (as seen in the sexual rebellion discussed below). As a consequence of the disillusionment with the aftermath of World War I—the failure of Versailles, the Red Scare, the Bolshevik Revolution, the rise of an ethic of moral relativism, etc.—Americans felt insecure, vulnerable to foreign and domestic threats, and had lost their previous certainties about religion and the goodness of their political order.[222] As the previous chapters indicate, this level of negativity and lost confidence in their country was new. It would be repeated in future decades, however, as we shall see.

We can see above one after another of the cultural norms of the Founding Era turned away from: temperance, sobriety, the restraint of the pursuit of luxury, frugality, thrift, the rejection of individualism, sacrificing in the present for the sake of the future, the value of a middle class culture, concern about the general welfare, a communal orientation, simplicity, and belief in a sound morality not fashioned by men.

Perhaps nowhere was the rebellion against the cultural past greater than in the area of sex. We refer to the upheaval here as the sexual "rebellion" to distinguish it from the more thorough-going sexual revolution of the 1960s, which reached across much of the population. Here too the rebellion was led by the intellectuals, among whom it had actually started before World War I. It seemed to be part of their broader rejection of Victorian respectability, which itself was part of their repudiation of middle class, "bourgeois" thinking,[223] another phenomenon that would be repeated in future times. David E. Kyvig says there was "a sharp rise in premarital sexual intercourse after World War I," though mostly it took place between partners who would eventually marry.[224] Still, there was also an increase in outright promiscuity, and probably in adultery as well.[225] By the time of World War II, there was an "upsurge" in teen-age and even pre-teen promiscuity.[226] This was all spawned by a decline in modesty and a general loosening of the norms of conduct in romantic relationships,[227] and encouraged by a preoccupation with sex (albeit, with more inhibitions than in the 1960s) in novels, magazines, and—until the Hays Code—the early movies.[228] It was justified by turning to Sigmund Freud's theories—as would be the case in the 1960s, pop psychology was the rage—and by the even then much-disputed anthropological writing of Margaret Mead about Samoan adolescents who she claimed engaged in sex without scruple or consequences.[229]

The new sexual norm almost certainly contributed to the problems of the family of the 1920-1945 period. As noted, the birth rate had already been declining in the nineteenth century. It was halved in that century. From 1900 to 1929, it declined another third on top of that. In the 1930s, with the increased pressures of economic dislocation, the population increase was the smallest of any generation in American history. Even before the 1930 Anglican Lambeth Conference—in which for the first time ever a Christian denomination accepted the moral liceity of contraceptive use (it accepted it in very limited situations)[230]—contraceptive use had become common among at least the upper middle classes, and contraceptives were readily available. This facilitated the 1920's sexual rebellion.[231] It was mentioned that the divorce rate had risen in the last decades of the nineteenth century. The 1920s saw a noticeable further increase, and some states made divorce easier to get. The rate declined at the beginning of the Depression, then picked up again as the 1930s wore on.[232] By the middle of the 1930s, the rate reached an unprecedented level. Kyvig also says that, in the absence of divorce, "abandonment rates soared" as well.[233] Family stability was hurt by other factors, as well: the new freedom of women, which was seen not only in sexual behavior but in the great increase of women—including more married women—in the workforce;[234] changed attitudes about marriage that had begun in previous decades, including the companionate notion (mentioned in Chapter 5), vague expectations of "emotional fulfillment" (another influence of the new pop psychology), and the notion that it was to be seen essentially as a contract and nothing more;[235] the weakening of parental authority and control over their children (this partly reflected the growing view—encouraged by family experts, who were being turned to more than ever—that "communication" should replace strict discipline);[236] and generally the culmination of a century of the sequential loss of previous family functions (economic, educational, even its focus as the center of other activities).[237] It was held by some authorities that marriage bonds could—and *should*—be severed, even when there were children, if there was an absence of true companionship and emotional fulfillment.[238] Next, starting in the 1920s a kind of cult of youth developed. There was a reversal of the historic understanding that youth should look to their elders for direction; now older people wanted to imitate the young. There was thus a weakening, in some sense, of the role of wisdom. As the Founders' belief in the need for a natural aristocracy in politics was buried in the Jacksonian Era, now the same attitude spread to the broader culture. During the World War II period, married women made up half of female workers and there was a problem with "unsupervised and undisciplined...'latch key children.'"[239] During the war, both juvenile delinquency and serious violent crime by adolescents increased substantially.[240] Crime generally increased during the 1920s.[241] Prohibition was an important factor, and for the first time organized crime syndicates arose.[242] In the World War II era, however, while juvenile crime sharply increased adult crime actually decreased[243] (maybe because so many young adult men were away at war). The experience of Prohibition had weakened public support for law.[244] In a roundabout way the Founders' central principle of the rule of law had been damaged—law based on moralism, instead of sound moral principles, had a deleterious effect. Moralism, as we have noted, was an old story in the U.S. Undercutting the rule of law was also not new, though the nexus of the two had not typically been seen before. We discussed previously how Prohibition was problematical in light of American Founding principles.

Most of the above pathologies indicate a decline in morality. Adams says that by the end of World War II, there was much discussion of a "moral breakdown" in the U.S.[245] Morality, of course, was viewed by the Founding Fathers as essential in sustaining a democratic republic. As we have seen, sexual morality was particularly strong in early America—and crucial for a stable political life. We have also frequently said how the strength and integrity of the family was a central feature of Founding culture. From the widespread new norm of accepting sex outside of marriage, to the embracing of a contraceptive ethic that by its nature undercut and implicitly denied that marriage was oriented to producing new life, to the increased sundering of marital unions by divorce, the family was being undermined. With the kind of sexual behavior now predominant, it also would be difficult to say that the spirit of the gentleman and the regimen of good manners that were so stressed in Founding culture had not been eroded. The norm of marital fidelity of the Founding culture was weakened with the explosion of divorce and increase in adultery. This was, of course, reflective of the individualism that had been so rejected by the Founding but had expressed itself in so many areas in the course of American history. The weakening of the family and of sexual morality was not new, but in the 1920s the departures from traditional norms noticeably increased and perhaps for the first time justifications for a break from traditional sexual morality gained currency in the culture.

The self-indulgence in consumption and sex showed that there was little attention to the Founding Fathers' stress on the importance of virtue per se. The late nineteenth century had showed the decline of economic virtue. In the 1920s, for the first time, the decline of virtue swept broadly over the sexual and family areas, while continuing in the economic. We mentioned moral relativism above. The English historian Paul Johnson says that with the 1920s what emerged was "a relativistic world"[246]—this was, of course, completely contrary to Founding principles and to the assumptions that underlay it. The groundwork for this was, of course, laid in the social evolutionary thought and philosophical pragmatism that took hold of American thought in the late nineteenth century (see Chapter 5).

We have repeatedly recalled the Founders' view about the necessity of religion. The above developments were all occurring at a time of growing secularization in the U.S.[247] In the 1920s, Americans became more interested in the here and now than the hereafter. Many still went to church—and they were concerned about their children receiving at least some religious instruction there—but the rituals became hollow (actually Kyvig says that formal church membership "vastly exceeded" the number who actually attended Sunday services). Sunday became more of a secular recreation day than a religiously focused one. It was not an era of reverence. People thought religion irrelevant to most of what went on in their lives. This accelerated a trend that started in the 1877-1920 period. People still engaged in the external practices of religion in the latter, even if the doctrines became less relevant. Now, increasingly people did not even practice. More, in the 1920s religion started to be used for opportunistic ends. In the manner of a cynical Calvinism, some businessmen actually used religion as a way to promote their businesses. In addition to the secularization of the culture, religion itself became increasingly secularized. Churches took on the functions of social centers, and tried to make themselves relevant to the concerns of the here and now. Regarding even some of the latter, other institutions started to displace the traditional role of churches of taking care of social welfare—and, of course, this practice expanded much more during the New Deal.[248] In short, if religion was so relatively unimportant to people in this period one cannot think of it playing the vital role for the American democratic republic that the Founders conceived. The 1920s were a further—but a sharp—leap in the growth of secularization that spanned the previous ninety years. It accelerated as that period went on, and by the 1920s it spread more broadly into the general population. Also, for the first time in a substantial way, its effects were noticeable in such areas of morality as sexual and reproductive matters. This simply built on and expanded the undermining of the marital relationship that had been slowly occurring (as we have previously seen) since the Revolutionary War.

As far as education was concerned, the percentage of people attaining higher levels of it was greater than ever in American history. The 17% of the population that was graduating from high school in 1920 was three times the number as in 1900, and by the end of the 1920s had increased more than another 10%.[249] The percentage of young people in college also doubled in the two decades before World War II.[250] There were also trends to consolidate schools, thereby eliminating local schools and producing larger ones. Kyvig says that this, plus growing bureaucratization, caused schools to become "increasingly impersonal."[251] Curricular change accompanied these developments. At the pre-college level, while English, history, math, and science were at the core, there was a growth of electives. Vocational education expanded considerably,[252] even more so during World War II.[253] This seems consistent with the kind of education that the Founders and Tocqueville found acceptable for most pupils (i.e., agricultural, technical, or commercial education),[254] but may not have met the Founders' emphasis on adequate education for citizenship. Adams says, for example, "that much education became shallow and vocation oriented."[255] This assessment seems consistent with the fact that education in both foreign cultures and foreign languages languished (probably partly as a consequence of the above suppression of language instruction in schools during and after World War I), and social studies education had become uncontroversial because of the "politically-correct" (for the time) doctoring of texts and programs mentioned above. This was a reason why Americans could not fully understand or appreciate why the U.S. was in World War II.[256] The latter reflected a confused notion of citizenship, which thought that good republican citizenship required only conformity (we spoke about the growth of the culture of conformity) and an uncritical stance about one's country, instead of a discerning eye aimed at recognizing blemishes and seeking their improvement (which would have been more in line with the Founders' stress on a liberal arts education). At the college level, standards declined and curricula "widened," as new majors, more specialization, and the elective system became the norm. The modern social sciences, with their often-positivistic assumptions, implanted themselves. Also, courses that supposedly provided "life skills" became available, like sex researcher Alfred Kinsey's popular marriage course at Indiana University in Bloomington.[257] All this meant that a liberal arts education, which began to decline as early as the 1840-1877 period, was now being eroded so much at the college level—where future leaders were being trained, who the Founders said needed such an education—that sham courses of questionable intellectual or moral value (like Kinsey's) appeared. The educational thought that was ascendant at this time was that of John Dewey, discussed in Chapter 5. He probably most influenced pre-college education, but it is likely that his philosophy of pragmatism created an intellectual ambiance that helped encourage more "useful" college studies and the wearing down of the liberal arts.

Finally, regarding socio-cultural developments, were the demographic changes of this period. As Leuchtenburg writes, "The United States in the 1920's neared the end of a painful transition from a country reared in the rural village to a nation dominated by the great metropolis." It was the first time in the country's history that less than half of the population lived on farms or in small villages.[258] By 1930, there were ninety-six cities of 100,000 or more people, which represented almost 45% of the population.[259] Also, the growth of the suburbs began in the 1920s.[260] The urban growth was, of course, a phenomenon of ongoing industrialization (including, especially, war production), and was also somewhat stimulated by the Negro migration to northern cities that had begun during World War I and continued throughout this period.[261] The decentralized norm of the Founding thus increasingly ebbed in the community situation most Americans lived in, in addition to their economic life. As big, impersonal mass culture grew, civic friendship—suffering already with the inter-group conflict above—became more difficult to forge. As they depended more on the inter-workings of the complex structure of urban life, the norms of independence and self-initiative of the Founding culture waned. We should recall, too, that the migratory tendencies of Americans since the earliest years of the Republic tended to weaken family and community ties. It is thus likely that they were a further contributing factor to the family problems of this period, and also indirectly helped contribute to the centralization of government because many people could not relate so readily to their local communities or states—which they had not been part of for long—but only to the national government. They became more nationally oriented.

Currents in Social and Political Thought. Probably the two most prominent American thinkers—what are now called "public intellectuals"—in the 1920-1945 period were John Dewey, who we discussed in Chapter 5 and whose writing encompassed many areas of thought, and the aforementioned Walter Lippmann. There were also a number of other significant, but lesser known, thinkers. Previously, we talked about Dewey's basic philosophical thought; here we discuss his political thought. Dewey was an emphatic defender of democracy, which despite the individualism at its core, he believed would actually be promotive of community if permitted to extend to all aspects of life. He was a positivist, however, and rejected a notion such as natural rights, which underlay the Founding. Like Thomas Hobbes, he believed that men obeyed law not because they believed it right—and correspondingly there was no basis for state authority in nature—but because of perceived consequences of disobedience. The state's legitimacy came merely from consent; it was not natural to man. Dewey believed himself to be a Jeffersonian. He saw Jefferson as a sensible individualist, localist, and promoter of freedom and equality. While in Jefferson's day laissez faire was the best way to achieve the latter, in the twentieth century it was through government regulation and action. Dewey saw democracy in association with the scientific method as the key to political freedom. To carry out democracy effectively—which included socialization of the means of production and democratic social planning (and social engineering)—citizens would have to be prepared by universal public education reshaped by his "progressive" educational theories, which stressed the shaping of students in a cooperative ethos and the encouraging of a critical examination of existing socio-political institutions. It also required communication, so that citizens could develop into a community and take an active part in public affairs. Like the Jacksonians, Dewey's thought demanded faith in the capabilities of the individual and in the possibilities for good of public opinion. At bottom line, Dewey was a relativist—at least he denied that there was any ultimate good, though he believed there were specific evils that presumably could be discerned from a social consensus or a vague self-evidence. He had a great faith in science, broadly understood, as being able to solve social problems—it could replace the age-old political understanding that compromise is necessary to avoid political conflict. In this sense, he was a scion of the Progressives in which period he actually began his career. He went a step further than them, however, in believing that science and scientific technique could not only provide the solution to political problems but also to moral ones. In fact, it might be more correct to say that he went several steps beyond them by believing that it could help man to "conquer himself" as well. Science effectively became for Dewey a substitute for religion, something that could perfect man.[262]

Many of Dewey's ideas were on a collision course with the Founding Fathers. His positivism and rejection of natural rights clashed with their emphasis on morality and the central place they gave to the tradition of natural law and natural rights. He embraced democracy and they republicanism. His belief that science could displace morality, religion, and politics would have been abhorrent to them—and, of course, it went against the basic elements that they said a democratic republic required. It also would have offended their realism. While Dewey's stress on education for sound government concurred with them, they would probably have not even recognized his version of it—it certainly left little room for the liberal arts. To be sure, his view of the need for community concurred with Founding cultural norms, but his notion of it seemed broad and unfocused, without the range of elements and mores that the Founding era believed had to be present to constitute it. It also seemed like an artificial construct, whereas for the people of the Founding Era it was second nature. Also, the family, central in Founding culture and maybe at the core of its understanding of community, is not mentioned in Dewey's discussion of community. His social planning and universal public education schema suggested heightened centralization and a dimension of coercion that would seemingly have offended the Founders' notions of federalism, decentralization, and liberty. Like other thinkers below, the central Founding notion of constitutional restraints on power, such as checks and balances, is absent from his thought. While he seems to believe that with the right scientific thinking political conflict could be eliminated, the Founders more wisely—and realistically—understood that it had to be *controlled* for the sake of the common good by having competing factions and the like. We can only observe that Dewey's anointing as "America's philosopher"[263] and his in some sense being the philosophical face of the New Deal—even if, as indicated above, he did not think it went far enough—shows how far the country had departed from the Founders' vision by the 1920s and 1930s.

Lippmann's views changed from those of a Progressive, "liberal democrat," and even a socialist, to a defender of the natural law and a believer in the need to restrain democracy. Originally, he espoused a philosophical position in which he saw man as essentially a creature of his passions and, in Hobbesian-Lockean fashion, saw the purpose of politics as the satisfaction of human desire. He rejected the notion of there being any intrinsic good, exalted the supremacy of the will, and like Dewey was a pragmatist.[264] He believed that TR had been the embodiment of political leadership *par excellence*. TR's aggressiveness and activism were the essential ingredients to refashioning the world—which he was fully confident that man was capable of doing—to good purposes (even though he did not believe in the good). While insistent about the need for leadership and experts shaping politics, he also believed that the masses—through Progressive mechanisms such as the referendum—helped to educate the leaders. Also like the Progressives and Dewey—exhibiting the outlook rooted in the Enlightenment, with its view of the possibility of human perfectibility and the automatic character of mechanistic-like laws even for human affairs—he believed that this dynamic of leadership and an enlightened public could lead to the elimination of the age-old tensions of politics and need for compromise.[265]

Lippmann gradually came to have doubts about this optimistic assessment of the capacity of a democratic public, however. He came to see that it was easily swayed by opinion—sometimes, not such sound opinion—so as to distort even the facts before it. Also, in a manner similar to John Stuart Mill's refinement of the thought of the earlier utilitarians, Lippmann modified his earlier view that pure passion and impulse motivated man, and started to hold instead that men could come to make mature choices—that is, he came to a balanced view about the capabilities of reason. With this changed view of human nature came a changed understanding of politics. He now distinguished the politician, who either seeks to satisfy people's desires or manipulate them, from the statesman, who nudged people along to seek better ends that he could discern from an objective assessment of the facts—in effect, to motivate them, as best as possible, to see truths that were there and really could be discerned.[266] The mature Lippmann stressed the importance of the rule of law, the virtues of the common law tradition, the value of an active private sector—"pluralism," he called it—and diffused power, the need for mechanisms such as separation of powers and checks and balances, the need for a "higher law" as a standard to judge human laws and eliminate the danger of arbitrariness, the belief that due process guarantees and the protections of bills of rights secure liberty more reliably than universal suffrage and, more, the dangers that mass opinion and democratically-driven legislative bodies pose to liberty. Reflecting the sweeping democratic condition of twentieth-century America, all the power was now in the hands of the latter. This happened partly because of the erosion of true authority, which included among other elements veneration (which seems to mean religion), prescription (which involves mores), and hierarchy (which in some ways is synonymous with natural aristocracy). The rejection of natural law was the cause of all of this, and if it were not recovered human dignity would be subverted.[267] In effect, Lippmann said—as Pope John Paul II was to do half a century later—a democratic republic cannot survive if it is disconnected from the truth.[268] All of the above from the mature thought of Lippmann obviously sounds very much like the principles of the Founding Fathers and their cultural norms.

Paul Elmer More avowedly sought to return to the natural aristocracy that Lippmann suggested. He saw a natural aristocracy, which embodied self-restraint and judiciousness, as a restraining force at once to democracy, the plutocracy of wealth that had begun to characterize America in the Gilded Age, and the intellectuals and cultural elites with their humanitarian sentimentality.[269] More was correct in criticizing the humanitarian sentimentality of the age. It had built up with the religious transformation and reform movements of the nineteenth century, deviating from the realism and spirit of moderation of the Founders and their era. He was correct, too, in observing that it now had come to envelop the elites of the time; the 1920s represented a kind of culmination of that whole progression.

Irving Babbitt sounded similar themes as Lippmann and More in insisting upon, in effect, a natural aristocracy to assume political leadership for the sake of implanting ethical restraints on human desire. He believed that modern democracy had been influenced by something like the general will of Rousseau and was characterized by the unleashing of desire. Political leaders must have a moral imagination—which has been defined as that faculty which ties together wisdom and moral virtue—and there needs to be institutional restraints, such as the Supreme Court, upon democracy and popular passion. Babbitt saw the democratizing developments of Jacksonianism, and even Jeffersonianism before it, as pejorative.[270]

Ralph Adams Cram was known primarily as an architect, but he wrote political philosophy as well. He squarely held that the Founding Fathers sought to establish an aristocratic republic. Their statesmanship had been replaced historically by mere politics. A neo-medievalist, he sought something like an elective constitutional monarchy and aristocracy to replace political parties and a majority rule system, along with functional representation of different occupations and groups in society. In accord with the Founding, he favored equality of opportunity, but rejected any more sweeping notion of equality.[271] He showed an awareness of the importance of mixed government (in some sense) and the cooperative spirit of Founding culture, but the U.S. was not medievalist and his advocacy of monarchy and dispensing with majority rule was profoundly at odds with the Founding.

George Santayana was an ardent opponent of Deweyite pragmatism, which he saw as collectivistic—subsuming the individual into simply a role for society. Like Cram, he supported equality of opportunity, but rejected any broader notion of equality and majority rule. Like many of these thinkers, he called for a kind of natural aristocracy, which he thought that a regime of equality of opportunity could bring about (by providing the opportunity for men of merit to emerge). Like Babbitt, he stressed the need to restrain desires. His concern about getting the "right people" to rule and so achieve moral progress, however, got him close to the eugenics movement since biological inbreeding played an important role in this scheme.[272] Santayana's concern for better rule makes one wonder if he was attuned to the danger of a domineering elite.

Taking an even more extreme stand against democracy were figures with fascist sympathies, such as Lawrence Dennis. Like Dewey, he was a relativist who rejected the notion of moral good, but unlike him was a critic of democracy. Like the other critics above he believed that some were better suited to rule than others, but unlike them he did not claim it was based on merit—he was just asserting the need for an elite to exercise social control. Also unlike Lippmann—and probably the other democratic critics, although they did not stress it as much as Lippmann—he was dismissive of such mechanisms as separation of powers, majority rule, federalism, constitutional norms, judicial review, and political parties (except for a controlling fascist party). He believed that pursuit of the common good was a central concern, but was best achieved by fascism since it promoted solidarity and the discipline needed to achieve it. Also like Dewey, although much more sweepingly, the effect of his theory was to subsume the individual into the social whole.[273]

James Burnham took the rejection of democracy in a different direction. He believed government to be too organizationally complex for popular rule, so what were needed—in the manner of the Progressives and Dewey—were technocrats. Such technocratic rule could be developed in a way that would insure liberty and the opportunity for political opposition, however. In spite of his suspicion of elites in general, his view established a new elite, which he somehow thought would be different. He downplayed the role that the populace, elected officials, and non-governmental leaders could play in checking power-aggrandizing elites, and seemed to think that a new elite of functional specialists—i.e., bureaucrats—was the main way to check the abusive elite currently in power. The problems of politics—we see the spirit of Progressivism here again—were to be solved by eliminating politics.[274]

Like the others, Thurman Arnold believed that democracy had become corrupted; it had become nothing more than a set of procedures to maintain popular control in some sense and had no moral vision. Like Dewey, he was a kind of pragmatist. The absence of leadership was a main problem, and he wanted to bring forth good men, a kind of natural aristocracy—although as a relativist (like Dewey and Dennis), he asserted no good or morality for them to be shaped by. Like Burnham, he paid insufficient attention to means to restrain power and was taken with the need to have organization be the central feature in reshaping politics.[275]

Like Dewey and Arnold, T.V. Smith saw no moral content behind democracy. As with many political scientists in the middle decades of the twentieth century, he saw it simply as a process. He stressed compromise—this is the central feature of democracy and the politician is best understood as a conciliator. Anticipating the secularist democratic and church-state commentators of today, but building on the late nineteenth-century separationists, truth and claims of conscience must be kept out of the public sphere because they are not given easily to compromise. Everything, when in the public sphere, must be subject to give-and-take. This position was utterly at odds with Lippmann—and later, Pope John Paul II—but also with the Founding Fathers. His position would leave little basis for the pursuit of justice in politics, since this presumes that there must be truth.[276]

A further version of the scientist-technocrat elite of Dewey and Burnham was seen with Harold Lasswell. He believed that social scientist researchers and administrators—masters of scientific technique—were the ones who could discern truth, even though he was vague about what that is and followed Dewey and others in being skeptical about ultimates. He maintained a positive view of democracy, claiming that it exalts human dignity, even while he also asserted that the mass of people really did not know what was in their interest. This was something that the scientists apparently had to point them toward. Opposite of T.V. Smith, he did not think that compromise could solve political problems; the scientific elite—which he seemed to believe would have to expand worldwide—provided the answer here. He had the confidence that this gnostic-type scientific elite could govern with limited coercion and not abuse its power.[277] We have seen such shallow optimism and readiness to embrace technocratic arrangements frequently enough in previous periods.

Finally, the Southern agrarians were a group of twelve writers from the South who were neo-populists of the 1920s and 1930s. They issued a manifesto in 1930 called *I'll Take My Stand*, which attacked industrialism, what they called the "gospel of progress," mass culture and "the barbarism of taste." They wanted to reemphasize the virtues of the agrarian way of life, and called for a turning away from a fixation on efficiency and a return to a small-scale economy. They viewed traditional religion as providing stability for men. They are considered conservative writers, but their focus was more cultural than political.[278] They were much in line with the Founding culture, but were insufficiently attuned to the political and institutional principles of the Founders. One also wonders if their apparent desire to sweepingly and decisively reverse economic life went against Founding realism. Also, the Founders accepted the higher realm where needed—i.e., strong national government—and realized that all things could not be adequately addressed locally. As we have said, without knowing the term the Founders were practitioners of the principle of subsidiarity.

While the critique of democracy and its effects of Lippmann and most of the above lesser-known thinkers concurred with the Founding Fathers—except for Dennis' fascism, which is simply incompatible with the Founding on many points starting from its core belief that ordered liberty is simply impossible—most ignored the fact that there was a democratic dimension, not just a republican one, to the Founders' notion of the American political order. In this sense, they were like certain democratic critics of the period from 1877 to 1920. The major strains of critical political and social thought of any period seem to focus on the perceived central cause of current social problems. In the 1877-1920 period it was laissez faire economics; in this period of a vastly expanded federal government to respond to Depression era popular demands it was democracy. What came from this was the attempt to put forth a new notion of ruling hierarchy. Only some of these thinkers pointed back to the Founders' natural aristocracy notion; others looked to a new technocratic elite (they followed Herbert Hoover's orientation, as noted earlier)—a perspective prepared, as noted, by the mentality of the Progressive Era but foreign to the Founding and impervious to its belief in the centrality of the political. Many of them departed from the Founders in failing to stress, if they did not outright dismiss, the importance of institutional mechanisms (e.g., separation of powers, checks and balances, an independent judiciary) in maintaining liberty and the character of a democratic republic. Perhaps also because most of them were lamenting the irresponsible individualism that had come to characterize America, they did not stress the importance of popular sovereignty and certain rights. While the upshot of the thought of most is the need for virtue (in fact, they are strong in suggesting the need for such virtues as self-sacrifice and temperance), most do not single out the need for religion as the Founders do—or an awareness that for most people inculcating virtue is connected with religious formation. Perhaps that reflects the progress of secularization in American thought over many decades before them. In short, while many of the political thinkers of this period embraced the Founding's rejection of democracy, individualism, moral relativism, intemperance, and mass culture, they did not capture its spirit of true but restrained rule by the people or a proper balance of liberty and order.

We come to the following conclusions about the implications of the above developments for the political order forged by the Founders. The period from 1920 to 1945 brought some changes in government that, we believe, permanently altered the American democratic republic: 1) Federalism was weakened (not only did the federal government take on roles formerly reserved to the lowers levels of government, but it now interfaced directly with citizens and thus a psychological change occurred with people now looking to the federal government to an unprecedented degree—in many respects, it became the "default" level of government—for assistance); 2) Considerable governmental centralization occurred—joining the earlier enhancing of centralized economic life with the growth of large corporations—because of the new federal economic regulatory role, the burgeoning of federal domestic programs, the Supreme Court's dispensing with standards for what is encompassed under "interstate commerce," and the precedent set by coercive federal control over individual behavior during Prohibition; 3) Increased bureaucratization of government occurred, with big government agencies now becoming the order of the day (as, again, bigness had come to dominate economic life); 4) The spirit of liberty was weakened by the new "conforming culture"; 5) Executive power was permanently enhanced in the 1930s, as the populace now expected the president to be a legislative leader (while this did not imperil separation of powers, it perhaps permanently weakened Congress as it was no longer as potent of a policy initiator); 6) Democratization had advanced to the point where, given the right conditions and with modern mass media and/or the capabilities of modern political organizations and the expectations that government deliver more and more largess to its citizenry, demagogues could readily emerge and gain a mass following; and 7) An ongoing significant public debt became *de rigueur* for the federal government (as did a heavier tax burden falling on an increasing number of people).

The continuing long-term trends of secularization and educational transformation minimized the effect of two social conditions that the Founding Fathers viewed as essential for maintaining a democratic republic: religion and the proper kind of education. Both the decline of liberal and even citizenship education had been going on for some time. A culmination of sorts of these trends occurred in the 1920s, and a secularized culture and an education embodying technical training and the outlook of liberalism (i.e., not the liberal arts) became the new norms.

On the other hand, the Supreme Court's actions throughout much of this period in nationalizing various Bill of Rights provisions gave greater force to the political-type rights and rights involving social matters that the Founders regarded as important—such as religious rights and rights protecting the integrity of the family (e.g., the right of parents to control the education and upbringing of their children). Their giving to the political branches greater leeway to engage in economic regulation did not compromise the Founders' stress on property rights, but was consistent with the balanced view of property and economics of their time and its norm of the social obligation of property (even though, as noted, it may have gone *too far* in some ways in lifting property protections to permit regulation). Furthermore, the demise of the substantive due process-property rights doctrine finally ended a crucial distortion of the Founders' traditional notions of natural law and natural rights.

While the loss of the Founders' belief in the need for a natural aristocracy was lamented by some thinkers of this period—as it was by some thinkers and reformers in the mid- and late-nineteenth century—the technocratic elite that some of them proposed was sharply at odds with the Founders' notion. Also, if America had long since settled into diminishing the republican side of her democratic republic, these anti-democratic thinkers of the 1920s and 1930s, like some of the earlier ones, tended to downplay the democratic side.

A substantial number of the cultural norms of the Founding Era seemed to be disregarded in the 1920-1945 period, in one or another area that has been discussed—or in multiple areas. In economics in the 1920s, such Founding cultural norms or conditions as a middle class culture, the universal destination of goods, avoidance of concentrated wealth and significant economic disparities, restrictions on economic freedom, civility, a cooperative spirit, a community of friendship, decentralization, equality, upholding of the general welfare, and avoidance of unproductive investment were weakened or ignored. Even though Hoover—normally viewed as the pariah of the Great Depression—embraced many of these norms in principle, his policies and the practice of his age did not. During the 1930s, with the FDR administration, there were attempts to somewhat restore certain of these norms, such as decentralization in economic life (with the NIRA and anti-trust efforts), a cooperative orientation (with the

NIRA), and checking the concentration of wealth—mostly with limited success. All told, the lack of a cooperative spirit continued to be the rule (e.g., in labor relations). Further, the problem of the lack of civility was possibly enhanced with FDR's attacks on the rich. The New Deal also challenged genuine liberty with some of its economic policies, as noted. In addition, the norms of initiative and courage were threatened by the new conformity culture of the New Deal and World War II periods. The war may have been the final force in cementing the mass culture—enmassment—that had gradually enveloped America since the nineteenth century.

The lack of civic friendship, civility, a cooperative spirit, and insufficient attention to the general welfare or common good appear repeatedly in this period, not only in economic life, but also in inter-group relations (the worst breakdown of this occurred with the Japanese internment) and, at least early in this period, in dealings with the U.S.'s Latin American neighbors (though this changed from the late 1920s onward). While these norms are not at their historical nadir during this period, their nagging insufficiency continued to plague America in a significant way from the Jacksonian Era onward. The lack of fair-dealing also manifested itself in such matters as the Japanese internment, dealing with neighboring countries, and how conscription was implemented.

Absence of the Founders' realism was poignantly evident in the 1920s in America's foreign affairs and with the whole Prohibition experiment—just as it had been when the latter was enacted and at Versailles at the end of the previous period. The same lack of realism was also seen in so many of the prominent social and political thinkers of this time with their strange confidence that the age-old problems of politics could be finally eliminated by the anointing of a new technocratic ruling elite. The momentum for an apolitical "politics" carried itself over from its Progressive Era origins, and the dynamic of a socio-political "unrealism" had begun—if we think back to Chapter 4—with the rise of the pre-Civil War reform movements. The abstract thinking about politics that began with the democratic theoreticians of the Jacksonian Era continued all the way to many of the thinkers of the 1920-1945 period. Actual policymaking based on such abstract notions finally took hold in the decade from 1919-1929 with, again, the likes of the Fourteen Points, Prohibition, and Kellogg-Briand.

Prohibition, by the way, may have left as a permanent undesirable legacy in America the weakening of popular respect for law and the rule of law.

There was little question that the 1920s reached an American historical high point to that time—i.e., a cultural *low point*—for self-gratification and imperviousness to such Founding cultural norms as temperance, sobriety, restraining of the pursuit of luxury, frugality, thrift, restraining of individualism, present self-sacrifice for a future good, simplicity, and a communal orientation. Although the 1930s provided a respite—the economic disaster simply ground much material self-indulgence to a halt—the country was later to return to consumerism. It seems that the 1920s decisively implanted this way of life into the American psyche.

The 1920s also permanently weakened the central norm of the Founding culture—and of much of nineteenth-century America—of family stability. It was the beginning of an "ongoing revolution" on matters of marriage, family, sex, and reproduction, which later on in post-1960s America even formed the main fault line in the country's politics and profoundly changed its culture.

The further enduring moral legacy of the 1920s, standing behind the latter developments but on the level of general attitudes and operating at a theoretical as well as practical level, was the embracing of moral relativism—at least by the country's intelligentsia, who are the opinion-shapers, but in time affected the broader culture's thinking. This struck at the very core of American Founding principles, since after all natural law and natural rights were axiomatic for the Founding Fathers. The predominant socio-political thinker of the period, Dewey, gave a philosophical justification for this departure (i.e., for the positivist state, whose actions were motivated primarily by amoral, pragmatic concerns) which, like the extreme church-state separationists of the 1870s tried to do with *their* novel theory, made it seem to fit into the American tradition. Most of the other thinkers of the 1920-1945 period—the mature Lippmann was an exception, and clearly most in line with the Founders—who wanted to recover what that tradition more accurately was grasped at only parts of it, or misunderstood key elements of it, or could not capture its splendid but essential balance.

It is striking that during the period from 1920 to 1945 one sees present more of the factors of the decline of cultures and political orders discussed in Chapter 1 than at any previous time in American history. All of the following are observed to a marked degree in this chapter: a turning away from religion; materialism or the excessive pursuit of luxury or runaway prosperity (actually, all three are clearly present); an excessive orientation to private pleasure or lack of control of the desires and passions (one sees this in the pursuit of luxury and, clearly, in the sexual rebellion); social conflict (seen especially in the ethnic and racial conflict and in the labor and economic-generated conflicts of the time, although it was not nearly as *intense* as the great sectional conflict of the Civil War or even the ethnic and nativist conflicts of the nineteenth century); the prevalence of a relativistic moral or ethical outlook (clearly more evident than at any previous time); the dissolution of the middle class—seen in the economic disparities noted above—and serious economic disorders (the Great Depression, of course, was the worst economic situation in U.S. history); the growth of a sense of purposelessness (observed vividly among the 1920's intellectuals); the breakdown of the family; excessive urbanization (as noted, greater than ever in U.S. history in this period) and the rise of mass culture (which continues in this period); the prevalence of liberalism, in most of the characteristics that the different thinkers on cultural decline have associated with it (specifically, an anti-traditional viewpoint, an excessively present-oriented state of mind, and moralistic sentimentality); the breakdown or neglect of the common good (noted in different contexts above, in varying degrees); and the corruption of sound philosophy (seen especially with the seeming triumph of pragmatism, but also perhaps in the realm of political and social philosophy with the stress on technocratic rule). To be sure, some of these conditions prevailed to greater or lesser degrees at different times during the period from 1920 to 1945; others, however, had become deep-seated, ongoing realities.

Finally, the possible weaknesses in the American Founding as discussed in Chapter 1 that perhaps are indicated by the period 1920-1945 were these: an incomplete public philosophy, lack of a sound understanding of all the principles of social ethics, lack of a sound understanding of the common good, and a sense of public purposelessness all due to insufficient philosophical reflection; the seeds of an expanded individualism; the seeds of positivism laid because the Church was excluded as an authoritative interpreter of the natural law (seen increasingly vividly with pragmatism and the sexual rebellion); no formal, reliable way to bring forth a natural aristocracy; no formal, reliable means to shape virtue; not enough of an emphasis on justice in the thought of the Founding; not enough emphasis on community in the thought of the Founding; the emphasis on a commercial republic led to more individualism and laissez faire; the Founders did not realize how much the hold of religion would weaken along with the morality fashioned by it (seen more vividly in this period than ever before); the failure to see the centrality of the family for the political order (despite the fact that there were such positive developments as the Supreme Court's protection of parental rights); the Founders did not see how powerful the courts would become (brought to a head with the court-packing plan); and how the stress on institutional and structural factors gave rise to bureaucratization. One wonders, too, with government now becoming intensely involved in securing the economic and social welfare of American citizens if the problem of an orientation to the higher things not being brought enough into the formal constitutional order did not begin to manifest itself.

Notes

1. William E. Leuchtenburg, *The Perils of Prosperity, 1914-1932* (Chicago: University of Chicago Press, 1958), 108.

2. Ibid., 178.

3. Ibid., 178-179. The quotations are from 179.

4. Ibid., 180-186.

5. Ibid., 190-193. The quotation is from 192-193.

6. Tindall and Shi, 1213.

7. Ibid., 1216; Leuchtenburg, *The Perils of Prosperity,* 178, 201.

8. Anthony J. Badger, *The New Deal: The Depression Years, 1933-40* (Chicago: Ivan R. Dee, 1989), 23.

9. Leuchtenburg, *The Perils of Prosperity,* 246.

10. Ibid., 246.

11. Tindall and Shi, 1215.

12. David E. Kyvig, *Daily Life in the United States, 1920-1940* (Chicago: Ivan R. Dee, 2002), 210, 236.

13. Sean Dennis Cashman, *America in the Twenties and Thirties: The Olympian Age of Franklin Delano Roosevelt* (N.Y.: New York University Press, 1989), 103.

14. Ibid., 44.

15. Badger, 30.

16. Cashman, *America in the Twenties and Thirties,* 44.

17. Tindall and Shi, 1220.

18. Ibid., 1221.

19. Leuchtenburg, *The Perils of Prosperity*, 245-246; Badger, 30.

20. Badger, 31.

21. David M. Kennedy, *Freedom From Fear: The American People in Depression and War, 1929-1945* (N.Y.: Oxford University Press, 1999), 66.

22. Tindall and Shi, 1221.

23. Ibid., 1219-1221.

24. David J. Goldberg, *Discontented America: The United States in the 1920s* (Baltimore: Johns Hopkins University Press, 1999), 78.

25. Ibid., 76.

26. Cashman, *America in the Twenties and Thirties*, 225.

27. Ibid., 228.

28. Goldberg, 73-76.

29. Leuchtenburg, *The Perils of Prosperity*, 111-112. The quotation is from 112.

30. Cashman, *America in the Twenties and Thirties*, 115.

31. Leuchtenburg, *The Perils of Prosperity*, 246; Cashman, *America in the Twenties and Thirties*, 110.

32. Tindall and Shi, 1201.

33. Ibid., 1206, quoting the article.

34. Ibid., 1200.

35. Leuchtenburg, *The Perils of Prosperity*, 102.

36. Ibid., 185.

37. Ibid., 130.

38. Kennedy, 82-84.

39. Ibid., 84-85.

40. Badger, 42.

41. Ibid.

42. Ibid., 42-43.

43. Goldberg, 172.

44. Ibid., 173.

45. Cashman, *America in the Twenties and Thirties*, 117-120.

46. See Tindall and Shi, 1239-1250.

47. "Executive Orders, Proclamations, Memoranda Issued by President Franklin D. Roosevelt, 1933-1945," http://www.conservativeusa.org/eo/fdroosevelt.htm; Internet; accessed March 30, 2009.

48. See ibid.

49. Tindall and Shi, 1238-1239.

50. Ibid., 1254; Kennedy, 290-291.

51. Cashman, *America in the Twenties and Thirties*, 235, 242.

52. Tindall and Shi, 1275-1276. On the restrictions imposed by the federal government on crop cultivation, even for consumption on the individual farm, see: "*Wickard v. Filburn*," http://en.wikipedia.org/wiki/Wickard_v._Filburn; Internet; accessed April 3, 2009.

53. Badger, 109-115.

54. Tindall and Shi, 1326.

55. Badger, 102-104. The quotation is from 102.

56. Kennedy, 278, 282. The quotation is from 278.

57. Badger, 105-106.

58. Cashman, *America in the Twenties and Thirties*, 235-236.

59. Kennedy, 293-296.

60. Cashman, *America in the Twenties and Thirties*, 236-237.

61. Ibid., 237-239; Rayback, 353-354.

62. Cashman, *America in the Twenties and Thirties*, 240-241.

63. Ibid., 244-246.

64. See Kennedy, 170-172, 263-264, 272.

65. Tindall and Shi, 1325-1328. The quotations are from 1327.

66. Sean Dennis Cashman, *America, Roosevelt, and World War II* (N.Y.: New York University Press, 1989), 199.

67. Robert Higgs, *Crisis and Leviathan: Critical Episodes in the Growth of American Government* (N.Y.: Oxford University Press, 1987), 229-230, 235-236.

68. Tindall and Shi, 1277.

69. Kennedy, 359.

70. Ibid., 365.

71. Higgins, 421. He gives a good, terse description of the paternalistic state (420-421).

72. Kennedy, 371.

73. Ibid., 214.

74. Ibid., 350.

75. U.S. Dept. of Labor, "Compensation and Working Conditions: Compensation from Before World War I through the Great Depression," http://www.bls.gov/opub/cwc/cm20030124ar03p1.htm; Internet; accessed April 2, 2009.

76. Tindall and Shi, 1327.

77. Ibid., 1199.

78. Ibid., 1199-1200, 1201, 1204.

79. Ibid., 1204.

80. Ibid., 1218-1219.

81. Badger, 245.

82. Ibid., 261.

83. Ibid.

84. See ibid., 264-271.

85. Ibid., 263, 266. The quotation is from 263.

86. Tindall and Shi, 1372.

87. Ibid., 1269.

88. Kennedy, 331.

89. Franklin D. Roosevelt, "Fireside Chat on Reorganization of the Judiciary, March 9, 1937," http://www.hpol.org/ fdr/chat/; Internet; accessed April 7, 2009.

90. William Manchester, *The Glory and the Dream: A Narrative History of America, 1932-1972* (Boston: Little Brown, 1974), 151; Kenneth D. Crews, "Introduction," in Kenneth D. Crews, ed., *Corwin's Constitution: Essays and Insights of Edward S. Corwin* (Westport, Conn.: Greenwood, 1986), 4-5; "Judicial Reorganization Bill of 1937," http://en.wikipedia.org/wiki/Judiciary_Reorganization_Bill_of_1937; Internet; accessed April 10, 2009.

91. Kennedy, 325.

92. Manchester, 152.

93. Tindall and Shi, 1269.

94. Ibid., 1270.

95. McCloskey, 185-186.

96. Ibid., 188. The citation for the *Curtiss-Wright* case is 299 U.S. 304.

97. The case in which the Japanese internment was upheld was *Korematsu v. U.S.*, 323 U.S. 214 (1944).

98. McCloskey, 186. The citation for the *Carolene Products* case is 304 U.S. 144.

99. "United States v. Carolene Products Company," http://en.wikipedia.org/ wiki/United_States_v._Carolene_Products_Co.; Internet; accessed April 9, 2009. This source directly quotes the opinion, as indicated.

100. Crews, 5; "Judicial Reorganization Bill of 1937."

101. See, e.g., Edward S. Corwin, "The Supreme Court and the Fourteenth Amendment" and "Social Planning Under the Constitution," in Alpheus T. Mason and Gerald Garvey, eds., *American Constitutional History: Essays by Edward S. Corwin* (Gloucester, Mass.: Peter Smith, 1970), 67-98, 109-125.

102. Michael Barone, *Our Country: The Shaping of America from Roosevelt to Reagan* (N.Y.: Free Press, 1990), 95-96, quoted in Kennedy, 285.

103. See Kennedy, 170-172; 263-264.

104. Ibid., 263-264.

105. Ibid., 265.

106. Scot Zentner, "New Deal," in Bruce Frohnen, Jeremy Beer, and Jeffrey O. Nelson, *American Conservatism: An Encyclopedia* (Wilmington, Del.: ISI Books, 2006), 620.

107. Kennedy, 262-263

108. Hamilton, Federalist 17, 103-104. The first and second quotations are from 103, and the third and fourth from 104.

109. See Hamilton, Federalist 23, 141-146. The complete quotation is from 146.

110. Michael C.C. Adams, *The Best War Ever: America and World War II* (Baltimore: Johns Hopkins University Press, 1994), 75. Eisenhower's warning about the dangers of the military-industrial complex came in his "Farewell Address," January 17, 1961 (see: http://www.americanrhetoric.com/speeches/ dwightdeisenhowerfarewell.html; Internet; accessed April 10, 2009). The term "permanent crisis" about the Cold War conflict between the Free World and communism comes from Kurt London, *The Permanent Crisis: Communism in World Politics* (N.Y.: Walker and Company, 1962).

111. See, e.g., David Riesman, *The Lonely Crowd: A Study of the Changing American Character* (New Haven, Conn.: Yale University Press, 1950); Bernard Iddings Bell, *Crowd Culture: An Examination of the American Way of Life* (N.Y.: Harper and Brothers, 1952); Sloan Wilson, *The Man in the Gray Flannel Suit* (N.Y.: Simon and Schuster, 1955), which was a novel and in 1956 was made into a 20th Century Fox movie.

112. See Tindall and Shi, 1170-1173.

113. Ibid., 872. The Indians were granted citizenship and, of course, with it the vote in 1924.

114. Leuchtenburg, *The Perils of Prosperity*,160.

115. Cashman, *America in the Twenties and Thirties*, 56; Kyvig, 25.

116. Kyvig, 4; Goldberg, 53.

117. Mason and Stephenson, 255.

118. Jefferson went ahead, although not without reluctance, to make the Louisiana Purchase even though he did not believe that the Constitution contained any provision for the purchase of additional territory by the federal government (as noted in Chapter 2). Jackson, as discussed in Chapter 3, went against the law and withdrew the government deposits from the Second Bank of the United States because he believed the Bank was unconstitutional—even though the Supreme Court had upheld it—and a threat to democracy, and this was the way he could help put it out of business.

119. Mason and Stephenson, 250.

120. Ibid., 581. The citation for the *Meyer* case is 262 U.S. 390, and for *Pierce* it is 268 U.S. 510.

121. Ibid., 383-384. The citation for the *Gitlow* case is 268 U.S. 652, and for *Near* it is 283 U.S. 697.

122. Ibid., 384. The citation for the *Powell* case is 287 U.S. 45.

123. See Cashman, *America in the Twenties and Thirties*, 288-290.

124. Tindall and Shi, 1333. The citation for the *Allwright* case is 321 U.S. 649.

125. Mason and Stephenson, 385. The citation for the *DeJonge* case is 299 U.S. 353.

126. Fred D. Ragan, "*Buck v. Bell*," in Hall, 97-98. The citation for the *Buck* case is 274 U.S. 200.

127. Mason and Stephenson, 581. The citation for the *Skinner* case is 316 U.S. 535.

128. Ibid., 542. The citation for the *Gobitis* case is 310 U.S. 586, and for *Barnette* it is 319 U.S. 624.

129. Cashman, *America, Roosevelt, and World War II*, 273. The citation for the *Jones* case is 316 U.S. 584, and for *Murdock* it is 319 U.S. 105.

130. Cashman, *America in the Twenties and Thirties*, 329-330.

131. Adams, 9-10.

132. Ibid., 154.

133. Ibid., 126.

134. Ibid., 75.

135. Cashman, *America, Roosevelt, and World War II*, 271.

136. Ibid., 272-273.

137. Ibid., 272; "Lawrence Dennis," http://en.wikipedia.org/wiki/Lawrence_Dennis; Internet; accessed April 29, 2009.

138. Cashman, *America, Roosevelt, and World War II*, 269, 271.

139. Ibid., 186.

140. See Jay, Federalists 3 and 4, 13-22.

141. Tindall and Shi, 1218.

142. Cashman, *America in the Twenties and Thirties*, 202-203.

143. Ibid., 209; "Conservative Coalition," http://en.wikipedia.org/wiki/Conservative_coalition; Internet; accessed April 15, 2009.

144. Cashman, *America in the Twenties and Thirties*, 215.

145. Ibid., 213-215. The quotation is from 213.

146. Kennedy, 341.

147. Ibid.

148. Ibid., 214.

149. "Wisconsin Progressive Party," http://en.wikipedia.org/wiki/Wisconsin_Progressive_Party; Internet; accessed April 14, 2009.

150. Kennedy, 220.

151. Ibid., 221.

152. Ibid., 224-225.

153. Ibid., 225-226.

154. Ibid., 231-232; Tindall and Shi, 1253. The quotation is from Kennedy, 231.

155. Kennedy, 229-234.

156. Ibid., 234.

157. Ibid., 235.

158. Badger, 292.

159. Ibid., 237; "Huey Long," http://en.wikipedia.org/wiki/Huey_Long; Inter- net; accessed April 14, 2009.

160. Kennedy, 236.

161. Kennedy, 238.

162. Ibid., 223, 290-296; Cashman, *America in the Twenties and Thirties*, 244-246.

163. Kennedy, 222; Badger, 290.

164. Badger, 295.

165. Ibid., 296.

166. Kennedy, 263.

167. See, e.g., "Jewish Socialism in the United States, 1920-1948," *My Jewish Learning*, http://www.myjewishlearning.com/history/Modern_History/1914-1948/American_Jewry_Between_the_Wars/Radical_Politics/Socialism.shtml; Internet; accessed March 23, 2010; Rudolph J. Vecoli, "Radicalism," in Salvatore J. LaGumina, Frank J. Cavaioli, Salvatore Primeggia, and Joseph A. Varacalli, eds., *The Italian American Experience: An Encyclopedia* (N.Y.: Garland, 2000), 523-527.

168. Theodore Roosevelt, FDR's distant relative, had tried to return to the office in 1912—after Taft's term—after having previously served almost eight years but actually being elected only once.

169. Higham, 267.

170. "Immigration Act of 1924," http://en.wikipedia.org/wiki/Immigration_Act_of_1924; Internet; accessed April 15, 2009.

171. Ibid.; Higham, 267-269, 272; Cashman, *America in the Twenties and Thirties*, 47-48. Stoddard was a lawyer-historian whose 1920 book, *The Rising Tide of Color*, raised fears that the Negroid and Mongoloid races, in the aftermath of the impairing of Caucasian solidarity in World War I, would shortly overwhelm the Caucasian world (Higham, 272).

172. Higham, 272, 273, 276.

173. Tindall and Shi, 1166-1168.

174. Cashman, *America in the Twenties and Thirties*, 76-77.

175. Kyvig, 170.

176. Kennedy, 342.

177. "Mass Racial Violence in the United States," http://en.wikipedia.org/wiki/Mass_racial_violence_in_the_United_ States; Internet; accessed April 15, 2009.

178. Tindall and Shi, 1332-1333. The quotations are from 1333.

179. Higham, 293.

180. Ibid., 280-285.

181. Cashman, *America, Roosevelt, and World War II*, 267-268. The quotations are from 267 and 268, in that order.

182. "MS St. Louis," http://en.wikipedia.org/wiki/SS_St._Louis; Internet; accessed April 16, 2009. This article says that the *MS St. Louis* affair was a set-up by the Hitler regime. The Nazis arranged for the refugees to board the ship headed for Havana, knowing that their visas would not permit them to enter. They further wanted to show that no other Western country would admit them either, implicitly agreeing with the Nazis that the Jews were a problem and that the Nazis were right to try to address it. FDR specifically refused to let any of the refugees enter the U.S. A small number did succeed in disembarking in Cuba and other Western European countries took small numbers of them. Germany later occupied most of the latter countries and many of the refugees were presumed to have perished later at the hands of the Nazis. In fairness to him, FDR did push for the convening of the Evian Conference in France the year before in 1938 to have nations discuss the problem of Jewish refugees, but it did not result in any plan to resolve it.

183. Cashman, *America, Roosevelt, and World War II*, 273.

184. See "United States Supreme Court Cases Involving Jehovah's Witnesses," http://en.wikipedia.org/wiki/United_States_Supreme_Court_cases_involving_Jehovah's _ Witnesses; Internet; accessed April 16, 209.

185. Tindall and Shi, 1228-1229.

186. "Hooverville," http://en.wikipedia.org/wiki/Hooverville; Internet; accessed April 16, 2009.

187. Tindall and Shi, 1228.

188. Cashman, *America in the Twenties and Thirties*, 248.

189. Leuchtenburg, *The Perils of Prosperity*, 106.

190. See Morgenthau, 423, 426, 433-435.

191. Leuchtenburg, *The Perils of Prosperity*, 107.

192. See Morganthau, 11, 189, 191-192.

193. Leuchtenburg, *The Perils of Prosperity*, 117.

194. Ibid., 107; "Nicaragua," http://en.wikipedia.org/wiki/Nicaragua; Internet; accessed April 17, 2009.

195. Federico G. Gil, *Latin American-United States Relations* (N.Y.: Harcourt Brace Jovanovich, 1971), 155, 163. The quotations are from 155.

196. Leuchtenburg, *The Perils of Prosperity*, 108.

197. Tindall and Shi, 1293-1294.

198. Cashman, *America in the Twenties and Thirties*, 531.

199. "Good Neighbor Policy," http://en.wikipedia.org/wiki/Good_Neighbor_ Policy; Internet; accessed April 17, 2009.

200. Kennedy, 390.

201. Ibid., 388-392.

202. Ibid., 423-424, 436.

203. See ibid., 394.

204. Ibid.

205. Ibid., 434, 446, 492, 505, 510; Tindall and Shi, 1307-1308; Cashman, *America in the Twenties and Thirties*, 587.

206. See Jay, Federalist 3, 13-17.

207. Kennedy, 392-393; Morgenthau, 99.

208. Adams, 81-82.

209. Kennedy, 743-744, 846-847; James Turner Johnson, *Can Modern War Be Just?* (New Haven, Conn.: Yale University Press, 1984), 111, 131.

210. Tindall and Shi, 1363.

211. For example, Kennedy suggests that the U.S. and Britain gave little attention to any preferences of the Polish government in exile in London in making decisions about post-war Poland (Kennedy, 801-802).

212. Paul Johnson, *A History of the American People*, 802. It should be pointed out, however, that there was much disagreement among the top military brass about Truman's conclusion that the use of the atomic bombs was militarily necessary—among the critics were Generals Dwight Eisenhower and Douglas MacArthur (Cashman, *America, Roosevelt, and World War II*, 368-369).

213. Kennedy, 743-744. This was also apparently the aim of the February 3, 1945 bombing of the center of the city of Berlin. Churchill viewed the Dresden firebombing in such a light and distanced himself from it. To be sure, there is historical disagreement about whether the Dresden bombing could have been justified because of industrial targets in the city and its transportation infrastructure that could have facilitated German military movements (see "Bombing of Dresden in World War II," http://en.wikipedia. org/wiki/Bombing_of_Dresden_in_World_War_II; Internet; accessed April 27, 2009).

Kennedy leaves little doubt about the intention, however, which was part of a British-initiated operation code-named Thunderclap which had crushing morale as its specific purpose.

214. James Turner Johnson, *Can Modern War Be Just?*, 16.

215. It is worth recalling Tocqueville's observation that if religious ties are weakened in a democratic republic, morality will weaken and the door would be open to its destruction (Tocqueville, I, ii, 294).

216. Quoted in Leuchtenburg, *The Perils of Prosperity*, 176.

217. Leuchtenburg, *The Perils of Prosperity*, 146, 155.

218. Ibid., 148, 174, 188.

219. Ibid., 149.

220. Ibid., 149-150.

221. Ibid., 151.

222. Ibid., 204.

223. Ibid., 144-145.

224. Kyvig, 134.

225. Leuchtenburg, *The Perils of Prosperity*, 171.

226. Cashman, *America, Roosevelt, and World War II*, 218.

227. Cashman, *America in the Twenties and Thirties*, 58.

228. Leuchtenburg, *The Perils of Prosperity*, 167-169.

229. Ibid., 165; Cashman, *America in the Twenties and Thirties*, 406.

230. "Birth Control," http://www.catholic.com/library/Birth_Control.asp; Internet; accessed April 20, 2009 (on the 1930 Lambeth Conference).

231. Kyvig, 137; Leuchtenburg, *The Perils of Prosperity*, 171.

232. Tindall and Shi, 1178; Kyvig, 135.

233. Kyvig, 227-228. The quotation is from 227.

234. Leuchtenburg, *The Perils of Prosperity*, 159-160;

235. Ibid., 159; Kyvig, 135.

236. Leuchtenburg, *The Perils of Prosperity,*162; Kyvig, 138. This deference to experts was curious in light of the fact that many of them were already showing themselves to be no friends of the family, had little confidence in the capability of parents to properly raise their children, and were increasingly espousing the view that child-rearing should be subjected to the close supervision of the state (see Carlson, 248).

237. Leuchtenburg, *The Perils of Prosperity*, 162.

238. Ibid., 135

239. Cashman, *America, Roosevelt, and World War II*, 219.

240. Ibid., 218.

241. Higham, 268.

242. Tindall and Shi, 1171-1172.

243. Cashman, *America, Roosevelt, and World War II*, 218.

244. Kyvig, 182.

245. Adams, 132.

246. Paul Johnson, *Modern Times: The World from the Twenties to the Eighties* (N.Y.: Harper & Row, 1983), 1, 4 (the entire first chapter is entitled "A Relativistic World").

247. Leuchtenburg, *The Perils of Prosperity*, 158.

248. Ibid., 188-189; Kyvig, 149-151, 155. The quotation is from Kyvig,149.

249. Kyvig, 144; Cashman, *America in the Twenties and Thirties*, 59.

250. Kyvig, 148.

251. Ibid., 145-146. The quotation is from 146.

252. Ibid., 146-147.

253. Adams, 127.

254. See Thomas Jefferson, correspondence to Peter Carr, Sept. 7, 1814, in Adrienne Koch and William Peden, eds., *The Life and Selected Writings of Thomas Jefferson* (N.Y.: Modern Library, 1944), 642; Tocqueville, II, i, 476-477.

255. Adams, 127.

256. Kyvig, 147; Adams, 126.

257. Cashman, *America in the Twenties and Thirties*, 59; Kyvig, 149. The first quotation is from Cashman and the second from Kyvig.

258. Leuchtenburg, *The Perils of Prosperity,* 225.

259. Cashman, *America in the Twenties and Thirties*, 50.

260. Ibid., 16.

261. Badger, 25; Tindall and Shi, 1329; Stanley Coben, *Rebellion Against Victorianism: The Impetus for Cultural Change in 1920s America* (N.Y.: Oxford University Press, 1991), 72.

262. Beitzinger, 474-479; "John Dewey," http://en.wikipedia.org/wiki/John_ Dewey; Internet; accessed April 21, 2009.

263. *The New York Times* made this description of Dewey on the occasion of his 90th birthday (mentioned in Larry Hickman, "The Lasting Legacy of John Dewey," http://www.brc21.org/themes/ed_hickman_dewey.htm; Internet; accessed May 3, 2009). Robert Horwitz says, "Dewey has been recognized as the foremost American philosopher of democracy of the twentieth century" (Horwitz, "John Dewey," in Strauss and Cropsey, 851).

264. Beitzinger, 540-541.

265. Ibid., 541.

266. Ibid., 542-544.

267. Ibid., 545-547.

268. See Pope John Paul II, *Centesimus Annus* (*The Hundredth Year*), #46.

269. Beitzinger, 516.

270. Ibid., 516. The definition of "moral imagination" is from Fred Hutchison, "The Moral Imagination, Politics, and Wisdom," Nov. 23, 2004, at the "Renew America" website, http://www.renewamerica.us/columns/hutchison/ 041123; Internet; accessed April 23, 2009.

271. Beitzinger, 516.

272. Ibid., 517-518.

273. Ibid., 522-523.

274. Ibid., 524.

275. Ibid., 524-526.

276. Ibid., 527.

277. Ibid., 531-532.

278. Lasch, 297; "Southern Agrarians," http://en.wikipedia.org/wiki/Southern_ Agrarians; Internet; "Old Right (United States), http://en.wikipedia.org/wiki/Old_Right_ (United_States); both accessed April 23, 2009.

CHAPTER 7

1945-1960: POST-WORLD WAR II AMERICA AND THE COLD WAR

The historian Paul Johnson says that the decade of the 1950s was the last "in which the traditional elements in American society held the cultural upper hand."[1] While we have seen how traditional norms were chipped away at in the nineteenth century and then challenged aggressively in the 1920s, Johnson's assessment is essentially correct. Nevertheless, as we shall discuss, there was much erosion of traditional culture beneath the surface in the 1950s—Johnson also says that "the portents of change were present"[2]—which was to have a profound effect on politics and American life generally in the 1960s and beyond. The 1950s was also a time when—due to the socio-economic conditions of post-War America and the threat of Soviet communism—there was a new manifestation of the middle class order and condition of civic friendship of Founding Era culture (with an absence of serious social conflict), and for the first time—with the rising Negro civil rights movement—such Founding principles as equality and political and legal rights had the promise of universal practical application for all citizens. It was also a time of new strains in the relationships among the branches of the federal government and consolidation of the federal-state relationship forged during the New Deal that had implications for the character of the American democratic republic. The period was especially noted for continuing and furthering the conformist culture that began in the 1930s. At the same time, the battle against fascism in World War II and the challenge of communism in the new Cold War motivated a renewed attention to traditional American political principles and religious commitment. For the analysis in this chapter, we examine the following seven areas: economics, economic and social welfare policy, and labor questions; foreign policy, the military, and espionage; race and Negro civil rights; constitutional and legal developments, relations among the three branches of the federal government, federalism, and the role of government in general; individual liberties and citizen rights; currents in political and social thought; and socio-cultural developments.

Economics, Economic and Social Welfare Policy, and Labor Questions. The first areas to consider concern economics, foreign policy, and Negro civil rights since they were the most important domains of public issues and policy during this period. The end of World War II and America's rapid demobilization (from eleven million to one million men at arms)—"the habitual American response to victory"—and conversion back to a peacetime economy brought expected problems.[3] Among the latter were unemployment—but not at the levels of the Great Depression—inflation, product (including food) shortages, a housing shortage, and a rash of strikes.[4] As soon as the war ended, both business and labor began to make demands and reverted to their typical mutually hostile relationship. In 1946, President Truman had wanted to extend the wartime Office of Price Administration (OPA) for an additional year to try to keep a lid on price increases while the conversion went on. However, Congress—which had a strong pro-business bias even though it was still controlled by the Democrats—would agree only to continuing the agency with much scaled down powers. In the face of the additional opposition of farmers—which featured even their withholding of meat from the market as a response to continued price controls—virtually all commodity price controls ended.[5] Actually, William Manchester says there was little popular support to continue wartime controls. The OPA had exercised overwhelming power during the war, when it utilized a large number of employees and volunteers to insure compliance down to the local community level (Manchester calls it an "intolerable tyranny").[6] As far as labor was concerned, some of its demands were extreme. Although Truman favored wage increases after the war to sustain purchasing power and thus avert a problem that helped cause the Depression, the UAW sought a massive 30% pay increase from General Motors and the UMW an 18.5-cent-per-hour increase (which was quite substantial, considering what wage rates were like at the time). Business also rebuffed the administration's call for wage hikes.[7] Truman often had to intervene in major labor disputes to try to forge a compromise. The UMW's redoubtable leader John L. Lewis, however, refused to cooperate and a resulting coal strike hurt the economy. Railroad union leaders also spurned intense efforts by Truman to convince them to moderate their demands. When a rail strike began, Truman proceeded to order a governmental seizure of the railroads and mused that he would ask Congress for authority to draft the strikers into the military. These actions brought the strike to a conclusion.[8]

Right after V-J Day, Truman put forth a legislative program that sought to continue and expand the New Deal's economic and social welfare initiatives. It eventually came to be called the "Fair Deal." He proposed: expanding unemployment compensation, increasing the minimum wage, regularizing the wartime fight against race discrimination in employment, a public works program, rent subsidies, urban renewal efforts, and the expansion of TVA-like development programs. He also supported a Keynesian-inspired bill that would have committed the federal government to declare that all Americans were "entitled" to full-time employment, and would have made it the "responsibility" of the federal government to "assure continuing full employment, that is, the existence at all times of sufficient employment opportunities" by means of "such volume of federal investment and expenditure as may be needed" to achieve it.[9] Most of this did not take off, and after the Republicans gained control of

Congress in 1946 and the nation became absorbed by early Cold War developments it was substantially sidetracked. Congress did pass a compromise Employment Act of 1946, which in a vague way made it federal policy "to promote maximum employment, production, and purchasing power," and established the Council of Economic Advisers for the president and a Joint Economic Committee in Congress to help generate legislation.[10] While the final legislation did not make commitments to specific policy, Tindall and Shi point out that federal officials and leading economists in an ongoing way in this period created in the American public not only an expectation that they "should not fear another economic collapse," but also of "perpetual economic growth" and a condition of "unending plenty."[11] In 1947 the Republican Congress passed, over Truman's veto, the Taft-Hartley Act, which forbade unfair labor practices by unions (such as secondary boycotts, refusal to bargain in good faith with management, and "featherbedding" or pay for work not done), banned the closed shop (in which hiring had to be restricted to union members), permitted states to pass "right to work" laws (in which workers could not be required to join a union after hiring), gave employers the right to sue unions for breaking contracts and to speak openly during campaigns to install unions in their companies (i.e., in opposition to them), and permitted the president to impose an eighty-day "cooling-off" period (i.e., suspension) on any strike he deemed detrimental to national health or safety.[12] Truman pledged never to invoke the latter provision, and when the 1952 steel strike threatened to jeopardize production during the Korean War he followed his railroad strike precedent and seized the steel mills instead. With Taft-Hartley's cooling-off provision available, the Supreme Court declared that he lacked the constitutional authority for such an action (discussed below).[13] Late in the Eisenhower administration, following Congressional investigations that exposed labor corruption, the Landrum-Griffin Act put further restraints on labor unions by giving states more freedom to regulate them, putting restrictions on secondary boycotts, requiring the filing of union financial reports with the U.S. Labor Department, creating minimum standards to be met before a union could discipline one of its members, and forbidding Communists from holding union offices.[14]

In spite of the above economic problems, Tindall and Shi tell us that the "dominant feature of post-World War II American society was its remarkable prosperity...the economy soared to record heights."[15] Eric F. Goldman says that the Korean War years brought "the boomingest America in all the prosperous years since V-J."[16] Major factors that helped bring this about were the following: the GI Bill, which subsidized college and vocational education and provided housing loans for the massive number of World War II veterans; the housing boom that followed from the latter; resumed high government defense spending stimulated by the Cold War and its "hot" manifestation in Korea (which affected not just war materiel industries, but related ones); new technological innovations that fueled substantial productivity increases; the unleashing of pent-up consumer demand following from the enforced restraint of the World War II years, and the forming of many new families as war veterans returned home.[17]

There was little new domestic economic or social welfare legislation during the second Truman term, but what little there was added to the New Deal-installed programs. For example, Social Security underwent its first comprehensive change since its enactment when such new groups as farmworkers, domestic servants, and small businessmen were added to it; the minimum wage was increased; and agricultural and public power programs were expanded.[18] That Keynesian views were well accepted was observed in the fact that during the economic downturn of 1949, the Truman administration readily resorted to deficit spending to "keep the pump primed."[19]

Paul Johnson says of the Eisenhower years that, "America...enjoyed unprecedented prosperity...It was the Twenties prosperity over again, but less frenetic and more secure, with a far wider social spread...The Fifties was the decade of affluence." The same was true of Western Europe, now rebuilt from the war (with the initial help of the Marshall Plan, discussed below).[20] Eisenhower's administration claimed that it represented business and industry, and undertook some reversals of the economic policies of FDR and Truman, such as abolishing the Reconstruction Finance Corporation, ending what remained of wage and price controls, reducing farm subsidies, and backing away from federal public power efforts. Cutting the budget was initially a high priority, and in his first term Eisenhower reduced federal expenditures by about 10%. When a business slowdown decreased federal revenues, however, he had to stress this less—demonstrating how ingrained a large federal government and federal programs had become, since a lot more revenue than in the past was needed.[21] By 1957, he submitted the largest peacetime budget in American history.[22] Tindall and Shi say that Eisenhower "chipped away at several New Deal programs," but retained "its basic structure and premises." There was no wholesale retreat of the federal government from social welfare programs. Social Security benefits increased and its reach was extended again (to professionals, clerical workers, and members of the military), the minimum wage was hiked, federal housing programs continued (though at a reduced level), federal public works spending continued—we have seen that this is an old practice dating back to the early years of the Republic—with the interstate highway system (a joint federal-state, but mostly federal, undertaking) and the St. Lawrence Seaway the most notable large-scale projects, some farm programs were actually expanded, federal education spending sharply increased, and an initial food stamp program was inaugurated. Eisenhower even proposed federal involvement in health insurance, but Congress did not agree.[23] Government had become, and remained during the 1950s, a major employer.[24]

As might be expected, the affluence of the period from 1945 to 1960 fueled a consumerist mentality and an intense pursuit of luxury. To some degree this could be expected since, as noted above, many consumer goods were not available during World War II. A kind of "consumer culture" developed, however.[25] As Leuchtenburg says, "consumers devoted much of their time to institutions that catered to their needs and whims."[26] This consumerism became "sophisticated...worldly...diversified," with Americans seeking goods from around the world.[27] Advertising to create consumer demand and credit buying ("[s]o easy...that scores of pawnshops were driven out of business") were important features of this consumer culture, as was the new-found purchasing power of youth who became "pacesetters for much of the popular culture."[28]

The economic growth and affluence of the period meant a "vastly expanded middle class," and increased financial security with the growth of fringe benefits, sharply increased pension funds, and for some unionized workers even a guaranteed annual income.[29] An increasing percentage even owned stocks.[30] Still, there were some disturbing problems: "extreme disparities in income distribution continued," particularly among various minority groups and farmers; the usually troubled farm sector overall suffered both economic and population decline; in spite of Social Security, a disproportionate percentage of the elderly were poor; a substantial minority of the population was able to save relatively little and had very limited liquid assets; throughout the 1950s a creeping inflation occurred that weakened the buying power and real income of many; and the personal and family debt problem grew.[31] Even with increasing income, vertical mobility did not necessarily occur because of attitudes fostered by the consumer culture. Many people preferred more material things to personal improvement in other ways—i.e., involving the immaterial things that were held important in Founding Era culture—that could have helped change class position (which is often a more central concern in vertical mobility than wealth).[32]

We make the following comparison of the economic life and policies of the 1945-1960 period with the Founding Era. While government economic controls did not necessarily violate the practices of that era—after all, we said that it featured much legal restraint of economic freedom—the centralization that it represented did. While as a wartime exigency they were not problematical, to continue them in peacetime—even the transition that Truman had in mind to insure economic stability—would have been. Continued controls could also have hurt initiative, an important Founding norm. The absence of the spirit of cooperation that was part of the Founding Era's mores was readily observable with the renewed labor-management conflict not long after V-J Day. While the conflict was not as intense or violent as it often had been in the past, the haste to stake out competing claims practically as soon as the war ended did not exactly bespeak abundant civic friendship. Moreover, the excessive demands of the unions flew in the face of such Founding norms as self-sacrifice and temperance. The provisions of the Taft-Hartley and Landrum-Griffin Acts were reasonable, and recognized that labor unions—not just management—could be abusive. The former's making "right to work" laws an acceptable state option, however, may have betrayed an insufficient awareness of the advantage in economic bargaining power of large corporations, which had been evident since the late nineteenth century. Truman's proposal to draft strikers both violated Founding notions of liberty and, more tangibly, the Thirteenth Amendment. The economy had long since stabilized into a situation of bigness and the modern corporate arrangement of the separation of ownership and control, so the pertinent Founding norms were gone for much of economic life. In popular discussion, there also seemed to be little attention to the question of morality in economic life; as mentioned, Keynesianism—with its amoral notions of government intervention and manipulation to secure prosperity—was in control. While the postwar expansion of the middle class certainly accorded with the Founding, the fact that significant poverty and substantial inequalities existed obviously did not. The norm of personal initiative and the spirit of independence and liberty of the Founding culture was somewhat compromised by the continuation—actually, as the discussion below makes clear, considerable enhancement—of an ethic of conformism. The new consumer culture and the growth of individual and family debt that accompanied it went against the Founding exhortation against luxury and its norms of thrift, sobriety, and temperance. The fact that even youth shared in the pursuit of luxury by itself perhaps showed a weakness in the family and its ability to form the young—we discuss more about the postwar family below—that was a central part of Founding Era life. The "cult of youth" of the 1920s reemerged in the 1950s and then swept over American life in the 1960s. On the government side, while Eisenhower began with the Founding spirit of restraint and concern about deficit spending, as time went on for all practical purposes he accepted the Keynesian government-spending-to-stimulate-the-economy perspective.

   Foreign Policy, the Military, and Espionage. The American demobilization after V-J Day was to be short-lived, due to the rise of the Cold War. While Cold War "revisionist historians" tried to claim that Truman ignited the conflict with the Soviets by taking "an unnecessarily belligerent stance" and trying "to create American spheres of influence around the world,"[33] by far the evidence is much stronger that the Soviet Union turned away from American hopes of continuing the wartime alliance, violated wartime agreements such as the Yalta Agreement, and aggressively sought to extend her control in Europe and elsewhere.[34] Even before V-E Day, the Soviets began to circumvent the Yalta Agreement by installing puppet governments in Eastern Europe backed up by the presence of Soviet occupation troops.[35] The Soviet promise to conduct free elections was discarded, pro-Soviet Communist governments were forcibly established in these countries, and eventually the Eastern Bloc emerged. Both FDR and Truman realized quickly that the Soviets were not upholding their pledges.[36] Things began to build from there. In 1946, the Soviets rejected Western attempts to establish international control over nuclear energy and weapons by a special UN commission, calling instead—probably not seriously, since they were secretly building an atomic bomb with the help of information provided them by U.S. spies (see below)—for an agreement to abolish nuclear weapons to be enforced by the UN Security Council, where they had an absolute veto.[37] The Soviet Union liberally used the veto in the early days of the UN to shield herself and her allies from international rebuke.[38] A Soviet-backed Communist guerrilla war had continued in Greece since the war's end, and the prospect of Greece falling into the Soviet orbit—with Turkey soon to follow—was very serious as 1947 wore on.[39] The nature of the danger was driven home further in 1947 by Ambassador George F. Kennan's famous "long telegram" and his anonymously published *Foreign Affairs* article in which he concluded that the Soviet government under Josef Stalin believed that the destruction of the Western way of life was the only way for their nation's power to be secure and to that end would expand wherever it could. He called for an American policy of "containment" that would oppose such expansionism. If this was pursued, in the long run he thought it might be possible for the West to moderate these Soviet tendencies.[40] The need to support Greece and Turkey and the acceptance of Kennan's proposal led to the Truman Doctrine, in which the President announced that wherever an anti-Communist government was threatened the U.S. was willing to supply political, economic, and military aid. The conviction was growing in the American public that not merely was another war threatened, but a conflict between two vastly different ways of life that involved the highest of stakes and the very future of civilization.[41] This readily led to public and Congressional support for the Truman Doctrine and, with the financial support for Greece and Turkey, the establishment of a precedent of the U.S. intervening for the first time in the affairs of nations outside of the Western Hemisphere in the absence of a "hot war."[42] This was followed by an even more massive commitment in the form of the Marshall Plan (the European Recovery Program), a major economic assistance plan to help the countries of Western Europe to rebuild after the war and get their economies functioning again (it was also offered to the Eastern Bloc—even though stabilizing Europe to help contain communism was a key objective of the Plan—but the Soviet Union rejected it).[43] 1948 brought the final events that cemented containment as the foundation of American foreign policy for almost the next three decades. A coup in Czechoslovakia ousted the last Eastern European non-Communist government and the Soviets—apparently because of their anger at the Marshall Plan and Allied intentions to allow the creation of the German Federal Republic—blockaded West Berlin in the hopes of "starving" it into joining the Eastern Bloc. This, of course, led to the famous Berlin Airlift, with the result that the Soviets abandoned this effort.[44] In 1948, the UN also agreed to the partitioning of Palestine between Palestinian Arabs and Jewish settlers and the establishment of the nation of Israel, an action that was strongly supported by both the U.S. and the U.S.S.R[45]—even though later the Soviets allied with the anti-Israel Arabs and the U.S. with Israel, and the Cold War was to stand not far in the background of Arab-Israeli hostilities for most of the next forty years.

In 1949, the North Atlantic Treaty Organization (NATO) was formed. It was a military alliance of the U.S. and Western European countries, in which all agreed to a joint military response in case of a Soviet attack on any one of them (in the mid-1950s, the Eastern Bloc nations countered by forming the Warsaw Pact alliance). Also in 1949, China fell to the Communists and the Soviets conducted their first nuclear test.[46] The Cold War was consolidated, the competition between the West and communism spread to Asia, and a nuclear and conventional arms race between the U.S. and the U.S.S.R. was underway. East-West hostility was to be the central reality of international politics for the ensuing four decades.

A Marshall Plan of sorts, much more sweeping in terms of the areas of the world it sought to help but less in terms of a financial commitment, was the Point Four Program, announced by Truman in his 1949 inaugural address. It aimed to provide economic aid to poor countries.[47] It was the first general American commitment to elevate the underdeveloped world.

The Cold War first became a "hot war" in Korea in 1950, and did so again in Vietnam in the 1960s. It is beyond our purposes here to discuss the particulars of the war. The pertinent point to make is that it was the first extended foreign military engagement that the U.S. undertook merely by presidential action, without a formal declaration of war. Moreover, Truman made the decision essentially unilaterally, after the North Korean attack on South Korea, without even consulting Congress. He also failed to consult American allies in either Asia or Europe, though a few days before when the North Korean attack commenced the U.S. had secured a UN Security Council resolution condemning the action that the U.S. then used as a kind of justification for its actions.[48] Later, after Communist China entered the conflict and the U.S. began facing battlefield reversals, the Truman administration pulled back on its stated intent to liberate North Korea and sought just to restore the status quo ante of South Korea's independence on a permanently divided Korean peninsula. When this change occurred, the American commander, General Douglas MacArthur, proved to be uncooperative and publicly criticized the decision, with the result that Truman took the unpopular step of removing him from command.[49] The war eventually ended, of course, after Dwight Eisenhower was elected president and negotiated an armistice that secured Truman's status quo objective.

Important institutional changes in the military resulted from the Truman administration and the first decade of the Cold War. The National Security Act of 1947 established the Cabinet-level Department of Defense to replace the former cabinet-level Departments of War and the Navy. Now the Departments of the Army, Navy, and newly established Air Force were sub-cabinet departments within Defense. The act also regularized the Joint Chiefs of Staff and established the National Security Council and the Central Intelligence Agency (CIA).[50] After a two-year hiatus, the military draft was also reinstituted. Congress enacted a new conscription statute in 1948, though inductions were limited until the outbreak of the Korean War. During the latter, Congress further tightened the law, and over 1.5 million men were drafted. The draft continued until the end of 1972. During the Eisenhower administration, a "complex system of deferments" was put in place and lobbyists sought to have deferments established for different constituency groups. The U.S. government also admitted that it was using the draft in an unprecedented fashion to motivate more men to voluntarily enlist (many preferred to do this and get a choice of a more desirable branch of service and military job).[51] Overall, Truman's expansion of the U.S. military establishment went well beyond previous peacetime precedents. More, with the massive increase in defense contracts for all sorts of new, advanced weapons large corporations became permanent parts of the "military-industrial complex," with the Department of Defense acting as a kind of industrial manager.[52]

Perhaps the other significant foreign policy development during the Truman presidency did not involve the Cold War, even indirectly. It was the war crimes trials in Nuremberg and Tokyo in the years right after World War II, which resulted in the executions and imprisonments of numerous Nazi and Japanese officials. Although such international tribunals trying persons for "crimes against humanity"—when they supposedly did not violate any criminal statutes in the countries where the offenses took place—were unprecedented, the trials were popularly supported. The support was not unanimous, however, as some in the U.S., led by the prominent Republican U.S. Senator Robert A. Taft of Ohio, criticized the ex post facto character of the charges and believed that it was unjust for the victors in a war to charge and sit in judgment on the vanquished.[53]

As regards communism, initially the policy of the Eisenhower administration seemed to be "rollback" or "liberation" of nations controlled by Communist governments. It did not seem to be satisfied with containment.[54] From the beginning, however, when Eisenhower moved quickly to secure the Korean armistice this seemed to be belied in practice. Later, even the containment policy was transformed into a milder coexistence policy for the sake of maintaining world peace.[55] Still, there was intense activity in the Cold War in the 1950s. Much of it involved covert operations. Stephen E. Ambrose and Douglas G. Brinkley assert that the Central Intelligence Agency (CIA) "had spies located throughout East Europe," but could not achieve anything at the scale of "toppling" Communist governments because the "secret police of the satellite governments were too well organized and too active."[56] It was much more successful along these lines in the underdeveloped world, which emerged as a major tug-of-war between the two sides in the Cold War. This was the case in Iran and Guatamala, where political leaders who had moved too close to the Communists were ousted in CIA-orchestrated coups. In the former, oil companies from U.S. and other Western countries benefited, and in the latter American fruit interests did.[57] These advantages or possible rationales for the coups, however, were likely only windfalls of actions geared primarily to stopping the expansion of Soviet influence. In 1954, the U.S. held back from intervening in Indochina—that was to come a decade later—when the French colonizers withdrew from the region following the Battle of Dien Bien Phu and the division of Vietnam into a Communist North and an anti-Communist South. This occasioned the Democrats to attack Eisenhower during the 1956 election campaign for not doing enough there.[58] The Middle East also became an area of East-West competition. As mentioned, the Soviets shifted from support of the Israelis to the Arabs, and the Eastern Bloc courted the Arab nations of the region with substantial aid packages. The Eisenhower administration initially countered by aiding Egypt in the building of the Aswan Dam, but early in 1956 withdrew its support. In retaliation, the Egyptian leader, Gamal Abdel Nasser, seized the Suez Canal and put his country on a collision course with Britain and France who ran the canal and depended on it for shipment of Middle East oil. The entire episode was to play a crucial role in developments in the Cold War later that year. Britain, France, and Israel joined forces to attack Egypt and get back the canal—without the U.S.'s approval or foreknowledge. At the same time, the de-Stalinization campaign in the U.S.S.R. fueled the fires of anti-Communist opposition in Eastern Europe, resulting in riots in Poland and the Hungarian Revolution. As a result, the Poles gained greater freedom and the Hungarians came close to breaking away from the Soviet orbit. With the prospect of twin rollbacks of their international influence and strength in Hungary and the Middle East, the Soviets brutally suppressed the Hungarians. After this, the U.S. actually joined the U.S.S.R. in pressuring the British, French, and Israelis to pull back in their campaign against Egypt and forego further efforts to take the canal. In the aftermath, for the better part of the next two decades the Egyptians moved close to the Soviets and instability convulsed Arab governments as struggles ensued between pro- and anti-Nasser—and, *a fortiorari*, pro- and anti-Soviet— elements. This motivated Eisenhower to seek authority from Congress to militarily intervene in the Middle East to support any country seeking help against attempted takeovers by Communist elements—which, of course, were supported by the U.S.S.R. This came to be called the Eisenhower Doctrine. He used that authority in 1958 in Lebanon.[59] While Western economic interests were certainly at stake in the region because of oil,[60] the U.S. probably also aimed to restrain the spread of Soviet influence for the sake of averting the U.S.S.R.'s gaining an enhanced geo-strategic position.

Episodes like the Soviets' launching of the first intercontinental ballistic missile (ICBM) and the first man-made satellite (*Sputnik*) led to the much-publicized Gaither Report of the Ford Foundation in 1957. It insisted that U.S. security was in peril because of massive Soviet military spending, and in response called for a sharp American defense build-up and an increase in the defense budget of nearly 10%. Eisenhower resisted this, however, apparently because he thought it would militarize American life. In fact, Ambrose and Brinkley tell us that throughout his second term "he warned of the danger of turning America into a garrison state," and in his farewell address cautioned about the growing military-industrial complex. He took a more restrained, prudent course, in light of more precise information from intelligence sources that showed that the U.S. had a substantial military advantage over the Soviet Union.[61] The Democrats—perhaps believing that they had to compensate for the Alger Hiss case (below), the falling of China to communism and the problems during the Korean War under Truman's watch, and criticisms and electoral reversals they suffered at the hands of Senator Joseph McCarthy (below) and others for being "soft on communism"[62]—claimed that the Republicans "were allowing their fiscal views to endanger national security."[63] They argued that there was a "missile gap" between the U.S. and the U.S.S.R.,[64] a theme that later became a campaign issue in the 1960 presidential race between Vice President Richard M. Nixon and Senator John F. Kennedy. Indeed, this defensiveness may have led to the Democrats, once in power in the 1960s, committing the U.S. to the long, unpopular conflict in Vietnam. Eisenhower believed, for the most part correctly, that the Soviets would be willing to negotiate with the U.S.; both he and the Soviet leader Nikita Khrushchev "were anxious to solidify the concept of peaceful coexistence." Eisenhower succeeded in preventing the Cold War from becoming "hot" again after Korea, but if he had any hopes of actually ending it that did not happen. In fact, his administration ended on a couple of sour notes with Communist Fidel Castro's seizure of power in Cuba and the scuttling of a Paris summit with Khrushchev and American embarrassment after the downing of a CIA U-2 spy plane over the Soviet Union.[65] These developments set the stage for an intensification of tensions over Cuba and Berlin—the latter was the planned topic of the summit meeting—in the early 1960s. Eisenhower authorized the CIA-directed Bay of Pigs invasion,[66] which failed in 1961 and paved the way for the most dangerous moment of the Cold War with the 1962 Cuban Missile Crisis.

The Cold War made espionage a major issue in the U.S. because of the substantial role of spying and covert operations on both sides. This question came to the fore shortly after World War II with the Alger Hiss case. Hiss, who had been an FDR administration official and was on the U.S. delegation to the Yalta Conference, had been exposed as a Soviet agent by former Communist Whittaker Chambers and convicted of perjury for lying during a 1948 Congressional investigation about it. Spokesmen for the Truman administration had initially defended Hiss, believing that he was being accused for political reasons.[67] In 1949, a number of U.S. Communist party officials were convicted of violating the Smith Act. The most stirring post-war espionage development was the revelation in 1950 that a spy ring active in both the U.S. and Britain had purloined atomic bomb secrets from the Los Alamos, New Mexico facility where the device had been developed and channeled them to the U.S.S.R. Julius and Ethel Rosenberg were executed in 1953 and others served long prison terms for their involvement. The dangers of espionage had led to the Truman administration's implementing a loyalty program for federal employees in 1947.[68] In 1953, Eisenhower instituted an even stricter program that covered federal contractors as well as employees.[69] The most celebrated and controversial element of the espionage saga of the post-war period, however, concerned the investigations and allegations of Senator McCarthy. From 1950 to 1954 McCarthy made a series of spectacular charges about Communists in various parts of the executive branch of the U.S. Government, including the State Department, the Voice of America, and the U.S. Army. His attacks began against the Truman administration, but continued against the Eisenhower administration even though he was a Republican. He also attacked and brought before his investigatory committees and subcommittees left-wing intellectuals. He even questioned the loyalty of such a prominent American statesman and military leader as General George C. Marshall (the shaper of the Marshall Plan) and sweepingly attacked Protestant ministers for supposedly supporting communism. While there had been espionage problems and penetration of Communist agents into the U.S. government[70]—the Hiss case was the preeminent example—and some irregularities in security clearance checks conducted of State Department employees, it does not seem as if McCarthy ever really substantiated his specific charges. Sometimes he twisted or stretched facts, as in the situation when evidence indicated that a certain figure had been ideologically inclined toward communism in some way and he claimed that the person actually was a Communist. He also seemed to assume that unverified hearsay about some person was actual fact. Some of the people he accused suffered considerable damage to their reputations and careers and one of McCarthy's main targets, Owen Lattimore, the China scholar and American advisor to Chiang Kai-Shek, was indicted for perjury and had to face three years of legal proceedings until finally having the charge dismissed.[71] McCarthy lost much popular support after his investigation of the Army (seen by millions on live television during the Army-McCarthy hearings in 1954), and later that year the Senate censured him for misconduct in carrying out his investigations.[72] A fellow Republican senator referred to his activities as "'witch-hunting, star-chamber methods, and the denial of...civil liberties.'"[73]

We now evaluate this category in light of the principles of the Founding and its culture. The first question that might be raised is whether America's assumption of the leadership in the struggle against the Soviets from early in Truman's presidency onward went against the traditional American principle of international impartiality and so was against the spirit of the Founders. In light of how Soviet communism was so anathema to Founding principles and how aggressively expansionistic the Soviets were, the answer certainly is no. Impartiality did not mean that the U.S. could not act to protect herself, and we must keep in mind that the Cold War, even while not featuring guns blazing at each other by the two major adversaries, was still a deep, intense, extended international conflict of the nature of a war in all other respects. If the U.S. had not faced down the U.S.S.R. as she did, there was every reason to believe that the Soviets would have militarily moved on the West. Having said this, the mere existence of the Cold War did not necessarily justify every action that the U.S. undertook as part of it. The American military interventions, the largest and most extended of which in this period was the Korean War, undertaken without a formal declaration of war—in spite of the stand-by Congressional authorization that justified the Eisenhower Doctrine and Congress's reluctance to cut off budget allocations for such actions—damaged the principles of separation of powers and, by extension (since Congress would have been an independent check on the wisdom of individual actions) checks and balances. Even if one would grant that the president has the freedom to deploy U.S. troops on his own in exigent circumstances, is very difficult to seriously claim that the ongoing war in Korea was in keeping with the constitutional requirement of a Congressional declaration of war. The Cold War also helped to enhance the longer-term trend toward greater centralized governmental power and expanded bureaucracy. What was said about the military-industrial complex indicates that it further solidified the predominant place of large-scale corporate entities in the economy, and continued—in fact, permanentized—the major federal economic role begun in the New Deal. All of these developments, of course, contravened the political and cultural norms of the Founding. The Cold War's requirements—and it certainly *was* necessary—of a large, standing military was certainly contrary to the practice of most of American history. While the Founding constitutional norm of civilian control of the military was not subverted—and ringingly reaffirmed by Truman's removal of MacArthur in Korea—an increasingly expansive military establishment was in a position to exercise more influence on American foreign and defense policy. (By the way, the accession to the presidency of a career military man who had been the top general in the Army did not constitute in any way a threat to civilian control of the military; it had happened before in the country's history and, after all, it was Eisenhower who was opposing the excessive militarization of American life.) The country did not become sweepingly militarized, but militarism—a factor in the decline of political orders—arguably advanced; the military now played a heightened, large-scale, ongoing role in American life. This was more the case because of the permanent peacetime draft, which put in arms many more members of the male population than would otherwise have been the case. Conscription extended from 1948 through this entire period, and while it did not ultimately end until 1973 its existence for the last twelve years of the 1945-1960 period already made it by far the longest draft in U.S. history. It is likely that the precedent of the peacetime draft established in 1940 made it easier to resume and regularize it with the beginning of the Cold War. Besides it being another indicia of a greater militarization of American life, a permanent peacetime draft also raised the question of a compatibility with American traditions of liberty (and the deferment arrangements mentioned above raised the further issue of hurting equal protection of the laws). Eisenhower's rejection of the Gaither recommendations, his warning about the military-industrial complex, and his striving for a policy of peaceful-coexistence with the Soviet Union all indicate that the militarism of American life had taken place to some extent and that it could have progressed onward to dangerous levels. Moreover, if the Gaither recommendations had been accepted, it would surely have driven the federal budget into a deeper deficit that would have been problematical in light of the Founding thinking about this. The Marshall Plan and the Point Four Program were magnanimous gestures to be sure, but the notion of major economic aid commitments to other countries spanning a period of years would have been completely foreign to the Founding Fathers. Further, even though the courts have not been willing to challenge the constitutionality of such foreign policy decisions the constitutional authority of the U.S. government's funding of other countries—which, by the way, became an ongoing practice with the foreign aid program—can only be viewed as dubious. Its benefit to the defense and general welfare of the U.S.—the Constitution gives the federal government the power to "lay and collect taxes...to...provide for the common defense and general welfare of the United States,"[74]—can only at best be said to be indirect. Defense might justify some measure of such spending, but it is doubtful that it could justify a large-scale or continuing scheme. As it was, while concerns about Soviet expansion partly influenced the shaping of the Marshall Plan (as noted above) and the foreign aid program afterwards was somewhat motivated by the Cold War and defense concerns,[75] humanitarian objectives from the beginning were prominent. It was also believed that the American economy could in some ways benefit.[76] While overseas humanitarianism is a lofty goal, whether it is a legitimate ground for federal spending is questionable. While government in the U.S. has long spent money to promote the U.S. economy, foreign aid is hardly on par, say, with internal improvements. Next, a policy of military intervention to topple unfriendly governments, even while understandable to stymie Soviet expansion, raised questions about civic friendship projected internationally, fair-dealing, and respect for popular sovereignty in the nations concerned. The

Guatemala incursion continued the long-standing problems in this regard with Latin American countries stretching back to the Mexican War. These were all Founding political or cultural principles, of course. Finally, Senator Joseph McCarthy's actions, even if they were motivated by the genuine danger of espionage and subversion within the U.S. government, had the effect of threatening freedom of speech and assembly (by calling people to task even for other than Communist associations), which were among the central rights stressed by the Founders. The often shrill, non-substantive, and irresponsible nature of his charges and the atmosphere of extreme caution, suspicion, and over-eagerness to accuse that they created in the country—where some people even wanted to root out library books and give pro-Communist interpretations to old works of literature[77]—showed a lack of moderation, civility, truth-telling, and fair-dealing at odds with the norms of the Founding. While identifying Communist subversion was surely critically important, that this approach and such reckless behavior would cause division and conflict in the country was foreseeable,[78] and thus showed imperviousness to the norm of civic friendship.

   Race and Negro Civil Rights. In race relations in the U.S., the period 1945-1960 brought a veritable upheaval. The odyssey of change in this area probably began with the growing Negro militancy during World War II mentioned in Chapter 6 and the very experience of the war itself, where America's battle against a regime ruthlessly committed to racial and ethnic purity highlighted our own grievous shortcomings, and the beginning of developments in the courts that would erode segregation and finally reverse the rule of *Plessy v. Ferguson* (discussed in Chapter 5). These actually probably began in the New Deal period with *Missouri ex rel. Gaines v. Canada* (1938), which held that a state could not refuse a Negro student admission to its state law school when it did not have an equivalent law school for Negroes even if it provided him funds to attend an out-of-state institution. The "white primary" case of *Smith v. Allwright* in 1944 was mentioned in Chapter 6. Alpheus Thomas Mason and Donald Grier Stephenson note, "A cluster of cases between 1948 and 1950 indicated that the separate-but-equal doctrine [of *Plessy*] would in the future be more difficult to apply in practice." These included: *Sipuel v. Oklahoma* (1948), which further refined *Gaines* by holding that a state had to permit Negroes to be admitted to its public law school or provide equivalent in-state education; *McLaurin v. Oklahoma State Regents* (1950), which held that a state could not segregate educational activities on a public university campus for admitted Negro graduate students (the student here had been admitted pursuant to a federal court order); and *Sweatt v. Painter* (1950), in which a state was ordered to admit a Negro student to its Caucasian-only public law school when he successfully showed that the quality of his education at the alternative public law school for Negroes was clearly not equivalent to the former.[79] These decisions did not constitutionally repudiate separate-but-equal, but narrowed the state's segregationist prerogatives and, by the time of *Sweatt*, set the stage for repudiation. Indeed, such cases were all part of a long-range strategy by the NAACP (National Association for the Advancement of Colored People) Legal Defense and Educational Fund, spearheaded by Thurgood Marshall (later the first Negro

Supreme Court justice), to gradually whittle away at it.[80] The direct attack, of course, came in the 1954 *Brown v. Board of Education* case, clearly the Fund's greatest victory. In that case, concerning the entire segregated public school system in the southern and border states, the Court unanimously held that "separate-but-equal" was unconstitutional and that separate educational facilities are *inherently* unequal.[81]

In the executive branch, Truman undertook a number of initiatives to break down racial barriers. After being enlightened about the plight of Negroes in the South in 1946 by a delegation of the National Emergency Committee Against Mob Violence who were concerned about lynching and the reemergence of the Ku Klux Klan, he appointed a Committee on Civil Rights. The latter called for the federal government to address the question of race relations, which had been considered a state prerogative since the end of Reconstruction (see Chapter 4), by doing the following: making permanent the Fair Employment Practices Committee set up by FDR (Truman proceeded to try to do this, but southerners in Congress stymied his effort); establishing a civil rights commission to investigate alleged violations of Negro civil rights; and, most boldly, denying federal aid—which was gradually becoming more important through grants-in-aid programs—to states that mandated segregation. Truman also sought anti-lynching legislation and the abolition of the poll tax, which was used in southern states to stop Negroes from voting, but again was stopped in Congress.[82] What he *did* succeed in doing, by executive order, was to ban racial discrimination in federal hiring and to desegregate the armed forces.[83] The latter action was well received in military ranks, and set something of an example and provided momentum for desegregation in the rest of the country. The end of the military color line was first tested in the Korean War where it was found that Negroes were as good as Caucasian soldiers in combat and that integration did not impede military effectiveness.[84]

If developments in the military in the late 1940s and early 1950s served as examples for the broader culture in race relations, so did those in the world of sport. The nearly sixty-year bar on Negroes playing in major league baseball was broken when the Brooklyn Dodgers signed Jackie Robinson to a contract. Tindall and Shi say that the Dodgers' owner, Branch Rickey, selected the college-educated (he never graduated) Robinson to break the barrier because of "his willingness to control his temper in the face of virulent racism." In fact, he routinely faced taunts, insults, abuse from other players, and refusals of service when traveling with the team. As time went on, he "won over many fans and opposing players through his quiet courage, self-deprecating wit, and determined performance." The result, according to Tindall and Shi, was that people came to see "that segregation need not be a permanent condition of American life."[85]

The Eisenhower years witnessed the full-fledged emergence of the Negro civil rights movement. A follow-up case to the *Brown* decision, usually known as *Brown v. Board of Education II* (1955),[86] addressed the question of the implementation of the Court's sweeping rejection of the separate but equal doctrine. It held that school desegregation should proceed "with all deliberate speed," which left it to lower federal courts to carry on the proceedings as cases came up to enforce the decree in accordance with local circumstances.[87] Late in 1955, the Montgomery bus boycott began when Rosa Parks refused to give up her seat on a Montgomery, Alabama bus when a Caucasian man asked for it. For the next year, the Negroes of Montgomery refused to ride the buses, and from the struggle Martin Luther King, Jr.—then just a young minister in Montgomery—emerged as the undisputed leader of the civil rights struggle in the South. After legal threats to Negro taxi drivers, the misuse of the state's criminal labor law provisions against King and other Alabama Negro leaders, futile attempts by the city leadership to stir discord within the ranks of the Negro community, and repeated violence against Negroes (which included the firebombing of King's house and four Negro churches), the city and the bus company backed down and desegregated the bus system.[88] As William H. Chafe says, due to its promotion of Negro solidarity and newly found courage and determination, "the Montgomery bus boycott laid the foundation for the civil rights movement of the 1960s."[89] The latter, of course, was to lead to sweeping legal and cultural change in civil rights and race relations in the U.S. The next major conflict in the Negro civil rights struggle of the 1950s was the desegregation of Central High School in Little Rock, Arkansas, pursuant to the order of a federal judge in compliance with *Brown*. When the new Negro students attempted to enter the school at the start of the 1957 school year, they were turned back by an angry Caucasian mob. Governor Orval Faubus had refused to use the National Guard to protect the students, but then Eisenhower federalized the Guard and also brought in regular U.S. Army troops to enforce the order. Afterwards Faubus closed the Little Rock public high schools for a year to stop desegregation, but finally resistance ended.[90] In 1960, the civil rights movement entered a new phase—obviously inspired by Rosa Parks' action—with the sit-in movement, which began in Greensboro, North Carolina, and spread throughout the South.[91]

Eisenhower overall was restrained in pressing a federal civil rights agenda. He supported addressing the denial of Negro voting rights in the South, but despite his Little Rock intervention did not assume federal leadership on school desegregation. He was reluctant to intervene to back up court-ordered school desegregation in other cases in the South, and was noteworthy for his unwillingness to use the presidential bully pulpit to promote the cause.[92] He did secure enactment of the Civil Rights Act of 1957, which concerned Negro voting rights and was the first federal civil rights legislation since Reconstruction, but it lacked effective enforcement provisions and actually did little to address the problem. He later supported the Civil Rights Act of 1960, which improved enforcement to some degree by giving federal judges more authority in voting rights cases.[93] He also supported establishing a permanent federal civil rights commission, but would not agree to granting the U.S. Justice Department the authority to initiate civil rights lawsuits.[94] Chafe states what may have been Eisenhower's chief reason for not being more assertive: "Central to Eisenhower's position was his conviction that the federal government should be passive on controversial social issues, and that Washington had no right to intervene in the affairs of local governments."[95]

While initially there was, except for a few major political figures, mostly resignation or low-key criticism about the *Brown* decision in the South, active resistance grew.[96] Chafe contends that it "mushroomed in direct correlation to the growing evidence that the federal government would do nothing to counteract it." Some state legislatures passed resolutions "calling for massive resistance." Most southern members of Congress signed a "Southern Manifesto," which promised resistance. Legal maneuvering was used in most southern states to insure *de facto* school segregation even without formally continuing to sanction *de jure* segregation.[97] There were mobs and violence in various parts of the South.[98] Chester J. Pach, Jr. and Elmo Richardson write that possibly "the most alarming manifestation of southern defiance was the growth of white citizens councils," which may have had a quarter of a million members at one point. They were a more respectable version (on the surface) of the Klan, and became "a potent political force." They were known for sponsoring white supremacy rallies and trying to engineer "social and economic retaliation against anyone who dared to breach the color line."[99]

Along with this resistance, legal and illegal, the racially-motivated crimes against individual Negroes—that so frequently there was no redress for— continued during this period, sometimes apparently prompted by small things, things that should have been addressed in a much different way, or things that were entirely legal and that people should have been free to do. For example, there was the execution-type slaying of fourteen-year-old Emmett Till for adolescent bravado-type flirting with a young married woman (the alleged perpetrators were acquitted despite the evidence, and a local grand jury refused to indict them on federal charges);[100] the murders of Negroes like Rev. George Lee and Lamar Smith just because they voted or sought to vote (the former case was not seriously investigated by the authorities, and in the latter legal proceedings against the likely perpetrator were dropped);[101] and the slaying of Samuel O'Quinn, possibly because he supposedly attended an NAACP convention in the North or had refused to sell properties he owned to Caucasians (the case was hardly investigated).[102] All these crimes occurred in Mississippi. David Halberstam writes that at the time, "Blacks in Mississippi seemed...outside the legal protection of the police."[103] It was not just Mississippi, however. As Manchester writes, if a Causcasian murdered a Negro, "[h]is peers, in large areas of the South, were likely to acquit him."[104]

How do we evaluate these developments in light of the Founding and its culture? First, for all the Founding Era's greatness, Caucasians and Negroes obviously were not treated equally under the law and certainly were not socially equal—even outside of the half of the country that did not have slavery. So, as mentioned above, Negroes moved closer to this basic principle of the Founding in the 1945-1960 period than at any previous time in U.S. history. It is evident, too, that the reactions to the *Brown* decision, to say nothing of the general treatment of the Negro population in the Jim Crow South, offended the most basic standards of civility and civic friendship. Moreover, there was certainly no true upholding of the common good when the well-being of a large minority segment of the population in that region was by and large ignored. The trumped-up charges against King and the other Negro leaders during the Montgomery bus boycott showed little regard for the Founding cultural norm of truth-telling. The resistance of so much of the southern Caucasian population to a regimen of basic civility toward the Negro precluded the melding of different groups and the spirit of cooperation that characterized the Founding Era's culture—although admittedly not including the Negro slaves south of the Mason-Dixon Line or even the free Negroes in either North or South. The Founding principle of popular sovereignty was weakened by the fact that the voting rights of Negroes were widely suppressed in the South, which also undercut the rule of law in light of the Fifteenth Amendment. The rule of law, in an even more fundamental way, was being routinely subverted by the practice of brushing off or at least not punishing serious crimes by Caucasians against Negroes. The key point about the present period was that these contradictions to Founding principles were decisively breaking down. Eisenhower's reluctance to involve the federal government in race relations in the states was too narrow of a reading of federalism. Federalism, we believe, never meant that the federal government could not act locally if there was a critical need to do so. Moreover, the enactment of the Fourteenth Amendment and the Reconstruction Era civil rights legislation gave the federal government a clear justification and precedent for that in the case of the treatment of the Negro—regardless of whether political considerations caused it to refuse to exercise that prerogative.

Constitutional and Legal Developments, Relations among the Three Branches of the Federal Government, Federalism, and the Role of Government in General. While there was only one formal constitutional change (i.e., constitutional amendment) during the period from 1945 to 1960, there were other significant constitutional developments in the form of important U.S. Supreme Court decisions. Some of the latter affected such other foci of this section as the relations between the executive and legislative branches and federalism. Some concerned civil liberties and the Bill of Rights, which will be taken up in this section and the next. The Twenty-second Amendment, which limited a person to being elected president twice and to a maximum of ten years in the office, was pushed through by the Republican-controlled 80th Congress in 1947 in the aftermath of FDR's four elections and was ratified and went into effect in 1951 (it did not apply to the incumbent Truman). Eisenhower, the first president affected by the Amendment, complained about "the erosion of a second-term president's power and influence, as the president becomes a political lame duck."[105] This has often been commented about over the years since, and one could argue that it weakens the presidency somewhat. As what we say below about presidential power during the Eisenhower period indicates, however, it is not likely that it caused any appreciable weakening of separation of powers. If anything, presidential power in the foreign affairs area expanded. Moreover, the George Washington-initiated "two-term tradition," which lasted until FDR—did not seem to have singularly weakened presidential power (although admittedly when even the *possibility* of a president running for a third term is foreclosed it would bring forth the changed perception that Eisenhower referred to). As we have seen in this book, there have been strong and weak presidents, and presidential power has waxed and waned at different times— although its constitutional prerogatives insure that it is always a powerful office.

As mentioned, presidential war-making powers reached a new high point during this period, with the extended "presidential" war in Korea and the Eisenhower Doctrine. It was now the era of war and military interventions without a Congressional declaration, which was to continue to the present day. Even apart from the commitment of forces when a conflict suddenly arose— where a president might claim that he needed the flexibility to respond because of an exigent circumstance—Truman began to do this without Congressional approval even when there was no conflict, as with his assigning troops to Europe as part of the implementation of the NATO treaty.[106] With this background, Halberstam says that the Eisenhower administration went on to erect a Cold War "national security apparatus" that could operate "without the unwanted...scrutiny of the Congress."[107] All this represented a subversion of both separation of powers and checks and balances. Congress was not playing the full participatory role in such decisions that Article I, Section Eight, Clauses Eleven and Fourteen of the Constitution indicated it should, and because of this it could not provide an adequate check on executive power. To be sure, the Supreme Court in this period put some limit on this exertion of presidential power—at least as far as it involved controlling the economy in the name of war-making. In the steel seizure case mentioned above, *Youngstown Sheet and Tube Co. v. Sawyer* (1952),[108] the Court held that the president did not have inherent executive power, in light of his constitutional role as commander-in-chief and irrespective of Congressional action, to assume governmental control of steel mills to keep them operating during a strike in the interest of continuing war production.[109] Congress would have to authorize this by legislation (as mentioned, Congress already had provided the Taft-Hartley Act to use in situations such as this). So, the Court stopped the president from claiming what was essentially a legislative function. Parenthetically, in safeguarding the separation of powers here, the Court also checked at least one aspect of centralization of economic activity that would have been contrary to Founding Era economic practice. There cannot be much doubt that in the post-World War II era, presidents were much more ready to reach for more power after the long experience of expansive executive power—which had seemingly become ingrained in American political thinking—during the Great Depression and the war.

If the Court was ready to set outward limits to presidential power in the interest of preserving Congressional prerogatives, this did not mean that it was prepared to allow Congress to overreach. In *Watkins v. U.S.* (1957),[110] the Court held that while Congress had the inherent power to conduct investigations as part of its Article I powers, this did not give it the prerogative to violate the due process rights of witnesses before it.[111]

With the New Deal, the president was now expected to regularly be a legislative leader. Truman exhibited this by putting forth many legislative initiatives—his legislative program, the Fair Deal, was in essence an expansion of the New Deal with an added emphasis on Negro civil rights[112]—even when Congress was not so receptive. He did not slip into FDR's cavalier attitude (indicated in Chapter 6), but worked to build better relations with Congress.[113] For his part, Eisenhower did not slink back into the traditional "hands-off" role of Republican presidents. As discussed below, he pushed numerous domestic policy initiatives, even if not as enthusiastically as the Democrat Truman. While projecting a public image of passivity—possibly deliberately to give himself more political flexibility and clout—Tindall and Shi say that he took an "active involvement in policy decisions" and was "an effective leader."[114] The presidential domestic role was now permanently expanded. As we said in Chapter 6, however, the expectation of presidential legislative leadership did not undercut separation of powers. It did not compromise this or checks and balances as the new presidential war-making power did.

The *Brown* decision also affected relations among the branches since the Court's power waxed as it injected itself into the center of one of the main political conflicts in the country. Indeed, *Brown* is generally regarded as having ignited the era of judicial activism, which has led many to believe that the judiciary has become the most powerful branch of the federal government. On one hand, the Court began to decisively act on the statement about its new role in Justice Stone's footnote #4 in the 1938 *Carolene Products* opinion (see Chapter 6) of protecting "discrete and insular minorities." On the other hand, its newly assumed power followed, as some have observed, from the inaction of the political branches in sufficiently addressing the Negro civil rights problem,[115] just as Chapter 4 said the Court's assertiveness in *Dred Scott* may have resulted from the diminishment of both Congressional and presidential power in the decade and a half before the Civil War.

Congressional or presidential abdication of responsibility cannot be said to be at fault for the Court's break from both judicial and historical precedent on religious establishment—which had the effect of advancing the secularizing trends in American life that, as we have seen, may have had their roots as far back as the Jacksonian Era but definitely since the 1870s. The Court elevated to the level of fundamental constitutional principle the church-state separationism that, as Chapter 4 discussed, was first vigorously asserted by secularists and even some religionists in the 1870s. In the 1947 decision of *Everson v. Board of Education*,[116] the Court both incorporated the First Amendment establishment clause and held that a "wall of separation" exists between church and state in the U.S. so that government cannot aid religion even in a sect-neutral manner.[117] The history of the clause and the Court's few earlier precedents, however, indicated that the clause simply sought to insure that there would be no sect preference; it did not mandate a kind of official neutrality between belief and unbelief.[118] The Court reinforced this new position the following year in *Illinois ex rel. McCollum v. Board of Education*,[119] when it held that public schools—a particular venue for its concerns about the encroachment of religion on the public arena—could not permit clergymen onto their premises to conduct religion classes in the sect of the parents' choice.[120] While the Court seemed to step back slightly in *Zorach v. Clauson* (1952) when it allowed early dismissal of public school students to attend religion classes off-campus[121]—the majority opinion even said that American "institutions presuppose a Supreme Being"[122]—it in no way reversed the separationist precedent of *Everson* and the 1960s and 1970s were to further ingrain and extend separationism into the fabric of American life and governmental practice.

While *Brown* would seem justified because it was consonant with the Founding principle of equality, as per the analysis in the previous section, some might be inclined to state that like *Dred Scott* it represented an attempt by the Court to inject itself into a troubling public policy question. In fact, however, it was just rectifying its problematical decision in *Plessy v. Ferguson*, and may have acted consonant with the view of the framers of the Fourteenth Amendment that the Amendment could be open to further constitutional development.[123] Clearly indicative of judicial excess was its new establishment clause jurisprudence, however, which it had little historical or precedential basis for and which cries out more for an accommodationist approach that the political branches are clearly more suitable for. Decisive damage was beginning to occur to separation of powers and checks and balances by a renewed thrust toward expansive judicial power. What had ceased with the New Deal began again in a different constitutional area. There is little doubt that the precedents established for it in *Dred Scott* and in the long era of substantive due process on economic questions made it easier for the Court to be activistic and push toward a preeminent place among the branches. Also, in the establishment clause decisions the Court was beginning to force on government an areligious stance completely at odds with the Founding principle that held religion as essential for a democratic republic. It was also contributing to the momentum for secularization of American life that was completely at odds with the Founding culture.

While the Court's decisions during the New Deal probably had the greatest judicial effect on federalism in the twentieth century—opening the doors, as stated in Chapter 6, for the federal government to legislate on a whole range of subjects in the name of regulating interstate commerce—there were a few decisions in the current period—in addition to the ones on Negro civil rights, which of course primarily affected state prerogatives—that had important implications for federalism. The effect was mixed. In the *Southern Pacific Co. v. Arizona* decision (1945),[124] the Court held that states could impose regulations in the interest of, say, safety and that could impede interstate commerce. It would determine if such regulations should stand on the basis of a balancing-of-interests test (i.e., whether the nature of a particular state regulation truly merits the interference with commerce).[125] In 1946, the Court both extended its doctrine of allowing the proprietary functions of state governments, such as liquor and mineral water sales, to be taxed by the federal government,[126] and refused to interfere in state reapportionment decisions about their Congressional delegations (that had to wait for the 1960s).[127]

Also during the 1945-1960 period, the Court affected federalism by its incorporation of other Bill of Rights provisions: the Sixth Amendment right to a public as opposed to a secret trial,[128] the Sixth Amendment right to learn the nature and cause of a criminal charge against oneself,[129] and the Fourth Amendment protection against unreasonable searches and seizures.[130] After this, the states' actions in these areas would be subject to federal court review.[131]

There were two Supreme Court cases during this period that *explicitly* reaffirmed the supremacy of the federal government's power pursuant to Article VI, Section Two of the Constitution (the "supremacy clause"). In 1946, in *U.S. v. Carmack*,[132] the Court held that the supremacy clause gave the federal government as the supreme level of government even the power to take state-owned land under eminent domain.[133] The *Cooper v. Aaron* decision (1958) resulted from the Arkansas state government's obstructionism regarding school desegregation in Little Rock. The Court held that since the Constitution under Article VI was the "supreme law of the land," the Court's interpretation of the Constitution as in *Brown* was—in light of *Marbury v. Madison's* precedent that the federal judiciary has the power to interpret the Constitution—also the supreme law of the land. As such, no state official may resist it.[134] Thus, the Court vigorously re-emphasized the point of its 1859 decision of *Ableman v. Booth*.[135]

Southern firebrands specifically opposed to desegregation were not alone in opposition to the Court's subjecting to federal oversight matters that were previously viewed as within the province of the states. In 1958, the Conference of State Chief Justices overwhelmingly adopted a report that criticized the Court's "'impatience with the slow workings of our federal system'" in general. They were concerned that this might be signaling a kind of legal arbitrariness.[136]

The Court's decisions were not the only way in which federalism was being challenged in this period, however. There was sharp growth in federal grants-in-aid programs; between 1940 and 1960 the number of such programs increased ten times. This happened even in the face of Eisenhower's expressing the same concerns about the weakening of federalism as the Conference of State Chief Justices. The largest of these new programs was the Federal-Aid Highway Act of 1956, whose aim was to build the interstate highway system mentioned above. This imposed on the states the rules of the Davis-Bacon Act, which required them to pay certain wage levels to road construction workers (and thereby caused increased state spending in addition to the large new highway expenditure commitment the federal government made).[137]As noted above, Eisenhower did not seek to roll back New Deal-initiated programs. Tindall and Shi say that with this approach, Eisenhower actually "[made] legitimate the New Deal" and probably insured the permanence of its major programs and its notion about the federal social welfare role.[138] While there was rhetorical support for a revitalized federalism and some reduction of centralized control under Eisenhower,[139] the post-1933 role of the federal government did not significantly change and, on balance, probably expanded.[140]

In addition to the above, there were developments in other areas of American law in the 1950s that would significantly affect federalism. A good example was the proposal by the Conference of Commissioners on Uniform State Laws of the Uniform Commercial Code in 1950. By the end of the decade, states had begun to enact it.[141] While it reflected the need to respond to a more national-oriented economy and the states acted freely in deciding to adopt it, in a certain way it represented a movement away from states making individual decisions about their commercial law. They now saw a need simply to conform to a national standard. Perhaps more fundamentally federalism was increasingly falling victim in some significant ways to nationalizing economic trends that started after the Civil War.

In sum, the weakening of federalism and the growth of centralized government that characterized the New Deal—contrary to the thinking of the Founding—advanced during the 1945-1960 period. The attitude of the public to look first to the federal government that took hold in the New Deal now became ingrained. It is not surprising that Eisenhower said that if any political party tried to eliminate programs like Social Security and federal labor laws "you would not hear of that party again in our political history."[142] The thrust of American constitutional jurisprudence and the acceptance of cooperative federalism—the federal-state partnerships we spoke of in Chapter 6, as carried out especially by the multiplying of grants-in-aid programs—were major factors in cementing a permanently diminished state status and a weakening of the principle of federalism. More fundamentally, what this signaled was a permanently enhanced role for government generally that eclipsed anything the Founding Era could have imagined, and which further meant bad portents for the Founding principle of avoiding excessive public debt. The growth of government and its programs also meant that more and more people worked for it, or worked because of it (e.g., contractors with the military-industrial complex), or depended on it (i.e., those who partook of its social welfare programs). In terms of compromising Founding principles: they became a substantial and growing faction that would become increasingly difficult to check; government would be prompted to address their interests and not necessarily the common good; while a big government bureaucracy makes rules pursuant to statute and regulates the activities of the population it is not so clear that *it* is being adequately regulated—that is, Who watches the watchman?—so there is a greater chance that the makers of the laws will not sufficiently be subject to them; and we know too well the cozy relationships forged and favoritism that regulated groups and elements often receive from government—i.e., the iron triangles and issue networks that political scientists often speak about[143]—which results in a measure of arbitrariness and dilutes the principle that there should be a government of laws and not men. Big government involved in so many things—by providing a range of benefits and by regulating so many activities—generally spawned the problems of "interest group government"—i.e., it had to become increasingly solicitous of interest group wishes and often was restrained from acting in a manner beneficial to the entire community—and harmed the common good on this score, weakened popular sovereignty, and at times even ignored morality and the natural law.[144]

Individual Liberties and Citizen Rights. The 1945-1960 period was a time of some significant decisions of the U.S. Supreme Court on civil liberties and Bill of Rights questions. We have noted some of these in the sections above.

While this period did not produce the number of precedential decisions that the 1960s were to do, there were nevertheless some important ones that not only influenced the nature of the rights that the Founders stressed as essential for a democratic republic, but also the cultural conditions that were needed to buttress it. We have already discussed the Court's new direction on religious establishment and its crucial Fourteenth Amendment decisions on Negro civil rights. Most of the other decisions concerned different aspects of First Amendment free speech rights, and all told were expansions of individual rights. The majority occurred, along with the establishment clause decisions, during the Vinson Court (i.e., the Court under the leadership of Chief Justice Frederick Vinson, which ended with his death in 1953) and not the Warren Court (under Chief Justice Earl Warren), which commenced in 1953. Most of the Warren Court's key decisions on civil liberties, the expansion of which it was especially known for, came during the 1960s (Warren was Chief Justice from 1953 to 1969).

The key free speech decisions of the Vinson Court follow. *Terminiello v. Chicago* (1949),[145] which established that a state—keeping in mind that this right had only been incorporated or nationalized in the 1920-1945 period—may not proscribe speech simply for the reason that it roused people to anger or caused unrest or invited public dispute.[146] *Feiner v. New York* (1951)[147] somewhat qualified this, in light of the Court's "clear and present danger test." The state in this case did not outright proscribe speech that could incite a reaction, but arrested a speaker giving an incendiary speech after repeated requests that he stop when a crowd was clearly being stirred to violence and criminal activity. The Court permitted his conviction to stand because he had gone beyond "the bounds of argument or persuasion" and was engaging in "incitement to riot."[148] In *Dennis v. U.S.* (1951),[149] the clear and present danger test was held to justify the Smith Act convictions of several American Communist party leaders for belonging to an organization advocating the overthrow of the government through force.[150] The Court in *Saia v. New York*[151] concerned the way speech was to be undertaken. A municipality's police chief was afforded apparently unfettered discretion to bar the use of sound trucks. The Court rejected this, since there were no standards to insure against arbitrariness.[152] The upshot was it was probably permissible for a municipality to regulate the use of or perhaps ban sound trucks or other such amplification equipment in at least certain circumstances—since such equipment can easily be disruptive—so long as clear standards were present. An official may not be given unfettered or undirected discretion that could result in his, say, forbidding such use based upon whether he just did not like the viewpoint or message. In *Beauharnais v. Illinois* (1952),[153] the Court addressed group libel. It held that the state may prohibit speech aimed at defaming groups if such speech would be libelous when directed strictly at an individual. This is because libelous utterances are not constitutionally protected.[154] In another dimension of free speech, the Court held in *U.S. v. Paramount Pictures* (1948)[155] that for purposes of First Amendment protection, movies were to be treated like the press.[156] In light of that, in 1952 the Court in *Burstyn v. Wilson*[157] held that the state could not ban the showing of a film just because it was blasphemous or sacrilegious.[158] A case that involved both freedom of speech and freedom of religion was *Kunz v. New York* (1951),[159] in which the Court reversed the petitioner's conviction for holding a religious meeting without the required permit from the municipal police department. He had been turned down when he applied for the permit on the basis of a belief by the authorities that disorder that had resulted from his previous public meetings would occur again. Again, the Court pointed to an unfettered discretion in a city official in deciding about granting the permits as a crucial factor in its decision, and said that such an action by government represented a "prior restraint" that it would not accept.[160] In a similar case, *Fowler v. Rhode Island* (1953),[161] the Court invalidated the application of a municipal ordinance that was used to forbid one sect (Jehovah's Witnesses) from peaceably meeting in a public park when other sects routinely were permitted to hold services there.[162]

Particularly noteworthy decisions of the Warren Court in the individual rights area, other than Negro civil rights, were *Yates v. U.S.* (1957),[163] *Roth v. U.S.* (1957),[164] *Trop v. Dulles* (1958),[165] and *Kingsley International Pictures v. Regents* (1959).[166] In *Yates*, which again concerned Smith Act convictions of Communist party officials, the Court reaffirmed *Dennis* but set down such a condition—i.e., a prosecutor would have to show that an accused person actually intended to urge people to violently overthrow the government, instead of just advocating it in the abstract—that convictions were thereafter very difficult to obtain.[167] In *Roth*, while the Court made clear that obscenity was not constitutionally protected speech, it set down such criteria for determining if material was legally obscene—"whether to the average person, applying contemporary community standards, the dominant theme of the material taken as a whole appeals to the prurient interest"—that in fact made it more difficult to legally suppress.[168] *Trop* held that Congress could not decree by law that a soldier be stripped of his citizenship and sent into forcible exile for desertion in time of war; it considered this "cruel and unusual punishment."[169] *Kingsley* expanded on the two film cases of the Vinson Court above and also began the application of the new *Roth* doctrine by striking down the decision of New York State's film censorship board to refuse to license the film *Lady Chatterley's Lover*, based on the D.H. Lawrence novel, which sympathetically portrayed adultery.[170] The Court rejected the state's action as unacceptable prior restraint and said the state could not make "the moral standards, the religious precepts, and the legal code of its citizenry" the grounds for suppressing the individual's right to advocacy of his views.[171]

Apart from Supreme Court decisions, probably the most serious issues of individual rights and liberties during the 1945-1960 period were presented by the McCarthy investigations above and the passage in 1950 of the McCarran Internal Security Act, which expanded on the Smith Act to make it unlawful to conspire to perform an act that would "substantially contribute" to the establishment of a totalitarian regime in the U.S. The McCarran Act also required Communist and Communist-front organizations to register with the Justice Department, and prohibited aliens who had been members of totalitarian political parties from emigrating to the U.S. It was passed over Truman's veto; he said that it represented government "thought control."[172]

By way of evaluation in light of the rights of speech and religion that the Founders regarded as essential we can say the following. The Court carved out a position in line with the Founders in the *Terminiello* and *Feiner* decisions: If free speech means anything, it cannot be prohibited just because people will be stirred up to dispute or even anger by it, but if it truly incites criminal conduct it can be restrained. While not every means to deliver speech (*Saia*) has to be accepted—some can be disruptive of good order and are in no way needed to put the message across—if free speech and the fair-dealing norm of the Founding Era are to be in force government cannot arbitrarily pick and choose which views it will allow people to express. By the same token, the Founders' notion of free speech did not likely include the right to advocate such a position as totalitarianism that would be destructive of all political freedom and limited government—much less a right of association (growing out of free speech) to advocate and work for that end, as with the Communist party. So, if legislation like the Smith Act sought to suppress totalitarian-oriented organizations like the Communist party it was on solid ground. Its broader reach, upheld by the Court, of criminalizing the advocacy—or association for the advocacy, as the case may be—of the overthrow of the government through force (at least in the absence of specific action toward that end) is very problematical in light of the Founding. It must be kept in mind that the Declaration of Independence said that when government no longer upholds its rightful ends "it is the Right of the People to alter or to abolish it" and after "a long train of abuses and usurpations" seeking to put people "under absolute Despotism," they have both the right and the duty to "throw off such Government." The fact that the Men of '76 took up arms and fought the American Revolution against the British leaves no doubt that "throwing off" despotic government could, at a certain point, involve the use of force.[173] Further, the Founders were defenders of natural law, and a sound natural law-based social ethics holds—despite its strong bias for maintaining order and authority, which is so crucial for a tolerable human existence and attainment of essential human ends[174]—that as a last resort, when "[a]ll legal and pacific means" of redress have been tried and the effort will "not engender worse evils," armed rebellion to overthrow an abusive and thus illegitimate government is justifiable.[175]

It does not seem per se that prohibiting group libel (*Beauharnais*) would be contrary to the Founders' notion of free speech—after all, they apparently even considered the suppression of seditious libel as legitimate, as Chapter 2 discussed—but it could be used as a club by groups embracing positions very much at odds with Founding cultural norms (such as homosexualist groups, when they became powerful in later decades) to stifle their critics. The Supreme Court's claim that blasphemy was protected speech would have been a foreign notion in the Founding Era, and arguably helped advance secularism and thereby undercut the importance the Founders placed on religion. It is, of course, doubtful that such a position could have been taken in the absence of the secularization and rise of the separationist perspective that had characterized the previous several decades. Further, it is doubtful that the Founders would have accorded free speech protection to an essentially entertainment medium such as movies given the accepted legal doctrine of their time that the prohibition of newspaper censorship did not automatically extend to books and pamphlets. The strict sexual morality of their culture and the existence in their time of morals laws, common law prosecutions for obscenity, and the absence of any evidence that the framers of the First Amendment intended it to protect obscenity makes evident that the conclusions of *Roth* and *Kingsley* were sharp deviations from the Founders on free speech.[176] Even more out of line with the Founding Era was the claim of the *Kingsley* opinion that a people's moral standards may not be the basis for censorship. With this, the Court came close to rejecting the idea that there should or can be a public morality—and thereby jeopardized the notion of the common good. Such a notion would have been unthinkable without the moral upheavals that occurred in the 1920s, the growth of pragmatism and positivism, and the Holmesian belief that ethics and law should not be intertwined (all previously discussed).

The understanding of freedom of religion of *Kunz* and *Fowler* was consistent with the Founders' view. In light of what was said above about suppressing totalitarian views, the McCarran Act likely did not offend the latter either. Prohibiting former or present Nazis, Communists, etc. from immigrating was even less questionable than the alien provisions of the 1790's Alien and Sedition Acts (see Chapter 2). We also noted the genuine problems of espionage that the U.S. faced. The Founders, it will be recalled, made order and security a central concern, and this certainly would be an attempt to do that. The McCarran Act, then, was hardly the exercise in thought control Truman alleged; it was national security legislation.

Overall, then, the Founders' conception of freedom of speech was not just expanded in this period, but also distorted. That distortion would proceed further in the 1960s, on the subject of obscenity (as Chapter 8 indicates). The Founders would not have even considered individual rights at stake in a situation such as the *Trop* case, much less viewing it as contravening a right crucial for republican government. After all, no one blinked an eye when Lincoln imposed exilic punishment on the Copperhead Clement Vallandigham during the Civil War. The Court apparently was not concerned about that, however. As Stuart Banner writes, it measured Trop's sentence "not against historical precedent, but against contemporary sensibilities."[177]

Currents in Political and Social Thought. There were numerous influential socio-political thinkers in the post-war period. In the aftermath of the horrors of World War II, there was a great deal of reflection about political life and men's relationship with each other and to the state. One of the most noted of these was the Protestant clergyman, theologian, and political thinker Reinhold Niebuhr. He became known from early in his scholarly and pastoral career as one who had come to believe that power was the overwhelming reality in modern socio-political life and who was intensely concerned about social justice. He was initially attracted to democratic socialism, seeking much more substantial socio-economic reform than the New Deal, but ended up rejecting the confidence of thinkers of both the 1877-1920 and 1920-1945 periods that scientific planning was salutary and instead stressed in Madisonian fashion that power must be checked with power. He came later to see the value of even the more piecemeal reform of the New Deal and of a practical approach to politics, and lined up with the early Cold War liberalism of the mainstream of the Truman-Adlai Stevenson Democratic party.[178] As a Christian theologian, he rejected the Marxist and utopian view that evil was the result of institutional arrangements; it was rather the result of self-love and could issue forth from any individual, and in some cases had social consequences. This, of course, was clearly in accord with the Founders and their era. He departed from the Founders, however, in criticizing natural law. He mistakenly melded together the Christian version of natural law (i.e., as identified with St. Thomas Aquinas and his modern disciples) and the modern Enlightenment version because he thought that both absolutized things—i.e., historical situations—that were in reality contingent. He failed to see that the Thomistic understanding preserved man's freedom and asserted that there could be basic political and social differences even while there had to be an underlying order in human affairs that transcended the historical arrangements of a time.[179] By the same token, his skepticism of a scientific and technocratic approach to social and political questions made him reject the view that somehow in near-utopian fashion scientific technique could bring about social and political harmony and human well-being.[180] Thus, he distanced himself from a strong stream of thought that, as discussed, began with the Progressive Era. He also took modern social scientists and psychologists to task for wrongly believing that evil somehow came out of religion and seeking its demise to achieve *their* notion of human redemption. Niebuhr stressed a kind of law of love that had its roots in the Christian idea, although as a realist he understood that this law did not work automatically and that with the inevitability of self-interest and power relations an arrangement was needed where power could counterbalance power.[181] In fact, the purpose of politics for him was not the achievement of love, but justice. This, too, probably followed from the Christian idea that charity must be given freely, whereas justice is something people have a right to and, in fact, requires a degree of coercion to achieve—something that only government can rightfully exercise. Still, love is not disconnected from politics, since for him laws and the attempts of the state to achieve justice had to be connected with love in order to even retain their character as justice. It is through justice and equality that his law of love is applied to actual human situations.[182] Democracy for him made more possible the reconciliation of the ubiquitous reality of self-interest with the interest of the community. It creates the opportunity in political orders for "peaceful self-correction."[183] This is certainly in accord with the thinking of the Founders. On one hand, relativism is suggested in his thought when he insists that in a democracy "no ultimate principle...should be above criticism." He does, however, indicate the *need* for such principles when he says that "society cannot make democracy or freedom its final end" and that social institutions cannot provide all that man needs for the true freedom of his soul.[184] The latter certainly conformed to the Founders' sentiment, but the relativism seen in the former did not. He sought a mixture of the Madisonian notion above with the Jeffersonian emphasis on liberty.[185]

Fr. John Courtney Murray, S.J. was, along with Orestes Brownson (see Chapter 4), probably the most significant political thinker ever produced by the American Catholic community. In a country with traditional Protestant roots that had historically questioned whether Catholics, with their supposed loyalty to a foreign potentate (the pope), Murray startled readers by his claim in his 1960 book, *We Hold These Truths: Catholic Reflections on the American Proposition*,[186] that by that time Catholics were the largest group still upholding basic Founding beliefs. This was because they still embraced the natural-law thinking that was behind the Founding at a time when an increasingly secular Protestant community rejected it. Murray reminded Americans about something that even our Founding Era paid insufficient attention to: "such American beliefs as constitutionalism, limited sovereignty, and the rule of law" had their origins in Catholic medieval England. He also emphasized that popular government, the notion of need for consent of the governed, and the distinction between state and society were not modern innovations but outgrowths of the great tradition of Western thought going back to the ancient Jews. He also commended the understanding of the Founders that virtue was necessary to secure and sustain these principles and conditions.[187] While he did not write specifically of all of them, it is clear that Murray embraced many of the Founders' principles for a democratic republic.

Erich Fromm lamented—echoing a theme that we stated had first appeared in the 1930s—that mid-twentieth-century man in advanced, capitalistic, democratic nations had lost his freedom and surrendered to a regimen of conformity. Influenced by Marx and Freud, he saw such man as utterly alienated and depersonalized. The capitalist ethos made him like a commodity to be sold, and his views and tastes are shaped by the economic and political forces of society. Such determinism would have been foreign to the Founders and their era. For Fromm there is nothing "higher and more dignified than human existence,"[188] but man is also the measure of all things. Human life for him seemed to be simply a matter of chance, it has no meaning other than that which man gives it "'by the unfolding of his powers.'"[189] While the Founders understood from their Christian outlook the unique dignity of man, they of course would have taken no part in Fromm's relativism and deification of man. Fromm, like Marx and unlike the Founders, believed that all evil issues forth from institutions instead of human nature. So, man can construct a perfect society, a utopia on earth, which for him is one that will allow "the fullest development of human capacities to reason and love." What these potentialities are is shown by the insights of the greatest teachers in history, the luminaries from many different traditions. This is Fromm's "'sane society.'" Its political arrangements would be along the lines of "communitarian participatory democracy," which would allow man to in some way "directly prescribe his institutions…[and] formulate policy."[190] His extreme optimism by now had a long tradition in American thought, going back to the Jacksonian Era. It would be an ultra-decentralized direct democracy, with all citizens taking an active part in discussion and decisionmaking. In economics, all workers would participate in the management and decisionmaking of their enterprises.[191] As Beitzinger points out, Fromm was a Rousseauian who simply substituted his participatory scheme for the general will and believed that institutional restraints could be dispensed with. This also rang of the Jacksonian Era; it was like the thinking of its extreme defenders of democracy. Like Rousseau, he believed that authority—at least in theory—could essentially be eliminated as well. This is all in direct opposition to the Founding Fathers and shows an obliviousness to the dangers of tyranny that they were so attuned to—so, as Beitzinger points out, Fromm said nothing about "institutional separation of powers, checks and balances, an enforceable bill of rights, and limited governmental powers."[192] They were hard-nosed realists; he was a starry-eyed utopian.

In his famous 1960 book, *The End of Ideology*, Daniel Bell presented a Deweyite perspective that was completely explicit about its relativism.[193] As Beitzinger puts it, he "recommended the rejection of all absolutes and the acceptance of pragmatism." Expressing the reality of 1950s-era political consensus seen above, he says that the widespread acceptance of the welfare state, decentralized power (even though, as noted above, the trend increasingly was toward the center in Washington), a mixed economy, and political pluralism means that politics as ideological conflict could now end—in fact, it was now irrelevant—and consensus was now the dominant political reality.[194] It seemed to be a superficial consensus, however, based as it was upon the absence of moral truths. It was also one at odds with the Founders, who stressed natural law, morality (indeed, Christian moral beliefs, which strongly stressed such truth), traditional virtue, and a definite enough of a notion of the common good or the general welfare. Dewey and American pragmatism were obviously the foundation of his thought, but it probably also had grounding in the push for technocratic government since the rise of the civil service movement in the nineteenth century.

Within American political science, the dominant perspective of the postwar period was behavioralism. Somewhat along Bell's lines, it focused its study on "the actual behavior of political actors"—individuals, groups, and institutions. As it developed, it became increasingly concerned about data collection, which behavioralists believed "guarantee[d] scientific objectivity." They "eschewed" normative positions or "value judgments."[195] They ignored what has been called a "moral or goals approach" to politics, because it would invite "wide disagreement." They were obliviousness to a "moral or teleological dimension" of politics.[196] At the very least they feared that the disagreement about this would be dangerous for political life, although their view probably also betrayed a deeper-seated relativism—that, as we have seen, slowly gained strength in American thought—that held that there either are not any certain moral positions to erect politics on or if there are man cannot know them for certain. Regarding practical political life, the political science behavioralists tended to be what are called "pluralists." They saw politics as a struggle among interests, with interest groups the dominant influencers of public policy in their particular area of concern. The aim of political decisionmakers was to forge an accommodation among interests, which was what the public interest would consist of. There was no more overarching public interest or good beyond that. While, as we have seen, the Founders saw the inevitability and even value of factions, they also believed in a public good beyond them.

C. Wright Mills laid an important intellectual groundwork for the 1960s New Left with his 1956 book, *The Power Elite*.[197] Unlike the pluralists, Mills held that all significant political decisions in America—whatever the subject matter—were made by "interacting business, military, and political elites." They "controlled and manipulated" American life.[198] Thus, America was elitist—with a small group in control—and not democratic. He claimed that the elites of these three groups had "a common worldview" and promoted a kind of militarism by "transforming the economy into a 'permanent war economy.'" He was influenced by the Marxian notion of class conflict, he believed that American life was "sharply divided and systematically shaped by the ongoing interactions between the powerful and powerless."[199] The Founders, as we have seen, did not embrace the outright democracy that Mills lamented the absence of (which, like the thought of so many others, was rooted in the Jacksonian perspective). While his detested elite was not of the character of the natural aristocracy the Founders saw as critical, there is little doubt that he would have had little use for such an element as well. While the Founders certainly understood the perennial reality of contending factions, particularly ones based upon differing levels of wealth, they did not characterize this as a situation of unmitigated class conflict, and certainly believed the competing interests could be reconciled and the common good upheld. Moreover, they had a political realism that would not be seduced by the far-fetched scenario that a small group of men controlled such a complex and diverse country as the U.S.

In sum, we can conclude that the drift of the socio-political thought of the 1945-1960 period—with the clear exception of Murray, and in varying degrees with the other major thinkers or schools of the time—showed a lack of the Founders' realism, a relativism and disregard of the natural law, and an unquestioned adherence to democracy that was sometimes to be carried out in unworkable ways. With Niebuhr joining Murray as the exceptions, we also witness a distinct lack of a belief in the possibility of a common or public good and the removal of any kind of religious dimension from politics.

Socio-Cultural Developments. What was said above about economics during the 1945-1960 period leads to the first point about its socio-cultural developments. There was the promotion of an ethic of *more*. The consumption culture that initially took shape in the 1920s resumed after the interlude of the Great Depression and World War II. Prosperity was viewed as being tied up with consumer spending. As a result, according to Tindall and Shi, "marketing specialists accelerated their efforts to promote rising expectations and self-gratification" and "[p]lanned obsolescence became a guiding principle for many manufacturers."[200] As noted above, to make such an ongoing regimen of purchasing possible a credit culture took root and debt increased.[201] It was also mentioned that—in the manner of the 1920s—such norms of Founding Era culture as temperance, sobriety, the restraint of the pursuit of luxury, frugality, thrift, and sacrificing in the present for the sake of the future were nudged aside. It could even be said that planned obsolescence and slick marketing offended the Founding norms of truth-telling and fair-dealing. At the same time, along with the substantial increase of the middle class (noted above) came an increase in "[t]he proportion of homeowners in the population...by 50 percent between 1945 and 1960."[202] These latter developments, of course, were consistent with the situation and norms of the Founding culture.

The family and sexual morality were significant areas of cultural change in this period, although not always perceptibly. While on one hand, there was a "pro-natalism" and sharp increase in the population—due to the baby boom when the returning servicemen married or returned to wives after the war—and a renewed focus on family life, on the other hand there were distinctive aspects of erosion of family strength and a deepening in the culture of the new sexual norms of the 1920s. Regarding the strengthening of the family were such developments as the following: There was a strong "pro-marriage" norm, with more people marrying. The mid-1950s recorded the highest rate in U.S. history of people in the population who were or at some time had been married.[203] While right after the war there was a jump in the divorce rate, throughout the 1950s it remained low—dipping to only 2.1 per 1,000 population in 1958.[204] The population increase in the 1950s was almost 28 million, the largest increase of any decade in U.S. history.[205] During the entire 1945-1960 period, the population increased almost 30%.[206] It was the baby-boom generation. The strong stress was on the wife as a full-time homemaker,[207] a reversal from the developments discussed during the 1920-1945 period. All too many women and households, however, coupled this with an embrace of the consumption, self-gratification, and luxury ethic above.[208] The troubling developments regarding the family and sexual morality included the following: The illegitimacy rate climbed steadily.[209] Parental permissiveness became apparent,[210] and a tendency that first appeared in the early nineteenth century and intensified in the 1920-1945 period of relying childrearing experts became common (e.g., Dr. Benjamin Spock).[211] The new cult of youth and youth participation in the consumerism of the time were noted above. There was also a decline in family togetherness—as seen in such things as its members pursuing their own activities and not even having dinner together as much, and teenagers going their own way because of the availability of the motor car—and an explosion of juvenile delinquency and crime (the latter included serious crime and gang activity).[212] In 1948 and 1953, the Kinsey studies throttled the country by revealing supposedly lax sexual behavior on the part of most Americans—including the claimed finding that half of American women had had sexual relations before marriage.[213] Only much later were Dr. Alfred Kinsey's data questioned and his intention—seemingly successful—to promote sexual permissiveness brought to light.[214] 1953 also saw the appearance of *Playboy* magazine, which not only brought female nudity and bawdiness into the mainstream, but also popularized a "lifestyle" obsessed with pleasure-seeking.[215] In 1957, the birth control pill became available, which reinforced the trends (mentioned in Chapter 6) toward acceptance of contraception that had been gaining momentum since early in the century.[216]

With the separation of sex from procreation—more fundamentally, the severing of the unitive and procreative dimensions of sex—the consequences unfolded during the coming decades: young people becoming sexually permissive because the oral contraceptive ("the pill"), which became widely available, removed the fear of pregnancy;[217] the increasing acceptance of a full range of sterile sexual practices ranging from fornication to homosexual activity (even to the point of a major push to gain legal and social recognition of same-sex "marriage"), and a world population implosion after 1960 with fertility rates going below replacement level in the developed world.[218] Finally, the seeds of the contemporary feminist movement—which aimed to liberate women from the supposed strictures of marriage and family—were planted by Simone de Beauvoir's book *The Second Sex*, published in 1953.[219]

The new sexual permissiveness bubbling up in the 1950s—which was to come to fruition in the 1960s—was expressed in popular culture, especially that enveloping the young, and in counter-cultural movements that would become ascendant in the 1960s. In literature, novels such as *Lolita* and *Peyton Place* became bestsellers, and Jeffrey Hart asserts that, "By 1955, certainly in literature, and to a considerable degree in society itself, pre- and extra-marital sex had lost their capacity to produce moral outrage."[220] A number of movies exhibited what Douglas T. Miller and Marion Nowak call a "new sexual frankness," and the Hays production code (a kind of self-censorship by the film industry) "was on its way out."[221] Actresses such as Marilyn Monroe and Brigitte Bardot splashed eroticism on the screen and, according to Hart, "represented a powerful new expression of female sexual freedom."[222] Perhaps the relaxing of sexual restraint in popular culture most affected the young through music. "Rock' n' roll" emerged in the 1950s. It had roots in Negro music and, in fact, the term had a sexual connotation in the Negro community. The performances of rockers such as Elvis Presley were not only sexually suggestive, but challenged adult culture and norms. It was an early expression of a youth rebellion that was to explode in the 1960s, one of whose "major vehicles" would be rock music.[223] With this challenge to established conventions, rock music had the aura of the counter-cultural. Even more decisively in that category—further laying the groundwork for the socio-cultural upheavals of the 1960s—were a group of artists, writers, and musicians known as the "Beats." They had their origins in the "bohemian underground" of New York City's Greenwich Village, and were characterized by: the outright rejection of existing cultural—even commonsensical—norms (without providing any alternative), moral latitudinarianism, the fashioning of a different kind of individualism—anticipating the 1960's "me generation"—even while vilifying the individualism of the consumer and corporate culture, the use of illicit drugs, attraction to Eastern thought and religion, and a desperate search for meaning.[224] They were direct descendants of the disaffected writers and intellectuals of the 1920s who previously had rejected middle class life, and in a certain sense harkened back to the escapist utopians of the Jacksonian Era.

The strong emphasis on the family in the 1945-1960 period mirrored the Founding Era, but its place was more tenuous and family stability weaker. The sliding sexual morality contrasted with that earlier era, and the new permissiveness that was starting to be preached and the growing acceptance of a weakened standard of sexual morality—the attitudes from the 1920s were now slowly spreading throughout the culture—affronted the Founding's notion of the need for virtue and a morality above human making. We have already mentioned how the new consumption ethic and ready recourse to credit deviated from Founding cultural norms. The Beats, who directly foreshadowed the 1960's counter-culture, were sharply contrary to Founding principles on a range of points: their lack of realism about life, extreme individualism and reluctance about limits on freedom, a corresponding false concern for the general welfare and communal focus, rejection of respect for morality and the need for virtue (especially in the crucial area of sex), need for religion, respect for law, and even scorn for such aspects of civility as good manners and gentlemanliness.

The ethic of conformity that took hold in the 1930s—coincident with the domination of big institutions in the major areas of American life—reached its height in the 1950s. The latter was the era of the emergence of the "corporate man" (with nearly 40% of the workforce by 1960 employed by entities that had more than 500 employees). The "strong-minded individual," characterized by "competitive ability and creative initiative" was superseded by "a new managerial personality and an ethic of cooperation and achievement"[225] (though the "cooperation" stressed was more going along and melding in and less the cooperative, communal spirit of Founding Era life). The suburban growth that exploded in the 1950s—as new housing was needed to accommodate the growing population and people sought to leave the cities[226]—additionally encouraged the conformity ethic, with people struggling for "companionship and a sense of belonging" amidst all the new faces around them and to reestablish communities to replace the ones they had left behind. Indeed, the very nature of suburbia with, in some cases, its similar houses in similar developments bespoke conformity and mass culture—but so did large apartment complexes in the urban areas left behind.[227] The greater mobility of people due to the increased tendency of companies to transfer employees also caused people to leave their old communities.[228] The consumer culture—with people purchasing mass-produced goods and developing similar buying habits (partly because of marketing practices aimed at creating demand)—also fostered conformity.[229] Even the reliance on childrearing experts above perhaps stimulated conformity, as some alleged that their aim was to produce supposedly responsible adults who would fit well into the new conformity-oriented culture.[230] The criticism of the regimen of conformity, from the standpoint of the Founding Era, which was made in Chapter 6 obviously applies here.

The developments in education during the 1945-1960 period did not do much to encourage a break from the conformity mold. At the pre-college level, "progressive education"—dating from the educational reformers of the Progressive Era (discussed in Chapter 5)—was very influential and continued to downplay book learning, the development of intellectual skills, the transmission of cultural heritage, and the strong authority of the classroom teacher[231]—all things that could have helped form minds that would have been more capable of challenging the prevailing pattern of things. In fact, a transformed progressive education after World War II fit in well with the conformity bent of the time: unlike the earlier reformers, the progressivists now promoted a utilitarian approach to education that stressed "social efficiency and social utility," instead of the earlier concern with social reform. Along with this came "a pretentious scientism" in which new innovations—such as teaching reading without phonics—were to be followed just because the "experts" (i.e., social scientists) favored them regardless of whether their effectiveness was proven.[232] On this, as with childrearing more generally, one witnessed the ascendancy of an elite of technical experts in the tradition of the Progressive Era that overstated the capabilities of social science—and also one that did not accept challenge or criticism well.[233] In light of this, it was not surprising that pre-college education was being accused of not teaching students to think and with promoting "trivial" studies.[234] Only a small percentage of schools (about 11% of high schools) after World War II even had a core curriculum.[235] There was substantial experimentation with new curricula,[236] and a big push for vocational education programs and non-academic "life-adjustment" education (i.e., insuring that education as much as possible be made "useful" for everyday living).[237] Along with this, the pattern begun in the 1877-1920 period of educational bureaucratization considerably advanced. Some claimed that the government schools were no longer accountable to the public.[238]

The Founding and the earlier American tradition may have judged this more "applied" kind of education as acceptable for most students, but it still probably failed on critical points. Shorn of a sufficient liberal arts emphasis it was not adequate for those who would be future leaders. Its ignoring of the importance of critical thinking and cultural transmission denied all of its students the wherewithal needed to become effective citizens of a democratic republic. The new educational elite, like the elites espoused by the various socio-political thinkers surveyed over time and the technical elite that first emerged in the late nineteenth century, was hardly a natural aristocracy in the Founders' mold. The weakening of genuine public control over the schools offended popular sovereignty.

The trends in higher education, to be sure, were not much different. Despite the claims that the unprecedented large number of students attending college "democratized higher education,"[239] the corporatization and bureaucratization of the universities resulted in control by a new breed of businessmen-administrators who often operated as an aloof elite.[240] As institutions made a new commitment to expanding enrollments—in the corporate spirit of ever expanding a business and seeking new markets—academic standards were lowered.[241] Russell Kirk states that the liberal arts were suffering, as colleges and universities were weakening in their commitment to helping students to question and reflect (i.e., lead "the examined life"), transmitting their nation's cultural tradition, and providing "the ethical preparation for leadership."[242] This diminishing of liberal arts education, it will be recalled, had its distant beginnings in the 1840-1877 period and picked up momentum in the 1877-1920 period. Now, in the face of a loss of a sense of purpose and a growth for growth's sake mentality,[243] this had become a rampant problem. The intellectual strength of programs flagged, curricula were watered down, degree requirements were lowered, such trendy programs as "Non-Western Studies" became popular, and with increasing size institutions became more impersonal.[244] These developments did not sweep as far as they were to do in the 1960s, but they definitely were occurring. Ideological intolerance and "political correctness" also did not advance as far as they would in coming decades, but they were there.[245] Similarly, the beginnings of a militant, intolerant secularism and anti-Christian hostility appeared on the campuses of non-denominationally-affiliated institutions; it too would become increasingly the reality in the decades ahead.[246]

The decline in the liberal arts at the college level, more pronounced than at any earlier time in American history, was especially troublesome in light of the Founding thinking about education. It was the colleges that were definitely training the future leaders. So while the developments in pre-college education were largely the same, the consequences of their taking place at the college level were more portentous. The fact that the higher education leadership seemed to have no real sense of its crucial mission and moved their institutions away from it meant that the problem would continue to perpetuate itself. Even though the notion of a natural aristocracy, as we have seen, had long since faded from the American socio-political landscape, the place from which at least a rough facsimile could hope to emerge was deteriorating. In a related fashion, the rising ideological and religious intolerance within precincts of the university did not bode well for keeping alive the understanding of the importance the Founders placed on religion for a democratic republic, nor for the vitality of the central rights of free speech and freedom of religion in American society in the future (as the coming chapters perhaps bear out).

There were interesting, and somewhat contradictory, developments in American religion itself during this period. The percentage of the population who were members of a church increased (from less than 50% in 1940 to 65% in 1960), the sale of Bibles "soared," religious themes were "pervasive" in popular culture (in spite of the problematical developments above), traditional religious figures such as Bishop Fulton J. Sheen and evangelist Billy Graham gained substantial media exposure and popular followings, Catholicism—which had more adherents than any single Protestant denomination in the U.S. by far[247]— may have reached a zenith both in terms of the fervor of its adherents and its social influence and public respect,[248] and there was a strong pro-religion tone generally in American life.[249] At the same time, however, many clergymen were telling people what they wanted to hear. Tindall and Shi put it this way: "the popular religious revival during the 1950s was upbeat and soothing...people...wanted to be reassured that their own comfortable way of life was indeed God's will."[250] Too much of American religion sought a rapprochement with the new age of affluence, and it began to mesh with psychology[251]—paving the way for what was often its outright envelopment and even substitution by pop psychology in the 1960s.[252] In spite of the upsurge of religion, it was not so clear that people had a deep religiosity, as they were— again, anticipating the 1960s—"profoundly anxious about the meaning of life."[253] The famous Jewish theologian and sociologist of religion Will Herberg claimed at the time that Americans were "simultaneously professedly religious yet very secular," most saying that religion was important to them but that it did not affect their ideas or conduct in affairs of business or politics.[254] Religious developments in this period were in line with the notion of progress—i.e., a positive spirit, always looking ahead—that we have seen has long been a part of American thinking,[255] and with the long-standing tendency of American religion to be weak on doctrine. In another respect, it was at odds with the religious spirit of the Founding Era's culture, which as we have seen was, by and large, genuinely devout and directed—however imperfectly—toward the service of God. Early America was a religious culture in more than a nominal or superficial way. Moreover, leading Christian religious thinkers of the 1945-1960 period justified fundamental departures from traditional Christian teaching. With his determined effort to promote tolerance, Niebuhr—"the most important Protestant theologian in America"—said that Christians should no longer seek the conversion of the Jews, and effectively rejected Christian universalism (i.e., the age-old teaching that Christianity was for all men, that the Gospel should be preached to everyone). According to Hart, Niebuhr sought a "henotheism...a move back...to the tribal theologies of the ancient world."[256] He also sought moral pluralism,[257] a likely enough outcome of rejecting both Christian universalism and, as noted before, natural law. This, of course, was sharply at odds with the Founding, but anticipated what would happen in America in the decades ahead. Perhaps, too, moral pluralism was an outgrowth of the non-doctrinal approach to religion that we have said was often seen in American history. When utilitarianism, pragmatism, and relativism became embedded in American thought and the culture became more secular, the jump to moral pluralism logically followed. Not only would such a functional deprecation of Christianity have been repudiated by the Founding Era, but it effectively rejected the Christian worldview that shaped its thinking about politics and society. On another level, however, the development and eventual spreading of moral pluralism in American culture may have been facilitated by the fact that most of American Christianity did not recognize the Catholic Church's magisterium as the authoritative moral teacher—a potential weakness in the Founding itself that we have suggested may have helped it to come undone. Thus, it lacked a stabilizing anchor. So, eminent theologians and other thinkers could become influential on such things and come to be regarded—along with governmental institutions such as the courts—as the de facto moral teachers. Another eminent Protestant theologian of the time who was also in light of traditional Christian teaching "doctrinally suspect" was the German émigré Paul Tillich. He saw himself as standing "between Christian tradition and modern secular culture." He did not believe in immorality, seemed to see revelation in some sense as continuing in the present time, and tended to de-divinize Jesus Christ.[258] Such creeping, but increasingly obvious, secularism would hardly have been expressed by the intellectual leaders of Founding Era Christianity, even if the forerunners of it had already appeared within the intelligentsia and even to some degree among a few of the Founders.[259] It should be mentioned that the new religious uncertainties and the lack of a sufficient religious commitment amidst the seemingly pervasive religiosity of the 1945-1960 period may have contributed to the weakening of families and increased juvenile delinquency mentioned above.[260]

Not only was juvenile crime a serious problem in the 1950s, so was urban crime. The substantial Negro migration from the South to northern cities that had begun in the 1920-1945 period increased in the present period; it was partially the result of technological innovation in cotton-farming that had eliminated the need for many agricultural workers and sharecroppers. Instead of finding work, however, the transplanted southern Negroes found themselves facing continued unemployment (resulting partly from race prejudice), congested slums (in which they were often exploited by greedy landlords), the disadvantages of continued illiteracy, and family breakdown. These conditions spawned, among other maladies, gang activity and crime. As Tindall and Shi state, "the great black migration produced a web of complex social problems that in the 1960s would burgeon into a crisis."[261] This would include even more crime in the 1960s, as well as considerable civil unrest (discussed in Chapter 8).[262] The Negro migration also had the effect of breaking down communities and leaving people with the difficult task of trying to construct new ones, when such things often have to happen over time organically (a similar problem as was seen by the period's suburbanization). This contributed to the social problems of the Negro during this time. If the 1945-1960 period presented the genuine promise of Negro equality for the first time, the lack of civic friendship, fair-dealing, and civility in the North (i.e., concerning treatment of the Negro) was at least a factor in creating this unfortunate situation. The norm of voluntary melding of the Founding obviously was not so readily embraced. The weakening of community—both for the Negro and the Caucasian middle class that had moved to the suburbs—in the eyes of the Founding Era would have represented a tearing of the social fabric. The new crime problems perhaps illustrated, too, a diminution of respect for law in at least some parts of the culture.

When we combine the above analysis of the 1945-1960 period in each of the areas examined, we can conclude the following about its comparison with Founding Era principles and conditions. In terms of institutional factors, separation of powers and checks and balances were weakened by the new expansive military prerogatives assumed by the presidency in the Cold War era. Further, judicial activism began and would ultimately have serious implications for these bedrock principles of the Constitution—with the federal judiciary in the next two decades seeming to become the most powerful branch of government. Civilian control of the military was intact, but was slightly compromised by the permanent larger role of the military during the Cold War and the growth of the military-industrial complex. Perhaps the most serious erosion of liberty was due to the Cold War military footing, as well: the ongoing peacetime draft. Federalism continued to weaken, as the federal government's domestic role continued to expand and "cooperative federalism" meant states carrying out functions according to federally imposed standards. Judicial decisions also limited the scope of state authority. The weakening of federalism was, of course, an aspect of the long-term centralizing trend in American life, going back to the Progressive Era. More basically, it was clear that the enhanced involvement of government at all levels in more and more endeavors was now a regular feature of American life. In terms of democratic principles and practice, we saw that popular sovereignty was ignored in such areas as Negro voting rights, interest group liberalism, control of public education, and in American treatment of other countries; and the respect for the common good in treatment of the Negro (even while change was beginning), the socio-political thought of the time, and—most crucially—in the regime of interest group liberalism. In the conduct of government, the renewed concern about the public debt early in the Eisenhower period was a positive development in comparison to the Founding, even though it was short-lived and ultimately it must be said that the subversion of the Founding principle of avoiding excessive government debt continued. Interest group liberalism also portended greater governmental arbitrariness and lack of accountability of government officials. We saw a distortion or compromising in different ways of such basic rights as freedom of speech, assembly, and religion—although they were not grievously harmed. Weaknesses in such Founding Era socio-cultural norms as the need for civility, civic friendship, community, temperance, fair-dealing (both domestically and internationally), truth-telling, concern for the general welfare, a close tie between ethics and economics, thrift, sobriety, an ethic of present sacrifice for the future good, the need to avoid luxury, lack of cooperation (e.g., between labor and management), sound sexual morality and strong families, sound education, and strong religion were seen in varying degrees—although on balance American life had more strengths in most of these areas than weaknesses, or the weaknesses would play themselves out fully and become consequential only in the following decade. As stated above, for example, the period was actually a time of considerable civic friendship. The loss of a spirit of liberty and initiative due to the conformity ethic and the troublesome ideas in most of the period's socio-political and religious thought also had implications that were not encouraging. While personal initiative was thus declining, the beginning of distortion about the role of the individual was also seen at the other extreme—individualism—in the luxury-orientation, thought, and counter-culture of the time. The foundation was being laid for an increasingly widespread moral relativism anathema to Founding principles and presuppositions that would begin to pervade American culture in the 1960s. The growth of the middle class and of property ownership were positive developments in moving the country closer to Founding ideals, even while the continued and even sharper growth of large, distant economic entities that separated ownership from control—with the economic sustenance of ever more people tied up with them—was opposed to Founding economic conditions. Another positive development was the movement toward a fuller realization of citizen equality, as seen in the racial question. Even where the period most departed from Founding norms, on political and economic centralization and the permanently enlarged role of government, the departure was not intolerable or extreme. Where the principle of liberty was constrained, as with the peacetime draft, it was limited to one area where some grounds of justification were possible. While belief in the need for a natural aristocracy and a limited franchise had long since vanished, there were still some legal, practical, and attitudinal limits to out-and-out democracy: the poll tax—which, to be sure, was abused in the South for racial discriminatory purposes—had not yet been outlawed; significant residency requirements for voting were still in place;[263] there were few presidential primaries and party nominees were still genuinely selected by the filtering device of national conventions and in some states party nominees for various offices were selected by state conventions; and people in Washington, D.C.—which as a federal enclave historically had been simply subject to the will of Congress and did not have the political prerogatives of the rest of the country, and where today much is made of the lack of Congressional representation—at that time had no vote at all even for local offices (and apparently many of them did not even mind).[264] All told, the 1945-1960 period emerges as one in which Founding principles were moderately well upheld, probably more so than in any period since before the Progressive Era. It is not surprising that the 1950s were considered by many to be a time of optimism.[265] Not too far out of view, however, decay was progressing in many areas and there were harbingers of deep future troubles.

    In considering the factors of regime decline that may have been operational at this time, we find that only a couple—overcentralization/excessive bureaucratization/bigness and mass culture/urbanization—are clearly evident, although perhaps not stiflingly so. Mass culture implanted itself in the 1920s, overcentralization and bureaucratization continued from the New Deal, and bigness and urbanization had been prominent since the late nineteenth century. One might even consider the movement to the suburbs to be a diminishment of urbanization. One witnesses most of the other factors, to be sure, but only in a growing or minor way—not enough (yet) to say decadence was afoot. Most apparent of these were materialism and the excessive pursuit of luxury. Social conflict was relatively muted, confined to the early civil rights revolution. Moral relativism stirred, but mostly among intellectuals. The turning away from religion was not happening, but the above makes apparent its slow weakening under the surface. The latter, plus the burgeoning consumerism and increasing concern with the here-and-now, were probably behind the growing sense of purposelessness noted above. A weakening of control of the passions began not only with the pursuit of luxury, but also the loosening of sexual restraint. While family breakdown did not become a serious problem until the 1960s, family integrity during the 1945-1960 period was fraying at the edges. America hardly experienced the militarism that characterized various European and Asian regimes in history, but there is also little doubt that it advanced as far as it ever had in her history during this first decade and a half of the Cold War. There was no massive breakdown of the rule of law, although it continued to be systemically flouted with respect to the Negro in many parts of the South (but, again, that was beginning for the first time in American history to be reversed). Respect for the common good was compromised as interest group liberalism advanced with the expanding role of government as regulator and provider and due to the disparate treatment of Negroes and Caucasians, but the former was not yet a crisis—as Theodore Lowi said it had become at the end of the 1960s[266]—and the latter, again, was beginning to be addressed. All told, we might conclude that there was an arresting of the cultural decline that seemed to occur in the 1920s; maybe—in spite of all the problems bubbling below the surface—the culture even actually improved.

The problems of the 1945-1960 period suggested the following possible weaknesses in the character of the Founding that may have given rise to them: lack of an awareness of all the principles of social ethics because of insufficient philosophical reflection and the lack of stress in the Founders' thought on the role of intermediary associations (seen in the continued overcentralization and bigness), lack of a sound understanding of the common good for the same reason (seen in how government and the concomitant interest group liberalism were allowed to grow), the seeds of an expanded individualism and how the commercial republic helped to stimulate it (seen especially in the period's consumption ethic and such new practices as planned obsolescence to keep consumerism going), the discerning of the natural law left to private judgment—instead of recognizing the Catholic Church as its authoritative interpreter—led to positivism (seen in the beginning of theological justification of moral pluralism, the relativism in socio-political thought, and the counter-cultural Beats whose influence would expand in the 1960s), the lack of a sense among the Founders about how religion would weaken and the absence of formal ways to bring forth a natural aristocracy and to shape virtue (the latter seen in the growing susceptibility of the population to slip away from sexual virtue), failure to see the central role of the family for the political order (although only to a degree in this era of renewed stress on family life); the Founders' inability to see how powerful the courts would become; and how the emphasis on institutional and structural factors eventually spurred bureaucratization. One wonders, too, if the Founding's failure to orient our constitutional republic to higher things did not help make possible—and the existence of the notion of a consumer republic compound—the condition of the this-worldly luxury orientation seen in the 1920s and again in the 1945-1960 period.

Notes

1. Paul Johnson, *A History of the American People*, 837.
2. Ibid., 840.
3. Tindall and Shi, 1381-1382; Eric F. Goldman, *The Crucial Decade—and After: America, 1945-1960* (N.Y.: Vintage Books, 1960), 36. The quotation is from Tindall and Shi, 1381.
4. Goldman, 20-27.
5. Tindall and Shi, 1384.
6. Manchester, 398.
7. Tindall and Shi, 1383.

8. Goldman, 21-24.

9. Tindall and Shi, 1384. The draft legislation is quoted in G.J. Santoni, "The Employment Act of 1946: Some History Notes," http://research.stlouisfed.org/publications/review/86/11/Employment_Nov1986.pdf; Internet; accessed May 14, 2009.

10. Tindall and Shi, 1384; 1385; Santoni.

11. Tindall and Shi, 1424.

12. Ibid., 1385-1386.

13. The decision was *Youngstown Sheet and Tube Co. v. Sawyer*, 343 U.S. 579 (1952).

14. Chester J. Pach, Jr. and Elmo Richardson, *The Presidency of Dwight D. Eisenhower* (rev. edn.; Lawrence, Kan.: University Press of Kansas, 1991), 212-213; "Labor Management Reporting and Disclosure Act," http://en.wikipedia.org/wiki/Landrum-Griffin_Act; Internet; accessed June 22, 2009.

15. Tindall and Shi, 1424.

16. Goldman, 182.

17. Tindall and Shi, 1424-1425.

18. Goldman, 182; 95.

19. Ibid., 96.

20. Paul Johnson, *Modern Times*, 613.

21. Tindall and Shi, 1465-1466.

22. Ibid., 1485.

23. Ibid., 1466-1467 (the quotation is from 1466); William H. Chafe, *The Unfinished Journey: America Since World War II* (3rd edn.; N.Y.: Oxford University Press, 1995), 139.

24. William E. Leuchtenburg, *A Troubled Feast: American Society Since 1945* (Boston: Little, Brown, 1983), 47.

25. Ibid., 58.

26. Ibid., 55.

27. Ibid., 61.

28. Ibid., 42, 65 (the first quotation is from 42, the second from 65); Manchester, 594.

29. Leuchtenburg, *A Troubled Feast,*, 48.

30. Manchester, 594.

31. Leuchtenburg, *A Troubled Feast*, 50-53; Manchester, 594.

32. Leuchtenburg, *A Troubled Feast*, 52.

33. Tindall and Shi, 1390.

34. For an impressive refutation of "Cold War revisionism," see Robert James Maddox, *The New Left and the Origins of the Cold War* (Princeton, N.J.: Princeton University Press, 1973).

35. Tindall and Shi, 1390-1391.

36. Ibid., 1391.

37. Ibid., 1392.

38. Goldman, 58.

39. Ibid., 57; Stephen E. Ambrose and Douglas G. Brinkley, *Rise to Globalism: American Foreign Policy Since 1938* (8th rev. edn.; N.Y.: Penguin, 1997), 8.

40. Tindall and Shi, 1492-1393.

41. Goldman, 61.

42. Ambrose and Brinkley, 82-83.

43. Ibid., 86-87.

44. Tindall and Shi, 1396-1397.

45. Ambrose and Brinkley, 100-101.

46. Tindall and Shi, 1398-1399, 1409-1410.

47. "Point Four Program," http://en.wikipedia.org/wiki/Point_Four_Program; Internet; accessed May 25, 2009.

48. Ambrose and Brinkley, 118, 116.

49. Ibid., 121, 123-125.

50. Tindall and Shi, 1387-1388.

51. "Conscription in the United States," http://en.wikipedia.org/wiki/ Conscription_in_the_United_States#Cold_War_and_Korean_War; Internet; accessed May 25, 2009.

52. See Ambrose and Brinkley, 123.

53. Tindall and Shi, 1389-1390; John F. Kennedy, *Profiles in Courage* (N.Y.: Harper & Row, 1955), 216-219.

54. Goldman, 249-250.

55. Ibid., 284-285.

56. Ambrose and Brinkley, 148.

57. Ibid., 148-149.

58. Ibid., 152.

59. Ibid., 153-158.

60. Ibid., 154, 159.

61. Ibid., 159-160, 164; "Military-Industrial Complex Speech, Dwight D. Eisenhower, 1961," http://coursesa.matrix.msu.edu/~hst306/documents/indust.html; Internet; accessed June 15, 2009. The quotation is from Ambrose and Brinkley, 164.

62. See Douglas T. Miller and Marion Nowak, *The Fifties: The Way We Really Were* (Garden City, N.Y.: Doubleday, 1977), 29-30, 33-34.

63. Ambrose and Brinkley, 160.

64. Ibid., 161.

65. Ibid., 164-166, 168. The quotation is from 164-165. Initially, the Eisenhower administration did not think that Castro was a Communist, but it was not long before that became apparent or that he moved in the direction of communism and the Soviet Union.

66. Ibid., 168-169.

67. Hiss continued throughout his life to maintain his innocence and he seemed to have convinced certain elements of the American media, but any lingering doubt was eliminated when "Hiss's guilt [was] finally established beyond argument by material from Soviet sources" after the Cold War ended (Paul Johnson, *A History of the American People*, 848.

68. Tindall and Shi, 1416-1418.

69. Miller and Nowak, 35.

70. Johnson, *A History of the American People*, 833.

71. "Joseph McCarthy," http://en.wikipedia.org/wiki/Joseph_McCarthy; In- ternet; accessed June 15, 2009. Other sources agree with this assessment of the lack of substantiation of McCarthy's specific charges (see: Tindall and Shi, 1418; Leuchtenburg, *A Troubled Feast*, 37; Manchester, 523-524). This is not to say that Communists were not present or even in significant positions in the U.S., even if they were not Soviet agents. As Jeffrey Hart of Dartmouth College writes: "[H]onest scholars can disagree over the importance of Communist influence on American policy making. What they cannot disagree about is the presence of actual Communists and proven Communist sympathizers in positions of great importance both inside and outside government" (Jeffrey Hart, *When the Going Was Good! American Life in the Fifties* [N.Y.: Crown Publishers, 1982], 188).

72. Manchester, 716-718.

73. Senator George H. Bender of Ohio, quoted in Manchester, 717.

74. U.S. Constitution, Art. I, Sec. 8, Clause 1.

75. "A Brief History of U.S. Foreign Aid," http://www.bcps.org/offices/lis/models/foreignaid/history.html; Internet; accessed June 16, 2009.

76. Graham Hancock, *Lords of Poverty: The Power, Prestige, and Corruption of the International Aid Business* (N.Y.: Atlantic Monthly Press, 1989), 69-70.

77. See Manchester, 580-582.

78. See ibid., 581; "McCarthyism," http://en.wikipedia.org/wiki/McCarthyism; Internet; accessed June 16, 2009.

79. Mason and Stephenson, 621. The citation for the *Gaines* decision is 305 U.S. 337; for *Sipuel*, 332 U.S. 631; for *McLaurin*, 339 U.S. 637; and for *Sweatt*, 339 U.S. 629.

80. Leuchtenburg, *A Troubled Feast*, 92; David Halberstam, *The Fifties* (N.Y.: Villard Books, 1993), 414-415.

81. Mason and Stephenson, 622.

82. Tindall and Shi, 1400-1401; "Fair Employment Practices Commission," http://en.wikipedia.org/wiki/Fair_Employment_Practices_Commission;Internet; accessed June 17, 2009.

83. Tindall and Shi, 1401.

84. Goldman, 184-186.

85. Tindall and Shi, 1402.

86. 342 U.S. 294.

87. Mason and Stephenson, 622; "Brown v. Board of Education (II)," http://www.oyez.org/cases/1950-1959/1954/ 1954_1/; Internet; accessed June 18, 2009.

88. Tindall and Shi, 1494-1495; Manchester, 741-743; Chafe, 161-165; "Montgomery Bus Boycott," http://en.wikipedia.org/wiki/Montgomery_Bus_Boycott; Internet; accessed June 18, 2009.

89. Chafe, 164-165. The quotation is from 164.

90. Tindall and Shi, 1497.

91. Chafe, 165-168.

92. Ibid, 154-155.

93. Tindall and Shi, 1496; "Civil Rights Act of 1957," http://en.wikipedia.org/wiki/Civil_Rights_Act_of_1957; Internet; accessed June 18, 2009.

94. Chafe, 156

95. Ibid, 155.

96. Chafe, 153.

97. Ibid., 157-158.

98. Manchester, 739.

99. Pach and Richardson, 145.

100. Halberstam, 431-441; Manchester, 738.

101. Ibid., 430-431.

102. Benjamin Greenberg, "The Legacy of a Murder," *Colorlines* (March-April 2008), http://www.scribd.com/doc/2410179/Legacy-Of-A-Murder-by-BenjaminGreenberg; Internet; accessed June 19, 2009.

103. Halberstam, 431.

104. Manchester, 738.

105. "Twenty-second Amendment to the United States Constitution," http://en.wikipedia.org/wiki/Twenty-second_Amendment_to_the_United_States_Constitution; Internet; accessed June 20, 2009.

106. Manchester, 556.

107. Halberstam, 372.

108. 343 U.S. 579.

109. Thomas E. Baker, "*Youngstown Sheet and Tube Co. v. Sawyer,*" in Hall, 950-951.

110. 354 U.S. 178.

111. Mason and Stephenson, 84. Two years later, however, in *Barenblatt v. U.S.*, 360 U.S. 109 (1959), the Court seemed unwilling to hold Congress to the rule enunciated in *Watkins*, although the precedent still stood.

112. Tindall and Shi, 1381, 1404, 1407-1408.

113. Chafe, 81.

114. Tindall and Shi, 1464-1465. The first quotation is from 1465 and the second from 1464.

115. See, e.g., Chafe, 153.

116. 330 U.S. 1.

117. Krason, *The Public Order and the Sacred Order*, 203.

118. See ibid., 214-216; Gerard V. Bradley, *Church-State Relationships in America* (Westport, Conn.: Greenwood, 1987), 135. He gives the historical evidence to back up this conclusion throughout the book.

119. 333 U.S. 203 (1948).

120. Krason, *The Public Order and the Sacred Order*, 203.

121. Ibid. The citation for *Zorach* is 343 U.S. 306.

122. 343 U.S., at 313.

123. *Plessy v. Ferguson* was discussed in Chapter 5 and the thinking of the framers of the Fourteenth Amendment in Chapter 4.

124. 325 U.S. 761.

125. Mason and Stephenson, 244-245.

126. *New York v. U.S.*, 326 U.S. 572, as discussed in Mason and Stephenson, 141.

127. *Colegrove v. Green*, 328 U.S. 549, as discussed in: Melvin I. Urofsky, "History of the Court—The Depression and the Rise of Legal Liberalism," in Hall, 395; "Colegrove v. Green," http://en.wikipedia.org/wiki/Colegrove_v._Green; Internet; accessed June 21, 2009.

128. *In re Oliver*, 333 U.S. 257

129. *Cole v. Arkansas*, 333 U.S. 196 (1948).

130. *Wolf v. Colorado*, 338 U.S. 25 (1949).

131. For the list of Bill of Rights provisions and the cases incorporating them and their dates, see Mason and Stephenson, 385.

132. 329 U.S. 230.

133. "U.S. v. Carmack," http://en.wikipedia.org/wiki/United_States_v._ Carmack; Internet; accessed June 22, 2009.

134. *Cooper v. Aaron*, 358 U.S. 1, 18-19.

135. 62 U.S. 506. *Ableman* and *Cooper* were, however, on opposite sides of the American race question.

136. Quoted and paraphrased in Felix Morley, *Freedom and Federalism* (Chicago: Henry Regnery [Gateway Edn.], 1959), 160.

137. Chris Edwards, "Federal Aid to the States: Historical Cause of Government Growth and Bureaucracy," *Policy Analysis* (May 22, 2007), 7-8.

138. Tindall and Shi, 1466.

139. See Chafe, 139; Morley, 240.

140. Eisenhower even established a Commission on Intergovernmental Relations to determine which governmental activities could be returned to the states. It identified few

such programs, and led to no changes. ("History of U.S. Federalism," http://www.cas.sc.edu/poli/courses/scgov/History_of_Federalism.htm; Internet; accessed June 22, 2009.)

141. Lawrence M. Friedman, *A History of American Law* (3rd edn.; N.Y.: Simon and Schuster [Touchstone], 2007), 563-564.

142. Quoted in Tindall and Shi, 1466.

143. See: Ryan J. Barilleaux, *American Government in Action: Principle, Process, and Politics* (Upper Saddle River, N.J.: Prentice-Hall, 1996), 168-172.

144. For a good discussion of the problem of "interest group government," see Theodore J. Lowi, *The End of Liberalism: Ideology, Policy, and the Crisis of Public Authority* (N.Y.: W.W. Norton, 1969).

145. 337 U.S. 1.

146. Paul C. Bartholomew, *Ruling American Constitutional Law, vol. II—Limitations on Government* (Totowa, N.J.: Littlefield, Adams, 1970), 79.

147. 340 U.S. 315.

148. 340 U.S., at 320, 321.

149. 341 U.S. 494.

150. Bartholomew, 52.

151. 334 U.S.558.

152. Bartholomew, 84.

153. 343 U.S. 250.

154. Bartholomew, 71.

155. 334 U.S. 131.

156. Bartholomew, 71.

157. 343 U.S. 495.

158. 343 U.S., at 506.

159. 340 U.S. 290.

160. 340 U.S., at 293.

161. 345 U.S. 67.

162. "Fowler v. Rhode Island," http://en.wikipedia.org/wiki/Fowler_v._Rhode_Island; Internet; accessed July 2, 2009.

163. 354 U.S. 298.

164. 354 U.S. 476.

165. 356 U.S. 86.

166. 360 U.S. 684.

167. Bartholomew, 58.

168. Ibid., 73.

169. Ibid., 304.

170. Ibid., 76.

171. 360 U.S., at 688.

172. Tindall and Shi, 1419.

173. Declaration of Independence. By the way, this issue came to the fore in the 1961 Supreme Court case of *In re Anastaplo*, 366 U.S. 82, which concerned a state bar's unwillingness to admit a candidate, who later on became a prominent scholar of political philosophy and law, to the bar essentially because he thought that in light of the Declaration of Independence a people had a "right of revolution" to throw off a government that became destructive of the rights to life, liberty, and the pursuit of happiness.

174. See Higgins, 464.

175. Ibid., 469.

176. See Krason, *Abortion: Politics, Morality, and the Constitution*, 262; Krason, *The Public Order and the Sacred Order*, 362.

177. Stuart Banner, *The Death Penalty: An American History* (Cambridge, Mass.: Harvard University Press, 2002), 237.

178. Beitzinger, 551-552.

179. Ibid., 554-555.

180. Ibid., 556.

181. Ibid., 556-557.

182. Ibid., 558.

183. Ibid., 558-559. The quotation is from 559.

184. Ibid., 559-560. The quotation is from 560.

185. Ibid., 559.

186. N.Y.: Sheed and Ward, 1960.

187. George H. Nash, *The Conservative Intellectual Movement in America: Since 1945* (N.Y.: Basic Books, 1979), 195. For an extensive elaboration about how these principles and conditions emerged from the Western cultural heritage going back to the ancients, see Kirk, *The Roots of American Order*. In this book (see 177-179), Kirk also discusses the importance of the medieval background and how appreciation of it was insufficient among America's Founding Fathers.

188. Beitzinger, 562-563. The quotation is from 563.

189. Fromm, quoted in Beitzinger, 563.

190. Beitzinger, 564.

191. Ibid., 565.

192. Ibid., 566.

193. Daniel Bell, *The End of Ideology: On the Exhaustion of Political Ideas in the Fifties* (Glencoe, Ill.: Free Press, 1960).

194. Beitzinger, 582.

195. John J. Schrems, *Principles of Politics: An Introduction* (Englewood Cliffs, N.J.: Prentice-Hall, 1986), 75.

196. Ibid., 62.

197. C. Wright Mills, *The Power Elite* (N.Y.: Oxford University Press, 1956).

198. Beitzinger, 584.

199. "C. Wright Mills," http://en.wikipedia.org/wiki/C._Wright_Mills; Internet; accessed July 1, 2009.

200. Tindall and Shi, 1429.

201. Ibid., 1430.

202. Ibid., 1427.

203. Miller and Nowak, 147.

204. Sally C. Clarke, "Advance Report of Final Divorce Statistics, 1989 and 1990," in *Monthly Vital Statistics Report* (Centers for Disease Control and Prevention/National Center for Health Statistics), vol. 43, no. 9, supplement (March 22, 1995), 9, http://www.cdc.gov/nchs/data/mvsr/supp/mv43_09s.pdf; Internet; accessed July 4, 2009.

205. Paul Johnson, *A History of the American People*, 941.

206. Tindall and Shi, 1426.

207. Ibid., 1440-1442.

208. See ibid., 1440.

209. Carlson, 6.

210. Tindall and Shi, 1431;

211. Ibid., 1430, 1449-1450.

212. Ibid., 1428, 1431-1432.

213. Judith A. Reisman and Edward W. Eichel (ed. John H. Court and J. Gordon Muir), *Kinsey, Sex, and Fraud: The Indoctrination of a People* (Lafayette, La.: Huntington House, 1990), 2; Hart, 52.

214. Reisman and Eichel, 7, 12, 21, 34, 57-82, 177-196, 219.

215. Hart, 52.

216. Ibid.

217. This was the assessment of the pill's effect by one of its developers, Dr. Minchuch Chang (cited in *Christchurch* [New Zealand] *Press*, Dec. 6, 1981).

218. Steven W. Mosher, *Population Control: Real Costs, Illusory Benefits* (New Brunswick, N.J.: Transaction, 2008), 4-7.

219. Hart, 47. Although French, de Beauvoir's writing apparently had considerable influence in American feminist and academic circles (see "Still the Second Sex?", *The Independent* [Jan. 9, 2008], http://www.independent.co.uk/news/world/europe/still-the-second-sex-simone-de-beauvoir-centenary-769122.html; Internet; accessed July 5, 2009).

220. Hart, 49-50, 52. The quotation is from 49.

221. Miller and Nowak, 325-327. The quotations are from 326.

222. Ibid., 51.

223. Tindall and Shi, 1433-1435; Hart 133. The quotation is from Tindall and Shi, 1435.

224. See Tindall and Shi, 1454-1457. The quotation is from 1455.

225. Ibid., 1440.

226. Ibid., 1435.

227. Ibid., 1439, 1448. The quotation is from 1439.

228. Ibid., 1443.

229. Tindall and Shi (439) mention this effect of the consumer culture on conformity, and by that they likely mean what is stated here.

230. Ibid., 1449-1450.

231. Diane Ravitch, *The Troubled Crusade: American Education 1945-1980* (N.Y.: Basic Books, 1983), 44.

232. Ibid., 46, 48. The quotations are from 46.

233. Ibid., 79.

234. Ibid., 75, 76.

235. Ibid., 67.

236. Ibid., 63.

237. Ibid., 56, 66. The quotation is from 66.

238. Ibid., 75.

239. Tindall and Shi, 1426.

240. See Russell Kirk, *Decadence and Renewal in the Higher Learning: An Episodic History of American University and College* (South Bend, Ind.: Gateway Edns., 1978), 26-29.

241. Ibid., 3, 25.

242. Ibid., 22.

243. Ibid.

244. Ibid., 23-25.

245. See ibid., 38-39.

246. Ibid., 63-64.

247. See the table on "Major Religious Bodies in the United States," in the article on "Religion" in the 1964 edn. of *The World Book Encyclopedia*, vol. 16, 212-213. The statistics were from a time in the early 1960s close enough to the period focused on in this chapter to be reflective of it.

248. Joseph A. Varacalli, *Bright Promise, Failed Community: Catholics and the American Public Order* (Lanham, Md.: Lexington Books, 2000), 61-62.

249. Tindall and Shi, 1443-1445. The quotations are from 1443.

250. Ibid., 1444.

251. Ibid., 1445.

252. On this point, see William Kirk Kilpatrick, *Psychological Seduction: The Failure of Modern Psychology* (Nashville: Thomas Nelson, 1983).

253. Tindall and Shi, 1445.

254. George M. Marsden, *Religion and American Culture* (2nd edn.; Belmont, Calif.: Wadsworth/Thomson, 2001), 225.

255. Tindall and Shi mention as the preeminent example of this brand of positive, upbeat religion Norman Vincent Peale, who they say followed "a long tradition of 'positive thinking' in American social and religious thought" (1444).

256. Hart, 261.

257. Ibid., 260.

258. Ibid., 262-263. The quotations are from 262.

259. See Marsden, 40-41; Kirk, *The Roots of American Order*, 340-343; Ahlstrom, 366-368.

260. Tindall and Shi, 1432.

261. Ibid., 1438.

262. Ibid. About the increase in crime in later decades, it should be noted that the overall U.S. crime rate doubled in the 1960s and tripled in the 1970s. From 1960 to 1990, there was a 560% increase in violent crime (see Paul Johnson, *A History of the American People*, 965).

263. William H. Flanigan and Nancy H. Zingale, *Political Behavior of the American Electorate* (6th edn.; Boston: Allyn and Bacon, 1987), 6.

264. On this last point, see Patrick J. Buchanan, *Right from the Beginning* (Washington, D.C.: Regnery Gateway, 1990), 131.

265. See, e.g., Frederick D. Wilhelmsen, "John Courtney Murray: The Optimism of the 1950's," in D'Elia and Krason, 20-32.

266. See Lowi.

CHAPTER 8

1960-1980: THE WELFARE STATE, CULTURAL UPHEAVAL, AND THE REIGN AND DECLINE OF LIBERALISM

The beginning of Chapter 7 quoted historian Paul Johnson as saying that the 1950s were still a time of traditional culture in the U.S., but there were portents of change. This change would flower in the 1960s; traditional culture would pass. Johnson further says that change began—in the 1950s—as "a sexual revolution," but "was to bring about revolutions in many other areas too."[1] Bruce J. Schulman says that the 1970s "transformed American economic and cultural life as much as, if not more than, the revolutions in manners and morals of the 1920s and 1960s. In race relations, religion, family life, politics, and popular culture, the 1970s marked...the beginning of our own time" (he writes in 2001).[2] These two quotations explain why it would almost be appropriate to treat 1960 to the end of the first decade of the twenty-first century as a single period to be discussed in one chapter. The 1960s represented, in an emphatic way, a new turn in American life, with what Paul Johnson calls "baleful consequences." The 1970s consolidated the changes of the 1960s, making them a part of the new American social fabric. While the decades that followed saw departures, even pronounced ones, on certain levels—such as in politics—they did not alter the developments in American life that the 1960s and 1970s wrought. There has been continuity from 1960 to the present that has had decisive implications for the character of the American democratic republic as envisioned by its Founders. Still, there is a rough division between, on the one hand, the 1960s and 1970s when the "new way" emerged and with its further expressions took root and, on the other, the 1980s to the present when its resiliency became apparent and its full implications came clearly into focus. This, along with the fact that the period since 1960 has seen an overwhelming number of crucial events, trends, and developments in different areas, argues for a treatment in two separate chapters. The topical areas considered (which are similar to those in previous chapters) for the 1960-1980 period are: economics and economic and social welfare policy; the role and powers of government, relations among the three branches of the federal government, and federal-state relations; political developments, trends, and reform; legal and constitutional developments and citizen rights; foreign and defense policy, war and international conflicts, and America's role in the world; relations and conflict among social groups, and immigration; socio-cultural developments; socio-political movements, trends in socio-political thought, and the influence of the intelligentsia.

To gain bearings, it is perhaps worth highlighting the major events and socio-politico-cultural trends and developments during the entire post-1960 period. Elaboration is provided as needed and other facts presented throughout this and the next chapter in order to carry out the analysis. The period began, of course, with the election of John F. Kennedy over Richard M. Nixon in 1960. This brought liberalism and the Democratic party back into power, but JFK's New Frontier legislative program did not make much headway in Congress. A tax cut that he had sought to stimulate the economy was passed under President Lyndon B. Johnson. While the ongoing Cold War in the early 1960s saw the Bay of Pigs invasion, the erection of the Berlin Wall, and the Cuban Missile Crisis, by far the most significant development was the Vietnam War. Probably the most throttling event for the national psyche was the JFK assassination of 1963. The landslide election of LBJ in 1964 and his Great Society legislative program signaled the expansion of the New Deal/Fair Deal agenda, but were paralleled by socio-cultural upheavals in the form of urban race riots, campus confrontations, the sexual revolution, and the emergence of a new wave of feminism that transformed the old liberalism of FDR and Truman. The pro-integrationist efforts of the civil rights movement reached their peak with the 1963 march on Washington and then the Civil Rights and Voting Rights Acts of the next two years. 1968 was the most tumultuous year in a decade of upheaval, with LBJ unexpectedly withdrawing from the presidential race, the assassinations of Rev. Martin Luther King, Jr. and the slain president's brother and 1968 presidential candidate Senator Robert F. Kennedy, racial and campus turmoil reaching their heights, a week of conflict inside the Democratic National Convention and violent clashes in the streets outside, pornography readily available in movie theaters and bookstores and the explosion of sex reaching even into mainstream entertainment, and finally the election of Richard M. Nixon as president. The 1960s concluded with a very different but epochal achievement, the landing of men on the moon.

The most dramatic political development of the first half of the 1970s was Nixon's final political odyssey: his reelection by the widest popular vote margin in U.S. presidential election history—the crowning achievement of his long political career—was followed less than two years later by his resignation on the heels of the Watergate scandal. In 1970, the student movement died after the National Guard shootings at Kent State and the environmental movement was born with the first Earth Day. 1973 was the culmination of a politico-legal effort to legalize abortion, which had gone on in some fashion for only about a decade, when the U.S. Supreme Court suddenly discovered that the Constitution forbade state laws prohibiting abortion—essentially at any stage of pregnancy.[3] The result within only a few years was the legal killing of million or more unborn children each year.[4] Nixon nominated House Republican Leader Gerald R. Ford to be the new vice president after Spiro T. Agnew had to leave office because of a bribery scandal, and he assumed the presidency with Nixon's resignation (becoming the only person to assume the presidency in U.S. history who had not been elected on a national ticket). His interregnum presidency was highlighted mostly by his full pardon of Nixon for any criminal charges he might have faced from Watergate, and the evident final failure of the long U.S. adventure in Southeast Asia with the fall of South Vietnam, Laos, and Cambodia to communism (and the ensuing extermination of about a third of the Cambodian population). The Republican disarray after Watergate propelled Jimmy Carter into the presidency narrowly in 1976, the year of the underwhelming celebration of America's bicentennial. The 1970s brought federal government regulation of more areas and activities in American life than ever before, as will be discussed below. Relations between the U.S. and the U.S.S.R. seemed to thaw with the policy of détente that began under Nixon. This was coupled with Nixon's dramatic opening to the other Communist giant, the People's Republic of China. In reality, the Soviets became more assertive in different parts of the globe and engaged in a military build-up that culminated with their invasion of Afghanistan in 1979.[5] By 1980, some thought that the U.S. no longer had the upper hand in the Cold War. Along with the takeover of the U.S. embassy in Iran and the holding of its staff hostage for over a year, the country's foreign policy was in deep trouble. While Carter could claim a measure of success in U.S. Middle East policy by helping to engineer a rapprochement between Israel and Egypt, foreign policy—along with continuing economic problems (see below)—proved crucial in Carter's 1980 defeat by Ronald W. Reagan.[6]

Reagan's victory not only brought the Republican party into control of the presidency, but also of a house of Congress for the first time since 1954. It also marked the greatest success of a conservative movement in American politics that began with the disastrous Barry Goldwater candidacy of 1964. Besides major economic efforts (cutting taxes in the manner of JFK to stimulate the economy and cutting the rate of increase in federal spending, which were termed the "Reagan revolution"), Reagan moved to build up the U.S. military to face the seeming renewed aggressiveness of the U.S.S.R. Soviet President Mikhail Gorbachev's *glasnost* (openness) policy was announced in 1988, and the next year communism fell in Eastern Europe and in 1991 the U.S.S.R. collapsed. Reagan was wounded but survived an assassination attempt early in his administration in March 1981. He was sweepingly reelected in 1984, losing only one state. In 1987 his administration found itself under attack by a rejuvenated Congressional Democratic party for providing military assistance, against confusing legal restraints (as discussed in Chapter 9), to the Contra rebels opposing the pro-Communist Sandinista government in Nicaragua.

Reagan's vice president, George H.W. Bush, was elected to the presidency in 1988, and the period of divided government (i.e., with the presidency in the hands of one party and both houses of Congress in the other) that began in 1986 continued for the next four years. Bush's presidency was noted for foreign policy developments: the disintegration of the Soviet Bloc (it happened early in his term and his policy decisions had little influence on it); "Operation Just Cause" in Panama, when the U.S. militarily deposed strongman ruler and drug-trafficker Manuel Noriega after he annulled the results of a free election for president of the country; the 1991 Persian Gulf War, which followed from the Iraqi invasion of Kuwait and trimmed the sails of but did not oust from power Saddam Hussein; and the push for a post-Cold War "New World Order" with such initiatives as the North American Free Trade Agreement (NAFTA) and the new General Agreement on Tariffs and Trade (GATT) treaty, which established the World Trade Organization (WTO) to lessen trade barriers between the U.S. and her neighbors and among nations generally. The specter of renewed racial tension was presented by the South Central Los Angeles riot of 1992, which followed from the acquittal of police officers who allegedly beat habitual criminal Rodney King after stopping his car.

Despite high popularity ratings after American success in the Gulf War,[7] Bush was hampered by domestic economic problems and lost his bid for reelection to William Jefferson "Bill" Clinton (the first baby boomer to become president).[8] Clinton quickly ran into difficulty with attempts to integrate homosexuals into the military and to establish a publicly funded national health care system. He continued the international trade initiatives of Bush, securing ratification in the Senate of the NAFTA and GATT treaties.[9] The Clinton administration solidly lined up the U.S. in favor of the advancement of international abortion rights at major UN-sponsored conferences.[10] The 1994 mid-term election saw a reaction against Clinton, and the Republicans gained control of both houses of Congress for the first time since 1954 and for only the third time since before the start of the New Deal (the Democrats had held both houses for fifty-two of the previous sixty-four years, and at least one house for sixty). The Republicans rode their so-called "Contract with America" to power, which called for reduced federal spending, welfare reform, a balanced budget, less federal regulation on the environment and other matters, and reform of Congress and Congressional term limits. Clinton responded by seeming to moderate his views by joining the Republicans in enacting a welfare reform law, embracing their budget concerns, and appealing for a rejection of extremism after the 1995 bombing of the federal building in Oklahoma City. Also, the Republicans overreached when they instigated a partial federal government "shut-down" to promote their fiscal objectives. Clinton secured reelection in 1996, riding the crest of a newly found economic prosperity.[11] His second term was dominated by his impeachment for perjury following the sex scandal involving a White House intern Monica Lewinsky. He, of course, maintained the office as the Senate refused to remove him. The Clinton impeachment is discussed in Chapter 9.

The new millennium brought to the White House for only the second time in American history the son of a former president. The disputed election of 2000, which was resolved only by a U.S. Supreme Court decision about the constitutionality of a ballot recount in Florida,[12] was the first time since 1888 that the winning candidate did not secure a plurality of the popular vote. That George W. Bush's presidency, like his father's, was to be foreign policy focused was insured by the September 11, 2001 attacks on the World Trade Center and the Pentagon by Islamic terrorists less than eight months after he took office. What followed quickly was the American invasion of Afghanistan that ousted the Taliban, who had harbored Osama bin Laden's al-Queda that was responsible for the attacks. Two years later, Bush ordered a military invasion of Iraq—joined in by numerous U.S. allies—that completed the task his father had begun in the Gulf War a dozen years before of toppling the tyrannical Saddam Hussein and his Bath party. Saddam had been constrained, but proved to be increasingly uncooperative with the restrictions put on him after the Gulf War. The younger Bush acted after claiming that Saddam was seeking to build weapons of mass destruction to threaten his neighboring countries and the West. This apparently was subsequently disproven, however,[13] and American officials gave such other reasons for the war as Iraq's financial support for the families of Palestinian suicide bombers, Iraqi government human rights abuses, and a need to impose democracy on the country.[14] One of Bush's major domestic initiatives was the 2003 expansion of Medicare to include a prescription drug benefit. Bush was reelected in 2004 by defeating Senator John Kerry of Massachusetts. He escaped an attempt to assassinate him during a 2005 visit to the nation of Georgia. He tried to push a major immigration reform bill in 2007 that would have regularized the millions of illegal immigrants in the U.S., but it evoked much public controversy and was defeated.[15] In the final months of his administration, the country faced a major crisis in its financial system, a sharp stock market downturn, and the onset of a serious recession. His administration secured a massive federal "bail-out" of major financial institutions.

In the 2008 presidential election, amidst the economic turmoil just mentioned, two sitting U.S. senators (Democrat Barack H. Obama and Republican John McCain) squared off against each other. It was the first time that had happened in American history, and only twice had a sitting senator been elected president. Obama's rise had been sudden. At the time of the 2004 presidential election, he had been an Illinois *state* senator, and had served in federal office for less than four years before being elected president. Riding the crest of deep public concerns about the economy, displeasure about the prolonged Iraq war, and the unpopularity of the Bush administration, Obama won election relatively easily. He won eight of the ten largest electoral vote states and virtually swept the Northeast, industrial Midwest, and West Coast.[16] His administration has pushed a policy agenda closely identified with the political left in America: major federal subsidies for economic stimulation, expanded federal "bail-outs" for troubled financial enterprises (and even outright, temporary federal take-over of a few enterprises), greater federal control of the financial sector, greater centralized control of health care, legislation making easier federal lawsuits for alleged employment discrimination on the grounds of sex, lining up the U.S. in favor of a controversial international climate control agreement, cap-and-trade environmental legislation (which would impose legal limits industrial emissions, with fines if they are not maintained), strong support for legalized abortion and federally-funded embryonic stem-cell research, support for increasingly authoritarian leftist governments in Latin America and outreaches to the Islamic world, and efforts to wind down the American involvement in Iraq and to deal with a Taliban resurgence in Afghanistan. He also appointed several "czars" to oversee various public policy areas, which was controversial because they were given substantial power despite not needing Senate confirmation and many were noted for their extreme leftist views. Most startling was the fact that Obama was named the winner of the Nobel Peace Prize after only nine months in office and no significant foreign policy achievements. He had served on the Senate Foreign Relations Committee, but had not been distinguished for international efforts in his short four years as a U.S. senator.[17] In fact, the nominations for the prize had closed only eleven days after Obama's inauguration.[18] The major legislative achievement of the first year-and-a-half of his administration was a controversial, major expansion of the federal role in health care.

Economics and Economic and Social Welfare Policy. In the 1960s and 1970s, there were a number of long-term developments in the American economy. In 1960-70, there was a doubling of the economic growth rate and a 5% annual increase in the real growth rate. As Henry C. Dethloff writes, however, "the bloom was fading on the bush." Inflation, unemployment, and interest rates were all rising in the 1960s.[19] The balance of payments deficit had been slowly rising, and the trade deficit suddenly shot up. The dollar came under pressure from the devaluation of the British pound sterling in 1967.[20] The Vietnam War and the increased social spending of the Great Society played a significant role in stimulating inflation in the 1960s. It continued to afflict the economy throughout the 1970s, when it was mostly at double-digit rates and was further spurred by energy prices[21] (the latter was quite a reversal from the entire decade of the 1960s, when a worldwide glut of oil kept prices low).[22] The country during this period was bedeviled by stagflation, which involved high inflation plus and an unacceptably high unemployment rate. When Carter came into office, he targeted the unemployment side more vigorously than Nixon and Ford had by increasing federal spending. Then he reversed course and tried to restrain government spending, and this caused more unemployment. The result, in Tindall and Shi's words, was that he "inherited a bad situation and left it worse" and the inflation rate reached a crunching 18% in 1980.[23] Besides the above, the increase in real median family income sharply dropped from 33% in the 1960s to only 6.5% in the 1970s—even with the growth of two-income families. The concern about the just wage of the Founding Era seemed to be in the background in the economic life and practice of the time. Corporate profit levels shrank, and capital investment and productivity growth stagnated in the 1970s. As Steven F. Hayward puts it, "[g]one was the economic stability and easy growth that had characterized the rest of the post-war era."[24]

American attitudes about economic life also changed—at least somewhat. In the 1960s, Dethloff says that people began to feel that they were overwhelmed by consumer goods, and "became somewhat less preoccupied with acquisition and more concerned about order, stability, and the quality of life."[25] All of the above economic problems of the 1970s created a situation where, in Schulman's words, "[f]or the first time since the Great Depression, talk of limits and diminishing expectations" was found widely among Americans.[26] Still, America did not retreat from being a consumer culture. As James T. Patterson says about the 1970s, "The more people bought, the more they seemed to crave. Wants became needs."[27] Thus, while there was at least a small resurgence of part of the spirit of the Founding culture of constraint, simplicity, and temperance in the area of material well-being, it would be difficult to say that there was a new dawning of that era's concern about avoiding luxury. As we see below, this new sense of constraint, such as it was, certainly did not manifest itself on sexual matters and manners—two other areas where it was so strong during the Founding Era. Moreover, even though government anti-poverty policy (see below) seemed to view poverty as a kind of static condition that could with sufficient effort be conquered, it really was relative and what an acceptable living standard was changed as economic growth occurred.[28] There were also further structural developments in the American economy. The trends toward economic concentration and the separation of management and ownership—so contrary to the conditions of the Founding Era—that we have said began to develop significantly in the late nineteenth century continued. Dethloff notes that there were "relatively fewer and larger firms." From the end of World War II, automation, mass-production, and a "mass-consumption society" stimulated the "enlargement in private plants and production." One of the main reasons that government power and private sector economic concentration both expanded, however, was because of war (including the Cold War).[29] Dethloff argues that while there were more constraints on them, on balance property rights continued to expand, and such entrepreneurial characteristics as individual opportunity, competition, and innovation were "more evident…than at any time in the past."[30] This spirit of entrepreneurship and the regulation and restraints on property use, as we have seen, conformed to the Founding Era—though the degree and manner of the latter, as noted below, did not.

Another aspect of what might be called a structural change in the economy—although in a different sense—occurring in these decades was the transition from a substantial manufacturing base to a more service-oriented economy. From 1970 to 1980, service jobs increased from an already high 60% of the economy to 70%. Many jobs, especially in manufacturing, moved abroad;[31] the remaining service jobs generally were lower paying.[32] Overall labor union membership also declined, from over 30% of the workforce in the mid-1960s to 23% in 1980 (its steady decline was to continue until it reached less 13% of the workforce in 2004).[33] The result was that labor unions lost strength[34] (except for public employee unions, which grew and became *more* powerful).[35] The combination of these developments doubtless helped to cause the just wage problem above.

Government economic policy, for the most part, was interventionist in the 1960s and 1970s, and the business community actually favored it to some degree. An era of heightened capital investment that began in the early 1960s demanded more employees, so business favored more liberal immigration laws (this happened in 1965), programs to address unemployment (which JFK and LBJ pushed), government training programs (like the Great Society's Job Corps), and a condition of social stability and calm (which Great Society social welfare programs implicitly promised, but as the 1960s wore on certainly did not deliver).[36] Facing the economic problems above, LBJ moved to try to stem the outflow of gold from the country and the movement in general of American investment and spending abroad even to the point of trying to tax foreign travel. He also imposed an income tax surcharge.[37] Late in his administration, he tried to stimulate the economy—and supposedly address a social problem—by pushing through a housing act that authorized the building of 1.7 million federally subsidized housing units over a three-year period. Thus, during the Nixon administration that began the following year the federal government built more units than in all previous administrations combined, although by his second term he suspended all subsidized housing programs. The program had witnessed persistent scandals, a situation where most of the benefit arguably was going to builders and lenders, the inability of many low-income people to qualify for the housing, and new owners who could not afford to keep up the properties. It also caused a housing glut and perhaps even aggravated slum conditions.[38] Other federal programs similarly benefited corporate interests, such as agricultural programs that encouraged large-scale agribusiness, federal highway spending and subsidized pipeline construction that helped the petroleum industry, and of course defense spending that profited many industries. The latter also played a major role in stimulating the economy of the Sunbelt, even as the Frostbelt economy declined.[39] This was all in the tradition of federal internal improvements, but on a much larger scale reaching to many more things than earlier in history. Federal spending in general grew faster under Nixon than under LBJ. In fact, Nixon massively increased domestic spending. He also imposed more regulation on the economy than any president since FDR. As Hayward points out, between 1970 and 1974 eight new independent regulatory agencies and eight other executive agencies were established, and another thirteen existing independent agencies and twenty-two other executive agencies gained additional powers. He concludes, "the regulatory revolution was...[his] most profound legacy."[40] It was another striking example that even Republican presidents who campaigned against increased federal power wound up going along with the twentieth-century trend towards centralization. Nixon made other economic regulatory moves that were hardly viewed as traditional, conservative, or restraintist: taking the country off the gold standard, devaluing the dollar and allowing it to gain its own valuation in international markets, and imposing—for a time—wage and price controls.[41] Carter tried to bring back JFK's "jawboning"—i.e., the use of moral suasion and arm-twisting to get business and labor to restrain price and wage increases—to control inflation, but was not very successful; nor was the Federal Reserve Board when it tried to do so by hiking interest rates. The economic problems of the time, then, occurred under a regimen of already substantial centralized economic control.[42] While businesses found the increased burden of regulation costly, to be sure, they came over time to strongly influence the government agencies that regulated them, and certain of their number often worked to get preferential treatment from them. Further, government agencies often had self-interest—involving in some way institutional or bureaucratic self-perpetuation—in keeping intact the business arrangements they were charged with regulating, even if the broader public interest was being hurt.[43] The 1970s also brought a new enthusiasm for national economic planning and government management of the economy—not to be paralleled again until near the end of the first decade of the twenty-first century—that reached its "high-water mark" with the passage of a watered-down Humphrey-Hawkins full employment act.[44]

While the mid-1960s brought a tax cut, the 1968 tax surcharge was the beginning of a heightened tax burden imposed on Americans throughout the 1970s at all levels of government. Between 1964 and 1980, the Social Security payroll tax increased eightfold. On the state and local levels, property taxes spiked upward. Thanks to inflation and higher energy prices, Americans in the 1970s saw increased taxes but a stagnation or decline in their real incomes. With many states running large budget surpluses, a tax revolt broke out in such states as California and Massachusetts and many other states enacted state spending caps.[45] While there was certainly no problem of "taxation without representation"—a great cry of immediate pre-Revolutionary America—the fact that taxes had gotten out of control suggests that the spirit behind that principle was perhaps diminished in the minds of American politicians and government officials in the 1970s.

The federal government's social welfare role expanded markedly during the Great Society. It brought such major new legislative initiatives as Medicare (government-funded health care for the elderly), Medicaid (government-funded health care for the poor), Head Start (government-funded pre-school programs for poor children to supposedly help them overcome obstacles they frequently face in achieving academic success in their school years), Legal Services (government-subsidized legal assistance for low income people in civil matters), the Elementary and Secondary Education Act (federal assistance to public education), the Higher Education Act of 1965 (which increased federal assistance to colleges and universities and provided grants and subsidized educational loans to college students), and perhaps most noteworthy LBJ's "War on Poverty." These programs and others, of course, were touted as necessary to help those in need, who were not able to have the same access to needed services and able to improve the quality of their lives as more advantaged people were. There is much dispute both as to whether that was the case and if they genuinely helped the people they were targeting. There were also unintended consequences. Allen J. Matusow writes that there is no evidence that Medicare significantly affected the mortality of the elderly, or that Medicaid provided more ready access to health care or a better quality of care for the poor than the previous charity care did. Congress appears just to have "theorized," without conclusive evidence, that "lack of income was a barrier to treatment."[46] The cost of health care had been increasing since private health insurance was instituted in the 1950s and as forms of insurance—but more universal—Medicare and

Medicaid added considerably to that. The reimbursement mechanism in the law further helped insure "galloping medical price inflation."[47] Their major economic effect was perhaps to "transfer...income from middle-class taxpayers to middle-class health care professionals."[48] Moreover, the Medicaid program created new inequalities in health care among states and among the welfare and the non-welfare poor and also witnessed fraud and abuses.[49]

The much-heightened federal regulatory and social welfare roles, of course, indicated an intensification of the twentieth century trend toward governmental centralization that was completely at odds with the Founding. While the concern for the less advantaged that, in some sense, motivated the new social welfare programs was in accord with the Founding culture's norm of being "thy brother's keeper," having government sweepingly take on this task would have been a foreign notion. Further, the effect of both allowing interest groups and certain segments—even well-off ones—to become advantaged at the expense of others simultaneously offended the norms of upholding the public good and heedfulness of the need for civic friendship (which, as seen below, suffered great stresses in the 1960s). Further, the fact that this perhaps unintended consequence happened and that at least some of these new programs—which were quite vast and expensive—may have been unnecessary hardly bespeaks the "shrewd practical intelligence," attention to frugality, and practice of promise-keeping of the Founding Era.

The reach of LBJ's War on Poverty is seen by this 1964 quote: "'We stand at the edge of the greatest era in the life of any nation. For the first time in world history we have the abundance and the ability to free every man from hopeless want...This nation...has man's first chance to create...a society of success without squalor.'"[50] This was what Peter Clecak called "the left-liberal view of the American future: freedom from the old ills of scarcity—poverty and exploitation—and genuine liberty and full equality of opportunity to pursue self-fulfillment in the new age of abundance."[51] Political commentator Richard Rovere said LBJ's view "'was evangelistic and almost utopian.'"[52] Matusow says that "the War on Poverty was destined to be one of the great failures of twentieth-century liberalism....[it] did little to diminish inequality and...failed measurably to reduce poverty."[53] Perhaps the Great Society's problem was that it did not have a proper understanding of equality in light of the Founding Fathers, or that it believed wrongly that government could effectively address poverty and inequality, or that it simply failed to grasp that poverty—as noted above—is a relative thing and one cannot likely solve it for all time. In any event, it did not embrace the realism of the Founders. The same was the case with federal education funding. Great Society planners apparently thought they could improve the academic achievement of poor children by simply pumping more money into public education; this theory, like the poor's putative lack of access to health care, was hardly questioned as the legislation was pushed. Very soon, it became apparent that the theory was not correct,[54] and educational research since that time has consistently proven that more money does not necessarily translate into better educational results.[55] Also, as with health care and housing, the new federal programs seemed to benefit primarily vested interests: school districts, teachers unions, and state educational bureaucracies. Again, it was not so clear that the public interest, instead of particularistic ones, was truly promoted. Matusow says that while Head Start did not meet early expectations, it was a "Great Society program that worked."[56] Other later evidence has raised doubts even about this program.[57] Legal Services helped the poor by providing routine legal assistance, but was not so successful in helping to bring about the institutional change its planners in the Office of Economic Opportunity (OEO) envisioned.[58] Moreover, government-supplied legal assistance has not always measured up to its promise, as illustrated by the serious deficiencies in the even more basic legal assistance provided to the poor in criminal matters, as guaranteed by U.S. Supreme Court decision and carried out through various public defender arrangements.[59] Most Job Corps enrollees did not complete the program, the costs of their training were exceptionally high, and follow-up studies did not show good results.[60] It seems that almost all the major Great Society domestic initiatives betrayed the lack of Founding realism and shrewd practical intelligence noted above.

As mentioned, Nixon sharply increased domestic spending. Among the new social welfare initiatives during his presidency were Supplemental Security Income (SSI), the institution of cost of living adjustments (COLA's) for Social Security recipients, and the expansion of the food stamp and Medicaid programs. His effort to provide a guaranteed minimum income for all citizens— the Family Assistance Program—failed in Congress.[61] Not only did the latter deviate from the Founding Era's sense about the reach of governmental power and responsibility, but also from its concern about promoting a just wage. If government has to provide grants to citizens because they cannot make ends meet, it probably signals that they are not receiving a just wage. Moreover, the perceived need for all the new social welfare programs discussed in this section illustrates how significant economic inequalities had become—which, it will be recalled, were largely absent during the Founding Era—even while the citizenry grew in affluence and America remained essentially the middle class society it had been then.

With the increased domestic spending during the 1960s and 1970s—to say nothing of the Vietnam War spending—it was not surprising that the federal budget deficit sharply increased. Beginning with LBJ and all the way through Carter, deficit spending became the order of the day.[62] The acceptability of this followed from the embracing of Keynesian economics—which, as we have said, was quite willing to accept deficits if government spending was needed to stimulate the economy—by American presidential administrations during this period.[63] This deviation from one of the principles the Founders thought needed to sustain a democratic republic had become routine and substantial.

The Role and Powers of Government, Relations Among the Three Branches of the Federal Government, and Federal-State Relations. With the new federal emphasis on social welfare during the 1960s, Hayward tells us "the third wave of the progressive administrative state began." The first had been the Progressive Era, when the federal government first tried to address the problems of industrialization. The second was the New Deal, which was motivated by the belief that substantial federal spending was needed to keep the economy churning. Building on these, the third wave concerned social engineering.[64] One thing built upon another. It was now believed that deep-seated social problems, and not just economic ones, should be tackled. The War on Poverty made apparent just how ambitious the aims and reach of government had become. We see the range of these aims above, which signaled that the scope of federal power was sharply increasing and that thus there was more political centralization. This third wave had great confidence in the burgeoning social science research that was taking place. There was a paradox: on the one hand, it had overwhelming confidence about success in tackling such seemingly massive and perennial problems as poverty, but on the other it saw public problems as more complicated than ever. Now, only "sophisticated legislation" and "extensive bureaucratic management" utilizing the tools of the new social science could achieve results. Public policy now seemed beyond the grasp of ordinary citizens. Hayward says that it made "the idea of citizen self-government seem quaint or obsolete."[65] It was an expanded version of the attitude that we saw in the Progressive Era of scientific administration supplanting politics, of public problems being seen as technical and not political matters. It will be recalled, however, that the roots of such a technocratic notion were way back with the transcendentalists.

The latter meant, of course, that the power of the federal bureaucracy was expanding. Since the Progressive Era, the president increasingly had lost control of parts of the executive branch of the U.S. Government. It was not just that some believed that the executive branch was now too large for the president "to control meaningfully" (this is discussed in Chapter 9), but by delegating so much policymaking authority to executive agencies the permanent bureaucracy had become a major legislative force itself.[66] In fact, while in theory career federal civil servants are subject to political (i.e., presidential) control and are expected to follow the policy direction of the administration in power, they are often not neutral in practice.[67] The above "third wave" necessarily gave more power to the federal bureaucracy. This sharp expansion of the power of the unelected federal bureaucracy, of course, continued the long trend discussed in previous chapters of reversing the Founding norm of decentralization, damaged (along with other developments below) federalism, and compromised the Founders' principle of popular sovereignty (which the above discussion of the third wave suggests was increasingly irrelevant to this period's policy innovators and reformers). More prerogative in the hands of unelected bureaucrats compromised both the democratic and the republican dimensions of the American democratic republic, and enhanced elite control which in no way could be considered anything like the natural aristocracy of the Founders. The narrow technical and functional expertise that people supposedly had to exhibit to become career civil servants was in no way equivalent to the wisdom, prudence, moral vision, public spiritedness, and capability of governance that the Founders saw in a natural aristocracy (as we have said before). Further, since these developments aggrandized more power in the executive branch—even while control over the bureaucracy kept slipping away from presidents, and

Congress made this aggrandizement possible by sweeping delegations of legislative-type power[68]—it compromised the principle of separation of powers (even apart from the actions of the presidents of the period, as discussed below).

In spite of his sharply expanding both federal spending and regulation, Nixon actually sought to cut many federal programs and attempted to get control of the bureaucracy. Watergate and probably just the sheer challenge of doing this resulted in his making virtually no progress, however.[69] The main ways that Nixon sought to do this were vetoes of domestic spending bills that he thought excessive (but Congress overrode some of these and, again, in the end domestic spending increased), executive reorganization (which Carter also tried later in the decade, and neither effort went hardly anywhere),[70] trying to focus as much domestic policymaking as possible in the White House staff and the Executive Office of the President (this just had the effect of further expanding another part of the bureaucracy—the part "close-in" to him, insulating him from sufficient discussion and getting needed diverse views, and perhaps unduly expanding presidential power),[71] and impounding appropriated funds for programs he opposed (which further unduly expanded presidential power and was almost completely rejected by the courts).[72]

These observations about expanding presidential power underscore another central development of the 1960s and 1970s: the shifting strength of the presidency vis-à-vis Congress. We have seen throughout this book the waxing and waning of the power of these two branches with respect to each other in the course of American history. In the 1960s and early 1970s, it was presidential power that was waxing, with the massive force build-up and extended conflict in Vietnam without a declaration of war, the explosion in the use of executive agreements in making American foreign policy commitments (circumventing the constitutional requirements for Senate approval of treaties),[73] and the fact that Congress almost rubber-stamped LBJ's Great Society initiatives (without, as stated above, sufficient evidence of their need). The Johnson administration tried to argue that the 1964 Gulf of Tonkin Resolution essentially performed the function of a declaration of war, although the Nixon administration later declared that it was irrelevant. Both administrations—Nixon's more avowedly—believed that the president had the inherent power to carry on such a prolonged military action, with or without Congressional approval.[74] Nixon also stretched presidential power even further than LBJ with impoundment, his constitutionally questionable usage of the pocket veto power (i.e., using it even during brief Congressional recesses),[75] and, during Watergate, his claim that executive privilege permitted him to withhold evidence even when needed for a criminal prosecution (which was also stymied by the courts, in the famous 1974 Supreme Court decision of *U.S. v. Nixon*[76]). These actions of LBJ and, even more, Nixon damaged separation of powers and checks and balances. It was only because of the judicial action that further erosion in a couple of these areas was checked.

After American forces were pulled out of Vietnam in early 1973 and, especially, once Watergate heated up, the shift of power went in the direction of Congress. Congress passed the War Powers Act in 1973, which put clear limits on the president's power to commit troops to hostilities without Congressional approval. It also passed the Budget and Impoundment Control Act of 1974, which was aimed at giving Congress further control over the annual budget process and disallowing outright presidential impoundment of appropriated funds (the president could still *request* that Congress rescind specific spending items, but it has seldom agreed to do so).[77] The Ethics in Government Act of 1978 subjected the executive branch—especially political appointees—to additional scrutiny beyond the normal Congressional committee investigations by making a provision for an independent counsel to be appointed to investigate alleged wrongdoing.[78] Although his status as an unelected president without a national political base probably was a factor, Ford had a higher percentage of his regular (i.e., non-pocket) vetoes overridden than any twentieth-century president[79] and Congress also stopped him from providing military aid to the collapsing South Vietnamese government.[80] Indeed, in the immediate post-Vietnam War era Congress gained an increased role in foreign policymaking generally.[81] While the "bleeding" of presidential power in foreign affairs to Congress stopped with the accession of Reagan, the War Powers Act—its main legislative legacy—continues in force, even though much question exists about whether it is an unconstitutional restraint on the president.[82]

While Congressional power waxed on foreign affairs, a problematical judicial interpretation restricted the power of individual members of Congress in another important, but much less noticed, way. Democratic Senator William Proxmire of Wisconsin, who was known for exposing wasteful federal government spending, started to give out what he called the "Golden Fleece Award of the Month" to highlight an instance of what he viewed as a poor use of taxpayer dollars. In one case, he gave the award to several federal agencies for funding one scientist's research on the behavioral patterns of certain animals. As was customary, he provided information of the award to the press and by newsletter to his constituents. The scientist sued Proxmire, and eventually the Supreme Court ruled that the speech or debate clause, which provides legal protection for members of Congress for their statements in Congress, did not extend to press releases and such newsletters (even though they just reported what he had said on the Senate floor about the award).[83] In a certain way, this decision weakened Congressional power, and indirectly weakened checks and balances because, first, Congress would have to be more guarded than before in how it conducted oversight over the executive branch, and second, its members were more limited now in how they could arouse public opinion to give more force to this central principle of the Founding.

The question of excessive power in one of the branches presented itself in the 1960s and 1970s at least as strongly with reference to the courts as the presidency. During these decades, the federal courts became embroiled in public policies and controversies such as school desegregation that evoked much criticism about their exceeding their constitutional role.[84] Perhaps nothing in this area enflamed public anger as much as judicially mandated busing of public school students in the 1970s—this involved the assignment of pupils to a school irrespective of parental preference and busing them there—which in many respects seemed to be less desegregation than forced integration aiming to achieve percentages of Caucasian and Negro students in public schools that the courts deemed desirable. Besides desegregation, this period witnessed judicial overreaching in such areas as legislative reapportionment (where in *Baker v. Carr*[85] and its progeny the Supreme Court essentially took over what had historically been a function of the political branches and the states and imposed a particular view of representation based only on relatively equal population levels), the spoils system (where it disallowed the firing of patronage employees[86]), obscenity and pornography (where for well over a decade it largely paralyzed legislative attempts—which had been routine in American history—to prohibit or regulate it[87]), criminal justice (where it imposed the exclusionary rule as a constitutional mandate, when it had long been a legislative decision and had not even been a part of the common law tradition[88]), capital punishment (where it began to put conditions on a practice that had previously been in the province of legislatures, and even suspended its imposition at all for four years in the 1970s),[89] religious establishment (where it increasingly took upon itself to regulate or even forbid religious expression within public contexts and governmental aide to religion that had previously been decisions of the political branches),[90] and of course abortion, where the Court (as discussed above) suddenly discovered a right to privacy that had the effect of striking down all existing state laws restricting abortion (it even held that neither an unborn child's father nor the parents of a pregnant minor could veto the abortion decision[91]). In addition to embellishing the role of the judiciary, the actions in these areas also had the effect of limiting the prerogatives of the states and thereby weakened federalism. As stated before in this book, excessive judicial power—to say nothing of judicial supremacy—was clearly outside of the Founders' intent. The period of the 1960s and 1970s saw the most consistently sweeping and substantial judicial power in the history of the Republic, the one in which the claim of a condition of judicial supremacy could be taken most seriously. (To be sure, the previous periods of judicial overreaching, such as the substantive due process era, made it much easier for the Court to act so boldly now—but they did not compare to the level of power the Court now assumed.) Moreover, unlike the overreaching of executive power that led to a reaction and reassertion of Congress, the sweep of judicial power was essentially unrestrained during this period. It was not surprising that prominent legal scholars produced books such as *Government by Judiciary*[92] and the deliberately ironically entitled *The Least Dangerous Branch*.[93] Judicial power represented the most obvious distortion in the period from 1960 to 1980 of the Founding's crucial principles of separation of powers and checks and balances. Regarding the latter, the Court was not only checking the political branches in many cases when it should not have, but there was essentially no response—i.e., no check imposed by those branches—to the expansive exercise of judicial power.

Further, by effectively making public policy unelected judges were adding to an undercutting of the democratic dimension of the American democratic republic. This happened even while decisions like *Baker v. Carr* effectively overemphasized the democratic dimension by embracing an extreme notion of political equality at odds with the Founders.

Federalism was also weakened during this period, as it had been previously in the twentieth century, by the federal government's grants-in-aid programs. Actually, this factor may have been more responsible for hurting federalism than in previous decades because of the increased number of such programs in more areas, the increased number of conditions attached by the federal government, and the fact that in the first part of LBJ's administration the federal government often bypassed the states to give categorical grants to local governments—which are legally treated as subdivisions of the states, controlled by them—directly.[94] In an ongoing way, the federal government continued to leapfrog the states and deal directly with big city governments to implement programs.[95] Indeed in the LBJ period, OEO originally sought to circumvent even local governments and to provide grants directly to community organizations (sometimes to challenge and change those very governments).[96] The federal government was now interfacing directly with citizens and citizen groups, which was a sharp change from its historical role. During the Great Society, the federal government clearly sought to centralize more domestic decisionmaking power. Federalism scholar Daniel J. Elazar writes that even while there was much state and local control over the grant programs, Washington was "willing to apply various forms of pressure...to get them to conform to its demands."[97] In general, the lower levels of government became more *financially dependent* on Washington during this period. Elazar writes in 1972 that the "overall trend" was "toward a larger federal role in financing governmental activities on all planes."[98] This was a long way from the understanding of federalism of the Founding Fathers.

While the federal role mushroomed, it must be understood that this was a part of a broader expansion of the role of government in general in American life in the twentieth century. As Elazar points out, since the New Deal state and local expenditures—apart from federal grant programs—increased "rapidly."[99]

The almost open-ended judicial interpretation of the interstate commerce clause that sharply increased the scope of federal power (discussed in Chapter 6) was even further applied in the 1960s to uphold federal civil rights legislation. Even if this was for a good end, it signaled more centralization and yet more weakening of federalism. Other statutory developments, constitutional changes, and judicial decisions—again, with a civil rights motivation—partially federalized voting and elections, which essentially had been a state function throughout American history.[100]

The increasingly direct interfacing of the federal government with citizens was noted above. The 1960s and 1970s brought a level of regulation to the private sector—including increasingly the nonprofit sector—that was unparalleled in American history and demonstrated the increasing sweep of federal power. This was seen in such subjects as education, the environment, consumer goods, private clubs, and even parental upbringing of their children. Probably the New Deal had opened the door to some of this, but the battle against racial segregation by the Civil Rights Act of 1964, with its ushering in of federal regulation—in the name of interstate commerce—of even small private businesses it had hitherto had nothing to do with, provided the momentum. In higher education the taking of federal grants for research or the mere participation in student loan programs backed by the federal government subjected a private—even a religiously-affiliated—institution to a massive number of federal regulations. It got to the point in the 1970s where a mere complaint to the federal educational bureaucracy brought the full force of the federal government upon a hapless institution and the former effectively forced aspects of affirmative action on colleges and universities.[101] The 1960s brought direct federal funding of public pre-college education, and with it came an increasing number of regulations. It even went to the point—irrespective of the First Amendment—of exerting pressure on school textbook publishers to eliminate supposed sex stereotyping in books.[102] Both federal and state courts also became heavily involved in education matters.[103] Broad unspecific mandates establishing such 1970s-era agencies as the Environmental Protection Agency and the Consumer Product Safety Commission resulted in their exercising such wide-ranging powers over so many things as had hardly been seen before.[104] In 1969, the Supreme Court went so far as to say that the 1964 Civil Rights Act applied to a private recreational facility in Arkansas because three of the four items sold at its snack bar had moved in interstate commerce.[105] Some states refused to give liquor licenses to private clubs whose membership was limited only to certain racial, ethnic, or religious groups.[106] Whether one agreed with these actions or not, it must be acknowledged that they represented a substantial new reach of government into private matters. In 1974, the Congress passed the Child Abuse Prevention and Treatment Act (CAPTA) which led to the construction of a nationwide system, directed and administered at the state and local level, which gave governmental agencies sweeping power to intervene into families putatively in the name of preventing child abuse and neglect. With almost universally vague laws about the meaning of those terms, the ease of making even conjectural or false reports anonymously via hotlines, and a perspective that prevention of a grave evil justifies easy preventative intervention, a massive number of American families found themselves investigated and their childrearing practices—that often in no way involved abuse or neglect—regimented by government.[107]

The open-ended interpretation of constitutional provisions like the commerce clause not only undercut federalism, but also compromised the principle of the rule of law. The same was true, of course, of the broad, unspecific, vague statutes and regulations that were being churned out. CAPTA in practice became an official back-door assault on the family that the Founding Era saw as so crucial—even as what is said below illustrates the many "unofficial," cultural assaults on it that were also taking place in the 1960s and 1970s.

Most of the above developments in one way or another compromised liberty and, when religiously-affiliated institutions were involved, freedom of religion—both central principles of the Founding.

While the perspective of the reigning liberalism no doubt encouraged the growth of government during this period, Dethloff points to two other factors.

He says, "[p]opulation growth and democratic values encouraged expansion in government services."[108] In other words, democratization, paradoxically, helped to cause bigger, more pervasive, and more centralized government. An aspect of this democratization is the overwhelming presence of interest groups at different levels of government.[109] Tocqueville foresaw this in some sense happening in a democratic political order. Of course, he did not know of the contemporary, sophisticated, often well-heeled organized interest group, but (as mentioned in Chapter 4) he saw how associational activity was necessary for people in a democratic republic—all standing as equal individuals with limited influence on their own—to accomplish things in politics and other spheres.[110] The influence of interest groups in the 1960s and 1970s context was noted above. As Theodore Lowi argued in his famous 1969 book, *The End of Liberalism* (referred to in Chapter 7), government expanded in the twentieth century because it responded to the demands of interest groups which, as the above indicates, gained more and more influence and—for all practical purposes—control over government. The "interest group government" discussed in Chapter 7 became more and more of a reality with the third wave above. This raised questions about whether the control of the effects of faction—the central theme of Federalist 10—was any longer adequately occurring. The progression of democratization since the Jacksonian Era that this book has repeatedly spoken about, then, had the seemingly paradoxical effect of stimulating increasingly distant government carried out by an increasingly larger number of unelected officials and operatives. Democratization over time, then, led to a diminishing of both the democratic and the republican side of the Founders' democratic republic.

That leads to the final point of this section about the 1960s and 1970s. The specter raised in Chapter 7 about how bigger government might have the effect of the makers of law not subjecting themselves to it—a basic principle stressed by the Founders to insure a democratic republic—became a reality in this period. Such statutes passed in the 1960s and 1970s as the Freedom of Information Act (FOIA), the Occupation Safety and Health Act (OSHA), the Employee Retirement Income Security Act (ERISA), and the Age Discrimination Act specifically exempted either Congress, the executive branch, or both.[111]

Political Developments, Trends, and Reform. Hayward writes that during the last three decades of the twentieth century, "America's thinking about social and political life…changed more than perhaps any nation in such a short time."[112] The basis for this change was the transformation of the liberalism, suggested above, that was so much in control for the middle five decades of that century. The changes that occurred in its general perspective affected matters that concerned both foreign and domestic policy. The decisive move of mainstream American liberalism into a solidly anti-Communist stance in the early years of the Cold War under Truman[113]—buttressed by liberalism's sense that it had to prove itself after the attacks it faced during the Hiss case and the McCarthy era (see Chapter 7)—was reversed in the 1960s. Although the damage done by McCarthy had caused doubts, the Vietnam War—engineered as it was by liberals in the JFK and LBJ administrations—finally brought anti-communism into disrepute among liberals.[114] In the midst of this, the outlook of liberalism changed from one of confidence and optimism to one of negativism, limits, scarcity, and an increasingly critical stance toward America herself. While the Vietnam War was perhaps mostly responsible for this, Hayward says that it also came to see that its easy belief that the state could solve all social problems and generate economic growth was unmerited.[115] This viewpoint persisted until the Obama presidency, when liberalism's 1960's outlook reasserted itself even more aggressively.[116] Most dramatically, liberalism—under the influence of the New Left[117]—changed from a doctrine basically concerned about the economic, social welfare, and labor matters that were part of the second wave above to one that now stressed "lifestyle" freedom and that saw the respect for liberty become an endorsement of personal autonomy (e.g., counterculture, sexual liberation, abortion, etc. [discussed below]).[118]

As liberalism moved left, the Democratic party took on a more leftist tinge. The party was increasingly taken over by leftist activists in the early 1970s,[119] reaching an early high point with the presidential nomination of Senator George S. McGovern in 1972. While the left suffered a major defeat that year, Watergate diminished the effects of that and in the long-term the Democratic party came to be inordinately driven by leftist "interest groups" of various kinds. Sociologist David Carlin writes that the left moved to dominance in the Democratic party with the decline and collapse of the old local political machines. There was a vacuum of political power, which was filled by ideologues and their more affluent supporters who were well placed in opinion-making circles throughout the country. The Democratic party became less a working class party and more of an educated, upper middle-class one.[120] The intelligentsia took a leading role both in liberalism and in the Democratic party.[121] What also became prominent in the Democratic party after 1972 were "cause groups" and identity politics,[122] in which different social groups (ethnic, racial, and sexual)—spearheaded by small numbers of activists—used the party to air their real or imagined grievances. Their causes were often given center stage. Identity politics put the focus squarely on certain elements—those who were in some sense considered "oppressed" minorities (although one of those groups, women, actually constituted a majority)—and their claims were being made, often quite aggressively, against the community. Often, the people making up the elements in question had at best a tenuous sense of cohesion or common identity, and did not necessarily support the claims various spokesmen made on their behalf. Identity politics seemed to stress the parts of the community as against the whole; it arguably focused on what divided people instead of unity.

Two points appear here that were sharply at odds with the Founders' conception of a democratic republic: Just as an elite—which in no serious sense could be said to be a natural aristocracy of the Founders' thinking—by occupying the bureaucracy and the courts gained an overwhelming influence on American government, it gained control of the Democratic party. Again, the democratic element of the American democratic republic was weakened. In the meantime, the republican element was not likely being strengthened since there was no certainty that this elite had any great wisdom as the Founders' natural aristocracy would have so that it would have had the capability of reigning in the democratic impulse with sound statesmanlike judgment. It was simply economically advantaged and ideologically driven. Its greater educational attainment was not for the most part of the nature of the sound, traditional liberal arts kind of education that the Founders viewed as essential for a successful democratic republic (as discussed earlier). Secondly, the divisions spawned by identity politics undermined the Founders' belief that part of the purpose of government was to promote the common good and did not seem to evoke the cooperative ethos and the concern about the community and the general welfare overall that was part of the Founding Era's culture. It also could be said that particularistic-oriented identity politics had the effect of weakening the republican side of our democratic republic because, after all, the term "republic" most fundamentally means "public concerns."[123]

If the new activists who came to dominate the Democratic party were an elite, the reforms that opened the door for them paradoxically represented a further democratization of sorts of American political life. After its raucous 1968 convention, which saw intense conflict between old-line party regulars—the machine politicians Carlin speaks about—and the ideologically-driven reformers and anti-Vietnam War elements, the Democratic party set up a commission whose co-chairman was McGovern to open up participation in the party's presidential nomination activity to more people.[124] A whole range of crucial changes were instituted or resulted from the commission's decisions. Since some of the changes required state legislation they also ended up affecting the Republican party as well.[125] These changes included: the requirement that *all* convention delegates be selected through procedures that insured that all Democratic voters could participate[126] (later the party modified this to permit Democratic officeholders to automatically become delegates[127]); the end of the unit rule, which required all a state's convention delegates at party conventions to cast their votes for the candidate supported by the majority of them;[128] the proliferation of presidential primaries;[129] the use of caucuses (or public meetings) in the absence of primaries to select most convention delegates;[130] and the abolition after 1972 of "winner-take-all" primaries, so that candidates would have to receive a number of delegates proportional to their share of the primary vote.[131] These changes were all in the Jacksonian spirit, and eliminated remaining obstacles to political democracy (at least electorally). In this area, the democratic element of the American democratic republic tilted even more lopsidedly away from the republican.

In a different direction politically, the late 1970s and the 1980s brought a resurgence of in the use of referendum and initiative devices—a kind of neo-populism—as part of a grass-roots tax revolt in some states.[132] This was occasioned by the increasing doubt about government programs and solutions above, the economic problems of the period, and tax formulas that led to a swelling of state budget surpluses (noted above) even while tax rates for financially pressed citizens continued to climb.[133] The 1960s and 1970s also saw "procedural hurdles" to voting increasingly cleared away (the aforementioned poll tax, residency requirements, and other obstacles). It was a further expression of democratization. It is interesting to note, however, that as this occurred voter turnout began a steady decline.[134] One other major effort, after the 1968 election, that did not succeed would have been the ultimate democratization of American presidential politics: the abolition of the electoral college. The Bayh-Celler constitutional amendment proposal in 1969, which would have substituted a system whereby the winner of the popular vote would win the presidency if he received at least 40% (with a national runoff if no candidate received at least that percentage), cleared the House of Representatives. It passed through the Senate Judiciary Committee and had majority support in the Senate, but was stopped by a filibuster (which meant it would not have commanded the necessary two-thirds vote).[135]

The Democratic party largely dominated the American political scene in the 1960s and 1970s. Besides controlling both houses of Congress during this entire period, two key elections—the Goldwater debacle of 1964 and the 1974 post-Watergate midterm election—gave them extraordinary majorities in both houses. They, of course, also controlled the presidency for twelve of the twenty years. Even while not in the presidency, they had a predominant position during the last year and a half of the weakened Nixon presidency and during the two and a half years of the Ford presidency.

Watergate saw a descent into an ugliness in political tactics that may not have been previously matched, with not just the notorious Watergate break-in but the longer standing practices of political spying and dirty tricks that were used in the 1972 campaign.[136] The 1960-1980 period also saw nasty political rhetoric and advertising. During the 1964 campaign the Democrats aired a television ad of a little girl pulling petals from a daisy while a nuclear explosion was superimposed in the background, suggesting clearly that Goldwater would be ready to head recklessly into a nuclear war.[137] In 1968, the Republicans ran a television ad that contrasted images of the "happy warrior" Democratic nominee Hubert H. Humphrey with suffering, impoverished people, suggesting that he was impervious to the latter. In the 1970 mid-term elections, the national Republican campaign, in the words of Manchester, followed a strategy that "blazed away at the least attractive aspects of...[an] opponent's record, ideas, mannerisms, and private life."[138] In the 1980 campaign, Carter claimed that Reagan would divide "black from white, Jew from Christian, North from South, rural from urban."[139] Although this had been observed, as we have seen, since the earliest days of American politics it perhaps reached one of its low points during the Nixon period, and certainly cannot be said to have upheld the norms of civility, good manners, and self-restraint of the Founding culture.

The political developments of the time helped to alter citizen attitudes about politics and their government. On the one side, there was a kind of "revolution of rising expectations" among groups such as the poor who the Great Society was supposed to help. They grew impatient and frustrated. On the other side, many in the public thought that much money had been wasted and were angry that such efforts had seemed to lead only to urban unrest and such phenomena as Black Nationalism.[140] In the 1970s this led, in Schulman's words, to "skepticism about large-scale efforts to remake the world."[141] Americans now were more prepared to turn away from government to the private sector for things, which seemed to accord with the norm of self-reliance of the Founding. People "applauded smaller government and accepted diminished services."[142] In fact, though, even if some services were cut back government really did not get smaller. A major transformation occurred in public attitudes toward government from the mid-1960s to the mid-1970s (after Vietnam, failed social programs, and a president and vice president who were forced to leave office): public trust in government sharply declined.[143] It is perhaps too much to say that this signaled a popular turning from the hopeful belief in man's possibilities that characterized Founding culture, but it perhaps showed an increasing cynicism that was not in its spirit.

As the Democratic party made reforms, the Democratic majority in Congress pushed through reforms of that institution's procedures and practices. The effect of this perhaps was the further eroding of restraints on the democratic impulse, and thus continuing the long-term alteration of the republican character of the American political order. The most significant of these reforms were: 1) the Senate's making it possible to invoke cloture—i.e., to shut down a filibuster—by a vote of three-fifths (normally, 60 members) of the Senate, instead of the more difficult two-thirds present-and-voting that had previously been required;[144] 2) House committee chairmen no longer received their seats on the basis on seniority, but now would have to be elected by the members of the respective committee if enough members insisted on that; 3) each House member was limited to serving on only one subcommittee, which effectively permitted more members to be involved in shaping policy;[145] 4) opening up committee meetings and hearings to the public in most cases and providing advance notice of them; 5) reducing the chairman's prerogatives to halt committee deliberations or bottle up legislation he disagreed with by allowing committee members to call up a bill or a majority to call a meeting of the committee; 6) requiring three days' time from when a committee reported a bill to the full House and when floor debate could begin; and 7) guaranteeing debate time on the floor for proposed amendments to bills.[146] Those among these changes that had the effect of opening up the legislative process to more public scrutiny perhaps can be understood as just helping to maintain the balance between the democratic and republican dimensions of the political order (i.e., by better helping insure the oversight of government by a free press and the citizenry; to make more difficult the quiet aggrandizement of power by a small number; by making unjust, hidden manipulation less likely; by encouraging better and more deliberation). Others, such as weakening the filibuster, ending the automatic seniority system, and even trimming some prerogatives of committee chairmen resulted in less insulation of Congress from the political passions of the moment—another example of increasing democratization. In a seeming contrast, ending seniority opened the door to more influence by the leftist elite that had taken control of the Democratic party since the more conservative, mainly southern, members of the party had been the prime beneficiaries of that practice. In short, the House became "far more liberal."[147]

Even while the left now seemed dominant in the Democratic party and Congress, in the wake of the above disillusionment with liberal governance in both domestic and foreign policy conservatism started to rise. Beginning decisively in 1968, the formerly one-party Democratic "solid South" began to move into the Republican camp. That helped make conservatism less an economically upper crust movement—as noted, this element was now increasingly seen in the Democratic party left—and gave it a more populist coloration.[148] Other developments occurred. Prominent young conservatives who had cut their teeth in the Goldwater campaign matured and became conservatism's leading activists, ideologists, commentators, and organizers. The "new right" emerged, with its concern about cultural decay and family issues.[149] Late in the 1970s, the newly politically active Protestant evangelicals formed the backbone of Rev. Jerry Falwell's Moral Majority.[150] Former "old liberals," who broke with liberalism as it made its jaunt leftward, became the neoconservatives and brought leading scholars and intellectuals and opinion journals into conservative ranks.[151] During the 1970s conservatism also built up a considerable infrastructure of organizations, activist networks, and fund-raising apparatus.[152] The new movement reached its zenith, of course, with the election of Reagan in 1980—the man who had been its acknowledged political leader for over a decade.

Legal and Constitutional Developments and Citizen Rights. This was a time of a veritable explosion of constitutional developments during the Warren and Burger eras on the Supreme Court. We have referred to some of these already: the further expansion of the understanding of "interstate commerce" to permit sweeping federal civil rights legislation; holding that the equal protection clause required that state legislative and Congressional districts have relatively equal numbers of people; the new abortion liberty based upon a penumbral right of privacy; and the functional legal protection accorded for a time to obscenity and pornography (even though the Court claimed that it never actually specifically protected it under the First Amendment[153]). The abortion decisions of the 1970s culminated a short line of cases beginning in 1965 that established the right of privacy pertaining to reproductive matters—starting out with holding that contraceptive use by married couples could not be prohibited by the state, then saying it could not be prohibited to unmarried persons, then holding that the right extended not just to preventing conception but to destroying the "product of conception" (i.e., the new human life), and finally saying that it precluded giving any say in the matter even to the man who made the conception possible or the parents of a pregnant minor girl. The case development, then, jumped from a right attendant to marriage to a right of the individual based upon mere personal preference and then almost unquestioningly across the obvious chasm from a right to stop potential generation to actually destroy it once begun. The elimination of legal strictures on pornography, contraception, abortion, fornication, and even adultery during the 1960s and 1970s was, of course, the result of the sexual revolution in American culture. The new reproductive privacy doctrine of the Court also represented a re-emergence of the notion of substantive due process, but with a different focus.[154] Like the older version (see

Chapters 5 and 6), it referred to rights—or at least applications of rights—not expressly found in the Constitution or even in the constitutional precedents or the legal or common law tradition, and represented something like a skewed understanding of natural law.[155] Both grew out of a shifting socio-cultural paradigm in the U.S. in their respective times and, even though both appealed to a right or an interpretation of a right above the written law—and in fact, were used by the Supreme Court to strike down legislative enactments—were actually stark examples of legal positivism. As such, of course, they clearly collided with the natural law tradition behind the Founding, although this new version of substantive due process was a more extreme departure from it than the old. Also, the Court's unwillingness to permit the state to protect the unborn child in abortion was a serious limitation of one of the most central of the rights in our Founding natural rights tradition, the right to life, mentioned in the Declaration of Independence and stressed by John Locke. It also arguably compromised the Founding notion of equality, which as stated partly meant that all persons are equal before the law, and so should be protected by it.[156] The Court probably was influenced to ignore the equality of the unborn child, at least in part, because of sweeping views that had taken hold in American culture about the equality of women, which went so far as to say that that equality demanded the right to abortion.

The Court's positivism, of course, could be traced back to the developments in American social and legal thought that we discussed in Chapter 5—and further back to its early stirrings in the second third of the nineteenth century and the *Dred Scott* decision.

These matters of sexual morality, of course, also concerned the family. Major change occurred in the area of divorce law in the face of the pressures of the sexual revolution. After California passed the first "no-fault" law (i.e., divorce just when either party seeks it) in 1970, most states followed suit within a few years.[157] After this, the number of divorces sharply increased throughout the decade, from about 14 per 1,000 married women in 1970 to about 23 in 1980 (during the first decade of the sexual revolution, 1960-1970, it had increased less, from about 9 to 14).[158] Legal historian Lawrence M. Friedman concludes, "Cheap, easy divorce was in itself a cause of dry rot in the family."[159] The Supreme Court—perhaps as much because of its egalitarian-like emphasis as the momentum created by the sexual revolution—in a series of decisions from 1968 to 1976 struck down most laws that legally discriminated between legitimate and illegitimate children.[160] Even a push for palimony—i.e., equitable property distribution between a cohabiting couple after they break up—began in the mid-1970s in California.[161] All this—easy divorce, the legal legitimization of non-marital sex, and the legal freedom to destroy one's offspring in abortion— meant, of course, the further—and by this time forceful—undermining of the family that the Founding Era had viewed as so central to a sound culture and political order.

Such other Supreme Court actions as striking down residency requirements to receive state welfare payments,[162] opening the door to aggressive public school desegregation plans even in the North (this gave rise to the busing controversies of the 1970s, mentioned above),[163] giving a judicial imprimatur to affirmative action (even while restraining outright "reverse discrimination"),[164] mandating bilingual education in public schools in some circumstances,[165] and largely holding gender-based classifications in law to be unconstitutional[166] were further expressions—and extensions—of the civil rights revolution and illustrated an attempt of the Court to fashion a quite sweeping condition of equality in American life. By the 1970s, the view of equality in American life went well beyond the ending of racial discrimination and equal treatment under law of citizens. Equality was increasingly transforming itself into egalitarianism—reaching to many more areas than ever before—at odds with the Founders. Its meaning was undergoing such an alteration that unequal treatment of some groups to the advantage of others—with the justification of claimed past disadvantages of the latter—was held to be dictated by the objective of greater equality.

The Warren Court of the 1960s also ushered in what has been called the "due process revolution."[167] This included the nationalization of various provisions of the Bill of Rights as they concerned the rights of criminal defendants: the protection against cruel and unusual punishments,[168] the assistance of legal counsel in non-capital cases[169] (it will be recalled that in 1932 the Supreme Court nationalized it in capital cases), the protection against self-incrimination,[170] the right to confront accusers,[171] the right to an impartial jury,[172] the right to compulsory process for appearance of witnesses,[173] the right to a speedy trial,[174] the right to a trial by jury in non-petty cases,[175] and protection against double jeopardy.[176] In addition, in what were perhaps the Warren Court's most controversial criminal justice decisions, it set down legislative-type mandates in *Mapp v. Ohio* and *Miranda v. Arizona*.[177] In the former (noted above), it forbade the submission of evidence in court that had been acquired in an illegal search and seizure (the exclusionary rule). In the latter, it required the reading of a suspect of his rights before interrogations (the Miranda warning) so as to give force to the right against self-incrimination.[178] Further, the Court restricted the nature and reach of legal searches without a warrant when it subjected wiretapping to Fourth Amendment restrictions and confined a search incident to a lawful arrest essentially to the person of the arrestee and the room he was in.[179]

Outside of the criminal justice area, the due process revolution during the Burger Court era reached to requiring hearings before entitlements could be cut off to persons,[180] on the occasion of public employee job dismissals,[181] and before certain disciplinary actions could be taken against public school students.[182]

Even though the criminal justice decisions were controversial, the Warren Court's concern for the most part conformed to the Founders' views about the necessity of protecting due process-type rights. The particular requirements of *Mapp* and *Miranda*—set down as matters of constitutional mandate—were judicial overreaching, since the common law made no such demands.[183] The extension of rights to due process proceedings in civil and school disciplinary matters were well outside any conception of the principle at common law that the Founders would have been aware of.

There were a number of noteworthy Supreme Court decisions during this period on freedom of speech and the press. In 1961, *the Scales v. U.S.*[184] decision essentially closed the door the Court had already barely left open in *Yates v. U.S.* (see Chapter 7) to the possibility of criminal convictions of persons for Communist party membership.[185] In *Brandenburg v. Ohio* (1969),[186] the Court essentially held that any viewpoint-based restrictions on speech to be unconstitutional, unless the speech is specifically directed to bringing about lawless action (even if it might otherwise have that effect).[187] Crossing into the area of obscenity law, the Court held that an utterance protesting public policy, even if done with an obscenity, is constitutionally protected.[188] The Court laid down clear constitutional grounds for civil law libel actions in the 1960s. In *New York Times Co. v. Sullivan* (1964),[189] it virtually eliminated the possibility of public officials successfully suing for libel by setting down the requirement of "actual malice."[190] Later, it extended this to "public persons" (i.e., people who were prominent but not public officials).[191] In the famous 1971 decision of *New York Times Co. v. U.S.* (the "Pentagon Papers" case),[192] the Court reinforced its prohibition against prior governmental restraint of material that a newspaper wants to publish.[193] The case involved classified documents leaked to the press about decisions within the U.S. Government that had led to the escalation of the Vietnam War.

Related to free speech, at least in the way the Court characterized it, were laws restricting campaign financing which gained renewed attention on the federal level and were beefed up after Watergate. While the Court had no problem upholding the new legal limits on citizen contributions to federal campaigns, it struck down as violative of free speech both limits on the amount that a presidential candidate could spend from his own personal funds and independent spending—i.e., unconnected to the campaigns or the parties—of individuals and groups on behalf of a presidential candidate.[194]

The above Supreme Court decisions on free speech and freedom of the press were mostly in conformity with the Founders, since they considered these rights as essential for a democratic republic. The Court perhaps was too sweeping in placing into the "protected" category membership in an organization—the Communist party—that aimed to destroy all political freedom and legal rights and in considering campaign spending the equivalent of speech (even though, as stated in Chapter 9, there were genuine free speech questions raised by later attempts to restrict campaign spending by public advocacy organizations). It clearly did not conform to Founding thinking in protecting salacious and obscene materials.

As mentioned in Chapter 7, a series of establishment clause decisions in the 1960s and 1970s enshrined a fairly rigid view of church-state separation into American law. More, they had the effect of both redefining "religion" to include even movements that were not theistic,[195] forcing government to be essentially neutral between belief and unbelief, largely removed religious expression from the public arena,[196] precluded governmental aid for such a secular activity as education if it is carried out by a religious institution even though it clearly contributes to the public good,[197] and displaced legislative judgment on this subject with its own and thus essentially insisted that only an absolutist-type resolution as opposed to compromise and accommodation was acceptable.[198] In this area, it also turned its back on traditional legal requirements and its own informal rules by permitting a constitutional challenge to a governmental action even if the suing party faced no direct harm.[199] At the same time, it brought constitutional protection of free exercise to its high point by permitting persons with religious-based objections to be absolved from the requirements of certain generally applicable laws.[200]

We make the same observation here as in Chapter 7 about the Court's separationist jurisprudence on the establishment clause: it ignored the Founders' understanding about how imperative religion is for a democratic republic and it helped further a secularization that would have been foreign to Founding Era culture. During this period its separationist bias hardened and extended to the point that it tried to limit the influence of religion on government-controlled activities—especially education—as much as possible. The vise clamped on by *Everson* sharply tightened in the 1960s and 1970s. Further, the Court's willingness to carve out an exception to the normal rules to establish a *prima facie* case and to make an exception to standing requirements in this one type of case compromised the crucial Founding principle of the rule of law. All this, of course, was the culmination of the separationist sentiment that had increasingly gathered steam since the mid-nineteenth century.

As the above also indicates, the Court's actions in such areas as sexual and reproductive privacy, the exclusionary rule and Miranda warnings, reapportionment and redistricting, and church-state issues—undertaken as they were with little or no constitutional basis—were, in effect, legislative efforts. This, of course, violated the central Founding principle of separation of powers.

The Voting Rights Act and the Twenty-fourth Amendment were mentioned above (in the text and notes). There were other legislatively initiated expansions of voting rights in other contexts during this period. The Twenty-third Amendment (1961) granted presidential election voting rights for the District of Columbia) and the Twenty-sixth Amendment (1971) granted voting rights for citizens between ages 18 and 21. While keeping in mind the fairly broad franchise at the time of the Founding, these developments nonetheless represented further democratization—and additional weakening of the republican dimension of the American democratic republic. Youth voting rights especially signaled how substantial the departure was from Founding thinking, since many people in that age group lack real property holdings or often even a permanent attachment to the communities they live in.

As mentioned in a previous section, among the federal government's new roles was environmental regulation and consumer protection. The amount of federal law in these areas exploded during the 1960s and 1970s.[201] The states were establishing new public policy in them, as well.[202]

Many of the constitutional and legal developments of the 1960s and 1970s aimed to vindicate an assortment of claimed rights of the individual, abstracted

from any natural or human-fashioned private supporting structures. As Mary
Ann Glendon observed about the U.S. and "modern legal systems" generally,
"The effect...is that, without any particular purpose to do so...[they] have come
close to realizing a dream of the French revolutionaries: that citizens would one
day stand in direct relation to the state, without intermediaries."[203] This period
did more than perhaps any previous one to move American law away from the
country's natural law tradition. Further, the entire notion of the citizen
interfacing only with the state, increasingly non-reliant on supporting social
structures, would have been foreign to the realities of Founding Era culture. For
all the supposed achievements of individual rights during the 1960s and 1970s,
such a new situation raised a danger of lost liberty because of heightening state
power that was diametrically opposed to Founding principles. The Founding
Era's sense of taking account of both of the dimensions of man as individual and
as person (mentioned in Chapter 1), which understood him to intrinsically be
part of a community that could help to make him better was lost sight of. Indeed,
the emphasis seemed to be mostly on the first dimension—which involved
especially his rights and the satisfaction of his physical needs and desires—to
the exclusion of man as person (the matters relating to his soul). This, too,
developed through the course of American history, with community gradually
ebbing and enmassment increasing, with the advance of individualism in the
different ways that we have chronicled, and with slow but steady secularization.

    *Foreign and Defense Policy, War and International Conflicts, and
America's Role in the World.* For the first decade or so of this period, most of
U.S. foreign policy was shaped by the Cold War. Until the doubts caused by the
Vietnam War, it pursued the containment policy fashioned after World War II.
Apart from the anti-war protests that increasingly erupted after 1965, some
sober-mined thinkers concerned about American traditions, such as Walter
Lippmann (who was profiled in Chapter 6), had for some time questioned the
containment policy. They re-emphasized the old notion that the major role for
the U.S. in the world should be giving an example to be emulated.[204] Under JFK,
the containment policy translated into a large conventional and nuclear arms
build-up and an ability to militarily intervene anywhere in the world if needed
(the "flexible response" policy).[205] Even as he took this position, JFK wanted the
underdeveloped countries (the "Third World")—the most likely targets of
intervention—to look to the U.S. in refashioning their governments and
societies.[206] So, he shared the notion of providing an example, but unlike
Lippmann and the earlier American understanding was not hesitant to back it up
militarily. Beyond the problem of interventionism itself being problematical,
JFK at least had a perspective about what kind of government to accept in these
countries that concurred with Founding Era realism: he wanted to see a
democratic republic, but found an anti-Communist despotic regime better than a
revolutionary one that was either Communist or might go that way. He figured
that he could prod the former toward providing more freedom later on.[207]
Ambrose and Brinkley say that the deepening American involvement in
Vietnam did not happen, as some claimed, because of a rising militarism (one of
the causes of regime decline, it will be recalled) or pressure from the military-

industrial complex that Eisenhower had warned against, but was the "logical culmination" of containment.[208] It was also responsible for such other American interventions in the 1960s as the Bay of Pigs and in the Dominican Republic (even while the latter apparently did not involve communism at all, and in a way helped to undo the results of its most recent presidential election).[209] While both her NATO allies and her Latin American neighbors supported the U.S. in the great facedown with the Soviets in the Cuban Missile Crisis, there were problems in the relationship with each. Some of the former became unhappy with what they saw as American dominance in the alliance and sought to reassert themselves, and (at least under LBJ) the U.S. had little regard for the preferences of the latter.[210] We can make the following observations in light of Founding political and cultural principles: 1) As stated in Chapter 7, one cannot say with the threat to those principles presented by Communist ideology that a policy of opposition to communism was problematical or that it in any way violated the principle of foreign policy impartiality; 2) the readiness to militarily intervene in neighboring countries to the south and LBJ's lack of regard for their sensibilities—not new phenomena, as previous chapters have showed—demonstrated to some degree a lack of communal, cooperative spirit and orientation to the hemispheric common good; and 3) the Dominican Republic intervention arguably helped thwart the preferences expressed in a free election, and as such showed disrespect for the norm of popular sovereignty. The U.S. could not easily be a good example abroad if she did not demonstrate commitment to her Founding principles.

There are several other things to say about the Vietnam War. First, in the early 1960s the U.S. ignored popular dissatisfaction with the Ngo Dinh Diem regime in South Vietnam, although later the CIA got involved in a plot to depose him and approved of his assassination.[211] At first, then, the U.S. was inattentive to popular sovereignty and afterwards it ignored sound morality—so stressed in the Founding Era—by supporting assassination.[212] Second, even though the JFK administration apparently understood that a war like this one, where the mass of people had to be won over, required a political and not just military approach, it and the two administrations following it in effect primarily stressed the latter.[213] This was not exactly an exercise of prudence that the Founders would have commended. Third, when under LBJ the U.S. first instituted the policy of bombing North Vietnam it was somewhat problematic from the standpoint of international law and just war thinking because the U.S. was not at war with that country and it had not been aggressive toward the U.S.[214] Since the North was supporting the Vietcong Communist insurgency against the South,[215] however, some action against the North could be understood as helping a vulnerable party and thereby judged morally acceptable. Even if analyzed in this way, the strategy could be held to have violated proportionality (one of the criteria to have a just war—*jus ad bellum*—in the first place).[216] Once the bombing policy was underway, avoiding civilian casualties was not the most important consideration. This was even more vividly seen by the fact that the option of the U.S.'s using nuclear weapons was seriously discussed.[217] Again, one of the most central principles of just war (*jus in bello*)[218] that is grounded in the natural law and Christian morality that was so fundamental a part of the Founding tradition was paid insufficient attention to. While there is dispute about how great the American-inflicted damage on Southeast Asia and the level of civilian casualties were,[219] there were nonetheless serious questions about proportionality (*jus in bello*) and discrimination (i.e., noncombatant immunity)—and thus not only serious moral issues, but problems of temperance and respect for the rule of law (international law, since the traditional principles of just war had become part of it[220]). Obviously, the North Vietnamese violated the Paris Accords that ended the American military presence and set up a cease-fire by attacking and finally overrunning South Vietnam in 1975. Ambrose and Brinkley, however, say that actually all sides seriously violated the Accords.[221] If that were the case—even while war and conflict are certainly not neat and the North Vietnamese were highly blameworthy—America's actions in this regard offended her Founding cultural norm of promise-keeping, just as did, say, her violations of the Treaty of Guadalupe Hidalgo that ended the Mexican War.

To be sure, the American effort in Vietnam was not just a series of affronts to Founding principles. As mentioned, it was not undertaken for reasons of economic self-interest and the containment policy was motivated by a concern about confronting an aggressive ideology utterly hostile to these principles. Moreover, as Ambrose and Brinkley point out, not only did the U.S. not financially gain from the war but "poured money into" the country. It also had no "territorial objectives" or desire to become a new colonizer.[222] For whatever its negatives, the war must be judged an example of the Founding cultural principle of willingness to practice present sacrifice for expected future good.

After the war, there was a common attitude of reluctance in the U.S. about getting into future similar engagements, although it expressed itself in two divergent perspectives. On the one hand, there was a neo-isolationism that held that she should never interfere in the internal affairs of another nation. On the other hand, a neo-hawkish view insisted that the U.S. should never commit herself unless it had the willingness to pursue total victory.[223] Both of these attitudes touched a chord with earlier American tradition. Tocqueville observed that democratic republics like America have a pacific spirit and are very reluctant to go to war,[224] and Americans have always been uncomfortable about being imperialistic.[225] Tocqueville also said, however, that once a democratic people decides to engage an enemy, it typically goes all out to win.[226]

In line with this new national sentiment, when Carter came to power he insisted that the U.S. "had to accept a more limited role in world affairs," even in principle backing away from the containment policy.[227] He did not seem to any longer view communism as the "chief enemy," and in fact seemed to downplay the threat it posed to the West.[228] Ambrose and Brinkley say that many of his foreign policy goals were "wildly impractical," and the trust he was willing to place in America's Cold War adversaries perhaps naïve. Among his goals were the enunciation of the ultimate objective of eliminating all nuclear arms, moving to decrease U.S. arms sales, and his famous human rights crusade. He thought that the U.S.S.R. would respond to a conciliatory approach based upon incentives instead of confrontation. The result instead was increasing Soviet aggressiveness, culminating in the 1979 invasion of Afghanistan. His human rights policy "contributed to the downfall of America's oldest and staunchest ally in the Middle East, the Shah of Iran." The U.S. undercutting of the Shah—which ushered in the contemporary Islamic revolution with all the consequences that has had for the Western world and U.S. foreign policy—followed from his belief that the U.S. should not be so supportive of "right-wing dictatorships."[229] While Carter's concern about human rights perhaps reflected the stress on rights, personal dignity, and civility of the Founding Era—and was, in some manner, in line with the sense of mission that from that time characterized American foreign policy of promoting principles consistent with republicanism[230]—the crusading and imposing character of the policy strikingly lacked Founding-type realism. By and large, as indicated, the Founders believed that they should teach the world about the value of republicanism by example.[231] The fact that Carter disliked "right-wing" regimes and more readily favored and supported leftist ones[232] also went against the impartiality norm of the Founders. This betrayed an ideological orientation in his foreign policy that contrasted with their pragmatism—as seen, for example, in their willingness to seek support from monarchical France in the Revolutionary War in the cause of establishing a republican form of government. (We have argued, on the other hand, that partiality would have been merited in the opposite direction from Carter's policy—i.e., a particular opposition to Communist regimes because they were so fundamentally hostile to all the principles of the American Founding. This would be a foreign policy based on a crusading moralism of a sort, but not one inconsonant with Founding realism.)[233] If Carter's undermining of the Shah of Iran showed a lack of realism and a blasé attitude about maintaining commitments (out of line with the Founding norm of promise-keeping), the remaining level of support for him—in a certain sense—did too, however, because of imperviousness to his deepening unpopularity among his people. As such, it also showed a lack of concern for the Founding principle of popular sovereignty. Moreover, the facts that American economic interest was an incentive for supporting his regime and that the U.S. helped sustain his notorious secret police operation, SAVAK,[234] were not exactly statements of such Founding norms of fair-dealing, civility, and a restraint on economic self-interest.

During the 1960-1980 period, Israel and Mideast Arab states fought two wars: the 1967 Six-Day War—in which the Israelis quickly and decisively crushed their adversaries and resulted in their occupation of neighboring Palestinian-inhabited territories that has since been a point of intense controversy—and the 1973 Yom Kippur War that could have led to a major East-West confrontation when the tide turned in Israel's favor.[235] The U.S. historically had tried to have good relations with both sides, but had given much support to Israel and saw it as its closest ally in the Mideast. The U.S. worked hard to broker an end to the Yom Kippur War and afterwards, with oil considerations important, the American support for Israel was "more restrained."[236]

Apart from the problems of international politics and military conflicts, a new trend developed in international economics in the 1960s and 1970s that followed American cultural trends. Americans became less focused on acquisition in this period, and as a result American business turned increasingly abroad to find new markets.[237] While this is, to be sure, how the market or business economy tends to work at times, the fact that American companies were turning to other places to sell goods—i.e., that were manufactured in the U.S. and so the developing of new markets benefitted the U.S.—that were not yet saturated with them meant that they were trying to create demand. One discerns, at least to some extent, both a lack of temperance and perhaps an excessive spirit of individualism—both tendencies at odds with the Founding.

Relations and Conflict Among Social Groups, and Immigration. We have spoken of the civil rights revolution. The 1960s were, of course, a time of intense racial conflict, perhaps without parallel in American history. In the early 1960s, one thinks of such events as the integration struggle at the University of Mississippi in 1962, when JFK sent troops to enforce a court order to permit Negro student James Meredith to enroll.[238] The next year, a similar episode took place at the University of Alabama. A high point in peaceful race demonstrations was perhaps reached in the spring and summer of 1963 when as many as 75,000 people took part, paving the way for the march on Washington. 1963 also, however, saw perhaps the apex of civil rights-related violence in the South. The aggression directed by southern authorities against Negroes was showcased for the entire country on television news in such cases as the notorious T.E. "Bull" Connor's unleashing of fire hoses and police dogs against Negro demonstrators in Birmingham, Alabama. Bombs targeting King and other civil rights leaders there helped to trigger the decade's first significant urban race riot, which became a frequent happening as the 1960s went on. That spring also witnessed the sniper slaying of the noted Mississippi NAACP leader Medgar Evers in Jackson.[239] In September was the infamous bombing of Birmingham's 16th Street Baptist Church that killed four young Negro girls.[240] The race riots began as the federal government was starting to address the civil rights question with legislation and continued through the rest of the decade. They rocked a substantial number of medium and large-sized cities. In 1966 alone, there were forty-three.[241] That was before the five-day-long Detroit riot of 1967, which was possibly the most destructive.[242] As such destruction continued, a so-called "white backlash" developed that expressed itself in the national elections of 1966 and 1968 when the Democratic party of LBJ's Great Society lost, first, massively in Congress and then the presidency. "Law and order" became an increasingly crucial political issue.

In the second half of the 1960s, the Negro desire for integration began to be transformed into what Matusow calls a "quickening impulse toward racial separatism." The slogan "Black Power" was frequently heard and helped ignite Negro violence and unrest.[243] As this kind of Black Nationalism (mentioned above) took hold, there was something of a rift in the civil rights movement (i.e., integrationists supporting non-violent tactics versus separatists willing to use violence) and also many active Caucasian supporters distanced themselves from the new militants. Blatantly anti-Caucasian and specifically anti-Jewish attitudes found expression among the militants.[244] This all developed in the context of the revolution of rising expectations mentioned above. According to Matusow, "liberal accomplishment in radical reform fell short of expectations," and a minority of Negroes—although a vocal, activist one—became "embittered."[245] It also occurred as Negroes increasingly climbed into the middle class, and many more Negroes than ever before moved into prominent and influential positions in the U.S.[246]

Law and order politics and Black Power were two contrasting expressions of the disillusionment with liberal reform ideas alluded to above.

Racial violence, although on a much smaller scale, continued into the beginning of the next decade—especially in smaller cities.[247] As the 1970s went on, however, racial rhetoric and open tensions lessened. The decade saw no race riots after 1970 and black radical groups (although not necessarily the belief in Black Nationalism and separatism) declined. Suddenly, the North became the region with the greatest racial polarization, as witnessed in the busing controversy above.[248] What did increase, however, was "public sensitivity about racial matters," as all kinds of picayune matters and seemingly insignificant comments and the like suddenly became evidence of racism and often were blown way out of proportion—sometimes, if involving prominent people, becoming even national issues.[249] What might be called inter-class or anti-established order violence accompanied the racial violence of the 1960s. Domestic terrorists, such as the Weathermen, bombed numerous corporate offices, banks, and government buildings in the late 1960s and radical-inspired attacks on police increased.[250] Another version of this kind of violence was the campus riots that hit numerous American institutions of higher learning from 1964 to 1970.

As mentioned, the notions of Black Nationalism and separatism retained their viability in the 1970s. A moderated form of "black cultural nationalism" took hold that featured a more distinctively Negro way of life, the rise of a Negro ethnic politics, and "the abandonment of the integrationist ideal."[251] By the end of the 1970s most Negroes were saying that they "had lost faith in the responsiveness of American institutions," and identified more with people in Africa—even though most really did not know much about them—than they did Caucasian Americans.[252] This intensified racial distancing—at least in attitudes and identification with other races—was heightened by the increasing "white flight" from urban areas after the 1960s.[253]

Negro cultural nationalism was joined by the same phenomenon among Mexican Americans, American Indians, and East Asian Americans. Among other things, Mexican Americans pushed for their own ethnic studies programs in universities (as Negroes and other groups were also doing), bilingual education, and more community control of the affairs in areas where their people were heavily concentrated. Militant American Indian organizations emerged, protesting against what they saw as unfair federal government practices against their tribes. The Indian actions turned violent at Wounded Knee, South Dakota in 1973. East Asians also pushed for ethnic studies programs and started cultural institutions and publications highlighting their heritage. The most significant achievement was their successful push to get the federal government to make amends for the internment of Japanese Americans on the West Coast during World War II. All of these groups joined the Negro in suddenly resisting integration and assimilation into what they saw as the predominant Caucasian culture.[254] Even among Caucasian ethnic groups, there was a new stress on ethnic identity and, as Schulman puts it, "demands for rights flourished."[255] Even many of the elderly began to see themselves as "a distinct community with a separate identity," and senior communities and the like began to flourish.[256] The rise of the new wave of feminism—beginning in the 1960s, but flowering in the 1970s (discussed below)—represented another fissure, of some women identifying themselves as a distinct element, in opposition to a predominantly male-shaped society.[257] Failed assimilation was also a frequent theme in 1970's arts and culture.[258] The new anti-assimilation ethic resulted in the fashioning of the notion of "diversity" that, according to Schulman, held that the supposed phenomenon of "unassimilable groups" was "a good to be valued." Public policy—in spite of the courts' push for mandated busing—subtly shifted from promoting integration to upholding diversity.[259] The U.S. was no longer seen as a "melting pot," but merely as "discrete peoples and cultures sharing the same places."[260] David Burner, Robert D. Marcus, and Thomas R. West write that by the end of the 1970s, the country "had broken into many subcultures."[261] Affirmative action seemed to become the norm,[262] although this arguably—but not conclusively—strained instead of improved relations among groups by allowing group identification instead of proven merit to be the basis for the advantage of some.[263] Political scientist Allan P. Sindler wrote the following in the 1970s about the question of race preferences: "Moral commitments and causes have their darker side...They often promote intense and emotional conflict, and the more extreme partisans may display an arrogant self-righteousness which polarizes the dispute and depresses opportunities for reasoned discussion and negotiation of differences....the moral cause of equal opportunity for minorities has certainly been marked by excesses."[264]

Both the outright racial conflict and violence of the 1960s and the more subdued identity politics and cultural separatism of the 1970s showed sharp division among an assortment of groups. In fact, if the division was more blatant with the race riots of the 1960s, it was more *widespread* in the 1970s since it involved many more social, racial, and ethnic groups. Group identity even became one more force among several tearing at the family, with its extending to women and the elderly. Moreover, how deep-seated it had become was illustrated by how the slightest episode or even statement could generate conflict and controversy (as noted above) and by the anger that continued to be generated by official policies advantaging one or another group, even if now to supposedly correct past injustices. Lack of civility among groups was a constant during this entire twenty-year period, even if it was not as evident in the 1970s as in the 1960s and some previous periods. The absence of the community of friendship which Founding Era culture strove for was striking. Perhaps underlying the lack of inter-group civility and friendship was an absence of a basic sense of justice and just dealings in many ways—clearly evident in the treatment of the Negro in the civil rights era, but more subtly so later. Even though on a certain level there was more voluntary melding (e.g., the number of interracial marriages increased,[265] and inter-ethnic marriages among Caucasians was hardly an issue anywhere), such developments as the dissolution of the integrationist ideal indicate that on other levels it was not so evident. The latter underscored a subtle sense of pessimism that had enveloped the country in the 1970s—seen further above with the disillusionment of Negroes about America generally—that went counter to Founding culture's strong belief in man's possibilities within the tempering context of a realism grounded upon its Christian worldview. Indeed, it was perhaps the receding of the latter—the 1960s and 1970s was an era of much increased secularism, as discussed below—that caused such a pessimistic outlook to take hold.

With this reference to religion, it is perhaps worth noting that the one area where inter-group tensions were relaxed during this period was among religious groups. While the period began with anti-Catholicism directed against JFK in the 1960 presidential campaign,[266] traditional religious conflict dissipated and a spirit of ecumenism prevailed.[267]

While the inter-group problems detailed above concerned mostly indigenous groups in the U.S., the new norms of diversity and non-assimilation of the 1970s laid the groundwork for an even larger problem than tensions among indigenous groups. This was because the Immigration Act of 1965, which sharply shifted the main source of immigration from Europe to Asia, Africa, and Latin America, diversified the U.S. ethnically and culturally to a much greater degree than in the past. This was even further accelerated by the steep rise in illegal immigration from south of the border, which began to occur at the same time.[268] The possibilities of more and more varied inter-group conflict loomed on the horizon, especially since little was now expected of the new arrivals in terms of becoming part of a distinctively American culture. Indeed, the new norms suggested that people coming into the country perhaps did not even have to embrace the basic American Founding principles discussed throughout this book and, in fact, developments later on indicated that at least some had a greater loyalty to the country of their origin than the U.S.[269] The matter of being committed to a political order's principles has considerable implications for its continued viability. Ethicians speak about any political order having to have a civic bond, which involves the citizens acting in union with each other in the striving for a common good acknowledged by all. If there is no such common good—and hence no civic bond—the cohesion of the political order becomes tenuous.[270] Apart from the array of new immigrants, this was perhaps the basic problem presented by all of these new divisions in American life. While, of course, conflict among groups was a repeated phenomenon in U.S. history, what was new—and disturbing—was the shift to a way of thinking that extolled the divisions and saw them as the new norm that should be accepted. For many, *e pluribus unum* no longer seemed to be the aim.

Socio-Cultural Developments. We have mentioned the transformation of the many aspects of American culture and the triumph of lifestyle freedom in this twenty-year period. It marked many areas: sexual morality, marriage, and the family (where perhaps the most pronounced changes occurred); the role and situation of women and youth; education; religion and the religious outlook; and crime. It was in the mid-1960s that the cultural upheavals began and the first signs of the social maladies that were to continue to plague America to the present time showed up.[271] The 1960s, as has previously been stated, saw a flowering of cultural trends that began in the 1920s and showed new signs of life in the 1950s after the interregnum of the Great Depression and World War II. These trends had at their core the impulses for consumption and indulgence.[272] This is what led Christopher Lasch to speak about the "culture of narcissism," in which a spirit of "competitive individualism" led people to pursue what they thought was their happiness only to be led "to the dead end of a narcissistic preoccupation with the self."[273] There was an erosion of "social discipline,"[274] which people saw "as emancipation from the repressive conditions of the past."[275] As Lasch puts it, people saw themselves "repudiat[ing] competitive ideologies" and "extol[ling] cooperation and teamwork"—witness the anti-capitalist ethos, avowed disdain for middle class culture, and affection for socialism of the New Left—when in reality they were utterly "acquisitive in the sense...[of having] cravings...with no limits...demand[ing] immediate gratification and lives in a state of restless, perpetual unsatisfied desire."[276] The diminishing of social discipline was seen not only in what Manchester calls the "abrasive" mood resulting from the above dissatisfaction and anger of so many groups,[277] but in the loss of any sense of deference—respect for experience, learning, position, wealth, office, or personality—and of the spirit of the gentleman.[278] The latter was seen in its most repugnant way in some of the sex propagandists of the time instructing men how to "use" women sexually, and in the denigrating attitude toward the "nice girl."[279] Another part of this from the female side was the decline of modesty, which was underscored in the early part of this period in the sharp turning away from tradition in terms of clothing—one dimension of the snubbing of experience—in the "mini-skirt rebellion" of the mid-1960s,[280] and then very shortly after in a big way with the full-blown sexual revolution. There were many other expressions (some of which are discussed below): the proliferation of obscenity as a usual part of speech (even among women); the sharp expansion of sexual promiscuity and the acceptance of sexual perversions as "normal"; the breakdown of restraint—especially on sexual and personal matters—in the entertainment industry, as long-standing standards and taboos began to be ignored; the decline of parental discipline and the weakening authority of the family; the widespread availability and use of marijuana; the rejection of the teaching authority of religions; the loss of respect (precipitated by the Vietnam War) for the military; falling productivity of workers; the increasing norm of open boastfulness by celebrities, such as athletes; and the burgeoning of a counterculture (e.g., the hippies, the rock music culture) that rejected many of the conventions and personal moral and behavioral norms that had historically governed American life.[281] Schulman contends that by the end of the 1970s, "A new ethic of personal liberation triumphed older notions of decency, civility, and restraint." Even those who did not go along with the countercultural upheavals of the previous decade "embraced this looser code of conduct"; it thus had become widespread.[282]

This cultural transformation developed in small ways over a number of previous periods of American history, and we observed more limited expressions of it. In the 1960s, however, it just exploded throughout the country.

Here we see that many of the cultural norms of the Founding were flaunted in the 1960s and 1970s: frugality, industry, temperance, willingness to sacrifice, the spirit of cooperativeness, true concern for the general welfare, rejection of self-serving individualism, sexual restraint, self-regulation for higher ends, good manners, the spirit of the gentleman, and, of course, the prevalence of sound morality grounded in the natural law.

The significance of the sexual revolution was indicated by the quote from Paul Johnson at the beginning of this chapter. It was, indeed, probably the most defining development of the 1960s and 1970s, and as he indicated many other matters were connected with it. The sexual revolution meant that the individual decided what his morality regarding sex would be, so long as there was no obvious harm to another person. Personal physical and emotional satisfaction— at least what people *thought* constituted their emotional satisfaction—were the key considerations. The standard became: "If it feels good, do it." The sexual revolution meant that pre-marital sex jumped sharply. The number of girls and young women who had taken part in it doubled during the 1960s. To illustrate how much the sexual ethic had changed, one study found that in some communities a girl was expected to have sexual relations with a steady boyfriend after she turned sixteen or she lost status.[283] By the early 1970s, less than half of the public said it believed that premarital sex was wrong, and a third said that marriage was obsolete.[284] A third of the college-age population said that having children was not very important.[285] The number of cohabiting couples increased over 3.5 times from 1960 to 1980 (in 1980, there were almost 1.6 million adult cohabiting couples).[286] This was aided by the availability of the oral contraceptive, which was approved by the Food and Drug Administration in 1960.[287] As noted in Chapter 5, one of its developers in the 1980s lamented that it had made young people sexually irresponsible. The publicity given to supposedly scientific sex experiments by such researchers as Masters and Johnson (the team of William Masters and Virginia E. Johnson), like the Kinsey studies of the 1940s and 1950s, helped provide momentum for the new sexual permissiveness. The readership of soft-core pornography, such as *Playboy*, sharply increased. [288] As mentioned above, judicial decisions made it difficult throughout the 1960s to prosecute pornography. It became widespread and a big business.[289] In spite of readily available contraceptives and increasingly (universally, after 1973) abortion, illegitimate births steadily increased from 224,300 in 1960 to 598,000 in 1979.[290] So did sexually transmitted diseases (STDs). In one year's time at the beginning of the 1970s syphilis increased 16%, and gonorrhea rose about 15% per year throughout the decade of the 1960s.[291] With abortion legalization, the number of abortions sharply increased,[292] as even human life—in spite of the efforts of the early pro-abortion movement to argue otherwise, there was no doubt about the unborn child's humanity[293]—was all too readily sacrificed on the altar of sexual liberation. The homosexualist ("gay rights") movement emerged in the late 1960s.[294] Homosexuality and homosexuals now came out into the open, and in the 1970s homosexuality gained rapid acceptance in the U.S.—helped along by the American Psychiatric Association's declaration in 1974 that it was no longer viewed as a mental disorder.[295] It hardly needs to be pointed out that these developments were completely contrary to the high standard of sexual morality and norm of family integrity that characterized Founding times.

Along with the sexual revolution came the latest wave of feminism. It probably helped fuel the economic and educational advance of women—even though these trends were already well underway when it made its appearance in the late 1960s. It also put considerable strains on the family by promoting the sexual revolution—holding that women should have the same illicit sexual freedoms as men—and telling women to be concerned about pursuing their own individual wants and desires. By its very nature, however, the family requires cooperation ahead of an individual orientation and a willingness to sacrifice for the sake of the good of the whole unit. As Clecak puts it, for many women feminism involved "a renegotiation of the terms of family and personal life."[296] In the 1970s, for the first time a majority of women worked outside the home. This included married women and even women with young children.[297] By the middle 1980s, more than half of the latter worked outside the home. Apart simply from jobs, women were entering careers at a rapid pace.[298] This naturally put additional pressures on the family as the duties of job and household often pull in different directions. As previously noted, when lower-class women in the nineteenth century had to work outside the home for reasons of economic sustenance, the result was that families suffered and juvenile crime and other problems increased. These new developments set the stage for the same problems. Feminist ideology often saw the family as an oppressive structure for women.[299] It also paved the way for a historically unprecedented attempt to redefine what a family is.[300] Mainstream thinking even began to minimize the natural differences between men and women, at least apart from the obvious biological ones.[301] This had the effect of undercutting the notion of the nurturing role of women and the belief that fathers and mothers each brought something different and unique to the formation of their offspring. This "me-first" perspective of feminism was reinforced by an increasing anti-natalism (alluded to above) and skepticism about children in the culture of the period generally[302] (indeed, this follows more generally from the narcissism that Lasch saw enveloping this period). The above makes apparent that in many ways feminism was another expression in these times of the self-serving individualism that the Founding culture sought to constrain and that had consistently served to weaken the family.

As mentioned, the divorce rate rose steadily. Between 1960 and 1980, the number of female-headed families more than doubled.[303] The 1970s saw a rise in the number of "latchkey" children.[304] All of the above maladies were even more pronounced among Negroes, the largest minority group at that time.[305] Legal developments—the ones mentioned above and others—in the 1970s also added to the weakening of marriage—and thereby the family—by ceasing to acknowledge its unique place and increasingly placing cohabitation on the same level as it in terms of legal rights and access to public benefits.[306] The youth rebellion of the 1960s—which had been foreshadowed in the 1920s—was another source of strain on families, as different generations confronted each other with sometimes sharply divergent views about personal conduct and the things that are important in life.[307] Illicit drug usage and a countercultural orientation were found widely among youth.[308] As had happened earlier in American history, parental authority weakened. As Jacques Barzun wrote, many of the youth of the time sought to destroy a culture that had pampered them. Their "sentimental education" had failed to equip them to sensibly criticize the aspects of it that merited criticism; all they could do was condemn.[309] Reason no longer seemed to govern in education, which had serious implications for a political order whose background presumed the primacy of reason (which was, of course, the foundation of the natural law tradition it emerged from).[310] As we see below, the problems of education were considerable during the 1960s and 1970s.

In short, the 1960s and 1970s considerably intensified family breakdown. As in the nineteenth century, family breakdown tends to result in more crime. By 1980, the crime rate in the U.S. was three times higher than it had been in 1960; there was a veritable explosion of crime.[311] Another part of the growth of crime in this period, of course, was both the unprecedented proliferation of illicit drug use and crimes that spun off from it.[312] The connection between family breakdown and crime has been further affirmed by contemporary social science studies. During the period beginning in the mid-1960s, data has shown that the rise in violent crime generally and the rate of violent teenage crime parallels the rise in abandonment of families by fathers. It has also shown that even in high-crime neighborhoods over 90% of children from "safe, stable homes" do not become delinquents, and that neighborhoods with a high degree of religious practice tend not to become high crime neighborhoods. Interestingly, social science data also show that there is no clear connection between economic circumstances and the tendency of people to commit crimes.[313]

The mention of religion and neighborhoods leads to two other socio-cultural developments in the U.S. in the 1960s and 1970s that not only probably had an effect on crime rates, but also showed how distant the culture had become from that of the Founders. This period was a time of deepening, even abrupt, secularization and religious skepticism. American culture did not exhibit the outright rejection of God, but rather a functional kind of disbelief—i.e., secularism—whereby many people carried on their lives as if God did not matter.[314] Traditional religious denominations often seemed eager to embrace the worldview and norms of the new secular culture, loosening up on traditional Judeo-Christian teachings on sexual morality and supporting such initiatives as the push to legalize abortion in the 1960s.[315] More radical theologians added their voices to the anti-traditionalists of the 1945-1960 period mentioned in Chapter 7.[316] As part of the melding into the secular culture, religion for people increasingly became a privatized phenomenon, and not only were traditional denominations looking increasingly secular but more and more people followed Eastern religions, New Age movements, and assorted gurus.[317] In the tumultuous years after Vatican Council II, an unprecedented fragmentation occurred within American Catholicism between the orthodox and the neo-modernist. Dissent from many basic doctrinal and moral teachings of the Church became pervasive, and the U.S. bishops often tolerated it and did not seek to impose discipline.[318] Clergy of different denominations became involved and often highly visible in political and social protest movements, such as the civil rights and anti-Vietnam War movements.[319] This was helped along by the increasing bureaucratization of church bodies—following the long-time drift of other American institutions— since it spawned a version of liberal religious activists who occupied positions in church agencies insulated from both the ideas of and the restraints imposed by the more traditional people in the pews.[320] It was also a time, however, where— like the late nineteenth century—there was a reaction to such religious liberalization by an upsurge of Protestant evangelicalism and fundamentalism.[321] Also, as Patterson says, in spite of secularization the U.S. "continued to be one of the most churchgoing nations in the developed world." Weekly church attendance by adults declined from 1960 to 1980, but still 40% attended[322] (although Marty tells us that "[t]he disproportionately youthful population apparently felt less need for religious affiliations…or believed churches failed to serve their needs").[323] In spite of these contrary points, this period was a time of a weakening of religion. This, of course, would have been seen by the Founders and a figure like Tocqueville as holding serious implications for the future of the American political order, which as we have seen they understood religion to be at the foundation of.

The growth of mass culture continued apace from its nineteenth century origins and the suburbanization of the 1945-1960 period accelerated as people now fled the racial problems of the cities and their rising crime (as noted above). This resulted in the increasing decay of old neighborhoods, which had helped provide a refuge and reference point for people and a means of exerting stability and social control. Community was thus breaking down. The difficulty of building new community cohesiveness in the suburbs that was mentioned in Chapter 7 now met with greater obstacles, in light of all the other social problems of this time. As noted above, community was one of the crucial foundations of Founding Era culture, and was a necessity for the political principles and arrangements set forth by the Founders. Actually, Schulman says that the 1970s were a time when people were turning inward and retreating from community life in various ways. Some of this would have been consistent with the ethic of self-reliance of the Founding Era culture, but some of it just paralleled the new group consciousness of the decade and was a turning away from that culture's orientation to a "public" local community—while people now embraced many kinds of newly constructed "private" local communities, like homeowners associations—and from the public spiritedness of the Founders.[324]

The final area of socio-cultural developments to consider is education. We have already discussed the greater governmental regulation of both higher and pre-college education that the 1960s brought. At the pre-college level, progressive education reasserted itself amidst the aggressive challenge mounted against so many aspects of American life. It combined a renewed critique of schools with a broader critique of society. It attacked such typical norms of public schools—and virtually all schools—as the need for competition (e.g., grading, class rankings, etc.) and order as it usually prevailed. The new progressives claimed that radical change in education was needed.[325] They introduced so-called "open education," and alternative schools of various kinds were set up. Among the features of open education, which caught on in varying degrees, were: allowing the classroom teacher and even the pupils to decide what the routine of the class day would be, stressing self-learning and children making their own educational choices, a de-emphasis of authority, melding work and play together, nontraditional approaches to learning, de-emphasis on grading, the elimination of course requirements, establishing coursework on the basis of pupil interest, the elimination of ability-grouping of pupils, and academic credit for non-classroom work such as community service.[326] Authority in schools came under increasing attack in the 1960s and 1970s—as it was in the broader culture—and the result was a heightening of disciplinary problems and an ensuing loss of confidence in public education.[327] The courts contributed to the decline of discipline by some of their decisions on students' rights.[328] Educational standards declined (both on the pre-college and college levels),[329] and from the standpoint of our comparative analysis with the Founding Era two developments that were part of this were particularly ominous: the success of American education in transmitting the country's cultural and intellectual heritage was substantially eroded,[330] and what became deeply implanted in it was a skeptical worldview issuing forth from the philosophical position of, as John S. Schmitt puts it, "the denial that the mind can with certainty know reality."[331] The latter, of course, undercut any notion of natural law and moral truth, which were assumed by the Founding. By the mid-1970s a reaction to the erosion of standards started to set in as a "back to basics" movement (i.e., calling for renewed stress on traditional basic subjects and intellectual skills in pre-college education) began to develop.[332] It did not significantly address the problems of failing to transmit heritage and fostering skepticism, however.[333]

There were additional problems in American higher education—that spawning ground for America's leaders—that developed in the 1960s and 1970s that are pertinent to this book's inquiry. One was the growth of the large, mass university campus whose impersonality and pressures for conformity—along with the deepening skepticism and value neutrality, intellectual confusion, and sense of meaninglessness of the educational enterprise—helped to encourage the break down of discipline and—in line with the broader culture—restraint on such matters as sex and drugs. Skepticism or outright denial of truth and value neutrality, of course, destroy any possibility of a liberal arts education, whose purpose after all is to enable the student to see truth more clearly. Another problem that was also applying pressure on the liberal arts was the new stress on the importance of practical training—even in higher education—and a new view of college as a place just to get a credential for a career. The university as a place for "academic leisure, dialogue, and reflective preparation"—all crucial elements for a successful liberal arts education—declined. The activism of 1960's politics became the norm of college students as well: action became more important than reflection. If in pre-college education pupil choice became a new norm, in higher education it was "relevance." This melded with the emphasis on activism—it was insisted that studies be immediately pertinent to the social and political concerns of the day. The reigning attitude of higher education was that the needs of students and their wants automatically converged, and this was one more nail in the coffin of the liberal arts. The result of all this upheaval in higher education was, to use Russell Kirk's term, the production of many "quarter-schooled" people—i.e., they received Barzun's sentimental education, above—who, with assorted big or little grievances, were easily drawn to the socio-political ideologies of the New Left.[334]

The decline of the liberal arts, the new emphasis on career training, the absence of a component of moral formation, the doubt about purpose, and most of all—at the root of these other developments—the loss of belief in truth were all contrary to what the Founders would have understood was needed for education to sustain a democratic republic (i.e., to shape its citizens, but especially to shape its leaders). The lack of discipline and restraint that was so evident in the college/university culture and among so many students added to the breakdown of reason and order that was necessary for sound education—and probably compounded the disorder of the broader culture. Some of these educational trends, as we have noted, were not new in the 1960-1980 period, but like so many other things became much more serious and widespread.

Socio-Political Movements, Trends in Socio-Political Thought, and the Influence of the Intelligentsia. The above has discussed developments in these areas to some degree already. We have spoken about such movements as the civil rights movement, the New Left, feminism, Black Nationalism, homosexualism, and grass-roots neo-populism. We have also examined the transformation of liberalism in the 1960s. We here make a few additional comments about these developments and speak about another movement that emerged from the radical politics and counterculturalism of the 1960s: environmentalism. We also say more about the conservative political movements that arose in the 1970s in reaction to these movements. The increasing influence of the intelligentsia was noted, both in the importance of social science research in shaping public policy in the 1960s and in the ascendancy of a new elite in the Democratic party in the early 1970s. We make a few additional observations about this in this section.

The New Left's origin dated to the Port Huron Statement of 1962. It was a kind of updated statement of Jacksonian democracy. Following C. Wright Mills (as noted in Chapter 7) and like many political scientists of the 1960s,[335] the statement lamented that there was a dissonance between democratic principles and practice, with elites really in control of major institutions and the average citizen powerless and apathetic. Government, corporations, labor unions, and universities were all targeted. It sought a kind of vague participatory democracy, in which people could live in decentralized communities, be out from under hierarchic institutions, and control their own lives. It provided an intellectual inspiration for the radical student movement of the 1960s by insisting that taking control of the universities was the first step, and then students could help influence the other socio-political movements of the time which would end in a rejuvenation of American democracy.[336] In fact, as time went on the New Left became authoritarian, egalitarian, zealous for redistribution, anti-intellectual, and sometimes anti-Jewish.[337] The New Left somewhat fizzled after the 1968 Democratic Convention, with its adherents going off into the particular social causes of the 1970s above. After 1968 or perhaps 1969, it was not so much outright political revolution that was sought—indeed, organizations like the Students for a Democratic Society (SDS) largely disbanded—but cultural revolution. As noted above, the influence of the 1960s counterculture expanded in the 1970s.[338] We mentioned that liberalism moved left under the influence of the New Left. Clecak contends that this happened because liberalism did not have "a controlling vision beyond the idea of a democratic, pluralistic culture," and so was "especially susceptible to cultural values, images, and ideas" from the counterculture and more leftist elements.[339] Indeed, the lack of a deeper philosophical-ethical foundation and overreaching sense of purpose about politics was illustrated even in the immediate post-World War II period when the best mainstream liberals could muster as opposition to communism was that it was anti-democratic.[340] By the end of the 1970s, Clecak says it had only "pieces of liberal dreams and fragments of liberal values...with no...compelling vision or...workable politics."[341] John J. Schrems says about the SDS—and, by extension, much of the New Left—while it stressed sweeping democracy it really had a "hidden centrism." More power would go to the center in order for it to achieve its objectives that were supposedly good for "the people."[342] On the one hand, its theory overembellished the democratic dimension of the democratic republic, while on the other its push for centralization—which involved a kind of authoritarianism—undercut the entire notion of a democratic republic. It was troubling, then, that the New Left significantly influenced liberalism in general in the 1960s.

As liberalism at the end of the 1960s became disillusioned with the possibilities of pursuing sweeping change, American social thought generally became less ambitious in what it reached for. The same discussion of limits, diminished expectations, and relative scarcity that one heard among average citizens during the economic problems of the 1970s became the prevailing assumptions of American social thought during that decade. This meant that redistributive-type schemes, far-reaching programs, and welfare-statist ideas became less popular.[343] Perhaps liberalism began to regain some sense of realism, but it also bought into the pessimism of the new decade and, as suggested above in another context, lost some sense of the Founding spirit of faith in man's possibilities. Also, even if its aims were not so lofty anymore, the result nevertheless was not a significant disengagement of government from various activities or governmental decentralization.

Environmentalism, whose beginning was mentioned above, became one of the most influential worldwide socio-political movements in the forty years that followed. Nourished by the radical critique of Western life and countercultural back-to-nature movement of the 1960s, it built upon and then went far beyond—and did not always co-exist so easily with—the conservation movement that began three-quarters of a century before. Some in the new movement went to the extreme of even claiming that other species had rights, in effect blurring the distinctions between men and the latter.[344] We mentioned above the sweep of new environmental legislation and how it expanded the reach of the federal government. The effect of this new area of legislation and this new movement—which became an increasing force in the decades ahead—was an increased centralization of power at odds with the Founding.

In reaction to these movements of the left and the increasingly leftist tilt of liberalism were new conservative intellectual and political movements in the 1970s. The neo-populism mentioned represented a changed view within part of conservatism, from a strong—but not unqualified—defense of the established order and a suspicion of grass-roots activism to a demand—previously often associated with liberalism—for wider participation and opposition to what it saw as elitism. To be sure, a conservative populism had been seen before during the 1950s when many average citizens initially provided a base of support for Senator Joseph McCarthy's campaign against domestic communism.[345] The New Right, which had its origins in the grassroots-generated Goldwater presidential campaign of 1964,[346] flowered in the late 1970s (as noted above). Some elements of the New Right were not hesitant about bringing theological presuppositions—especially from evangelical Protestantism, which as noted had an upsurge in the 1970s also as a reaction to the period's trends—into the public arena.[347] The neoconservatives were more of an intellectual movement of Eastern-based opinion-makers, without a grassroots orientation. As noted, they were mostly old liberals who emphasized pre-Vietnam War liberalism's strong anti-communism, the value of the market economy but with a belief in the need for reasonable but restrained government regulation, a limited welfare state, and—but less prominently and uncompromisingly than the New Right—the importance of sound morality for culture.[348] Amidst these developments, there was a fading of support in public discussion for the so-called "Modern Republicanism" of the Eisenhower period, which was the term associated with the Republican party's acceptance of the New Deal's role of government but in a more moderated way (see Chapter 7).[349] While on the one hand this conservative upsurge represented an attempt to restore Founding notions, on the other its populist character—like the original populists—perhaps tilted the balance in the democratic republican equation too far in a democratic direction (the problems of which were perhaps seen in the McCarthy period earlier).

Finally, we have noted the enhanced role of the intelligentsia in the Democratic party and liberalism generally in this period. We have also noted the role of social science research in shaping policy and its claimed unique capability—ringing of neo-gnosticism—in addressing what it saw as highly complex social problems. Moreover, the 1960s also saw the rise of what Lasch called the "psychological man" as modern psychology was heavily turned to in order to give meaning to life for arch-individualistic, ultra-secular man.[350] Modern psychology emerged, then, as a kind of substitute religion and even influenced religious adherents.[351] Psychologists became almost priestly figures in the new therapeutic order, getting substantial attention in the media, on talk shows, in popular publications, etc. As part of this, sociologists such as Philip Rieff spoke about "the triumph of the therapeutic," meaning that therapy—the method of applied psychology—aimed to bring about what had become the aim of contemporary Western culture: "better living," instead of "the good life" the classics had sought. As part of this, "virtue gives way to value, and what is of value is whatever conduces to the well-being of the individual."[352] Thus, therapy and modern psychology generally were major re-enforcers of the deep-seated relativism of the age (i.e., "values"—the norms to live one's life by—are simply fashioned by the individual and anyone's are as good as anyone else's). Therapy in this scheme in essence is something that gives comfort to the individual about his value choices and helps assure him that they will give him personal meaning. Further, an attitude increasingly took hold in American life that if people acted waywardly or even criminally it was because of psychological factors or different pathologies; somehow it was not because of their free choice.[353] Hayward writes that in the 1960s, "the prestige of intellectuals had never been higher."[354] What we see here with this rise of the influence of intellectuals and secular psychology particularly is a lack of realism, a weakening of true religion, a decline in the belief in free will that underscored the Founders' worldview, and a continuation—but reaching a high point—of the anti-democratic ethos of rule by functional specialists that began in the Progressive Era (i.e., thwarting the democratic side of the democratic republic)—all at odds with the Founding. Furthermore, the intellectuals of this period were another elite that in no way could be considered the equivalent of a natural aristocracy as promoted by the Founders. We have discussed how this gnostic element—with its intrinsic elitist, anti-democratic ethos—has manifested itself repeatedly in American history. Ironically, it has typically asserted itself in the name of democracy, beginning in the Jacksonian Era, running through the Progressive Era, and seen in this period under the guise of the democratic rhetoric of the Port Huron Statement, the social science-inspired legislation (for the people's welfare, of course) of the Great Society, and the leftist upper-crust Democrats of the 1970s reforming their party to make it more democratic.

In bringing together the above comparisons of 1960-1980 period with Founding principles and culture, we observe that there are a mountain of deviations—and many fewer points of conformity. On the conformity side (and we can see many caveats even here), America remained a middle class culture; such central rights as freedom of speech and freedom of the press were upheld (even if these rights were stretched and turned in a direction the Founders did not intend); the norm of foreign policy impartiality was mostly upheld, but not as much under Carter; the concern about promoting principles in foreign policy was seen, although irregularly and went to a moralistic extreme under Carter;

commercial efficiency and industry were implicit in the entrepreneurial spirit of the time; the concern about being thy brother's keeper was present, but too often translated itself simply into more government social welfare programs; the need for limits on economic freedom and the social use of property were stressed in some sense, but this often meant excessive government control; there was a decline of conflict among social groups in some areas (e.g., greater inter-religious understanding) and even a melding in some ways (e.g., routine inter-ethnic and even more interracial marriage), but this was in contrast to a more pervasive reality of division and incivility; religion remained a strong force for many people and there was some measure of religious revival, but this was against the backdrop of its general weakening and the judiciary minimizing it in the public square; there was a realism in American foreign policy in the early part of this period (only to be succeeded by a policy lacking realism near the end of it); and there were also in noteworthy ways in American life the evident practice of such Founding cultural norms as self-reliance, self-restraint, temperance, simplicity, and a willingness to sacrifice in the present for a future good (e.g., the American commitment in Vietnam)—nevertheless, the general trends were in the opposite direction.

We now list, by the different general topics discussed in this chapter, the principles, practices, and cultural norms that the Founding Era understood as essential for a democratic republic that we stated were departed from, subverted, or ignored in the 1960-1980 period. In "Economics and Economic and Social Welfare Policy," these were the following: economic decentralization, ownership and management of enterprises routinely in the same hands, the avoidance of substantial economic inequalities (the overturning of these first three all continued long-term trends originating in the nineteenth century), a proper understanding of equality generally, the general maintenance of a just wage for workers, the avoidance of excessive government debt, governmental decentralization (seen in the increasing federal—i.e., centralized—role in these policy areas, supported by both political parties), simplicity, frugality, self-restraint, promise-keeping, shrewd practical intelligence, an orientation to the public good, civic friendship, and realism. While there was at least to a limited extent a new reserve about consumerism, there was no reversal of the consumer culture or the desire for luxury that Founding Era saw as a danger. While the basic principle of taxation without representation was not violated, the practices of state governments of the 1970s that triggered the tax revolt suggest that its spirit was not always upheld, or what we might consider a related problem of something like taxation irrespective of public preference observed. Thus, popular sovereignty was compromised. In the area of the "Role and Powers of Government, Relations Among the Three Branches of the Federal Government, and Federal-State Relations," we witnessed the weakening of the following: governmental decentralization and federalism (probably the principle/practice that was battered the most); separation of powers and checks and balances (harmed most in an ongoing way by the ascent of judicial power, but for many years also the aggrandizement of power in the executive); popular sovereignty (with more power going to the federal bureaucracy); the need for a natural aristocracy (instead there was a functional specialist elite in the form of government bureaucrats and judges—this, as we have shown, continued a long-term development in the U.S.); the compromising of the rule of law (with the increasing number of vague and overly broad statutes and regulations); liberty (which in different ways was increasingly a victim of more government regulation and regimentation in an expanding number of areas); the control of faction (as interest groups increasingly played a crucial role in shaping public policy to their benefit); the makers of the laws being subject to them like other citizens (as Congress began to exempt its members from some of the laws it passed); and the importance of family and freedom of religion (both of which were threatened by some of the policies implemented during this period). On the subject of "Political Developments, Trends, and Reform," we saw a damaging or disregarding of the following Founding Era norms: the need for a natural aristocracy (an economically and educationally—in terms of amount of schooling—elite took control of the Democratic party); orientation to the common good and concern with the general welfare; a cooperative spirit; civility, good manners, and self-restraint (all compromised in the politicking and politically-inspired scheming of the time); the restraint of democracy and the popular impulse (seen by the Democratic party reforms, Congressional reforms, and the emergence of neo-populism); and the spirit of hope in man's possibilities. On the subject of "Legal and Constitutional Developments and Citizen Rights," we observed in the constitutional jurisprudence of the time and in other legal change an undercutting, transformation, or damaging of: natural law; the Founding notion of natural rights; the Founding notion of equality (seen most markedly with the unborn child's and the woman's rights on the abortion question, and in legislative reapportionment); the family (with such constitutional developments as legalized abortion and changed laws on divorce, etc.); due process (the expansion of its reach by the Supreme Court); liberty (the judicial expansion of its meaning to embrace a rank individualism in certain areas, the narrowing of its meaning in American thinking to concern only legal rights instead of "man as person," and the general expansion of state power); the rule of law (by the Supreme Court's emptying the commerce clause of meaning to permit seemingly unlimited federal legislative authority, and its relaxing of standing requirements in establishment clause cases); religion (the Court's pushing of it out of the public square by the latter decisions); and, of course, separation of powers and checks and balances due to an substantial overreaching of the judicial role. In the category of "Foreign and Defense Policy, War and International Conflicts, and America's Role in the World," we saw that the norms of communal and cooperative spirit, concern for the common good, popular sovereignty, promise-keeping, fair-dealing, civility, temperance, restraint on individualism and self-interest, and respect for the rule of law (i.e., international law) were compromised in American dealings with different nations. Further, American foreign policy at different times did not uphold the norms of prudence and respect for morality and the natural law, and did not exhibit Founding Era realism or always maintain the central principle of impartiality among nations. In the area of "Relations and Conflict Among Social

Groups, and Immigration," the main deviations were in the Founding Era cultural norms of civility, respect for the common good, and the maintenance of strong community. The sense of pessimism that developed from the troublesome inter-group relations undercut the hopeful spirit of human possibilities of the Founding. In a small way, we noted that even the family was harmed by developments in this area. It was because of what was happening in the next area, however, that the family was most harmed: "Socio-Cultural Developments." In fact, of all Founding Era cultural norms the essentiality of strong family life perhaps suffered the most damage from these developments, which included the decline of sound sexual morality and restraint (and morality generally) and a massive upsurge of individualism. The enveloping of American culture by moral relativism—expressing itself most sweepingly and emphatically in areas of "individual morality"—was a harsh rebuke to the natural law tradition of the Founding. It also went hand-in-hand with the decline of religious belief and adherence (in addition to the official efforts to minimize public religious influence above). Even within religious bodies, as noted, excessive centralization occurred; it was yet another departure from the Founding spirit of decentralization. Along with moral decline came the decline of such related Founding norms as self-restraint and reserve, temperance, good manners, the spirit of the gentleman, and simple decency (another word for all these norms is mores). We also noted the general decline of such other individual virtues as frugality, industry, and—despite the *national* commitment to it in Vietnam and the Cold War in the first part of this period (JFK even spoke about America "bearing any burden")[355]—the willingness to sacrifice for a future good. On the social plain, as in some of the other areas above, such norms as civility, cooperativeness, concern for the general welfare, public-spiritedness, and the stress on strong community suffered. Education for both good citizenship and to maintain sound culture—i.e., insuring the transmission of the American cultural heritage—and to bring forth good leaders—i.e., the liberal arts—experienced perhaps its most serious crisis in American history. Finally, on the subject of "Socio-Political Movements, Trends in Socio-Political Thought, and the Influence of the Intelligentsia," we recounted that the following Founding principles and norms were challenged or ignored: restrained democracy (both the New Left and conservative neo-populism promoted more democratization); decentralization; equality (the New Left, which significantly influenced liberalism, pushed egalitarianism); realism, free will (which underlay the entire tradition of reason behind the Founding), and religion (all these were either wanting or absent in the thinking of the era's intellectuals); and (with the increasing disillusionment about liberalism) another expression of a loss of hope in man's possibilities.

In sum, there were few of the principles, practices, and norms that the Founders and their era held to be essential to a democratic republic that were not subverted, missing, or at least compromised during the 1960-1980 period. Such central rights as *habeas corpus*, freedom of assembly, the prohibition of bills of attainder, and trial by jury were left unaffected—though the latter would be seriously compromised in the post-1980 period, as we see in Chapter 9. Of the cultural norms and practices, there were almost none.

When we think back to the conditions in the 1945-1960 period, we have to conclude that the 1960-1980 period was a decisive one in shifting the U.S. away from the Founders' vision of a democratic republic. The U.S. increasingly became a centralized, bureaucratic state with expansive—and convoluted— notions of rights, but less liberty—and which featured a culture and a way of life entirely unlike that of the Founding Era. This meant the domination of big, centralized, distant entities shaping people's lives even outside of government, in economic and other domains, and the diminishing or outright debilitation of the underlying cultural imperatives needed to sustain a democratic republic. To be sure, many of these conditions were present earlier in the twentieth century, and the U.S. had gone back after World War II to a situation that in many ways conformed to the Founding Era. It will be recalled that Paul Johnson said that the element in the 1950s that began to stir in a different direction—in effect, against Founding culture—concerned sexual morality, and this went on to lead to the other changes that the 1960s would bring. One wonders if perhaps what he meant was simply that it signaled the beginning of the breakdown of internal order generally—i.e., the order within the human soul—that, as Russell Kirk points out, is the basis for the external order of the political society.[356] Or perhaps, he meant very precisely that the decline of the virtue and mores of the citizenry in this crucial area of sex helped to stimulate decline in other virtues and mores—and then the political and social decline that followed. We must recall (see Chapter 1) the advantage that the Patriots of 1776 had over the British because of sexual virtue, and what Tocqueville says about how social convulsions have their origins in the corruptions within marriage.

Next, we state, as we have throughout this book, conditions and factors of cultural decline—as identified by the important thinkers noted in Chapter 1— that manifested themselves in the 1960-1980 period. This chapter makes clear that more of these factors were seen in this period than at any previous one (in fact, virtually all of them were present in some degree): a turning away from religion; materialism or the focus on luxury (in spite of some reconsideration of this way of life in wake of 1960's cultural criticism); the excessive concern with pleasure or lack of control of the passions (seen readily in the sexual revolution); social conflict and turmoil; the prevalence of moral relativism; overcentralization and excessive bureaucratization; serious economic problems (seen in the 1970s), even while the middle class continued to predominate (the middle class, however, came under strong attack from the New Left and the counterculture in the 1960s); the loss of will (seen in the American reluctance to assert herself internationally after the Vietnam War) and a sense of purposelessness (seen in the growing skepticism about truth, the loss of purpose in education, and people's turning to modern secular psychology, therapy, and the like in order to find meaning in their lives); the continuation of mass culture that grew from the nineteenth century; the prevalence of liberalism—in control for much of this period—and the ascendancy—more sweepingly than at any previous point in American history—of anti-traditional views (e.g., on sex, family, morality); politics becoming a struggle for power (even though the political movements of the 1960s and their socio-cultural progeny of the 1970s had substantive objectives—as problematical as they often were—the often ugly politics indicated that power was more often than not the overriding aim); the weakening of the rule of law; the neglect or imperviousness to the common good or general welfare (mentioned in many contexts); and the corruption of sound philosophy (clearly seen with the pervasive skepticism about truth and moral relativism).

Finally, the following possible inherent weaknesses in the Founding are suggested by the experience of the 1960-1980 period: lack of awareness both of all the principles of social ethics and of a good understanding of the common good due to insufficient philosophical reflection (seen in such things, respectively, as the obliviousness to the principle of subsidiarity by the much heightened governmental centralization and the rise of identity politics); the ready collapse of the natural law into natural rights (suggested by the excessive stress on rights that characterized this period); the presence of the seeds of an expanded individualism; the lack of enough emphasis on community (suggested by the many expressions of individualism, the balkanization caused by identity politics, the retreat of many from a community-orientation in the 1970s, and the phenomena of people increasingly interfacing directly with government because of the lack intermediary support structures); the related lack of stress on intermediary associations in Founding thought (clearly seen by the latter and simply by how government had come to take on so much responsibility for people's needs); the lack of a formal, reliable way to shape virtue and the downplaying of it in politics (suggested by the excessive rights emphasis, the obvious absence of public discussion of the importance of virtue, and the substitution of a relativistic notion of values for it); the emphasis on a commercial republic, which led to more individualism and laissez faire (America continued to be a consumer culture in this period); the failure to see the centrality of the family for the political order (it was under a probably unprecedented attack on many fronts); the inability to see how powerful the courts would become (the indication of which is starkly witnessed in this period, as the courts reached the zenith of their political power); the stress on institutional and structural factors gave rise to bureaucratization (the growth of centralized government bureaucracy accelerated with the third wave); no formal way to bring forth a natural aristocracy (what was clearly seen was an elite of functional experts and upper-crust activists in politics, who could not be said to have been shaped in wisdom); the failure to orient the constitutional order to higher things (this was the most secular time in American history, and government distanced itself more from the transcendent than ever); the Founding cultural problem of monitoring people too closely in the community (seen here in government's increasing intrusiveness into more areas of people's lives); and finally the leaving of the task of discerning what constitutes the natural law to private judgment and the sowing of the seeds of positivism by the refusal to recognize the Catholic Church as the authoritative moral interpreter (in this period, moral relativism was more pervasive than ever, positivism more deeply ingrained in notions of law, and with the ascendancy of the Supreme Court a mere human institution now, effectively, decided about basic moral issues in the public context—and as the abortion decisions, among others, made clear, did not do a very good job of upholding morality).

Notes

1. Paul Johnson, *A History of the American People*, 841.

2. Bruce J. Schulman, *The Seventies: The Great Shift in American Culture, Society, and Politics* (N.Y.: Free Press, 2001), xii.

3. See Krason, *Abortion: Politics, Morality, and the Constitution*, 13-39. It is frequently claimed that the main 1973 decision, *Roe v. Wade*, 410 U.S. 113, only declared unconstitutional restrictions on abortion during the first or second trimester of abortion. The *Wade* decision must be read in conjunction with its companion case, *Doe v. Bolton*, 410 U.S. 179, however. The Court held in *Wade* that after the point of fetal viability—which at that time was viewed as roughly about the end of the second trimester of pregnancy—the state interest in the unborn child—what it referred to as "potential life"—becomes "compelling" and so it may prohibit abortion, except when it is necessary to preserve "the life and health of the mother" (at 163-164). It proceeded to say in *Bolton* that "health" related to "physical, emotional, psychological, familial [factors] and the woman's age" (at 192). With that broad definition, it is clear that the Court for all practical purposes legalized abortion until birth for virtually any reason.

4. See statistics from the Centers for Disease Control and the Alan Guttmacher Institute, cited at http://www.nrlc.org/abortion/facts/abortionstats.html; Internet; accessed Oct. 3, 2009.

5. See Paul Johnson, *A History of the American People*, 911-912, 926-927.

6. Roger Matuz (ed. Bill Harris), *The Presidents Fact Book* (N.Y.: Black Dog and Leventhal Publishers, 2004), 676-677.

7. Berkin, Miller, Cherny, and Gormly, 974.

8. Stephen J. Wayne, *The Road to the White House, 1996: The Politics of Presidential Elections* (N.Y.: St. Martin's, 1996), 280-281.

9. Berkin, Miller, Cherny, amd Gormly, 994-995.

10. See Richard G. Wilkins and Jacob Reynolds, "International Law and the Right to Life," unpublished paper delivered at 2005 conference of University Faculty for Life, 28-29.

11. Berkin, Miller, Cherny, and Gormly, 997-998; Tindall and Shi, 1674.

12. *Bush v. Gore* (531 U.S. 98 [2000]).

13. "2003 Invasion of Iraq," http://en.wikipedia.org/wiki/2003_invasion_of_ Iraq; Internet; accessed Oct. 3, 2009.

14. "Iraq War," http://en.wikipedia.org/wiki/Iraq_War; Internet; accessed Oct. 3, 2009.

15. See: "Just 22% Favor Stalled Immigration Bill," Rasmussen Reports, http://www.rasmussenreports.com/public_content/politics/current_events/immigration/just_22_ favor_stalled_immigration_bill; and "Comprehensive Immigration Reform Act of 2007," http://en.wikipedia.org/wiki/Comprehensive_Immigration_Reform_Act _of_2007 (both Internet and accessed Oct. 4, 2009).

16. See "United States Presidential Election, 2008," http://en.wikipedia.org/wiki/ United_States_presidential _election, _2008; Internet (accessed Oct. 6, 2009).

17. See "Barack Obama," http://en.wikipedia.org/wiki/Barack_Obama; Internet; accessed Oct. 9, 2009.

18. "How the Nobel Peace Prize Is Awarded," http://www.foxnews.com/politics/2009/10/09/look-nobel-peace-prize-process/; Internet; accessed Oct. 9, 2009. Political scientists Fred I. Greenstein of Princeton and Stephen Wayne of Georgetown said, respectively, that Obama's getting the award was a "'premature canonization'" and given for "'his rhetoric and his orientation.'" Historian Allan Lichtman of American University said that the award was given "'to encourage rather than to recognize an accomplished fact.'" ("Obama's Nobel Is Premature, Historians and Political Scientists Say," http://www.foxnews.com/politics/2009/10/09/nobel-prize-obama-embarrassment-process-expert-says/; Internet; accessed Oct. 9, 2009.)

19. Henry C. Dethloff, *Americans and Free Enterprise* (Englewood Cliffs, N.J.: Prentice-Hall, 1979), 281.

20. Steven F. Hayward, *The Age of Reagan: The Fall of the Old Liberal Order, 1964-1980* (N.Y.: Forum [Prima], 2001), 193.

21. Tindall and Shi, 1501-1502.

22. Ambrose and Brinkley, 209.

23. Tindall and Shi, 1599-1600. The quotation is from 1600.

24. Hayward (2001), 610.

25. Dethloff, 281.

26. Schulman, 8.

27. James T. Patterson, *Restless Giant: The United States from Watergate to* Bush v. Gore (N.Y.: Oxford University Press, 2005), 6.

28. Allen J. Matusow, *The Unraveling of America: A History of Liberalism in the 1960s* (N.Y.: Harper & Row, 1984), 219.

29. Dethloff, 280.

30. Ibid., 281.

31. Patterson, 62-63.

32. Myron A. Marty, *Daily Life in the United States, 1960-1990: Decades of Discord* (Westport, Conn.: Greenwood, 1997), 5.

33. Source: Union Sourcebook 1947-1983 (U.S. Bureau of Labor Statistic), http://www.workinglife.org/wiki/Union+Membership:+Overall+(1948-2004); Internet; accessed March 2, 2010.

34. Patterson, 78.

35. Marty, 100.

36. David Burner, Robert D. Marcus, and Thomas R. West, *A Giant's Strength: America in the 1960s* (N.Y.: Holt, Rinehart and Winston, 1971), 101.

37. Hayward (2001), 196-197.

38. Matusow, 233-237.

39. Schulman, 112-113.

40. Hayward (2001), 230, 257. The quotation is from 257.

41. Dethloff, 315.

42. Hayward (2001), 521, 523.

43. Dethloff, 295-296.

44. Hayward (2001), 518.

45. Schulman, 210-212.

46. Matusow, 230-231.

47. Ibid., 228.

48. Ibid., 232.

49. Ibid., 231.

50. Lyndon B. Johnson, quoted in Peter Clecak, *America's Quest for the Ideal Self: Dissent and Fulfillment in the 60s and 70s* (N.Y.: Oxford University Press, 1983), 66.

51. Clecak, 66.

52. Quoted in Burner, Marcus, and West, 98.

53. Matusow, 220.

54. Ibid., 223-224.

55. See, e.g., "Buffalo News Series Confirms That More Money Does Not Equal Better Education," http://www.bcnys.org/whatsnew/2005/0503buffalonews.htm; Internet; accessed Oct. 10, 2009; William J. Bennett, "20 Troubling Facts about American Education," *School Reform News* (Oct. 1999), http://www.heartland.org/publications/school%20reform/article/11200/20_Troubling_Facts_about_American_Edu-cation.html; Internet; accessed Oct. 11, 2009.

56. Matusow, 266.

57. See, e. g., Lindsay Burke, "Does Universal Preschool Improve Learning?: Lessons from Georgia and Oklahoma," *Education Matters* (July-Aug. 2009), 1; Lindsay Burke, "Head Start Lags Behind," *Education Matters* (March 2010), 3.

58. Matusow, 266-267.

59. See. e.g., Bob Kemper, "*Gideon*: Right to Counsel?" *Washington Lawyer* (Sept. 2009), 25-30.

60. Frank Stricker, *Why America Lost the War on Poverty—And How to Win It* (Chapel Hill, N.C.: University of North Carolina Press, 2007), 65.

61. "Richard M. Nixon," http://www.britannica.com/EBchecked/topic/416465/Richard-M-Nixon/214055/Domestic-policies#; Internet; accessed Oct. 11, 2009.

62. Hayward (2001), 261, 514.

63. Hayward (2001), 193-196; "Richard Nixon," http://en.wikipedia.org/wiki/Richard_Nixon; Internet; accessed Oct. 17, 2009; W. Carl Biven, *Jimmy Carter's Economy: Policy in an Age of Limits* (Chapel Hill, N.C.: University of North Carolina Press, 2002), 27; Timothy Tregarthen and Libby Rittenberg, *Macroeconomics* (2nd edn.; N.Y.: Worth, 2000), 358.

64. Hayward (2001), xxv-xxvi. The quotation is from xxvi.

65. Ibid., xxvii.

66. Ibid., 383, 365.

67. Ibid., 364.

68. Roger H. Davidson and Walter J. Oleszek, *Congress and Its Members* (2nd edn.; Washington, D.C.: CQ Press, 1981), 337.

69. Hayward (2001), 363-364; 383.

70. Ibid., 363.

71. Ibid., 363; Fred I. Greenstein, "A President Is Forced to Resign: Watergate, White House Organization, and Nixon's Personality," in Allan P. Sindler, ed., *America in the Seventies: Problems, Policies, and Politics* (Boston: Little, Brown, 1977), 70.

72. Hayward (2001), 369; Arthur M. Schlesinger, Jr., *The Imperial Presidency* (Boston: Houghton Mifflin, 1973), 397.

73. Schlesinger, *The Imperial Presidency*, 312-313.

74. Ibid., 181-183; 187, 189.

75. "Richard M. Nixon," http://www.presidentprofiles.com/Kennedy-Bush/Richard-M-Nixon-Prerogatives-and-power.html; Internet; accessed Oct. 13, 2009.

76. 418 U.S. 683.

77. "Congressional Budget and Impoundment Control Act of 1974," http://en.wikipedia.org/wiki/Congressional_Budget_and_Impoundment_Control_Act_of_1974; Internet; accessed Oct. 12, 2009.

78. Schulman, 48.

79. 25% of his vetoes were overridden (see Thomas E. Cronin and Michael A. Genovese, *The Paradoxes of the American Presidency* [2nd edn.; N.Y.: Oxford University Press, 2004], 172).

80. "Gerald Ford," http://en.wikipedia.org/wiki/Gerald_Ford; Internet; accessed Oct. 13, 2009.

81. Ambrose and Brinkley, 251.

82. See "War Powers Resolution," http://en.wikipedia.org/wiki/War_Powers_Resolution; Internet; accessed Oct. 13, 2009.

83. See *Hutchinson v. Proxmire*, 443 U.S. 111 (1979).

84. David L. Kirk, "School Desegregation in San Francisco, 1962-76," in Sindler, 154.

85. 369 U.S. 186 (1962).

86. *Elrod v. Burns*, 427 U.S. 347 (1976).

87. See the discussion in Krason, *The Public Order and the Sacred Order*, 355-375.

88. *Mapp v. Ohio*, 367 U.S. 643 (1961).

89. See Mason and Stephenson, 412-413.

90. See ibid., 538-541.

91. *Planned Parenthood of Central Missouri v. Danforth*, 428 U.S. 52 (1976).

92. Raoul Berger, *Government by Judiciary: The Transformation of the Fourteenth Amendment* (Cambridge, Mass.: Harvard University Press, 1977).

93. Alexander M. Bickel, *The Least Dangerous Branch: The Supreme Court at the Bar of Politics* (Indianapolis: Bobbs-Merrill, 1962).

94. Thomas E. Cronin, "The War on Crime and Safe Streets, 1960-76: Policymaking for a Just and Safe Society," in Sindler, 237.

95. Daniel J. Elazar, *American Federalism: A View from the States* (2nd edn.; N.Y.: Thomas Y. Crowell, 1972), 81.

96. Matusow, 244, 246.

97. Elazar, 52, 70. The quotation is from 70.

98. Ibid., 64.

99. Ibid., 62, 64. The quotation is from 62.

100. This was seen not only with the Voting Rights Act of 1965, which aimed to protect the voting rights of southern Negroes, but also with the proscribing of the poll tax in federal elections by the Twenty-fourth Amendment and in even in state and local elections by Supreme Court decision (*Harper v. Virginia Board of Elections*, 383 U.S. 663 [1966]).

101. Ravitch, 301-301.

102. Ibid., 299.

103. Ibid., 312-313.

104. Hayward (2001), 255-256.

105. Mason and Stephenson, 255. The case was *Daniel v. Paul*, 395 U.S. 298.

106. See, e.g., *Ludington [Mich.] Daily News*, April 14, 1971, http://news.google.com/newspapers?nid=110&dat=19710414&id=SY4KAAAAIBAJ&sjid=C0wDAAAAIBAJ&pg=5364,780651; Internet; accessed Oct. 15, 2009.

107. See: Krason, *The Public Order and the Sacred Order*, 155-188; Stephen M. Krason, "Child Abuse and Neglect: Failed Policy and Assault on Innocent Parents," in *The Catholic Social Science Review*, vol. x (2005), 215-231; Stephen M. Krason, "The Critics of Current Child Abuse Laws and the Child Protective System: A Survey of the Leading Literature," in *The Catholic Social Science Review*, vol. xii (2007), 307-350.

108. Dethloff, 280.

109. See ibid., 296.

110. See Tocqueville, II, ii, 513-517.

111. See "Laws That Do Not Apply to Congress," http://www.rules.house.gov/ Archives/jcoc2ai.htm; Internet; accessed Oct. 17, 2009.

112. Hayward (2001), xxxii.

113. See Krason, *The Public Order and the Sacred Order*, 517-521.

114. Hayward (2001), xxvii.

115. Ibid., xxvii, 519.

116. For example, when Obama announced his candidacy for president, he talked about such sweeping aims as finally ending poverty in America, solving the health care "crisis," ending the country's dependence on oil, and changing the governmental system. (See Kesler, 14.)

117. Matusow, 344.

118. Hayward (2001), xxix, xxxiii.

119. Ibid., 339.

120. David Carlin, *Can a Catholic Be a Democrat?: How the Party I Loved Became the Enemy of My Religion* (Manchester, N.H.: Sophia Institute Press, 2006), 44-46. As an example, it is interesting to consider how unrepresentative the delegates to the 1972 Democratic convention were: 31% earned $25,000 or more (a large salary at the time), compared to 5% of the entire population, and a "disproportionate number had advanced degrees" (Hayward [2001], 353).

121. Burner, Marcus, and West, 54; Carlin, 48-49.

122. Hayward (2001), 355, 308.

123. Kirk, *The Roots of American Order*, 415.

124. Austin Ranney, "The Democratic Party's Delegate Selection Reforms, 1968-76," in Sindler, 204.

125. Stephen J. Wayne, *The Road to the White House: The Politics of Presidential Elections* (N.Y.: St. Martin's, 1980), 87.

126. Ranney, 182.

127. Wayne (1980), 98.

128. Ranney, 163.

129. Ibid., 197-198.

130. Wayne (1980), 88.

131. Ibid.

132. Robert E. DeClerico, *Voting in America: A Reference Handbook* (Santa Barbara, Calif.: ABC-CLIO, 2004), 43.

133. Schulman, 210.

134. DeClerico, 31.

135. "Electoral College (United States)," http://en.wikipedia.org/wiki/Electoral_ College_(United_States)#The_Bayh-Celler_Amendment; Internet; accessed Oct. 21, 2009.

136. Hayward (2001), 336.

137. "United States Presidential Election, 1964," http://en.wikipedia.org/wiki/ United_States_presidential_election,_1964; Internet; accessed Oct. 21, 2009.

138. Manchester, 1218.

139. Hayward (2001), 699.

140. Burner, Marcus, and West, 58.

141. Schulman, xv.

142. Ibid., 215.

143. Hayward (2001), 515.

144. "Filibuster," http://en.wikipedia.org/wiki/Filibuster#20th_century_and_the_ emergence_of_cloture; Internet; accessed Oct. 22, 2009. This rule change occurred in 1975.

145. Norman J. Ornstein, "The Democrats Reform Power in the House of Representatives, 1969-75," in Sindler, 14.

146. Ibid., 21.

147. Hayward (2001), 385.

148. Schulman, 114.

149. Ibid., 195-197; Stephen M. Krason, *Liberalism, Conservatism, and Catholicism: An Evaluation of Contemporary American Political Ideologies in Light of Catholic Social Teaching* (rev. edn.; St. Louis: Catholic Central Verein of America, 1994), 150.

150. Schulman, 202.

151. Ibid., 203-204.

152. See ibid., 196-199.

153. Mason and Stephenson, 484.

154. See, e.g. Richard A. Epstein, "Substantive Due Process by Any Other Name: The Abortion Cases," *The Supreme Court Review* (1973), 159-185. This is also suggested in Archibald Cox, *The Role of the Supreme Court in American Government* (London: Oxford University Press, 1976), 51-55.

155. About the lack of a constitutional or legal basis for these new sexual and reproductive rights established by the Court, see Krason, *Abortion: Politics, Morality, and the Constitution*, 246-268. Friedman says that the Court's right of privacy applying to sexual and reproductive matters is "a concept (one must admit) that has only the flimsiest connection with the actual text of the Constitution" (Friedman [3rd edn.], 570).

156. That the right to life would seem to have applied to unborn children is suggested by William Blackstone's *Commentaries on the Laws of England* (Book I), when he says that the right of personal security that includes the right to life "begins in contemplation of law as soon as an infant is able to stir in the mother's womb." While the inadequate biology of his time thought that such movement—"quickening"—signaled the beginning of life, the point is that the right attached as soon as it was understood that life was there. The meaning of this is that when the biological knowledge improved and it was realized that life begins at conception, the right would logically have been understood to be in force at that point. Indeed, that better understanding is what motivated the change in the laws in both England and America in the nineteenth century that forbade abortion throughout pregnancy. It should be pointed out that Blackstone had a great influence on American legal and political ideas in the eighteenth and nineteenth centuries. (Krason, *The Public Order and the Sacred Order*, 123.)

157. Friedman (3rd edn.), 579.

158. "Divorce Rates [from monthly vital statistics reports]," http://www.bsos.umd. edu/socy/vanneman/socy441/trends/divorce.html; Internet; accessed Oct. 25, 2009.

159. Friedman (3rd edn.), 580.

160. Mary Ann Glendon, *The Transformation of Family Law: State, Law, and the Family in the United States and Western Europe* (Chicago: University of Chicago Press, 1989), 282-283. She lists the numerous decisions in a note.

161. Ibid., 280. The case was the famous celebrity *Marvin v. Marvin* case, 557 P.2d 106 (Cal. 1976).

162. Hayward (2001), 235. The decision was *Shapiro v. Thompson*, 394 U.S. 618 (1969).

163. See: *Swann v. Charlotte-Mecklenburg Board of Education*, 402 U.S. 1 (1971); *Keyes v. School District of Denver*, 413 U.S. 189 (1973).

164. Schulman, 69. The decision was *Regents of the University of California v. Bakke*, 438 U.S. 265 (1978).

165. Schulman, 70. The decision was *Lau v. Nichols*, 414 U.S. 563 (1974).

166. Mason and Stephenson, 627 The decisions were: *Reed v. Reed*, 404 U.S. 71 (1971); *Frontiero v. Richardson*, 411 U.S. 677 (1973); and *Craig v. Boren*, 429 U.S. 190 (1976).

167. Mason and Stephenson, 386.

168. Ibid., 385. The decision was *Robinson v. California*, 370 U.S. 660 (1962).

169. Ibid. The decision was *Gideon v. Wainwright*, 372 U.S. 335 (1963).

170. Ibid. The decision was *Malloy v. Hogan*, 378 U.S. 1 (1964).

171. Ibid. The decision was *Pointer v. Texas*, 380 U.S. 400 (1965).

172. Ibid. The decision was *Parker v. Gladden*, 385 U.S. 363 (1966).

173. Ibid. The decision was *Washington v. Texas*, 388 U.S. 14 (1967).

174. Ibid. The decision was *Klopfer v. North Carolina*, 388 U.S. 213 (1967).

175. Ibid. The decision was *Duncan v. Louisiana*, 391 U.S. 145 (1968)

176. Ibid. The decision was *Benton v. Maryland*, 395 U.S. 784 (1969).

177. 367 U.S. 643 (1961) and 384 U.S. 436 (1966), respectively.

178. Mason and Stephenson, 402, 410-411.

179. Ibid., 405, 403. The decisions were *Katz v. U.S.*, 389 U.S. 347 (1967) and *Chimel v. California*, 395 U.S. 752 (1969)

180. Ibid., 336. The decision was *Goldberg v. Kelly*, 397 U.S. 254 (1970).

181. Ibid. The decision was *Perry v. Sindermann*, 408 U.S. 593 (1972).

182. Ibid., 337. The decision was *Goss v. Lopez*, 419 U.S. 565 (1975).

183. See Mason and Stephenson, 402 (on *Mapp*). There is, of course, no question about the common law background to the Fifth Amendment's right against self-incrimination, which (as noted) is what was involved in *Miranda* (see Leonard W. Levy, *Origins of the Fifth Amendment* [N.Y.: Macmillan, 1986], 301-334). There was, however, no obligation at common law for law enforcement authorities to inform an accused person of his right to remain silent and to have an attorney present. Nevertheless, there is a certain logic to the rules established by the Court in these cases: if there should not have been a search in the first place because there was no legal authority to conduct one, then the evidence found should be treated as if it were not found; if a suspect during interrogation said something that would implicate him because he was unaware of his right to remain silent and no effort was made to inform him of that right, it follows that his statements should be considered as if he had never made them. Still, the logic—and reasonableness—of these rules does not establish that it was within the Court's authority to lay them down. Since such requirements do not appear in the Constitution and were not found at common law it would have been the province of legislatures, not the courts, to establish them.

184. 367 U.S. 203.

185. See Mason and Stephenson, 476.

186. 395 U.S. 444.

187. Mason and Stephenson, 476-477.

188. Ibid., 478. The decision was *Cohen v. California*, 403 U.S. 15 (1971).

189. 376 U.S. 254.

190. Mason and Stephenson, 483.

191. Ibid. The decision was *Curtis Publishing Co. v. Butts*, 388 U.S. 130 (1967).

192. 403 U.S. 713.

193. Mason and Stephenson, 482-483.

194. Ibid., 189-190. The decision was *Buckley v. Valeo*, 424 U.S. 1 (1976).

195. See *Torcaso v. Watkins*, 367 U.S. 488 (1961).

196. On these latter two points, see Krason, *The Public Order and the Sacred Order*, 191-228.

197. See *Lemon v. Kurtzman*, 411 U.S. 192 (1971).

198. See Krason, *The Public Order and the Sacred Order*, 191-228.

199. *Flast v. Cohen*, 392 U.S. 83 (1968).

200. See: *Sherbert v. Verner*, 374 U.S. 398 (1963); *Wisconsin v. Yoder*, 406 U.S. 205 (1971).

201. See Friedman (3rd edn.), 556-557, 565.

202. See: ibid., 565; John M. Scheb and John M. Scheb II, *Criminal Law* (5th edn.; Belmont, Calif.: Wadsworth, 2009), 279.

203. Glendon, 295.

204. Ambrose and Brinkley, 216-217.

205. Ibid., 175-176.

206. Ibid., 172.

207. Ibid., 206-207.

208. Ibid., 194.

209. Ibid., 206-208.

210. Ibid., 183, 187, 208.

211. See ibid., 197.

212. James Turner Johnson, an expert on the ethics of warfare and the Western just war tradition, says that "the difficulty of separating assassination from murder, which is universally taboo, has kept this extreme from being reached in the moral and legal traditions on war." (Johnson, *Can Modern War Be Just?* [New Haven, Conn.: Yale University Press, 1984], 146.)

213. Ambrose and Brinkley, 206.

214. See ibid., 202.

215. See "Viet Cong," http://en.wikipedia.org/wiki/Viet_Cong; Internet; accessed Oct. 27, 2009.

216. See James Turner Johnson, 25.

217. Ambrose and Brinkley, 203, 227. They say that the nuclear option, however, "was never very tempting" for military and domestic and international political reasons, and because of the fear of nuclear retaliation against South Vietnam by the U.S.S.R. or China (227).

218. See James Turner Johnson, 27.

219. See, e.g., Ambrose and Brinkley, 222-223; Hayward (2001), 300.

220. James Turner Johnson, 21.

221. Ambrose and Brinkley, 249.

222. Ibid., 241.

223. Schulman, 221.

224. See Tocqueville, II, iii, 648-649.

225. Tindall and Shi, 1043.

226. Tocqueville, II, iii, 662.

227. Ambrose and Brinkley, 284.

228. Ibid., 281.

229. Ibid., 281-282, 284-285. The first two quotations are from 282, and the third is from 281.

230. See Diamond, Fisk, and Garfinkel, 558-560.

231. Ibid., 560. They say that while "[m]any argued that America was obliged to befriend actively the cause of republicanism everywhere, to give diplomatic and military aid to republican revolutionaries"—e.g., supporting the revolutionary cause in France (see Chapter 2)—this policy was not the one adopted in the crucial early years of the Republic, and it is quite unclear anyway that had it been adopted it would have embraced moral crusading or interventionism to the degree that has sometimes been seen in American policy since World War I (ibid.).

232. See Ambrose and Brinkley, 290.

233. Gerhart Niemeyer argues from the perspective of a foreign policy realist that shaping a foreign policy specifically in opposition to an evil ideology like communism is a moralistic approach to foreign policy that is not only merited, but necessary. He contrasts it to a foreign policy, like Carter's or Wilson's, which is shaped by a moralistic approach per se. He calls the latter "universal moralism," whereas the kind of foreign policy approach he endorses would be a "selective moralism" (see Niemeyer, "Foreign Policy and Morality," *The Intercollegiate Review*, vol. 15, no. 2 [Spring 1980], 77-84).

234. See Ambrose and Brinkley, 293-294.

235. See "Yom Kippur War," http://en.wikipedia.org/wiki/Yom_Kippur_War; Internet; accessed Jan. 12, 2010.

236. See Tindall and Shi, 1587, 1618. The quotation is from 1587.

237. Dethloff, 281.

238. Matusow, 83-85.

239. Ibid., 86-90.

240. "16th Street Baptist Church Bombing," http://en.wikipedia.org/wiki/16th_Street_Baptist_Church_bombing; Internet; accessed Nov. 8, 2009.

241. See Manchester, 1064-1065.

242. "1967 Detroit Riot," http://en.wikipedia.org/wiki/1967_Detroit_riot; Internet; accessed Nov. 8, 2009.

243. Matusow, 345; Manchester, 1076-1077. The quotation is from Matusow, 345.

244. See Manchester, 1076-1078.

245. Matusow, 345.

246. Manchester, 1078.

247. Ibid., 1198.

248. Schulman, 114.

249. Hayward (2001), 611-612; Schulman, 60. The quotation is from Hayward (2001), 612.

250. Manchester, 1166, 1199; "Weather Underground Organization," http://en.wikipedia.org/wiki/Weather_Underground_Organization; Internet; accessed Nov. 8, 2009.

251. Schulman, 60-61.

252. Ibid., 58.

253. Ibid., 56.

254. Ibid., 66-67. On the growth of ethnic studies programs in universities, see "Ethnic Studies," http://en.wikipedia.org/wiki/Ethnic_studies; Internet; accessed March 7, 2010.

255. Schulman, 81.

256. Ibid., 87.

257. Burner, Marcus, and West, 137-138.

258. Schulman, 83.

259. Ibid., 68.

260. Ibid., 71.

261. Burner, Marcus, and West, 136.

262. Schulman, 69.

263. See, e.g.: Thomas Sowell, "Affirmative Action Around the World," *Hoover Digest*, No. 4 (2004), http:// www.hoover.org/publications/digest/3010426.html; Internet; accessed Feb 8, 2010; "Race and Affirmative Action: An Interview with Professor Glenn Loury of Harvard University (1985)" (in *Education Update*), http://www.ourcivilisation.com/cooray/rights/chap17.htm; Internet; accessed Feb. 8, 2010; John M. Ellis, "On Discarding Affirmative Action," *Academic Questions*, vol. 8, no. 4 (Fall 1995), 68-69; Russell K. Nieli, "The Changing Shape of the River: Affirmative Action and Recent Social Science Research," *Academic Questions*, vol. 17, no. 4 (Fall 2004), 20-34.

264. Allan P. Sindler, "Equality of Opportunity: Preferential Admission to Law School for Minorities," in Sindler, 236.

265. "Interracial Marriage in the United States," http://en.wikipedia.org/wiki/Interracial_marriage_in_the_United_ States; Internet; accessed Dec 4, 2009.

266. Theodore H. White, *The Making of the President* 1960 (N.Y.: Atheneum, 1961), 107-108, 259-262; Jay Dolan, "The Right of a Catholic to Be President," *Notre Dame Magazine* (Autumn 2008), http://magazine.nd.edu/ news/1155/; Internet; accessed Feb. 27, 2010.

267. Marty, 53.

268. Patrick J. Buchanan, *State of Emergency: The Third World Invasion and Conquest of America* (N.Y.: St. Martin's [Thomas Dunne Bks.], 2006), 238-240.

269. See, e.g., ibid., 107-114.

270. See Higgins, 352, 425.

271. Hayward (2001), 10.

272. Matusow, 306.

273. Christopher Lasch, *The Culture of Narcissism: American Life in An Age of Diminishing Expectations* (N.Y.: W.W. Norton, 1979), 21.

274. Matusow, 306.

275. Lasch, 21.

276. Ibid., 23.

277. Manchester, 1166.

278. Paul Johnson, *A History of the American People*, 846.

279. See Judith A. Riesman, *"Soft Porn" Plays Hardball: Its Tragic Effects on Women, Children and the Family* (Lafayette, La.: Huntington House, 1991), 58-67.

280. This was the name of a ABC-TV special about this sweeping new fashion development, which aired on Feb. 28, 1967. For a fuller understanding of how sweeping of a repudiation of fashion tradition this represented, see: Anne Hollander, "Drawing the Line," *Slate* (June 4, 1998), http://www.slate.com/id/3106/; Internet; accessed Nov. 12, 2009.

281. Matusow, 306; Manchester, 1107; Hayward (2001), 312, 8, 151; Matusow, 302; Schulman, 17.

282. Schulman, xv.

283. Manchester, 1109.

284. Hayward (2001), 291.

285. Schulman, 16.

286. Cheryl Wetzstein, "Real Drawbacks of Cohabiting" ("On the Family" column), *The Washington Times* (Sept. 20, 2009), 16 (Family Section), citing Census Bureau data.

287. Ibid., 150.

288. See Hayward (2001), 150.

289. See Manchester, 1107-1108, 1193.

290. *Family Almanac '72* (N.Y.: New York Times, 1971), 494; Patrick Mondout, "Super70s Statistics: Illegitimate Births," (citing Centers for Disease Control and Prevention statistics); http://www.super70s.com/Super70s/Timeline/Stats/Illegitimate Births.asp; Internet; accessed Nov. 12, 2009.

291. *Family Almanac '72*, 306.

292. Hayward (2001), 316-317.

293. See Krason, *Abortion: Politics, Morality, and the Constitution*, 337-349; Geraldine Lux Flanagan, *The First Nine Months of Life* (N.Y.: Simon and Schuster, 1962, 1965).

294. Schulman, 179-180.

295. Hayward (2001), 311.

296. Clecak, 216.

297. Schulman, 161.

298. George Guilder, "Women in the Work Force," *The Atlantic* (Sept. 1986), http://www.theatlantic.com/doc/198609/women-work-force; Internet; accessed Nov. 14, 2009.

299. See, e.g., the summary of the views of various leading feminist writers of the period in Andreas J. Köstenberger, "Feminism, Family, and the Bible: A Biblical Assessment of Feminism's Impact on American Families," *The Religion & Society Report* (online edition; vol. 23, no.1), http://www.profam.org/pub/rs/rs.2301.htm#Recent _Developments_in_Feminists'_Stance_Toward_the_Family; Internet; accessed Nov. 14, 2009.

300. Ibid.; see also: Bryce J. Christensen, *Utopia Against the Family: The Problems and Politics of the American Family* (San Francisco: Ignatius Press, 1990), 35-39.

301. Schulman, 165.

302. See, e.g., Cheryl Wetzstein, "Generation X's Rough Childhood" ("On the Family" column), *The Washington Times* (Sept. 6, 2009), 14 (Family Section).

303. Christopher Jencks, "Is the American Underclass Growing," in Christopher Jencks and Paul E. Peterson, eds., *The Urban Underclass* (Washington, D.C.: Brookings Institution, 1991), 59, citing *Current Population Reports*.

304. Kelly Boyer Sagert, *The 1970's* (Westport, Conn.: Greenwood, 2007), 49.

305. See Matusow, 213.

306. See Glendon, 282-284.

307. Schulman, 9, 16.

308. See: Matusow, 302; Schulman, 16-17.

309. Jacques Barzun, *The House of Intellect* (N.Y.: Harper and Brothers, 1959), discussed and quoted in Kirk, *Decadence and Renewal in the Higher Learning*, 82-83.

310. See Paul Eidelberg, "Karl Marx and the Declaration of Independence: The Meaning of Marxism," *Intercollegiate Review* (Spring/Summer 1984), 3-11.

311. Hayward (2001), 611.

312. See "Drugs and Crime: Behavioral Aspects - The Drugs-Violence Connection," http://law.jrank.org/pages/1031/Drugs-Crime-Behavioral-Aspects-drugs-violence-connection.html; Internet; accessed Feb. 7, 2010.

313. Patrick F. Fagan, "The Real Root Causes of Violent Crime: The Breakdown of Marriage, Family, and Community," *The Backgrounder* (March 17, 1995), 2. This contrasts with what was said about crime in the middle decades of the nineteenth century.

314. See: Ahlstrom, 1087, 1091; David Carlin, *The Decline and Fall of the Catholic Church in America* (Manchester, N.H.: Sophia Institute Press, 2003), 12, 106.

315. William A. Donohue, *Secular Sabotage: How Liberals Are Destroying Religion and Culture in America* (N.Y.: Faith Words, 2009), 206; see also: Krason, *Abortion: Politics, Morality, and the Constitution*, 16-39.

316. See Ahlstrom, 1082-1087.

317. Ahlstrom, 1050; Schulman, 96-100.

318. See, e.g., Whitehead, Kenneth D., "The Cost of Dissent," *The Catholic World Report* (June, 2003); and Kenneth D. Whitehead, "How Dissent Became Institutionalized in the Church in America," *Homiletic & Pastoral Review* (July, 1999).

319. Burner, Marcus, and West, 137, 166.

320. Ibid., 137.

321. Schulman, 92-96; Tindall and Shi, 1608.

322. Patterson, 142-143. The quotation is from 142.

323. Marty, 170.

324. See Schulman, 246-249.

325. Ravitch, 235, 237.

326. Ibid., 240-241, 250-251.

327. Ibid., 251.

328. Philip N. Marcus, "Evidence of Decline in Educational Standards," in William J. Johnston, *Education on Trial: Strategies for the Future* (San Francisco: ICS Press, 1985), 11.

329. See, e.g., Marcus, 11-12; Ruth B. Love, "Educational Standards: A Public Educator's View," in Johnston, 42-43; Kirk, *Decadence and Renewal in the Higher Learning*, 107, 166.

330. John Agresto, "The Failure of American Education As Both a Radical and a Conservative Enterprise," in Stephen M. Krason, ed. *The Recovery of American Education: Reclaiming a Vision* (Lanham, Md.: University Press of America, 1991), 6-8.

331. John S. Schmitt, "The No Longer Ask the Big Questions," in ibid., 10-11.

332. Ravitch, 255.

333. This is seen by the fact that Agresto and Schmitt write about these continuing problems in the late 1980s and early 1990s.

334. Kirk, *Decadence and Renewal in the Higher Learning*, 92-93, 122-123, 132-133, 147; the first quotation is from 132 and the second is from 133.

335. See Schrems, 221-228. Mills thought that the elite was composed of a very small group of interlocking people in different leading sectors of U.S. society, whereas most political scientists were among the "pluralists" discussed in Chapter 7 who believed that the numbers of the elites were much larger and were different in different fields of endeavor. Whether it was a very small or much larger group, and whether they were interconnected or just controlled decisions in their specific area of endeavor, both sides believed that the American life was characterized by elite domination.

336. Matusow, 312-313.

337. Clecak, 78-79.

338. Schulman, 13-14, 17; Matusow, 342.

339. Clecak, 74.

340. Krason, *The Public Order and the Sacred Order*, 518. A good example of a work that evinces such a perspective is Arthur M. Schlesinger, Jr., *The Vital Center: The Politics of Freedom* (Boston: Houghton Mifflin, 1948).

341. Clecak, 75.

342. Schrems, 123.

343. Clecak, 68-69.

344. Schulman, 90-91.

345. See: Robert J. Bresler, "The Roots of Conservative Populism," *USA Today* (Society for the Advancement of Education), http://findarticles.com/p/articles/mi _m1272/is_n2612_v124/ai_18274636/pg_3/?tag=content;col1; Internet; accessed Feb. 8, 2010; "McCarthyism," http://en.wikipedia.org/wiki/McCarthyism#Popular_support; Internet; accessed Feb. 8, 2010.

346. "New Right," http://en.wikipedia.org/wiki/New_Right#United_States; Internet; accessed Nov. 17. 2009.

347. See: Max Schulz, "Moral Majority," in *American Conservatism: An Encyclopedia*, 590, and Raymond Wolters, "New Right," in ibid., 625.

348. Schulman, 204.

349. Ibid., 195.

350. Lasch, 22.

351. See, e.g.: Kilpatrick; Paul C. Vitz, *Psychology As Religion: The Cult of Self-Worship* (Grand Rapids, Mich.: Eerdmans, 1977).

352. "Philip Rieff," http://en.wikipedia.org/wiki/Philip_Rieff; Internet; accessed Nov. 17, 2009.

353. See: Ernest van den Haag, *Punishing Criminals: Concerning a Very Old and Painful Question* (N.Y.: Basic Books, 1975), 122-123; James Q. Wilson and Richard J. Herrnstein, *Crime and Human Nature* (N.Y.: Simon and Schuster, 1985), 504-506, 518-522.

354. Hayward (2001), xxvi.

355. John F. Kennedy, Inaugural Address (Jan. 20, 1961), in *Inaugural Addresses of the Presidents of the United States: From George Washington, 1789 to John F. Kennedy, 1961* (Washington, D.C.: U.S. Government Printing Office, 1961), 268.

356. See Kirk, *The Roots of American Order*, 3-10.

CHAPTER 9

1980-PRESENT: THE UPSURGE OF CONSERVATISM, ECONOMIC TRANSFORMATION, AND POST-COLD WAR AMERICA

We have already presented an overview of the history of the period since 1980. The post-1980 period has been a time, as we see below, when conservatism became a major force in American politics and Ronald Reagan was the most successful and respected of the period's five presidents. As was the case during the administrations of the previous Republican presidents after 1945, however, the Democratic-generated welfare state showed its durability. It was also a time of changed economic life due to globalization. The sudden, unexpected collapse of the Cold War was the greatest international development of the period, and ushered in a new foreign policy emphasis for the U.S. that focused heavily on the Middle East/Central Asia and Islamic terrorism—but continued a policy of interventionism, although often under a multi-lateral umbrella, under presidents of both parties. The cultural transformation of the 1960s and 1970s largely continued, and in fact many aspects of it became deeply ingrained into American life. Some of the trends presented a serious challenge to the principles and conditions of the American Founding and its culture, although not as starkly as in the 1960-1980 period and not without political and intellectual resistance. The areas that we examine are similar to those that were considered for the 1960-1980 period: Economics and Economic and Social Welfare Policy; The Role and Powers of Government, Relations Among the Three Branches of the Federal Government, and Federal-State Relations; Political Developments, Trends, and Reform; Legal and Constitutional Developments and Citizen Rights; Foreign and Defense Policy, War and International Conflicts, and America's Role in the World; Relations and Conflict Among Social Groups, and Immigration; and Socio-Political Developments and Intellectual Trends.

Economics and Economic and Social Welfare Policy. We mentioned the serious economic problems of the 1970s. When Ronald Reagan came to power in 1981, he made economic policy the main focus of the first year of his presidency. His policy was a combination of budget-cutting—actually, it was reducing the size of the federal budget increase—and "supply-side" economics. The latter essentially involved tax cuts, which would stimulate more investment and entrepreneurial activity and so spur economic growth and increase personal income—which would result in larger tax collections (i.e., lower tax rates, but more inflow of tax dollars to government).[1] The tax cut which he successfully marshaled through Congress cut federal income taxes 23% over three years, reduced the top marginal rate from 70% to 50%, and also cut rates in the lower brackets. The budget cuts that were enacted were in domestic spending means-tested programs (e.g., public assistance, food stamps), paring a half a million people from the Social Security disability program, and eliminating the Comprehensive Employment and Training Act (CETA) that had provided 300,000 jobs.[2] He realized that there was no possibility of actually *ending* major New Deal-Great Society entitlement programs, however. His conclusion was similar to the one Eisenhower made in the 1950s (noted in Chapter 7). As Patterson says, Reagan understood the conflicting attitude Americans had about government: "they distrusted…[it but] expected important services from it." He also came face to face with the power of interest groups to sustain big government. There were actually incremental increases in key federal social welfare programs in the 1980s.[3] In his first term, after the initial budget cuts, Reagan strikingly proposed significant increases in expenditures for a number of social welfare programs.[4]

At various times in the 1980s, there were different types of economic developments. Some of these probably resulted from federal economic policies. The federal deficit increased in the 1980s, owing to these domestic increases (especially such programs as Medicare and Social Security, which as entitlements could not be cut in the annual federal budget), the rise in the federal civilian workforce, and Reagan's military buildup. It was true that the tax cuts increased revenue, but this was more than offset by the higher spending. During the decade, the federal deficit shot up from 33% to 53% of GDP. Reagan's most ambitious politico-economic initiative was his proposed Economic Bill of Rights, which helped frame the debate on controlling federal spending in the next decade but ultimately did not get off the ground. It called for the following constitutional reforms: a federal spending limit, a line-item veto (whereby the president could veto specific appropriations in legislation without vetoing the entire bill), a mandated balanced budget, a prohibition on wage and price controls, and a requirement for a two-thirds majority in each Congressional chamber to pass tax increases.[5] In spite of his tax-cutting preferences, Reagan found himself going back and forth during his two terms in upping and reducing various federal taxes.[6] In fact, in the decade the U.S. switched from being the largest creditor nation to being the largest debtor nation as the trade deficit sharply increased.[7] Massive government spending was not limited to the federal level; the spending of all levels of government combined made up 36% of GNP at the beginning of the 1980s.[8] The high rates of inflation in the 1970s gave way to recession in 1981-82. Consumer spending remained high during the latter— possibly because of the initial tax cuts—and throughout the decade real disposable income rose. When the economy picked up again a large variety of consumer goods hit the market. The consumerism that began in a more limited way in the 1920s, resumed in the 1950s, continued (in spite of economic difficulties) in the 1960s and 1970s, and boomed in the 1980s. Patterson writes that people bought more, but kept wanting still more and remained personally unfulfilled. A further consequence was that they were burdened by deepening debt—just as the federal government was burdened by a deepening deficit.[9] Again, the teaching of the Founders of avoiding excessive public debt went unheeded by the national leadership (despite Reagan's good intentions), as did the Founding cultural norms of frugality, temperance, and simplicity by the American public.

Other key Reagan economic policies included the reduction of the number of antitrust actions by the Department of Justice and more permissive merger guidelines. This followed a changed thinking in the years before that about anti-trust in certain circles, which held that previous policy had been "arbitrary, capricious, and economically counterproductive." The result was that there was an increase in corporate mergers in the 1980s.[10] Reagan also tried to push regulatory reform, to reduce the amount of federal regulation that business was subject to. Congress was reluctant, so the administration tried to rein in regulations as best it could through administrative means. It really did not succeed in rolling back regulations. As with the budget, where it reduced the rate of growth, it reduced the rate of promulgation of new regulations. Still, almost 90% of proposed regulations formulated in the federal bureaucracy were accepted unscathed by the administration. The latter's efforts to reduce regulations in such areas as the environment, civil rights, meat packing, and banking went nowhere.[11] Again, Reagan discovered the difficulty of reversing the direction of the federal government since FDR.

Such deregulation as did occur (actually, the limiting of regulations over such matters as pricing and competition in certain industries), which actually began in the 1970s,[12] is singled out by Gil Troy as one of the causes of an unruly situation in the corporate world in the 1980s. Other causes were corporate "raiding" (i.e., hostile takeovers aimed at increasing the value of stock shares to enrich the raiders or eliminate a company for some other reason), "24/7 traders" (who created instability in the stock market), insider trading (which resulted in some of the biggest economic scandals of the decade), the rise of "junk bonds" that enabled clever traders to get inordinate returns at the risk of harming companies and throwing people out of work, and a general decline in corporate ethics.[13] It was also a time when CEO salaries mushroomed—even arguably beyond what they would have been under an already problematical supply and demand standard—which perhaps rewarded business managers too much. This, of course, further perpetuated income inequalities—something that the Founding Era had held in check. As government and individual citizens spent beyond their means, such behavior was publicly extolled by the likes of the increasingly prominent junk bond investment king, Michael Milken, who urged people not to even pay off their mortgages but just get the value out of their home purchases and walk away. He made greed and irresponsibility outright economic virtues.[14] We see here an outright flouting of numerous Founding Era norms: promise-keeping, frugality, sobriety, a willingness to practice present sacrifice for future good, honesty, avoidance of individualism, self-restraint, concern for the general welfare (since almost anyone could see that actions such as these could not help but harm it), and just general personal responsibility. On the positive side, deregulation may have helped spur creativity among inventors and a greater willingness among investors to take risks—as manifested by the significant technological innovations of the 1980s—and encourage a sense of empowerment among corporate managers and stockholders. It also lowered prices and heightened competition in some industries.[15] Still, it must be remembered that government economic regulation was not infrequent in the Founding Era, although centralized regulation was unknown and an *excessive* amount of economic regulation in any case would have been unacceptable. The 24/7 trading and the explosion of computer trading that was part of it—and which led to considerable speculation—was probably the main cause of the substantial stock market crash of October 19, 1987 (although the bull market returned a year later and consumer spending was not much affected).[16] We have seen repeatedly that speculation was at the root of many economic crises in American history, and it represented an embracing of the ethic of individualism at odds with the Founding. It was not in the spirit of early America's endorsement of everyone having the opportunity of wealth accumulation without clear limits—indeed, it would have contravened the public-spiritedness and concern for the general welfare of the Founding—although that very spirit of unlimited accumulation and the strong focus on the notion of a commercial republic in the Founding may have helped give rise to it.

    In the 1980s, some sectors of the economy declined due to new technology, failure to adapt, and corporate-style bureaucratic inertia. For example, Troy comments that the American auto industry "had grown too big, bureaucratic, and staid" in the 1970s, and as a result did not realize that buyers wanted fuel-efficient cars that they could only get from Japan.[17] They struggled in the early 1980s and rebounded after getting the Reagan administration to put some trade restrictions in place.[18] Still, after the early 1980s recession and despite the country's continued transition to a service-oriented economy, the manufacturing sector actually increased.[19] This indicated that American manufacturing could not just be written off. As part of the stress on investment, wealth accumulation, and less socially activist government during the decade, Americans "accepted greater economic insecurity in return for the possibility of greater personal property."[20] Even as the real income of Americans was increasing, the gap in wealth between the richest and the poorest expanded.[21] This, of course, was counter to the relative economic equality of the Founding Era, and continued a long-run trend that—as discussed—began as far back as the end of the first quarter of the nineteenth century.

Most of the one-term presidency of George H.W. Bush witnessed a lengthy recession, the longest since the Great Depression to that time. During 1991, 20% of the country's workforce was unemployed at some point. The recession struck white-collar workers disproportionately, as many companies were downsizing and reducing the size of their middle management to cut costs. Besides declining sales and profits, the federal deficit deepened still more and the foreign trade imbalance continued.[22] Median family income actually dropped during the Bush years and the income gap above continued.[23] Concern about the deficit motivated Bush to break a pledge he had made in his nomination acceptance speech at the 1988 Republican Convention that he would not consider imposing new taxes, which proved to be a "political disaster" for him.[24] Beyond this, there were no significant economic policy initiatives from his administration. Government social programs, such as unemployment compensation and welfare, increased.[25] This signaled that a just wage, stressed in the Founding Era, was absent for at least some people (and possibly also, the ethic of industry was not there for some).

In contrast to Bush, when Clinton came into office he quickly proposed a program to reduce the deficit—with tax increases and spending reductions—and to stimulate the economy with investment in public works and social welfare spending[26] (even though the latter had never proven to stimulate the economy directly—except perhaps by increasing the number of government workers— and had played a significant role in increasing the deficit). He also secured approval, in spite of division within his party, of the North American Free Trade Agreement (NAFTA)—the negotiations had begun under Reagan, but the agreement reached under Bush—which eliminated trade and investment barriers among the U.S., Canada, and Mexico.[27] He also got a renewed GATT (General Agreement on Tariffs and Trade) treaty ratified by the Senate. Both agreements were in line with his desire to maintain the U.S. as "the world leader inside the global economy."[28] Along with this, Clinton normalized trade relations with the People's Republic of China, believing that in the long run it would pave the way to political and economic freedom.[29] NAFTA seemed to cause some job loss in the U.S. manufacturing sector—although not as much as U.S. labor unions had feared (hence a major reason for the opposition within the Democratic party to it)—and also strengthened management's hand in staving off union organizing efforts with threats to move plants to Mexico.[30] This illustrated an absence of such Founding norms as the sense of social obligation for the use of property, a sense of justice, concern for the general welfare, the restraint of individualism, and limits on economic freedom. The fact that public policy permitted this underscored the departure in economic thinking from the Founding Era when laws such as those involving trade restrictions were found. Also, the contentiousness between management and labor and management's cavalier attitude in light of NAFTA about the situation of American workers had a long history in the U.S., becoming especially pronounced after the mid-nineteenth century (as we have seen).

Clinton's major social welfare initiatives were a Family and Medical Leave Act, which required all but small employers to provide three months' unpaid leave for births and serious family illnesses, his failed attempt to provide universal medical coverage for every citizen and legal resident (although he did secure a measure mandating that employees changing jobs could continue to keep and pay for their previous insurance), and increases in the federal student loan program, other education programs (including Head Start, which was noted in Chapter 8 as being of questionable effectiveness), and the minimum wage. Going in a different direction, Clinton joined with the Republican-controlled Congress in 1996 in a major welfare reform measure that turned the main federal assistance programs over to the states (with continued federal subsidization) and put limitations and work requirements on recipients.[31]

By the latter part of the 1990s, the economy was generally booming with reasonably high growth rates and a low level of unemployment. Over nineteen million new jobs were created in the decade, with improvements occurring even in the situation of blue-collar and unskilled workers. By 1998, there was a surplus in the annual federal budget (although this did not include entitlements and Clinton quickly moved to use the surplus to shore up spending for various programs).[32] Still, with the overall upbeat economic outlook, there were many serious problems with the economy—some of which were structural. Corporate downsizing continued, and computerization and advanced automation of factories and other workplaces caused the loss of many jobs that had fit in with older technologies.[33] Throughout the decade, there was a significant mal-distribution of wealth. William C. Berman says that this differential "had been accelerating since the 1980s," and "there had been no appreciable improvement in real wages since the early 1970s."[34] The gap between Caucasians and Negroes was especially striking: the typical Caucasian family earned double the typical Negro family, and the latter's net worth was only *one-tenth* that of the former.[35] Under Clinton, there was also a deepening trade deficit and—previous chapters have made it clear that this was hardly new—an increasing susceptibility of the U.S. to economic problems abroad as part of the burgeoning global economy. Also, the personal debt problem of the 1980s was reaching new depths. Berman says that 'the ratio of household debt to after-tax income" shot up from 59% in 1984 to a whopping 83% in 1997. Corporate debt rose also. As Berman observes, "the boom of the 1990s was driven to a considerable extent by an enormous expansion of corporate and consumer debt."[36] He also argues that the weakened state of the American labor movement "contributed to the persistent wage inequality." With not even 15% of America's workforce unionized—and a good chunk of that was in the public sector—it had "a radically weakened position vis-à-vis corporate America."[37] We see here the deviation from a number Founding norms and conditions: frugality, thrift, sobriety, self-restraint, temperance, avoidance of luxury (the consumer debt occurred partly because people sought this), willingness to practice present sacrifice for future good, economic inequality, and lack of a just wage. The ongoing existence of large corporations dominating the economy underscored the long-term departure from the Founding norms of economic decentralization and the merging of ownership and management.

In the first decade of the twenty-first century, during the presidency of George W. Bush, unemployment first rose, then dropped, and then rose again to its highest rate in fifteen years as he was leaving office.[38] There is some dispute about whether median household income slightly increased or slightly dropped during this period. The national debt shot up a full 100%.[39] There seemed to be almost obliviousness to the Founding admonition to avoid excessive public debt. In September 2008, when the economy was already in recession, a serious financial situation developed from the upheaval in the sub-prime mortgage market and the other factors below. This led to the collapse or near-collapse of Fannie Mae and Freddie Mac (the nicknames for the federal government enterprises that back up mortgage-lending institutions), the Bear Stearns and Lehman Brothers investment banks, American International Group (AIG), and other large and small financial institutions, and also triggered a very sharp decline in the housing market and in housing values. In addition to this, the country experienced a soaring of oil prices, a declining dollar value, and an extremely tight credit market since lending institutions that had sufficient capital were unwilling to lend because of the tumultuous situation. This had the effect of stymieing job creation and deepening the recession.[40] The Bush administration responded with a massive economic stimulus plan, wherein the federal government bought up the debt related to the bad mortgages held by (especially) some of the largest lenders, outright took over the operation of Fannie Mae and Freddie Mac, and even invested in such companies as AIG—effectively nationalizing them.[41] The latter practice was expanded somewhat when Barack Obama came into the presidency the following year. Bush had "advocated...[an o]wnership society, premised on the concepts of individual accountability, smaller government, and the owning of property"—and probably the main economic initiative he had previously undertaken was tax cuts—but with the new developments he pushed for an unprecedented level of federal intervention in financial sector.[42] So even though his stated principles echoed the Founding Era, his policy actually furthered a centralization opposed to it. Many factors—usually involving the government or corporate practices—have been pointed to as helping to bring on the serious situation of 2008, including the widespread mortgage speculation that accompanied the sharp increase in housing values of the previous decade; excessively easy credit conditions that encouraged homeowners to refinance their mortgages (which had adjustable rates) followed by a shift upwards in interest rates by the Federal Reserve Board that caused homeowners to be unable to handle new higher payments; sub-prime lending that saw financial institutions—following federal regulations aimed at promoting more homeownership especially among minorities and those of modest income, and in poor neighborhoods—making loans to people who were probably credit risks; predatory lending, in which homeowners got mortgages at seemingly low rates when there were really hidden or unclear provisions that required them to pay a great deal more down the road; financial innovation that spawned new possibilities for potentially troublesome speculative behavior and the failure of government regulation to keep pace with it; the continuation—and, in fact, acceleration—of the private debt problem of the 1980s and 1990s (above) and the deepening debt of financial institutions; a related confusion about how to understand the level of risk that should be associated with many of the new financial products that had appeared; the increasing use of alternative financial institutions other than banks ("the shadow banking system") whose financial strength was often in doubt; a sharp increase in commodity prices, especially oil, which adversely affected economic growth; problems of unproductive investment (i.e., excessive investment in the financial sector instead of in other areas of the economy that would have involved actual goods and other services) due to a combination of the deregulation that had occurred in the financial sector, long-term decline in GDP growth rates, and the oversaturation of markets previously with too many—perhaps unnecessary— goods and services; the related problem of imperviousness to the genuine value of the goods and services produced by companies and instead artificially propping up stock share prices; and increasing irresponsibility by top corporate management and boards of directors, which resulted partly from the ongoing problem—now probably more pronounced than ever—of separation of ownership from management.[43]

Behind these causes of the economic problems of 2008 was the old scourge of speculation. As such it again illustrated the departure from Founding Era morality and virtuous conduct concerning economics. The other norms it represented a deviation from were all too familiar in the period of 1960 to the present: avoidance of individualism, the social obligation of property (which included wealth in general), temperance, frugality, the avoidance of luxury (the latter three seen vividly with the substantial part of the public that simply sought *too much*), promise-keeping, willingness to sacrifice for a future good, shrewd practical intelligence, concern for the general welfare (ignored especially by the big corporate and governmental entities—i.e., Fannie Mae and Freddie Mac— that were involved), and decentralization (both in economics and government). While government economic regulation, again, was in the spirit of the Founding Era, the excessive regulation that seemed to be part of the problem here was not.

Probably the three most noteworthy social welfare initiatives of the George W. Bush administration were the No Child Left Behind Act, the enactment of a Medicare prescription drug program, and Social Security reform. The first of these—a sweeping federal education measure—will be discussed later. The second was a major expansion of the Medicare program, which provided prescription drug coverage exclusively through private insurance companies involving substantial out-of-pocket expenditures. It also provided a federal subsidy to employers to help them continue to offer prescription drug benefits as part of retiree health insurance plans. The program was just enacted in 2004, and the early experience with it has led to projections that it will be much more of a financial burden on the federal government than originally thought.[44] Bush's Social Security reform proposal, for which he campaigned vigorously but unsuccessfully in 2005, had as its main focus permitting citizens to invest a portion of their Social Security tax in certain private investments of their choice.[45] This would have been a small decentralizing initiative; as it was all that happened was more governmental centralization with the new drug scheme and a likely deepening of the federal debt.

In his first year in office, Obama took a strongly activist, interventionist stance on the economy. He pushed through another economic stimulus bill, which aimed to create jobs mostly by funding infrastructure and public school building construction and renovation and assistance to state governments that enabled them to keep up the levels of public employment in difficult economic times. It also increased funds for unemployment compensation, food stamps, and health care. It was thus a funding bill heavily focused on the public sector and social welfare spending.[46] He also signed legislation expanding the State Children's Health Insurance Program, although this was just a legislative stalking horse for his major first-year initiative of enacting the kind of universal health insurance program that had eluded Clinton. He also put in place temporary subsidy programs for car purchases and some home improvements, a tax credit for home purchasing, effectively nationalized part of the auto industry for a time, further buttressed the financial sector by having the federal government buy up depreciated real estate assets, imposed CEO pay limits on companies that the federal government had "bailed out" during the serious 2008 financial situation,[47] and in his second year pushed through new financial sector regulation.[48] The stock market improved in his first year and there was more consumer buying, but (despite the tax credit) home sales lagged, lenders were still reluctant to make business loans, and unemployment continued to climb.[49] While Obama's stress (like his immediate predecessor) on the value of home ownership, limits on economic freedom, and economic regulatory laws certainly conformed to the Founding Era, his heightening (beyond any of his predecessors) of the federal role in that—i.e., with unprecedented nationalizations—was sharply at odds with two norms whose violation we have repeatedly noted in this section: governmental decentralization (which also implied respect for federalism) and avoiding excessive public debt (which clearly his substantial new initiatives would deepen).[50] They also represented an expansion of government social welfare programs that would likely make even the middle class—still predominant in the U.S.—more dependent on government, and thus weaken such Founding norms as household independence and liberty. What's more, with the considerably heightened level of taxation and mandates (e.g., respecting health care) that would likely be imposed on business, including small business, they could suppress the entrepreneurship so touted by Founding culture.

Probably the most significant expansion of the federal social welfare role— and of centralized governmental power (with its undercutting of federalism)— under Obama occurred in his second year in office, with the enactment of his health care reform act (the Patient Protection and Affordable Care Act). This massive piece of legislation included unprecedented legal mandates on U.S. citizens and legal residents to purchase health insurance (assisting some with tax credits), legal mandates on insurance companies to provide certain medical services free of charge and sharply increased federal regulation of them (which had traditionally been a state function), heightened regulation of private health care facilities, and the expansion of Medicaid and consequent new unfunded mandates on state governments.[51] This return to big social welfare schemes indicated that within the ranks of liberalism, and probably also in at least a sizable enough of a portion of the population, there was a renewal of the confidence of the 1960s in the viability of such an approach.

The Role and Powers of Government, Relations Among the Three Branches of the Federal Government, and Federal-State Relations. A number of the points made above about economic policy illustrated how expansive the federal government's role had become by the post-1980 period: efforts at trimming federal rules and regulations had limited success; its role in health care seemed to be expanding significantly; expenditures for existing social welfare and other domestic programs expanded; and the experience of massive federal intervention into the economy since 2008, including not just economic stimulus packages and subsidies to consumers but also unprecedented nationalizations. The significant area that the federal government pulled back on was public assistance, with the welfare reform of 1996—but the federal government was still involved with it by way of subsidies to states and the setting of new rules and standards. Such additional expansion of the federal role and powers as: criminal justice (with a one-third increase in the number of federal crimes on the books since 1980),[52] education (with George W. Bush's No Child Left Behind Act),[53] unprecedented and sweeping federal disability rights regulations (with the Americans With Disabilities Act [ADA]),[54] federal "hate crimes" legislation,[55] gun control (the Brady Law and assault-weapons ban under Clinton and the judicially-nullified Gun-Free School Zones Act),[56] Internal Revenue Service revocation of tax exemptions of private religious institutions for even very limited doctrinally-based racial discrimination (the ban on interracial dating at Bob Jones University),[57] domestic violence (the Violence Against Women Act, also struck down by the U.S. Supreme Court),[58] and disaster relief (the federal government played a large role in the aftermath of Hurricane Katrina in New Orleans, even though it was heavily criticized for supposedly not doing enough and the local and state authorities were insufficiently aggressive in their efforts).[59] The latter underscored the attitude and expectations of much of the American public, media, and other opinion-makers that the federal government was supposed to address almost all public problems, that it was the level of government that people turned to almost by default. Not surprisingly, if the federal government did not disengage from many of the tasks taken on since the New Deal and Great Society or reduce domestic spending under the ideologically conservative and anti-centralization Reagan it certainly did not under either Bush.[60] Even apart from the political clout of entrenched special interests, public opinion really did not support such disengagement.[61] The American experience since the New Deal, then, confirmed Tocqueville's assertion that democratic republics would see enhanced central authority because people would develop the tendency to turn to the state as protector and provider. Except for public assistance, one of the few other areas in which the federal government retreated from asserting itself concerned sexual morality, reproductive rights, and public decency. Abortion, of course, had been ensconced as a constitutional right by the Supreme Court in 1973, but the federal government had gone back-and-forth on such related, ancillary matters as governmental support for abortion and fetal experimentation since that time. While direct federal funding of most abortions through the Medicaid program had been barred since the late 1970s by the Hyde Amendment, the Obama health care reform law held out the prospect of paying for some abortions through certain provisions.[62] Obama, following Clinton, also funded through the USAID (Agency for International Development) international NGOs that performed or promoted abortion, such as IPPF (the International Planned Parenthood Federation).[63] He also broadened federal funding for embryonic stem cell research.[64] Further, from the Reagan period onward the Federal Communications Commission took what Patterson calls a "laissez-faire attitude" about sex and violence in television programming. Producers took advantage of this and "boldly featured" both.[65] The level of federal pornography prosecutions went back and forth—less during Democratic administrations than Republican ones, generally[66]—but overall, even on the state and local level, pornography was not prosecuted extensively.[67] Most of the governmental decentralization that occurred, then, seemed to be on matters that would have affronted Founding Era morality.

Republican Senator Howard Baker of Tennessee, who became Majority Leader in 1981, said that the pace of Congressional legislating was altering the traditional status of the Senate as a great deliberative body. Insisting that fewer federal laws were needed, he said that the important issues of the time were no longer being debated on the Senate floor as they had been earlier in American history; he said there was more debate in the corridor outside his office door than on the floor.[68]

The federal government was not the only level of government that was either entering or expanding legislative, regulatory, and funding activity in different topical areas and regimenting more and more areas of people's lives during the period since 1980. Besides what was mentioned in Chapter 8, in the decades since 1960 such activity exploded on the state and local level in such areas as: animal welfare,[69] occupational licensing,[70] public school spending (whose levels were constantly increasing,[71] even though as stated previously more funding does not necessarily improve educational attainment), eminent domain (whose expansive use was given constitutional imprimatur in the Supreme Court's *Kelo v. New London* decision)[72] zoning,[73] historic preservation (this also effectively received a judicial imprimatur, even when it concerned a church building),[74] aesthetics (even to the point of regulating the kind of vegetation on one's private property),[75] the expansion of criminal law into new areas or areas that were only in the realm of tort previously,[76] and even adding more traffic laws (e.g., requiring people to wear seat belts, put their children into car seats, and turn on their headlights whenever it rains). Tocqueville's prediction (see Chapter 1) that a democratic republic would increasingly control the everyday aspects of life and usher in a gentle despotism seemed to be borne out. The principle of liberty enshrined in the Founding, of course, was a casualty. The implications go further, however. It has been said that the

Founding Fathers wanted to create a governmental structure where what we today call the "political class" would be absorbed in competing with each other and whose ambitions would check each other off (Federalist 10) and thereby protect the citizenry. As government got involved in more and more things, however, the citizenry would become more vulnerable.

Besides the substantial growth of areas that the federal government was regulating, federalism continued to be weakened in the same way as it had been for almost a hundred years: by grants-in-aid programs. Although the number of these programs was cut during the Reagan administration and there were modest reductions when the Republicans took control of Congress in 1995 on the basis of firm commitments to reduce federal spending and programs, in general they sharply increased after 1990 and their expansion in the long haul has continued. By the second half of the first decade of the twenty-first century they had become the third largest item in the federal budget after Social Security and defense. While limits were put on unfunded mandates by legislation and judicial decision, the grants-in-aid programs—which state and local governments developed an increasing budgetary dependence on—were a major factor in shaping and constraining state actions.[77]

It is evident, then, that neither federal power nor governmental power generally was restrained—nor the contemporary liberalism that pushed it along truly reversed (in spite of the difficulties it had)—even under the most rhetorically anti-government president since the 1920s. What Reagan did succeed in doing, Hayward tells us, is to at least get some debates going about it. Still, his assessment implicitly suggests that Reagan failed to adequately carry out—or maybe even appreciate—the educative function of politics. This would have involved his building a systematic, well-structured case about why these developments went against the American constitutional spirit (i.e., went against the Founding), constantly explaining this, driving it home as a matter of course to the media and the public, and from there building a kind of infrastructure that would insure consistent follow-through long after he was gone. Hayward implies that such a thing, if done, might have begun to wear down deep-seated convictions about the fundamental need for an expansive, activist government.[78] We are inclined to believe that this would only have been one of the necessary ingredients—and in no way one of the most fundamental. Such a problem is not primarily a rhetorical or even solely an ideological one (as important as these considerations are). It grows out of long-existing social, cultural, and economic conditions (e.g., the increasing bigness and remoteness of economic enterprises and the lack of sufficient support structures to provide people with economic and other forms of security, whose void government programs have been enacted to fill) that we have noted are at odds with the culture of the Founding Era that spawned our constitutional arrangements.

The period of 1980 to the present featured noteworthy developments in the relations among the three branches of the federal government with respect to a consideration of respect for the principle of separation of powers. The Iran-Contra affair, the Clinton impeachment and accompanying judicial proceedings, the question of executive privilege, and the various presidential wars and acts of committing troops to hostilities abroad are pertinent to Congressional-presidential relations. Selected Supreme Court decisions, of course, are pertinent to relations between the judicial branch on the one hand and the legislative and the executive branches on the other. Regarding Iran-Contra, the putative scandal involved senior Reagan administration figures agreeing to facilitate the sale of arms to a hostile Iran in order to secure the release of American hostages in the Mideast and to fund the Contra rebels who were opposing the Marxist Sandinista regime in Nicaragua. Even though this circumvented a U.S. arms embargo with Iran, the major focus was on the alleged violation of the Boland Amendment that forbade U.S. support in overthrowing the Sandinista government. When the effort, which Reagan did not know about, became public there were televised Senate hearings, a special commission set up by Reagan (the Tower Commission) to investigate, and the appointment of a special prosecutor (which resulted in convictions of several of the figures involved, none of which held up).[79] Initially, the Reagan administration was providing funding assistance to the Contras that it believed was within the confines of the amendment.[80] Later, the amendment was tightened up, but it did not prohibit the raising of funds from independent sources for such assistance (in fact, one version of it gave a "green light" to soliciting aid from foreign nations).[81] While there was a question raised about the constitutionality of the limits the Amendment put on the president's conduct of foreign policy, we think that it was in line with the Founders' intent, as seen in several parts of Article I, Sections 7 and 8 of the Constitution regarding Congressional powers: to make appropriations, to declare war, to raise and support armies, and to make rules for the government and regulation of the land and naval forces. As Hayward says, however, "whether it could restrain the president from supporting the Contras in other ways, such as soliciting private support or support from other nations, is doubtful."[82] In seeming to think that it could, Congress was probably genuinely interfering with legitimate presidential prerogatives. Hayward recounts the partisan press coverage of the affair,[83] salivating of Democrats to "get" the Reagan administration with the thought that another Watergate might have emerged,[84] readiness to appoint a special prosecutor even though the Boland Amendment prescribed no penalties, aggressiveness of the Senate Democrats during the hearings,[85] and the fact that there had for some time been quite a bit of partisanship and leftist ideological opposition on the Contra aid issue.[86] The push to attack and even topple the Reagan administration in light of all this indicated a lack of civility, civic friendship, and concern for the common good (as opposed to mere partisan advantage) at odds with the Founding Era culture.

The Clinton impeachment also showed a lack of civility, although from the other side. While Berman indicates that an objective analysis would conclude that Clinton's untruthfulness in his testimony in the Paula Jones sexual harassment suit against him was damaging to the rule of law and the integrity of the judicial process and deserved a strong response, the Republicans in the House of Representatives rejected a strong censure resolution that almost certainly would have received bi-partisan support in order to push for impeachment as a way of expressing "their implacable hostility to Clinton."[87]

While, to be sure, the offense in question would not have been out of the realm of what would have been considered a grounds for impeachment under the Constitution,[88] the impeachment vote proved to be sharply on partisan lines, was motivated in part by political considerations, and was unpopular with the public.[89] Berman also argues that Clinton's impeachment proceedings, even though he easily staved off removal in the Senate, "continued the long-term loss of presidential prestige that began with Lyndon Johnson's presidency."[90] The effect, then, was like what followed the attempted presidential impeachment of Andrew Johnson. The further problem from an ongoing institutional standpoint—as the Founders foresaw would be the case with a mechanism for impeaching a president—is that it may have harmed presidential independence. This was perhaps even more so because the Clinton matter was not an extreme or open-and-shut case and, as the above indicates and the public perceived, got mixed up with partisanship. Weakening presidential independence, of course, meant threatening the separation of powers. The Supreme Court's decision in *Jones v. Clinton*—Paula Jones' case against Clinton—that a sitting president could face civil suit for actions arising from his unofficial conduct was,[91] we think, a further weakening of the power of the presidency as established by the Founders,[92] and opened a door to the possibility of serious abuses (e.g., politically-motivated lawsuits aimed at bringing down a future sitting president). A similar problem was possibly present with the independent prosecutor law, which was upheld by the Supreme Court in 1988[93] but generated controversy during the investigation leading up to the Clinton impeachment. While under the law the counsel's office is subject to some supervision by a federal court, it has been criticized as being a kind of fourth branch of government.[94] This arguably weakens the president by taking an executive function out of his hands—the prosecutorial power, which on the federal level is normally carried out by his Department of Justice—and thus separation of powers. More, it perhaps strengthens the hand of Congress vis-à-vis the president, since such prosecutors are funded by it and report to it. A further problem of independent counsels, both for separation of powers and the rule of law, was observed in the Clinton investigation: the tendency of the independent counsel to widen the investigation well beyond the subject that was the basis for the counsel's appointment in the first place. While support, in some sense, by the attorney general and approval of a judicial panel was required for such a widening of the investigation,[95] the grants of power to a prosecutor are often very broad and such additional approval can easily be perfunctory (much like the ease with which a regular prosecutor can secure an indictment from a grand jury, mentioned below). This opens the door to arbitrariness, which arguably was becoming disturbingly typical of prosecutorial conduct generally in post-1980 America (as seen below). It also could encourage politically-motivated attacks that would weaken the presidency. Indeed, this was frequently alleged during the Clinton investigation and the long-continuing Iran-Contra investigation (although the latter involved an independent prosecutor appointed by the attorney general instead of pursuant to the law).[96]

Executive privilege, as mentioned in Chapter 8, was a critical question during Watergate. Since that time, as Ryan Barilleaux and Mark J. Rozell point out, "Some administrations have shown great reluctance to exercise executive privilege for fear that any such claim will immediately be equated with a Nixonian abuse of power." Reagan attempted to exert claims of executive privilege several times regarding the disclosure of documents to Congress, but backed off.[97] George H.W. Bush succeeded in withholding certain information from Congress, but did not make executive privilege claims. As Barilleaux and Rozell say, "the doctrine of executive privilege has fallen into political disrepute."[98] Perhaps the inability of presidents to effectively assert executive privilege anymore (which, in the sense of meaning that presidents believed that they could withhold some types of information from Congress, was an old practice in the history in the American Republic[99]) is one indication of the long-term loss of presidential prestige that Berman noted. With it comes a further loss of executive power and harming of separation of powers.

If separation of powers was hurt to the detriment of the executive in the above areas, it continued to be hurt to the disadvantage of Congress in the area of war-making during the decades after 1980. The existence of the War Powers Act and the experience of the Vietnam War perhaps motivated presidents to consult Congress more often before foreign military interventions—although this has perhaps been mostly of the nature of notification of Congressional leaders, and has never meant "an equal exchange of ideas or balance of power"[100]—but did not deter them from carrying them out. From 1980 to 2003, there were American military actions in Lebanon, Grenada, Libya, Panama, Iraq and Kuwait (the Gulf War of 1990-91), Somalia, Haiti, Bosnia, Afghanistan and Sudan (the Clinton-ordered missile strikes in 1998), Iraq a second time (a brief bombing campaign by Clinton in 1998), Kosovo, and the major wars in Afghanistan and Iraq after the September 11, 2001 terrorist attacks. In not a single one of these was there a formal declaration of war. While the Founders may not have viewed that as imperative for all kinds of engagements, it certainly is more readily indicated in the cases of extended engagements and those involving massive troop build-ups (such as the Gulf War, and the Afghanistan and Iraq wars). The language of the Constitution mentioned above certainly indicates Congress's role in military activity. Ryan C. Hendrickson argues the following: "[I]t is inaccurate to conclude that the Constitution gave the president unilateral powers as commander in chief. The vast majority of the recorded evidence points to a Congress that was to be the final arbiter in determining when force was used."[101] Even apart from not seeking formal declarations of war, the presidents of this period failed to get Congressional approval for their foreign military actions or, if they did so in some manner, insisted that it was not necessary. Reagan, like the previous Cold War era presidents, acted unilaterally.[102] George H. W. Bush did seek Congressional approval before actually starting hostilities against Iraq in 1991, but made it clear that he was not required to.[103] Clinton "claimed essentially unilateral powers as commander in chief...[and] employed the *rhetoric* of 'consultation' to appease members of Congress."[104] Clinton's seeking the sanction of the UN Security Council for a number of his military actions obscured his unilateralism. Such unilateralism in these cases followed the steps of President Truman in the Korean War. Even though when the U.S. joined the UN President Truman had assured Congress that it had "the right to prevent U.S. participation in UN [military] operations"—and Congress even enacted statutory language "guaranteeing its role"—this did not stop him from committing U.S. troops to South Korea "without specific legislative approval."[105] The two extended wars of George W. Bush's presidency were undertaken after passage of supportive resolutions of Congress, although (again) without formal declarations of war. The Afghan War gained almost unanimous agreement of Congress, but the Iraq war saw much opposition.[106] Hendrickson says that, in spite of the War Powers Act and the constitutional language, Congress has been partly responsible for presidential unilateralism in war-making—and, *a fortiori*, in the damaging of separation of powers and checks and balances—because it has continued the practice of deferring to the president and has refused to sufficiently assert itself.[107]

Yet another dimension of the excessive deference to the executive was seen in the aftermath of the 9/11 events. The federal government's approach to providing greater protection to the country—which certainly was its role—followed the pattern of its addressing domestic problems since the Progressive Era, and especially since the New Deal. It established new, additional agencies in the executive branch—new large bureaucracies—such as the Department of Homeland Security and the Transportation Security Administration.[108] In one sense, this was a curious response because bureaucratic failure played some role in the federal government's failing to thwart the 9/11 hijackers' plan before it could be launched.[109] That the establishing of new agencies was not necessarily the best way to fight the War on Terror and provide protection was seen further with the near bombing of a U.S. commercial airliner over Detroit on Christmas Day 2009. President Obama said a few days later that the incident was the result of a systemic failure of the agencies involved in homeland security, including an inadequate sharing of information received beforehand about the terrorist would-be bomber, the potential threat he posed, and the failure to place him on the "no-fly" list.[110] What has happened over the years since September 11, 2001 has itself indicated problems with the bureaucratic response to terrorism: it has expanded the no-fly list to a staggering 700,000 or more names, and a large number of outrageous cases have occurred where completely innocent people have been stopping from boarding airliners.[111] It seemed as if the homeland security bureaucracy's response to airline security was like that of the child protective bureaucracy to stopping child abuse: if everyone is seen as a potential terrorist (or every parent a potential child abuser), then the real terrorists (or child abusers) get lost in the shuffle and do not get stopped.[112] This underscored the failure of excessively centralized, bureaucratic power; bureaucracy often lacked the realism and the shrewd practical intelligence that characterized the Founding. The result was, in varying degrees, a loss of citizen liberty and failure to promote the common good—as government could not even provide something as basic as protection.

We have discussed how in American history there was a pattern of periods where presidential and Congressional power waxed and waned with regard to each other. What has happened during the post-1980 period has been that both branches have suffered damage to their rightful prerogatives at the hands of the other. While some might see that as a desirable checking or restraining of each, separation of powers in some sense has been compromised.

Finally, on the topic of the relations among the branches after 1980, we consider the courts and their relationship to Congress and the president. Although the courts stepping into the policy arena was an ongoing issue, the period was one of considerably less judicial activism than in the decades before it. The Supreme Court was "activistic," in a certain way, in: first, attempting to restore *some* limits as to how far the federal government could go in intruding on state prerogatives and, second, in trying to recover *some* standards about what constitutes interstate commerce so the federal government would not continue to have a veritable blank check in it. The invalidating of the Gun Free School Zones Act of 1990 and the Violence Against Women Act, above, were the two main decisions regarding the latter. The Court has so far not gone any farther, however, and Congressional leeway to legislate on these grounds remains vast. Perhaps the most direct conflict between the Court and the political branches came in the wake of the Court's narrowing the reach of the free exercise clause of the First Amendment by holding that it does not require that persons be exempted from the application of general laws for religious reasons.[113] Congress responded by overwhelmingly passing (unanimously in the House and 97-3 in the Senate) the Religious Freedom Restoration Act (RFRA) in which it restored such an exemption—the Court had overturned its previous precedents on this—under its powers to enact legislation to enforce the Fourteenth Amendment under the little used Article 5 of the Amendment. The Court then proceeded to declare RFRA, as applied to state and local governments, unconstitutional.[114] To be sure, Congress did not just roll over and accept this—at least in certain areas. In 2000, it passed a different law—the Religious Land Use and Institutionalized Persons Act—that limited the reach of state and local land use regulations (the topic of the case in which RFRA's application was ruled unconstitutional).[115] That statute has so far not faced a constitutional challenge,[116] but it represented a willingness by Congress to resist the Court in at least a limited, indirect way—a mild assertion of its power to check the courts to uphold separation of powers.

Political Developments, Trends, and Reform. To some degree, the above spoke about political developments. We expand upon those in this section somewhat and discuss some others that bear on our comparative analysis with the Founding. In the 1980s a significant political reality was a kind of consolidation of the ideological polarization between the two major parties that had begun to manifest itself in the 1960s and early 1970s.[117] By the mid-1980s the partisan polarization in Congress was, in Hayward's words, "more raw than ever."[118] Such matters as political and, especially, judicial appointments became subjects of intense ideological struggles[119]—partly because such socio-cultural conflicts as abortion had become prominent in the public arena. John Ehrman argues that the Reagan sweep of 1980 did not signal that "Americans had swung to the right"; they retained their "centrist moorings" but were willing to "experiment with the alternatives he offered" after the failures of liberalism in the 1970s.[120] As we have noted, that was the culmination of a decade-long period of increasing public frustration with, and turmoil within, liberalism. As Ehrman puts it, the 1980 election made it clear that liberalism "had collapsed as a governing ideology," but it was not clear that the majority of the electorate "now embraced conservatism."[121] Reagan's aforementioned inability to make major reversals in the domestic role of the federal government due to a lack of public support confirms this. Still, as Hayward said, debates began about the role of government, and there was some reorientation of American politics—seen in a continuing skepticism about big government, the repeated efforts at tax-cutting, the ongoing concern about federal deficits (it even became part of the rhetoric of the Democratic party), and some of the slight restraints above that were put on federal power by the Supreme Court. As Troy puts it, while the welfare state remained, through successive presidents after Reagan "America seemed further away from the Great Society."[122] When Obama went in the opposite direction and moved to sharply expand the federal role in health care, a fairly consistent majority of the public opposed it throughout the extended debate in 2009-2010.[123] After its enactment in March 2010, a majority of voters favored its repeal.[124] Perhaps one of the reasons that Clinton commanded public support was because he tapped into this "moderate" approach to government, even while he was personally not well regarded.[125] This all indicated that at least some measure of sentiment against big, centralized government and in favor of the limited government norm of the Founding became ingrained after 1980, even if it did not result in much actual change and, as stated above, sweeping federal power later reasserted itself forcefully with Obama.

Hayward mentions three other political achievements of Reagan's, which were certain if not earthshaking. He says that he transformed his party—i.e., by making it more attached to conservative political principles—and, in doing this, he built upon the previous failures of liberalism by "frustrating and deflecting the course of the rival party."[126] Even if the Republicans could not end the regime constructed by liberalism, it was no longer fashionable for the party to absorb its fundamental principles and become "Democrats-lite."[127] There was no purge of non-conservatives from the party and even while in practice he ruled in moderate fashion and political "pragmatist" types permeated his administration, in the end it became and remained a more conservative party—"Reagan became the standard against which to measure Republicanism."[128] Second, even if we accept Berman's assessment of the presidency's prestige being in a long-term decline, Reagan inspired a renewed belief that the occupier of the office was not simply overwhelmed by it and the vast governmental apparatus around him, and so could still be a responsible executive. Third, by the debates he engendered and the somewhat changed perspective about government that he influenced, he helped alter in the minds of many the notion dating back to the Progressive Era that political and social reform necessarily meant making the federal government more powerful. The notion of reform being identified with a smaller and less powerful federal government now became respectable.[129] If he was not as successful as he perhaps could have been in restoring the educative function of politics (as stated above), he was not without influence in encouraging some redirection of popular thinking. Reagan's consistent optimism, upbeat manner, and status as the "Great Communicator" no doubt helped this effort.

Reagan's latter effort probably had something to do with the support that most of the public maintained in the 1980s for American political ideals and her historic entrepreneurial spirit. His anti-big government rhetoric also probably helped to stimulate the ambivalent attitude above that it displayed about government: distrustful of it, but wanting the services and programs it provided.[130] Still, by the late 1990s, long after Reagan was out of office, confidence in the federal government in general did not run high very with the public. Only about a third of Americans believed it was making their life better, and two-thirds believed that people they knew were angrier because of it. Many also believed its officials were simply not honest with them.[131] By a decade later, these views were shared to some extent by an overwhelming majority of the public, with only 5% saying that Washington was giving them the information they should have about its spending practices. Almost 70% believed that all levels of government were not responsible in their spending or honest about how the money was being used.[132] To be sure, the public can exhibit fickleness about this and its views can be affected by recent developments and short-term circumstances. Nevertheless, the frequency with which such low ratings have appeared over a long period of time (going back to the 1960s) and the substantial number of people sharing negative views at various times (seen above) readily prompt the conclusion that the public has had a significant amount of distrust in the federal and perhaps other levels of government for some time. (Interestingly, the public assessment of government per se improved during the Reagan administration, even though the dislike of *big* government increased.) John Samples of the CATO Institute says that periods of activist government have been especially prone to result in loss of public confidence.[133]

George H.W. Bush may not have been aware of the problems of confidence engendered by activist government. Probably his personal political perspective, approach to governance, pragmatism, and awareness of the need for a period of "policy consolidation" after Reagan were more responsible for what Barilleaux and Rozell call his "incrementalism" as president. With the exception of the ADA, he certainly seemed to avoid activist government and "visionary" programs domestically.[134] Barilleaux and Rozell say that Bush's type of presidential leadership would be considered unsuccessful from the standpoint of so many presidential scholars who have made "activist-presidential leadership" in promoting a liberal policy agenda the model of presidential power. In fact, they have insisted that the president act not only as a policy leader, but also tackle a whole range of problems and act as a kind of national moral instructor. This perspective distorted the role the Founding Fathers had in mind for the presidency.[135] If they meant it to be a powerful office, they did not mean it to be an engine for national salvation. So even if presidential prestige was in a long period of sustained decline, Bush's incrementalism—and Reagan's assertiveness in tying the office to reducing the policy role and thus the size of the federal government—was much more in accord with the Founders' idea for the office, to say nothing of, again, limited government. Indeed, in order to further the cause of the latter, along with restraining ambitious new programs they both at least rhetorically promoted the development of non-governmental social support efforts (Reagan, with the strong commendation of mediating institutions in the 1984 Republican Platform,[136] and Bush even more emphatically with his encouraging of voluntarism through the Points of Light Initiative[137]). Where they fell short, as suggested above, was in not seeing that to truly roll back the welfare state would require the development of more ubiquitous, substantial, and permanent, social support structures such as characterized Founding culture. In that sense, there was an insufficiency of Founding realism in their perspectives, even while one could say that their understanding of what they *could do politically* in the circumstances that they were in—i.e., Bush's gradualism and Reagan's moderate rule, in spite of frequent impatience by conservative activists[138]—exhibited Founding realism and prudence.

Three other political developments of the post-1980 period that are pertinent to our analysis are the large increase in the cost of campaigns, the influence of monied interests and the political corruption it caused, and the frequent nasty political rhetoric and interactions. Both presidential and Congressional campaigns became very expensive and the cost kept increasing.[139] As a result, candidates have had to aggressively seek funds. So, massive amounts of money are poured into politics—especially from well-heeled individuals and PACs (political action committees) representing various (especially economic) interests that have an ongoing relationship with government (i.e., either receiving benefits or being subject to regulation). In the post-1980 period, government's role as subsidizer, contractor for its many endeavors, and regulator was a fixture of American life. "Subsidizing" politicians and campaigns had become a routine part of the business activity of many of those interests. While sometimes these activities have been illegal or at least questionable under legislative ethics rules—as in the Abramoff scandal[140] and the favored treatment afforded to some members of Congress by outfits like Countrywide Mortgage[141]—mostly they were strictly legal, although sometimes by what W. Lance Bennett calls "creative interpretations of the Federal Election Campaign Act."[142] Examples of the influence of big money in recent presidential administrations were: the Team 100 club before and during the George H.W. Bush administration, made up of people from business interests dealing with Washington;[143] PAC contributions to incumbent Congressmen in 1990 that enabled them to outspend their election opponents over three to one;[144] and, much more on the legal edge, huge contributions to the Democratic party under Clinton by overseas Chinese interests, the "blatant peddling of access" to Clinton, and his "renting out the Lincoln Bedroom for a night to well-heeled donors."[145] Nor was such massive infusion of money into politics confined to the federal level. State-level campaigns are getting more and more expensive and PAC's are playing an increasingly heavy role in funding them.[146] The result of all of this has often been what the money-suppliers hoped for, from both parties:

preferable policy outcomes for the interests they represent.[147] To be sure, we have seen that favored treatment for monied interests has a long history in the U.S., going back to the early years of the Republic—there were now just many more interests (reflecting the larger role of government) and a lot more money. The post-1980 period also has seen major reform efforts, such as Bipartisan Campaign Reform Act (the McCain-Feingold law) of 2002. This was especially noted for prohibiting "soft money" in campaigns (i.e., unregulated contributions to national political parties and also funds spent by independent organizations that do not specifically advocate the election or defeat of candidates and are not contributed directly to candidate campaigns).[148] There were also reforms in several states to limit contributions at that level.[149] McCain-Feingold and the state laws obviously took the 1970's campaign finance legislation as their starting point; the notion of using law to regulate campaign financing and its problems had taken deep hold among American policymakers. Such laws have been criticized, however, as being unduly complicated, damaging to political parties, protective of incumbents against challengers, ineffective in controlling the costs of campaigns, and infringing on free speech.[150] On the latter, the Supreme Court in 2007 held unconstitutional the above provision of the law pertaining to the spending by independent organizations,[151] and then in 2010 held that McCain-Feingold's ban on spending by corporations—whether for-profit or nonprofit—to support or oppose candidates (not to contribute to their campaigns) was also unconstitutional. The effect of the latter had been to restrain advocacy even by organizations, like the one in question in the case, set up for public issue advocacy.[152]

When one thinks of interest groups and money in politics in light of the Founders' principles, one recalls their concern about factions insufficiently controlled that are acting against the common good.

How much American politics had come to be shaped by the influence of organized interest groups was seen in the Obama administration's health care proposal. Even though, as seen above, most of the public opposed it, he was particularly fastidious in lining up interest group support—whose opposition he believed had thwarted Clinton's health care initiative—and was able to push it through a Democratic-controlled Congress.[153] The interest group government that Lowi wrote about in the 1960s certainly has in no way changed in the post-1980 period.

As far as political thinking during the 1980s was concerned, both parties were influenced by policy-oriented strains of thought. The rise of the conservative movement in the 1970s has been discussed. Think tanks such as the Heritage Foundation supplied the Reagan administration with many policy ideas.[154] Probably the most influential new movement within conservatism during the Reagan and both Bush administrations was neoconservatism, discussed in Chapter 8. Neoconservatives occupied key positions in those administrations. Neoconservatism, while not embracing the liberal version of the welfare state, favors a significant social welfare role for government. It strongly supports the market economy and, while rejecting liberalism's notion of massive governmental interventionism, sees a role for some government regulation.

While certainly favoring legal and political equality, it strongly opposes economic leveling and the view that all cultural norms are equally good. It also vigorously opposed communism during the Cold War.[155] Later, it tended to be ready to support military interventionism, and has sought to promote democracy around the world.[156] It conforms to the Founding in favoring restrained economic regulation, but not in being willing to have it done from the center. Its welfare state role for government, while less sweeping than with liberalism, is still more pronounced than characterized the Founding Era. Its balanced view of equality corresponds to Founding principles. Its interventionist orientation and tendency to crusade for worldwide democracy collide with the norm of foreign policy impartiality and Founding realism, as Wilsonianism did. "Democracy," as they understand it, essentially seems to mean representative government and respect for popular sovereignty—which, of course, coincide with the Founding—but they may not be concerned enough with making the proper distinctions and so go along with the problematical historic trend of democratization that we have discussed.

Social conservatives also became an important element, especially during the Reagan period. The Protestant evangelicals mentioned in Chapter 8, along with other religiously inspired conservatives, were a major component of this group. They got involved in politics to combat such issues discussed in this chapter as legal abortion, pornography, homosexualism, and government's perceived role in the decline of morality generally. They became a force with which the Republican party regularly had to reckon. Their basic perspective about politics was in line with—and perhaps rooted in—a school of conservative thought that might be called "cultural conservatism."[157] Their concern about morality, especially sexual morality and with it implicitly the family, echoed the Founding culture.

In the Democratic party, the neoliberals emerged in the early 1980s. They were pro-entrepreneurship and skeptical of Keynesianism, big bureaucratic government, entitlement programs, and "large-scale government intervention" generally.[158] They seemed to emerge out of the 1970's disillusionment with liberal solutions. They influenced the Democratic party in the 1980s and early 1990s, most notably when Clinton—calling himself a "new Democrat"—adopted many of their ideas.[159] However, after that they faded. By the time of Obama, the Democratic party had returned with a vengeance to its 1960's view of the federal government as "provider," repository of all solutions, and arch-economic interventionist. We have previously seen the problems of contemporary liberalism in light of the Founding.

A significant philosophical defender of the contemporary, leftist, rights-oriented, social welfare state embodied by Democratic presidents since LBJ in varying degrees was Harvard professor John Rawls. Rawls claimed that justice—which for him was an almost exclusive goal for society—was violated by any public policy that failed to benefit even one person, even if that person was not damaged by it. This had the potential of undoing the Founders' belief that majority rule should prevail, even while minority rights—true rights, natural rights—should be upheld. Rawls effectively—at least in theory—would give a single individual the right to veto a public policy he disliked.[160] In practice in American constitutional law, this was what the post-1960 era had sometimes permitted (as mentioned about establishment clause cases in Chapter 8). By the way, it was doubtful that Rawls' notion of justice followed that of the natural law/Western philosophical tradition that had shaped the Founding.[161]

We mentioned that the Republican party began to take on an uncustomary populist complexion in the 1960s. This was seen in the 1970s and 1980s with many of the social conservatives above and, at the end of the first decade of the twenty-first century, the Tea ("*t*axed *e*nough *a*lready") Party movement. The latter was made up of mostly average citizens turned political activists who opposed excessive public spending and bloated government. While on one hand, populism—as previously discussed—always suggests enhanced democratization, on the other the Tea Partiers seemed to be oriented to the norms about deficit spending, limited government, decentralization, and popular sovereignty (with the concern about public decision-makers not paying heed to their average constituents) of the Founding.

A representative sampling of the nasty political rhetoric and relations of the period, which became *de rigueur*—and probably partly had its roots in the increasing polarization discussed above—were these: In the last chapter, we mentioned Carter's repeated, strident, extreme attacks on Reagan during the 1980 campaign, calling him a "warmonger" and one who would "pit Americans against one another along racial, religious, and sectional lines" and attempting to portray him as a dangerous, even fanatical, ideologue;[162] the ugly Democratic attacks against the Republicans in the House of Representatives in the 1980s over Nicaragua policy;[163] the aforementioned House Republicans' attitude toward Clinton during the impeachment proceedings of the late 1990s; the seeming upsurge of an array of campaign "dirty tricks" in this period;[164] and the increase of so-called "negative campaigning" in elections at all levels.[165] The latter has led some states to adopt fair campaign practices codes and even enact laws banning, under penalty of fines, false campaign statements.[166] Even though there is dispute about its seriousness and pervasiveness, Larry J. Sabato and Glenn R. Simpson stated in the mid-1990s that even the outright criminal activity of voter fraud was increasing with each election cycle.[167] While ugly, untruthful political attacks and dirty tricks have had a history in American politics, going back even to the earliest years of the Republic, for different reasons they may have become more common in the politics of the present.[168]

The depths of nastiness to which American politics descended in the post-1980 period was also seen in federal appointment politics. The notion of "borking" someone took shape with the confirmation hearing of the respected legal scholar and federal appellate judge Robert H. Bork, whom Reagan had nominated to the Supreme Court in 1987. Borking involves a deliberate and even extreme distortion of a nominee's record and a scurrilous attack on him with the direct intention of bringing about his defeat.[169] Hayward says, "the demagogic nature of the public campaign against...[Bork] made it a watershed moment in American politics."[170] It ushered in what David Plotz called "an era of appointments warfare."[171] To be sure, there had been unreasonable and unfounded attacks on nominees before then,[172] but the practice intensified after the Bork nomination.

As we have said before in this book, such nasty politics affronts the Founding norms of civility, good manners, and self-restraint. The new recourse of trying to pass laws against it, however, is like the effort to solve certain campaign finance problems: a challenge to free speech. The fact that law has been turned to as a way of securing civility and manners underscores the current expanded notion of the role of government in contrast to the Founding Era (even while we said that sometimes monitoring of the individual could be excessive in some places then).

As the Obama administration progressed, actions of some high public officials made one wonder if the rule of law was a sufficient guide to their actions. For example, when the Obama health care proposal was in danger of defeat, important Democratic leaders in the House of Representatives planned to enact it by just having a vote on a rule for its consideration be tantamount to its actual passage (i.e., adopting a "rule" that said that the Senate-passed version of the bill—resisted by many in the House—was passed, never actually voting on the bill, and on the basis of the adoption of the rule deeming the bill to have been passed and then send it to the president).[173]

Even worse was the scene of pressure politics applied to members of Obama's own party in Congress if they were reluctant about supporting the proposal. The reports indicated that this included blatant examples of offering substantial favors for support, making campaign funds conditional on support, and such intimidation tactics as leaking supposedly scandalous information and threatening to open ethics investigations against reluctant Congressmen. Some of these alleged actions were also illegal.[174] This was another ugly kind of politics that offended the same Founding Era norms as borking did and also, if some actions were illegal, also undercut the rule of law.

Legal and Constitutional Developments and Citizen Rights. Developments in this area during the post-1980 period presented disturbing threats to such basic Founding principles and conditions as: religion (especially its public role), the right to trial by jury, the expectation of due process, the need for civic friendship, the stress on the common good, the need for virtue and morality, popular sovereignty, the tradition of natural law and natural rights, equality (although there were also developments concerning this that were in line with the Founding), and the very rule of law itself. In the constitutional law area, specifically, the U.S. Supreme Court gave some renewed hope—even if slight— for a strengthening of federalism (seen above) and for reinvigorating the Founding notion of equality, but at the same time it continued to bar government from protecting human life *in utero*, made slightly portentous gestures about freedom of speech, extended the pro-democratic bias of its *Baker v. Carr* line of cases (see Chapter 8), and—along with developments in law more generally— weakened religious liberty and property rights, and arguably helped to further erode sexual morality and the vitality of the family.

Some of the major deleterious legal developments have been the following. In the area of undercutting the rule of law, we see: the increasing number of vague statutes and government regulations, so that citizens and businesses are not really sure of what is expected of them; the erosion of the requirement of *mens rea* in order to sustain a successful criminal prosecution (i.e., diminishing the necessity of fault for criminal liability); the expansion of the reach and scope of such traditionally all-purpose crimes as conspiracy (which can be applied even when an action in question is not a crime) and mail fraud; the growth of prosecutions based on speculation and theorizing instead of evidence; the multiplication of laws that punish action or inaction on the basis of speculative instead of actual harm; the widespread use of sting operations that set people up for criminal activity that effectively constitutes entrapment;[175] the trend to hold parents liable for the offenses of their children (another example of the decline of a fault-based standard);[176] and the contradictory nature of provisions, especially in regulatory law, which sometimes results in the almost literal impossibility of individuals and businesses being able to meet legal requirements.[177] On the weakening of the right of trial by jury, we have witnessed the utter explosion of plea-bargaining, to the point where 90-95% of criminal cases at all levels are decided in this manner and without trials, and with the result that truth is apparently often brushed aside, the innocent are increasingly convicted, and defendants are often at the mercy of their lawyers' negotiating skills.[178] Due process has been compromised by such developments as the weakening of attorney-client privilege through prosecutorial pressure; the growth of the retroactive application of law (against at least the spirit of the constitutional prohibition of ex post facto laws) in the environmental area;[179] the growing practice of using psychological pressure tactics on defendants to secure guilty pleas;[180] the routine and easy manipulation of grand juries by prosecutors so that some have contended that this institution is no longer a protector of persons suspected of crimes;[181] and the authorization of trials based on secret evidence in the federal Counter-Terrorism Act of 1995.[182] Related to due process have been the starting up of such questionable search and seizure and surveillance practices as those found in President G.W. Bush's Surveillance Program to combat terrorists, which permitted the monitoring of phone calls, e-mails, Internet activity, and text messaging by parties outside the U.S, even to parties in the U.S., without warrants.[183] Liberty was weakened, at least in the associational area, by such state policies as forbidding or making difficult the operation of single-sex private clubs and fraternal organizations.[184] Civic friendship and the common good have been harmed by the increasing tendency of law to absolutize the rights claimed for one or another group, as seen in disability rights legislation that often seems impervious to the costs placed on the public at large and on the burdens often put on other groups of people.[185] Instead of needed accommodation among different groups, there has been an excessive tilting in one direction. Such legal changes have helped to spawn an explosion of lawsuits as people try to assert the absolutist notions of rights that such legislation has granted them. The result has been, according to social and legal critic Philip K. Howard, to make America "a nation of enemies."[186]

The corrosive legal developments of previous periods respecting the family and sexual morality have continued and, in fact, accelerated. The trends involving parental rights and authority in law of the 1960-1980 period continued intact and probably even intensified in such areas as children's health.[187] This further weakened the family. The family and sexual morality (which is discussed more below)—both of which, of course, were so central in Founding culture— also suffered with the legislative and judicial moves in a number of states to legalize homosexual "marriage," or such a close substitute as civil unions (which essentially provide all the legal benefits of marriage to same-sex partners).[188] The legalizing of homosexual "marriage" by the high courts of two states—Massachusetts and California—further was a direct assault on the Founding principle of popular sovereignty. The assault continued when after the California electorate overturned its decision in a popular referendum, a federal judge declared the referendum in violation of the U.S. Constitution.[189] It had nothing to do with restraining democratic impulses to protect traditional constitutional or common law or natural law-based rights, which was the traditional rationale for American courts to intervene in matters involving the individual against the state. This was more like a policy matter—but not *really* that, in light of the Founding. Homosexual "marriage" for the Founders would have been unthinkable as a public-policy option because it is contrary to the very nature of things. They and their culture understood axiomatically that two persons of the same sex simply do not have the capacity to marry, legally or realistically; whatever their relationship may be, it cannot be marriage.[190] The push for homosexual "marriage" and the aggressive and intolerant activism of the homosexualist movement began to genuinely threaten the liberty—including religious liberty—of some who opposed it, such as the Boy Scouts of America that the State of New Jersey under its public accommodations law tried to force to have homosexual scoutmasters (the U.S. Supreme Court sided with the Scouts),[191] the Christian demonstrators at a pro-homosexual festival in Philadelphia who were arrested (and faced over forty years in prison), and people who states sued for not providing business services for homosexual "weddings" or renting their apartments to homosexual partners.[192] What essentially has been happening in American law is that it was now, particularly on sexual matters, imposing on citizens a moral pluralism (mentioned in Chapter One)—with legal consequences if they refuse to accept it. This was a blatant disregard of the natural law tradition behind the Founding and of the Founding Era's understanding that without it liberty and free government could not exist. It has also signaled a complete disregard for civic friendship—all in the name of the ideological objective of sexual freedom.

Government infringed or tried to infringe on the liberty of religious bodies in other ways. Even if it did not always succeed, the attempts demonstrated an attitude of increased hostility toward religion or at least a belief that religion did not contribute significantly to society. This, of course, probably grew out of an increasingly widespread secular worldview. For example, there was a brief legislative attempt in Connecticut—motivated partly by the hierarchy's opposition to homosexual "marriage" legislation in the state—to actually have the state take control of the Catholic Church's internal budgetary decisions.[193] In the wake of highly publicized revelations during the first decade of the twenty-first century of many cases of clerical sex abuse in the Catholic Church in the U.S. involving mostly teenage boys—occurring primarily in the 1960s and 1970s, a quarter-century or more before the revelations—the district attorney of Philadelphia announced a sweeping investigation of all such allegations among the Archdiocese's clergy, no matter how far back in history and regardless of whether any statutes of limitation were involved. She seemed to exploit an opening given her by the revelations throughout the country, and made no similar searching investigations into other kinds of institutions even if they had had similar experiences of abuse.[194] In some communities, religious bodies were stopped by historic preservation ordinances from enlarging their church buildings to meet their needs, as noted above. A Protestant congregation in Manchester, Massachusetts was forbidden to erect a live nativity scene outside its church building because it sits on the town common.[195] Local zoning laws are increasingly being used to stop church expansion, to stop churches from being built at all, or even to stop religious meetings in private homes. Sometimes churches are forced by their local governments to pay for mandated public improvements near their properties as an apparent roundabout way to extract monies from tax-exempt bodies. Some local officials even declare that congregations should be limited in their number of people. There is some indication that churches that are strong about bringing an evangelization message into their communities are given a particularly difficult time.[196] The U.S. Supreme Court's decisions of *Employment Division v. Smith* (1990) and *City of Boerne v. Flores* (1997), discussed above, gave something of an imprimatur to some of these actions by holding that religious belief did not legally absolve a person or a religious body from abiding by laws of general application (i.e., those that do not specifically try to interfere with religious activity). Effectively, the Court narrowed the free exercise of religion by these decisions. The governmental actions mentioned above cannot but be understood as interfering with religion. The inveterate litigiousness (usually over small matters that involve no coercion of unbelievers) of organizations hostile to religion in the public sphere or even religion at all, such as the American Civil Liberties Union (ACLU), Americans United for Separation of Church and State, and the Freedom from Religion Foundation, hardly bespeaks civic friendship.[197]

The Court also contributed during the post-1980 period to the banishment of religion from the public square by its establishment clause decisions that further isolated public schools from any expression of it[198] and forbade public-sponsored religious displays (e.g., Nativity scenes on public property) unless they were in a significant way secularized.[199] This is a reasonable conclusion about the Court even if its jurisprudence was sometimes inconsistent, and it was more willing to permit some state assistance to sectarian pre-college-level schools than in the 1970s.[200]

Law has also exhibited an increasingly utilitarian, end-justifies-the-means perspective. This was seen in the *Bob Jones University v. U.S.* case, mentioned above, when the Supreme Court went along with the IRS's decision to revoke the conservative Christian university's tax exemption because of its religious belief-based ban on interracial dating on campus[201]—even though the Internal

Revenue Code gave it no authorization to do so and was silent about racial belief as a basis for a tax exemption (the University easily met the stated criteria). The desire to achieve a certain end—even if desirable—appeared to be the IRS's motivation, and it essentially arbitrarily decreed it to be law.[202] This was not fundamentally different from the Supreme Court's stretching the commerce clause in the 1960s—in one case, mentioned previously, drastically stretching it—to uphold and insure sweeping applications of federal civil rights legislation. Both effectively compromised the rule of law. Paul Craig Roberts and Lawrence M. Stratton contend that in recent decades, due to trends such as those described, the American legal system has increasingly embraced a utilitarian perspective of the sort identified with the nineteenth century English thinker Jeremy Bentham. Bentham disdained traditional common law protections, which he believed stood in the way of needed social change.[203] This obviously also compromised the natural law/natural rights tradition of the Founding.

On equality, the Supreme Court edged back in the direction of the Founding vision of equal opportunity without expecting equal results and the belief that all should be judged simply by their individual character and attainments. It limited the reach of federal affirmative action programs, saying they had to be "'narrowly tailored'" to serve a "'compelling national interest.'"[204] Later, the Court accepted a more limited version of affirmative action in state university admissions, which had an avowed purpose of achieving a more diverse student body (i.e., was "narrowly-tailored") so long as it did not involve a quota system.[205] The Court also restrained attempts to apply affirmative action principles to drawing up Congressional districts so as to increase Negro electoral clout,[206] even though its rejection of gerrymandering (for the first time)[207] was an extension of the *Baker v. Carr* "one man-one vote" outright democratic perspective that expressed a transformed view of equality from that of the Founding. The most noted political development about affirmative action was Proposition 209 in California, where a statewide voter referendum amended the state's constitution to prohibit all public institutions from making decisions on the basis of race, sex, ethnicity, or national origin.[208] These developments followed the earlier efforts of the Reagan administration.[209]

The Reagan administration also tried to get the Supreme Court to overturn its 1973 abortion decisions. It did not succeed, and the decisions were reaffirmed in the 1992 *Planned Parenthood of Southeastern Pennsylvania v. Casey* decision[210] (the Court, however, has permitted some tangential restraints on abortion, such as a short waiting period, parental consent for minors, and a prohibition of "partial-birth" abortions [where a child is killed when partially out of the womb during the birth activity][211]). Thus, the Court continued to embrace a position unsettling to the family and tolerant of a sexual ethic at odds with the Founding.

The slight portent in the free speech area concerned the Court's giving a green light to the hate crimes legislation mentioned above—such laws raise a genuine concern about inhibiting free speech[212]—and the fact that it has made it difficult for government to check obscenity and pornography on television and the Internet[213] (that latter is now a main source of it[214]). These developments served to subvert the Founding notion of free speech and helped to further weaken sexual morality and the family. The major focus of obscenity prosecution in recent years has been child pornography,[215] which the Court specifically upheld[216] but has been more reluctant to permit when it concerns the Internet[217]—and thereby possibly has undercut such efforts. Freedom of political speech, at least for organizations, got a boost with the Court's 2010 corporate campaign advocacy decision above. Freedom of the press was not compromised in this period; it might even be argued that it expanded. The Warren Court's standards for libel were kept in place. In fact, the Court even held that parodies that are plainly false and intended to cause emotional distress are constitutionally protected.[218] The Federal Communications Commission's repeal of the Fairness Doctrine that required television and radio broadcasters to provide equal time for opposing points of view, and Reagan's veto of a Congressional attempt to restore it by statute, were a boon for the electronic media and, according to Hayward, "pave[d] the way for the rise of conservative talk radio."[219] While Barilleaux and Rozell suggest that George H.W. Bush's policy of restricting press reporting during the Gulf War was excessive,[220] it had precedents in earlier U.S. wars and so was not genuinely a threat to press freedom.

The threat to the Founding norms of family integrity and sexual ethics presented by homosexualism and the push for same-sex "marriage" was added to by the Supreme Court's action in giving constitutional protection to sodomy in 2003.[221]

The Court's biggest blow to private property rights came in the *Kelo* eminent domain decision, mentioned above.

An encouraging development during the Reagan administration was the starting up of a debate about the original intent of the Founding Fathers as the proper basis for constitutional adjudication.[222] Although this standard has certain drawbacks—such as the difficulty of knowing the Founders' intent about the meaning of every constitutional provision and the obvious need to make some adaptation of certain provisions to different circumstances[223]—it seems like a necessity if basic Founding principles are to remain viable. It was another crucial debate ignited about American government during the Reagan presidency. For whatever erosion occurred in the constitutional area in the post-1980 period, such a renewed reflection on the Founders offered hope for the future.

Foreign and Defense Policy, War and International Conflicts, and America's Role in the World. We have mentioned the most significant American military engagements in the post-1980 period and have explored presidential war-making powers. As far as American foreign policy generally is concerned, the period might be divided into three parts: the engagement with the Soviet Bloc during the final decade of the Cold War, the new American role in the post-Cold War world, and the engagement with Islamist terrorism springing forth especially from the Mideast. There can be little doubt that the quick, breathtaking collapse of the U.S.S.R. and European communism in 1989-91 was the most significant international affairs development since World War II. It was also one that neither the American intelligence community nor political science scholars had foreseen.[224] Reagan, however, came into office with the sense that the U.S.S.R. was on the way to collapsing.[225] Pursuant to this, about two years into his administration Reagan signed NSDD 75, which promulgated what came to be called the Reagan Doctrine: "contain and over time reverse Soviet expansionism," promote—within the limited means available to the U.S.— change in the U.S.S.R. to "'a more pluralistic political and economic system,'" and negotiate "to reach agreements that would enhance American interests."[226] Hayward writes that NSDD 75 "called specifically for 'exploiting Soviet weaknesses and vulnerabilities,'" and that due to economic problems, "'the loss of ideological commitment'" to Marxism, and the succession activity then underway after the death of long-time leader Leonid Brezhnev (there was, of course, no anticipation that two more Soviet leaders would die within the span of two years), the administration believed that "circumstances in the Soviet Union might be conducive to rapid change."[227] Reagan's policy in Nicaragua, the Grenada invasion, and aid to the Afghan Mujihadeen who were resisting Soviet occupation and anti-Communist rebels in Africa were expressions of this aggressive resistance to Soviet expansion. So was his military build-up. So were his tough negotiations with Soviet leader Mikhail Gorbachev on arms limitation during four summit meetings. So was his Strategic Defense Initiative (SDI), a space-based anti-missile defense system that represented a reversal of the Cold War mutually assured destruction (MAD) policy as the deterrent to a Soviet-initiated nuclear war. SDI, in theory, was in accord with traditional just war principles—*jus ad bello*—and the MAD policy was completely against it.[228] There were indications that Pope John Paul II collaborated with Reagan in helping to bring down communism by assisting opposition elements in Eastern Europe, especially Poland.[229]

Reagan's foreign policy was characterized by realism, which of course was in line with the Founders. While liberals took a soft line out of fear that an "uncontrollable war" would break out and conservatives were wary that arms control could mean appeasement, Reagan "fuse[d] both viewpoints." He matched his military build-up and "tough anti-Soviet rhetoric" with openness to negotiating with America's Cold War adversary.[230] Even SDI, which Hayward says "[f]riends and critics alike ascribe…to his Hollywood-fueled imagination," was not counter to such realism; as Reagan proposed it, the idea was quite practical.[231] What's more, SDI retrospectively "is nowadays considered a political and diplomatic masterstroke that contributed significantly to the arms reduction breakthroughs of the late 1980s and the eventual end of the Cold War."[232] Indeed, it "deeply shook" the Soviet leadership.[233]

We have said previously that because of what Soviet communism represented, gearing American foreign policy against it could hardly be considered as contrary to the principle of neutrality/impartiality in foreign dealings that the Founders enunciated. The same question should be asked about Israel. We have noted the following: The U.S. strongly supported the establishment of the nation of Israel in 1948, but so did the U.S.S.R. and many other countries; the U.S. long regarded Israel as its closest Mideast ally;

Eisenhower strongly opposed the Israeli-British-French action over Suez in 1956; the U.S. over the decades tried to have friendly relations with both the Israelis and the Arab states; despite the closeness of the U.S. and Israel, the U.S. helped forge a mutual settlement of the 1973 war and was less supportive of Israel afterwards; and the U.S. helped engineer the Camp David Agreement for a more permanent peace between Israel and Egypt. As far as Reagan was concerned, he harbored "strong pro-Israel sentiments" but his administration still put strong pressure on the Israeli government over its Lebanon intervention,[234] made overtures to the Palestinians and proposed a self-governing Palestinian entity in the occupied territories,[235] and took a hard line in the case of Jonathan Pollard (who spied on the U.S. for Israel). George H.W. Bush resisted Israeli claims over East Jerusalem and convened the Madrid Conference to get all sides to negotiate for peace.[236] Clinton brought together Israeli Prime Minister Yitzak Rabin and Palestine Liberation Organization Chairman Yasser Arafat to sign an agreement that laid the legal basis of Palestinian home rule (the Oslo Accord).[237] George W. Bush became the first American president to call directly for a Palestinian state.[238] He insisted that UN Security Council resolutions pertinent to the Israeli-Palestinian conflict be balanced.[239] All this suggests that while U.S. policy has certainly exhibited favor toward Israel in the post-1980 period and before, it has been relatively even-handed. It is not so clear that the Founders' impartiality principle has been compromised here; if it has been, it has not been so massively.

Further on the subject of impartiality in foreign policy, there was much question raised about whether Presidents George H.W. Bush and Clinton—and much of Congress—took a sufficiently impartial stance toward the People's Republic of China. This was especially evident with the willingness to allow human rights concerns to be subordinated to good trade relations— and in Bush's case, even the refusal to impose significant penalties on the Chinese government after its massacre of dissidents at Tiananmen Square.[240] Barilleaux and Rozell argue that one must understand this approach as reflecting Bush's prudence and realism in foreign policy—he preferred private, diplomatic ways of dealing with other nations that he believed would better further long-term American interests. They say that this was confirmed when Bush was able to enlist China in the anti-Saddam Gulf War coalition the year after Tiananmen.[241] On the other hand, one could wonder if Bush's downplaying support for popular government and human rights in China could have compromised, in some sense, the spirit of the Founders' belief that America should be an example in such matters for the world—that is, it is difficult to be such an example if American leadership conveys the impression that it is impervious about such things. Clinton can be given much less slack: the Chinese campaign contributions mentioned above may have influenced his thinking—in fact, it may have motivated a policy change even on a national security matter.[242] This directly collided with the Founders' concern about the dangers of foreign influence on the U.S.

Partiality and foreign influence were not the only Founding Era principles in this area that may have been compromised by Clinton. Berman suggests that the central principle of civilian control over the military may have been weakened because he was unwilling to exert his authority over military commanders fully enough.[243] That principle may have been weakened in another way, as well—from the opposite direction. That is, Clinton may have been responsible for politicizing the military—in the sense of forcing on it policy changes to satisfy political agendas (e.g., allowing homosexuals into the military, opening up more roles in the services for women)—which can both limit the rightful range of freedom that military people must have to make their own command decisions and compromise military respect for presidential authority.[244] (It should be noted, however, that the other presidents of this period did not substantially restrain such politicization and social experimentation in the military, as seen with the ongoing integration of women into the ranks,[245] leaving in place Clinton's policy of letting "closet" homosexuals serve,[246] and the apparent unwillingness to even root out potentially dangerous Islamists— e.g., the Hasan case at Ft. Hood—possibly because of fear of political criticism.[247]) In any event, the things mentioned about Clinton do not speak well for his realism. His foreign policy impartiality can also possibly be questioned on another front: his decision, with Congressional approval, to bring former Eastern Bloc countries into NATO. It seemed to cause strains in U.S.-Russian relations.[248]

Next, we consider as we have in previous chapters how the main American military interventions—apart from those representing a genuine resistance to communism, which has already been discussed—of the post-1980 period squared with Founding moral and cultural principles. The Reagan intervention in Lebanon was actually a commitment of a contingent made up primarily of U.S. Marines—along with French and Italian troops—as peacekeeping forces, in the aftermath of an American brokered withdrawal of Israeli forces after the Israel-Syria war in the country in 1982. The peacekeeping effort was shattered by the killing of 241 American military personnel in a suicide bombing in 1983.[249] Unlike other interventions that have been chronicled, the U.S.'s effort was hardly an expression of incivility and narrow self-interest. On the contrary, the Reagan administration was working cooperatively with other countries to try to promote cooperation, peace, and civility in Lebanon and the region. Grenada and even Nicaragua, contrary to efforts to portray the latter as such, were not in the typical mold of past American interventions in Latin America. In Grenada, a brutal, extreme Marxist element ousted and executed the sitting prime minister, also a Marxist who they viewed as too moderate. Even Fidel Castro had called the new leader "the Pol Pot of the Caribbean." The new rulers had refused to allow the evacuation of the American citizens on the island (there was especially a sizable contingent of medical students) and there was reason to believe they were in danger.[250] There was also clear evidence of Soviet involvement, which would have had the effect of their securing an additional, threatening foothold in the Western Hemisphere (along with Cuba). Further, the Organization of Eastern Caribbean States had appealed for a U.S. invasion (and joined in it), since these neighboring Caribbean countries thought they might be endangered by the new regime. Most Grenadians supported the intervention.[251] The previous comments about resisting communism apply here, and these facts hardly betray a lack of civic friendship, civility, cooperation, and respect for the common good of a nearby country. Moreover, while social ethics dictates that nations have a right of non-intervention, that right is not absolute, especially when the regime becomes tyrannical or may be threatening to its neighbors.[252] Perhaps it was a preemptive attack—which *could* be problematical from a just war standpoint (as in Iraq, below)—but the threats to the Americans there and the perception of a threat to them by the other countries were real enough.

The Reagan Nicaragua policy, which was discussed above, may have been seen as interference with a close-by country, particularly because it did not seem as threatening in the region as Grenada did. Nevertheless, Soviet Communist influence was involved, and the Marxist Sandinista government was engaging in subversion against El Salvador and Nicaragua's other neighbors felt threatened.[253] The regime was also becoming increasingly authoritarian, as well.[254] The latter would not axiomatically justify America's policy, however, since many countries in the world were in the same category. Still, it is apparent that the U.S. policy was not without justification. Also, the U.S. cannot so readily have been accused of lacking civic friendship toward Nicaragua, since the Sandinista regime came into power with disdain for the U.S.

The George H.W. Bush intervention in Panama, unlike U.S. actions in Latin America in previous times (including Panama, as indicated in Chapter 5), was not geared to furthering U.S. economic interests or securing a regime that would protect them. The action was a response to the illicit seizure of power by a strong-arm general who refused to allow the duly-elected presidential candidate to take power, was involved in the international drug trade, and was known for human rights abuses.[255] The U.S. intervention, which rectified the election nullification, was in line with notions of justice and fair-dealing, and arguably could be said to have actually helped to promote the Founding concern about a community of friendship.

The 1990-91 Persian Gulf War, on one hand, emerged as an attempt by the U.S. to promote the cause of justice, the common good, and the general welfare of international society since the U.S.-led coalition came to the aid of a small country that had been a victim of unprovoked aggression. On the other hand, the intemperance and individualism of economic self-interest may have loomed large because of the likely adverse effect on the flow of Mideast oil. Still, much harm could have occurred to many nations internationally if a tyrannical, aggressive power had been permitted to dominate the region and control a major lever of the international economy. While the Gulf War, then, was not pristine in terms of upholding Founding principles, it bore out Founding realism.

Clinton's action against Haiti had the effect of restoring the elected president, Jean-Bertrand Aristide, a defrocked Catholic priest and proponent of Marxist-inspired liberation theology. Aristide's election had apparently been fair, although after his party's control of the parliament collapsed in a no-confidence vote he attempted to rule alone. This prompted a coup and new elections were scheduled, although they were then cancelled—possibly under American pressure. The top army general became the *de facto* head of the government, and his regime became more and more repressive and led to increasing numbers of Haitian refugees seeking asylum in the U.S. (which led to a negative political reaction in the U.S.).[256] Later, it became apparent that, especially after he returned to power, Aristide became financially and politically corrupt and was responsible for human rights violations. Despite having had a strong following among the large poor population in Haiti, he was later forced from the country again in 2004 without much popular lament.[257] He was thus not much different from previous Haitian rulers. Clinton's action can be contrasted with the above interventions when considering Founding cultural principles. While it is not so clear that interventions south of the border generally bring about better regimes—since there is such a history of corruption and self-serving rule—it is clear that in this specific case restoring Aristide to power hardly promoted such Founding principles as concern for the common good, civic friendship, civility, honesty or sobriety in government, or justice. Any advantage to be gained in this regard from deposing the military rulers was thus lost with Aristide's return. Moreover, it is also doubtful that the common good *within the U.S.* was a driving consideration for Clinton, as there are many indications that political considerations were significant is his decision.[258] His insistent favoritism for Aristide also hardly bespoke foreign policy impartiality.

Clinton's Bosnia and Kosovo engagements appear somewhat more positive, or at least ambiguous, when evaluated in light of Founding principles. The Serbian regime that emerged in its part of the former Yugoslavia prosecuted a policy of "ethnic cleansing" against Bosnians, who were predominantly Moslem.[259] To be sure, there had been age-old suspicions and hostilities among ethnic groups that had made up Yugoslavia and while the American-led NATO intervention in 1995 did not enhance civic friendship, it did stop the Serbian government's repression and atrocities and led to an agreement (the Dayton Peace Accords).[260] In 1998-1999, the Serbian military activity in Kosovo initially sought to suppress the move for independence by the Kosovar Liberation Army (KLA) that followed from repression of the mostly Albanian Kosovars by the Serbian government. American-spearheaded NATO bombing against the Serbs took place in 1999 after Western attempts to diplomatically end the conflict failed. The airstrikes actually had the effect of worsening the situation, emboldening the Serbs to extend their ethnic cleansing policy to Kosovo by forcing the Kosovars out of the country and creating a massive refugee problem in eastern Europe. Nevertheless, with Russian help, the Serbian government accepted a negotiated settlement.[261] There had been concern about the actions leading to Islamist terrorist activity in the Balkans. A Congressional Research Service study of the subject in 2005, however, concluded that while there have been some home-grown terrorist attacks on Serbian civilians in Kosovo, there has been little connection with international Islamic terrorists. Also, efforts by the latter to recruit in both Bosnia and Kosovo have been unsuccessful.[262] The more secular outlook of the Moslems in these areas may be one reason for this.[263] Also, NATO interventions apparently helped create pro-American sentiment among Moslems in both Bosnia and Kosovo.[264] So, while the U.S. did not foster civic friendship among the parties involved, it did in the end help to secure justice and make them act with at least a reluctant civility toward one another. Achieving that outcome, however, came only after U.S. actions initially caused more incivility and breakdown of civil order and justice in Kosovo.

The best way to analyze the main interventions of George W. Bush (Afghanistan and Iraq) is to evaluate what came to be called the Bush Doctrine, or what Lamont Colucci called "crusading realism."[265] It espoused three objectives and three general strategies. The former were combating and defeating terrorism, constructing strategic relationships with the other great powers, and encouraging free political societies. The latter were prevention, preemption (anticipatory self-defense and preventive war), and defense of the homeland. If necessary, the U.S. would be prepared to act unilaterally—both in a military sense and in her general foreign policy—and to force regime change.[266] The Afghanistan invasion, a month after September 11, could be characterized as a defensive action. The attacks on the U.S. were orchestrated by al-Qaeda, and the Islamist Taliban regime in that country was harboring al-Qaeda and its leadership. The U.S. wanted to eliminate the terrorist movement that had attacked her and the regime that gave them a base of operations, both as reasonable retaliation and to protect herself from further attacks. Thus, the essence of the Bush Doctrine as *crusading* realism—i.e., deliberately aiming to change the character of regimes and promoting democracy, in some sense—would not necessarily have to come into play.

The Iraq War that commenced in 2003 is much harder to justify in defensive terms, since there was no significant connection between Saddam Hussein's regime, as much as it detested the U.S., and al-Qaeda or other Islamic terrorist organizations; the Iraqis had not attacked nor given support to an attack on the U.S.; and—after the initial claims of the regime's attempts to develop weapons of mass destruction were apparently shown to be untrue[267]—there was no serious *likelihood* that it would attack the U.S. There was the possibility that it might have sought to sponsor an attack on U.S. interests closer to its own homeland, but no evidence that it had previously done that. In just war theory, a preventive war is not excluded. However, the possibility of aggression by the nation attacked cannot be remote or unlikely.[268] The latter seemed to have been the case with Iraq in 2003, however. The Iraq War showcased the Bush Doctrine. Colucci claims that this doctrine corresponded precisely to the Founding tradition. He says the following: 1) "The Founders were…products of the western Enlightenment," and as such they believed in progress, which included at the same time "the idealism of 'human rights' and the pragmatism of national interest."[269] 2) Idealism is thus good in a foreign policy, but too often in American history it has signaled the compromise of security (i.e., "pragmatism"). With the Bush Doctrine, both came together (i.e., "crusading realism").[270] 3) The Bush Doctrine understood that "America was and is a revolutionary state"—i.e., it was a democratic revolution—and "the time is now ripe to export that revolution."[271] 4) The Founding also embodied natural law principles, which are universal and include principles like respecting human dignity and the need for freedom. Thus, the Bush Doctrine had "a comprehensive quality" (i.e., was understood as seeking to promote universalistic principles everywhere on the globe). Bush also saw principles such as these representing a nexus of Lockeanism and Christian morality, which he viewed as joined together at the foundation of the Republic. 5) The means to achieve this supposedly idealistic end would have to be realistic—"the heavy use of military force and covert operations," if needed. 6) There were many precedents in American history for the Bush Doctrine, such as Manifest Destiny, the "walk softly but carry a big stick" approach of Theodore Roosevelt, and the Reagan policy against Soviet communism.[272]

Despite the supposed realism of the Bush Doctrine, as characterized by Colucci, it was actually *unrealistic* in believing that it could aggressively promote these principles around the world. It was also unrealistic in believing that democratic republics could be imposed militarily. In truth, it offended the realism of the Founders. Further, contrary to its belief, the Founders did not advocate crusading—especially not militarily—to promote the American form of government abroad. As stated earlier, the Founders believed that they would influence the rest of the world *by example*. While the natural law tradition that was part of the Founding would indeed have held that such matters as human dignity and freedom were universal, it would have recognized that there are legitimately some differences in how freedom is understood in different cultures. With the theory of political realism in modern-day international politics scholarship, it would not have insisted that one nation's conception of freedom is synonymous with freedom per se. Also like that theory, it would have viewed crusading zeal in a foreign policy—whether a Bush Doctrine or Wilsonianism— as a troubling kind of *moralism*, not realism.[273] The natural law tradition behind the Founding would not have insisted that democracy, or any one form of government, was best for all peoples. It tended to follow Aristotle, believing that while some forms are perverted forms and should be rejected there are certain others that are good forms.[274] In fact, if the democracy that the Bush Doctrine sought to export was understood to mean outright power in the hands of the masses, then that tradition would have held it not to be one of the good forms, or at least to have been problematical[275]—nor would the Founders themselves, as we have noted repeatedly in this book. If Bush was so sure that he was promoting traditional American moral precepts, it would have been well for him to have considered that the notion of using military force to achieve even good ends such as the promotion of human rights is a utilitarian (end-justifies-the-means) perspective that would have been anathema to Founding Era morality. Finally, it may be correct as Colucci says that the Bush Doctrine was like major American foreign policy approaches of the past. As we have shown in this book, however, some of these approaches have not squared with Founding political and cultural norms. The ones involving interventionism for less than noble purposes—which have been frequent enough in American history, as discussed in this book—and Woodrow Wilson's moralism no doubt made it easier to develop something like the Bush Doctrine. Many historical precedents had cleared the path.

During the post-1980 period, American foreign policy gyrated back and forth between unilateralism and multilateralism, in varying degrees. Reagan tended toward the former, although in the Grenada invasion it was different. George H.W. Bush and Clinton inclined toward multilateralism—with the U.S. being the initiator—although Clinton acted unilaterally in Haiti. George W. Bush sometimes inclined to multilateralism, at least believing that coalitions of nations had to be forged for the interventions in Afghanistan and Iraq. Obama has an orientation toward multilateralism.[276] The attitude thus began to develop in the period that the proper course for the U.S. was multilateralism—that the U.S. should consult with other nations or pertinent international organizations before undertaking a military action. The latter was an expression of the same outlook that was seen above in legal developments—identified especially with liberalism in the U.S. and European Union internationalism in Europe—of downplaying national sovereignty. This, of course, would have been incomprehensible to the Founders, who saw themselves as building a "new order for the ages" instead of following the path of the Old World.

In sum, the post-1980 period was one in which Founding principles as they affected foreign affairs were at times upheld and at times not: sometimes Founding realism prevailed (especially under Reagan and the first Bush), sometimes moralism; mostly there was attention to the problems of impartiality and foreign influence, but on some occasions not (the Clinton-Chinese connection, however, was one of American history's most egregious violations of these norms); the civil-military relationship was strained, in an ongoing way, by political pressures and influences; the reasons behind most of the interventions, unlike often in the past, were not against Founding cultural norms (in fact, such Founding cultural norms as a cooperative spirit, civility, justice, and the promotion of the common good were often—not always—the result); and the sovereign power of the nation to commence war (mentioned even in the Declaration of Independence) was increasingly downplayed. On balance, it must be concluded that in spite of a foreign policy that often had good intentions some views and practices were becoming deeply implanted that were contrary to Founding thinking.

Relations and Conflict Among Social Groups, and Immigration. Next, as with previous historical periods, we inquire into how relations among different groups in the time since 1980 have measured up to such norms of the Founding Era culture as civic friendship and civility. We have already discussed the conflicts caused by the push to enact the homosexualist agenda. The culture wars also spawned conflict involving the abortion issue, as the mid-1980s to mid-1990s saw a substantial amount of anti-abortion non-violent "direct action" (i.e., sit-ins and blockading of abortion clinics) with thousands of arrests and some anti-abortion violence (including bombings of clinics and some physical assaults and murders).[277] There was an increase in racial tensions on campuses, resulting in significant part from affirmative action programs (even while the courts, above, put some limits on the programs). Such programs created tensions between Caucasian and minority students because the former believed that standards were being lowered and the latter, after being heavily recruited, were given little academic or other support and became alienated.[278] Also, the attitudes of "political correctness" that gripped many campuses engendered what Paul Johnson calls a "witchhunt" atmosphere where non-leftist political and social views were suppressed and Negro, Hispanic, and female students were encouraged to report comments by professors and fellow students that they subjectively considered derogatory.[279] That comments, even if innocent, would stimulate racial and other controversy was an outgrowth of the extreme sensitivities that developed in the 1970s.

Overall, however, there were no major racial troubles in the 1980s. However, the existence of racial and ethnic conflicts was seen in the following: some well-publicized incidents (e.g., the Bernhard Goetz shooting of four Negro youths in a New York City subway in 1984 when they threateningly asked him for money,[280] the 1986 Howard Beach (Queens) attack by a Caucasian gang on a group of Negroes and resulting protests,[281] the racial tensions incited by Tawana Brawley's false gang rape story (also in the New York City area),[282] and the clubbing death of a Chinese American man near Detroit by two Caucasian autoworkers who were angry at Japanese auto competition (they thought him to be Japanese, and blamed him for their layoffs[283]); a strident newly-emerging racial demogoguery by some self-proclaimed civil rights leaders (which sometimes took on an anti-Jewish tone);[284] and troubling attitudes of average Negroes about Negro victimization by the Caucasian culture (e.g., the views of Atlanta Negroes, who were convinced that the string of Negro child murders there in the late 1970s and early 1980s—committed, it turned out, by a young Negro man—was not getting addressed for racial reasons[285] and the willingness of most American Negroes to want to dismiss the evidence against football legend O.J. Simpson in the murder of his Caucasian ex-wife and her friend in the 1990s[286]); and Negro leaders who seemed ready to excuse Negro criminal activity (e.g., the eminent psychologist Kenneth B. Clark, who justified Negro muggings of Caucasians, as in the Goetz case, as "an act of social protest").[287] If previously the Jim Crow South eviscerated the rule of law in its treatment of Negroes, now racial partisanship trumped it in the attitudes of many Negroes. In spite of these realities and the routine criticisms of Reagan by Negro leaders,[288] Ehrman says that it was "by no means clear that race relations were worse at the end of the Reagan years than at the start," since there was "greater tolerance and inclusion"[289] and the country was "inch[ing] along toward 'diversity.'"[290] Negroes continued to move up the economic scale and into the suburbs, and this economic progress continued into the new century.[291] The early 1990s produced a feared harbinger of a return to the destructive racial conflict of the 1960s with the South Central Los Angeles race riot of 1992, and several smaller-scale race riots around the country. They followed from the acquittal in court of four police officers accused of beating repeat criminal Rodney King, who was then out of prison on probation, after a high-speed chase. During the Los Angeles riot, Negro and Hispanic rioters especially targeted business establishments owned by East Asians. There was some confusion about whether there actually had been police brutality and the some of the attacks by the rioters on innocent persons were outright savage.[292] Concern about the rule of law, so central of a principle of the Founding, dissipated during and after the riot—not only by the very lawlessness of the event itself, but also because of the facts that the Los Angeles police for a time were ordered not to intervene and then later the U.S. Justice Department prosecuted the acquitted officers for civil rights offenses[293] (i.e., a *de facto*, even if not *de jure*, case of double jeopardy because of the apparent political calculation that it was necessary to check further unrest). There were, however, no further such riots in the years that followed. In fact, the movement of Negro attitudes toward separatism of the late 1960s and 1970s was reversed. Negroes increased their presence in elective office and government.[294] This culminated, of course, with the election of Obama, who American Negroes think of as one of their own, but who is actually of mixed race (sub-Saharan African, Caucasian, and American Indian).[295] Patterson indicates that there was much acceptance by Americans by the end of the twentieth century of different racial and ethnic groups and cultures in the country.[296] The rate of interracial (Caucasian-Negro) marriages significantly increased.[297] This, of course, was even well beyond the extent of the voluntary melding of groups in the Founding Era, when most Negroes in the U.S. were slaves.

If the period witnessed the ugly episode of an attack on a man wrongly thought to be Japanese (above), it also featured the Japanese-American Redress Act that sought to rectify the wrongful internment of Japanese-Americans during World War II (see Chapter 6). It gave reparations to the survivors and their heirs.[298] Patterson tells us that socio-economic class diminished as a point of conflict and division in American life in the 1980s. This was because while the wealthy "advanced most rapidly, the real disposable income of every stratum of the population rose."[299] We already mentioned the rise of Negroes, who historically had been on the lower end of the economic scale. Patterson also mentions that birth and religion ceased to be "determinants of social mobility."[300] The enhanced social mobility, of course, coincided with conditions in the Founding Era. As the above indicates, however, religious conflicts—or, at least, hostility toward religion—did not cease, although it was now not so much hostility toward certain religions but by secularist elements or the secular culture toward traditional religion. In fact, when the points above are considered it might be said that religion and religious bodies were under greater pressure than at any time in American history. This, of course, built up from the early expressions of secularism in first half of the nineteenth century, to the beginnings of the move for separationism after the Civil War, to the secularization of the intelligentsia and a segment of the culture after World War I, to the Supreme Court's mandated neutrality between belief and unbelief after World War II, to the sweeping secularization of American life in the 1960s and 1970s. At each stage the rejection of religion as a formative force for American life deepened. Also, some of the political rhetoric of the Obama period has suggested that hostility directed toward higher economic classes had not disappeared.[301] While labor conflicts were in no way as intense as earlier in U.S. history, Berman says that NAFTA helped to create labor-management tensions (as perhaps was suggested by the above).[302] Also, while sectional differences paled as compared to much of the past, there was anger and political backlash in the western U.S. about environmental policies and the like imposed by the far-away federal government and "'elitist eastern bureaucrats.'"[303]

Perhaps the main area of inter-group stress in the post-1980 period has been in the area of immigration. We mentioned how the liberalized Immigration Act of 1965 changed the complexion of U.S. immigration. It also accelerated legal immigration beyond what had been expected[304] and, as noted, its aftermath brought a considerable increase in illegal immigration. In 1986, another reform bill—supported by Reagan—granted amnesty to what had become by then millions of illegal immigrants living in the U.S.[305] By the first decade of the twenty-first century it was clear that illegal immigration had harmed order and civility in some parts of the country. This was due to the vicious gang activity and substantial number of criminals it had brought in.[306] Recalling what was said about the civic bond problem, the Mexican nationalistic ideology that came along with the illegal immigration helped create divisive and even separatistic feelings in the Southwest.[307] This was contrary to the spirit of civic friendship and concern for the general welfare of the Founding. Some Hispanic immigrant elements have sometimes demonstrated a radicalism, strident rhetoric, and (despite being in the U.S.) anti-Americanism.[308] This was different from what had historically happened in the U.S., when immigrants ardently wanted to become "American."[309] This new attitude was doubtless an outgrowth of the identity politics that took hold in the 1970s. Part of the civic bond that holds a nation together involves "'emotional ties and core understandings about the world and common experience.'"[310] These facts suggest that this is lacking, which has portentous implications for inter-group relations and social stability—and shows a weakening of the common good. If Americans had become more accepting of the many cultures now in their midst, it thus did not seem that many immigrants and their spokesmen reciprocated.[311] Added to this was a continuation of the movement toward bilingualism that had begun in the 1970s, with obliviousness to the conflicts among social groups that this typically causes in a nation.[312] The Mexican government has even sought to stir up Mexican nationalistic feelings among *legal* immigrants who had become American citizens.[313] It has also encouraged its citizens to violate American immigration laws to come north and has interfered in internal American political affairs in places like California and Arizona to secure public policy decisions favorable to Mexican immigrants.[314] All this, of course, violates the civic friendship, spirit of fair-dealing, and respect for its general welfare owed by a country to its neighbor—to say nothing of interfering with the sovereignty of another nation. Further, the frequent unwillingness of government at different levels in the U.S. to enforce the immigration laws[315]—for political and ideological reasons—flies in the face of respect for the rule of law.

Early in his administration, before the events of September 11, 2001, George W. Bush had seriously considered proposals for an amnesty, like the one in 1986, for illegal immigrants.[316] When immigration liberalization ultimately was considered in Congress in 2007, as mentioned, it got nowhere.

In sum, the above indicates that while the post-1980 period was mostly devoid of major inter-group confrontation and there was heightened socio-economic mobility for most groups and much inter-marriage and other voluntary melding, tensions were still on a "low-burn"—and thus civic friendship was still lacking. The absence of such confrontation also did not mean that there was an absence of incivility. This also indicated an insufficient orientation to the common good. Except for the 1992 race riots, the immigration question seemed to cause the greatest amount of conflict with Founding principles.

Socio-Cultural Developments and Intellectual Trends. While socio-cultural change in the U.S. during the post-1980 period was not as dramatic as in the 1960s and 1970s, as indicated it continued many of the same trends and implanted them more deeply into American life. First, we consider religion. In the 1980s—not unlike the 1970s, in spite of the general cultural drift of that decade—there was something of a religious revival. About a third of Americans reported that they had had some kind of a religious experience that changed the direction of their lives. About 95% said they believed in God, and nearly two-thirds were affiliated with a church or synagogue. Still, the 40% who attended worship services weekly was considerably less than the 49% high point (since surveys started) in 1958—and much less than what were almost certainly the levels of earlier in American history. Also, the majority of Americans did not seem to want their religious beliefs to influence others or the culture, as they practiced a "privatized, nonjudgmental" faith.[317] This, of course, was not the kind of religious spirit that built the Christian culture of the early American Republic that Tocqueville commented about. The religiosity of the 1980s, such as it was, did not seem to last. By the end of the first decade of the twenty-first century, church attendance still seemed to be at this 1980's level, but the percentage of Americans who defined themselves as Christian—even if nominally—had declined to a little over 75%—down from over 90% after World War II—mostly because of the growth of the number of people who claimed no religion.[318] Also, according to a 2009 *Newsweek* poll, about 70% believed that religion was losing its hold on American life.[319] Actually, as we have seen, these developments were part of a long-term secularization trend in American life. Most disturbing perhaps is Paul Johnson's observation that, "For the first time in American history there was a widespread tendency, especially among intellectuals, to present religious people as enemies of freedom and democratic choice."[320]

The decline of religion in the entire period of post-1960 America was an important factor in the decline of the family and the growth of illegitimacy.[321] The increase in the latter in the 1960-1980 period continued after 1980.[322] Among Caucasians, the illegitimacy rate increased almost six times over what it had been in 1960 (to almost 30%); among Negroes, it tripled (to 65%).[323] By 2000, 22% of all families with minor children were headed by women without husbands present.[324] The conditions that caused this, illegitimacy and a continued high divorce rate—40% of all marriages ended in divorce in 2000[325]—resulted in much damage to children and the family.[326] Cohabitation massively increased in the aftermath of the sexual revolution of the 1960s; from 1960 to 2005, the rate went up over 1,000%.[327] Since couples that marry after cohabiting have a stronger likelihood of divorcing,[328] this was another serious stress on the family. So contrary to the Founding culture, there were now "a variety of family styles."[329] We saw that as early as the nineteenth century, with lower class women having to work outside the home to supplement their husbands' low wages and sustain their families, their children did not receive the attention they needed. The same stresses on the family were evident in the post-1980 period, but probably enhanced. Myron A. Marty writes that mothers working outside the home had become so common that when they quit to stay home with their children it became newsworthy.[330] The latchkey children phenomenon spoken about before became increasingly common, and older children had to care for younger ones at earlier ages.[331] The percentages of men and women who never married almost doubled between 1970 and 1990,[332] and by 2000 had climbed to 24% of adults.[333] Chapter 8 mentioned the growth of anti-natalism. Maggie Gallagher, a noted writer on marriage and family questions, says that in the post-1980 period this attitude "has slowed…but not died."[334] Carlson, with reference to the attitudes of young women, writes that "[m]otherhood had lost its aura,"[335] and notes that by the late 1980s wives aged 18 to 34 were having an average of just 1.5 children, "with employed women moving toward a one-child norm."[336] This signaled, in a somewhat different sense than with the foregoing developments, that the family was not as fundamental in American life as in the past. The sexual revolution of the 1960s and 1970s continued in other ways.[337] As suggested by the above, it played a significant role in the post-1980 decline of the family. The decline of sexual morality was also fed by an increasingly vulgar popular culture, that openly "placed sex and violence…in the public square."[338] Troy says that by the 1980s, "all subtleties were lost," with sadomasochistic lyrics in rock music, the emergence of "shock jocks," "a host of shameless sinners who combined various pathologies in twisted ways," and the injecting of "graphic images into mainstream culture."[339] Besides featuring a standardless—even nihilistic, "anything goes"—morality, the popular culture of the period betrayed a dearth of good manners and hardly a remnant of the spirit of the gentleman—such conditions, of course, would have been unimaginable to the Founding Era. The entertainment and communications industry, at once, helped to undermine the family, spurned the possibility that moral norms could have any possible effect on people's behavior, and showed its lack of a sense of social obligation when its spokesmen claimed that they should not be held blameworthy for peddling this brand of pop culture because, after all, contemporary American youth simply could not practice self-control anyway. Additionally, this was a laissez faire version of cultural and moral formation that did violence to the Founders notion of education for virtue and good citizenship. When the industry's leaders and celebrity spokesmen claimed repression and censorship because parents' groups sought nothing more than warning labels on records, akin to the movie rating system, it showed how convoluted the understanding of liberty had become among a major element of opinion-makers, and how far prudence and moderation had departed from the country's public discussion. How little a sound public morality still meant for some political leaders was seen by their unwillingness to criticize the industry because they sought its financial contributions for their political campaigns.[340]

The music lyrics controversy was an example of the culture wars above that had become so common and increasingly bitter in the post-1980 period,[341] and often saw liberals—who, it will be recalled, had embraced an anti-traditional culture agenda—and conservatives lining up on opposite sides.[342] This division was one dimension of the political polarization that we said above had remained a feature of American life since the 1960s. It was one more indicia of the lack of civic friendship.

Nevertheless, Patterson notes a number of commentators, *both* conservative and liberal, in the 1990s who looked at developments such as the above and concluded that America was in a state of general moral decline.[343] If any one perspective or intellectual trend was at the root of them it was individualism. Troy says that not only were religion, family, and morality pushed aside for many Americans, but so were community, tradition, authority, and duty. They "were no longer sure what kind of happiness they even wanted to pursue." As the above suggests, this "confusion caused much individual misery and social dysfunction."[344] The nihilism seen in some aspects of popular culture in a subdued way afflicted American life generally: it was "'a world without fixed rules.'"[345] The 1980s continued the trend of the 1960-1980 period of Americans being "more open, tolerant, and individualist."[346] Troy says that the one ethical commandment of the 1980s was: do not judge.[347] The general attitudes, then, paralleled the predominant direction of American religious attitudes above. Perhaps this is why Ehrman says that cultural change in the 1980s continued to go in a "liberal" direction—despite a conservative trend in American politics and a more assertive public presence of traditional Christians.[348] Indeed, many self-proclaimed conservatives "celebrated the moral life without actually living it."[349] People tended to live for the moment, and no presidents regardless of their political stripe—including Reagan—"demanded that Americans solve social problems through individual or collective sacrifice."[350] This, of course, was completely the opposite of what the Founding Era knew was necessary. Further, in spite of his strong traditional-sounding positions on many questions, Reagan never "tr[ied] to impose drastic changes on existing social arrangements" any more than he tried to roll back the welfare state.[351] When the Clinton administration came to power, they actually worked to *further* the anti-traditional culture agenda (e.g., abortion rights, including vetoing a federal partial birth abortion ban; homosexualism; the greater tolerance of pornography noted above, although he signed legislation restraining its dissemination to minors).[352] Obama was even more aggressive in doing this (e.g., federal funding of embryonic stem cell research; expanding the federal hate-crime law to "sexual orientation" and "gender identity;"[353] seeking to repeal the federal Defense of Marriage Act—enacted under Clinton—which protected reluctant states from having to recognize homosexual "marriages" from other states;[354] calling himself "a fierce advocate for gay and lesbian Americans"[355]).

It should be stated that in addition to the promotion of homosexualism being an obvious affront to the sexual morality, traditional cultural orientation, and norm of eschewing of individualism of the Founding Era, it represents a convolution of the Founding notion of equality that this book has frequently discussed. Even the promotion of homosexual "marriage" does not capture the extent of this. In early 2010, eighteen U.S. senators wrote to the Food and Drug Administration, pursuant to demands from the homosexualist movement, urging it to end its lifetime ban on blood donations from men who engage in sexual activity (i.e., sodomy) with other men. Somehow, they saw this as unjustly discriminatory—a violation of equality—even though active homosexual men have a prevalence of deadly HIV (human immunodeficiency virus) sixty times higher than the general population and so the safety of blood recipients could be at stake.[356]

The individualism of the post-1980 period also manifested itself in the consumerism, irresponsible use of credit, excessive corporate compensation, and shady business practices discussed above. As noted, too, the consumer culture left Americans restlessness and unfulfilled. Even children were swept into the consumer culture, with media marketing often directed specifically at them.[357] It indicated: a lack of frugality, sobriety, simplicity, willingness to make present sacrifices for future good, and attention to the norms of avoiding debt and excessive luxury of the Founding culture.

Another socio-cultural area that we have examined throughout American history is crime. In the last two decades of the twentieth century the crime rate declined, but still remained high (this is apart from the increasing problem of innocent persons being convicted, which was discussed above).[358] Crime was particularly high among the Negro population.[359] Also, the U.S. prison population grew steadily, approaching 2.4 million in 2008, by far the largest number in the world and about 24% of the world total.[360] The post-1980 period also featured shocking mass murders that had become almost routine.[361] It was mentioned that the continued high crime rate since the 1960s has coincided with the breakdown of the family and religion. The decline of what Paul Johnson calls a "moralistic culture"—i.e., one stressing traditional morality and being clear and emphatic about right and wrong—is another factor.[362] Three important factors in sustaining a democratic republic, then, also emerge as crucial just for order (i.e., family, religion, and morality)—with crime by its nature implying in some measure the absence of order.

Finally, we consider the situation of education in the post-1980 period. We saw the troubling developments in it in the 1960s and 1970s. In higher education, we have already mentioned the political correctness. Besides the increasing intolerance on many campuses, ideology reduced the academic quality of higher education.[363] These ideological influences sometimes had their roots in destructive intellectual trends. One of these was deconstructionism, which "taught that written words never can be assigned fixed meanings and, as a result, that close readings of texts can reveal ambiguities, hidden meanings, contradictions, and indications of repressive political relationships." Since, then, texts could be "open to innumerable interpretations, no absolute values can be said to exist" and there are "no…universal experiences." Interpretations are just the results of "social constructions."[364] This was beyond even moral or cultural relativism; like some of the pop culture of the time, it was nihilism. As is apparent, the echo of Marxism was also there. This and the general cultural trends discussed easily helped give rise to group identity politics on campuses, although that development probably had its roots in the particularistic, group-specific studies that had taken hold in universities since the 1960s. We alluded to this in Chapter 8. The basic philosophy behind these studies was to break down "the common identities of society by emphasizing the differences of ever smaller, ever more particular groups."[365] These influences accelerated and deepened the subversion of the liberal arts that had been occurring since the middle of the nineteenth century. Well-publicized episodes at such leading universities as Stanford and Yale seemed to evince hostility to studies in Western culture.[366] Across the academy, the nature of core curriculum requirements and the amount of attention to Western culture—the basic substance of most traditional liberal education—was much debated.[367] Allan Bloom's famous book, *The Closing of the American Mind* (1987), lamented the displacement of the Great Books from university and college curricula, which had long been a backbone of a liberal arts education.[368] Many learned commentators decried the continued unwillingness of higher education to transmit the cultural heritage behind America (and thus not provide a sufficient rooting in our tradition that is part of the basis for good citizenship); its exultation of race, class, gender, etc. (as seen above) and dismissal of universal, perennial truths; its falling prey to the consumerism of the larger culture; and its decimation of academic standards. A corrosive youth culture, with distant origins in the 1960s, seemed to pervade the campus scene.[369] This usually included alcohol, drugs, sex, and even sexual violence (i.e., sexual assaults on female students after they had been plied with alcohol or drugs).[370] We have traced an ongoing, even progressive, decline over American history of the kind of education the Founders believed necessary to sustain a democratic republic. Bloom said that higher education had come to "impoverish" students' souls;[371] it was clear that it seemed to contribute little to the moral formation that the Founders believed all-important for republican citizens. With the politicization and increasing irrationalism of the higher learning its condition, in that sense, was perhaps the most critical ever. Deconstructionism and group identity studies as they were pursued denied, in essence, the commonality among persons; as such, they were incompatible with the entire notion of nature behind the Founding—and the natural law/natural rights tradition that it embraced. They conveyed utter intellectual disorder to students that could only give rise to practical disorder, in their lives as students and afterwards.

The above makes clear that the skepticism that had overwhelmed higher education in the 1960-1980 period—and undercut the very liberal arts that the Founders viewed as especially important for leaders—continued intact. John S. Schmitt writes that such skepticism actually afflicts present-day education from the time that young children begin their schooling.[372] David Lowenthal says that another consequence of the ensuing decay of liberal education is that it leaves students, when they become citizens, "more susceptible to irrational ideologies appealing to idealism, morality and heroism"[373]—that is, to moralistic sentimentality.

Along with troublesome philosophical presuppositions, pre-college education was also afflicted by the group identity politics seen in higher education. This was manifested in the introduction of bilingual instruction (already discussed), the related push for Ebonics—or the street language of the Negro underclass—in some schools (which would have massively "dumbed down" their educational quality),[374] and the increased emphasis on "multicultural" programs—some of which were politically charged—that undercut "the long-standing monocultural emphasis in American public education" that was aimed at shaping a common American culture and producing good citizens.[375] The serious implications for the American democratic republic of group identity politics and education discussed previously are also certainly applicable here. One other aspect of group identity politics—again, following developments at the college level—was the attempt to increasingly "raise teacher consciousness" about alleged gender "stereotyping" and discrimination, which was said to manifest itself in fewer girls going on to studies in science and engineering fields, boys getting more teacher attention than girls, and socially-determined roles for boys and girls[376] (the latter claim, of course, comes directly from 1970's feminism, as previously noted).

In pre-college public education, the trends of the 1960-1980 period of more federal involvement continued, and in fact increased. State oversight over local districts also intensified. In seeming contrast to the simultaneous ingraining of group identity politics and the like, the nature of educational reform changed from the progressivist stream to a "back-to-basics" emphasis and more classroom structure.[377] Probably a momentum created by Reagan's National Commission on Excellence in Education's report entitled *A Nation at Risk* aided this,[378] as well as his own open support for such reform.[379] Local and state politicians pushed reforms,[380] and the Reagan administration provided block grants—which meant less federal control—to help make it possible.[381] State governments adopted requirements for teacher competency testing as a criterion for certification and statewide mandates for pupil proficiency testing.[382] As the post-1980 period continued, however, the federal role—and control—expanded, perhaps more under Republican than Democratic presidential administrations. It was under George H.W. Bush that the ADA and the Individuals with Disabilities Education Act became law,[383] which have had the effect of placing substantial constraints and burdens on public education.[384] Much more regimentation, as suggested above, came with George W. Bush's No Child Left Behind Act of 2001, which was another of a long line of grant programs that impinged on federalism because of the conditions on states to receive federal funds. The act prescribed teacher qualifications, pupil proficiency testing, the right of pupils to transfer from schools that fail to meet certain standards, supplemental services for pupils, and provisions for changing staff and state takeovers of supposedly failing schools.[385] Clinton had adopted a "killing us softly" approach to state powers on education: he called for national goals, standards, and testing, but wanted the states to voluntarily adopt them. He also had some sweeping objectives that would have offended the realism of the Founders, such as expecting every child to read and use the Internet competently and believing that every high school graduate could go to college.[386]

Two final, quite specific socio-cultural topics deserve to be mentioned because they provide striking contrasts with Founding Era norms. One concerns the growth, even if often quietly, of euthanasia. Most attention in the U.S. has been given to the legalization of physician-assisted suicide, where physicians are permitted to outright deliver a lethal dose of drugs to a patient who requests it to bring about his death. By 2010, this was legal in three states: Oregon, Washington, and Montana.[387] More typical, however, has been the refusal to provide even ordinary medical treatment (e.g., antibiotics to combat an infection) or normal care (i.e., nutrition and hydration) to a person who has a terminal or serious chronic illness. Sometimes this is done pursuant to a living will, in which people can specify years in advance of the onset of any condition that they do not want what they think would be "futile" medical treatment—even if their intentions when actually ill are not so clear[388]—or if another person charged to make medical decisions for them decides it, even if their own wishes may have been different (e.g., the Terri Schindler Schiavo case),[389] or even because medical decisionmakers—sometimes even against the wishes of patients or their next-of-kin—make such decisions.[390] Often, the criterion used to make such decisions has been one of "quality of life" (i.e., this person would not want to live because his quality of life would not be very good in his condition). Besides offending the right to life, as with abortion, this signals a utilitarian ethic that would have been anathema to the morality the Founders that is the foundation of a democratic republic. Doubtless, the growing acceptance of euthanasia followed from the increasingly widespread practice of abortion—that began in the 1960s—since both fundamentally involve a devaluing of the lives of vulnerable, dependent persons at the edges of life who are unwanted or held not to be able to contribute to society.

Finally, in the 1980s the issue of homelessness gained much attention in the U.S., as there was a record number of people without a regular abode sleeping on sidewalks, in public parks, or under bridges. One significant reason for this was the decision of state governments to adopt "deinstitutionalization" policies for mentally ill asylum residents, and the failure to provide adequate follow-up attention and care for them in community-based, outpatient programs.[391] Female homelessness, sometimes also involving a woman's children, was often the result of family breakdown in some manner, including physical abuse by a husband-father or cohabiting partner.[392] Addiction (to alcohol or drugs) and economic problems are also causes of homelessness.[393] The problem showed that the Founding norms of "being thy brother's keeper"—by both government and the public—and a communal orientation were to some degree lacking, probably because of individualism and the growth of impersonal mass culture. The entire notion of deinstitutionalization was another development that would have affronted Founding realism; it would have been seen as the kind of utopian scheme the Founders and their culture would have had no use for. Female homelessness above was another manifestation of the breakdown of the family and sexual morality, the forging of public policies such as easy divorce that we said before have damaged the family, and of the submersion of such Founding Era norms as responsibility, marital fidelity, willingness to sacrifice, promise-keeping, and simply men conducting themselves according to the code of the gentleman. Addiction as a factor underscored the general decline of individual virtue that was so stressed in Founding times. That economic problems are a cause further illustrates the continued problem—expressing itself in so many ways since the nineteenth century—of the breakdown of the sense of the social obligation of property, and of the notions that everyone should have a sufficiency of goods and equal economic opportunity.

To conclude, it is probably in this area of socio-cultural developments that the post-1980 period has deviated the most from the Founding Era. It is also probably the decline of religion, the family, education, and morality that are most responsible for the weakening of the other principles and practices associated with the Founding in the socio-cultural realm (since the moral formation that is involved with them is crucial for the latter): manners, the spirit of the gentleman, avoidance of individualism and the related norm of a communal orientation, self-restraint, prudence, civic friendship, unwillingness to sacrifice in the present for the future, the avoidance of luxury, frugality, sobriety, simplicity, promise-keeping, the social obligation of property, being one's brother's keeper, and liberty. The old story of the continued growth of mass culture further urged on many of these developments. We also saw the growth of more governmental centralization in this socio-cultural realm specifically in education (even while the greater the back-to-basics emphasis was more in the spirit of the Founding Era). Even more problematical was the weakening of a common American culture that included a commitment to many of the principles discussed in this book.

In terms of an overall conclusion about the period from 1980 to the present, we say the following. The period was not as sweepingly at odds with so many Founding Era principles and practices as was 1960-1980. This was perhaps because certain of the socio-political trends of that period receded somewhat. It is very clear that the post-1980 period brought renewed attention—to at least some degree—to a number of those principles and practices, even if it is doubtful that they were restored to a substantial degree. While there was a limited reemphasis on federalism, there was no significant decentralization of governmental power—in fact, the U.S. seemed to be on the verge of an unprecedented centralization with the Obama administration—and certainly no retrenchment of the overwhelming role of government in general in the lives and affairs of American citizens. Especially noteworthy, in light of this and some troubling legal/constitutional trends, was that liberty and the rule of law suffered. While civility and civic friendship may not have suffered so egregiously as during the racial upheavals of the 1960s, in a subtler but perhaps more pervasive and ongoing way these norms and a corresponding respect for the common good continued to be lacking in America. The major reasons were individualism, a convolution of the Founding notion of equality, and an embracing of a regime of ersatz rights that departed from the natural law-natural rights framework of the Founding. Ersatz rights waxed, while such basic, central rights that the Founders believed essential for a democratic republic as religious liberty came under probably unprecedented attack. In economics, many of the conditions of the Founding Era continued to be absent as they had for a long time. Most striking here was the substantial economic centralization and bigness, heavy (in fact, unprecedented) levels of government debt, the predominance of an ethic of luxury and a lack of temperance, and persistent significant economic inequalities. To be sure, the value of entrepreneurship, traditional American household independence, and some sense of the need for morality and virtue in economics and the necessity of limits on economic freedom were stressed, but these positive elements seemed to be overwhelmed by all the departures from Founding Era practice. In foreign affairs, this period saw an impartiality and realism—especially with Reagan—but also a crusading "unrealism" and the compromising of many Founding cultural norms in dealing with other countries in the years after him. Especially troubling was the historic low point in terms of spurning Founding fears of letting foreign influences shape American policy reached with the Clinton-Chinese connection. Finally, it was in the socio-cultural area where there was the most complete turning away from pertinent Founding norms—e.g., religion, education, morality (especially sexual morality), marital fidelity and the family, avoidance of individualism, and self-restraint, etc.—many of which were, as this book has indicated, the foundation of Founding political principles. As previous chapters have shown, this was not new, but how much staying power the new troublesome cultural norms had was seen in the fact that even as openness to the older political and constitutional principles appeared little ground was gained in restoring these norms. In fact, as discussed, the conflicts in this area became bitterer than ever as they assumed the character of social and intellectual warfare—"culture wars"—and contributed significantly to the loss of the norms of civility and civic friendship. Although most people apparently could not discern this, developments in this area were an obstacle to a possible restoration of many of the other principles. For example, if morality, moral formation, and virtue were deemphasized the state would have to become more powerful and expand its role in order to control people who had made up their minds not to control themselves. If religion—the basis for most people's conceptions of morality—no longer had a hold on people, and the family—the initial and most basic means of inculcating such morality—was in decay, the same problem appeared. In addition, the state's role would expand because people would look to it to fill the gap in providing social welfare and social support that the family and religious bodies would normally mostly take care of. Further, it was not surprising that the natural law-natural rights tradition seemed lost and confusion about rights and equality reigned among public decision-makers and leading legal figures since the character of their liberal arts education had been so eviscerated. It was also not unexpected that a popular commitment to traditional American principles would decline in light of the lack of a focus on cultural transmission and citizenship formation in education.

Now we ask the question: How have the elements of cultural and regime decline been apparent in the post-1980 period? Despite some signs of revival, it can only be said that religion continued its long-term decline in the U.S., and this was affected also by the attacks on it. Materialism and the pursuit of luxury did not abate. The sexual revolution of the 1960s and the accompanying pattern of marital break-up had ingrained themselves into the culture, indicating—along with the luxury orientation—that the drive for pleasure was still overpowering and passions for many not readily restrained. The accompanying factor of family breakdown was also widely seen. The further weakening of the family and its crucial role for culture would inevitably be the outcome of the experimentation with different—i.e., "untraditional"—family forms, the increasing momentum to equate same-sex attraction and homosexual practice with normal male-female relations, the continued anti-natalism, and the routine encroachment on parental rights. The relativism in education, the utilitarian ethic in law and human life questions, the decline of morality in sex and other areas, the evident standard of moral pluralism on some matters, and the decline of attention to moral formation because of family breakdown and educational trends indicated a strong undercurrent of relativism overall in the nation's ethical outlook. This is so even while it was blunted to some degree by the conservative upsurge, renewed political and judicial attention to Founding principles, and the struggle of the defenders on the traditional side in the culture wars. In spite of some reversals, governmental over-centralization continued to be the order of the day, and economic bigness and centralization were standard. Mass culture continued unabated. The sense of purposelessness of the 1960-1980 period continued to be evident—and, in fact, was emphasized with a vengeance by trends such as deconstructionism in the academy and the nihilism in popular culture—even while the conservative and traditional revival, again, gave some indication of a countervailing trend. While the U.S. seemed to recover from the loss of will in international dealings of the post-Vietnam period in Reagan's battle against communism and George W. Bush's taking up the struggle against Islamist terrorism after September 11, 2001, a new lagging of will was strikingly apparent in the Obama tendency to apologize for so many supposed failings of the U.S. around the world,[394] and in his and contemporary American liberalism's tendency to suddenly perhaps want the country to be a follower of European-style social democracy instead of a shaper of governmental trends and practice.[395] In spite of reversals, liberalism was still strong, and—like the 1960-1980 period—continued to dominate the thinking of the opinion-makers and movers of the major sectors of American political society. We observed such specific dimensions of this liberalism—as discussed by the writers on decadence—as the intolerance of disagreement (viz., political correctness) and moralistic sentimentality in the realm of education. The nasty politics, massive amounts of money floating around in it, and heavy role of interest groups in shaping public policy along lines favorable to their members give a picture of politics as, in many ways, essentially a power struggle. We mentioned a weakening of the rule of law, due to various legal, constitutional, and political developments—even though in a small way the Supreme Court's attempt to recover reasonable standards of federalism and interstate commerce could be considered steps to restore it in these areas. The interest group politics, group identity politics in education, promotion of a "nation of enemies" mentality by certain legal developments, continued low-level suspicion among groups, the immigration issues mentioned, and other points discussed showed serious damage to the common good—which, it will be recalled, is another indicia of regime decline. The utilitarian perspective, views about morality (especially on sexual and reproductive matters), inattention to Founding natural law-natural rights thinking, and chaos in educational ideas all suggested a continuation of a deep underlying corruption of philosophy. To sum up, while the specific indicators of politico-cultural decay—mentioned throughout this book—were not as deep or encompassing as in the 1960-1980 period, most were quite evident. It should be understood here, as when these factors have been discussed in all previous historical periods, that they did not sweep across the entire culture and include everyone or all activities but they reflected general trends and conditions.

Finally, the following possible weaknesses in the Founding are suggested by the experience of the post-1980-period: lack of awareness of all the principles of social ethics (seen in the lack of attention to the principle of subsidiarity by ongoing centralization) and a sound understanding of the common good (seen in the many ways that we said the common good was ignored) and also the prevalence of public purposelessness because of insufficient philosophical reflection; the seeds for an expanded individualism were present; an incomplete public philosophy due to insufficient philosophical reflection (observed in the Obama period with his administration's attempts to emulate Western European politics, showing a lack of awareness of the uniqueness of American practice and traditions); the discerning of the natural law left to private judgment, and so the seeds of positivism were present without the Catholic Church as the authoritative moral interpreter (seen in the domination of moral relativism—and the appearance even of nihilism—and the complete absence of discussion of natural law in the American public arena); the orientation to the higher things not being brought formally into the constitutional order (government both reached to address more matters concerning the here and now for people and in crucial parts of this era became more rankly secular and scornful of the higher things than ever); no formal reliable way to shape virtue and a downplaying of it as a concern of politics (to be sure, the law was used routinely to shape behavior on matters that were beyond its traditional concerns—e.g., sex discrimination, seat belt use—but what was involved was not necessarily the promotion of virtue [i.e., moral excellence by nature]); the lack of emphasis on intermediary associations (seen, again, in centralization and the continued trend of government, even distant government, interfacing directly with the citizen); the failure to see the family as central to the political order (seen in the continued cultural and legal pressures on it, and the abundant evidence of its breakdown); the lack of sufficient emphasis on community (seen in the many faces of individualism mentioned); the downplaying of statesmanship (seen in the moralism of the Bush Doctrine); the emphasis on the notion of the commercial republic led to increased individualism and laissez faire (witnessed in the developments in economic life in the 1980s, business attitudes in the wake of NAFTA, and the housing speculation that led to the 2008 financial turmoil); the Founders did not realize how much the hold of religion would weaken and how this would change morality and the worldview of the Founding Era; the Founders did not see how powerful the courts would become (as mentioned, they were less activistic than in the 1960-1980 period, but their actions still overreached in many areas); the emphasis on institutional and structural factors helped lead to bureaucratization (the course of governmental centralization continued as it had since the Progressive Era); and the Founding cultural problem of the too close monitoring of people by the community (seen in the increasing intrusiveness and regimenting of people by government).

At the end of Chapter 8, we offered a suggestion of what the American nation had become after two hundred years. In spite of some anguished reflection about that and glimmers of restoration in a few areas during this period, things had not changed much. It now behooves us to bring together our conclusions and consider whether the American political order still has the character and the vitality of the democratic republic fashioned by the Founding Fathers.

Notes

1. Patterson, 154-155.

2. Ibid., 157.

3. Ibid., 163, 165. The quotation is from 163.

4. Gil Troy, *Morning in America: How Ronald Reagan Invented the 1980s* (Princeton, N.J.: Princeton University Press, 2005), 136.

5. Steven F. Hayward, *The Age of Reagan: The Conservative Counter-revolution, 1980-1989* (N.Y.: Crown Forum, 2009), 586.

6. Patterson, 165-166; Hayward (2009), 470.

7. Troy, 223.

8. Ibid., 40.

9. Patterson, 168-169.

10. Hayward (2009), 214-215. The quotation is from 215.

11. Ibid., 218.

12. Ibid.

13. Troy, 212, 215, 229-230.

14. Ibid., 212.

15. Ibid., 211, 215, 216.

16. Hayward (2009), 576, 580.

17. Troy, 211.

18. Hayward (2009), 185, 217, 307.

19. Ibid., 364; Troy, 223.

20. John Ehrman, *The Eighties: America in the Age of Reagan* (New Haven, Conn.: Yale University Press, 2005), 208.

21. Troy, 223.

22. Tindall and Shi, 1658; William C. Berman, *From the Center to the Edge: The Politics and Policies of the Clinton Presidency* (Lanham, Md.: Rowman and Littlefield, 2001), 31.

23. Berman, 31.

24. Ryan J. Barilleaux and Mark J. Rozell, *Power and Prudence: The Presidency of George H.W. Bush* (College Station, Tex.: Texas A&M University Press, 2004), 33-34. The quotation is from 34.

25. Ibid., 35; "George H.W. Bush," http://en.wikipedia.org/wiki/George_H._W._ Bush; Internet; accessed Dec. 24, 2009.

26. Tindall and Shi, 1663.

27. "North American Free Trade Agreement," http://en.wikipedia.org/wiki/North_ American_Free_Trade_Agreement; Internet; accessed Dec. 24, 2009; Internet; accessed Dec. 24, 2009.

28. Berman, 30.

29. Ibid., 112.

30. Ibid., 29-30.

31. Tindall and Shi, 1663, 1664-1665, 1675-1676, 1678; Gerald L. Gutek, *American Education 1945-2000: A History and Commentary* (Prospect Heights, Ill.: Waveland, 2000), 297.

32. Berman, 74, 76, 87-88.

33. Ibid., 31.

34. Ibid., 31, 61. Both quotations are from 61.

35. Ibid., 106.

36. Ibid., 77, 82. Both quotations are from 82.

37. Ibid., 32.

38. "George W. Bush," http://en.wikipedia.org/wiki/George_W._Bush; Internet; accessed Dec. 26, 2009.

39. "Economic Policy of the George W. Bush Administration," http:// en.wikipedia.org/wiki/Economic_policy_of_the_George_W._Bush_administration; Internet; accessed Dec. 26, 2009.

40. See: "Financial Crisis of 2007–2009," http://en.wikipedia.org/wiki/Financial _crisis of_2007%E2%80%932009; Internet; accessed Dec. 26, 2009; "George W. Bush"; "Economic Policy of the George W. Bush Administration."

41. "Economic Policy of the George W. Bush Administration."

42. Ibid.

43. "Financial Crisis of 2007-2009."

44. "Medicare Prescription Drug, Improvement, and Modernization Act," http: //en.wikipedia.org/wiki/Medicare_Prescription_Drug,_Improvement,_and_Modernization _Act; Internet; accessed Dec. 27, 2009; "Medicare Drug Benefit May Cost $1.2 Trillion," *The Washington Post*, Feb. 9, 2005, p. A01, http://www.washingtonpost.com/wp-dyn/articles/A9328-2005Feb8.html; Internet; accessed Dec. 27,. 2009.

45. "George W. Bush."

46. "Obama Signs Stimulus Into Law," *The Wall Street Journal* (Feb. 18, 2009), http//online.wsj.com/article/SB123487951033799545.html; Internet; accessed Dec. 28, 2009.

47. "Barack Obama," http://en.wikipedia.org/wiki/Barack_Obama; Internet; accessed Dec. 28, 2009; "Expanded First-Time Home Buyer Tax Credit Becomes Law," *U.S. News and World Report*-Money (Nov. 6, 2009), http://www.usnews.com/money /blogs/ the-home-front/ 2009/11/06/expanded-first-time-home-buyer-tax-credit-becomes-law.html; Internet; accessed Dec. 28, 2009; "Obama Sets Executive Pay Limits,"

CNNPolitics.com (Feb. 4, 209), http://www.cnn.com/2009/POLITICS/02/04/obama. executive.pay/index.html; Internet; accessed Dec. 28, 2009.

48. "Financial Overhaul Signals Shift on Deregulation," *The New York Times* (July 15, 2010), http://www.nytimes.com/2010/07/16/business/16regulate.html; Internet; accessed Oct. 1, 2010.

49. See: "Consumer Spending Rises, but Home Sales Drop," *The New York Times* (Dec. 23, 2009), http://www.nytimes.com/2009/12/24/business/economy/24 econ. html; Internet; "Banks Still Reluctant to Lend," http://money.cnn.com/2009/08/17/news/economy/fed_senior_loan_officer_survey/; Internet; Trading Economics, http://www.tradingeconomics.com/Economics/Unemployment-Rate.aspx?Symbol=USD; Internet; all accessed Dec. 28, 2009.

50. In Obama's first year-and-a-half in office, the federal government debt was rising $4.9 billion per day, or a total of $2.4 trillion (the total of the overall federal debt was $13 trillion). This was a sharp increase from the $1.7 billion per day under the George W. Bush administration. (*The Washington Times*, June 2, 2010, http://www. washingtontimes.com/news/2010/jun/2/federal-debt-tops-13-trillion-mark/?page=1; Internet; accessed Sept. 27, 2010). New federal spending under Obama was only a part of this, to be sure, but it also did not involve the expected substantial new spending from his health care reform (below) that would kick in only in coming years.

51. See: "Major Provisions of Health Care Reform Legislation," (Tues., March 23, 2010), http://www.uscatholic.org/news/2010/03/major-provisions-health-care-reform-legislation Internet; accessed March 30, 2010; Kathryn Nix, "Top 10 Disasters of Obamacare," *Heritage Reports* (March 30, 2010), http://www.heritage.org./Research/Reports/2010/03/Top-10-Disasters-of-Obamacare; Internet; accessed March 30, 2010.

52. Gene Healy, "Introduction," in Gene Healy, ed., *Go Directly to Jail: The Criminalization of Almost Everything* (Washington, D.C.: Cato Institute, 2004), xiii.

53. Robert Draper, *Dead Certain: The Presidency of George W. Bush* (N.Y.: Free Press, 2007), 294.

54. Barilleaux and Rozell, 40.

55. Ibid.

56. Tindall and Shi, 1666; Mason and Stephenson, 143 (the Supreme Court case in question was *U.S. v. Lopez* [514 U.S. 549 (1995)]).

57. Hayward (2009), 225-227.

58. Mason and Stephenson, 143-144 (the case was *U.S. v. Morrison* [529 U.S. 528 (2000]).

59. See Draper, 314-333.

60. See Barilleaux and Rozell, 148-149; Hayward (2009), 636, 639.

61. Hayward (2009), 638.

62. See President Obama Signs Pro-Abortion Health Care Bill, Ignores Executive Order," *LifeNews.com*, March 23, 2010, http://www.lifenews.com/nat6180. html; Internet; accessed Sept. 27, 2010.

63. "Barack Obama," http://en.wikipedia.org/wiki/Barack_Obama; accessed Dec. 29, 2009; "Mexico City Policy," http://en.wikipedia.org/wiki/Mexico_City_Policy; Internet; accessed Dec. 29, 2009.

64. "Barack Obama." As of the fall of 2010, his action was being contested in federal court (see "U.S. Urges Stem-Cell Funding Stay by Appeals Court," *Bloomberg Business Week*, Sept. 27, 2010, http://www.businessweek.com/news/2010-09-27/u-s-urges-stem-cell-funding-stay-by-appeals-court.html; Internet; accessed Sept. 27, 2010).

65. Patterson, 184.

66. See, e.g.: Josh Gerstein, "Porn Prosecution Fuels Debate," *Politico* (Dec. 31, 2009), http://www.politico.com/ news/stories/0709/25622.html; Internet; accessed Feb. 5, 2010; Nicholas Confessore, "Porn and Politics in a Digital Age," *Frontline* (Feb. 7, 2002), http://www.pbs.org/wgbh/pages/frontline/shows/porn/special/politics.html; Internet; accessed Feb. 5, 2010; Jason Krause, "The End of the Net Porn Wars," *ABA Journal* (Feb 2008), http://www. abajournal.com/magazine/article/the_end_of_the_net_porn_wars/; Internet; accessed Feb. 5, 2010.

67. William A. Stanmeyer, *Clear and Present Danger: Church and State in Post-Christian America* (Ann Arbor, Mich.: Servant, 1983), 144; Gerard V. Bradley, "Moral Principles Governing Legal Regulation of Pornography," unpublished paper presented to the Witherspoon Institute consultation on "The Social Costs of Pornography," Dec. 11-13, 2008, 20; http://www.winst.org/family_marriage_and_democracy/social_costs_of_pornography/consultation 2008.php; Internet; accessed Dec. 30, 2009.

68. Roger H. Davisdon and Walter J. Oleszek, *Congress and Its Members* (3rd edn.; Washington, D.C.: CQ Press, 1990), 172.

69. See "Animal Cruelty Facts, Statistics and Trends," http://www.gevha.com/component/content/article/25-violence-to-animals-general/814-hsus.html; Internet; accessed March 14, 2011.

70. See: James Bovard, *Lost Rights: The Destruction of American Liberty* (N.Y.: St. Martin's, 1994), 86; *Education Matters* (Feb. 2011), 7.

71. Ibid., 124.

72. See ibid., 41-46. The citation for *Kelo* is 545 U.S. 469 (2005).

73. Bovard, 18.

74. See ibid., 28-33. The Supreme Court decision in question was *City of Boerne v. Flores*, 521 U.S. 507 (1997).

75. Bovard, 20.

76 Krason, *The Public Order and the Sacred Order*, 425.

77. Chris Edwards, "Federal Aid to the States: Historical Cause of Government Growth and Bureaucracy," *Policy Analysis* (May 22, 2007), 10-11, http://www.scribd.com/doc/13673543/-Federal-Aid-to-the-States-Historical-Cause-of-Government-Growth-and-Bureaucracy-Cato-Policy-Analysis-No-593-; Internet; accessed Dec. 31, 2009. On judicial limitation on unfunded mandates, see, e.g., *School District of Pontiac v. U.S. Secretary of Education*, No. 05-2708 (6th Cir., 2008). It should be pointed out that a question has been raised about how effective the federal legislation restricting unfunded mandates on the states has been (see: http://www.ncsl.org/StateFederalCommittees/BudgetsRevenue/MandateMonitorOverview/tabid/15850/Default.aspx; Internet; accessed Dec. 31, 2009).

78. See Hayward's (2009) comments, 638-639.

79. See "Iran-Contra Affair," http://en.wikipedia.org/wiki/Iran-Contra_affair; Internet; accessed Dec. 31, 2009.

80. Hayward (2009), 268.

81. See "Boland Amendment," http://en.wikipedia.org/wiki/Boland_Amendment; Internet; accessed Dec. 31, 2009; Hayward (2009), 516 (the quotation is from this page).

82. Hayward (2009), 536.

83. Ibid., 531.x

84. Ibid., 532.

85. Ibid., 540.

86. See ibid., 518-519.

87. Berman, 91-92. The quotation is from 92.

88. See Raoul Berger, *Impeachment: The Constitutional Problems* (Cambridge, Mass.: Harvard University Press, 1973), 59-78.

89. Berman, 91-92.

90. Ibid., 123.

91. Mason and Stephenson, 18. The citation for the case is 520 U.S. 681 (1997).

92. See the discussion in Krason, *The Public Order and the Sacred Order*, 568-570.

93. The decision was *Morrison v. Olson*, 487 U.S. 654.

94. See Mason and Stephenson, 87; "United States Office of Independent Counsel," http://en.wikipedia.org/wiki/United_States_Office_of_the_Independent_Counsel; Internet; accessed Jan. 1, 2010. Both these sources indicate that among its critics on this point has been Supreme Court Justice Antonin Scalia.

95. Berman, 80.

96. See "United States Office of Independent Counsel."

97. Barilleaux and Rozell, 91.

98. Ibid., 92.

99. Ibid., 91.

100. Ryan C. Hendrickson, *The Clinton Wars: The Constitution, Congress, and War Powers* (Nashville: Vanderbilt University Press, 2002), 17, 18. The quotation is from 18.

101. Ibid., 8.

102. Ibid., 20.

103. Ibid., 18.

104. Ibid., 161. Emphasis is in the original.

105. Ibid., 10.

106. See: Amy Goodman, "Opposition to War in Afghanistan Grows," *Rabble.ca* (Sept. 21, 2009), http://www.rabble.ca/columnists/2009/09/opposition-war-afghanistan-grows; Internet; accessed March 31, 2010; "Opposition to the Iraq War," http://en.wikipedia.org/wiki/Opposition_to_the_Iraq_War#Congressional_opposition; Internet; accessed March 31, 2010.

107. Hendrickson, 173.

108. Even though it was set up only in 2001, the Department of Homeland Security now has the third largest workforce of any federal agency (see: "United States Department of Homeland Security," http://en.wikipedia.org/wiki/United_States_Department_of_Homeland_Security; Internet; accessed Jan. 9, 2010).

109. The Inspector General of the CIA was strongly critical of the agency for not sharing information it had about two of the hijackers with the FBI and for not stopping them from entering the country (see: "September 11 Attacks," http://en.wikipedia.org/wiki/September_11_attacks#9.2F11_Commission; Internet; accessed Jan. 9, 2010). There was also, for example, some question about whether information from local FBI field offices about the terrorists' flying training did not get passed up the agency's bureaucracy (see: "Complete 9/11 Timeline," *History Commons*, http://www.historycommons.org/timeline.jsp?the_alleged_9/11_hijackers=complete_911_timeline_alleged_hijackers_flight_training&timeline=complete_911_timeline; Internet; accessed Jan. 9, 2010).

110. "Northwest Airlines Flight 253," http://en.wikipedia.org/wiki/Northwest_Airlines_Flight_253#U.S._political_fallout; Internet; accessed Jan. 9, 2010.

111. "No-Fly List," http://en.wikipedia.org/wiki/No_Fly_List; Internet; accessed Jan. 9, 2010.

112. See Mary Pride, *The Child Abuse Industry: Outrageous Facts About Child Abuse and Everyday Rebellions Against a System that Threatens Every North American Family* (Westchester, Ill.: Crossway, 1986), 55.

113. The decision was *Employment Division v. Smith*, 494 U.S. 872 (1990).

114. Mason and Stephenson, 543-544; "Religious Freedom Restoration Act," http://en.wikipedia.org/wiki/Religious_Freedom_Restoration_Act; Internet; accessed Jan. 1, 2009. The decision was *City of Boerne v. Flores*, cited above.

115. Mason and Stephenson, 545; Michael W. McConnell, John H. Garvey, and Thomas C. Berg, *Religion and the Constitution* (2nd edn.; N.Y.: Aspen, 2006), 158-160.

116. See "Religious Land Use and Institutionalized Persons Act," http://en.wikipedia.org/wiki/Religious_Land_Use_and_Institutionalized_Persons_Act; Internet; accessed April 3, 2010.

117. See Hayward (2009), 359. On the increasing polarization of the parties and the electorate in the 1960s and 1970s, see Norman H. Nie, Sidney Verba, and John R. Petrocik, *The Changing American Voter* (Cambridge, Mass.: Harvard University Press, 1976), 144, 199, 201-205.

118. Harward (2009), 388.

119. Ehrman, *The Eighties*, 210.

120. Ibid., 6-7.

121. Ibid., 48.

122. Troy, 342.

123. See "Health Care Reform," Jan. 4, 2010, *Rasmussen Reports*, http://www.rasmussenreports.com/public_content/politics/current_events/healthcare/september_2009/health_care_reform; Internet; accessed Jan. 5, 2010.

124. See "Health Care Law," Sept. 27, 2010, *Rasmussen Reports*, http://www.rasmussenreports.com/public_content/politics/current_events/healthcare/health_care_law Internet; accessed Sept. 27, 2010.

125. Berman, 107, 123.

126. Hayward (2009), 6.

127. Ibid., 7.

128. Ibid., 9-10. The quotation is from 10.

129. See ibid., 14-15.

130. Patterson, 168, 163.

131. Scripps Howard New Service/Ohio University poll, discussed in *The Washington Times* (July 5, 1997), A2.

132. GovernmentExecutive.com (Feb. 20, 2008), http://www.govexec.com/daily fed/0208/022008rb1.htm; Internet; accessed Jan. 6, 2010.

133. See John Samples, "Americans Don't Trust Big Government on the Home Front, Says ABC Poll, cato.org (Jan. 31, 2002), http://www.cato.org/pub_display.php?pub_id=3383; Internet; accessed Jan. 6, 2010.

134. See Barilleaux and Rozell, 155.

135. Ibid., 155-156.

136. See "Security for the Individual," 1984 Republican National Convention Platform.

137. Barilleaux and Rozell, 30.

138. See Hayward (2009), 10.

139. See: W. Lance Bennett, *The Governing Crisis: Media, Money, and Marketing in American Elections* (N.Y.: St. Martin's Press, 1992), 92; *The Washington Post* (Oct. 3, 2004), A08, http://www.washingtonpost.com/wp-dyn/articles/A2935-2004Oct2.html; Internet; accessed Jan. 6, 2010.

140. See "Capitol Crimes," *Bill Moyers Journal* (Aug. 1, 2008), http://www.pbs.org/moyers/journal/08012008/profile.html; Internet; accessed Feb. 5, 2010.

141. Glenn Setzer, "Two Senators Appear to Be 'Friends of Countrywide,'" *Mortgage News Daily* (June 16, 2008), http://www.mortgagenewsdaily.com/6162008_Friends_of_Mozilo.asp; Internet; accessed Feb. 5, 2010.

142. W. Lance Bennett, 91-92.

143. Ibid., 93.

144. Ibid., 94.

145. Berman, 67-68. The first quotation is from 67, and the second from 68.

146. Ann O'M. Bowman and Richard C. Kearney, *State and Local Government* (4th edn.; Boston: Houghton Mifflin, 1999), 133-134.

147. See, e.g., Kevin Phillips, *Arrogant Capital: Washington, Wall Street, and the Frustration of American Politics* (Boston: Little, Brown, 1994), 99-101.

148. "Campaign Finance Reform," http://en.wikipedia.org/wiki/Campaign_finance_reform#Criticisms_of_campaign_finance_reform; Internet; accessed Jan. 6, 2010.

149. See Bowman and Kearney, 134-135.

150. "Campaign Finance Reform."

151. The decision was *Federal Election Commission v. Wisconsin Right to Life, Inc.*, 551 U.S. 449.

152. The decision was *Citizens United v. Federal Election Commission*, 558 U.S. 50.

153. See "'Special Interests' in Both Sides in Health Fight'" (Aug. 19, 2009), http://www.msnbc.msn.com/id/32479506/ns/politics-health_care_reform/; Internet; accessed Jan. 7, 2010.

154. Hayward (2009), 47-48.

155. Krason, *Liberalism, Conservatism, and Catholicism*, 149, 171, 183-184, 191.

156. John Ehrman, "Neoconservatism," in *American Conservatism: An Encyclopedia*, 614.

157. See Krason, *Liberalism, Conservatism, and Catholicism*, 139-140, 156-158.

158. See Ehrman, *The Eighties*, 76-77; Hayward (2009), 362-363. The quotation is from Hayward, 363.

159. Ehrman, *The Eighties*, 76.

160. Paul Johnson, *A History of the American People*, 962-963.

161. For a short summary of the basic understanding about justice in that tradition, see Krason, *The Public Order and the Sacred Order*, 3-21.

162. Ehrman, *The Eighties*, 46.

163. See Hayward (2009), 356-358.

164. See Larry J. Sabato and Glenn R. Simpson, *Dirty Little Secrets: The Persistence of Corruption in American Politics* (N.Y.: Times Books, 1996), 153-154.

165. Bowman and Kearney, 131.

166. Ibid., 132.

167. Sabato and Simpson, 275, based on a study they conducted in specific parts of the country. Other studies in selected states, however, have concluded that voter fraud is infrequent (see Demos, "Securing the Vote: An Analysis of Election Fraud," 17, www.michiganelectionreformalliance.org/EDR_Securing_the_Vote.pdf-; Internet; accessed Jan. 7, 2010).

168. See Sabato and Simpson, 153-154.

169. "Robert Bork," http://en.wikipedia.org/wiki/Robert_Bork; Internet; accessed Feb. 4, 2010.

170. Hayward (2009), 568.

171. David Plotz, "Advise and Consent (Also Obstruct, Delay, and Stymie)," *Slate* (March 20, 1999), http://www.slate.com/id/22067/; Internet; accessed Feb. 4, 2010.

172. See Benjamin Wittes, "Borking Predates Bork," *The Washington Post* (July 30, 2006), B04, http://www.washingtonpost.com/wp-dyn/content/article/2006/ 07/28/AR200 6072801470_pf.html; Internet; accessed Feb. 4, 2010.

173. "House Democrats Looking at 'Slaughter Solution' to Pass Obamacare without a Vote on Senate Bill Updated," *The Washington Examiner* (March 10, 2010); http://www.washingtonexaminer.com/opinion/blogs/beltwat-confidential; Internet; accessed March 11, 2010.

174. See: Jeffrey T. Kuhner commentary in *The Washington Times National Weekly* (March 22, 2010), 31.

175. Krason, *The Public Order and the Sacred Order*, 421. There is a discussion about many of these developments at 421-440.

176. Ibid., 432.

177. Ibid., 423-424. The regulations of the federal Occupational Safety and Health Administration are good examples of this.

178. Ibid., 429-430.

179. Ibid., 421.

180. Ibid., 430.

181. Ibid., 427-428.

182. Berman, 126.

183. "NSA Warrantless Surveillance Controversy," http://en.wikipedia.org/wiki/ NSA_warrantless_surveillance_controversy; Internet; accessed Jan. 23, 2010.

184. Mason and Stephenson, 481.

185. Krason, *The Public Order and the Sacred Order*, 424-425.

186. This is the title of section III of Philip K. Howard's *The Death of Common Sense: How Law Is Suffocating America* (N.Y.: Random House, 1994). His other book that further develops these themes is *The Collapse of the Common Good: How America's Lawsuit Culture Undermines Our Freedom* (N.Y.: Ballantine Books, 2002).

187. See Krason, *The Public Order and the Sacred Order*, 387-389.

188. For the states that permit either homosexual "marriage" or civil unions—all put in force since 1990—see: "Civil Union," http://en.wikipedia.org/wiki/Civil_union# United_ States; Internet; accessed Jan. 21, 2010.

189. See "Perry v. Schwarzenegger," http://en.wikipedia.org/wiki/Perry_v._ Schwarzenegger; Internet; accessed Sept. 28, 2010.

190. Even though he does not mention the Founders, Professor Gerard V. Bradley captures well what their logic would have been (see Bradley, "The Case Against Same-Sex 'Marriage,'" *The Catholic Social Science Review*, vol. vi [2001], 88).

191. See Mason and Stephenson, 481-482. The decision was *Boy Scouts of America v. Dale*, 530 U.S. 640 (2000).

192. See: "Judge Drops Charges Against Repent America Protestors," *Baptist Press* (Feb. 17, 2005), 30, http://www.bpnews.net/bpnews.asp?ID=20165; Internet; accessed Jan. 21, 2010; "Christian Photographers to Appeal N.M. Court's Discrimination Ruling," Church Executive (Dec. 28, 2009), http://www.churchexecutive.com/newsprint. asp?print=1&mode=4&N_ID=2305; Internet; accessed Feb. 5, 2010; Julia Seward, "Media Black Out Discussion of California Same-Sex 'Marriage' Implications," http://www.cultureandmediainstitute.org/articles/2008 /20080530185505.aspx; Internet; accessed Fed. 5, 2010.

193. Donohue, *Secular Sabotage*, 129.

194. "Philadelphia D.A. Launches Witch Hunt Against Philadelphia Archdiocese," Catholic League for Religious and Civil Rights news release (April 24, 2002).

195. "Anti-Christmas Gang in High Gear," Catholic League for Religious and Civil Rights news release (Nov. 30, 2009).

196. Jonathan D. Thoburn, "Zoning as a Threat to Religious Liberty," Acton Institute for the Study of Religion and Liberty, http://www.acton.org/publications/randl/rl_article_111.php; Internet; accessed Jan. 21, 2010.

197. See: William A. Donohue, *The Twilight of Liberty: The Legacy of the ACLU* (New Brunswick, N.J.: Transaction, 1994), 114-120; Donohue, *Secular Sabotage*, 128; "Freedom From Religion Foundation," http://en.wikipedia.org/wiki/Freedom_From_Religion_Foundation; Internet; accessed Jan. 23, 2010;

198. See, e.g., *Lee v. Weisman*, 505 U.S. 577 (1992) and *Santa Fe Independent School District v. Doe*, 530 U.S. 290 (2000).

199. See *County of Allegheny v. ACLU*, 492 U.S. 573 (1989).

200. See Mason and Stephenson, 539, 540-541.

201. 461 U.S. 574 (1983).

202. See William Bentley Ball, *Mere Creatures of the State? Education, Religion, and the Courts: A View from the Courtroom* (Notre Dame, Ind.: Crisis Books, 1994), 112-116. The Supreme Court upheld the IRS's action, and upon reading Ball's analysis, one has the sense that that too may have been an end-justifies-the-means action.

203. See Paul Craig Roberts and Lawrence M. Stratton, *The Tyranny of Good Intentions: How Prosecutors and Bureaucrats Are Trampling the Constitution in the Name of Justice* (Roseville, Calif.: Forum [Prima], 2000), 37-38, 42-44, 106.

204. Tindall and Shi, 1682, quoting from *Adarand Constructors v. Pena*, 515 U.S. 200 (1995).

205. *Grutter v. Bollinger*, 539 U.S. 306 (2003).

206. See Mason and Stephenson, 187.

207. *Davis v. Bandemer*, 478 U.S. 109 (1986).

208. Tindall and Shi, 1682.

209. Hayward (2009), 223, 228.

210. 505 U.S. 833.

211. See: Mason and Stephenson, 585-586; *Gonzales v. Carhart*, 550 U.S. 124 (2007).

212. See "Dems Undermine Free Speech in Hate Crimes Ploy," *The Washington Examiner* (Oct. 13, 2009), http://www.washingtonexaminer.com/politics/Dems-undermine-free-speech-in-hate-crimes-ploy-8371517-64046162.html; Internet; accessed Feb. 5, 2010.

213. See *U.S. v. Playboy Entertainment Group*, 529 U.S. 803 (2000) and *Reno v. ACLU*, 521 U.S. 844 (1997), respectively.

214. See Kirk Doran, "The Economics of Pornography," unpublished paper presented to the Witherspoon Institute consultation on "The Social Costs of Pornography," Dec. 11-13, 2008, 1-61; http://www.winst.org/family_marriage_and_democracy/social_costs_of_pornography/consultation 2008.php; Internet; accessed Feb. 5, 2010.

215. Mason and Stephenson, 484.

216. *Ferber v. New York*, 458 U.S. 747 (1982).

217. See *Ashcroft v. Free Speech Coalition*, 535 U.S. 234 (2002).

218. Mason and Stephenson, 483. The decision was *Hustler Magazine v. Falwell*, 485 U.S. 46 (1988).

219. Hayward (2009), 586-587. The quotation is from 587.

220. See Barilleaux and Rozell, 84-90.

221. *Lawrence v. Texas*, 539 U.S. 558.

222. Hayward (2009), 413-414.

223. See Russell Kirk, *The Conservative Constitution* (Washington, D.C.: Regnery Gateway, 1990), 103-104.

224. Patterson, 194; George W. Carey, "Political Science: A Split Personality," *Modern Age*, vol. 34, no. 2 (Winter 1992), 110.

225. Hayward (2009), 114.

226. Ibid., 257, quoting the second point from NSDD 75.

227. Ibid., 257-258, quoting NSDD 75.

228. On the immorality of MAD and counter-population targeting generally, see James Turner Johnson, *Can Modern War Be Just?*, 37, 124. Regarding a plan such as SDI, Johnson indicates that since it was a defensive strategy it would be moral, but the period of its development and implementation could have proven to be destabilizing by undermining MAD—the principle upon which up to that time nuclear stability was based—and thereby make nuclear war more likely. That would have meant that it would have raised moral questions in practice (James Turner Johnson, *Can Modern War Be Just?*, 93). That fear, of course, was not tested as SDI never got close to implementation and the Cold War soon came to an end (what is said in the text below indicates that the prospect of SDI's development may actually have contributed to bringing that end about).

229. See Carl Bernstein, "Cover Story: The Holy Alliance," *Time* (Feb. 24, 1992), http://www.carlbernstein.com/magazine_holy_alliance.php; Internet; accessed Jan. 9, 2010.

230. Hayward (2009), 284.

231. Ibid., 291-293, 296. The quotation is from 291.

232. Ibid., 296.

233. See ibid., 295, 297-298, 631. The quotation is from 298.

234. Ibid., 268-269. The quotation is from 268.

235. Thomas L. Friedman, *From Beirut to Jerusalem* (N.Y.: Doubleday [Anchor Books], 1989), 171.

236. "Israel-United States Relations," http://en.wikipedia.org/wiki/Israel_%E2%80%93_United_States_relations#Bush_administration_.281989.E2.80.931993.2; Internet; accessed Jan. 12, 2010.

237. Berman, 37.

238. Yitzhak Benhorin, " Bush: Two-State Solution Will Be Realized," *Israel News* (Dec. 6, 2008), http://www.ynet.co.il/english/articles/0,7340,L-3634085,00.html; Internet; accessed Jan. 12, 2010.

239. "Israel-United States Relations."

240. Berman, 37, 68, 111; Barilleaux and Rozell, 27-28.

241. Barilleaux and Rozell, 27-28, 30.

242. Berman, 68.

243. Ibid., 23.

244. Berman says that Clinton's homosexual initiative in his first weeks in office "was the beginning of a strained relationship" with the military brass (ibid.).

245. See Brian Mitchell, *Women in the Military: Flirting with Disaster* (Washington, D.C.: Regnery, 1998), 115-117, 121, 124-127, 224-231; "Women Rising to Higher Positions in the Military," *About.com: U.S. Military* (April 3, 2005), http://usmilitary.about.com/od/womeninthemilitary/a/dodwomen.htm; Internet; accessed Feb. 6, 2010.

246. The policy—a kind of compromise—that was put in place after the scuttling of Clinton's plan to allow open homosexuals into the military was "don't ask, don't tell"

(i.e., recruiters would not inquire whether a person had same-sex attraction, and enlistees were not required to say).

247. See Melik Kaylan, "Analyzing Major Nidal Hasan," *Forbes.com* (Nov. 13, 2009); http://www.forbes.com/2009/11/12/major-nidal-hassan-fort-hood-muslim-opinions-columnists-melik-kaylan.html; Internet; accessed Jan. 17, 2010.

248. Berman, 83-84.

249. Hayward (2009), 313-314, 317, 322-323.

250. Ibid., 316.

251. Ibid., 317, 321-322; "Invasion of Grenada,"http://en.wikipedia.org/wiki/Invasion_of_Grenada; Internet; accessed Jan. 14, 2010.

252. See Higgins, 538-539, 544-545.

253. A good source on these points is Robert F. Turner, *Nicaragua v. United States: A Look at the Facts* (Cambridge, Mass.: Institute for Foreign Policy Analysis, 1987).

254. See Humberto Belli, *Breaking Faith: The Sandinista Revolution and Its Impact on Freedom and Christian Faith in Nicaragua* (Garden City, Mich.: Puebla Institute, 1985), 50-70, 93-97.

255. Barilleaux and Rozell, 28; *The New York Times* (Sept. 29, 2009), http://www.nytimes.com/2009/09/30/world/americas/30endara.html; Internet; accessed Jan. 15, 2010.

256. Hendrickson, 45; "Jean-Bertrand Aristide," http://en.wikipedia.org/wiki/ Jean-Bertrand_Aristide; Internet; accessed Jan. 16, 2010.

257. "Jean-Bertrand Aristide."

258. Hendrickson, 49; Berman, 36.

259. Hendrickson, 70.

260. See ibid., 70, 85-86.

261. Berman, 96-99.

262. Steven Woehrel, "Islamic Terrorism and the Balkans," CRS Report for Congress (July 26, 2005), www.fas.org/sgp/crs/terror/RL33012.pdf: Internet; accessed Jan. 26, 2010; 4, 7-8.

263. Ibid., 1.

264. Ibid., 11.

265. Lamont Colucci, *Crusading Realism: The Bush Doctrine and American Core Values After 9/11* (Lanham, Md.: University Press of America, 2008), 1.

266. Ibid., 20-21.

267. "Report: No WMD Stockpiles in Iraq" (Oct. 7, 2004), CNN.com, http://www.cnn.com/2004/WORLD/meast/10/06/iraq.wmd.report/; Internet; accessed Feb. 6, 2010; "WikiLeaks Iraq War Logs: No Evidence of Massive WMD Caches," *CBS News World* (Oct. 24, 2010), http://www.cbsnews.com/8301-503543162-20020542-503543.html; Internet; accessed March 24, 2011. The latter article indicates that there were apparently some residual chemical agents from the regime's past stockpiles, but they were very limited and probably not even operational.

268. Higgins, 544-545.

269. Colucci, 209.

270. Ibid., 212.

271. Ibid., 209.

272. Ibid., 210-211. The quotations are from 211.

273. See Morgenthau, 13-16, 584-586.

274. See Carnes Lord, "Aristotle," in Leo Strauss and Joseph Cropsey, eds., *History of Political Philosophy* (3rd edn.; Chicago: University of Chicago Press, 1987), 139.

275. For example, Plato, Cicero, St. Thomas Aquinas, and Edmund Burke agreed with Aristotle about this. (See [all in Strauss and Cropsey]: Leo Strauss, "Plato," 62-64; James E. Holton, "Marcus Tullius Cicero," 163; Ernest L. Fortin, ""St. Thomas Aquinas," 256; Harvey Mansfield, Jr., "Edmund Burke," 695-696.)

276. See David Rothkopf, "Obama's Six-Month Foreign Policy Report Card: Solid A- for the Team," *Foreign Policy.com* (Jan. 17, 2010), http://rothkopf.foreign policy.com/posts/2009/07/31/obama_six_month_foreign_policy_report_card_a_solid_a-_for_the_team; Internet; accessed Jan. 17, 2010.

277. Paul Johnson, *A History of the American People*, 964-965.

278. Ehrman, *The Eighties*, 194.

279. Paul Johnson, *A History of the American People*, 959.

280. Troy, 179-180.

281. Ibid., 183; *The New York Times* (Jan. 22, 1987), B3, http://www.nytimes.com/1987/01/22/nyregion; Internet; accessed Jan. 24, 2010.

282. Troy, 184.

283. Patterson, 172.

284. Troy, 183-184; Ehrman, *The Eighties*, 189-192.

285. Troy, 86-87.

286. Patterson, 311-312.

287. Troy, 181. The phrase is Troy's.

288. Ibid., 184.

289. Ehrman, *The Eighties*, 192.

290. Troy, 184.

291. Ehrman, *The Eighties*, 193; Patterson, 306.

292. See "1992 Los Angeles Riots," http://en.wikipedia.org/wiki/1992_Los_Angeles_riots; Internet; accessed Jan. 27, 2010.

293. Ibid.

294. Patterson, 305-306.

295. "Barack Obama."

296. Patterson, 304.

297. Ibid., 309-310.

298. Ibid., 172.

299. Ibid., 168.

300. Ibid.

301. See, e.g.: Michael G. Franc, "Obama, the Other Huey Long," *National Review Online* (April 2, 2009), http://article.nationalreview.com/390257/obama-the-other-huey-long/michael-g-franc; Internet; accessed Jan. 28, 2010; "Senator John Thune: Obama Seeks to Spark 'Class Warfare' with Populist Rhetoric," *The Daily Caller* (Jan. 22, 2010, http://dailycaller.com/2010/01/22; Internet; accessed Feb. 6, 2010.

302. Berman, 30.

303. Patterson, 176.

304. Ehrman, *The Eighties*, 185.

305. Hayward (2009), 464.

306. See Buchanan, 18-27.

307. Ibid., 105-113, 119-130.

308. Ibid., 110-111.

309. Ibid., 13, 28, 133, 135.

310. Ibid., 264, quoting Stanley Renshon, *The 50 Percent American: Immigration and Identity in an Age of Terror* (Washington, D.C.: Georgetown University Press, 2005), 7.

311. Ibid., 112, 132-133.

312. Paul Johnson, *A History of the American People*, 962.

313. Buchanan, 128-130.

314. Ibid., 130-132.

315. See ibid., 17, 22-26, 78.

316. Draper, 374-375.

317. Troy, 155.

318. Frank Newport, "This Christmas, 78% of Americans Identify as Christian," Gallup (Dec. 24, 2009), http://www.gallup.com/poll/124793/this-christmas-78-americans-identify-christian.aspx; Internet; accessed Jan. 30, 2010. See also: "Religion in the United States," http://en.wikipedia.org/wiki/Religion_in_the_United_States; Internet; accessed Jan. 30, 2010.

319. Audrey Barrick, "Poll: Most Americans Still Christian; Half See Religion as Solution," The Christian Post (April 8, 2009), www.christianpost.com/article/20090408.html; Internet; accessed Jan. 30, 2010.

320. Paul Johnson, *A History of the American People*, 968.

321. Ibid., 971.

322. Patterson, 184.

323. Marty, 249.

324. Patterson, 271.

325. Ibid. While remaining high, the rate apparently did not climb further after its sharp rises in the 1970s (183).

326. See: Paul Johnson, *A History of the American People*, 971; Paul C. Vitz, "Family Decline: The Findings of Social Science," in Paul C. Vitz and Stephen M. Krason, eds., *Defending the Family: A Sourcebook* (Steubenville, O.: Catholic Social Science Press, 1998), 1-23.

327. "Cohabitation in the United States," http://en.wikipedia.org/wiki/Cohabitation_in_the_United_States; Internet; accessed Jan. 30, 2010.

328. Marty, 249.

329. Patterson, 271.

330. Marty, 251.

331. Ibid., 248.

332. Ibid., 247.

333. Patterson, 271.

334. Maggie Gallagher, *Enemies of Eros: How the Sexual Revolution Is Killing Family, Marriage, and Sex and What We Can Do About It* (Chicago: Bonus Books, 1989), 82.

335. Carlson, 57.

336. Ibid., 129.

337. Marty, 299.

338. Troy, 267.

339. Ibid., 274, 276-277. The first two quotations are from 276, the third from 277, and the fourth from 276.

340. Ibid., 273-275.

341. Ehrman, *The Eighties*, 210.

342. Troy, 275.

343. See Patterson, 254-256.

344. Troy, 231.

345. Ehrman, *The Eighties*, 204, quoting Alan Wolfe, *One Nation, After All* (N.Y.: Viking, 1998), 129.

346. Ehrman, *The Eighties*, 205.

347. Troy, 299.

348. Ehrman, *The Eighties*, 172-173, 211.

349. Troy, 299.

350. Ibid., 339.

351. Ehrman, *The Eighties*, 206.

352. Berman, 126; "Bill Clinton," http://en.wikipedia.org/wiki/Bill_Clinton; Internet; accessed Feb. 1, 2010.

353. "Barack Obama."

354. "Obama Backs Marriage Act Repeal," *The Washington Times* (Aug. 18, 2009), http://www.washingtontimes.com/news/2009/aug/18; Internet; accessed Feb. 1, 2010.

355. "As Pressure Grows, Obama Addresses Gay Rights Group," *The Washington Post* (Oct. 11, 2009), http://www.washingtonpost.com/wpdyn/content/article/2009/10/10/AR2009101000627.html?sid=ST2009101100127; Internet; accessed Feb. 1, 2010.

356. *The Washington Times National Weekly* (March 8, 2010), 19. The senators supported a greatly relaxed limitation of accepting donations from men who have abstained from such sexual activity for a period of twelve months, though it is likely that this would result in more HIV-corrupted blood being donated.

357. Troy, 218.

358. See: Troy, 86; Eli Lehrer, "Looking for the Key to Declining Crime Rate," *The Washington Times* (Nov. 18, 2000), 12A.

359. Paul Johnson, *A History of the American People*, 966-967.

360. "Incarceration in the United States," http://en.wikipedia.org/wiki/Incarceration_in_the_United_States; Internet; accessed Feb 2, 2010.

361. See: "Are We Numb to Mass Murder?" *CBS Sunday Morning* (April 5, 2009), http://www.cbsnews.com/stories/2009/04/05/sunday/main4920311.shtml; Internet; accessed Feb. 2, 2010.

362. Paul Johnson, *A History of the American People*, 967.

363. Ibid., 959.

364. Ehrman, *The Eighties*, 196.

365. Ibid., 197.

366. See: Troy, 265-266; "Yale to Expand Teaching of Western Civilization," *The New York Times* (Sept. 13, 1995), http://www.nytimes.com/1995/09/13/us/yale-to-expand-teaching-of-western-civilization.html; Internet; accessed Feb. 2, 2010.

367. Gutek, 318.

368. Troy, 271.

369. Ibid., 271-272.

370. Gutek, 319.

371. The subtitle of *The Closing of the American Mind* is *How Higher Education Has Failed Democracy and Impoverished the Souls of Today's Students*.

372. John S. Schmitt, "They No Longer Ask the Big Questions" in Krason, *The Recovery of American Education*, 9-15.

373. David Lowenthal, "Liberal Education, Originally and Today," in Krason, *The Recovery of American Education*, 73.

374. See: Paul Johnson, *A History of the American People*, 962; "District to 'Affirm' Ebonics" (July 18, 2005), *World Net Daily*, http://www.wnd.com/news/article.asp?ARTICLE_ID=45334; Internet; accessed Feb. 2, 2010;

375. Gutek, 301-302. The quotation is from 301.

376. Ibid., 307-308. The quotation spans both pages.

377. Ibid., 272.

378. See ibid., 278-279, for the Commission's basic conclusions and recommendations.

379. Ibid., 274, 279-280.

380. Ibid., 274.

381. Ibid., 275-276.

382. Ibid., 287.

383. Marty, 263.

384. See: Krason, The Public Order and the Sacred Order, 425; "Individuals with Disabilities Education Act," http://en.wikipedia.org/wiki/Individuals_with_Disabilities_Education_Act#Criticisms_from_schools; Internet; accessed Feb. 2, 2010.

385. Suzanne Whitney, "Parent's Guide to No Child Left Behind," Wrightslaw, http://www.wrightslaw.com/info/nclb.parent.guide.heath.htm; Internet; accessed Feb. 2, 2010.

386. Gutek, 296-297.

387. "Assisted Suicide in the United States," http://en.wikipedia.org/wiki/Assisted_suicide_in_the_United_States; Internet; accessed Feb. 2, 2010.

388. See, e.g., Deborah S. Sturm, "The 'Quality of Life' Ethic and the Push for 'Living Wills,'" The Catholic Social Science Review, vol. xi (2006), 48-49, 54.

389. "Terri Schiavo's Brother Says the Press Is Still Lying About His Sister" (Jan. 22, 2010), CBSNews.com, http://www.cnsnews.com/news/article/60230; Internet; accessed Feb. 7, 2010; Diana Lynne, "The Whole Terri Schiavo Story," World Net Daily (March 23, 2005), http://www.wnd.com/news/article.asp?ARTICLE_ID=43463; Internet; accessed Feb. 7, 2010.

390. "Hospital Fights Parents' Wish to Keep Life Support for a 'Brain Dead' Child," The New York Times (Feb. 12, 1994), 16, http://www.nytimes.com/1994/02/12; Internet; accessed Feb. 7, 2010; Wesley J. Smith, "License to Kill: Hospitals Reserve the Right to Pull Your Plug," International Task Force on Euthanasia and Assisted Suicide Update, vol. 16, no. 1 (2002) (originally appeared in San Francisco Chronicle, [Dec. 2, 2001]), http://www.internationaltaskforce.org/iua24.htm#59; Internet; accessed Feb. 9, 2010.

391. Marty, 269.

392. "Homeless Women in the United States," http://en.wikipedia.org/wiki/Homeless_women_in_the_United_States; Internet; accessed Feb. 4, 2010. Interestingly, the article states that family breakdown is also a significant cause of male homelessness.

393. Roger Gaddis, "The Homeless in the United States," from: Associated Content, http://www.associatedcontent.com/article/351165/the_homeless_in_the_united_states.html; Internet; accessed Feb. 4, 2010.

394. See, e.g., "The Obama Apology Tour Continues: No U.S. Flag in Haiti," The Foundry (March 16, 2010), http://blog.heritage.org/2010/03/16/the-obama-apology-tour-continues-no-u-s-flag-in-haiti/; Internet; accessed June 5, 2010.

395. Some writers have suggested that Obama and contemporary liberalism are attracted to and seeking to promote such a European social democratic-type agenda (see: Ross Douthat, "The Pursuit of Social Democracy," The Atlantic [March 4, 2009], http://rossdouthat.theatlantic.com/archives/2009/03/the_pursuit_of_social_democrac.php; Eric Etheridge, "Obama Is a Social Democrat, Not a Socialist," Opinionator [The New York Times, The Opinion Pages - March 10, 2009], http://opinionator.blogs.nytimes.com/2009/03/10/obama-is-a-social-democrat-not-a-socialist/; Charles Krauthammer, "The Obamaist Manifesto," The Washington Post [Feb. 27, 2009], http://www.washingtonpost.com/wp-dyn/content/article/2009/02/26/AR2009022602908.html; all Internet; all accessed March 14, 2011).

CHAPTER 10

ANALYSIS AND CONCLUSION: HOW AND WHY THE AMERICAN DEMOCRATIC REPUBLIC HAS BEEN TRANSFORMED

The Characteristics of Contemporary America in Comparison to the Founding Era: A Summary

Is the democratic republic of the Founding still intact? What kind of political order is the United States today? As we consider our inquiry in the last two chapters, we have seen that contemporary America exhibits the following characteristics that deviate, in some cases sharply, from Founding principles and norms: The relationship between the federal government and the states has changed substantially. Federalism has been considerably weakened since political power and public policy-making have been increasingly centralized. Government at all levels has sharply expanded and intervened into more and more areas of American life, but the expansion of the federal government particularly has been marked. With the activism and interventionism of government has been a corresponding decline of individual, family, and private institutional liberty. While, to be sure, the Founding principle was ordered liberty, there is much indication today that today's restraints on liberty go well beyond what good order requires. Even traditional liberties that were held so central by the Founding, such as religious liberty, are imperiled. This weakening of liberty has been aggravated by the compromising of the rule of law due to such developments that have been discussed as vague and contradictory laws, outrageous prosecutorial tactics, the open-ended meaning of constitutional provisions because of judicial interpretation, the unwillingness to enforce some laws because of political and ideological considerations, the excessive use of law to address some activities that are more appropriately in the realm of manners, an increasing end-justifies-the-means (utilitarian) approach to law, and the weakening even of due process guarantees. The notion of equality has been distorted and carried to an extreme so that it not only has gone in an egalitarian

473

direction, but also has been applied to subjects and conditions that were never intended by the Founders and the tradition behind them. The notion of rights, such a central feature of a traditional understanding of liberty, has been convoluted as ersatz rights (e.g., the rights to abortion and to engage in sodomy) receive legal protection, while such traditional, natural law-based rights as parental rights have come under unremitting attack. Even traditional rights, like free speech, are now stretched in ways that would have been unrecognizable to the Founders (e.g., protecting salacious literature and entertainment). This distortion has resulted partly because of the confusion about equality, but it also reflects the almost complete subversion in American law and public discourse of the natural law-natural rights tradition underlying the Founding. Moral pluralism has become the predominant public ethical perspective, although it has been applied quite selectively by influential opinion-makers to such matters as sex and human life issues even as a dogmatic absolutism—grounded in ideology— prevails in such questions as civil rights and equality. This is sharply at odds with the sound, Christian-based morality that the Founders and their era stressed as a central feature of the life of a republic. As religious liberty has been attacked, religion itself has never been more marginalized as a force in the public arena. The Supreme Court has twisted the meaning of the establishment clause so that not only may there not be any official endorsement of the Christian culture of the Founding Era, but government may not even support the religious perspective that the Founders saw as crucial and must actually be neutral between religion and irreligion. American education continued to go down its long-term path of subverting the liberal arts, so that future leaders would not be properly shaped in the intellectual—and often the moral—virtues, and the next generation generally would not be properly formed with the knowledge of American government and history and the country's cultural heritage necessary for good citizenship. The decline of religion, sound morality, and solid education—and the deepening hold of ideology and the moral sentimentality that took their place—probably all combined to cause the loss of Founding realism that we noted was exhibited in various contexts. One of these was foreign policy, where the Founding norms of realism, impartiality, and even, under Clinton, resisting foreign influence were compromised. The Founding notion of a natural aristocracy was long gone, but what had come to replace it was: first, heavy influence by opinion-makers in different important areas of American life who neither exhibited the virtue and public-spiritedness of the greatest of the natural aristocracy of the early Republic—the Founders themselves—nor a commitment to many of their principles; and second, policy-making and ever increasing control and regulation of so many activities by distant, unelected bureaucrats (a technocratic elite) and judges. Ironically, it was the waxing of the democratic dimension of the American democratic republic that paved the way for the latter as an increasingly democratized populace demanded more and more from government, and government had to keep expanding and regimenting more of American life to respond to this. The irony was further evident by the fact that this development signaled the erosion of the principle of popular sovereignty. It has been further eroded by the rise of interest group government, which (as discussed) had its root in the very political equality found in embryonic form in the Founding itself and brought to fruition by the Jacksonian Era. Contrastingly, we live in a time when no public official and hardly any commentators dare to say that our political order is anything but an outright democracy, and we have discussed efforts in the last few decades to break down any remaining obstacles to a political regime of completely equal participation (in theory, at least) and institutional restraints on translating the popular passions of the moment into public policy (e.g., making it easier to stop filibusters in the U.S. Senate). The federal debt has skyrocketed to unprecedented heights, and there has been a seeming imperviousness to the Founders' warning about the dangers to liberty posed by it. Separation of powers and checks and balances have stayed intact, but listed as the federal judiciary has frequently overreached without facing serious opposition from the political branches and in the long run more and more power has accrued to the executive branch. Matthew Spalding summed up the latter: "The national legislature is increasingly a supervisory body overseeing a vast array of administrative [i.e., executive branch] policymakers and rulemaking agencies."[1] The mixed government the Founders embraced retains its form, but was watered down first by the engraining of the democratic ethos of the Jacksonian Era, then for a time by the weakening of the presidency in the post-Civil War period, then by the democratizing of the Senate through the Seventeenth Amendment, and then after 1932 by and large in an ongoing way by the growth of presidential and, more broadly, executive branch power, and finally by the continued accretion of sweeping power in the judiciary. In sum, every single principle of the Founding Fathers for the sustenance of a democratic republic, as laid out in Chapter 1, stands today as either no longer in force or compromised to at least some degree.

Nevertheless, the decimation of the cultural norms of the Founding Era—the informal norms, practices, and cultural conditions that stood beneath the principles—probably has been even more pronounced. To be sure, one of the most central of these, the maintenance of a strong middle class, remains intact—even if significant income disparities have remained a feature of American economic life since the first half of the nineteenth century and the middle class in various ways has come under increased pressure. This leads to a mention of the economic norms of the Founding Era, where the departure—for a long time—has been especially striking. Where small-scale enterprise and decentralization was universal then, we are now in an era of bigness and centralization. With continuing entrepreneurial activity, one cannot say that the norms of independence, self-directedness, initiative-taking, industry, and commercial efficiency are absent, but they are not as strong or widely seen as in that earlier time. The sense of the social obligation of property as an ethical principle, as we have repeatedly said, became weak through the course of American history. It is perhaps because of this that what was a typical feature in the Founding Era, laws regulating the use of property, has now become the overwhelmingly predominant means of promoting the social use of property (i.e., government regulation has become excessive). Such regulation has also become increasingly centralized, part of the centripetal movement of governmental power so much at odds with the Founding. We have commented about how such other Founding Era norms related to economics as thrift, sobriety, temperance, simplicity, frugality, a willingness to make present sacrifices for future good, and the avoidance of luxury are not widely practiced in contemporary American life.

A number of the above economic-related norms relate to personal qualities, and we have noted the decline as well of others of these that directly affect relationships with other persons and attitudes about the community. These are self-restraint, self-reliance, a willingness to cooperate with others, good manners, a general sense of decency, the spirit of the gentleman, truth-telling about others (a common failing in recent decades in the political realm), a concern about being one's brother's keeper, public spiritedness, avoidance of individualism, and orientation to the common good. This, in turn, has often been the cause of the loss of civic friendship and civility that recent decades have seen. It has even helped to create the conditions of (either open or subdued) social conflict that was so absent at the Founding and has been so evident—in spite of greater melding among groups in some ways—in recent times. If there were more acute periods of social conflict in American history in the past (e.g., the antebellum sectional conflict and the Civil War), arguably it is today more widespread than ever with the tribalism and identity politics discussed.

Perhaps at the root of these deteriorating Founding cultural norms—since the departure from so many of them involves the absence of proper personal formation (i.e., the shaping of the soul)—is the increasing breakdown, which we have chronicled, of three other Founding Era norms that were talked about so emphatically by Tocqueville: marital fidelity, the importance and integrity of the family, and—referred to above—the adherence to religion. It is clear from Tocqueville and the Founders that the latter was not just anything that called itself that, but *traditional*—i.e., before many parts of it were influenced by the secularizing thought and forces of the nineteenth and twentieth centuries— Christianity (see Chapter 1).

What the above means is that almost all of the principles and conditions that the Founders held to be necessary to maintain a democratic republic and the cultural practices and conditions that the *American* democratic republic was grounded upon currently are absent, not in force, or weakened to various degrees. What of the state of regime and cultural decline in America? The answer is also suggested by the above, since so many of the factors of decline discussed overlap with or are indicated by the deterioration of Founding norms: the decline of religion, moral relativism, the growth of materialism and preoccupation with pleasure, social conflict, over-centralization and bureaucratization, the growth of mass culture, the growth of liberalism (i.e., an anti-traditional perspective, moral sentimentality, and increasing intolerance of disagreement with such views), the weakening of the rule of law, the neglect of the common good, the corruption of sound philosophy (we noted that this was strikingly seen in the rejection of the very possibility of truth), politics as increasingly a power struggle, the loss of will, the spread of a sense of purposelessness, and severe economic problems. All of these are observed to different degrees—most substantially, some less so—in contemporary America. The only factors not seen are the dissolution of the middle class (in spite of its facing economic pressures) and the growth of militarism. True, we have seen that these signs of decline were present at one time or another earlier in American history and the political order nevertheless has continued. Still, we said at the beginning of this book that it has been transformed—and such a transformation of character is what is often meant by regime decline. A complete collapse where, say, a nation is conquered from without by a foreign power, is not the only thing meant by the term. We do not know where the decline will go from here, if it continues. The most likely direction would be a further transformation of the character of the political order (perhaps in a more authoritarian direction?). Indeed, Abraham Lincoln believed that if the American political order collapsed, it would not be at the hands of a foreign conqueror—he said that the U.S. was too powerful for that—but from within, by which he seemed to mean the very thing we are inquiring into: a change in the character of the political order away from a constitutionally grounded democratic republic.[2] The troubling reality that could be the harbinger of further change is the very fact that during the period of contemporary America—since 1960, fifty years ago—most of the signs are evident.

Is Contemporary America Still a Democratic Republic?

So, we return to the question with which we opened this chapter: What kind of political order is the United States today? Judge Robert Bork recently wrote the following: "America today is only partially a republic and, beginning about 50 years ago, has steadily become less of one."[3] We believe that his assessment is correct, and his time frame also concurs with our study. As we said near the end of Chapter 8, after 1960 there was a decisive shifting away from the Founders' vision of a democratic republic. The character of the government changed—not without a background leading up to this (we conclude below from this book's historical investigation what the most crucial developments in this transformation were)—and so did the culture and way of life. What America has become is, in part, what we will recall Tocqueville foresaw: a gentle despotism where people continue to elect their leaders, but increasingly see their everyday lives regimented, liberty reduced, and governmental power centralized. We noted how both the Founders and Tocqueville were suspicious of centralized government; Tocqueville, it will be recalled, went so far as to speak of the "extreme evils" that result from it. As suggested by Spalding above, an administrative state has taken precedence over the republican features of the political order. In many respects, people are now managed and not expected to exercise much self-government—or even in many areas responsibility for themselves—in the interest of utilitarian ends fashioned by considerations of equality, ideology, interest group preference, and their own needs and wants.

One cannot underestimate how much a striving for equality is part of this: Through the influence of democratic elections, people pressure government to give them not only what they need—which they may or may not be able to attain for themselves if they made changes in their lives—but also often what they want, so that they can be on a more equal plane with others. The attitude has long since become deeply ingrained that government is where people turn to address these things—indeed, an expanding number of things are even considered entitlements. These demands, as stated above, necessitate an increasingly expansive and activist government to address them, and so it is that the bureaucratic elites discussed have come to handle much public decision-making and, of course, the ensuing policy implementation. Even though they act according to enabling law, they are given such leeway and authority that law gives way to arbitrariness—and how could it happen otherwise, when government is called upon to control or regulate such a multitudinous number of human activities and endeavors? Even more troublesome is the fact that these elites espouse or at least operate in a utilitarian ambiance, where the limits set by the natural law tradition are inoperative and a runaway pragmatism, whose ends at best are fashioned by ideology or moral sentimentality, is the order of the day. With this kind of situation, and with the other ways that it has been weakened, the rule of law that is so central to a republic has been seriously compromised. They—and the elected officials who pass the laws in the first place for them to implement—are supposed to be acting for the people. In fact, they may be acting without a true concern for the people and according to what *they* think is good for them—often without even knowing the people very well or more basically understanding human nature or thinking themselves constrained by or even believing in moral truths. So, we have the bitter irony of more and more democratization issuing forth in a potentially more and more absolutistic elite—due to the weakened constraint of both positive law, and natural law on it—and less popular sovereignty. The diminishing of popular sovereignty axiomatically means that the character of a political order as a democratic republic has changed.

To be sure, it is not inevitable that opinion-makers, bureaucratic elites, and cynical politicians manipulate and control the masses, but the decline of the cultural norms of the Founding Era—which made possible a virtuous and enlightened citizenry and an expectation that leaders in early America would uphold a Christian worldview[4]—has made that more likely. Indeed, the recent emergence of the Tea Party movement and repeated expressions of conservative populism have been examples of resistance to such a development. Interestingly, a reason that Founding cultural norms in some sense have been eroded was because of a further kind of democratization that has occurred in recent decades, which was suggested by the phenomenon of moral pluralism that we spoke of. There is a now democratization in the realm of belief and way of life in America, like the condition of democracy that Plato discussed in *The Republic*: all beliefs and tastes are held to be equally good,[5] so sound cultural and moral norms such as those in Founding times do not hold so much weight. We cannot at the most basic level put the blame all on democratization, however. The reason why a condition of practical moral relativism and an elevation of all tastes, no matter how base, to a level of equal acceptability prevails in contemporary America is for the same reason Plato said that it happened: the inadequate shaping of the soul. This is due, in turn, to the decline of the factors we noted above that Tocqueville said were critical: religion, marriage, and the family. His insight was not original, however: the classics were well aware of these formative influences in producing good citizens and a sound political order.

A democratic republic also features the old standard of "majority rule, but with minority rights." What this means, of course, is that the majority will is what shapes public policy, but within the limits prescribed by constitutional norms and that those who do not join the majority will have their basic rights and dignity respected—again, because of constitutional limitations and the restraints imposed by sound morality, the natural law. As we have seen, the force of the majority is broad and often tenuous, as specific policies and much law is increasingly shaped not by the people's representatives but by unelected bureaucrats and judges, responding to or embodying the views of the elite opinion-makers discussed. It is also driven by particularistic-oriented special interests. If the majority agrees, it is often vaguely and broadly and its views are untutored and usually influenced by the attitudinal ambiance created by the opinion-makers and interests. In fact, instead of minority rights simply being upheld, it is often minorities—again, supported by elite opinion-makers—who shape policy, often in the name of their rights (which are often distorted or ersatz rights). Where the majority in some sense does prevail, or at least where majority opinion or sentiment has refashioned not just the politics but also the culture—after having its thinking shaped by minority opinion-makers or cultural movements (e.g., feminism, pro-abortionism, homosexualism)—it is too often contrary to the solid cultural and moral norms buttressing republicanism such as prevailed in Founding times. The bottom line here is that both parts of the basic republican notion of majority rule, but with minority rights are convoluted in contemporary America.

Republicanism—in its most basic sense of "public concerns"—has also been undercut in present-day America. We have observed the loss of the orientation to the common good, the weakening of community, the dissipating of public-spiritedness, and rampant individualism. As we have said, to have an orientation to the common good, to have true community, and to understand human nature so as to distinguish, say, between the proper respect for the individual and individualism requires a sound philosophical and moral framework. This has been largely lost.

Republicanism also means that there is a limitation of political power. The growth of centralization has weakened more localized centers of governmental power. Private decision-making authority has been curtailed in innumerable areas by the projection of government control and regulation. Separation of powers and checks and balances are intact but, as we have said, eroded (especially as respects judicial and executive power). Democratization has had a further pejorative effect on institutional restraints on power. The imperatives of democratic opinion can override institutional restraints. This can be so even if that opinion has been fashioned and in some cases manipulated by elite influence—and even if it does not constitute a *majority* but just the coalescing of forceful minorities with strong support of governmental and opinion-making elites (as with the 2010 health care reform). This is, of course, even more the likely scenario when for utilitarian ends public decision-makers no longer *wish to uphold* constitutional or institutional restraints (e.g., the Supreme Court's mostly open-ended interpretation of the commerce clause since the New Deal to permit federal legislation in one area after another).

The weakening of the American version of mixed government because of democratization and the twentieth-century growth of judicial and executive power is a significant indicia of a change in the character of the political order, since a mixed government is a historic characteristic of a republic, especially one fashioned in the Roman tradition.[6]

We said above that democratization—i.e., the demands and pressures of an increasingly democratic electorate—has been a major cause of the massive expansion of government and the concomitant growth of elite power that we behold today. This has often occurred in American history, as Robert Higgs noted, because of some event or crisis.[7] Indeed, it has almost seemed in the media age as if such a development does not even have to be so serious or affect a large number of people to evoke some new governmental regulation or increased level of regimentation. Knowledge of it is disseminated quickly and the population reacts, often without even realizing the nature and seriousness of what has happened. A new problem or crisis is *perceived*, the mentality of "something's got to be done" and "there oughta be a law" quickly kicks in, and the popular passions of the moment—which politicians and interest groups with corresponding causes are only too ready to oblige—push government to act. What often happens, however, as our historical discussion has pointed out, is that the expansion of government power that results brings about new problems and abuses and unforeseen consequences down the road. More, it often does not truly solve the problem it is supposed to address, but does create a permanent role or sub-role for government and a further reduction of liberty (both in limiting some sphere of citizen action and the likelihood of its erosion in the long-run due to more public debt to pay for the new governmental activities). Here again, we see the effects of democratization—not just in the obvious way of legislators and other public officials being readily subject to popular pressures, but in their all too frequent lack of prudence and in their allowing political considerations to simply crowd out prudential ones. If careful deliberation and prudential judgment were allowed to be uppermost, the possible problems of some new governmental action, adverse long-run effects, etc. might be avoided. When we speak here about the great political virtue of prudence, of course, we are talking about statesmanship. Democratization, as might be expected, has weakened the possibility of sound statesmanship for the simple reason that it left public decision-makers more exposed to the pressures of the moment and less of a sphere of freedom for prudent deliberation. It led to institutional changes like the Seventeenth Amendment that furthered such tendency. It also helped generate an ever-increasing set of demands on government. Government is now called upon to respond and produce solutions to more and more problems. The lost notion of a natural aristocracy means that there are insufficient filters for popular demands and, more basically, few public figures of known virtue, public-spiritedness, high capability, and who are widely trusted who embody the political order's essential moral principles, help it to avoid straying far from them, and who work to mold public thinking to continually support these principles. Jacksonian democracy probably spelled the end of any vestige of a natural aristocracy, and Progressivism supplanted it with the beginnings of the elite we have today—functional experts who treated government like a technical problem and so tried to abstract it from the very political "stuff" that made up the character of the American democratic republic: the principles and norms of the Founders and their era. As time went on, spurred by public demands and aided by the vague ideology of the twentieth century welfare and regulatory state and socio-political liberalism, the central administrative state became more powerful and its operatives more and more remote from both the popular will and the principles restraining that will. Both the democratic and republic dimensions of the American democratic republic declined.

With democratization having transformed the democratic republic of the Founders, the democratic demands arising from the decline of the principles and practices of the Founding Era pertaining to economic life are understandable. The Jacksonians themselves, it will be recalled, were only partially attuned to that decline and some of their actions helped to advance it. It was in the Gilded Age that the effects of this economic transformation came to a head, as people became increasingly vulnerable to economic and industrial currents and faced considerable insecurity and dislocation. If these developments had not occurred—i.e., if industrialization had proceeded with the norms of economic ethics of the Founding still in force—the excesses of democratization and the Progressive Era might have been avoided. Also, if something like an arrangement of subsidiary private bodies to regulate economic life had developed—perhaps along the lines of the old guilds, but updated to meet the realities of the modern economy—on the local and state levels and appropriately expanded as the economy became more interstate and national in scope, it might have averted much of the tendency to turn to government as the regulator. If that development could have been limited, then perhaps much of the social engineering in other realms that characterized the third wave of the administrative state (see Chapter 8)—and relied on governmental economic regulation as its precedent—could also have been checked later on. It is true that the ideological winds blowing in the Western world would have made it unlikely that the regulatory state could have been entirely avoided—for example, Progressivism was influenced by the German bureaucratic welfare state fashioned by Bismarck[8] —but it would not have been needed or welcomed very much if an existing arrangement had avoided many of the excesses and injustices of nineteenth-century economic liberalism.

What Were the Crucial Periods and Developments in Transforming the American Democratic Republic?

The above has already suggested a partial answer to our next question: Where did the changeover occur? When could it be said that the U.S. was no longer a democratic republic in the Founders' vision? While after 1960 a decisive shift occurred, a review of the historical study in this book points to some watershed, pivotal periods and developments that laid the foundation part-by-part and paved the way for the undermining of that vision.

The first crucial period was the Jacksonian Era, comprising the major part of the 1817-1840 period. The central development of that era, of course, was democratization—the embracing of democracy in place of the republicanism of the Founding. The odyssey discussed above essentially began then. As part of this, any remaining vestiges of a natural aristocracy or belief in its importance disappeared. Secondly, we have stated how this era featured the distant beginnings of official religious indifferentism (i.e., neutrality between belief and unbelief), which paved the way for the secularization of government and culture and the undermining of the role and hold of religion. The combination of democratization and a decline of religion were bound to have fateful consequences. Tocqueville echoes the Founders when he said, "Religion is...needed...in democratic republics most of all," because the freedom that characterizes such political orders can easily become destructive unless it is constrained by morality (i.e., the shaping of the soul that Plato spoke of above)—and that for most people requires religious faith. As Tocqueville puts it, "And what can be done with a people master of itself if it is not subject to God?"[9] He refers to a democratic republic, but he was writing during the Jacksonian Era and witnessed this phenomenon of increasing democratization. How much more what he says about a republic would apply when the American political order tilted in an even more democratic direction. Third, the age of Jackson provided the initial precedent for the embellishing of executive power. Fourth, the Jacksonian Era provided the first significant precedents for the compromising of the rule of law. Fifth, it saw for the first time an open public embracing by a major political movement—the Jacksonians—of the individualistic idea, with its support for laissez faire economics. Related to this is the appearance for the first time of a significant break in the connection between ethics and economics. Seventh, also related to economic individualism (which accompanied the period's early industrialization), was the initial emergence of significant social cleavages, gaps in wealth, and numbers of have-nots. Eighth, the Jacksonian Era saw the beginnings of mass culture and the weakening of community that was so strong in the Founding period. Industrialization, democratization, and economic individualism all influenced this. Ninth, the Jacksonian Era featured the first examples of social engineering—a phenomenon that would become familiar in the twentieth century. Finally, there were two other developments that began in the early part of the 1817-1840 period, even before Jackson's time. The first was the beginning of the significant governmental role in internal improvements. It signaled the establishing of the precedent that government (including the federal government) was looked to for economic well-being, and thereby also in a theoretical sense—although it would not emerge in actual terms for some time— laid the groundwork for the expanded economic regulatory and social welfare roles of government and an ongoing domestic commitment by government that heralded the massive public debt conditions of the future. The second development would in time become connected with the first: the emergence of interest groups that, with government in the business of economic development and eventually economic and other regulation, would come to it increasingly to get something or do something—always, of course, in the name of its helping the public. A part of this development of interest groups was the appearance of advocacy-type organizations, and the absolutist, uncompromising, moralistic approach that they took. We mentioned that the temperance movement of that time (which soon became the absolutist prohibition movement) was the paradigm for many more such organizations in the future.

The period 1840-1877 yielded only a few important developments leading to the ultimate transformation of the American democratic republic. Secularism advanced, and for the first time the notion of the U.S. as an outright secular state that required official neutrality between religion and irreligion was actively promoted. Major voices began to call for rigid separation of church and state, which in the long run would remove religion as a significant factor in American public life. Not unrelated was the beginning of open, forceful advocacy of moral relativism. Finally, the initial decline of the liberal arts education that the Founders believed so essential for the leaders of a democratic republic was apparent.

The Gilded Age/Progressive Era/World War I period was, after the Jacksonian Era, the next most crucial period in laying the groundwork for the decisive transformation later in the twentieth century of the democratic republic of the Founders. In fact, the changes of this period directly propelled the U.S. to that point: 1) The Gilded Age brought about the emergence and increasing domination of great, centralized economic power and bigness became the norm in the economy; 2) The connection between ethics and economics was decisively severed and the sense of the social obligation of property use mostly lost, and economics hereafter was seen as a strictly technical endeavor; 3) The presence of a significant economic underclass became a standard, ongoing feature of American life; 4) Due substantially to such economic developments— although racial and ethnic attitudes were also a factor—a condition of enduring division and tension among different social groups and lack of civic friendship took hold; 5) In further reaction to these developments and later world war, centralized government became firmly implanted and a key constitutional change of the period, the Sixteenth Amendment (income tax), insured that it would be sustained in the long run; 6) Within the expanded federal government, the earlier precedents for enlarged executive power of Jackson and Lincoln were built upon and became almost permanent in the Progressive Era; 7) The unelected part of the executive branch became a permanent feature and, as the decades went on, kept expanding and expanding from this beginning of the regulatory state. A new era of bureaucratization firmly took hold. Most significantly, what this bureaucratization meant was that—with the almost concurrent institution of the national civil service system—a sizable managerial, technically-oriented, officially apolitical elite became a fixture in American government. This was the embryonic development of the centralized administrative state that America would evolve into; 8) Separation of powers and checks and balances came to be even more strained in an ongoing way by the rise of judicial power. From this period forward, excessive power in the courts became a standard feature of American political life; 9) Also in terms of law, during this period positivistic jurisprudence gained the foothold from which it was to expand to predominance; 10) With respect to basic rights stressed by the Founders, the precedent was established during World War I for the significant, large-scale violation of citizen rights; 11) A further trend in thought at odds with the Founding became permanently entrenched, especially among the crucial intelligentsia: the philosophy of pragmatism. It signaled the decisive erosion of the natural law-natural rights tradition of the Founding; 12) The Progressive Era brought to a virtual culmination the large-scale democratization effort begun in the Jacksonian Era with the Seventeenth Amendment (direct election of U.S. senators) and Nineteenth Amendment (expanding the essentially universal adult manhood suffrage to universal adult suffrage by granting women the vote); 13) This period marked the beginning of the federal grants-in-aid programs to the states that within several decades became a major force thwarting the central Founding principle of federalism; 14) Carelessness about the federal government debt became the norm in this period, and of course has persisted most of the time since; 15) The church-state separationism that as noted above emerged in the 1840-1877 period seemed to become an accepted principle in American political thinking and in a few decades would become enshrined in constitutional thinking with the eventual consequences mentioned; 16) With the World War I mobilization, a permanently expanded standing army became the norm, although nothing compared to World War II and Cold War levels. The Founders admonition against standing armies was all but forgotten.

With the New Deal, America took a giant step past this toward a centralized administrative state. Very strong executive power now became a permanent feature of American government. A further, sweeping expansion of federal economic regulatory power and bureaucratization occurred and became permanent. This centralization during the New Deal permanently weakened federalism. The essentially open-ended authorization given it by the Supreme Court after 1936 by interpretations of the commerce clause and other constitutional provisions and the ongoing nationalization of Bill of Rights provisions powerfully assisted in this development. It bears repeating that the Founders' notion of federalism did not have to be understood in such an absolutist fashion as to preclude federal action when it was truly merited, but the blank check written by the Court allowed for ongoing centralization irrespective of a true need for federal intervention. Ultimately, attitude and perspective is what shapes governmental practice. It was during the New Deal that a nationalizing orientation became predominant in the minds of U.S. citizens. The federal government now emerged as the "default" level that citizens turned to; the 1960s brought a consolidation of this attitude as the federal role was to expand even further then. Indeed, as government—and especially the federal government—did more for citizens, they began to expect more and more from it; as it got involved in more areas, people expected it to be able to provide more solutions. As that happened, it also brought about an unexpected consequence that had not often been present in earlier American history: it cleared the way for demagogues and an uglier version of populism. It was during this time that the massive federal deficit spending that we are so familiar with first became routine. A few important cultural developments that had been taking shape for a long time became lasting during the 1920s, leading up to the Depression: secularization reached an important watershed in the post-World War I period, as the opinion-making element was substantially lost to religion or at least traditional religion; the ongoing decline of liberal arts education came to a point from which a restoration of its traditional character seemed unlikely; and the U.S.—despite the interregnum of the Great Depression and World War II—permanently became a consumerist culture. Finally, beginning with Wilson's Fourteen Points in 1917 just before the start of this period, the lack of Founding Era realism was more apparent than in any previous period, especially in foreign policy. From this period forward, this lack of realism has continually reappeared in both foreign and domestic policy.

This brings us to the next crucial time: post-1960 America. This is when the political order conclusively changed (especially during the 1960-1980 period). The third wave that we have mentioned represented the consolidation of the administrative state. Government regulation—or more accurately, regimentation—reached levels and concerned activities (e.g., social, cultural) never before seen. The future discerned by Tocqueville of the liberties of republican citizens being curtailed in so many of the areas of their day-to-day lives became a reality. As mentioned, never before had there been a departure from *so many* principles of the Founding and Founding Era cultural norms. From the standpoint of governmental institutions, judicial power reached its height, as court decisions sweepingly changed American law and altered American life. This raised very troubling questions about the viability of separation of powers and checks and balances. For the first time in American history, it has been said that the judiciary had become the most powerful branch of government. Since it is unrepresentative and unelected, this situation is incongruous with the notion of a democratic republic. This is even more the case when one considers that in many things the courts reflect the views of the opinion-making strata of American political society instead of the broader public.[10] The judiciary was perhaps the main source—or at least the prime instigator—of both: 1) the drastic twisting of such basic liberties as speech and press and of a convoluting of the notion of rights in a manner never before seen, and 2) a distortion of the notion of equality into areas and to a degree the Founding Era could never have envisioned. Court decree insured that these sharp departures from Founding thought would become ingrained into American politics and life. The already permanent expansiveness of executive power—

both presidential and bureaucratic—was further fueled by the third wave. The reality of "interest group government" emerged in a full-blown way after 1960, helped along by both the rise of the military-industrial complex in the 1940s and 1950s and the welfare state and far-reaching regulatory role of government in the 1960s. In the area of cultural norms, the most striking development—which, again, was unleashed in the 1960s—was the breakdown of sexual morality (following from the new ethic of sexual freedom) and of the family. This was to a degree unparalleled in American history. It was accompanied by a general decline in religion and morality that, unlike in earlier periods, spread throughout the population. Secularization and the public marginalization of religion reached their zenith—and, as stated, for the first time in American history the opinion-making strata had come to see religion as threatening to the good of the political society. This was a complete turnabout from the perspective of the Founding. Along with these developments in morality and religion was probably the most acute crisis in the long decline of American education, which featured a veritable upheaval on the campuses in the 1960s and an ongoing aftermath in which intellectual formation has often degenerated into an endeavor hostile to reason. The movement of liberalism in an outright leftist direction was a significant factor in prodding the country in the more statist, morally relativistic direction seen above. A condition of suspicion and conflict among different social groups became widespread as never before in the country's history, even if after the 1960s it was mostly subdued. There was a kind of institutionalization and regularization of the conflict with government policies, following an often-distorted notion of civil rights, sustaining and even encouraging it. The lack of knowledge of and commitment to the Founding principles discussed in this book has perhaps reached a nadir in contemporary America. As we have suggested, ideology (especially among opinion-makers and the intelligentsia), the failure— or unwillingness (for ideological reasons)—of American education to transmit the country's political and cultural heritage, and to a lesser degree the lack of support for those principles of many new immigrants are all factors in this. This development is especially troubling, in light of the fact that loss of will and a sense of purposelessness are main reasons for the decline of political orders. As it is often said, "ideas have consequences."[11] One should take pause to consider that the decline of the reigning Communist ideology underlying the Soviet state predated its political collapse by not too many years.[12] This weakening of belief in the country's fundamental principles among the opinion-makers is also evident in the widespread view among legal scholars and many judges that the intent of the Founders, where it can be discerned, about constitutional provisions does not have to govern and it can just be readily altered to meet changing views (i.e., the original intent question alluded to in Chapter 9).[13] Chapter 9 also made clear that regard for the rule of law—when one considers the range of areas affected—has perhaps been compromised to an unprecedented extent in contemporary America.

The Weaknesses in the Founding as a Springboard to the Transformation of the American Democratic Republic Over Time

In Chapter 1, we suggested and explained at length the nature of possible weaknesses in the Founding vision itself that may have laid the groundwork for its ultimate transformation. At the end of each historical chapter, we have pointed to different of those weaknesses that developments indicated may have been factors in the deviation from Founding principles and cultural norms. Here we briefly consider which of these putative weaknesses shown through most frequently in the different periods of American history and those that seemed most evident in the fifty-year period since 1960 when the transformation of the political order decisively occurred. This enables us to conclude which were especially critical. It must be emphasized that, as when these have been discussed throughout this book, these are just reflections based upon an understanding of the essential character of the Founding and the thought of the Founding Fathers. We have not proven or documented the connections between these putative weaknesses and the actual developments in the different periods of American history, nor are we suggesting that they are the fundamental cause of the ultimate transformation of the political order. Indeed, such connections would be difficult to clearly make when so many intervening historical factors have come into the picture. That is why we continually have used qualifying terms when discussing this (e.g., possible, probably, perhaps, apparent, likely, etc.). Nor is such a cause-effect relationship between Founding principles themselves—the very thing that defined the American democratic republic—and the ultimate transformation the focus of this book. We have put this forth as something to think about in the midst of our basic inquiry of *whether* the American political order has changed from the democratic republic the Founders aimed—very successfully—to establish. Other scholars may choose to make it the specific subject of future research.

Upon reviewing our historical study through the different periods, one finds that the most frequent putative weaknesses in the Founding perspective in possibly paving the way for transformation—in effect, for the undoing of that very perspective—pertained to the spawning of individualism. We repeatedly indicated that one or the other (or most) of these have shown through: the seeds of an expanded individualism, the Founding emphasis on a commercial republic as opening the way to more individualism and laissez faire, and the related lack of a sound understanding of the common good (due to insufficient philosophical reflection), and lack of enough emphasis on community in the Founders' political thought. This set of deficiencies very likely left America more prone to succumb to the pragmatism and utilitarianism that first reared their heads in the late nineteenth century. We also see in numerous periods how the non-recognition of the Catholic Church as the authoritative interpreter of the natural law—the problem Brownson pointed to—seemed to be crucial for American public life. We said that it helped to spawn the legal positivism that we showed became abundantly apparent with the developments in American law and jurisprudence (also) from the late nineteenth century onward. The Church was not there as a moral backstop to check these developments or to restrain the exultation of individual judgment as the arbiter of morality (the Protestant notion of individual interpretation of Scripture had led to individual decisions about religious belief generally and that, in secular times, led to individual decisions about what is moral). As we said in Chapter 1, the latter could not work; Brownson rightly saw it as a prescription for chaos. Since the Church was not in the picture, a human institution had to be turned to as the authoritative voice about, in effect, how natural law applies to the American public order. That became the courts, and we have noted how in U.S. history—especially since the late nineteenth century—the Founders' inability to see how powerful they would become was an obvious shortcoming. Even when the courts have eschewed an avowed reliance on natural law, their constitutional interpretation often in fact has been a determination about its applicability and has shaped the moral course of American life. Next, we recall that the Founders' failure to see how the hold of religion—along with the worldview and morality that it shaped—would decline over time is also seen extensively, especially beginning in the twentieth century. There is no doubt that this development mightily encouraged the growth of individualism and the attendant philosophical trends above. Insufficient philosophical reflection by the Founders, we argued, was the cause of a number of the putative weaknesses—including the one pertaining to the common good, and thus individualism. So, while the Founders' great success in fashioning a regime of ordered liberty was due to the fact that they were practical men of affairs,[14] instead of speculative, ideologically-driven men like the French Revolutionaries,[15] they may have needed more philosophical formation to enable their undertaking to avoid some of the pitfalls that the winds of history would bring forth.

The other putative weaknesses in the Founding that seemed to be suggested most frequently by historical developments were: 1) the absence of a formal, reliable way to bring forth a natural aristocracy (which seems to cry out in every single historical period, as we have often seen the problems of an absence of a natural aristocracy); 2) the fact that there was no formal, reliable means to shape virtue and a downplaying of it as a concern of politics (this is tied up with: the Founders' failure to see the decline of religion, which they viewed as perhaps the prime source of moral formation; the lack, again, of a natural aristocracy that could have helped inspire people to virtuous conduct and kept American public life focused on good ends; and the stress on the commercial republic above, that turned people's attention away from virtue to the pursuit of mundane individual-focused ends); 3) the Founders' lack of a theoretical understanding—despite the strong stress on it in the era's culture—of the centrality of the family for a political order, which may have occurred, again, because of their insufficient philosophical reflection and perhaps had the result both of the nation's fundamental law not affording it adequate protection (we have seen the readiness with which American law permits state intrusion into the family and the undercutting of parental authority) and its public policies and practice over time not doing enough to assist it and insure its integrity and independence (e.g., with economic policies that would insure adequate financial resources for the family so mothers of young children would not need to enter the workforce to make ends meet[16]); and 4) the lack of a stress on intermediary associations in Founding thought, which probably made easier the growth of economic individualism with the ensuing dislocations, conflicts, and injustices, and ultimately paved the way for a response that excessively embellished the role and power of government. A stronger presence of such associations, as mentioned above, might have helped to keep intact the economic perspective and practices of the Founding culture and limit the adverse effects of a commercial republic.

As far as the crucial time from 1960 is concerned, we find that only a few of the putative weaknesses mentioned in Chapter 1 are not suggested by developments. The problems we have said may have grown out of insufficient philosophical reflection (an incomplete public philosophy, lack of awareness of all the principles of social ethics, lack of a sound understanding of the common good, and a sense of public purposelessness); the related insufficient emphasis on community in the Founders' thought (which, ironically, may have contributed as historical change occurred to the undoing of the actual character of community in the Founding Era); the collapse of natural law into natural rights (even though natural rights have long since given way to an excessive focus on rights with no grounding in human nature, the excessive fixation on rights in contemporary America perhaps grew out the Founding's giving too much attention to rights even with the sound earlier perspective); the planting of the seeds of an expanded individualism; the Founders' emphasis on the notion of a commercial republic, which likely was a specific stimulant of individualism; eliminating the Catholic Church's magisterium as the authoritative interpreter of the natural law, and leaving it essentially to private judgment (which in a fundamental way helped spawned individualism because when the universal adherence to Christian morality that Tocqueville noticed dissipated, people came to believe that they could be their own moral arbiters—at least in areas where the pressure of public attitudes did not constrain them); the failure to see the decline of religion, which caused that very dissolution of a public moral consensus; the failure to see how powerful the courts would become—especially a feature of this time—which, as stated, may have happened partly because they became the alternative to the Catholic Church's magisterium; the fact that the formal constitutional order was not oriented enough to the higher things (that is, was focused almost exclusively on the things of the here-and-now, without much attention to the transcendent order) and to the shaping of virtue, and provided no reliable way to bring forth the natural aristocracy that we have discussed so much; the failure to understand the centrality of the family for a political order (the implications of this were most acute after 1960, of course, because family decline was so overwhelming); the inattention to the importance of intermediary associations (so evident at a time that government grew to unprecedented proportions to, in effect, check the problems resulting from individualism); how the perhaps too close monitoring of citizens in the

Founding culture led to a later unwarranted intrusion into their daily lives and activities (the development that Tocqueville foresaw that became so obvious after 1960, then, could have had its roots right in the Founding Era); and how the Founding stress on institutional and structural factors led to bureaucratization (which became overwhelming after 1960).

How Can the Democratic Republic of the Founders Be Restored?

The purpose of this book has been to trace if and how the American democratic republic has been transformed from the Founding Fathers' vision. The question of restoration is not something that can be focused on much here. It is, of course, a difficult, multi-faceted question, which would require several books to explore in depth. In a previous book, we gave it some attention: in one chapter, we put forth many specific ideas—focused on the restoration of the basic principles of the Founding discussed in this book—that heavily involved suggesting change in contemporary attitudes about and approaches to government. There were proposed changes in law and public policy, and ideas about education, as well.[17] Those ideas—which were numerous, but hardly exhaustive, and they certainly could be improved upon by other scholars or commentators—were shaped in accordance with the Founding principles and cultural norms under discussion in this book. They were also fashioned with reference to sound philosophical principles, the thought of great Western political thinkers, and the principles of Catholic social teaching. Some of these principles were discussed in Chapter 1, and some have been briefly referred to in other places in this book. The reader who wishes to see those ideas or to read at length about the thought and principles they are inspired by can consult our other book. What we offer here is nothing so extensive or with such an elevated aim of asserting the many kinds of changes that true restoration would involve nor put forth without any particular regard for the possibility of adoption any time soon. Rather, we present a small number of modest proposals that could *begin to forge a foundation* for restoration—with the full awareness that the American political order *grew* out of a heritage rather than being invented,[18] and that building up even lesser entities, to say nothing of a nation, is a much more difficult and long-term activity than that of tearing them down (and even the latter in the case of America unfolded over a considerable period of time).

One must first ask this question: Is restoration even possible? We can think back to Chief Justice Marshall's sober assessment about the decline of the Constitution—and implicitly America's constitutional order—at the beginning of this book, which was made less than fifty years after it went into effect. We can also consider the many thinkers, mentioned in Chapter 1, who traced the decline of political orders and cultures; this book has noted the presence in America of the factors of decline they pointed to. As indicated, the trends and cultural conditions are not particularly encouraging. We saw how even President Reagan, occupying the country's highest office and having a clear picture of some of the most serious political and constitutional troubles, could not effect much change. One of the thinkers surveyed about decline was Russell Kirk; but nevertheless he was always upbeat—even while thoroughly realistic—and always emphasized the chances for cultural renewal.[19] We must also realize that none of us knows what the future may bring or what unanticipated or uncontrollable developments may happen that shift human attitudes—even of masses of people—or open people up to proceeding in directions that could hardly have been foreseen. As Kirk understood, nations do not have to deeply decline or collapse for renewal to occur. Man is a rational creature, and he can choose to make changes in the way he does things, to improve, to act differently and in a better manner. Also, one can never dismiss the possibility of the miraculous or the power of prayer to change even big things,[20] or the fact that Divine Providence has a plan to unfold—and we must be humble enough to realize that we do not know all the developments that will take place as God does.

Many of the suggestions made here are very simple and focus mostly on regular citizens. They have their aim better intellectual and moral formation of the citizenry—so that people can learn about, come to appreciate, and gain a renewed commitment to the Founding principles and cultural norms discussed. "The fish rots from the head," and at bottom line the current troublesome condition of America has its roots mostly in problematical attitudes and beliefs. So, there is a need to alter and correct attitudes, which is not a quick task. Moreover, since practices affect attitudes some practices have to be tried and win people's confidence on a small scale so they can then expand and help to restore some of the key cultural conditions of the Founding Era that provided the foundation for the Founders' notion of a constitutional order. First, people should watch television less, and instead read good, old books—from the era before political correctness and erroneous revisionism—such as short historical studies of the forming of the Constitution, biographies of the Founding Fathers, and even fictional works such as *Johnny Tremain* (these instruct in a basic, often indirect way about America's heritage and basic principles). They should also watch old movies, say, from the 1930s to the 1950s because they convey the sense of personal restraint and propriety that must be re-instilled to begin the rebuilding of a culture like that of the Founding (cultures, of course, are constructed from the personal level upward). Even more basically, people need to reorient themselves—make sure of their own moral compass—and also make sure their children have the proper sense of correct attitudes and conduct for life (which, after all, is what characterized Founding culture). Turning to good books can help here again. When Allan Bloom wrote *The Closing of the American Mind*, he said that the Great Books were always available to help college students get themselves back on track in terms of the intellectual and moral formation referred to above. We do not expect the general population to sink their teeth into the heavy works that, frankly, only certain college students can handle well, but there are others that are more appropriate. A good suggestion is a book like William J. Bennett's noted edited volume, *The Book of Virtues: A Treasury of Great Moral Stories*.[21] When we speak about children, concerned parents these days—and parents who are not concerned enough are perhaps the ones who may especially need to reorient their moral compasses—simply have to be prepared to do a lot of educating of their children on their own. Homeschooling is a good solution for parents who can undertake it—there is little doubt, by the way, about how successful homeschooling has been in academic formation[22]—but those who cannot, must closely monitor what their children are being taught in schools and supplement and provide what they are not receiving. Parents should be prepared to get together to provide such additional instruction through group study in such areas as American history, government, and heritage. Such informal, cooperative arrangements would be good for parents themselves as a way to further their own citizenship education (e.g., study groups on the Constitution).

We have seen that there are many current developments that are challenging constitutional principles and other traditional practices. There is much reporting on and discussion of public issues surrounding these. American citizens must resolve to take the time and make the effort—actually, not a great amount of either is required—to seek more information about them from more sources, so they can make a more correct assessment of them as citizens. Too often, public decisions are driven by public sentiment and opinion fashioned by vague impressions of things or incomplete information (e.g., the popular outrage generated by some event or perceived new crisis above)—and sometimes the result, or the result over time, undercuts traditional constitutional principles (e.g., more centralized government action, which ideologically-driven elites are only too happy to accommodate). To simply seek more information is itself an example of the enhanced citizenship education that is needed today, and it happens merely by self-initiative. Along with this, Americans concerned about restoration must take the next step—at least once in awhile—of letting public officials know their views. Today, it is as simple as an email. When enough citizens communicate with them on something, it likely will affect their actions on most things—in spite of what we said about how the health care legislation of 2010 was passed despite consistent majority opposition. It almost goes without saying that citizens must then take the next—also fairly simple—step after that: voting. Even though it may seem that one person's vote makes little difference, that cannot not be an excuse; a citizen in a republic simply must vote.

We mentioned above that to restore sound culture Americans have to become reoriented to virtue—indeed, getting a renewed sense in an age of confusion what the full range of the virtues consist of and going through the (admittedly) arduous effort of leading virtuous lives. An important part of this, when we think back to the Founding Era with its admonition against luxury and its appropriate restraints on economic freedom in the name of the common good, is to seek less in the way of material goods and be more restrained in their spending and willingness to incur debt. Americans could do well to take to heart the urging of Pope John Paul II to live more restrained "lifestyles"—that is, to have and use material goods in a reasonable, but not excessive or superfluous, manner.[23] Related to this is the need for Americans to restrain themselves about what they seek from government. In an era of entitlements, they should take as little as they have to from it. Not only will this help in developing more self-restraint, but also enhance household independence and self-sufficiency. Moreover, it will be a small but important step in helping to restrain runaway government.

Since most people gain their moral formation through religion, religion was crucial in the Founding scheme, and a turning from religion is a factor in cultural decline, there is unlikely to be a serious cultural rejuvenation without the resurgence of religion. Since religious belief is fundamentally personal, this must start with each individual. Piety is, of course, a virtue—the classics recognized this and for Christianity the highest virtues are the theological ones, one of which is faith. A virtue is a habit, and habits must be developed. As stated in Chapter 1, as essential as religion is for the sustenance of a democratic republic the Founders did not view it in a utilitarian fashion; the spirit in which they spoke about religion viewed it as something good in itself and good for all persons. So, Americans need to develop the habit of religious practice—for their political order and mostly for themselves. Like all habits, it requires discipline—not an overwhelming amount, but at least a modicum. They need to make at least a little time daily—perhaps just a few minutes—for prayer; they will not be able to avoid an excessive fixation on material things or a veritable servitude to the here-and-now without making room for the transcendent. The discipline also involves their attending church. This is crucial for their moral formation, their being clear about what the moral formation requires, and their placing religion in its proper context of communal worship of God by men who share a common "createdness" and thus an essential equality (the latter is at the core of the entire Founding conception). Moreover, they need to find a traditional church or congregation to worship in—that is, one that has not sought to accommodate itself with the socio-intellectual trends that this book has made clear have played a large role in undermining Founding principles and cultural norms.

There is another aspect of discipline that the ordinary citizen needs to exert. We discussed the corrupted, nihilistic popular culture of contemporary America, which has eviscerated almost any vestige of such Founding Era norms as sexual morality, gentlemanliness, civility, and good manners. Much of this, of course, comes from the artistic community. Its sustenance depends in large part on people watching its television shows, going to its movies, reading its books, periodicals, and tabloids, and attending its plays. Curiosity, even for gossipy and lurid information, a desire to experience what others are talking about, and simply boredom motivates people to indulge in this popular culture. Persons who see the problem with the popular culture should discipline themselves not to indulge in it, and encourage others to follow the same course. In fact, they could in their own small ways make alternatives for themselves and their families, such as we see with such activities as Civil War era balls and cotillion dances that groups of parents in local communities organize for teenagers and pre-teens that provide a setting to develop some of the very inter-personal norms that the popular culture spurns.

To in a small way help to restore the central place of the family and norms of marital fidelity and family stability of the Founding Era spouses should simply take their marriage vows seriously, and work to be the best spouses and parents that they can be.

Those of a more intellectual cast should rightfully plan to "go deeper." College students should seek out sound professors (i.e., who have a good formation, are not taken with political correctness, and are committed to the principles of the Founding and the cultural traditions behind them) and take pertinent courses (e.g., history, political science, literature) from them wherever possible. They should take courses wherever possible that will enable them to read the Great Books. Such professors, or even the students themselves, can form the kinds of informal study groups, with a more academic cast perhaps, that were mentioned above to enable college students to learn about sound philosophy, the Western cultural heritage, and the Constitution when formal courses are not available. As future leaders in American political society in the public and private sectors, college students could do no better than focus some of their informal study attention on Tocqueville, if they cannot find actual college courses that include a focus on his thought. They can take advantage of the (often free) programs of the Intercollegiate Studies Institute—whose specific mission is to aid in the intellectual formation of college students to better understand the very principles and traditions this book has discussed[24]—and related groups.

The latter professors and other professionals could form speakers bureaus in local communities and make themselves available—as a free, public-spirited service—to citizen groups and other institutions to speak on the Constitution, the Founding Fathers, the ideas of the Founding, etc. They can work with local businessmen and other concerned citizens to restore the great American Revolutionary Era tradition of pamphleteering in order to re-educate their fellow citizens about the same, and can simply do things like showing up at parades and public events on national holidays to distribute them, make them available on library public information racks, leave them in places where free literature can be picked up, etc. With the financial help of businessmen, they could mail them, say, to the people listed on selected pages in local phone books (maybe even a few very wealthy national business leaders could be convinced to help bankroll a larger effort). They can offer free adult education and informal courses for college and high school students on basic logic and reasoning correctly, since so much present-day confusion comes just from people not knowing how to think clearly about how to understand and approach issues and problems.

People—everyday people or the more intellectually inclined—who understand the importance of the principles we have discussed should commit themselves to openly and forthrightly—but also kindly and patiently—defending them to others. They would be demonstrating, in a small way, the courage and civility that were Founding Era norms. A small amount of courage, by many people day in and day out, can have significant results, and showing that truth can be spoken in the spirit of love of neighbor can go a long way toward promoting civility. It can also be a ready witness that—contrary to the church-state separationists and moral relativists—asserting public truths does not inevitably bring intolerance and oppression in its wake.

This book has discussed how as American history progressed the growth of both big, centralized government and large, increasingly distant economic entities were encouraged by the lack of sufficient support structures to enable people to better control their economic destiny and provide economic and other forms of security. Such trends are very far advanced, and cannot easily be reversed. Indeed, no citizen or group of citizens can make that happen. What people can do, however, is to focus more attention on sustained volunteer efforts, work to build up intermediate groups to help each other and their fellow citizens in need, and undertake—in cooperation with each other, if needed— more very small scale and cottage industries. If such things could catch on, over an extended period of time people might begin to see that the American populace does not have to be a simple victim, without any recourse at all, of global economic trends and that government is not the only or best entity to help them. A few examples might be expanded cooperative efforts of various kinds among small businesses in the same field, the organizations set up by certain groups of active Christians to pool funds to help each other with health care expenses, and the special clinics set up by some physicians that offer a full range of health care services to people without insurance for a low flat monthly "membership-type" fee. These are modest efforts, but if enough such things were put in place and proven to be successful it could gradually shift people's attention toward a more small-scale, localized, non-governmental approach to social welfare and, even to some extent (especially if more people are also working to restrain their runaway demand for material possessions), economic activity. This would be more in line with the situation of Founding culture. Moreover, such efforts of citizens to assist each other might help, in a small way, to rebuild the sense of community that has been so compromised in an era of mass culture. To be sure, prevailing law may be an obstacle to some of these citizen initiatives (e.g., in the health care area). Citizen organizations and small businesses have to be as aggressive as possible in resisting, politically and legally, governmental efforts to over-regulate and regiment them. Lawyers who share the concern about the transformation of the political order that has occurred need to step up in larger numbers to join small-government public interest legal advocacy organizations or simply act on their own to offer free or low-cost voluntary legal help to such citizens and groups.

That brings us to our final admonition to citizens who are intent upon returning to Founding principles. They must, in general, oppose strongly every unreasonable attempt to limit their liberties more, and seek to reverse or minimize the effects of such limits already in place. Frequently communicating views to public decision-makers, mentioned above, is important here. We are at the point now, however, where this demands increasingly assertive—although entirely legal and peaceful—efforts to prod government to respect citizen liberty. Average citizens, who may have little experience in political activism or protest, must increasingly be prepared to take to the streets in protest rallies and marches—and do so in a sustained way—to "get government to back off" of one or another particular initiative or policy. The effectiveness of this was seen in France in the 1980s when to oppose government initiatives to put more restraints on Catholic and other private education, a million people took part in a massive rally—most of whom probably were not drawn from the sector of French society most accustomed to public protesting—and the government beat a hasty retreat.[25] In this sense, the Tea Party movement has been an encouraging development, though it still has to show it can maintain its momentum, attract more people to its ranks, and prove successful in the long run.

What about those who are in public office or have the inclination to seek it and who share these concerns about restoring Founding principles? This is a very large question, and one could go on at great length about it. Moreover, even though we are talking about restoring principles one always has to keep in mind that that is not incompatible with prudence and compromise—both of which are fundamental in politics. Maintaining or aiming to restore sound principles (i.e., those identified with the Founding) does not mean a cavalier, intransigent attitude that excludes reasonable accommodation of the many perspectives and interests that make up American political society. This is suggested by the very need to promote the civic friendship identified with the Founding Era. There obviously are baseline principles that must not be compromised, however. That was implied by what we said in Chapter 1 about the statesman always keeping intact a sound moral vision and trying to nudge the political order toward it. As such, what is needed among those running for office or those who have actually become public officials is courage in asserting and upholding the Founding principles—even if it means they may lose election and see their public careers sidetracked or even ended. Here, the example of Senator Edmund Ross and his small number of colleagues discussed in Chapter 4 is worth heeding. Many little examples of such political courage, far from being as dramatic as the latter, will over time help to transform American politics. If courage by average citizens above will have a good influence, even more will courage by public officials.

Restoring Founding principles and—where possible, cultural conditions—will require in some, or even many, cases for officeholders (especially legislators and top elected executives) to commit themselves to a course of gradual disengagement from public policies and practices that may have become deeply ingrained. (We say "gradual disengagement" because prudence requires that changes be made so as to minimize disruption, and the educational function of politics will have to become operative to convince many in the country of the necessity of changes). This is a crucial commitment they must be prepared to make; we have seen in this book how it has seldom happened in the last century or so even when some public-spirited officials have realized its necessity. To do this will require even *more* political courage.

Further, truly public-spirited officeholders must habitually practice self-limited power. One important way this needs to be done nowadays is by limiting—on their own—their tenure in office. We need to see more officeholders who are willing to spurn the financial benefits and prestige of becoming career politicians. They must realize that what they are doing is truly a public *service*—it is for the community and their fellow citizens, and not for themselves. While it may certainly be a legitimate concern of good men in office that they stay there so that bad men—or at least lesser men—do not replace them, perhaps what they should do instead of just perpetuating themselves is to bring forth and cultivate other good men to replace them. A recent good example of such a self-limiting act of stepping aside was Senator Sam Brownback of Kansas who, despite continued popularity, upheld his pledge to not stay in the Senate for more than two terms.[26]

An even more exemplary act—and one that is even more difficult, given the constraints of elective politics—is for public-spirited politicians to do what they can to avoid becoming dependent for campaign contributions on well-heeled individuals and various interests that seek pecuniary benefits from government. Such dependence often results in a kind of indebtedness. As much as possible—admittedly, this is easier in local, state legislative, and U.S. House of Representatives campaigns than in statewide ones—they should rely on small donations from average citizens and try new less-costly campaign approaches (e.g., more grassroots "pressing the flesh" and door-to-door canvassing). Along these lines, the developments in direct mail and Internet money appeals are encouraging.

It goes without saying, in the first place, that those entering political life need to be well schooled in the Founding principles in the first place. It is not enough to have good intentions; they need to be well formed as citizens before entering political life. They must also bring to politics what Edmund Burke called "the well-placed sympathies of the human breast";[27] that is, they must truly learn about the people they will represent and serve—the things that are important to them, their needs, their difficulties, the way they live their lives, and the things that are truly valuable and meaningful to them. One of the best ways to do that is to "stay connected" to average citizens, to be constantly aware of the realities of *their* lives. This requires a cultivation of genuine humility to avoid becoming part of a detached political class and fall prey to the temptations of privilege. While this focuses on strengthening the democratic side of the American democratic republic, those entering public office who are concerned about our Founding tradition must also remember the republican side. While being attentive to the people's wishes, they must also realize that they are not mere reflexive mouthpieces of the popular will, but must exercise good judgment in their public decision-making so as to further the common good—even if at times it goes against immediate public preferences. In Burkean fashion, they must exercise not just actual but also virtual representation.[28] This, again, requires the virtue of courage—and, once again illustrates how the restoration of the American democratic republic depends mostly upon sound, basic conduct by individual citizens in many walks of life. Such good judgment also requires that public officials not be beholden blindly to ideological prescriptions, but instead always study a question well, make a careful assessment of existing realities—their close connection with average citizens will help here—and ponder the likely and even unforeseen effects of the legislation and policies they must consider. If this is the approach that truly ethical, public-spirited representatives and government officials would take, it would help to restore the advantages accrued from America's long-lost natural aristocracy.

Regarding our criticism of, say, large distant government and economic entities and discussion of restoring the decentralized arrangements of the Founding Era, some would say that this is unrealistic, that it is no longer the Founding Era (indeed, the essence of the argument about not paying attention to the original intent of the Constitution is that it must be changed to meet the supposed needs of a different time). We are certainly aware that there is a role for larger economic entities and—in line with what we have said about the principle of subsidiarity and the flexibility of the Founding notion of federalism—there are times the federal government must act. We also have stated that the Founders provided a Constitution that did not preclude reasonable adaptation within the context of respect for original intent. Still, it is a truism— not backed up by sound argument or evidence—to say that the Founding Era is simply passé, or that its conditions—much less the principles of the Founding Fathers—are no longer viable for American life. One cannot say that the developments that have occurred in the periods of American history that have especially weakened the character of the American democratic republic are set in stone, or claim that they were or are inevitable.

The above are just a few suggestions and reflections. As stated, they are very small—but *doable*. The effort at reviving the Founders' thinking about the principles and conditions needed to sustain a democratic republic must start somewhere, and the only reasonable place to start is with concerned, public-spirited citizens who are at least aware of the problem and *want* to do something about it. When one thinks about it, that is not a bad place to start—*ultimately, a democratic republic can exist, be sustained, and flourish only when there is a deep commitment to it in the minds and hearts of its people.*

Can the Founders' vision of a democratic republic be restored if, indeed, there were shortcomings in the Founding itself, as suggested? Even if it is inevitable that political orders—like all things, St. Augustine of Hippo reminded us—decline,[29] there was nothing inevitable about the particular course of transformation of the American democratic republic. It was the result of a long series of developments, as this book has traced. This book has also demonstrated that the Founding and its culture, though not without imperfections, were not just sound, but exemplary—indeed, it was not supercilious to call it "a new order for the ages." The Founders knew of their greatness and of the greatness of the experiment they were undertaking, but they also knew of its fragility and the uncertainty about its future prospects. If its transformation, then, was not inevitable, it is not inevitable that it remain in its current condition and that the possibility of restoration is foreclosed.

Notes

1. Matthew Spalding, "A Republic If You Want It," *The Insider* (Winter 2010), 5.

2. See Abraham Lincoln, "The Perpetuation of Our Political Institutions: Address Before the Young Men's Lyceum of Springfield, Illinois, January 27, 1838," in Roy P. Basler, ed., *Abraham Lincoln: His Speeches and Writings* (Cleveland: World Publishing Co., 1946), 77, 82-83.

3. Robert Bork, "Keeping a Republic: Overcoming the Corrupted Judiciary," *The Insider* (Spring 2010). The article was based on his Joseph Story Lecture at the Heritage Foundation, Washington, D.C., Oct. 15, 2008.

4. Kirk, *The Roots of American Order*, 342.

5. See Plato, *Republic*, I.

6. See: *Encyclopedia Britannica*, 1966 edn., s.v."Republic"; Kirk, *The Roots of American Order*, 100.

7. Higgs, 17-18, 260-261.

8. Thomas Leonard, "American Economic Reform in the Progressive Era: What Beliefs Inclined the Progressives to Eugenics?" www.princeton.edu/~tleonard/papers/otherbel.pdf; Internet; accessed May 17, 2010, 8.

9. Tocqueville, I, ii, 294.

10. See, e.g., Robert H. Bork, *Slouching Towards Gomorrah: Modern Liberalism and American Decline* (N.Y.: HarperCollins [Regan Books], 1996), 321; Michael J. Klarman, "Court, Congress and Civil Rights," University of Virginia School of Law Public Law and Legal Theory Research Paper Series, no. 02-12 (Dec. 2002), 8-9; http://papers.ssrn.com/sol3/papers.cfm?abstract_id=353363; Internet; accessed June 10, 2010.

11. See, e.g., Sullivan, 94-95; Richard M. Weaver, *Ideas Have Consequences* (Chicago: University of Chicago Press, 1948).

12. This author recalls two episodes in his graduate student days at the State University of New York at Buffalo in the late 1970s and early 1980s, a decade or so before the collapse of Soviet communism, that made him realize the ideological transformation that was quietly going on in the U.S.S.R. One was when a graduate school colleague mentioned that a Russian exile friend of his—another graduate student, who had been one of the Russian Jewish émigrés from the U.S.S.R. in the 1970s—had talked about the decline of Communist ideology in his former country. The other was when the exiled Soviet dissident journalist and poet Aleksandr Ginzburg gave a lecture on campus. During the question-and-answer period after the talk, one member of the audience asked Ginzburg how many Communists there were in the Soviet Union. He replied—through an interpreter—that there were none; they were all in places like France and the U.S.

13. See: Robert H. Bork, *The Tempting of America: The Political Seduction of the Law* (N.Y.: Free Press, 1990), 187; Robert H. Bork, *A Time to Speak: Selected Writings and Arguments* (Wilmington, Del.: ISI Books, 2008), 256-259; "Original Intent," http://legal-dictionary.thefreedictionary.com/Original+Intent; Internet; accessed June 10, 2010.

14. Richard Hofstadter, "The Founding Fathers: An Age of Realism," in Horwitz, 73.

15. See Kirk, *The Roots of American Order*, 395-401.

16. In his encyclical *Laborem Exercens* (*On Human Work*) (1981), sec. 19, Pope John Paul II mentions a few noteworthy general policies and practices that could be put in place in modern states to advance these ends.

17. See Krason, *The Public Order and the Sacred Order*, chap. 45.

18. See Kirk, *The Roots of American Order*, 9.

19. This is why the small educational and research center established after his death at Kirk's long-time home in Mecosta, Michigan was called the Russell Kirk Center for Cultural Renewal.

20. Consider, e.g., the religious circumstances surrounding the Battle of Lepanto (1571) and the ending of the post-World War II Soviet occupation of Austria in 1955. Lepanto was one of the most famous and decisive naval battles in history. Pope St. Pius V had called for all of Europe to pray the rosary to save the continent from the invading Islamic Ottoman Turks. The outmanned European Christian forces, mostly from Catholic southern Europe, won a sweeping victory. Even though he was nowhere near the battle and there, of course, was no rapid communication at the time, Pope Pius is said to have proclaimed at the point of the final victory in the battle that the Christian fleet had won. (See: Fr. Ladis J. Cizik, "Our Lady and Islam: Heaven's Peace Plan," http://www.ewtn.com/library/mary/olislam.htm; Internet; accessed June 12, 2010; "Battle of Lepanto," http://en.wikipedia.org/wiki/Battle_of_Lepanto; Internet; accessed June 12, 2010). Regarding the second case, years of negotiations had done nothing to move the Soviets to withdraw from lower Austria, including Vienna, when the Franciscan Fr. Petrus Pavlicek began to mobilize large crowds, reaching to the hundreds of thousands and including leading Austrian politicians, to join in nightly rosary processions. In the years before this, he had played a major role in the post-war religious revival in Austria. Suddenly, on April 13, 1955—an anniversary of one of the apparitions of the Virgin Mary at Fatima—the Soviets announced that they were accepting the indemnity offered them and leaving Austria. (See "Freedom through Prayer," ttp://www.world-prayer-for-life.org/pg026.html; Internet; accessed June 12, 2010).

21. William J. Bennett, *The Book of Virtues: A Treasury of Great Moral Stories* [N.Y.: Simon and Schuster, 1993].

22. See, e.g., "Academic Statistics on Homeschooling," http://www.hslda.org/docs/nche/000010/200410250.asp; Internet; accessed July 4, 2010.

23. Pope John Paul II, Encyclical *Centesimus Annus* (*The Hundredth Year*) (1991), #58.

24. See Intercollegiate Studies Institute website, http://www.isi.org/about_ isi.html; Internet; accessed June 4, 2010.

25. See: "Jean-Marie Lustiger," http://en.wikipedia.org/wiki/Jean-Marie_Lus-tiger; Internet; "Alain Savary," http://en. wikipedia.org/wiki/Alain_Savary; Internet; both accessed June 11, 2010.

26. "Sam Brownback," http://en.wikipedia.org/wiki/Sam_Brownback; accessed Sept. 21, 2010.

27. Edmund Burke, *Reflections on the Revolution in France*, in Edmund Burke and Thomas Paine, *Reflections on the Revolution in France* and *The Rights of Man* (bound together in a single volume; Garden City, N.Y.: Anchor Press/Doubleday, 1973), 77.

28. See Schrems, 13-16.

29. St. Augustine of Hippo, *The City of God*, I, Preface 1.

SELECTED BIBLIOGRAPHY

Chapter 1

Bennett, William J., ed. *Our Sacred Honor: Words of Advice from the Founders in Stories, Letters, Poems, and Speeches.* N.Y.: Simon & Schuster, 1997.

de Tocqueville, Alexis. *Democracy in America* (ed. J.P. Mayer). Garden City, N.Y.: Doubleday (Anchor Books), 1969.

Evans, *The Theme is Freedom: Religion, Politics, and the American Tradition.* Washington, D.C.: Regnery, 1994.

Hamilton, Alexander; James Madison; and John Jay. *The Federalist.* N.Y.: Modern Library, n.d.

Kirk, Russell. *The Roots of American Order.* Malibu, Calif.: Pepperdine University Press, 1974.

Krason, Stephen M. *Preserving a Good Political Order and a Democratic Republic: Reflections from Philosophy, Great Thinkers, Popes, and America's Founding Era.* Lewiston, N.Y.: Edwin Mellen Press, 1998.

_____. *The Public Order and the Sacred Order: Contemporary Issues, Catholic Social Thought, and the Western and American Traditions.* Lanham, Md.: Scarecrow Press, 2009.

Meyers, Marvin, ed. *The Mind of the Founder: Sources of the Political Thought of James Madison.* Indianapolis: Bobbs-Merrill, 1973.

Nettels, Curtis P. *The Roots of American Civilization: A History of American Colonial Life.* 2nd edn. N.Y.: Appleton-Century-Crofts, 1963.

Padover, Saul K., ed. *The Complete Jefferson.* N.Y.: Duell, Sloan and Pearce, 1943.

Wood, Gordon S. *The Creation of the American Republic 1776-1789.* N.Y.: W.W. Norton, 1969.

_____. *The Radicalism of the American Revolution.* N.Y.: Vintage, 1991.

The Works of John Adams. Boston: Little & Brown, 1851.

Chapter 2

Beitzinger., A.J. *A History of American Political Thought.* N.Y.: Dodd, Mead, 1972.

Elkins, Stanley and Eric McKitrick, *The Age of Federalism.* N.Y.: Oxford University Press, 1993.

Faulkner, Harold U. *American Political and Social History.* 6th edn. N.Y.: Appleton-Century-Crofts, 1952.

Fehrenbacher, Don E. *The Era of Expansion, 1800-1848.* N.Y.: John Wiley and Sons, 1969.

Howe, Daniel Walker. *What Hath God Wrought: The Transformation of America, 1815-1848.* N.Y.: Oxford University Press, 2007.

May, Henry F. *The Enlightenment in America.* N.Y.: Oxford University Press, 1976.

Miller, John C. *The Federalist Era, 1789-1801.* N.Y.: Harper, 1960.

Smelser, Marshall. *The Democratic Republic, 1801-1815.* N.Y.: Harper & Row, 1968.

White, Leonard D. *The Federalists: A Study in Administrative History—1789-1801.* N.Y.: Free Press, 1948.

Chapter 3

Beitzinger., A.J. *A History of American Political Thought.* N.Y.: Dodd, Mead, 1972.

Dangerfield, George. *The Awakening of American Nationalism: 1812-1828.* N.Y.: Harper and Row, 1965.

Fehrenbacher, Don E. *The Era of Expansion, 1800-1848.* N.Y.: John Wiley and Sons, 1969.

Howe, Daniel Walker, *What God Hath Wrought: The Transformation of America, 1815-1848* (N.Y.: Oxford University Press, 2007.

Schlesinger, Arthur M., Jr., *The Age of Jackson.* Boston: Little, Brown, 1945.

Larkin, Jack. *The Reshaping of Everyday Life, 1790-1840.* N.Y.: Harper Perennial, 1988.

Sellers, Charles. *The Market Revolution: Jacksonian America, 1815-1846.* N.Y.: Oxford University Press, 1991.

Wilentz, Sean. *The Rise of American Democracy: Jefferson to Lincoln.* N.Y.: W.W. Norton, 2005.

Wiltse, Charles M. *The New Nation: 1800-1845.* N.Y.: Hill and Wang, 1961.

Chapter 4

Beitzinger., A.J. *A History of American Political Thought.* N.Y.: Dodd, Mead, 1972.

Brown, Richard D. *Modernization: The Transformation of American Life 1600-1865.* Prospect Heights, Ill.: Waveland Press, 1976.

Foner, Eric. *Reconstruction: America's Unfinished Revolution, 1863-1877.* N.Y.: Harper & Row, 1988.

Hamburger, Philip. *Separation of Church and State.* Cambridge, Mass.: Harvard University Press, 2002.

Howe, Daniel Walker, *What God Hath Wrought: The Transformation of America, 1815-1848.* N.Y.: Oxford University Press, 2007.

McPherson, James M. *Ordeal by Fire: The Civil War and Reconstruction.* 3rd edn. N.Y.: McGraw-Hill, 2001.

Volo, James M. and Dorothy Denneen Volo, *Family Life in 19th Century America.* Westport, Conn.: Greenwood, 2007.

Wilentz, Sean. *The Rise of American Democracy: Jefferson to Lincoln.* N.Y.: W.W. Norton, 2005.

Chapter 5

Bullough, William A. *Cities and Schools in the Gilded Age: The Evolution of an Urban Institution.* Port Washington, N.Y.: Kennikat, 1974.

Cashman, Sean Dennis. *America in the Gilded Age: From the Death of Lincoln to the Rise of Theodore Roosevelt.* 3rd edn. N.Y.: New York University Press, 1993.

Cochran, Thomas C. and William Miller, *The Age of Enterprise: A Social History of Industrial America.* Rev. edn. N.Y.: Harper & Row, 1961.

Friedman, Lawrence M. *A History of American Law.* N.Y.: Simon and Schuster (Touchstone), 1973.

Ganley, Albert C. *The Progressive Movement: Traditional Reform.* N.Y.: Macmillan, 1964.

Hamburger, Philip. *Separation of Church and State.* Cambridge, Mass.: Harvard University Press, 2002.

Higham, John. *Strangers in the Land: Patterns of American Nativism 1860-1925.* N.Y.: Atheneum, 1975 (originally published by Rutgers University Press, 1955).

Hofstadter, Richard. *The Age of Reform: From Bryan to F.D.R.* N.Y.: Vintage, 1955.

_____. *Social Darwinism in American Thought.* Rev. edn. Boston: Beacon Press, 1955.

Husband, Julie and Jim O'Laughlin, *Daily Life in the Industrial United States, 1870-1900.* Westport, Conn.: Greenwood Press, 2004.

Rayback, Joseph G. *A History of American Labor.* Rev. edn. N.Y.: Free Press, 1966.

Tindall, George Brown and David E. Shi, *America: A Narrative History.* 5th edn. N.Y.: W.W. Norton, 1999.

Urofsky, Melvin I. *A March of Liberty: A Constitutional History of the United States.* N.Y.: Alfred A. Knopf, 1988.

Chapter 6

Adams, Michael C.C. *The Best War Ever: America and World War* II. Baltimore: Johns Hopkins University Press, 1994.

Badger, Anthony J. *The New Deal: The Depression Years, 1933-40.* Chicago: Ivan R. Dee, 1989.

Beitzinger., A.J. *A History of American Political Thought.* N.Y.: Dodd, Mead, 1972.

Cashman, Sean Dennis. *America in the Twenties and Thirties: The Olympian Age of Franklin Delano Roosevelt.* N.Y.: New York University Press, 1989.

_____. *America, Roosevelt, and World War II.* N.Y.: New York University Press, 1989.

Goldberg, David J. *Discontented America: The United States in the 1920s.* Baltimore: Johns Hopkins University Press, 1999.

Kennedy, David M. *Freedom From Fear: The American People in Depression and War, 1929-1945.* N.Y.: Oxford University Press, 1999.

Kyvig, David E. *Daily Life in the United States, 1920-1940.* Chicago: Ivan R. Dee, 2002.

Leuchtenburg, William E. *The Perils of Prosperity, 1914-1932.* Chicago: University of Chicago Press, 1958.

Manchester, William. *The Glory and the Dream: A Narrative History of America, 1932-1972.* Boston: Little Brown, 1974.

Mason, Alpheus Thomas and Donald Grier Stephenson, Jr. *American Constitutional Law: Introductory Essays and Selected Cases.* 14th edn.; Upper Saddle River, N.J.: Pearson/Prentice Hall, 2005.

Tindall, George Brown and David E. Shi, *America: A Narrative History.* 5th edn. N.Y.: W.W. Norton, 1999.

Chapter 7

Ambrose, Stephen E. and Douglas G. Brinkley. *Rise to Globalism: American Foreign Policy Since 1938.* 8th rev. edn. N.Y.: Penguin, 1997.

Chafe, William H. *The Unfinished Journey: America Since World War II.* 3rd edn. N.Y.: Oxford University Press, 1995.

Goldman, Eric F. *The Crucial Decade—and After: America, 1945-1960.* N.Y.: Vintage Books, 1960.

Halberstam, David. *The Fifties.* N.Y.: Villard Books, 1993.

Johnson, Paul, *A History of the American People.* N.Y.: HarperCollins, 1997.

Kirk, Russell. *Decadence and Renewal in the Higher Learning: An Episodic History of American University and College.* South Bend, Ind.: Gateway Edns., 1978.

Leuchtenburg, William E. *A Troubled Feast: American Society Since 1945* Boston: Little, Brown, 1983.

Manchester, William. *The Glory and the Dream: A Narrative History of America, 1932-1972.* Boston: Little Brown, 1974.

Mason, Alpheus Thomas and Donald Grier Stephenson, Jr. *American Constitutional Law: Introductory Essays and Selected Cases.* 14th edn. Upper Saddle River, N.J.: Pearson/Prentice Hall, 2005.

Miller, Douglas T. and Marion Nowak. *The Fifties: The Way We Really Were.* Garden City, N.Y.: Doubleday, 1977.

Tindall, George Brown and David E. Shi, *America: A Narrative History.* 5th edn. N.Y.: W.W. Norton, 1999.

Chapter 8

Ambrose, Stephen E. and Douglas G. Brinkley. *Rise to Globalism: American Foreign Policy Since 1938.* 8th rev. edn. N.Y.: Penguin, 1997.

Burner, David, Robert D. Marcus, and Thomas R. West. *A Giant's Strength: America in the 1960s.* N.Y.: Holt, Rinehart and Winston, 1971.

Clecak, Peter. *America's Quest for the Ideal Self: Dissent and Fulfillment in the 60s and 70s.* N.Y.: Oxford University Press, 1983.

Dethloff, Harry C. *Americans and Free Enterprise.* Englewood Cliffs, N.J.: Prentice-Hall, 1979.

Hayward, Steven F. *The Age of Reagan: The Fall of the Old Liberal Order, 1964-1980.* N.Y.: Forum (Prima), 2001.

Krason, Stephen M. *Abortion: Politics, Morality, and the Constitution: A Critical Study of* Roe v. Wade *and* Doe v. Bolton *and a Basis for Change.* Lanham, Md.: University Press of America, 1984.

Manchester, William. *The Glory and the Dream: A Narrative History of America, 1932-1972.* Boston: Little Brown, 1974.

Marty, Myron A. *Daily Life in the United States, 1960-1990: Decades of Discord.* Westport, Conn.: Greenwood, 1997.

Mason, Alpheus Thomas and Donald Grier Stephenson, Jr. *American Constitutional Law: Introductory Essays and Selected Cases.* 14th edn.; Upper Saddle River, N.J.: Pearson/Prentice Hall, 2005.

Matusow, Allen J. *The Unraveling of America: A History of Liberalism in the 1960s.* N.Y.: Harper & Row, 1984.

Patterson, James T. *Restless Giant: The United States from Watergate to* Bush v. Gore. N.Y.: Oxford University Press, 2005.

Schulman, Bruce J. *The Seventies: The Great Shift in American Culture, Society, and Politics.* N.Y.: Free Press, 2001.

Sindler, Allan P. ed., *America in the Seventies: Problems, Policies, and Politics.* Boston: Little, Brown, 1977.

Chapter 9

Barilleaux, Ryan J. and Mark J. Rozell. *Power and Prudence: The Presidency of George H.W. Bush.* College Station, Tex.: Texas A&M University Press, 2004.

Berman, William C. *From the Center to the Edge: The Politics and Policies of the Clinton Presidency.* Lanham, Md.: Rowman and Littlefield, 2001.

Bovard, James. *Lost Rights: The Destruction of American Liberty.* N.Y.: St. Martin's, 1994.

Draper, Robert. *Dead Certain: The Presidency of George W. Bush.* N.Y.: Free Press, 2007.

Ehrman, John. *The Eighties: America in the Age of Reagan.* New Haven, Conn.: Yale University Press, 2005.

Hayward, Steven F. *The Age of Reagan: The Conservative Counter-revolution, 1980-1989.* N.Y.: Crown Forum, 2009.

Hendrickson, Ryan C. *The Clinton Wars: The Constitution, Congress, and War Powers.* Nashville: Vanderbilt University Press, 2002.

Howard, Philip K. *The Death of Common Sense: How Law Is Suffocating America.* N.Y.: Random House, 1994.

_____. *The Collapse of the Common Good: How America's Lawsuit Culture Undermines Our Freedom.* N.Y.: Ballantine Books, 2002.

Johnson, Paul, *A History of the American People.* N.Y.: HarperCollins, 1997.

Mason, Alpheus Thomas and Donald Grier Stephenson, Jr. *American Constitutional Law: Introductory Essays and Selected Cases.* 14th edn.; Upper Saddle River, N.J.: Pearson/Prentice Hall, 2005.

Patterson, James T. *Restless Giant: The United States from Watergate to* Bush v. Gore. N.Y.: Oxford University Press, 2005.

Tindall, George Brown and David E. Shi, *America: A Narrative History.* 5th edn. N.Y.: W.W. Norton, 1999.

Troy, Gil. *Morning in America: How Ronald Reagan Invented the 1980s.* Princeton, N.J.: Princeton University Press, 2005.

INDEX